Black Flame

Black Flame

The Revolutionary Class Politics of Anarchism and Syndicalism

Lucien van der Walt
and
Michael Schmidt

Counterpower Volume 1

AK PRESS
EDINBURGH · OAKLAND · WEST VIRGINIA

Black Flame: The Revolutionary Class Politics of Anarchism and Syndicalism
by Lucien van der Walt and Michael Schmidt

ISBN 978 1 904859 16 1
Library of Congress Number: 2006933558

Cover Design: Vincent Chung
Layout: JR

AK Press
674-A 23rd Street
Oakland, CA 94612
www.akpress.org
akpress@akpress.org
510.208.1700

AK Press U.K.
PO Box 12766
Edinburgh EH8 9YE
www.akuk.com
ak@akedin.demon.co.uk
0131.555.5165

The production of this book was made possible in part by a generous donation from the
Anarchist Archives Project.

Printed in Canada on 100% recycled, acid-free paper by union labor.

Don't let anyone tell us that we—but a small band—are too weak to attain unto the magnificent end at which we aim. Count and see how many there are who suffer this injustice. We peasants who work for others, and who mumble the straw while our master eats the wheat, we by ourselves are millions.

We workers who weave silks and velvet in order that we may be clothed in rags, we, too, are a great multitude; and when the clang of the factories permits us a moment's repose, we overflow the streets and squares like the sea in a spring tide.

We soldiers who are driven along to the word of command, or by blows, we who receive the bullets for which our officers get crosses and pensions, we, too, poor fools who have hitherto known no better than to shoot our brothers, why we have only to make a right about face towards these plumed and decorated personages who are so good as to command us, to see a ghastly pallor overspread their faces.

Aye, all of us together, we who suffer and are insulted daily, we are a multitude whom no one can number, we are the ocean that can embrace and swallow up all else. When we have but the will to do it, that very moment will justice be done: that very instant the tyrants of the earth shall bite the dust.

Pyotr Kropotkin, "An Appeal to the Young," 1880

Contents

Part 3 Social Themes

Chapter 9 The Class Character and Popular Impact of the Broad Anarchist Tradition   271

Chapter 10 Anarchist Internationalism and Race, Imperialism, and Gender   297

Chapter 11 Conclusion to Volume 1 and Prologue to Volume 2   347

Preface

Stuart Christie

To use the metaphor of plant life, the seeds of anarchism have been around since time immemorial, but the plant itself—the ideas and the movement as we understand them today—first germinated in September 1869 during the fourth general congress of the First International in Basel, in Switzerland. They quickly began to spread, take root and bloom in towns, cities and villages across Europe, the Americas and, later, throughout Asia and into Africa. The most immediate manifestations of this were the Lyons uprising of September 1870 and the Paris Commune of March 1871.

The subsequent 138 years of the movement's history have been characterised by egalitarian dreams, the pursuit of justice, and a never-ending propagandistic cultural and educational activity punctuated by violent and nonviolent direct actions, strikes, insurrections, and aborted and frustrated revolutions.

This anarchist presence in political and social life has not gone unnoticed. Since that first meeting in Basel, anarchists have acquired a reputation for honesty, integrity, selflessness, sacrifice, and struggle. Anarchism's enemies, on the right and on the left, highlight, in contrast, the anarchists' so-called "easy" recourse to assassinations and other dramatic headline-grabbing direct actions, with exaggerated, black-and-white images that have influenced historians, media commentators, and politicians.

Since those early days, the red and black flag of anarchism has been—and continues to be—followed by varied and wide sections of the population. Some historians, such as the Marxist Eric Hobsbawm, believe this is something rather abnormal and atypical. "Normality," in their view, is that the "scientific doctrine" the proletariat needed was Marxist "socialism"; what they found "abnormal" was the extent to which anarchism and its offshoot, syndicalism, had succeeded in putting down roots in some of the most industrial and modern cities in Europe, cities such as Barcelona, and elsewhere, working-class strongholds where Marxist and parliamentary socialism never achieved striking success. In fact, in electoral terms, of all the cities in Western Europe it was only in Germany that an influential mass socialist party managed to consolidate itself.

Anarchism and anarcho-syndicalism are by no means "exceptional" or "extraordinary" phenomena in the history of political-social movements; it was only after the First World War with the co-option or seduction of "socialist" trade unionism and "socialist" parties into the parliamentary political system that—with the notable exceptions like Spain, Argentina, and Sweden—the influence of anti-political, anti-statist, and direct-action oriented revolutionary syndicalism began to fade elsewhere in the world.

Even though anarchism and anarcho-syndicalism have proved less stable and robust than anarchists could have hoped for—characterised as they have been by both chronological and geographical discontinuity—they nevertheless still bloom when and where least expected. Often disappearing from view and written off by historians such as George Woodcock, they then reappear, unannounced, with explosions of protest.

The present work, however, is neither obituary nor panegyric; it is the first of a two-volume critical analysis of the ongoing evolution of anarchist ideas and movements, the social project for freedom and how best to transform and organise a coercion-free future society based on the principles of communitarianism, direct democracy—and consistency between means and ends.

Nor is it an anthology of anarchist writings or a history of libertarian movements; it is an attempt to define anarchism within the framework of classical Marxism, economic liberalism, and the ideas of P. J. Proudhon, and assess the impact—or not—of these anarchist and syndicalist ideas, and rethink ways to implement these ideas and practices in the global economy of the twenty-first century.

The work is not only an invaluable reference source, it is thought-provoking, insightful and encyclopaedic in scope, synthesizing as it does, a global history of the movement and the ideas which drive it, while at the same time challenging, constructively, many commonly-held views and misconceptions about anarchism and revolutionary syndicalism.

Stuart Christie is a Scottish anarchist journalist, writer, and translator, born in 1946, who has been active in the movement since the age of sixteen. Having hitchhiked into fascist Spain in 1964 with the intention of assassinating dictator Francisco Franco, Christie and accomplice Fernando Carballo Blanco were arrested. Christie was found in possession of explosives and faced grim execution by garrote, but he was freed three years later after an international campaign for his release by the likes of Jean-Paul Sartre. Back in Britain, he helped reestablish the Anarchist Black Cross for the support of political prisoners in Spain and elsewhere—one of the movement's longest-surviving initiatives—and the journal *Black Flag*. In 1972, he was acquitted of involvement in the Angry Brigade's sabotage campaign after one of the longest criminal trials in British history. He went on to found Cienfuegos Press and later Christie Books, and remains an active militant contributing to the broader anarchist movement.

Acknowledgments

In any project of this sort, the authors are fundamentally indebted to the aid, advice, ideas, information, encouragement, and help of a wide range of people. We would like to acknowledge and thank all of those who made this work possible in numerous ways over the many years we have been at work. Particular thanks go to Shelomi Augustine and Nicole Ulrich. We also want to express our gratitude to Bert Altena, Ann Beech, Jon Bekken, Harald Beyer-Arnesen, S. B., Phil Bonner, Toby Boraman, Wilstar Choongo, Laura Cibelli, François Coquet, Martín Dalto, José Antonio Gutierrez Dantón, Colin Darch, Allison Drew, Acracia Fernandez, Andrew Flood, Allison Drew, Marianne Enckell, Brahim Fillali, Shane Freeman, João Friere, Rául Gatica, Antony Gorman, Jack Grancharoff, Rochelle Gunter, Joni Gunter, Ken Haley, Nick Heath, Steve Hirsch, Martin Howard, Dongyoun Hwang, Jon Hyslop, Mieke Ijzermans, Kadoya Shiomi, Reza Kalani, Brenda Keen, Ilham Khuri-Makdisi, Sam Mbah, Iain McKay, Nestor McNab, Juan Carlos Mechoso, Nelson Méndez, Marie-Christine Mikhaïlo, Mitch Miller, Frank Mintz, Mandy Moussouris, Chuck Munson, Leny Olivera, Jonathon Payn, Barry Pateman, James Pendlebury, Payman Piedar, Henk Poeze, Joni Purmonen, Peter Rachleff, Antti Rautianen, Hartmut Rubner, Sal Salerno, Ilan Shalif, James Sotros, Wayne Thorpe, Reiner Torsdoff, Matthew Turner, and Marcel van der Linden. Several institutions have played a major role as well, and we extend our gratitude to the Centre for International Research on Anarchism, the Institute for Anarchist Studies, the International Institute of Social History, the Kate Sharpley Library, and the University of the Witwatersrand, with special thanks to all the staff at the University's Inter-Library Loans section. Finally, we would like to thank Charles Weigl of AK Press for making this project a reality. We are, of course, solely responsible for any errors, and we do not claim that those who aided or inspired us necessarily endorse all of our claims or interpretations.

Mikhail Bakunin (1814–1876)

Russian émigré, international revolutionary and key figure in the emergence of anarchism and syndicalism in the First International. A profound thinker and tireless, skilled activist, his reputation has suffered from an unsympathetic historiography, but he laid the foundations of the broad anarchist movement with his emphasis on a disciplined core of militants providing the leadership of ideas within trade unions and other mass working-class organisations.

Picture courtesy of the International Institute of Social History

Lucy Parsons (1853–1942)

Life-long American anarchist activist, a founder of the International Working People's Association, activist in the syndicalist movement in Chicago in the 1880s, and a co-founder of the Industrial Workers of the World in 1905. Lucy Parsons was buried in Waldheim Cemetery near her husband, Albert Parsons. Albert Parsons, a leading figure in the first wave of syndicalism in the 1870s and 1880s, was one of the Haymarket anarchists executed in 1887.

CHAPTER 1

Introduction

Let's start this book with a few sketches. From September 6 to 12, 1869, seventy-five delegates gathered in Basel, Switzerland, for the fourth general congress of the International Workingmen's Association, better known as the First International. Representing working-class organisations in Austria, Belgium, Britain, Germany, France, Italy, Spain, Switzerland, and the United States, they came out in favor of the common ownership of property. Prominent among the delegates was Mikhail Bakunin, a Russian émigré and revolutionary whose name was legendary across Europe.

On November 11, 1887, four men—unionists and activists—were hanged in Chicago, Illinois. Mounting the scaffold, August Spies declared, "There will come a time when our silence will be more powerful than the voices you are strangling today!" Half a million people filled the funeral cortége, a crowd of twenty thousand surged around the cemetery, and May Day was adopted as an international day of remembrance for the Chicago martyrs and their fight for an eight-hour day.

On June 19, 1918, a mainly African crowd of several thousand people gathered on Market Square in Johannesburg, South Africa, in the shadow of the mine dumps that girdle the city. Addressed by African and white radicals, the crowd roared its approval for proposals for a general strike for a one-shilling-a-day pay rise. Although the strike was called off at the last moment, several thousand African miners came out and clashed with armed police.

In 1923, in the wake of the chaos following the Great Kantō Earthquake, the union militant Ōsugi Sakae, the activist Itō Noe and a six-year-old relative were arrested by the military police in Tokyo. They were beaten to death, and several days later their bodies were found in a well.

On July 18, 1936, Spanish generals announced the formation of a military government. When troops moved into position in Barcelona, they were confronted by armed workers' patrols and immense crowds, and were overwhelmed. Within a few months, millions of acres of land and thousands of industrial enterprises were under the direct control of workers and peasants.

In October 1968, a quarter of a million workers and students gathered on the great plaza in Mexico City in antigovernment protests. Addressing the crowd, a speaker attacked the regime of Gustavo Díaz Ordazo and invoked the memory of the famed Mexican revolutionary Ricardo Flores Magón, who died in 1922 in

5

a Kansas prison: "Was Flores Magón a sell-out?" Two hundred and fifty thousand voices shouted back "No!" Later, helicopters and troops moved against the crowd, leaving hundreds of dead in their wake.

The calm of quiet Seattle in the United States is shattered on November 30, 1999, when hundreds of thousands of activists, environmentalists, protesters, and unionists arrived to contest the opening of the World Trade Organisation conference. The sea of humanity forced the cancellation of the World Trade Organisation's opening ceremonies, and millions of viewers worldwide witnessed the escalation of the demonstrations into dramatic confrontations. By the end of "N30," a state of civil emergency was declared; by the next morning the city resembled an armed camp.

What do these sketches have in common? What binds figures like Bakunin, Spies, Ōsugi, and Flores Magón together, and links the First International, the martyrs of Chicago, the revolutionary unionists of Tokyo, the militants in Johannesburg and Mexico City, the revolutionaries of Barcelona, and many of the protesters in Seattle? They are all part of the story of the broad anarchist tradition—influenced by the tradition that forms the subject of our two volumes.

"Anarchism" is often wrongly identified as chaos, disorganisation, and destruction. It is a type of socialism, and is against capitalism and landlordism, but it is also a *libertarian* type of socialism. For anarchism, individual freedom and individuality are extremely important, and are best developed in a context of democracy and equality. Individuals, however, are divided into classes based on exploitation and power under present-day systems of capitalism and landlordism. To end this situation it is necessary to engage in class struggle and revolution, creating a free socialist society based on common ownership, self-management, democratic planning from below, and production for need, not profit. Only such a social order makes individual freedom possible.

The state, whether heralded in stars and stripes or a hammer and sickle, is part of the problem. It concentrates power in the hands of the few at the apex of its hierarchy, and defends the system that benefits a ruling class of capitalists, landlords, and state managers. It cannot be used for revolution, since it only creates ruling elites—precisely the class system that anarchists want to abolish. For anarchists the new society will be classless, egalitarian, participatory, and creative, all features incompatible with a state apparatus.

Now, "every anarchist is a socialist, but not every socialist is an anarchist."[1] Since its emergence, socialism has been divided into two main tendencies: libertarian socialism, which rejects the state and hierarchy more generally; and political socialism, which advocates "a political battle against capitalism waged through ... centrally organised workers' parties aimed at seizing and utilising State power to usher in socialism."[2] Anarchism is an example of the first strand; classical Marxism is an example of revolutionary political socialism, while social democracy stands for a peaceful and gradual political socialism.

For anarchism it is a struggle by the working class and peasantry—the "popular classes"—that can alone fundamentally change society. These two groups constitute the great majority of humanity, and are the only ones with a basic interest in changing society as well as the power to do so. The emancipation of the popular classes—and consequently, the creation of a free society and the emancipation of all human beings—must be undertaken by those classes, themselves. Struggles against the economic, social, and political injustices of the present must be waged from below by "ordinary" people, organised democratically, and outside of and against the state and mainstream political parties.

In stressing individual freedom, and believing that such freedom is only realised through cooperation and equality, anarchism emphasises the need to organise the popular classes in participatory and democratic movements, and the significance of direct action. It is critical to build movements that are able to develop a counterpower to confront and supplant the power of the ruling class and the state. At the same time, it is essential to create a revolutionary popular counterculture that challenges the values of class society with a new outlook based on democracy, equality, and solidarity.

The most important strand in anarchism has, we argue, always been syndicalism: the view that unions—built through daily struggles, a radically democratic practice, and popular education—are crucial levers of revolution, and can even serve as the nucleus of a free socialist order. Through a revolutionary general strike, based on the occupation of workplaces, working people will be able to take control of production and reorient it toward human need, not profit. Syndicalism envisages a radically democratic unionism as prefiguring the new world, and aims to organise across borders and in promotion of a revolutionary popular counterculture. It rejects bureaucratic styles of unionism as well as the notion that unions should only concern themselves with economic issues or electing prolabour political parties.

There are many debates and differences within anarchism and syndicalism, but there are core ideas that are sufficiently coherent to be thought of as a shared "broad anarchist tradition." While the tradition shares common principles and aims, it is characterised by wide diversity, and major debates over tactics, strategies, and the features of the future society. To struggle in the present, learn from the past, and create the future, anarchism invokes rationalism, critical thinking, and science, and couples it with a passion for justice and for the creation of one world and a universal human community, free of economic and social inequalities and hierarchies.

The broad anarchist tradition stresses class, but this should not be mistaken for a crude workerism that fetishises male factory workers in heavy boots and hardhats. The working class and peasantry are understood in expansive terms: the working class includes all wageworkers who lack control of their work, whether employed in agriculture, industry, or services, including casual and informal workers as well as their families and the unemployed; the peasantry includes all small farmers who are subject to the control and exploitation of other classes, including sharecroppers and labour tenants.

The stress on class also does not mean a narrow focus on economic issues. What characterises the broad anarchist tradition is not economism but a concern with struggling against the many injustices of the present. As the popular classes are international, multinational, and multiracial, anarchism is internationalist, underscoring common class interests worldwide, regardless of borders, cultures, race, and sex. For anarchists, a worker in Bangalore has more in common with a worker in Omsk, Johannesburg, Mexico City, or Seoul than with the Indian elite. Karl Marx's ringing phrase "Working men of all countries, unite!" is taken in its most literal and direct sense.

To create a world movement requires, in turn, taking seriously the specific problems faced by particular groups like oppressed nationalities, races, and women, and linking their struggles for emancipation to the universal class struggle. There is a powerful anti-imperialist, antimilitarist, antiracist, and feminist impulse—"feminist" in the sense of promoting women's emancipation—in the broad anarchist tradition, all within a class framework.

Our Project

We want to look at the ideas and history of the broad anarchist tradition since it initially emerged. It is a tradition rich in ideas, and one that has had an enormous impact on the history of working-class and peasant movements as well as the Left more generally. While the broad anarchist tradition has received more attention in recent years due to the prominent role of anarchists in the "antiglobalisation" movement and the rebirth of significant syndicalist union currents, its ideas and history are not well known today. In many cases, a proper appreciation of the ideas and activities of the movement have been obscured by unsympathetic scholarship and media, but the problem goes deeper than that. Even sympathetic accounts often misunderstand the core ideas and underestimate the historical reach of the broad anarchist tradition.

In our two volumes, we will undertake several key tasks: challenging many commonly held views about anarchism and syndicalism, reexamining the ideas of the broad anarchist tradition, and synthesising a global history of the movement. In doing this, we are motivated in part by a concern with demonstrating that an understanding of the role of anarchism and syndicalism is indispensable to the understanding modern history. It is simply not possible to adequately understand the history of, for instance, unions in Latin America or peasant struggles in East Asia without taking anarchism and syndicalism seriously. The history of the broad anarchist tradition is an integral—but often forgotten—part of popular and socialist history. Besides, it is a fascinating body of thought and history.

The first volume concentrates on several main areas. First, it defines anarchism and outlines its main ideas, developing the case that anarchism is a form of revolutionary and libertarian socialism that initially arises within the First International. This volume then examines the relationship between anarchism and other ideas, particularly the views of Pierre-Joseph Proudhon (1809–1865), the classical Marxists, and economic liberalism. Third, it explores the relationship between anarchism and syndicalism. It then looks at the major strategic and tactical debates in the movement. Next, the first volume discusses some of the major historical themes in the history of that tradition, such as its class character, along with its role in union, peasant, community, unemployed, national liberation, women's emancipation, and racial equality struggles. Sixth, it argues that the broad anarchist tradition was an international movement that cannot be adequately understood through the focus on Western anarchism that typifies most existing accounts. And finally, it suggests that an understanding of the broad anarchist tradition can play an important part in informing progressive struggles against contemporary neoliberalism.

We reject the view that figures like William Godwin (1756–1836), Max Stirner (1806–1856), Proudhon, Benjamin Tucker (1854–1939), and Leo Tolstoy (1828–1910) are part of the broad anarchist tradition. Likewise, we reject the notion that anarchist currents can be found throughout history: the anarchist movement only emerged in the 1860s, and then as a wing of the modern labour and socialist movement. If we exclude Godwin and the others, for reasons that will become apparent, we include under the rubric of the broad anarchist tradition syndicalists like Daniel De Leon (1852–1914), James Connolly (1868–1916), and William "Big Bill" Haywood (1869–1928). The key figures in defining anarchism and syndicalism were, however, Bakunin (1814–1876), and Pyotr Kropotkin (1842–1921).

The broad anarchist tradition was profoundly influenced by both Proudhon and Marx, but its outlook went far beyond the ideas and aims of both, was centred on an internationalist politics that sought to address a wide range of social issues in a class framework, and was historically primarily a movement of the working class even if peasants also played an important role. If we pay a great deal of attention to syndicalism in our work, it is because syndicalism is central to the story of the broad anarchist tradition. When we speak of syndicalism, we mean a revolutionary union movement capable of a wide range of tactics and actions: syndicalism should not be narrowed down to the politics of forming brand-new unions, for many syndicalist unions were created through capturing and revolutionising existing unions.

Contrary to the view that anarchism was "never more than a minority attraction," the poor cousin of other Left traditions, we demonstrate that mass anarchist and syndicalist movements emerged in a number of regions, notably parts of Europe, the Americas, and East Asia.[3] Having laid out this framework in this volume, we turn in volume 2 to developing a global history of the broad anarchist tradition. Volume 1 looks at the class politics that fuels the black flame of the broad anarchist tradition, and examines how that flame was lit. Volume 2 explores the global fire of anarchist and syndicalist struggles over the last 150 years.

Throughout both volumes, we use a basic distinction between principles (the core ideas of the broad anarchist tradition), strategies (broad approaches to implementing the anarchist agenda), and tactics (short-term choices made to implement strategy). What we aim to do in the two volumes is, in short, to weave together a story and an analysis that examines the politics of the broad anarchist tradition, discusses the lives and struggles of anarchists and syndicalists as well as their movements, and demonstrates the historical importance of the broad anarchist tradition.

Beyond Capitalism: History, Neoliberalism, and Globalisation

We are also influenced by the view that the 150-year history of anarchism and syndicalism is of interest to many people in the world of today—a world marked, on the one hand, by appalling injustices, gross inequalities, and political hypocrisies, and on the other hand, by millions of people looking for an alternative. What exists now will one day be history; it is the duty of those who long for something better to make sure that the future is an improvement on the present. The dismal record of the old East bloc regimes, the decline of the welfare state, and the economic and environmental crises afflicting the world complicate the search for alternatives.

The 1990s' mantra "There Is No Alternative" to neoliberal capitalism has, in the wake of Seattle and other struggles, been replaced by the more optimistic slogan "Another World Is Possible." But what type of world, and how is it to be created? We believe that the ideas and history of the broad anarchist tradition have much to contribute to progressive movements in the years to come. A multiracial and international movement with a profound feminist impulse, a movement with an important place in union, worker, and rural struggles, prizing reason over superstition, justice over hierarchy, self-management over state power, international solidarity over nationalism, a universal human community over parochialism and separatism—anarchism and syndicalism is this, and much more.

The twenty-first century is a world of extremes. One of its most striking features is a spiralling increase in inequality between and within countries. In 1996, the combined wealth of the world's 358 richest people, all billionaires, was equal to the total income of 45 percent of the world's population, around 2.3 billion people.[4] The share of world income held by the top 20 percent rose from 70 percent in 1960 to 85 percent in 1991.[5] The United States, the most powerful state and industrial economy in history, has a higher level of inequality than struggling Nigeria, and income inequality is at its highest since the 1920s.[6] Wealth is overwhelmingly concentrated in the hands of a few, with the top 1 percent having an income equal to that of the bottom 40 percent; "America has a higher *per capita* income than other advanced countries ... mainly because our rich are much richer."[7] The collapse of the centrally planned economies in the old East bloc saw the number of people in these regions living in extreme poverty shoot up from 14 to 168 million.[8] Inequality has deepened in Asia and Latin America (with 350 million in abject poverty in China alone).[9] And most of Africa is marginalised from the world economy, with average incomes lower than in colonial times.[10]

In 1996, almost a billion people were either unemployed or underemployed worldwide; the unemployment was highest in the agromineral and semi-industrial countries, but many highly industrialised economies had unemployment rates over 10 percent.[11] Enormous pressures on the peasantry, particularly the evolution of landlords into agricultural capitalists, had led to massive and unprecedented urbanisation; for the first time, the world's population is now predominantly urban. At least a third of the world's three billion urban dwellers currently live in slums, with perhaps 250,000 slums worldwide, and it is estimated that by 2020, half of the total urban population might live in severe poverty on a "Planet of Slums."[12] The modern working class has grown enormously, becoming the largest single class in history, in part due to the industrialisation of large parts of Eastern Europe and Russia, East Asia, Southern Africa, and Latin America. There are at present more industrial workers in South Korea alone than there were in the entire world when Marx and Friedrich Engels wrote *The Communist Manifesto* in 1848, and industrial workers are only one part of the working class.[13] With perhaps two billion members, the working class is now arguably the largest single class in human history.[14]

Underlying the growing class divisions is a larger set of processes of international restructuring. From the 1930s to the 1970s, the world could be fairly neatly divided into three main zones: the "First World" of advanced capitalism, based increasingly on mixed economies and the Keynesian welfare state; a "Second World" of centrally planned command economies that described itself as "socialist"; and the "Third World," comprising much of the former colonial world, where policies of import-substitution industrialisation and closed economies, promoted by nationalist and populist regimes, held sway. Starting in the mid-1970s, and gathering momentum in the 1980s and 1990s, all regions of the world began to converge around a single model of capitalist accumulation, known as neoliberalism.

Drawing directly on the free market ideas of classical and neoclassical economics pioneered by Adam Smith—that is, the tradition of economic liberalism— neoliberals argued that the relentless pursuit of profit would create growing economies as well as free and equitable societies.[15] In other words, crude self-interest could, through a free market, create major social benefits. There had to be a strong and lean state, able to enforce law and order as well as property rights, prevent monopoly, issue currency, and deal with externalities and public goods where necessary, but there was no place for restrictions like minimum wages, extensive welfare systems, price controls, progressive taxation, state-provided old-age homes, strong unions, and so forth.[16] In the context of a global economic crisis starting in the 1970s, the increasing integration of different national economies, and a crisis of the Left arising from the decline of the East bloc and the inability of social democracy and import-substitution industrialisation to restore economic growth, neoliberalism became a dominant economic policy model worldwide.

That such policies—variously known as economic rationalism, monetarism, shock therapy, Reaganomics, Thatcherism, and structural adjustment—should increase inequality is hardly surprising: they are associated with the casualisation of labour, the commodification and privatisation of public goods and natural resources, free trade and deindustrialisation, the expansion of transnational corporations including agrobusinesses, rising unemployment, and substantial cutbacks in state-provided services, all creating, in Pierre Bourdieu's words, a "utopia of endless exploitation."[17]

The importance of the broad anarchist tradition, in this context, is clear. It is striking to observe that no coherent radical, popular alternative to neoliberalism has yet emerged. The impact of neoliberalism on the popular classes, and the massive social polarisation along with the vast growth of the working class and the urban population with which it is associated, might be expected to lead to widespread class struggles and a radical, even revolutionary popular politics. This has not taken place. From the start, neoliberalism attracted popular opposition: the anti-International Monetary Fund (IMF) "riots" of Africa and Latin America in the 1980s, the Zapatista uprising in Mexico in 1994, the mass strikes in France and elsewhere in the years that followed, and the antiglobalisation movement that captured the public consciousness in 1999 in Seattle. Such protests demonstrate growing disenchantment with the current state of the world, and increasingly show a visceral opposition to capitalism unseen in decades, but they have not been linked to a systematic project to replace neoliberalism or the capitalism that underlies it with a different social order.

In many cases, for "the moment at least, the agenda is one of reform rather than revolution."[18] Struggles in Africa against the structural adjustment programmes designed by both the IMF and World Bank in the 1980s and 1990s, for example, rejected neoliberal measures and their effects, but focused their attention on demands for parliamentary democracy. But while the movements had a good deal of success in winning political reforms, they never had much in the way of a socially transformative politics; their concern was winning a framework for democratic debate, yet they did not have real positions to articulate within that framework. All too often, the popular movements, headed in many cases by unions, ended up electing new parties to office on vague platforms—parties that, in practice, simply continued to implement the neoliberal agenda.

The collapse of much of the former Second World, the East bloc, offers a partial explanation for the lack of substance to a popular politics. These developments shook a whole generation that identified socialism with the Soviet model. At the same time, social democracy suffered a severe blow from the manifest inability of Keynesian welfare states to restore economic growth, reduce unemployment, or effectively finance welfare, and most social democratic parties drifted toward neoliberalism by the 1990s. Across the postcolonial world, the import-substitution model began to crumble from the 1970s on; unable to deliver jobs and a modicum of welfare, the old nationalist and populist regimes either collapsed, or else embraced structural adjustment and the IMF.

In short, the statist politics that had dominated the popular classes from the 1930s to the 1970s proved unable to resolve the international economic crisis. The era of neoliberalism was associated with the rapid integration of economies across the world, and this underlay the second failure of the old approaches: the reliance on the state management of relatively closed economies. Central planning, the Western welfare state, and import-substitution industrialisation were all singularly ill-suited to deal with an increasingly globalised capitalism. In a memorable paper, the conservative writer Francis Fukuyama described the period after the collapse of USSR as the "end of history," the "unabashed victory of economic and political liberalism," and "the end point of mankind's ideological evolution." There are numerous problems with his analysis, but it cannot seriously be disputed that the 1990s were characterised by a "total exhaustion of viable systematic alternatives to Western liberalism."[19] The older left and nationalist projects were no longer desirable nor feasible.

The enabling state was crippled, its alternatives to liberal economics were found wanting, and as a result, popular opposition to neoliberal politics remained unable to effectively confront the neoliberal order. On the one hand, the crisis of popular progressive politics has enabled the neoliberal agenda to continually accelerate; an effective radical politics may have been able to fundamentally disrupt the neoliberal agenda from its inception. On the other hand, it has meant that anti-neoliberal struggles tend to be primarily defensive, directed against the effects of neoliberalism, rather than addressing its causes and developing an effective, lasting solution. These struggles thus tend to be limited, sporadic, and at best sidetracked into moderate (if important) reforms that do not stop neoliberalism, such as prodemocracy movements.

For all their limitations, the prodemocracy movements of Africa, Asia, and Latin America as well as post-1999 East Europe are at least broadly progressive in outlook. The dark side of the general crisis of progressive popular politics has been the frighteningly rapid rise of mass right-wing nationalist and religious movements, like Christian and Hindu fundamentalism, radical Islam, and neofascism. Antidemocratic, antimodern, and antisecular in orientation, these movements can deliver nothing but endless ethnic and racial conflicts, authoritarian regimes, and an epoch of reaction comparable to the darkest years of the mid-twentieth century. Their rise is made possible precisely by the collapse of progressive alternatives; that some self-declared leftists can defend and even work with these reactionary currents, describing them as "anti-imperialist," is itself a sign of the climate of the Left's crisis.

It is here that the broad anarchist tradition can make a real contribution. It provides a rich repertoire of ideas and actions that are particularly appropriate to the present period. For one thing, it can play a key role in the renewal of the socialist project. That the East bloc model failed in many respects is no longer widely disputed on the Left. It was not democratic, egalitarian, or emancipatory; looking back, there can be little doubt that it was based on a class system enforced by ongoing repression. It does not follow, however, that capitalism, particularly in its neoliberal form, offers anything better, that it is capable of solving the massive social problems that confront humanity—alienation, inequality, injustice, and poverty—or that it can avert the terrible spectre of the planet of slums.

Taking the great promises of the Enlightenment (egalitarianism, individual freedom and democracy, rationalism and progress) seriously, and providing an analysis, strategy, and tactics to realize that promise, the broad anarchist tradition can make many contributions to the current impasse of peasant and working-class movements. The broad anarchist tradition emerged as a movement of the peasantry and working class, as mentioned earlier, and there is much that contemporary struggles against neoliberalism can learn from an examination of its ideas and history. Without a progressive Left alternative, contemporary struggles against neoliberalism will inevitably be unable to fundamentally challenge the capitalist system that gave rise to neoliberalism.

By rejecting the "frequent assumption that revolutionary Socialism is by and large covered by the term 'Marxism-Leninism,'" it becomes possible to rediscover alternative, libertarian socialist traditions like anarchism and syndicalism.[20] To "recall anarchism, which Leninist Marxism suppressed," Arif Dirlik contends, is to rethink the meaning and possibilities of the socialist tradition, and "recall the democratic ideals for which anarchism ... served as a repository."[21] In a world where nationalism and racial prejudice seem endemic, not least among many on the Left, the consistent internationalism of the broad anarchist tradition is worthy of rediscovery as well.

This means a rediscovery of libertarian socialism more generally. Social democracy, or parliamentary socialism, the moderate wing of political socialism associated with bodies like the Labour Party in Britain and the Socialist Party in France, aimed at a "piecemeal settlement by means of organisation and legislation" rather than "universal, instantaneous and violent expropriation."[22] It embraced John Maynard Keynes's theory of managed capitalism from the 1930s onward and was associated with the implementation of comprehensive welfare states in Western countries. Yet economic globalisation, declining economic growth, and a drive by the ruling classes to implement neoliberalism have undermined the basis for the social democratic reforms of the post–World War II era: an economic boom able to fund redistribution, a closed economy that could be managed on Keynesian lines, and a ruling class willing to make major concessions to the popular classes. By the 1990s, social democratic parties had for the most part embraced neoliberalism.

Finally, it is worth noting that the "glorious period" of anarchism and syndicalism from the mid-1890s to the mid-1920s took place in an earlier phase of globalisation, marked by high levels of international economic integration and free trade, immigration, rapid advances in telecommunications and transport, and the rise of supranational institutions, including early transnational corporations.[23] This is a period distant in time, but in many ways not so different from the twenty-first-century world of neoliberalism, and the ways in which the broad anarchist tradition responded to this earlier period of globalisation speak directly to current antiglobalisation concerns, particularly when the statist approaches that have dominated much of the twentieth century have been found so very wanting.

Rethinking the Broad Anarchist Tradition

There has been a resurgence of syndicalism following the reestablishment of the anarcho-syndicalist National Confederation of Labour (CNT) in Spain in 1977, and a rapid growth of anarchism in the 1990s, notably in the contemporary antiglobalisation movement, where it provided the main pole of attraction for many.[24] By 2004, the syndicalist General Confederation of Labour (CGT) in Spain represented nearly two million workers in terms of that country's industrial relations system.[25]

Even so, syndicalism and anarchism are not always taken seriously, and are often misunderstood. In this book, we reject the view that the broad anarchist tradition is an atavistic throwback to the precapitalist world, and argue that it was a response to the rise of capitalism and the modern state, that its origins were as recent as the 1860s, and that it emerged within and was an integral part of modern socialist and working-class movements. We also challenge the view that any philosophy or movement that is hostile to the state, or in favour of individual freedom, can be characterised as anarchist. Anarchism is part of the libertarian wing of socialism, and dates back to the First International, which lasted from 1864 to 1877. If classical Marxism had Marx and Engels, anarchism and syndicalism were above all shaped by two towering figures, Bakunin and Kropotkin.

We take issue with the common view that anarchism "became a mass movement in Spain to an extent that it never did elsewhere."[26] This is the common "Spanish exceptionalism" argument. Mass movements in the broad anarchist tradition developed in many countries, and the Spanish movement was by no means the largest. The twentieth-century Spanish syndicalist unions, which represented only half of organised Spanish labour, when considered in relation to the size of the working class and the organised labour movement, were *smaller* than movements in Argentina, Brazil, Chile, Cuba, France, Mexico, Peru, Portugal, and Uruguay, where the broad anarchist tradition dominated almost the entire labour movement.

Justifying his pioneering research on anarchism in the early 1960s, James Joll suggested that it was a mistake to think "it is the causes which triumph that alone should interest the historian."[27] What we assert is that there were many moments of "triumph" for the broad anarchist tradition, and it is a mistake to assume that anarchism was always the poor cousin of socialist traditions like classical Marxism and social democracy. The thesis of "Spanish exceptionalism" took Western Europe and North America as its point of comparison, but ignored many important movements in these areas, as well as elsewhere, thereby diverting a great deal of energy into trying to explain a "Spanish" peculiarity that did not exist.[28]

Social Base and Global Reach

Rather than see the broad anarchist tradition as an expression of some sort of vague yearning, "a timeless struggle," we stress its novelty and relatively recent roots.[29] Against the view that anarchism was "not a coherent political or philosophical movement," and was full of "contradictions and inconsistencies," without a "fixed body of doctrine based on one particular world view," we stress the coherence of its ideas.[30] And crucially, an opposition to capitalism and landlordism, and a politics of class struggle, is integral to anarchism and syndicalism: the state is certainly a target of the anarchist critique, but views that hold that anarchists see the state as "responsible for all inequality and injustice," or "as the root of all evil," seriously distort the anarchist position, and purge it of its socialist content and origins.[31] The notion of "anarcho-capitalism," used by some writers, is a contradiction in terms.[32]

In place of the stereotype of anarchism as a movement and secular religion for a petty bourgeoisie of artisans and peasants ruined by modernity, "social classes that were out of tune with the dominant historical trend," "thrust aside by ... industrial progress," and "threatened" by "industry and mechanisation," led by ruined aristocrats and composed of declining peasants and craftspeople only rarely "involved in centralisation or industrialisation," and hankering for a premodern past, we demonstrate that the movement was historically based predominantly among the modern working class, or proletariat.[33]

It was, above all, among the urban working class and farm labourers that the broad anarchist tradition found its recruits, and it found them in the millions. Contrary to the common view that syndicalism was a movement comprised of skilled artisans, the syndicalist unions were primarily made up of groups of people like casual and seasonal labourers, dockworkers, farmworkers, factory workers, miners, and railway employees, and to a lesser extent white-collar workers and professionals, notably teachers. Issues of de-skilling and work restructuring played an important role in attracting some to syndicalism, but the movement as a whole drew in a great many unskilled and semiskilled workers.

The broad anarchist tradition also had a significant appeal to the peasantry, and there were large anarchist peasant movements—fighting the power of landlords, rural capitalists, and the state, particularly where rural commercialisation was taking place—but its largest constituency was the working class. Because anarchism did not dismiss the peasantry, peasants were crucial to at least three major attempts at making an anarchist revolution: the Ukrainian Revolution (1917–1921), the Kirin Revolution (1929–1931), and the Spanish Revolution (1936–1939). Anarchists were also a central force in other peasant struggles in eastern and southern Europe, East Asia and Latin America.

In short, the broad anarchist tradition is certainly not a revolt against the modern world by declining classes. It is above all a dynamic, modern, and predominantly working-class movement that seeks to collectivise and self-manage production, and replace the modern state with international self-management. It had a large peasant constituency historically, but even this emerged precisely where capitalism was penetrating and changing the countryside. The broad anarchist tradition is a movement that aims to harness modern technology for human emancipation: it does not, contrary to the stereotype, advocate "crude village communism" or aim to "turn the clock back."[34]

Syndicalism is very much a part of the story of anarchism. Many accounts have presented syndicalism as a movement distinct from—or even hostile to—anarchism. In this vein, many works present Georges Sorel, a retired French engineer and former Marxist, as "the theorist of anarcho-syndicalism," "the leading theorist of Revolutionary Syndicalism," and "syndicalism's foremost theoretician."[35] To the contrary, we demonstrate that syndicalism was always part of the broad anarchist tradition. It is often assumed that syndicalism emerged for the first time in the 1890s in France: we show, however, that it was Bakunin in the 1860s, not Sorel forty years later, who was the key theorist of syndicalism, and that a whole first wave of syndicalism took place in the 1870s and 1880s.

Syndicalism is a *variant* of anarchism, and the syndicalist movement is part of the broad anarchist tradition. This point is applicable to all the main variants of syndicalism: anarcho-syndicalism (which explicitly situates itself within the anarchist tradition), revolutionary syndicalism (which does not make so explicit a connection, due to ignorance or a tactical denial of the link to anarchism), De Leonism (a form of revolutionary syndicalism that claims to be Marxist), and rank-and-file syndicalism (a form of syndicalism that builds independent rank-and-file groups that overlap with, but are independent of, orthodox unions). Syndicalism, in essence, is an anarchist *strategy*, not a rival to anarchism. When we use the term syndicalism without prefixes or qualifications, we use it in an inclusive manner to describe all variants of syndicalism.

Here, it should be stressed, we make the case that the Industrial Workers of the World (the IWW, or "Wobblies"), a radical union current that emerged in 1905 in the United States and spread worldwide, was an integral part of a second wave of syndicalism that started in the 1890s. We specifically reject the notion that the history of the IWW is separate from that of syndicalism, and the view that the IWW arose from endogenous U.S. radical traditions or Marxism.[36] The historical IWW was syndicalist in outlook, drew heavily on the legacy of first-wave syndicalism and the broad anarchist tradition more generally in the United States, and was inspired and influenced by the rebirth of syndicalism elsewhere.

The IWW split in 1908 into two main wings: first, the well-known "Chicago IWW," which was important in the United States, Australia, Chile, and elsewhere, was associated with figures like Haywood, and was strictly opposed to any participation in government elections; and second, the smaller "Detroit IWW," which had an influence in Britain, South Africa, and elsewhere, was associated with De Leon and Connolly, and advocated a conditional use of elections. We argue that both currents were and are syndicalist—and therefore form part of the broad anarchist tradition. That some syndicalists described themselves as Marxists or rejected the anarchist label does not invalidate their place in the broad anarchist tradition; we do not use self-identification but rather ideas as the basis for inclusion in the broad anarchist tradition.

Some of the consequences of these arguments are quite striking and force a rethinking of the canon of the broad anarchist tradition. Following a tradition established by Paul Eltzbacher's *Anarchism: Exponents of the Anarchist Philosophy* published in 1900, the conclusions of which "have been incorporated into almost every study of the subject up to the present day," the standard works on anarchism and syndicalism have spoken of the "Seven Sages" of the movement: Godwin, Stirner, Proudhon, Tucker, Tolstoy, Bakunin, and Kropotkin.[37] For Eltzbacher, these sages could be "taken as equivalent to the entire body of recognised anarchist teachings."[38]

According to Eltzbacher, the sages shared an opposition to the state, for "they negate the State for our future."[39] He was aware that "the negation of the State" had "totally different meanings" for his sages.[40] It nonetheless followed that anyone who held an antistatist position must be an anarchist, even if they disagreed over fundamental issues like the nature of society, law, property, or the means of changing society.[41] This minimalist definition of anarchism overlapped with the tendency of many anarchists and syndicalists to invent myths about their own history. Kropotkin was not alone in constructing an imagined prehistory for the anarchist movement, a supposed genealogy of anarchist ideas and movements that dated back to the antiquity of Asia and Europe.[42] These anarchist narratives, which remain common, centred on listing a range of actors and ideas that purportedly shared the basic concerns of the anarchist movement, ranging from Lao-tzu in ancient China (the founder of Taoism), to late medieval Anabaptists, to Bakunin in nineteenth-century Europe. The aim of such mythmaking was to legitimise anarchism by providing it with a lengthy pedigree, and claiming many famous and respected figures. The most important study from within the movement, Max Nettlau's (1865–1944) nine-volume history of anarchism, spent the first volume dealing with events *before* the 1860s, starting from ancient China and Greece.[43]

There are obvious problems here. If an anarchist is someone who "negates" the state, it is by no means clear how anarchism differs from the most radical economic liberals, like Murray Rothbard, who envisage a stateless society based on private property and an unrestrained free market. Likewise, classical Marxism's ultimate objective is a stateless society without alienation and compulsion. Using Eltzbacher's definition, both Rothbard and Marx could arguably earn a place in the pantheon of anarchist sages; it would be arbitrary to exclude them. In other words, Eltzbacher's definition fails the basic task of clearly delineating anarchism from other ideas and therefore cannot be regarded as adequate.

The tendency to project anarchism onto all of human history has related problems: on the one hand, no serious examination of Lao-tzu, the Anabaptists, and Bakunin can maintain that they shared the same views and goals, so it is not clear why they should be grouped together; and on the other hand, if anarchism is a universal feature of society, then it becomes very difficult indeed to explain *why* it arises, or to place it in its historical context, to delineate its boundaries, and analyse its class character and role at a particular time. To claim that anarchism is universal is a useful legitimising myth for an embattled movement; to take such a claim seriously, however, does little to advance the analysis and activities of that movement. It fails to historicise the broad anarchist tradition, or explain why it arose as well as why it appealed to particular classes.

The obvious temptation is to take refuge in psychological explanations. Peter Marshall, for example, claims that the "first anarchist" was the first person who rebelled against "authority," and that anarchism was rooted in human nature, "a timeless struggle" between "those who wanted to rule and those who refused to be ruled or to rule in turn," premised on a "drive for freedom," a "deeply felt human need."[44] The radical environmentalist and libertarian socialist Murray Bookchin made the same argument, adding a Freudian touch: anarchism is a "great libidinal movement of humanity to shake off the repressive apparatus created by hierarchical society" and originates in the "age-old drive" of the oppressed for freedom.[45]

Yet there is no real evidence for this line of argument, and it fails to explain why anarchism has been significant in some periods and almost entirely absent in others. If anarchism is a human drive, why have its fortunes varied so dramatically over time? Only a historical and social analysis can really explain the rise and fall of anarchism, and this requires recourse to social science, not psychology. The "seven sages" approach that grouped a wide range of thinkers with little in common, and the anarchists' own mythmaking, stunted any analysis of the broad anarchist tradition.

For all of these reasons, we have found it imperative to use a narrower, more clearly delineated, and more historicised and historically accurate understanding of anarchism and syndicalism. Of Eltzbacher's sages, only Bakunin and Kropotkin may be considered anarchists. Godwin, Stirner, and Tolstoy have no place at all in the broad anarchist tradition; Proudhon and his disciple Tucker represented an approach, mutualism, that influenced anarchism profoundly—along with Marxism, Proudhonism provided many ingredients for the broad anarchist tradition—but that cannot truly be called anarchist. There are many libertarian ideas —ideas stressing individual freedom—but not all libertarians are also socialists. It is in the context of the rise of the modern state and capitalism—and concomitantly, the modern working-class and socialist movement—that anarchism first emerged.

By arbitrarily grouping together figures that have, as shown in this book, little in common, as the key thinkers in anarchism, the seven sages approach inevitably creates the impression that anarchism is contradictory as well as unfocused, and renders the theoretical analysis of anarchism a frustrating task at best. This apparent incoherence is the result of a problematic analysis of anarchism, not of the poverty of anarchism itself. A sweeping and loose definition of anarchism tends to group quite different ideas together, and does not historicize anarchism; by presenting anarchism as vague and rather formless, it also makes it difficult to consider how the broad anarchist tradition can inform contemporary struggles against neoliberalism.

What Is the Broad Anarchist Tradition?

Using a narrower definition, we believe we have been able to bring the broad anarchist tradition along with its ideas and history into sharper focus, and thus are able to present a fairly thorough and systematic examination of anarchist and syndicalist ideas, debates, and developments. In our analysis, anarchism is presented as a definite and clear set of positions. In examining the history of the broad anarchist tradition, we likewise sacrifice apparent breadth for real depth. Many accounts spend a great deal of time discussing figures like Stirner, Tolstoy, and the Anabaptists. We regard these people as extraneous and largely irrelevant to an account of the broad anarchist tradition.

Nor do we use terms like "philosophical anarchism" (often used in reference to Godwin), "individualist anarchism" (often used in reference to Stirner, but sometimes also for Proudhon and Tucker), "Christian anarchism" (for Tolstoy), or "lifestyle anarchism" (sometimes used to refer to contemporary forms of individualism), as we do not regard these currents as part of the broad anarchist tradition. The point is not to dismiss other libertarian ideas and the wide range of antiauthoritarian ideas that have developed in many cultures but to suggest that we need to differentiate anarchism and syndicalism from other currents, including libertarian ones, the better to understand both anarchism and these other tendencies. "Class struggle" anarchism, sometimes called revolutionary or communist anarchism, is not a type of anarchism; in our view, it is the *only* anarchism. We are aware that our approach contradicts some long-standing definitions, but we maintain that the meaning of anarchism is neither arbitrary nor just a matter of opinion—the historical record demonstrates that there is a core set of beliefs.

Many writers have drawn a supposed distinction between "anarchist communism ... perhaps the most influential anarchist doctrine" and "another doctrine of comparable significance, anarcho-syndicalism."[46] We reject this approach as a misleading analysis of the broad anarchist tradition. Not only is this alleged distinction absent from the bulk of anarchist writings until recently, but it also simply does not work as a description of different tendencies within the broad anarchist tradition. Moreover, the vast majority of people described in the literature as "anarchist communists" or "anarcho-communists" championed syndicalism, including Kropotkin, Alexander Berkman (1870–1936), Flores Magón, and Shifu. On the other hand, the majority of syndicalists endorsed "anarchist communism" in the sense of a stateless socialist society based on the communist principle of distribution according to need. It is difficult to identify a distinct "anarchist-communist" strategy or tendency that can be applied as a useful category of anarchism.

Insurrectionist Anarchism, Mass Anarchism, and Syndicalism

Instead, we develop a distinction within the broad anarchist tradition between two main strategic approaches, which we call "mass anarchism" and "insurrectionist anarchism." Mass anarchism stresses that only mass movements can create a revolutionary change in society, that such movements are typically built through struggles around immediate issues and reforms (whether concerning wages, police brutality, high prices, and so on), and that anarchists must participate in such movements to radicalise and transform them into levers of revolutionary change. What is critical is that reforms are won *from below*: these victories must be distinguished from reforms applied from above, which undermine popular movements.[47]

The insurrectionist approach, in contrast, claims that reforms are illusory, that movements like unions are willing or unwitting bulwarks of the existing order, and that formal organisations are authoritarian. Consequently, insurrectionist anarchism emphasises armed action—"propaganda by the deed"—as the most important means of evoking a spontaneous revolutionary upsurge. What distinguishes insurrectionist anarchism from mass anarchism is not necessarily violence as such but its place in strategy: for insurrectionist anarchism, propaganda by the deed, carried out by conscious anarchists, is seen as a means of generating a mass movement; for most mass anarchism, violence operates as a means of self-defence for an *existing* mass movement.

This line of argument raises questions about the anarchist canon. Having rejected the seven sages, we do not ourselves develop a new canon, except to suggest that it must centre on Bakunin and Kropotkin, and include key figures from the broad anarchist and syndicalist tradition both within and beyond the West. If Godwin, Stirner, and Tolstoy have no place in the canon, people like Pyotr Arshinov (1887–1937), Juana Belem Gutiérrez de Mendoza (1875-1942), Camillo Berneri (1897–1937), Luisa Capetillo (1880–1922), Connolly, Christian Cornelissen (1864–1942), Voltairine de Cleyre (1866–1912), De Leon, Elizabeth Gurley Flynn (1890–1964), Praxedis Guerrero (1882–1910), Emma Goldman (1869–1940), He Zhen (born He Ban [n.d.]), Petronila Infantes (1920–?), Itō, Kōtoku Shūsui (1893–1911), Li Pei Kan (1904–2005, also known by the pseudonym Ba Jin), Maria Lacerda de Moura (1887–1944), Liu Sifu (1884–1915, also known as Shifu), Errico Malatesta (1853–1932), Flores Magón (1874–1922), Nestor Ivanovich Makhno (1889–1934), Louise Michel (1830–1905), Ferdinand Domela Nieuwenhuis (1861–1919), Ōsugi (1885–1923), Albert Parsons (1848–1887), Lucy Parsons (1853–1942), Fernand Pelloutier (1867–1901), Enrique Roig de San Martín (1843–1889), Juana Rouco Buela (1888–1968), Rudolph Rocker (1873–1958), Lucia Sanchez Saornil (1895–1970), Shin Ch'aeho (1880–1936), and others are all serious candidates as people who made significant intellectual contributions to the movement. This list is not exhaustive, and is only indicative of the possibilities.

Without discounting the importance of the relatively well-known movements of Italy, France, Spain, and the United States, we also believe it necessary to stress the centrality of movements in Asia, Africa, Eastern Europe, Latin America, and the Caribbean, asserting that a truly global history of anarchism and syndicalism provides a crucial corrective to Eurocentric accounts, and demonstrates that the notion that anarchism was "never more than a minority attraction" has little basis in fact.[48] The commonly held thesis of Spanish exceptionalism, and the notion that only in Spain did anarchism become "a major social movement and ... threaten the State," are among the views that are challenged as a result.[49]

At the heart of the mass anarchist tradition is the view that it is necessary to build a popular revolutionary movement—centred on a revolutionary counterculture and the formation of organs of counterpower—in order to lay the basis for a new social order in place of capitalism, landlordism, and the state. Such a movement might engage in struggles around reforms, but it ultimately must aim to constitute the basis of a new society within the shell of the old, an incipient new social order that would finally explode and supersede the old one. Insurrectionist anarchism is impossibilist, in that it views reforms as impossible and futile; mass anarchism is *possibilist*, believing that it is both possible and desirable to win, to *force* reforms from the ruling classes, and that such concessions strengthen rather than undermine popular movements and struggles, and can improve popular conditions. Through direct action, for example, progressive changes in law can be demanded and enforced, without the need for participation in the apparatus of the state.

Syndicalism is a powerful expression of the mass anarchist perspective. Historically, it was above all syndicalism that provided the anarchist tradition with a mass base and appeal. Not all mass anarchists were syndicalists, however. Some were supporters of syndicalism, but with reservations, usually around the "embryo hypothesis": the view that union structures form an adequate basis for a postcapitalist society.[50] There were other mass anarchists who were antisyndicalist, for they did not believe unions could make a revolution. Here we see two main variants: those who rejected the workplace in favour of community struggles, and those who favoured workplace action with some independence from the unions.

Syndicalism is caricatured as a form of economistic or workerist unionism by Marxists like Vladimir Ilyich Lenin and Nicos Poulantzas.[51] However, embedded in larger popular movements and countercultures, linked to other organised popular constituencies, taking up issues that went well beyond the workplace, playing a central role in community struggles, and at the heart of a project of revolutionary counterculture, including the production of mass circulation daily and weekly newspapers, the historical syndicalist unions were social movements that never reduced the working class to wage earners, or the aspirations of the working class to wages. Economism and workerism are particularly inappropriate labels for syndicalism.

The view that insurrection was something that "trade unions seem never to organise" also cannot be reconciled with the history of syndicalism.[52] Syndicalist unions were involved in general strikes that assumed an insurrectionary character in Mexico in 1916; Spain in 1917, 1919, and 1936; Brazil and Portugal in 1918; Argentina in 1919; and Italy in 1920. In many cases syndicalists helped organise workers' militias, including in the United States in the 1880s, Ireland from 1913, Mexico beginning in 1916, Argentina in 1919, Italy in 1920, and Spain from 1936.

Historically, syndicalism was a revolutionary union movement that was part of a larger popular movement of counterpower and counterculture, and care should be taken not to set up an artificial divide between syndicalist unions and the larger anarchist movements of which they formed an integral part. This reminds us that union numbers and formal structures provide only a partial estimate of the impact of anarchism and syndicalism; while we have used these criteria to critique the notion of Spanish exceptionalism, we are mindful that they are limited guides to anarchist and syndicalist strength.

Syndicalism shares many features with the "social movement unionism" that emerged in a number of late industrialising countries like Brazil and South Africa, in that syndicalist movements historically formed alliances beyond the workplace, and raised issues that went well beyond immediate concerns over wages and working conditions, but there are important differences.[53] Like social movement unionism, syndicalism engages struggles both within and beyond the workplace, and also seeks major reforms. Unlike social movement unionism, however, syndicalism is explicitly anticapitalist, antilandlordist, and antistatist, and envisages the union structures as the building blocks of a self-managed, stateless, socialist order. From this perspective, immediate struggles are important in themselves, but also because they contribute to the confidence, organisation, and consciousness of the working class that syndicalists believe is essential to *revolution* from below.

In many cases—not least Brazil and South Africa—social movement unions have allied themselves with mainstream political parties and even engaged in an industrial strategy to help strengthen the "national" economy. Syndicalism, in contrast, typically rejects linkages to such parties, stressing the significance of building popular counterpower outside of and *against* the state apparatus; an industrialisation strategy is not its concern, for a revolutionary workers' movement can take no responsibility for the salvation of capitalism. Strong unions are critical, but that strength is to be measured in terms of the participation and politicisation of the members, and the extent to which the union is able to fight immediate battles and ultimately form the basis for workers' self-management of the means of production. It is not simply a question of numbers.

Organisational Dualism

One of the key debates we discuss in this volume is the question of whether anarchists and syndicalists need political groups dedicated to the promotion of the ideas of the broad anarchist tradition, and if so, what form such groups should take. When the editors of the Paris-based anarchist newspaper *Dielo Truda* ("Workers' Cause") issued the *Organisational Platform of the Libertarian Communists* in 1926, they were met by a storm of controversy.[54] Some anarchists saw the editors' advocacy of a unified anarchist political organisation with collective discipline as an attempt to "Bolshevise" anarchism and accused its primary authors, Arshinov and Makhno, of going over to classical Marxism. We argue, on the contrary, that the *Platform* and "Platformism" were not a break with the anarchist tradition but a fairly orthodox *restatement* of well-established views.

From the time of Bakunin—who was part of the anarchist International Alliance of Socialist Democracy, which operated within the First International—the great majority of anarchists and syndicalists advocated the formation of specific anarchist political groups *in addition* to mass organisations like syndicalist unions.

In other words, most supported organisational dualism: the mass organisation, such as unions, must work in tandem with specifically anarchist and syndicalist political organisations. Moreover, most believed that these groups should have fairly homogeneous principled, strategic, and tactical positions as well as some form of organisational discipline.

War, Gender Issues, and Anti-Imperialism

While the broad anarchist tradition historically tied itself closely to class, it also engaged with questions of social oppression that were not necessarily reducible to class. It was an international movement and an internationalist one: rejecting nationalism and the state, consistently opposing national oppression and racial prejudice, the broad anarchist tradition was at the forefront of attempts to organise the popular classes across the barriers of nationality and race. It developed as a movement with supporters from among almost all the nationalities and races of the world, with organisations across the world, and played a key role in struggles for equal rights and against segregation (for instance, in Cuba, Japan, Mexico, the U.S., and South Africa), in anti-imperialist struggles and national liberation movements (for example, Bulgaria, Cuba, Korea, Macedonia, and the Ukraine), and in opposing militarism and war between peoples and states.

Antimilitarism was a central feature of the history of the broad anarchist tradition, including mass revolts within the major powers against imperialist aggression such as the Japanese occupation of Korea, Manchuria, and China, Spain's colonial wars against Cuba, Morocco, and the Philippines, and Italian attacks on Abyssinia, Libya, and Albania. In 1914, the Labour and Socialist International (also known as the Second International) collapsed with the outbreak of the First World War, with all the major parties supporting the war efforts of their respective states. (The Labour and Socialist International, formed in 1889, was dominated by classical Marxism and social democracy; the key affiliate was the great Marxist bastion of the time, the Social Democratic Party [SDP] of Germany, which Marx and Engels helped found in 1875). Contrary to the view that Lenin alone rallied antiwar opposition, the radical opposition to the war was largely confined to the anarchists and syndicalists.

Gender was another important concern. We admit to a certain discomfort with the tendency of many writers to label women anarchists and syndicalists "anarchist-feminists" or "anarcha-feminists." There is no doubt that women played a critical role in promoting a feminist analysis in anarchism, but it is problematic to assume that women activists in the movement were necessarily feminists or that they should primarily be defined by feminism. The feminist elements of anarchism and syndicalism were neither the exclusive province of women activists, nor should the activities of women activists in the broad anarchist tradition be reduced to an advocacy of a feminist perspective. The broad anarchist tradition, on the whole, championed gender equality, rejected the patriarchal family, and sought a means to link up feminist concerns with the larger project of class struggle and revolution. Anarchists and syndicalists differed among themselves on the implications of women's emancipation, and there were certainly many anarchists and syndicalists whose views and lives contradicted gender equality. The important point is that such equality was a principle of the broad anarchist tradition.

At the same time, anarchist and syndicalist women like Choi Seon-Myoung, Luisa Capetillo, Voltairine de Cleyre, Elizabeth Gurley Flynn, Emma Goldman, He Zhen, Petronila Infantes, Lucy Parsons, and Itō Noe should not be reduced to gender activists. They played a wide range of roles in the movement, as writers, unionists, strike leaders, community organisers, and militia members, and saw themselves as part of a larger movement of the popular classes that crossed gender boundaries. Like their male counterparts, they argued that the class system and other forms of oppression were integrally linked, and that only a universal and unifying popular movement against all domination and exploitation could create a new social order.

Anarchism and Marxism

Finally, the broad anarchist tradition is important as an alternative to the other major revolutionary class-based movement: classical Marxism, also known as Bolshevism, and associated with Marx, Engels, Karl Kautsky, Lenin, Leon Trotsky, Joseph Stalin, Mao Tse-tung, and others. For classical Marxism, the capitalist state must be destroyed, replaced by a revolutionary state, "a political transition period, whose State can be nothing else but *the revolutionary dictatorship of the proletariat*," a "centralised organisation of force, of violence," of "undivided power."[55] This regime would control the means of production and be headed by a revolutionary party. The "revolutionary dictatorship of a proletarian party" was an "objective necessity" due to "the heterogeneity of the revolutionary class."[56] And "without a party, apart from a party, over the head of a party, or with a substitute for a party, the proletarian revolution cannot conquer."[57] A person who refuses to recognise that the "leadership of the Communist Party and the state power of the people's dictatorship" are necessary for revolutionary change "is no communist."[58]

In practice, regardless of the intents or the emancipatory aims of classical Marxism, these politics provided the basic rationale for the one-party dictatorships of the former East bloc. The view that "Marx's socialism was simultaneously anti-statist and anti-market" is rather misleading.[59] There are many tensions and ambiguities in Marx's thought, but the predominant element—and the historical record of Marxism in practice—has been overwhelmingly authoritarian and statist.

The creation of the gulag system in the USSR, which placed tens of millions into concentration camps based on forced labour, was an integral part of the Soviet system, but was probably not part of Marx's plan.[60] The harsh circumstances under which the Russian Revolution and the establishment of the USSR took place obviously also left a profound imprint. The features of the USSR and the later Marxist regimes cannot, then, simply be reduced to Marxist politics.

Yet this does not exonerate classical Marxism from a good deal of responsibility for the oppression and inequities of the old East bloc. Marxist ideology was a central influence on these regimes, and the heavy emphasis that Marx and his successors placed upon the need for a highly centralized state, headed by a communist party, controlling labour and the other forces of production and claiming to be the sole repository of "scientific" truth, was absolutely critical to the evolution of

Marxism in the twentieth century into an ideology of dictatorship after dictatorship. Marx and Marxism cannot be exonerated by attributing the consistently repressive character of Marxism in power to the force of circumstances, or a misreading of Marx's texts by "more or less faithless successors."[61]

The history of Marxism in the third of the world once ruled by Marxist regimes is a part—the major part—of the history of Marxism, and there is a direct link between Marx's strategy of a centralised dictatorship headed by a vanguard party as the agent of revolution and the one-party dictatorships established in Russia, China, and elsewhere. Even Trotsky, a vehement Marxist critic of Stalin, envisaged socialism as "authoritarian leadership ... centralised distribution of the labour force ... the workers' State ... entitled to send any worker wherever his labour may be needed," with dissenters sent to labour camps if necessary.[62] The Communist movement failed to emancipate humanity and discredited socialism for hundreds of millions, and its rise and fall are central to the current problems facing the Left.

By contrast, libertarian socialism always rejected the view that fundamental social transformation could come about through the state apparatus or that socialism could be created from above. Its rejection of capitalism is part of a broader opposition to hierarchy in general, and part of a larger understanding of the freedom and development of the individual as the aim of socialism. Classical Marxism from the beginning was a form of political socialism, but it is crucial to note that there were also libertarian Marxists. These included the council communists Herman Gorter, Anton Pannekoek, and Otto Rühle, who held views close to syndicalism and were openly hostile to Bolshevism.[63] More recently, an "autonomist" Marxism has emerged that it is often antiauthoritarian in its outlook.

Above all, though, libertarian socialism was represented by the broad anarchist tradition, which combined a commitment to the view that individuals should be free, provided that this does not undermine the freedom of others, with a critique of the economic and social inequities that prevented this freedom from being exercised. Liberty, Bakunin argued, required "social and economic equality," "established in the world by the spontaneous organisation of labour and the collective ownership of property by freely organised producers' associations, and by the equally spontaneous federation of communes, to replace the domineering paternalistic State," "from the bottom up."[64] Many of the ideals and practices associated with the broad anarchist tradition—direct action, participatory democracy, the view that the means must match the ends, solidarity, a respect for the individual, a rejection of manipulation, a stress on the importance of freedom of opinion and diversity, and an opposition to oppression by race, nationality, and gender—are precisely those that appeal to millions of people in the post-Soviet age.

These anarchist ideals and practices were consciously designed to avoid the fate that overtook classical Marxism. By stressing antiauthoritarian values, maximising democracy, and valorising self-management, the broad anarchist tradition sought to prevent the emergence, from within popular struggles, of new ruling elites. Bakunin and Kropotkin warned that the classical Marxist strategy would, regardless of its good intentions, culminate in the perpetuation of economic and social inequality and oppression. The state, Kropotkin insisted, "having been the force to which the minorities resorted for establishing and organising their power over the masses, cannot be the force which will serve to destroy those privileges."[65]

Before We Start

Before moving on to the main account, a few final points are in order. One is that a work like this is, by necessity, based primarily on a synthesis of the existing literature and the assistance of people with expertise from across the world. The eclipse of the broad anarchist tradition in the mid-twentieth century by statist politics—classical Marxism, social democracy, and nationalisms of various sorts— froze research on the subject as political socialism came "nearly to monopolise the attention of those who write on labour and radical history."[66] This situation changed from the 1960s. The rise of the New Left, which questioned official Marxism and reexamined alternative radical traditions, was particularly important in laying the basis for new scholarship on anarchism and syndicalism. The resurgence of anarchism from the 1960s onward and the collapse of much of the East bloc from 1989 to 1991 led to another upsurge in relevant scholarly work.

The growing body of studies on anarchism and syndicalism promises to fundamentally reshape our views about the past. In China, for example, where the history of socialism has long been reduced to the "progressive evolution of a correct socialism under the guidance of Mao Zedong or the Communist Party," the central role of anarchism in the first four decades of the twentieth century is being rediscovered.[67] In Cuba, where the broad anarchist tradition has "largely been ignored or misrepresented," with an "almost complete lack of historiography," its critical part "in the political and economic development of the country" is increasingly recognised.[68] Likewise, the "historical amnesia" regarding "the appeal of anarchism to Koreans" has started to be challenged.[69] While the implications of the growing research have not yet been as widely accepted as might be hoped, there is no doubt that many researchers are now taking anarchism and syndicalism seriously.[70]

Our two volumes have relied heavily on the growing scholarship, supplemented in some cases by "movement" publications and in a few instances by interviews with key figures. Doubtless there are some materials we have missed, but our general analysis and account is, we believe, an accurate portrayal of the broad anarchist tradition. Although every attempt has been made to ensure the accuracy of the facts and figures presented, it is possible that some of our sources have errors of their own; we take responsibility for any other errors. Doubtless there are also important issues we have left out of our analysis of the core themes in the history and politics of the broad anarchist tradition. Readers are directed to the notes and bibliography for sources and further reading.

For the most part (although not exclusively) we have used English-language sources. This can introduce two main biases: we may have overlooked some crucial works in other languages; and some areas and issues are better covered in the English-language literature than others. We have tried to be as comprehensive as possible. Certainly, some of the arguments presented here will be controversial. This is to be welcomed: good scholarship proceeds through debate, rather than the creation of orthodoxies. If this book succeeds in promoting new research into anarchism, even if that research contradicts our arguments, we consider our work well done. Similarly, we believe that debate is essential to the development of any political tradition, and we hope that this work is a fruitful contribution to sharpening perspectives within the broad anarchist tradition.

In terms of naming conventions, we have generally used the English-language version of the names of organisations for the purposes of clarity. When using acronyms for organisations, however, we have preferred the most commonly used ones, wherever possible; these are typically, but not always, derived from the home language of the organisation. Thus, the Macedonian Revolutionary Clandestine Committee is referred to as the MTRK, in reference to its original name, but the Interior Revolutionary Organisation of Macedonia and Adrianopole is referred to as VMRO, the French acronym that is most commonly used. When referring to the titles of periodicals or books in other languages, we have used the original names of the publications, but provided translations of the titles in brackets.

Finally, a few words about the origins of this book are in order. It began as a brief and rather didactic booklet in the late 1990s, and simply grew and grew. We were, frankly, rather amazed by the rich history of the broad anarchist tradition; expecting to fill in a few gaps, we found our eyes opened to an unexpected world, a global history unknown to many of the anarchists and syndicalists themselves. It was an evocative and intriguing history, replete with sacrifice, tragedy, suffering, and sometimes even humour and pathos, but shot through with heroism, creativity, beauty, and achievement. It also became clear to us that we were not simply writing an obituary of a movement or an antiquarian account but discussing a living tradition of interest to many people who want to change the world. As such, this is also a work about the future, and it is to a better world and a better tomorrow that we dedicate it.

Notes

1. A. Fischer, "Adolph Fischer," in *Anarchism: Its Philosophy and Scientific Basis*, ed. A. R. Parsons (1887; repr., New York: Kraus Reprint Co., 1971), 78.

2. W. Thorpe, *"The Workers Themselves": Revolutionary Syndicalism and International Labour, 1913–23* (Dordrecht: Kulwer Academic Publishers, 1989), 3.

3. R. Kedward, *The Anarchists: The Men Who Shocked an Era* (London: Library of the Twentieth Century, 1971), 120.

4. United Nations Development Programme, *Human Development Report* (New York: United Nations, 1996), 13.

5. K. Moody, *Workers in a Lean World: Unions in the International Economy* (London: Verso, 1997), 54.

6. M. D. Yates, "Poverty and Inequality in the Global Economy," *Monthly Review* 55, no. 9 (2004): 38.

7. P. Krugman, "For Richer," *New York Times Magazine*, October 20, 2002.

8. M. Davis, "Planet of Slums: Urban Involution and the Informal Proletariat," *New Left Review* 26 (2004): 22.

9. Yates, "Poverty and Inequality in the Global Economy," 42.

10. J. S. Saul and C. Leys, "Sub-Saharan Africa in Global Capitalism," *Monthly Review* 51, no. 3 (1999): 13–30.

11. Moody, *Workers in a Lean World*, 41.

12. Davis, "Planet of Slums," 5, 13–14, 17.

13. C. Harman, *A People's History of the World* (London: Bookmarks, 1999), 614–15.

14. Ibid.

15. See A. Smith, *An Inquiry into the Nature and Causes of the Wealth of Nations*, vol. 2, *The Glasgow Edition of the Works and Correspondence of Adam Smith* (1776; repr., Indianapolis, IN: Liberty Fund, 1981).

16. Key twentieth-century statements of this position include L. von Mises, *Socialism* (1922; repr., Indianapolis, IN: Liberty Classics, 1981); F. A. von Hayek, *The Road to Serfdom* (London: Routledge, 1944); M. Friedman with R. Friedman, *Capitalism and Freedom* (Chicago: University of Chicago Press, 1962).

17. P. Bourdieu, "Utopia of Endless Exploitation: The Essence of Neo-liberalism," *Le Monde Diplomatique* (December 8, 1998): 3.

18. A. G. Hopkins, "The History of Globalisation—and the Globalisation of History?" in *Globalisation and World History*, ed. A. G. Hopkins (London: Pimlico, 2002), 19.

19. F. Fukuyama, "The End of History?" *National Interest* (Summer 1989): 3, 4, 12.

20. D. Schechter, *Radical Theories: Paths beyond Marxism and Social Democracy* (Manchester: Manchester University Press, 1994), 1–2.

21. A. Dirlik, *Anarchism in the Chinese Revolution* (Berkeley: University of California Press, 1991), 3–4; see also 7–8.

22. E. Bernstein, *The Preconditions for Socialism*, ed. and trans. H. Tudor (1899; repr., Cambridge: Cambridge University Press, 1993), 158.

23. The "glorious period" is a phrase from H. Beyer-Arnesen, "Anarcho-syndicalism: A Historical Closed Door ... or Not?" *Libertarian Labor Review* (Winter 1997–1998): 20. From 1870 to 1914, for example, world trade and output grew steadily at 3.5 and 3.45 percent, respectively, with major powers developing trade to gross domestic product ratios exceeding 35 percent (around 44 percent in the case of Britain). The ratios of 1913 were generally not reached by the mid-1990s. In this earlier period, capital exports (both direct investments in production and portfolio investment) took place on a scale that had not been matched by the end of the 1990s. See, inter alia, E. Hobsbawm, *The Age of Capital, 1848–1875* (London: Abacus, 1977), 66ff; P. Hirst, "The Global Economy: Myths and Realities," *International Affairs* 73, no. 3 (1997): 411.

24. B. Epstein, "Anarchism and the Anti-Globalisation Movement," *Monthly Review* 53, no. 4 (2001): 1–14 ; see also D. Graeber, "The New Anarchists," *New Left Review* 13 (2002): 61–73

25. Following the union election process in the public and private sector in 2004, it represented around one million workers through elections to industrial committees, a further 600,000 workers in collective bargaining, and 300,000 in the smaller subcontracting shops, with an average of 560 workers in the workplaces where it was active. This made the CGT the third-largest union federation in Spain; "Espagne: La CGT s'affirme comme la troisième organisation syndicale" (Spain: CGT Is Now the Third Biggest Union," trans. N. Phebus), *Alternative Libertaire*, November 2004.

26. J. Joll, *The Anarchists* (London: Methuen and Co., 1964), 224.

27. Ibid., 11–12.

28. For a survey of such attempts, see J. Romero Maura, "The Spanish Case," in *Anarchism Today*, ed. D. Apter and J. Joll (London: Macmillan, 1971). Even Murray Bookchin's groundbreaking examination tends to explain the role of anarchism in Spain by reference to the peculiarities of Spanish culture and society; see M. Bookchin, *The Spanish Anarchists: The Heroic Years, 1868–1936* (New York: Harper Colophon Books, 1977), especially chapters 1 and 2.

29. P. Marshall, *Demanding the Impossible: A History of Anarchism* (London: Fontana Press, 1994), xiv, 3–4.

30. Joll, *The Anarchists*, 173, 275; Marshall, *Demanding the Impossible*, 3.

31. Kedward, *The Anarchists*, 6; M. Statz, introduction to *The Essential Works of Anarchism*, ed. M. Statz (New York: Bantam, 1971), xiii.

32. See, for example, Marshall, *Demanding the Impossible*, 53–54, 422, 443, 544–45, 500–1, 559–65; T. M. Perlin, *Contemporary Anarchism* (New Brunswick, NJ: Transaction Books, 1979), 109.

33. G. M. Stekloff, *History of the First International*, rev. ed. (London: Martin Lawrence, 1928), 312; E. Yaroslavsky, *History of Anarchism in Russia* (London: Lawrence and Wishart, ca. 1937), 26, 28, 41, 68–69; E. Hobsbawm, *Primitive Rebels: Studies in Archaic Forms of Social Movement in the 19th and 20th Centuries*, 3rd ed. (Manchester: Manchester University Press, 1971); E. Hobsbawm, *Revolutionaries* (London: Abacus, 1993); G. Woodcock, *Anarchism: A History of Libertarian Ideas and Movements*, rev. ed. with postscript (London: Penguin, 1975), 444–45; Kedward, *The Anarchists*, 24–26; C. M. Darch, "The Makhnovischna, 1917–1921: Ideology, Nationalism, and Peasant Insurgency in Early Twentieth Century Ukraine" (PhD diss., University of Bradford, 1994), 57.

34. For a contrary view, see Darch, "The Makhnovischna," 70.

35. Joll, *The Anarchists*, 207; Schechter, *Radical Theories*, 28, 25; J. Jennings, "The CGT and the Couriau Affair: Syndicalist Responses to Female Labour in France before 1914," *European History Quarterly* 21 (1991): 326.

36. A sophisticated version of this view may be found in M. Dubofsky, "The Origins of Western Working-Class Radicalism," *Labour History* 7 (1966): 131–54; M. Dubofsky, *We Shall Be All: A History of the IWW* (Chicago: Quadrangle Books, 1969), 5, 19–35, 73, 76–77. It was also accepted by some anarchists; see, for example, R. Rocker, *Anarcho-Syndicalism* (Oakland: AK Press, 2004), available at http://www.spunk.org/library/writers/rocker/sp001495/rocker_as6.html (accessed November 12, 2000). An excellent overview and critique of this approach can be found in S. Salerno, *Red November, Black November: Culture and Community in the Industrial Workers of the World* (New York: State University of New York Press, 1989).

37. P. Eltzbacher, *Anarchism: Exponents of the Anarchist Philosophy* (1900; repr., London: Freedom Press, 1960); M. Fleming, *The Anarchist Way to Socialism: Elisée Reclus and Nineteenth-Century European Anarchism* (London: Croom Helm, 1979), 19.

38. Eltzbacher, *Anarchism*, 188.

39. Ibid., 189, 201.

40. Ibid., 189, 191.

41. See ibid., 184–96.

42. Most notably in a celebrated article on anarchism written for the *Encyclopaedia Britannica*; P. Kropotkin, "Anarchism," in *Kropotkin's Revolutionary Pamphlets: A Collection of Writings by Peter Kropotkin*, ed. R. N. Baldwin (1905; repr., New York: Dover Publications, 1970).

43. On Nettlau's research, see the editor's notes to M. Nettlau, *A Short History of Anarchism* (1934; repr., London: Freedom Press, 1996).

44. Marshall, *Demanding the Impossible*, xiv, 3–4.

45. Bookchin, *The Spanish Anarchists*, 17.

46. R. Graham, preface to *Anarchism: A Documentary History of Libertarian Ideas, Volume 1: From Anarchy to Anarchism, 300 CE to 1939*, ed. R. Graham (Montréal: Black Rose, 2005), xiii.

47. R. J. Holton, "Syndicalist Theories of the State," *Sociological Review* 28, no. 1 (1980): 5.

48. Kedward, *The Anarchists*, 120.

49. Marshall, *Demanding the Impossible*, 453.

50. Nettlau, *A Short History of Anarchism*, 277–78.

51. See Holton, "Syndicalist Theories of the State," 5–7, 12–13, 18–19.

52. J. Krikler, *Rand Revolt: The 1922 Insurrection and Racial Killings in South Africa* (Cape Town: Jonathon Ball, 2005), 153.

53. On social movement unionism, see, inter alia, Moody, *Workers in a Lean World*.

54. P. Archinov, N. Makhno, I. Mett, Valevsky, and Linsky, *The Organisational Platform of the Libertarian Communists* (1926; repr., Dublin: Workers Solidarity Movement, 2001).

55. K. Marx, *The Gotha Programme* (1875; repr., New York: Socialist Labour Party, 1922), 48; V. I. Lenin, "The State and Revolution: The Marxist Theory of the State and the Tasks of the Proletariat in the Revolution," in *Selected Works in Three Volumes*, ed. V. I. Lenin (1917; repr., Moscow: Progress Publishers, 1975), volume 2, 255.

56. L. Trotsky, *Writings of Leon Trotsky, 1936–37*, 2nd ed (New York: Pathfinder Press, 1975), 513–14.

57. L. Trotsky, *The Lessons of October* (1924; repr., London: Bookmarks, 1987), 72.

58. Mao Tsetung, "On the People's Democratic Dictatorship: In Commemoration of the Twenty-eighth Anniversary of the Communist Party of China," in *Selected Readings from the Works of Mao Tsetung*, ed. Editorial Committee for Selected Readings from the Works of Mao Tsetung (1949; repr., Peking: Foreign Languages Press, 1971), 371.

59. As claimed by D. McNally, *Against the Market: Political Economy, Market Socialism, and the Marxist Critique* (London: Verso, 1993), 3.

60. See G. M. Ivanova, *Labor Camp Socialism: The Gulag in the Soviet Totalitarian System* (New York: M. E. Sharpe, 2000).

61. For a contrary view, see D. Guérin, "Marxism and Anarchism," in *For Anarchism: History, Theory, and Practice*, ed. D. Goodway (London: Routledge, 1989), 109, 125.

62. Trotsky, quoted in Thorpe, "*The Workers Themselves,*'" 128, 132.

63. See S. Bricianer, *Pannekoek and the Workers' Councils* (St. Louis, MO: Telos Press, 1978); J. Gerber, *Anton Pannekoek and the Socialism of Workers' Self-Emancipation, 1873–1960* (Dordrecht: Kluwer Academic Publishers, 1989); R. Gombin, *The Radical Tradition: A Study in Modern Revolutionary Thought* (London: Methuen and Co., 1978); M. Shipway, "Council Communism," in *Non-Market Socialism in the Nineteenth and Twentieth Centuries*, ed. M. Rubel and J. Crump (Basingstoke, UK: Macmillan, 1987); M. Shipway, *Anti-Parliamentary Communism: The Movement for Workers' Councils in Britain* (Basingstoke, UK: Macmillan, 1988); D. A. Smart, ed., *Pannekoek and Gorter's Marxism* (London: Pluto Press, 1978). Rühle characterised Lenin as the pioneer of fascism; O. Rühle, *The Struggle against Fascism Begins with the Struggle against Bolshevism* (1939; repr., London: Elephant Editions, 1981), 10–11, 13, 20.

64. M. Bakunin, "The Paris Commune and the Idea of the State," in *Bakunin on Anarchy: Selected Works by the Activist-Founder of World Anarchism*, ed. S. Dolgoff (1871; repr., London: George Allen and Unwin, 1971), 262, 263.

65. P. Kropotkin, "Modern Science and Anarchism," in *Kropotkin's Revolutionary Pamphlets: A Collection of Writings by Peter Kropotkin*, ed. R. N. Baldwin (1912; repr., New York: Dover Publications, 1970), 170.

66. Thorpe, "*The Workers Themselves*," x.

67. Dirlik, *Anarchism in the Chinese Revolution*, 15, 27, 170; see also P. Zarrow, *Anarchism and Chinese Political Culture* (New York: Columbia University Press, 1990).

68. K. R. Shaffer, "Purifying the Environment for the Coming New Dawn: Anarchism and Counter-cultural Politics in Cuba, 1898–1925" (PhD diss., University of Kansas, 1998), vii, 2.

69. J. M. Allen, "History, Nation, People: Past and Present in the Writing of Sin Ch'aeho" (PhD diss., University of Washington, 1999), 4, 263–64.

70. A fuller discussion of this point falls outside the scope of this work, but two examples are illustrative. Writing in a recent issue of the *Journal of World-Systems Research* on the history of labour internationalism and its relevance to the present, Dimitris Stevis concluded that "labour unions, therefore, are confronted with the need for a modicum of syndicalism decades after the latter's premature demise"; see D. Stevis, "International Labor Organizations, 1864–1997: The Weight of History and the Challenges of the Present," *Journal of World-Systems Research* 4, no. 1 (1998): 66. Likewise, exploring the creation of mass slums over the last century, Mike Davis drew attention to the importance of anarchism and syndicalism as key factors in the development of militant working-class communities in the early twentieth century; see M. Davis, "Planet of Slums," 28, 30–32.

1
THEORY AND ANALYSIS

Pyotr Kropotkin (1842–1921)

Russian émigré, scientist, and revolutionary. After Bakunin, Kropotkin was the most influential and widely read anarchist worldwide, with a profound influence on popular class movements in Europe, the Americas, and Asia. His book *The Conquest of Bread* (1892) is a classic and remains one of the soundest expositions of anarchist-communist ideas.

Mikhail Gerdzhikov (1877–1947) of the Macedonian Clandestine Revolutionary Committee (MTPK), established in 1898.

In 1903, the MPTK staged a revolt against the Ottoman authorities in Thrace, to coincide with a rising by the Interior Revolutionary Organisation of Macedonia and Adrianople (VMRO). Anarchists like Gerdzhikov believed that the struggle for national liberation was an integral part of the struggle for libertarian communism.

CHAPTER 2

Socialism from Below: Defining Anarchism

The aim of this chapter is twofold: to develop an understanding of the doctrine of anarchism and its origins; and to outline the core features of anarchist doctrine. As noted in chapter 1, we stress anarchism's coherence and strength. We have also already suggested that anarchism is a revolutionary and libertarian socialist doctrine: advocating individual freedom through a free society, anarchism aims to create a democratic, egalitarian, and stateless socialist order through an international and internationalist social revolution, abolishing capitalism, landlordism, and the state.

In this chapter, we explain why we define anarchism in this way. Anarchism is commonly defined as an opposition to the state, or as an opposition to the state because it constrains the individual. It is also sometimes argued that anarchism sees the state as "responsible for all inequality and injustice."[1] We do not find these assertions to be useful. For one thing, they strip anarchism of its class politics and socialist content.[2] They also do not adequately address the specific features of the anarchist understanding of individual freedom.

For anarchists, individual freedom is the highest good, and individuality is valuable in itself, but such freedom can only be achieved within and through a new type of society. Contending that a class system prevents the full development of individuality, anarchists advocate class struggle from below to create a better world. In this ideal new order, individual freedom will be harmonised with communal obligations through cooperation, democratic decision–making, and social and economic equality. Anarchism rejects the state as a centralised structure of domination and an instrument of class rule, not simply because it constrains the individual or because anarchists dislike regulations. On the contrary, anarchists believe rights arise from the fulfilment of obligations to society and that there is a place for a certain amount of legitimate coercive power, if derived from collective and democratic decision-making.

The practice of defining anarchism simply as hostility to the state has a further consequence: that a range of quite different and often contradictory ideas and movements get conflated. By defining anarchism more narrowly, however, we are able to bring its key ideas into a sharper focus, lay the basis for our examination of the main debates in the broad anarchist tradition in subsequent chapters, and see what ideas are relevant to current struggles against neoliberalism.

Another consequence of defining anarchism loosely is the notion that anarchism is a movement existing throughout history, possibly rooted in human nature. We argue, though, that anarchism should be considered a relatively recent phenomenon. Specifically, it emerged from the 1860s onward within the context of the modern working-class and socialist movement, within the womb of the First International. There have certainly been libertarian currents throughout history, not to mention a great many struggles for individual freedom; these are an important part of humankind's heritage, and challenge contemporary views that human nature is inherently greedy or capitalist. Yet this libertarian history should not be conflated with the history of anarchism. Defining anarchism more narrowly and historicizing it makes it possible to identify the crucial moments in the broad anarchist tradition as it evolved over the last 150 years, the way in which anarchist and syndicalist ideas were applied in the real world, and the relevance of that tradition for the present.

The Meaning of Anarchism: Debating the Literature

We begin with a survey of the way in which anarchism and syndicalism have been defined in the literature. Studies of anarchism and syndicalism have often suffered from an unclear definition of their subject matter. As mentioned in the previous chapter, one problem is the popular view of anarchism as a synonym for chaos, destruction, and the breakdown of all order.[3] This is flawed, as anarchism is a social doctrine with a positive programme; opposed to the existing social order, it advocates a new one.

A second problem has been the tradition of defining anarchism as an outlook marked by its hostility to the state, as mentioned above. Roderick Kedward is representative of this dominant tradition. He asserts that the "bond that united all anarchists" was "antagonism to any situation regulated by imposition, constraint, or oppression," and that this was the basis for anarchist antistatism.[4] Corrine Jacker similarly claims that anarchists have a "romantic approach" and maintain that "the individual must be completely free; there must be no authority to dictate his behaviour or its limits"; anarchists oppose the state, continues Jacker, because "rules are an attempt to restrict an individual's freedom," and "another term for anarchism is *antistatism*."[5]

For Robert Hoffman, anarchists hold that "government creates and perpetuates both disorder and violence," and "*any* imperative authority, even that of a popular socialist government or the joint decision of an egalitarian community, must violate individual liberty," "justice," and "community." A person should "obey the dictates of his free will only."[6] Marshall Statz contends that anarchism aimed at a society organised through free association, without imposed order, and was a "positive social doctrine" that embodied a "critique of human society as it exists and a vision of a better form of social order." Statz, however, reduced the "positive" programme to a variety of schemes to replace the state; anarchism allegedly regarded "political authority, and its modern embodiment the state, as the root of all evil."[7]

Terry Perlin put forward a similar argument, and introduced the supposed "anarchists of the 'right,'" "anarcho-capitalists," whose quest for individual freedom from the state shares the "common anarchist quest: for the freedom of the individual."[8] These "anarcho-capitalists" essentially took free market ideas to the most extreme conclusions. Traditional economic liberalism, including neoliberalism, stressed the benefits of a free and unrestricted market, based on the relentless pursuit of individual self-interest, for individual liberty and economic efficiency. But it also stressed the need for a minimal state to enforce law and order, provide military defence, provide public goods, and deal with externalities. By contrast, "anarcho-capitalists," like the late Murray Rothbard, advocated the transfer of *all* the services provided by the state—including law and order—to private firms and associations.[9]

It may seem odd to place such figures alongside one another as part of a single movement and tradition, but it is entirely consistent with a definition of anarchism as an opposition to the state. The work that really established this definition as the dominant one was Paul Eltzbacher's *Anarchism: Exponents of the Anarchist Philosophy*, which appeared in 1900 and sought to identify the key features of anarchist thought. The conclusions of this work, one of the first academic studies of anarchism, "have become such a commonplace that they have been incorporated into almost every study of the subject up to the present day."[10]

Eltzbacher, a German judge, was interested in understanding anarchism, which appeared to his contemporaries as something quite new and mysterious.[11] In trying to develop a definition and analysis of anarchism, he started off well: his aim was to identify a number of thinkers as representative examples of anarchists, and then derive the key principles of anarchism from an examination of their ideas. This use of a deductive method is probably ideal, but its analysis is always shaped by the representativeness of the data. It was when Eltzbacher made his selection of prominent anarchists that the problems arose. He made his choices "not upon the basis of any objective criteria, but rather examined the thought of those who the (informed) public opinion of the time regarded as the principal exponents of anarchism."[12] The "(informed) public opinion" to which Eltzbacher turned was that of his close associates, who already assumed that anarchism was defined mainly by antistatism. Eltzbacher did not, concomitantly, make enquiries within the self-described anarchist movement of the time.

The result was the fairly arbitrary selection of seven figures as the "recognised" anarchist teachers: Godwin, Stirner, Proudhon, Bakunin, Kropotkin, Tucker, and Tolstoy.[13] These are the figures subsequently identified, as mentioned in chapter 1, as the seven sages of anarchism.[14] Having made his selection in this way, Eltzbacher then faced the problem of definition: what did these individuals have in common? Following an extensive and lucid analysis of each sage by Eltzbacher, the answer, it seemed, was very little.[15]

Godwin, a forgotten Enlightenment thinker, derived a generally antistatist position from utilitarian principles in the 1790s.[16] He argued that humans could be perfected through reason and education, and that government would wither away when all people had become sufficiently reasonable to exercise full personal autonomy, by which he meant the application of a utilitarian calculus to all activities.

In Godwin's view, "Every well-informed friend of mankind" would "look forward to ... the dissolution of political government, of that brute engine, which had been the only perennial cause of the vices of mankind."[17] He opposed class inequality on the same grounds: both poverty and wealth distracted people from the pursuit of pure reason.[18] Godwin also opposed cooperation between people because it hampered the development and exercise of utilitarian reasoning.[19] "Everything that is usually understood by the term cooperation, is, in some degree an evil," claimed Godwin, and it followed that all unnecessary interaction should be carefully avoided, including "common labour and common meals," "co-habitation," and the "institution of marriage."[20] While Godwin was on the Left, inasmuch as he defended the French Revolution, he believed that state coercion was a necessary evil until general rationality could be reached.[21]

In contrast, Stirner was an extreme individualist of the 1840s, asserting the right of the individual to do whatever she or he pleased.[22] The mind must be freed of "spooks" and "wheels," meaning any and all abstract principles that impede individual gratification, including the notions of "the cause of mankind, of truth, of freedom, of humanity, of justice," the "cause of my people, my prince, my fatherland," and finally, "even the cause of Mind." Unbridled self-interest was the only true value; the only valid criterion for action was individual satisfaction; the only limit was the power of a given individual; even truth was the product of individual choice and thus entirely relative: "You alone are the truth, or rather, you are more than the truth, which is nothing at all before."[23] Stirner did not actually advocate the abolition of the state.[24] "My object is not the overthrow of an established order but my elevation above it, my purpose and deed are not ... political or social but ... directed toward myself and my ownness alone ... an egoistic purpose and deed."[25] He advocated a "cult of unlimited self-will."[26] Reason was irrelevant, and the state was objectionable inasmuch as it halted the individual's pursuit of pleasure and power. The state constrained the individual, but there was nothing wrong with one individual constraining another.

Tolstoy, the famous Russian novelist, derived his principles from Christian scriptures and favoured a withdrawal into a simple life of religious contemplation.[27] Taking Jesus Christ's admonition to "turn the other cheek" seriously, Tolstoy became a pacifist, and thus an advocate of nonviolence and nonresistance in the face of conflict and force. His opposition to the state arose from two sources: the conviction that government was inherently violent, and the view that divine law must always be superior to both secular law and human reason. At the heart of Tolstoy's thinking was Christian mysticism, a quest for inner freedom through religious obedience and divine revelation, requiring withdrawal, wherever possible, from the evils and temptations of the world. His wish to withdraw from contact with the state followed, as did his dislike of private property and advocacy of chastity.

In short, even at the most basic level, there was not much in common between the first three sages discussed so far: Godwin was a rationalist, Stirner was an epistemological relativist, viewing truth as a matter of opinion, with the most widely accepted "truth" that imposed by the most powerful people; Tolstoy was a believer in divine revelation; Godwin and Tolstoy were ascetics, and Stirner was a libertine; Godwin opposed the class system for preventing the exercise of reason, Stirner disliked modern industry for mechanising life, and Tolstoy complained that capitalism replaced wholesome rural labour with the factory system and the quest for profit impeded salvation. The remaining four sages add more variation, falling into two main groups: Proudhon and Tucker, on the one side, and Bakunin and Kropotkin, on the other.

Proudhon, a self-taught French artisan of peasant stock, was somewhat influenced by the early nineteenth-century "utopian" socialist Charles Fourier (1772–1837), who advocated cooperative labour, communal ownership and living, sensual pleasure, and gender equality.[28] Proudhon used a broad labour theory of value—an approach that argued that only labour created new wealth, and that the price at which goods and services were sold corresponded to the amount of labour time that they embodied—to criticize capitalism.[29] This idea was not new, and can be found in the works of Smith and other early economic liberals. In Proudhon's hands, it became a tool for social critique: if labour created all wealth, why did the labouring classes remain impoverished, while those classes that did not labour—made up of, say, bankers, landlords, and merchants—continually accumulated wealth?

For Proudhon, exploitation—in which the popular classes were not remunerated according to their labour, and the unpaid surplus accrued to other classes—took place through a range of mechanisms in the market, including interest, rent, and patent fees. Banks, for example, did not actually produce value but continually accumulated it by compelling the producers to pay interest. In turn, the state defended exploitation and undermined justice. Proudhon's strategy for change was gradualist: he favoured the development of a noncapitalist sector, based on small individual proprietors as well as cooperatives that would undermine and then overwhelm capitalism. Proudhon placed great emphasis on the need to form a nonprofit and cooperative People's Bank, funded by the producers that would lend money without interest, and envisaged a sort of "market socialism," based on competition, in which producers would receive the full value of their labour.[30]

Eventually, the state would become redundant, as self-government was carried out by the noncapitalist sector: "No longer having need of legislator or of sovereign, the *atelier* [workshop] will make the government disappear."[31] "Socialism," Proudhon argued, "is the opposite of governmentalism.... We want these associations to be ... the first components of a vast federation of associations and groups united in the common bond of the democratic and social republic."[32] The market was really a means to an end, and would be controlled and leveled by society as needed.

Proudhon's ideas, often known as mutualism, were widely influential in socialist and popular circles between the 1840s and 1880s in Europe and the Americas.[33] Tucker was the "leading American apostle of Proudhon's doctrines," which he called "individualist anarchism."[34] He described himself as an "individualist anarchist" or a "philosophical anarchist," and was also influenced by U.S. thinkers such as Josiah Warren, whose ideas were remarkably similar to those of the French activist. Like Godwin, Proudhon and Tucker were rationalists and atheists, and like him, they saw reason as a necessary means of securing social change. Unlike Godwin, they had a concrete strategy for change, favoured the creation of new institutions that would prefigure the desired future order, and saw society as the necessary matrix for individual freedom.

Let us move now to Bakunin and Kropotkin. Bakunin was the eldest son of a minor Russian noble. He studied in Russia and Germany in the 1840s with an academic career in mind, but became increasingly radicalised, met Marx and Proudhon, and was driven out of several countries for his political activities.[35] Arrested and returned to Russia, Bakunin received a life sentence, which was later commuted to exile in Siberia, and escaped in 1861. The first phase of Bakunin's career was characterised by pan-Slavic nationalism, but with the failure of the 1863 Polish uprising Bakunin moved toward a class struggle and internationalist position. His views were shaped by debates in Italy (where he founded the secret, socialist International Brotherhood), followed by participation in the pacifist League for Peace and Freedom, and then the First International. By this time, Bakunin had helped form the International Alliance of Socialist Democracy, which applied to join the First International en bloc. The First International's secretariat insisted that the Alliance dissolve and its sections join separately, but it seems certain that the Alliance continued to operate underground. There was nothing "imaginary" about Bakunin's "secret societies."[36]

Like Bakunin, Kropotkin was from the Russian aristocracy—he was no less than a prince—and embarked on a military career, including ten years in the Russian civil service, mainly in eastern Siberia.[37] Increasingly disillusioned with the government, Kropotkin concentrated on scientific work and developed a formidable reputation as a geographer. Resigning his government post, he visited Switzerland, where he joined the anarchists. In Russia he promoted revolutionary ideas in the Chaikovsky Circle, part of the revolutionary *narodnik* ("populist") movement. Jailed in 1874, Kropotkin escaped, going to Switzerland and then to France, where he was jailed for three years for membership in the First International. After his release, Kropotkin moved to England, where he spent most of his remaining years, helping to found Freedom Press and the journal *Freedom*, both of which are still active. In 1914, the elderly Kropotkin came out in support of the Allies in the First World War, alienating himself from the great majority of anarchists and syndicalists, the "most unhappy event of Kropotkin's life," one of his "darkest moments."[38] In 1917, he returned to Russia. His funeral in 1921 was the last mass anarchist demonstration for many years in that country.

Despite the common presentation of Kropotkin as a gentle "anarchist saint" compared to Bakunin, the two did not differ on any substantial issues.[39] Both were advocates of social revolution through class struggle to abolish the state, capitalism, and economic and social inequality, and create a self-managed socialist economy and society, without a state, in which individual differences could flourish on the basis of social and economic equality. Their ideas will be discussed in more depth below, yet suffice it to say, both men were rationalists (indeed, atheists) and advocates of cooperation rather than Stirnerite individualism. They shared the mutualist opposition to capitalism, admiring Proudhon and sharing his view that freedom was a social product rather than something exercised in opposition to others, but saw exploitation as taking place in production (rather than through the market), advocated international class war (rather than gradual change), and favoured an economy planned from below (in place of the market mechanism); both described themselves as socialists.[40]

Faced with such a diverse group of thinkers as a consequence of his method of choosing representative anarchists, Eltzbacher was in a quandary. He aimed to derive anarchist principles from an examination of their ideas, but he had ended up with a selection of people with radically different ideas. Rather than rethink his choices, however, Eltzbacher persevered and ended up with a definition of anarchism based on the lowest common denominator: an opposition to the state.[41]

This definition is even more nebulous than it may seem at first glance, for Eltzbacher admitted that his seven sages gave "totally different meanings" to "the negation of the State."[42] As our account has shown, there was certainly little agreement between the supposed sages on the reasons for opposing the state, or on the question of whether the state should be abolished, and if so, how. In some cases, for example, the opposition to the state follows from an opposition to hierarchical relationships between people (here we may include Proudhon, Tucker, Bakunin, and Kropotkin); in others, the state is opposed but authoritarian relationships are not (Stirner); and in still others, the opposition to the state is part of a withdrawal from a sinful world (Tolstoy).

Eltzbacher's approach, as noted above, was nonetheless influential, and his conclusion reinforced a common view that anarchism was simply antistatism.[43] The trend toward a vague definition of anarchism received a further boost from the anarchists themselves: there was a tendency, emanating from within the broad anarchist tradition, to present the movement as a universal feature of human history. From the early twentieth century onward, prominent anarchists produced a number of historical narratives of the movement. In these narratives, anarchism was typically described as present throughout human history, starting in ancient Asia and Europe, moving through the medieval period, and then heading into modernity.

Like other movements, the anarchists had begun to create what can only be considered a legitimising myth for the movement: portraying anarchism as common to all places, peoples, and times, this metahistory helped undermine charges that anarchism was alien, bizarre, or contrary to human nature. The cast on this universal stage included ancient philosophers like Lao-tzu, religious heretics like the Anabaptists, and thinkers like Godwin and Stirner, followed by movements from the First International onward, including syndicalism. To group these together, one must have a fairly loose definition of anarchism; the overlap with Eltzbacher's approach is fairly clear, and it is worth noting that Kropotkin was impressed with Eltzbacher's treatise.[44]

Given his prestige, Kropotkin's claim that the "tendency" toward anarchism "had always existed in mankind" was widely accepted, particularly when it appeared in the 1910 edition of the *Encyclopaedia Britannica*.[45] The anarchist historian Max Nettlau gave further weight to this line of thinking in a series of works from 1925. Born in Austria, his father a gardener for the royal family, Nettlau became an anarchist around 1881, and earned a doctorate in linguistics. Unexpectedly inheriting a small fortune in 1892, he devoted his life to research on anarchism, writing an extensive *Bibliography of Anarchism* (1897), a multivolume biography of Bakunin, and a nine-volume history of anarchism, appearing from 1925 onward, and summarised in a companion volume, *A Short History of Anarchism*.[46] He also helped found Freedom Press.

The companion volume to Nettlau's history dealt extensively with anarchism's historical development *before* 1864, and Nettlau believed that while "few people have yet attained a true understanding of the anarchist idea," the "anarchist concept" and "anarchist principles" could be found in ancient Greece as well as among utopian and scientific writers of the eighteenth century (including Godwin), utopian socialists like Fourier, his great disciple Victor Considérant (1808–1893), Proudhon and other nineteenth-century writers including Stirner, Anselme Bellegarrigue (ca. 1820–1865?), and Joseph Déjacque (1821–1864).[47] It is only in chapter 8 (of Nettlau's eighteen chapters) that we come to a discussion of the period of Bakunin's role in the First International.

The same general approach could be found in other anarchist writings, such as those of Rudolf Rocker in the 1930s. Born in Mainz, Germany in 1873, Rocker was a bookbinder by trade, and active as a youth in the German SDP.[48] Anarchism made occasional appearances in the SDP, and Rocker was involved with a left-wing faction, the *Jungen* ("Young Ones"), which had libertarian leanings.[49] In 1890, Rocker was expelled from the SDP, became an anarchist, and ended up in London in 1895, where he was active among Jewish immigrant communities, editing the Yiddish-language anarchist paper *Arbayter Fraynd* ("The Workers' Friend") and taking an active role in unionism. Interned as an "enemy alien" in 1914, Rocker was deported to Germany in 1918, where he became a leading figure in the syndicalist unions. In 1922, he was elected secretary of the newly formed syndicalist International Workers' Association (IWA), but had to leave Germany in 1933 following the Nazi takeover, passing away in the United States in 1958. The IWA was a continuation of prewar initiatives for a syndicalist international, and its member unions were drawn mainly from Latin America and Europe.

In his classic *Anarcho-Syndicalism*—one of the best single accounts of anarchism and syndicalism—Rocker claimed that "anarchist ideas are to be found in every period of known history," before repeating roughly the same narrative as Kropotkin and Nettlau.[50] In 1944, George Woodcock—later known for his scholarship on anarchism, but then an ardent anarchist—likewise found in Taoism the "first anarchistic doctrine," and discovered "anarchism before the rise of an anarchist movement" in the views of the radical Diggers sect in seventeenth-century England as well as Godwin and Proudhon.[51]

Given this backdrop, it is not surprising that many of the standard works on anarchism—we have in mind those of Roderick Kedward, James Joll, Peter Marshall, David Miller, and Woodcock—insist that there was something necessarily incoherent about anarchism. Both Miller and Woodcock speak of anarchism's "singular disagreement" on "revolutionary methods" and the "economic organisation" of the future.[52] Miller even suggests that anarchism is not in fact an ideology but a "point of intersection of several ideologies."[53] The same view of anarchism allows writers like Paul Feyerabend, an advocate of epistemological relativism and an opponent of scientific method, to describe his "anything goes" philosophy as an "anarchist" approach to knowledge.[54] Grouping Stirner with Bakunin unavoidably suggests incoherence—but is such grouping justified?

The Need for a New Approach

Having outlined the ways in which anarchism is generally discussed in the literature, we would like to draw attention to some of the problems associated with these approaches. It is here that our discussion of the seven sages approach is particularly pertinent. An outline of figures like Godwin, Proudhon, Stirner, Bakunin, Tucker, Kropotkin, and Tolstoy demonstrates clearly that they cannot be taken as representative of a single doctrine, unless that doctrine is defined at a general level that obscures the radical differences between these thinkers.

On one level, the result is that a number of writers see nothing odd about grouping extreme individualists like Stirner, radical economic liberals like Rothbard, and revolutionary socialists like Bakunin and Kropotkin into a single tradition. If these figures form a single tradition, however, that tradition *must* lack a coherent theoretical corpus, suffer from major internal contradictions, and prove a manifest inability to find common ground on the meaning of and rationale for individual freedom and antistatism.

One problem with such an approach is that it fails to provide an effective definition. Definitions should identify the common features of the subject under definition; this approach fails to do so, and suffers from internal incoherence. Definitions should also be able to clearly delineate the category being defined from other categories. It is on this external level, the level of the boundary, that the vague definition of anarchism as antistatism also fails. It is eminently logical, using this definition, to include classical Marxism within the anarchist category, given that this doctrine's ultimate objective is a stateless society without alienation and compulsion.

The Communist Manifesto, for example, stressed that the final stage of history, the communist society, would be stateless—"the public power will lose its political character"—and based on individual freedom—"we shall have an association in which the free development of each is the condition for the free development of all."[55] This communist society, in the classical Marxist tradition, is the final result of history. According to Lenin, the "dictatorship of the proletariat ... will begin to wither away immediately after its victory"; "We do not at all differ from the anarchists on the question of the abolition of the state as the *aim*."[56] Likewise, Nikolai Bukharin claimed that the "State will die out ... the proletarian State authority will also pass away."[57]

If anarchism can encompass economic liberals, Marxists, radical Christians, Taoism, and more, it is hardly surprising that the standard works on anarchism describe it as "incoherent." Such an approach is not useful. Given that there are few intellectual traditions that do not have at least some negative comments about the state and some positive views on the individual, it is not easy to specify an upper limit on the traditions that may be assimilated, in some form, to the anarchist category. Eltzbacher only had seven selections, but there is no real reason to stop there: once Eltzbacher's definition is accepted, it is a short step to Marshall's work, where the "anarchist" gallery includes the Buddha, the Marquis de Sade, Herbert Spencer, Gandhi, Che Guevara, and Margaret Thatcher. And if the notion of anarchism can cover so vast a field—and let us not forget that the case can be made to include Marx and his heirs—then the definition is so loose as to be practically meaningless.

It is, moreover, striking to note the consistent absence of the classical Marxists from these works on anarchism. If it is logical to include Stirner and Rothbard, it is surely so to include Marx, Engels, and their successors. Accepting Eltzbacher's definition of anarchism, applying it consistently, must mean that Mao and Stalin have every right to a place among the sages; the logic is inescapable, for both wanted to "negate the State for our future."[58] Yet none of the standard works on anarchism includes the duo; on the contrary, classical Marxism is always presented as the absolute antithesis of anarchism. This is a most revealing point.

The obvious reason for excluding classical Marxism—and for presenting it as the antithesis of anarchism—would be its strategy of the proletarian dictatorship. Indeed, some writers do try to suggest that this strategy helps to define anarchism, with Marshall observing that "most anarchists" believe that the means of change must prefigure the ends desired.[59] Again, however, we quickly run into difficulties. *Strategy* is specifically excluded as a defining feature of anarchism in the standard works and presented as the area where anarchists disagree most. For Eltzbacher, the "seven teachings here presented have nothing in common" regarding the means to "negate the State."[60] The anarchists, Hoffman argued, lacked "the agreement about doctrine and programme that have generally united men in comparable movements," while Derry Novak claimed it is "the nature of anarchism" to lack a "general programme" and a coherent theory.[61] Even Marshall is careful to stress that he is not speaking about all anarchists in relation to the means shaping the ends, and his account labels as anarchist a number of figures who were in favour of a transitional state, not least Godwin and Gandhi.[62] This is not so different from classical Marxism.

Yet even if the argument that the means must prefigure the ends was accepted as a binding criterion for inclusion in the anarchist camp, there remain other striking and unexplained absences from the tradition as constructed by Eltzbacher, Nettlau, and others. A notable example is the tradition of council communism, a libertarian form of Marxism that rejects the state as a revolutionary instrument, and advocates international and self-managed working-class revolution from below. Why is council communism not, then, included under the anarchist umbrella? It cannot be simply that the council communists refused to accept an anarchist label, for the standard works on anarchism include many figures who did not adopt the anarchist name, among them Godwin, Stirner, and Tolstoy.

Above, we said that the exclusion of classical Marxism from standard accounts of anarchism would be revealing. We believe that we have shown this to be so in several ways. First, the consistent exclusion of classical Marxism only makes sense if the writers of the standard works implicitly apply criteria like strategy to their definition of anarchism, and this in turn means that these works have conceded that there are serious difficulties in defining anarchism merely as an opposition to the state. Second, the tendency of the standard works to continually expand the field covered by the term "anarchism" to vast proportions, while arbitrarily excluding both classical Marxism and libertarian strains like council communism, demonstrates that the definition is vague, inadequate, and inconsistently applied. Marshall's account illustrates these points well: having insisted that anarchism "is anti-dogmatic" and "does not offer a fixed body of doctrine based on one particular world view," he goes on to suggest that so-called "anarcho-capitalists" are not really anarchists because they ignore the anarchist "concern for economic equality and social justice," notwithstanding the fact that the latter "concern" is not part of his own definition of anarchism.[63]

In short, the mainstream definition of anarchism fails some of the most basic requirements of a definition, lacking the ability to effectively exclude from the category phenomena deemed external to those being examined. At the same time, the pattern of continual but implicit modifications to the definition by writers who define anarchism as antistatism shows that even these analysts find this definition of limited value. The effect of these modifications is, however, to muddy the waters even further.

A good definition is one that highlights the distinguishing features of a given category, does so in a coherent fashion, and is able to differentiate that category from others, thereby organising knowledge as well as enabling effective analysis and research. The usual definition of anarchism fails on all these grounds. So far we have argued that it has criteria that are simply too vague to really distinguish anarchism from other bodies of thought and action, resulting in anarchism being defined so loosely that it is not clear what should be included and what should not, and why some things are included and others are not.

Definitions, however, serve an important purpose besides simply classifying data. They provide the basis for analysis and research, and here the standard definition of anarchism is also not effective. Second, there is the problem of explanation. Presenting anarchism as a universal feature of society makes it difficult indeed to explain why it arises in particular historical contexts, to delineate its boundaries, or analyse its class character and role at a particular time. What, after all, did the Taoists have in common with the anarchists of the First International? If we group such radically disparate moments and movements under the heading of anarchism, we can do little to identify the social basis of anarchism or the reasons for its rise and fall in particular situations.

A tendency to project anarchism on to a wide range of disparate figures also results in serious problems for the theoretical analysis of the tradition. If the anarchists include figures as different as the seven sages, or practically every figure in the past who could somehow be construed as advocating antistatism or individual freedom, then anarchism *must* seem incoherent and therefore cannot be subjected to a rigorous theoretical interrogation. This was the problem Eltzbacher faced, and it remains real today.

Consider April Carter's *The Political Theory of Anarchism*, which proves less a demonstration that there is some sort of anarchist political theory than an account of how the supposed sages were at odds on basic issues such as the nature of society, the use of violence, class struggle, industrialisation, urbanisation, and democracy.[64] In the end, the book is really a series of monographs on different themes—federalism, the individual, and so on—each drawn exclusively from a single theorist, with no explanation of why these theorists should be thought to share a larger paradigm.[65] If we wish to consider anarchism as a set of ideas relevant to current progressive struggles against neoliberalism, we must have a clear understanding of what ideas we mean by anarchism.

Starting Again: Socialism, Bakunin, and the First International

We suggest that the apparently ahistorical and incoherent character of anarchism is an artefact of the way in which anarchism has been studied, rather than inherent in anarchism itself. Using a deductive method, but taking more care in our selection of the representatives of anarchism, we can develop a different, more accurate, and more useful understanding of anarchism.

Where, then, to start, and how should the anarchists be selected? It is Eltzbacher's approach that perhaps ironically provides a guide. Eltzbacher's interest in anarchism emerged against the backdrop of the rise of a self-described anarchist movement in the late nineteenth century. A "general awareness of an 'anarchist' position did not exist until after the appearance of its representatives in the late 1870s," and anarchism "initially appeared to contemporaries to be a new phenomenon."[66]

It was precisely this development, this "new phenomenon," that led to the first studies of anarchism. While the movement was seen at first as a harmless revival of older utopian ideas, it was increasingly viewed as a sinister and subversive force, and explained in criminological and psychological terms; only in the early twentieth century did anarchist ideology itself become a serious object of enquiry, with Eltzbacher blazing the trail and shaping the course of twentieth-century accounts.[67] This, in turn, opened the door to a series of historical accounts of anarchism, both by scholars and anarchist ideologues.[68]

That the anarchist movement only emerged as an identifiable and self-identified current, a social movement, and a political force from the late 1860s onward is beyond any serious dispute. Eltzbacher himself stressed that anarchism was a new phenomenon.[69] Notwithstanding their claims that anarchism can be found throughout history (and seemingly unaware that they were contradicting themselves), both the standard works on the subject and the mythological histories developed by some of the anarchists made the same point, dating anarchism to the First International, Bakunin, and the Alliance.

Joll stated that it was only after 1848 that the "modern revolutionary movement begins," and that it was "in the 1860s that the anarchist movement began to be a practical political force."[70] Kedward spoke of the "great age of the anarchists in Europe and America ... between 1880 and 1914."[71] Miller referred to the "eruptions of anarchist activity occurring throughout Europe from the 1860s," and traced the "origins of anarchism as an organised political force" to splits in the First International.[72] Woodcock wrote that the "anarchist movement" arose in the First International, and was the "creation" of Bakunin.[73] It was in the First International that the "central Marxist-Bakuninist conflicts over political action and the state" were established, and the "great schism" between classical Marxism and anarchism took place.[74] Even Marshall, who used an extremely loose definition of anarchism, argued that it was Bakunin who "turned anarchism into a theory of political action, and helped develop the anarchist movement" into a popular force.[75]

The same starting point is also conceded in works that propound the legitimising myth of universal anarchism. While making a claim for the universality of anarchism, Kropotkin also noted that anarchism was the outgrowth of nineteenth-century socialist and democratic movements, and was "the no-government system of socialism."[76] It was in the First International that socialism moved from "Governmentalism" to a new conception, "formulating itself little by little in the Congresses of the great Association and later on among its successors," and so "modern anarchism" was born.[77] For Rocker, in "modern anarchism we have the confluence of the two great currents which during and since the French Revolution have found such characteristic expression in the intellectual life of Europe: Socialism and Liberalism."[78] It "was with the rise of Mikhail Bakunin that revolutionary anarchism emerged as a social doctrine and that an anarchist movement grew in Europe and became the vanguard of revolutionary endeavour."[79]

It is therefore reasonable to take the 1860s and the First International as the womb of the anarchist movement; it is also reasonable to take Bakunin, the key figure in the movement at that time, and Kropotkin (after Bakunin's death, "unquestionably the most widely read and respected anarchist theorist" in the world) as suitable representatives of the anarchist tradition, and the basis from which to identify the main ideas of anarchism.[80] By doing so, we can also delineate which figures and movements should be included within the broad anarchist tradition.

In particular, it is crucial to note that it was within the *socialist* milieu that the ideas identified with Bakunin, Kropotkin, and the anarchist movement emerged, and given that the First International was a working-class movement, that it was in the *working-class* movement and the unions that anarchism was born. This is a significant point, one that draws attention to a key consequence of Eltzbacher's position: he removed class struggle and anticapitalism from anarchism. As Marie Fleming observes, "The importance of the socialist impulse within the thought of the European anarchists" was consistently ignored, an approach that is still commonly expressed by the tendency of scholars to juxtapose the terms anarchist and socialist.[81] It is this that allows Woodcock to describe the question of capitalism as merely a "limited region" over which anarchists had no consensus, Miller to suggest that while the anarchists opposed "existing economic systems" they differed on the question of whether to abolish capitalism or institute a resolutely free market, and Marshall to speak of "anarcho-capitalists."[82] Once it is recognised that anarchism was and is part of the socialist movement, it makes no sense to use phrases like "a fusion of anarchist and socialist ideas."[83]

The First International was founded in London in 1864, largely at the hands of disciples of Proudhon and some English unionists. While he was not involved in the initiative to establish the organisation, Marx was invited to sit on its general council. He did not represent any major section of the First International, but was a hard worker and impressive thinker, and was able to take control with the aid of his followers along with political socialists of various types, and the mutualists soon lost any substantial influence in the central section.

It was only with the entry of Bakunin and his circle that Marx's domination began to be challenged. The Alliance, though formally dissolved, continued to operate, and provided the pole around which a growing number of people and currents critical of political socialism began to cohere. The Belgian delegate César de Paepe, the Swiss James Guillaume (1844–1916), Adhémer Schwitzguébel (1844–1895), and the French activist Jean-Louis Pindy (1840–1917) were among those who, along with Bakunin, played a key role in formulating the anarchist conception at the meetings of the First International. Guillaume was a schoolteacher and historian who took an energetic part in the First International, worked closely with Bakunin, withdrew from political activity in 1878, later resurfaced in 1903 as a prominent figure in French syndicalism, and died in 1916.

Bakunin and the Alliance made their first appearance at the 1869 Basel congress of the First International, which Bakunin dominated with his striking oratory and personal force. Bakunin's victory over Marx—centred on the relatively trivial issue of inheritance rights—opened the struggle with Marx in earnest, for Marx had been challenged successfully for the first time on matters of policy and doctrine.[84] This meeting saw important early discussions of syndicalism by Pindy, and a crucial debate on the state by de Paepe and Schwitzguébel.[85]

By 1871, the First International was divided into Marxist and Bakuninist sections, and it split the following year along these lines. Both factions subsequently claimed to be the real First International, although the anarchists, who were the large majority of the First International's adherents and sections, and counted among its ranks the largest national federations of sections, certainly had the stronger grounds for their claim. Not every group affiliated with the Bakuninist section was anarchist, but the anarchists were the majority in what became known as the "Saint-Imier International," which lasted until 1877. The Marxist-led faction, headquartered in New York, lingered on until 1876. Bakunin died in 1876, and was buried in Berne, Switzerland.

This new movement, this self-consciously "anarchist" tradition, defined itself from the start in a clear manner, with a detailed social analysis along with strategies and tactics to change society. The new doctrine had none of the incoherence often attributed to it. In terms of its intellectual influences, only Proudhon, out of Eltzbacher's other sages, influenced anarchism. Marx, too, was an important influence, although the bitterness between the anarchists and the Marxists led many to downplay his ideas. Godwin and Tolstoy played no role.

While the key figures in the anarchist movement were Bakunin and Kropotkin, neither claimed to be the originator of anarchism, insisting—like subsequent anarchists—that their philosophy stemmed directly from the experiences of the working class and peasantry. Such an identification of the anarchist idea with great individuals has been regarded by anarchists as suggesting infallible texts or teachers, undermining the collectivist nature of anarchism as a social creed rather than an individual revelation, and deifying individuals. When the *Fraye Arbeter Shtime* ("Free Voice of Labour"), an American Jewish anarchist paper, planned to publish a supplement of Kropotkin photographs, Kropotkin himself objected on the grounds that he refused to be made into an icon.[86]

Both Bakunin and Kropotkin defined anarchism as an anticapitalist ideology and a form of socialism. Bakunin's writings before 1870 tend to use the term revolutionary socialism rather than anarchism, and sharply distinguish his collectivist and antiauthoritarian approach from the authoritarian socialism of Marx. Kropotkin is equally emphatic: "We are communists," but "our communism is not that of the authoritarian school; it is anarchist communism, communism without government, free communism."[87] This identification with the socialist movement is extremely significant. Later, of course, many anarchists rejected labels like socialist and communist because of their associations with social democracy and Communism, but this should not be understood to mean that anarchism was not socialist.

In place of capitalism and centralised state control, the anarchists favoured a stateless, self-managed, and planned economy in which the means of production were controlled by the working class and peasantry, class divisions had been abolished, and distribution took place on the basis of need. This would provide a situation of social and economic equality that would enable genuine individual freedom to exist. There was no sign of any hankering after the premodern era; the anarchists aimed at a rational, democratic, and modern society.

Against Hierarchy

The basic premise of all of the anarchist arguments was a deep and fundamental commitment to individual freedom. For the anarchists, however, freedom could only exist, and be exercised, in society; equally, inegalitarian and hierarchical social structures made freedom impossible. It followed that the anarchist ideal was a society based on social and economic equality as well as self-management, in which individual freedom could truly exist. Bakunin declared that the anarchist "insists on his positive rights to life and all of its intellectual, moral and physical joys" because "he loves life and wants to enjoy it in all of its abundance."[88]

It is simply not true to claim, like E. H. Carr in his rather hostile biography, that Bakunin was an extreme individualist influenced by Stirner.[89] Bakunin envisaged freedom as a product of society, not a revolt against society by individuals, arguing,

> Society, far from decreasing ... freedom, on the contrary creates the individual freedom of all human beings. Society is the root, the tree, and liberty is its fruit. Hence, in every epoch, man must seek his freedom not at the beginning but at the end of history.... I can feel free only in the presence of, and in relation with other men....
>
> I am truly free only when all human beings, men and women, are equally free, and the freedom of other men, far from negating or limiting my freedom, is, on the contrary, its necessary premise and confirmation.[90]

He saw the struggle against extreme individualism as an essential part of the anarchist project: "In every Congress" of the First International, "we have fought the individualists ... who claim, along with the moralists and bourgeois economists, that man can be free ... outside of society.... He is ... a social animal.... Only in society can he become a human being ... freedom ... is the product of the collectivity."[91]

Along similar lines, Kropotkin rejected the "misanthropic bourgeois individualism" he identified with people like Stirner.[92] This approach, of every person for herself or himself, was not freedom at all but simply the right of the strong to oppress the weak. What Kropotkin favoured instead was "true individuality," which could only be developed "through practising the highest communist sociability." It "is easy to see" that Stirner's approach was simply a "disguised return" of "privileged minorities." The "privileged minorities" could only survive if backed by a state power, and so "the claims of these individualists necessarily end in a return to the state idea and to that same coercion which they so fiercely attack."[93]

In other words, genuine individual freedom and individuality could only exist in a free society. The anarchists did not therefore identify freedom with the right of everybody to do exactly what one pleased but with a social order in which collective effort and responsibilities—that is to say, obligations—would provide the material basis and social nexus in which individual freedom could exist. This is entirely at odds with Stirner's views. Stirner believed that "the egoist" thinks "only of himself," only of "*my* cause" and not of anything more, whether that be "the Good Cause, then God's cause, the cause of mankind, of truth, of freedom, of humanity, of justice; further, the cause of my people, my prince, my fatherland; finally, even the cause of Mind, and a thousand other causes." The "name of egoist" must be applied to the "man who, instead of living to an idea,—*i.e.* a spiritual thing," is always "sacrificing it to his personal advantage."[94]

Between the notion of freedom articulated by Stirner and that of the anarchists lies an abyss. For Bakunin, a person's "duties to society are indissolubly linked with his rights."[95] The watchwords of popular emancipation were freedom and solidarity. Such solidarity was "the spontaneous product of social life, economic as well as moral; the result of the free federation of common interests, aspirations and tendencies." Most important, he emphasised, it "has as its essential basis *equality and collective labour*—obligatory not by law, but by the force of realities—and collective property."[96] Kropotkin likewise insisted that "all must be put on the same footing as producers and consumers of wealth," and "everybody" must contribute to "the common well-being to the full extent of his capacities."[97]

Such, in short, was the aim of anarchism: not "misanthropic bourgeois individualism" but a deep love of freedom, understood as a social product, a deep respect for human rights, a profound celebration of humankind and its potential, and a commitment to a form of society where a "true individuality" was irrevocably linked to "the highest communist sociability." This interlinking of rights and duties opens the door to the exercise of a degree of *legitimate* coercive power in an anarchist society—an issue that will be examined below.[98]

The anarchist view that freedom was exercised through and implied obligations to society was not shared by Godwin, who saw society as a threat to freedom and looked forward to a world of isolated rational individuals. Stirner was also an individualist, but of rather a different sort than Godwin. He believed that unbridled self-interest was the only true value, and saw idealism as a cynical mask, celebrated criminals, and claimed might made right: "Everything over which I have might that cannot be torn from me remains my property; well, then let might decide about property, and I will expect everything from my might!"[99] Here, freedom was not a withdrawal from society but a doctrine of revolt against others.

Against Capitalism and Landlordism

The anarchists aimed, said Bakunin, "to organise society in such a manner that every individual, man or woman, should find, upon entering life, approximately equal means for the development of his or her diverse faculties and their utilization in his or her work."[100] And "freedom," he wrote, is "above all, eminently social, because it can only be realised in society and by the strictest equality and solidarity among men."[101] "A person who is dying from starvation, who is crushed by poverty, who every day is on the point of death from cold and hunger and who sees everyone he loves suffering likewise but is unable to come to their aid, is not free; that person is a slave."[102]

But such a free society did not exist yet. Every individual did *not* find "upon entering life" equal access to the means of life but instead a world scarred by inequality and privilege; for the wealthy few, life could be a joy, but for the mass of the people, for the working class and peasantry, it was a struggle to survive, a world of destitution among plenty. "True individuality" simply could not exist for ordinary people under the existing social conditions, for equality and solidarity did not exist.

At the heart of the problem were typically interlocked systems of class domination and exploitation. Most obviously, there were the systems of capitalism and landlordism. For the anarchists, the capitalists or bourgeoisie were powerful in the modern world, but where economies were less developed, older precapitalist landowning elites (generally hereditary aristocracies or nobilities) also played an important role. It is not possible to understand the anarchist position on the peasantry unless it is noted that the socialist impulse in anarchism was not simply an anticapitalist one but entailed a critique of landed wealth as well.

The capitalists and landlords were two elites that could easily coexist—indeed, many of the great landholders developed into rural capitalists—and it is in this context that the common use of the term "middle class" to refer to capitalists in nineteenth-century anarchist writing must be understood. They did not use the term middle class in either of the ways common in the twentieth century—to signify relatively comfortable layers of society, or to refer to the middling layers of professionals, small business people, and middle management—but rather to distinguish the new capitalists from the aristocrats. The same usage may also be found in older Marxist writing, yet has generally fallen away in later years.

The landlords and capitalists made up a substantial part of the ruling class of the modern world, but there was a third element to this class, according to the anarchists: the managers of the state apparatus. This "bureaucratic aristocracy," these "cynical bureaucratic martinets," were also "enemies of the people," and just as involved in the domination and exploitation of the popular classes.[103] From this perspective, presidents, kings, generals, members of parliament, directors, and mayors were as much a part of the ruling class as the industrialists.

Landlordism and capitalism were directly responsible for making the "strictest equality and solidarity" impossible. Anarchists identified the peasantry as victims of landlordism: because the peasantry did not generally own their own land, they were compelled to pay rents in the form of labour, produce, or money where a landlord or corporation held title, or pay taxes where the state or the peasant held land title. In both cases, the peasantry were compelled to turn over a significant part of their produce to the dominant groups for the right of farming the land on which they lived. And in order to survive, the peasantry were often compelled to borrow money, particularly in lean seasons, and sell goods on the market at low prices in good seasons with bumper harvests; many were, in addition, compelled to enter wage labour to make ends meet.

Trapped in a web of domination and exploitation, the peasantry constituted an oppressed class. As Kropotkin declared,

> But the golden age is over for the small farmer. Today he hardly knows how to make ends meet. He gets into debt, becomes a victim of the cattle-dealer, the real-estate jobber, the usurer; notes and mortgages ruin whole villages, even more than the frightful taxes imposed by State and commune. Small proprietorship is in a dreadful condition; and even if the small farmer is still owner in name, he is in fact nothing more than a tenant paying rent to money-dealers and usurers.[104]

Bakunin noted the peasants' "instinctive hatred of the 'fine gentlemen' and ... bourgeois landlords, who enjoy the bounty of the earth without cultivating it with their own hands."[105] Kropotkin complained of the injustice of a system in which a person may only farm if "he gives up part of [the] product to the landlord."[106]

The system of landlordism was as intolerable as capitalism, which oppressed the working class. The problem with capitalism was not its use of modern technology, for the anarchists were greatly in favour of new technologies that could eliminate drudgery and reduce working time. The problem was the pervasive social injustice and oppressive hierarchy embedded in the class system. In other words, the problems lay in the economic and social relations under which technology was used, not with the technology itself.

Capitalists and state officials controlled the means of production and dominated capitalist production. Asked Bakunin, "Is it necessary to repeat here the irrefutable arguments of Socialism which no bourgeois economist has yet succeeded in disproving?" "Property" and "capital" in "their present form" meant that "the capitalist and the property owner" had the power and the right, guaranteed by the state, to "live without working," while the worker was already "in the position of a serf."[107] (In comparing the worker to a serf, Bakunin was referring to the unfree peasants of feudal Europe who were legally bound to particular estates and unable to move freely).

This was a system of exploitation, which the anarchists evidently understood as the transfer of resources from a productive class to a dominant but unproductive one. Exploitation in the capitalist system took place at work and through the wage system. The worker was paid a wage that in theory covered one's basic needs. Yet the actual value produced by the worker at work was always higher than the wage received by the worker; a baking worker, for example, might help produce several hundred loaves of bread per day, but would receive the cash equivalent of perhaps two loaves of bread per day. The difference went to the capitalist who owned the bakery.

Unlike the serf, the worker was controlled in part through the labour market; lacking property on which to subsist, the worker was forced to work for another, and as Bakunin put it, the "terrible threat of starvation which daily hangs over his head and over his family, will force him to accept any conditions imposed by the gainful calculations of the capitalist." Private property in the means of production therefore meant, for Bakunin, "the power and the right to live by exploiting the work of someone else, the right to exploit the work of those who possess neither property nor capital and who thus are forced to sell their productive power to the lucky owners of both."[108] For Kropotkin, "Owing to our wage system" the "sudden increase in our powers of production ... resulted only in an unprecedented accumulation of wealth in the hands of the owners of capital; while an increase in misery for great numbers, and an insecurity of life for all, has been the lot of the workmen." It was a "sad mockery" and a "misrepresentation," said Kropotkin, to call the labour contract a "free contract," for the worker accepted the contract from "sheer necessity," the "force" of need.[109]

The serfs at least had direct control over the work process and managed many of their affairs through the village. The wageworker did not. The drive to maximise exploitation was always wedded to authoritarian workplace regimes. For "once the contract has been negotiated," Bakunin argued, "the serfdom of the workers is doubly increased," because the "merchandise" that the worker had "sold to his employer" was "his labour, his personal services, the productive forces of his body, mind, and spirit that are found in him and are inseparable from his person—it is therefore himself":

> From then on, the employer will watch over him, either directly or by means of overseers; every day during working hours and under controlled conditions, the employer will be the owner of his actions and movements. When he is told: "Do this," the worker is obligated to do it; or he is told: "Go there," he must go. Is this not what is called a serf?[110]

Finally, domination through both the labour market and labour process was often supplemented by various forms of extraeconomic coercion that were used to control and bond labour: debt, controls over movement, forced labour, and so forth.

Linked to these issues was the question of distribution. Under capitalism, goods and services were distributed through the market; they were commodities that had to be bought before they could be used. Access was conditional on the ability to *pay*, rather than on actual need. An unemployed person without a wage had no specific right to the goods or services one needed to survive, while the wages of the employed workers were at best just able to cover one's basic needs. One result was an apparent situation of "overproduction": more goods and services were produced than could be sold, because the working class, a sizable part of the population, had such limited purchasing power. Another was war and imperial conquest. Kropotkin argued that a system where workers were "unable to purchase with their wages the riches they are producing," an artificial situation of overproduction, resulted in "wars, continuous wars ... for supremacy in the world market," as each country sought new markets for its surplus goods and services to the elites of other countries.[111]

From the above it is quite clear that the class issue—what Bakunin called the "social question"—was uppermost in the minds of the anarchist movement. The anarchists, consequently, viewed class struggle as a necessary part of social change, and saw in the victims of class domination and exploitation—the working class and peasantry—the agents of that change. Capitalism was no mere "limited region" of "economic organisation" over which the anarchists could not agree, as Woodcock suggests.[112] It was, and remains, at the heart of the anarchist critique of the modern world. Miller's assertion that while the anarchists opposed "existing economic systems" they differed on the question of whether to abolish capitalism or institute a resolutely free market is equally problematic, as is Marshall's attempt to find a home in the anarchist tradition for those extreme liberals who adopt the oxymoron "anarcho-capitalist."[113]

Economic liberalism, with its belief that a competitive free market based on maximising self-interest produces optimal results for most people—the idea central to its current incarnation as neoliberalism—is not anarchist. Stirner, who translated into German Smith's *Wealth of Nations* and the writings of Smith's French disciple, J. B. Say, was not an advocate of the free market, despite Marshall's claim to the contrary.[114] What he shared with economic liberalism, however, was the notion that the unrestricted pursuit of personal advantage is a virtue in itself, a basic sentiment of laissez-faire capitalism.

The anarchists, by contrast, had nothing but contempt for capitalism and loathed economic liberals. Bakunin referred to economic liberals as the "passionate lovers of all freedom which they can use to their advantage" who "demand the unlimited right to exploit the proletariat and bitterly resent state interference."[115] Kropotkin rejected the "middle class economists" who promoted the doctrine of the free market, in which the state should refrain from involving itself in the economy. "While giving the capitalist any degree of free scope to amass his wealth at the expense of the helpless labourers, the government has *never* and *nowhere* ... afforded the labourers the opportunity to 'do as they pleased.'" In a class system, the free market was nothing but a means to exploitation, something to be put aside whenever it suited the ruling class: "'Non-interference,' and more than non-interference,—direct support, help and protection,—existed *only* in the interests of the exploiters."[116]

Against the State

For the anarchists, the class system, affecting the majority of people, was the most fundamental obstacle to true individuality. Many commentators, both hostile and sympathetic, have nonetheless reduced anarchism to antistatism. According to Engels, the anarchists argued that "it is the state which has created capital, that the capitalist only has his capital by grace of the state ... the state is the chief evil ... which must be done away with and then capitalism will go to blazes of itself."[117] This approach fails to understand *why* anarchists opposed the state. It cannot be claimed that anarchists rejected the state simply because it imposed social order and rules, nor that they attribute all social ills to the state.

Rather, the anarchist critique of the state arises partly from an opposition to hierarchy and partly from a class outlook. The state is seen as a defender of the class system and a centralised body that necessarily concentrates power in the hands of the ruling classes; in both respects, it is the means through which a *minority* rules a majority. It follows that the abolition of the state is one of the preconditions for a libertarian and socialist order. The view that the state was an organ of class domination was one that anarchists shared with Marxists. But there were also critical differences between the traditions. The state, Bakunin argued, has always been the patrimony of some privileged class or other; a priestly class, an aristocratic class, a bourgeois class. And finally, when all the other classes have exhausted themselves, the state becomes the patrimony of the bureaucratic class and then falls—or, if you will, rises—to the position of a machine; but it is absolutely necessary for the salvation of the state that there should be some privileged class devoted to its preservation.[118]

For Kropotkin, the state was nothing but the concentrated power of the ruling class, and in the modern period, "the chief bulwark of capital."[119]

Bakunin was certainly convinced that a parliamentary system was preferable to a dictatorship because it allowed more scope for individual freedom and popular self-activity:

We are firmly convinced it is true that the most imperfect republic is a thousand times better than the most enlightened monarchy. In a republic there are at least brief periods when the people, while continuously exploited, is not oppressed, in the monarchies, oppression is constant. The democratic regime also lifts the masses up gradually to participation in public life—something the monarchy never does.

Yet, for Bakunin, while a parliamentary system was an important reform that benefited the popular classes, it still did not create a means to remove the basic inequalities of power and wealth in society:

Nevertheless, while we prefer the republic, we must recognise and proclaim that whatever the form of government may be, so long as human society continues to be divided into different classes as a result of the hereditary inequality of occupations, of wealth, of education, and of rights, there will always be a class-restricted government and the inevitable exploitation of the majorities by the minorities. The State is nothing but this domination and this exploitation, well regulated and systematised.[120]

The establishment of a parliamentary government did not change the basic class character of the state: it was as much a form of "class-rule" as "absolute monarchy."[121] Laws created by the state were, in general, not a means providing equal rights and protection for all but served the interests of those who thrived on inequality and oppression; all "legislation made within the state," Kropotkin insisted, "has to be repudiated because it has always been made with regard to the interests of the privileged classes."[122] Only laws forced on to the state *from without*, by the direct action of the popular classes, could benefit the masses. Even these laws were compromises that restrained the ruling class yet did not overthrow it. The field of law must then be understood as shaped by class struggles, yet dominated by the ruling class, and unable to provide the means of popular emancipation.

In the classical Marxist tradition, the state is defined in fairly simple terms as a "body of armed men" serving the dominant class, from which it can be concluded that the working class, led by the revolutionary party, must form its own dictatorship of the proletariat to change society.[123] This state would later wither away, but it was a necessary intermediate stage between capitalism and the free communism of the future. For the anarchists, this strategy failed to take account of the fact that the state was not simply a "body of armed men" but also and always a highly centralised structure that inevitably concentrated power in the hands of a directing elite. "It would be obviously impossible for some hundreds of thousands or even some tens of thousands or indeed for only a few thousand men to exercise this power."[124] A strong state could have "only one solid foundation: military and bureaucratic centralisation."[125]

If that was the case, then even the most radical government must perpetuate the rule of a (class) minority over a (class) majority. One effect was a crippling of popular self-activity and self-organisation, with the state "a vast slaughterhouse or enormous cemetery, where all the real aspirations, all the living forces of a country enter generously and happily," but are "slain and buried."[126] A "centralised government" concentrated power in "parliament and its executive," and was also unable to deal with the concerns of ordinary people, "all the numberless affairs of the community."[127]

If "state ... and capitalism are inseparable concepts ... bound together ... by the bond of cause and effect, effect and cause," then even a revolutionary state must generate a capitalist system of some sort.[128] Just as an economically dominant class entails a state, a state entails an economically dominant class. State centralisation was not accidental but rather followed from the role of the state as an instrument of the dominant minorities—of ruling classes—which could only rule if administrative power was concentrated in their hands. The State was both a defender of the class sytem, and itself a central pillar of ruling class power.

The emancipation of the working class and peasantry required a radically democratic form of social organisation that maximised popular self-activity and self-management—and this was entirely at odds with the state. The state, argued Kropotkin, "having been the force to which the minorities resorted for establishing and organising their power over the masses, cannot be the force which will serve to destroy those privileges."[129] This critique of the state as both a ruling-class organisation and the destroyer of individual freedom is quite different from the rejection of the state as an enemy of individual autonomy—the view, again, held by Godwin, Stirner, and Tolstoy.

The Rejection of State Socialism

The political conclusion that followed was that the state was as much an obstacle to the abolition of the class system as landlordism and capitalism. While opposed to economic liberalism, the anarchists did not look to increased state intervention as a solution. The choice between the market and the state was an empty one. The state was not, and could not become, an instrument of fundamental social change. Regardless of their ideology, intent, or social origins, those who held state power would always be part of a dominant class. Bakunin commented that "the people will feel no better if the stick with which they are being beaten is labelled the 'people's stick.' ... No State ... not even the reddest republic—can ever give the people what they really want."[130]

A strategy premised on the capture of state power—whether by electoral action or revolution—would, in other words, simply repeat the social evils present in the existing states: class domination through authoritarian centralisation. It is in this context that Bakunin described universal suffrage as an "immense fraud" and a "puerile fiction," at least with regard to the distribution of power and wealth in society: "The day after election everybody goes about his business, the people go back to toil anew, the bourgeoisie to reaping profits and political conniving."[131] When decision making occurs without the "intervention" of the people, the "people are committed to ruinous policies, all without noticing." The results of the election of a new government, even one openly committed to advancing the interests of the majority, would be "very moderate," and the ruling party would become part of the machinery of class domination, adopting patriotism in place of internationalism, forming alliances with "bourgeois liberal" parties, and restricting its aspirations to minimal reforms that do not upset the ruling class.[132]

Instead of the ruling party changing the state, the state would change the ruling party. Bakunin argued that parliamentarians would be corrupted by their "institutional positions" and unaccountable to their constituencies, and it is a "characteristic of privilege and of every privileged position to kill the hearts and minds of men."[133] This would apply regardless of the mandates given to the party, the wages paid to the parliamentarians, or the existence of other mechanisms to keep the parliamentarians accountable to their constituents. Paying parliamentarians a worker's wage or making provision for constituents to recall "bad" parliamentarians between elections would not change the situation.

When Bakunin wrote, widespread suffrage was a rarity everywhere, including in Europe. By Kropotkin's time there had been real changes, yet the situation still seemed to bear out Bakunin's views. "Much hope of improvement," remarked Kropotkin, "was placed ... in the extension of political rights to the working classes," but "these concessions, unsupported by corresponding changes in economic relations, proved delusions."[134]

The anarchists also rejected the classical Marxist strategy of the proletarian dictatorship as a means to destroy class society. The use of the state, a centralised instrument of power, would mean a small revolutionary elite would operate as a ruling group, replicating an important feature of the class system that anarchists wished to destroy: rule by minority. Further, freedom could not be introduced from above but required self-emancipation through cooperation and struggle. "I am above all an absolute enemy of revolution by decrees," said Bakunin, "which derives from the idea of the revolutionary State, i.e., reaction disguised as revolution." Why "reaction disguised as revolution"? Simply because authoritarian means could not be used to promote emancipatory ends: "decrees, like authority in general, abolish nothing; they only perpetuate that which they were supposed to destroy."[135]

Even if a revolutionary dictatorship crushed the older elites, the new regime would itself be a class system, fundamentally as bad as any that preceded it. For "the proletariat," Bakunin wrote, "this will, in reality, be nothing but a barracks: a regime, where regimented workingmen and women will sleep, wake, work, and live to the beat of a drum."[136] For Kropotkin, such a state would be "as great a danger to liberty as any form of autocracy" because government would be "entrusted with the management of all the social organisation including the production and distribution of wealth."[137]

Bakunin and Kropotkin repeatedly suggested that revolutionary "socialist" governments would, in fact, be forms of state capitalism. Bakunin spoke of the opportunities for the "shrewd and educated," who would "be granted government privileges," and the "mercenary-minded," who would be "attracted by the immensity of the international speculations of the state bank, [and] will find a vast field for lucrative, underhanded dealings."[138] "The State, having become the sole proprietor" of the means of production, "will then become the only banker, capitalist, organiser, and director of all national labour, and the distributor of its products."[139] The spectre of "centralised state-capitalism," "preached under the name of collectivism," a "form of the wage system," always haunted Kropotkin's writings.[140]

Slavery within would be matched by slavery without, as the revolutionary state competed with other states, forcing the new ruling elite to become patriots, warmongers, and aspiring imperialists; thus, a Marxist regime in Germany would become the bearer of a new pan-Germanism, and Marx would become the "Bismarck of socialism." After a twentieth century that has seen the invasion and military occupation of Eastern Europe by the USSR, border clashes between the USSR and the People's Republic of China (which led to more troops being deployed by the USSR along the Chinese border than the border with Western Europe by the 1970s), and war between the self-described socialist regimes of Cambodia and Vietnam, many would say that Bakunin was right.

For anarchists, the repression, social inequalities, and militarism of the self-described regimes of "actually existing socialism" and "people's democracies" of the twentieth century are not temporary "distortions" or a "degeneration" of an otherwise-emancipatory Marxist practice. They are the logical outcomes of an authoritarian and statist politics. The means shape the ends; an authoritarian strategy, based on centralisation, dictatorship, and militarisation, necessarily leads to a centralised, dictatorial, and militarised regime. A self-managed and popular revolution from below, on the contrary, has the real potential to create a new and radically democratic society. The need for the means to match the ends, and the possibility of a radical anticapitalist politics that rejects the state, are two of anarchism's major insights for contemporary struggles.

Elements of the Social Revolution

How, then, did these anarchists propose to change society? They did not always agree on the best strategy—an issue that we will explore in later chapters. Consequently, strategy cannot be a defining feature of anarchism. What anarchists did share, however, were a set of principles to frame strategy and tactics: class struggle, internationalism, self-determination, antistatism, and antiauthoritarianism.

The Popular Classes

As is clear from the preceding discussion, anarchists saw the struggle of the popular classes—the working class and peasantry—as the basic motor of change. It would be futile to expect the ruling class to act against its own vested interests in the current system. Even when ruling classes were oppressed by other ruling classes and powerful states, their interests lay in expanding their *own* scope for exploitation and domination. A class struggle from below, assuming a radically democratic form and taking place outside of and against the state, and aiming to replace capitalism and the state with collective ownership of the means of production, collective and participatory decision-making, and an international, federal, and self-managed socialist system is at the heart of anarchism.

Bakunin emphasised that "the only two classes capable of so mighty an insurrection" as was required to remake society are "*the workers and the peasants*."[141] It was essential that ordinary people, working class and peasant alike, organise as a bloc of oppressed classes independently of their class enemies. Bakunin and Kropotkin had immense faith in the "flower of the proletariat," the great "rabble of the people," the "underdogs," the "great, beloved, common people," the masses.[142] It was in the "great mass of workers ... unable to obtain a better station in life" that the "will" and "power" needed to make the revolution was to be found.[143] The enormous growth of the working class in modern times, the continued existence of the peasantry, and the increasing class divisions of the present signal that the historical agents identified by Bakunin and Kropotkin remain a force with which to reckon.

Anarchism's stress on the revolutionary potential of the peasantry differentiated it from the views of the early Marxists. Marx and Engels predicted the demise of the peasantry, and argued that the peasantry were inherently unable to organise, for their "mode of production isolates them from one another, instead of bringing them into mutual intercourse"; they "do not form a class" capable of "enforcing their class interests in their own name."[144] This supposedly predisposes peasants to seek salvation from above by an "unlimited governmental power" that "sends them rain and sunshine from above."[145] The agrarian question had to be resolved as a secondary part of the "proletarian" revolution, and it could not be resolved without the leading role of the working class.

The appropriate agrarian strategy was fiercely debated among classical Marxists, and the SDP was deeply divided on the issue of the peasantry. While some activists were keenly interested in winning the peasantry, the party majority followed Kautsky's view that the peasantry constituted a declining class and was relatively unimportant to the party's fortunes, and that the party should not adopt a programme of reforms aimed at the peasantry.[146] Kautsky, the "pope of socialism," did "more to popularise Marxism in western Europe than any other intellectual" besides Engels.[147]

Kautsky's views on the agrarian question were designed for industrial Germany, and he believed that a different approach was needed for less developed countries like Russia where capitalism was not yet dominant. Here, the task of the day was a bourgeois democratic revolution: the capitalist class must take power, uproot feudal barriers to trade and industry, and undertake agrarian and legal reforms. The peasantry could aid this process, although they would be destroyed by the subsequent development of capitalism.[148] Capitalism, in turn, was a necessary step towards socialism.

Lenin agreed with Kautsky, arguing that as a "bourgeois revolution expresses the needs of capitalist development," it was "*in the highest degree advantageous to the proletariat*."[149] Operating in backward Russia, where urban industry was an island in a vast peasant sea, the Bolsheviks naturally looked to the peasants for allies, but proposed that the peasants take their lead from the working class, itself led by the vanguard party.[150] In the thought of Mao, the leader of the Chinese Communist

Party (CCP), the peasantry were regarded as critical to the bourgeois democratic revolution against the imperialist and "feudal forces" that hampered capitalist development.[151] Again, however, the peasants must be "led by the working class and the Communist Party," with the latter, Mao contended, structured as an armed guerrilla formation (a "people's army") given the Chinese conditions.[152] In the context of colonial and semicolonial countries, the bourgeois democratic revolution was termed a *national* democratic revolution to stress its anti-imperialist character.

The two-stage approach to the revolutionary process in the less developed colonial and semicolonial countries—first, a national democratic revolution, and only later a proletarian one—was codified by the Communist International (Comintern, or sometimes called the Third International) in the late 1920s.[153] Yet this strategy followed from the classical Marxist view that capitalism was a necessary evil that would create the working class that could install the dictatorship of the proletariat as well as the advanced industries that made socialism viable—positions that we will discuss in more depth in the next chapter. Classical Marxists, in short, traditionally saw the peasantry as a doomed class, unable to make a revolution without outside leadership, whether by capitalists or Communists.

By contrast, the anarchists always identified the peasantry as a potentially revolutionary class and the natural ally of the working class. Bakunin admitted that peasants were frequently "egoistic and reactionary," full of "prejudices" against the revolution, often fiercely attached to private property, and quite possibly harder to organise than urban workers.[154] But the peasants had a history of struggle, a deep hatred of their oppressors, and a common cause with the working class. Steps must be taken to draw the peasants into the revolutionary movement by applying the "determined treatment of revolutionary socialism" to the "rash of measles" of reactionary sentiment.[155]

The peasants could be won over to the struggle for social transformation through agitation, joint organisation with the working class, and a revolutionary programme. The key was not a programme of reforms under the present system but one of radical redistribution of "state and Church lands and the holdings of the big landowners," and the suspension of "all public and private debts."[156] By the end of the twentieth century, it certainly seems clear that the classical Marxist rejection of the peasantry was flawed. Anarchists can point to the importance of the peasants in the major social upheavals of the last few centuries—including the Russian and Chinese revolutions—and the existence of radical peasant currents that have gone far beyond the narrow politics that Marxism would suggest.

Anarchists can also point to the continued significance of the peasantry, for even by the most severe calculations there are perhaps still two billion peasants and petty commodity producers, while half of the world's population lives in regions numerically dominated by the peasantry—China, South Asia and continental Southeast Asia, sub-Saharan Africa, and Central America.[157] Indeed, in some parts of Africa and Latin America there has even been some "re-peasantisation" as industrial workers retrenched during the current economic decline and neoliberal restructuring have returned to farming.[158]

The peasantry and working class, then, are the anarchists' engines of revolution—not a political party, a revolutionary vanguard party, a benevolent government, or a great leader. It was necessary, Bakunin insisted, to unite the working class and peasantry, so often divided by their cultures, ways of life, and the machinations of the powerful. There was "no real conflict of interest between these two camps."[159] On the contrary, they had a common class interest in rebellion—just as landlords, capitalists, and state managers formed an alliance of the oppressors, so too should the working class and peasants form a front of the oppressed in a revolutionary struggle.

This class politics is another point of difference between the anarchists and people like Godwin, Stirner, and Tolstoy. Godwin pointed to an equitable, nonclass system, but had no model of how such a society would operate, assuming that "both production and distribution can be an entirely personal matter." He maintained that cooperation undermined rationality, favoured "gradual" change, and rejected "the possibility of any sort of working-class organisation which might be used to spread the ideas of justice and equality."[160] Both Godwin and Tolstoy were great believers in individual reason, and assumed that all rational people must necessarily come to the correct conclusions if confronted with clear arguments and supporting evidence. Thus Tolstoy wrote to both the Russian czar and prime minister, urging them to introduce radical reforms. The mutualists saw society in class terms, but did not envisage change as coming through class struggles.

Clearly, it is necessary to reject the view that anarchists did not favour class struggle, or reduce social evils to the state. It has also sometimes been claimed that Bakunin was hostile to the industrial working class, seeing students, intellectuals, criminals, and the long-term unemployed as a better revolutionary element. This claim has been made by many scholars, including the esteemed historian of anarchism, Paul Avrich, the translator of the standard edition of Bakunin's *Statism and Anarchy*, Marshall Shatz, and E. H. Carr, biographer of Bakunin.[161] Activists who draw deeply on the anarchist tradition, but who see class struggle as no longer relevant, like the late radical environmentalist and libertarian socialist Murray Bookchin, have also repeated it.[162]

There is no basis for such claims. Bookchin's notion that Marx placed his hopes in the formation of a stable industrial working class while Bakunin "saw in this process the ruin of all hopes for a genuinely revolutionary movement" is a caricature.[163] Bakunin did, it is true, voice suspicions of the "upper strata" of workers in "certain better paying occupations" who had become "semi-bourgeois."[164] He also contrasted this "little working class minority," the "aristocracy of labour," the "semi-bourgeois" workers, with the "*flower of the proletariat*," the great "rabble of the people," the "underdogs," the "great, beloved, common people," who he believed Marx, perhaps unfairly, dismissed as a criminal lumpenproletariat.[165]

Nevertheless, Bakunin stopped short of formulating any clear theory of a "labour aristocracy"—a theory of the sort that suggests that a privileged layer of workers betrays the working class as a whole. Even while speaking of an "aristocracy of labour," he stated that there were "rare and generous workers," "true socialists," in its ranks.[166] He actively sought to recruit skilled and well-paid workers to the anarchist movement, having a great deal of success among the watchmakers of the Jura region in Switzerland, and commended these workers for their stance:

> In my last lecture I told you that you were privileged workers ... you
> are better paid than workers in large industrial establishments, you have
> spare time, you are ... free and fortunate ... not absolutely so but by
> comparison.... And I hasten to add that you deserve so much the more
> merit to have entered the International.... You prove thereby that you are
> thinking not just of yourselves.... It is with great happiness that I bear
> this witness.

He believed that the progress of capitalism—specifically the mechanisation of
industry—would ultimately undermine the situation of all "privileged workers," and
saw solidarity between the skilled and unskilled as therefore critical:

> But let me tell you that this act of unselfish and fraternal solidarity is also
> an act of foresight and prudence ... big capital [will] ... overrun your
> industry.... And so you, or at least your children, will be as slavish and
> poor as workers in large industrial establishments now.[167]

For Bakunin, the basic logic of the capitalist system was not to create secure
layers of privileged workers but rather to pit the "slavish and poor" against those
who were more "free and fortunate," inevitably undermining the conditions of the
latter. It is understandable, from this perspective, why Bakunin always regarded the
relatively privileged workers as only a small layer, a "little working class minority,"
and clear that he believed them incapable of single-handedly defending their conditions against the onslaught of the ruling class. Bakunin's position was at odds with
the view, held by many modern-day nationalists, that capitalism and the state could
co-opt large sectors of the working class; the "aristocracy of labour" were a besieged
minority, and Bakunin believed that only through the broadest possible class unity
could the interests of the popular classes *as a whole* be defended and advanced.

The notion of a "labour aristocracy" has generally not been important to anarchism, which has tended to argue that the interests of the popular classes are essentially the same worldwide. It was through the "association" of the workers in
"all trades and in all countries" that the vision of "full emancipation" becomes possible.[168]

Internationalism, Social Equality, and Anti-imperialism

Anarchism is an internationalist movement. Just as the working class and
peasantry were international, and just as capitalism and landlordism existed internationally, it is necessary to wage and coordinate struggles across national boundaries. The state was a tool of the wealthy and powerful, not a voice of a people or
nation, and therefore the struggle should not be confined to state borders; the basic interests of the popular classes were essentially alike everywhere, and thus the
struggle cannot be confined to one country; isolated struggles can no more succeed
in one country than they can in one trade.

As Bakunin asserted: "The question of the revolution ... can be solved only
on the grounds of internationality."[169] It was necessary to forge the most powerful
"ties of economic solidarity and fraternal sentiment" between the "workers in all
occupations in all lands."[170] He saw in international bodies such as the First International the nucleus of an international movement and the basis of a new international
order. Such a body could eventually "erect upon the ruins of the old world the free

federation of workers' associations," "the living seeds of the new society which is to replace the old world."[171] Again and again, Bakunin argued for a "serious international organisation of workers' associations of all lands capable of replacing this departing world of *states*."[172]

Bakunin believed that there "exists only one law which is really obligatory for all members, individuals, sections and federations of the International," and that was "the international solidarity of the toilers in all trades and in all countries in their economic struggle against the exploiters of labour." He continued: "It is in the real organisation of this solidarity, by the spontaneous organisation of the working masses and by the absolutely free federation, powerful in proportion as it will be free, of the working masses of all languages and nations, and not in their unification by decrees and under the rod of any government whatever, that there resides the real and living unity of the International."[173]

Such "real and living unity" required unity between skilled and less skilled workers as well as the unity of the popular classes around the world. For Bakunin, the division between the urban working class and the peasantry was the "fatal antagonism" that has "paralysed the revolutionary forces"—a problem that any serious revolutionary project had to defeat.[174] While Bakunin was by no means free of prejudices of his own, he made a principle of popular unity across the lines of race and nationality: "What do we mean by respect for humanity" but "the recognition of human right and human dignity in every man, of whatever race" or "colour"?[175] "Convinced that the real and definitive solution of the social problem can be achieved only on the basis of the universal solidarity of the workers of all lands; the Alliance rejects all policies based upon the so-called patriotism and rivalry of nations."[176]

Despite an occasional tendency to stereotype the Germans and praise the Slavs (understandable perhaps given his commitment to the decolonisation of Eastern Europe), Bakunin hoped for a situation where "the German, American and English toilers and those of other nations" would "march with the same energy towards the destruction of all political power."[177] He had "no doubt that the time will come when the German proletariat itself" would renounce statist politics and join the international labour movement, "which liberates each and everyone from his statist fatherland."[178] In his view, despite the differences between the German kaiser, the Russian czar, or the French emperor, all were fundamentally united in their determination to maintain the class system.

This is one of the great insights of the broad anarchist tradition: if the ruling classes practice international solidarity with one another on fundamental issues, so should the popular classes. This is a remarkably early statement of the idea of "globalisation from below" to change the world.

For Bakunin and Kropotkin, it was the state system that artificially inflamed national hatreds and rivalries, and consequently, "the necessarily revolutionary policy of the proletariat must have for its immediate and only object the destruction of states." How could anyone "speak of international solidarity when they want to keep states—unless they are dreaming of the universal state, that is to say ... universal slavery like the great emperors and popes—the state by its nature being a very rupture of this solidarity and a permanent cause of war"?[179] Anarchists, however, go beyond simply making abstract calls for an end to prejudice and hatred; as we shall see in chapter 10, the broad anarchist tradition generally believed that the struggle for popular unity *also* required a struggle against institutionalised discrimination and oppression on the basis of race and nationality.

This follows from the anarchist commitment to freedom and equality, and is also expressed in the broad anarchist movement's feminist impulse. There were certainly anarchists and syndicalists who paid only lip service to women's emancipation, and the early movement often failed to challenge the sexual division of labour that confined women to particular occupations and roles. In principle, however, the anarchists wanted to unite men and women in the class struggle, and championed equal rights for women as well as measures to improve women's position in society. Bakunin's stance on women was "far ahead of that of most of his contemporaries."[180] He noted that the law subjected women to men's "absolute domination," women were not given the same opportunities as men, and the "poor underprivileged woman" suffered most. Given his class politics, though, Bakunin believed that working-class and peasant women's interests were "indissolubly tied to the common cause of all exploited workers—men and women"—and were quite different from those of the ruling classes, the "parasites of both sexes."[181]

It was through the revolution that the final "emancipation of all" would be achieved: women would no longer be economically dependent on men, as their basic needs would be provided by society, and they would therefore be "free to forge their own way of life." The abolition of the state along with the creation of social and economic equality would see the "authoritarian juridical family" disappear, to be replaced by free and consensual relationships and the "full sexual freedom of women."[182] The Alliance's programme stressed that it sought "above all" the "economic, political and social equality of both sexes." The "children of both sexes must, from birth, be provided with equal means and opportunities for their full development, i.e. support, upbringing and education," for "next to social and economic equality" this measure was critical for creating "greater and increasing natural freedom for individuals, and [would] result in the abolition of artificial and imposed inequalities."[183]

Bakunin also declared "strong sympathy for any national uprising against any form of oppression," stating that every people "has the right to be itself ... no one is entitled to impose its costume, its customs, its languages and its laws."[184] He doubted whether "imperialist Europe" could keep the subject peoples in bondage: "Two-thirds of humanity, 800 million Asiatics asleep in their servitude will necessarily awaken and begin to move." Decolonisation was perfectly acceptable: "The right of freely uniting and separating is the first and most important of all political rights."[185] Given his commitment to class struggle and socialism, however, he asked, "In what direction and to what end" would and should such struggles evolve?[186] For Bakunin, national liberation had to be achieved "as much in the economic as in the political interests of the masses." If the national liberation struggle is carried out with "ambitious intent to set up a powerful State," or if "it is carried out without the people and must therefore depend for success on a privileged class," it will become a "retrogressive, disastrous, counter-revolutionary movement." He believed that "every exclusively political revolution—be it in defence of national independence or for internal change ... —that does not aim at the immediate and real political and economic emancipation of people will be a false revolution. Its objectives will be unattainable and its consequences reactionary."[187]

Bakunin maintained that the "statist path involving the establishment of separate ... States" was "entirely ruinous for the great masses of the people" because it did not abolish class power but simply changed the nationality of the ruling class. Where local capitalists and landlords were weak at independence, a new ruling elite could quickly coalesce through the new state itself. Bakunin illustrated this with a striking discussion that remains relevant. In Serbia, which had broken free of Turkey, there were "no nobles, no big landowners, no industrialists and no very wealthy merchants" at independence; a "new bureaucratic aristocracy," drawn from the educated young patriots, soon emerged as the ruling class in the new state. The "iron logic" of their position transformed them into "cynical bureaucratic martinets" who became "enemies of the people," a ruling class.[188] This is a point that would seem to be confirmed by the experience of many postcolonial countries, where the leading cadres of the independence movements used state power and developed into new ruling classes—often proving as repressive as their colonial forebears.

The rhetoric of independence, freedom, and national unity would become a cover for the activities of the new rulers, and a cudgel to beat the working class, the peasantry, and the poor. Bakunin observed that "the bourgeoisie love their country only because, for them, the country, represented by the State, safeguards their economic, political and social privileges.... Patriots of the State, they become furious enemies of the mass of the people." Thus, for Bakunin, national liberation without social revolutionary goals would simply be an elite transition, transferring power from a foreign to a local ruling class.[192]

Moreover, newly independent states would continually re-create the problem of conquest and national oppression: "to exist, a state must become an invader of other states ... it must be ready to occupy a foreign country and hold millions of people in subjection."[190] For Bakunin, the state system would continually generate war, to which Kropotkin added the point that wars were also waged in the economic interests of ruling classes: "men fight no longer for the good pleasure of kings; they fight to guarantee the incomes and augment the possessions of their Financial Highnesses, Messrs. Rothschild, Schneider and Co., and to fatten the lords of the money market and the factory."[191]

It was precisely because capitalism tended to produce more than could be sold, argued Kropotkin, that ruling groups clashed in search of sources of raw materials and new markets:

> What Germany, France, Russia, England and Austria are struggling for at this moment, is not military supremacy but economic supremacy, the right to impose their manufactures, their custom duties, upon their neighbours; the right to develop the resources of peoples backward in industry; the privilege of making railways through countries that have none, and under that pretext to get demand of their markets, the right, in a word, to filch every now and then from a neighbour a seaport that would stimulate their trade or a province that would absorb the surplus of their production....
>
> The opening of new markets, the forcing of products, good and bad, upon the foreigner, is the principle underlying all the politics of the pres-

ent day throughout our continent, and the real cause of the wars of the nineteenth century.[192]

Later anarchists held similar views. Rocker claimed that it was "meaningless to speak of a community of national interests, for that which the ruling class of every country has up to now defended as national interest has never been anything but the special interest of privileged minorities in society secured by the exploitation and political suppression of the great masses." For behind nationalist ideas, wrote Rocker, are "hidden ... the selfish interests of power-loving politicians and money-loving businessmen for whom the nation is a convenient cover to hide their personal greed and their schemes for political power."[193]

Grigori Petrovitch "G. P." Maximoff (1893–1950) contended that "so-called national interests ... are in fact the interests of the ruling classes" for whom the right "to independent sovereign existence, is nothing but the right of the national bourgeoisie to the unlimited exploitation of its proletariat." Furthermore, the new national states "in their turn begin to deny national rights to their own subordinate minorities, to persecute their languages, their desires and their right to be themselves," and in "this manner 'self-determination' ... also fails to solve the national problem" itself; "it merely creates it anew."[194] Maximoff, who graduated as an agronomist in 1915 in Petrograd, became involved in the revolutionary movement of his day.[195] He played a key role in the Union of Anarcho-syndicalist Propaganda and the subsequent Confederation of Russian Anarcho-syndicalists, and edited the weekly *Golos Truda* ("Voice of Labour"). The paper had been initially published in the United States as the organ of the anarcho-syndicalist Union of Russian Workers, a group with around ten thousand members.[196] In 1917, it was transplanted to revolutionary Russia. Maximoff was forced into exile from Russia in 1921, but he remained an important part of the anarchist movement in Germany, France, and the United States.

For Bakunin, then, the achievement of national liberation had to be linked to the broader struggle for an international revolution. If nationality was separate from the state and a natural feature of society, it did not need the state for emancipation, and as Bakunin argued, the unity of a nationality could only occur naturally, and could not be created from above through statist projects of "nation-building."[197] Equally, if liberation from national oppression involved class struggle, then it could not stop at the borders of a state or even a nationality but had to be part of a broader international struggle. A social revolution must be international in scope, and oppressed nationalities "must therefore link their aspirations and forces with the aspirations and forces of all other countries."[198] Given this perspective, most (but by no means all) anarchists were hostile to nationalism: "All nationalism is reactionary in nature, for it strives to enforce on the separate parts of the great human family a definite character according to a preconceived idea."[199]

The anarchist stress on the importance of creating substantive equality through a new social order that was both libertarian and socialist, and on internationalism, also differentiates anarchism from the ideas of people like Godwin, Stirner, and Proudhon. Both Godwin and Stirner made an abstract individual the centre of their analysis, and generally paid little attention to the social context that made freedom possible. Godwin wanted an end to private property because it hindered the development of reason, while Stirner did not see socialism as a goal. Proudhon was an outspoken misogynist and antifeminist who believed that a "woman knows enough if she knows enough to mend our shirts and cook us a steak."[200] His views were also infused with nationalist and racial prejudices. We will examine the broad anarchist tradition and its relationship to issues of race, imperialism, and gender in more depth in chapter 10.

Counterpower and Counterculture

For the anarchists, class struggle had to be antistatist and antiauthoritarian; it had to be a self-managed struggle conducted outside of and against the state, as noted earlier. The state was an instrument created for the domination of the few over the many, and Bakunin argued that anarchists sought the "destruction of the state" as an "immediate" goal, for the "state means domination, and any domination presupposes the subjugation of the masses" and a "ruling minority." [201] It was also particularly important that the struggle for a new society embody within itself the seeds of the new order, so that the basic framework of the new society would have already been created within and through the struggle against the old order of things.

The character of the revolution was in large part *prefigured* by the ideas and practices of the movements of the popular classes that preexisted it, and its course was shaped by the actions of those movements. This required the creation of organs of counterpower able to supplant the organs of ruling class power, and the creation of a revolutionary counterculture that rejected the values of the status quo. If organisations and ideas are crucial, and they come together through direct action, and if the struggle must prefigure the future society, then the organisations, actions, and ideas have to be consistent with anarchism.

The anarchists maintained that the means shape the ends. The movement for revolution had to contain all the key values of anarchism: internal democracy, self-management, and as far as possible, social and economic equality, and its goals could not be achieved through authoritarianism and hierarchy. Such a movement could obviously not take the form of a political party aimed at taking state power, an elite vanguard party aimed at establishing revolutionary dictatorship, or a guerrilla movement aimed at imposing itself on the masses.

What was critical was a movement for self-emancipation by and for the working class and peasantry, an expression of the organised will of the popular classes, which would themselves be the architects of the new order rather than the passive recipients of salvation from above. The revolution, Kropotkin argued, could only be "a widespread popular movement" in "every town and village," in which the masses "take upon themselves the task of rebuilding society" through associations operating on democratic and antihierarchical principles.[202] To look above to leaders or the state for freedom was simply to prepare the ground for the rise of a ruling class. "Free workers require a free organisation," and this organisation must be based on "free agreement and free cooperation, without sacrificing the autonomy of the individual to the all-pervading influence of a state," asserted Kropotkin.[203]

The "material conditions" and "needs" of the popular classes generated, contended Bakunin, a fundamental antagonism to capitalism and landlordism as well as the state, and a desire for "material well-being" and to "live and work [in] an atmosphere of freedom" created the potential to remake the world through revolution.[204] Yet this was not enough. The popular classes were "poverty-stricken and discontented," but in the depths of the "utmost poverty" often "fail to show signs of stirring."[205] What was missing was a "new social philosophy," a "new faith" in the possibility of a new social order and the ability of ordinary people to create such a society.[206] A revolutionary counterculture embodying the "new faith" was vital, according to Kropotkin, and it distinguished revolutions from sporadic outbreaks and revolts:

> A revolution is infinitely more than a series of insurrections ... is more than a simple fight between parties, however sanguinary; more than mere street-fighting, and much more than a mere change of government.... A revolution is a swift overthrow, in a few years, of institutions which have taken centuries to root into the soil, and seem so fixed and immovable that even the most ardent reformers hardly dare to attack them in their writings....
>
> In short, it is the birth of completely new ideas concerning the manifold links in citizenship—conceptions which soon become realities, and then begin to spread among the neighbouring nations, convulsing the world and giving to the succeeding age its watchword, its problems, its science, its lines of economic, political and moral development.[207]

This brings us to the complicated issue of the use of force and violence in the revolution. For Bakunin and Kropotkin, the revolution would certainly always involve some violence, the result of the resistance of the old order to the new. It would thus, sadly but unavoidably, be necessary to organise for the armed self-defence of the masses; the alternative would be brutal counterrevolution. The two anarchists believed that military action had to reflect libertarian forms of organisation as far as possible, and that the functions of self-defence had to be carried out by a large proportion of the population in order to prevent the emergence of a separate armed and hierarchical force that could be the seed of a new state. In place of a modern hierarchical army, they advocated a militia, democratic in content and popular in character, in which officers would be elected and should have no special privileges. This would not be a dictatorship of the proletariat in the classical Marxist sense but the armed self-defence of the organs of revolutionary counterpower created by the popular classes; it was not a state, at least as the anarchists understood the term.

Bakunin stressed the need for the "dissolution of the army, the judicial system ... the police," to be replaced by "permanent barricades," coordination through deputies with "always responsible, and always revocable mandates," and the "extension of the revolutionary force" within and between the "rebel countries."[208] The workers and peasants, he declared, would unite by "federating the fighting battalions," so that "district by district" there would be a common coordinated defence against internal and external enemies.[209]

Most anarchists and syndicalists seemed to accept this general approach. Some certainly hoped that the revolution would be as peaceful as possible, and many underestimated the extent of armed resistance that the ruling classes would certainly mount. There were, however, some among the syndicalists who believed that the revolutionary general strike would enable a peaceful revolution; there were also a small number of pacifist anarchists who believed that violence in any form was both unnecessary and unacceptable, in that it generated a new apparatus of privilege and power. We will discuss the debates on the defence of the revolution in more detail in chapters 6 and 7.

What is important to note at this stage is that the broad anarchist tradition accepted a measure of coercion. This is a key issue, ignored by approaches that reduce anarchism to individualism and antistatism, or define anarchism as an opposition to any constraints on any individual. A basic distinction is drawn, usually implicitly, in anarchist thinking between *hierarchical* power and exploitation, which exercises force and coercion to perpetuate a basically unjust and inequitable society, and legitimate coercive power, derived from collective and democratic decision making used to create and sustain a libertarian and socialist order. The former category refers to the *repressive* actions of the dominant classes and their institutional complexes; the latter refers to *resistance* and emancipatory direct action.

These two simply should not be collapsed as undifferentiated "authoritarianism," as Engels suggested. He believed the anarchists to be hypocritical in opposing "authority" while advocating revolution: "A revolution is certainly the most authoritarian thing there is; it is an act whereby one part of the population imposes its will upon the other part."[210] But this confuses the violence and coercion used to create and maintain an unjust situation, and the violence of resistance. It is somewhat akin to treating murder and self-defence as identical.

It is on this point that anarchists differed sharply from Tolstoy's doctrine. Tolstoy advocated non-resistance. But even anarchist pacifists practice resistance and seek to coerce the class enemy, albeit peacefully. For Tolstoy, religious contemplation, rather than direct action, was key. As for Stirner, his message was "personal insurrection rather than general revolution."[211] Indeed, he had no real interest in the actual abolition of the state: "My object is not the overthrow of an established order but my elevation above it, my purpose and deed are not ... political or social but ... directed toward myself and my ownness alone ... an egoistic purpose and deed."[212] Stirner's own project, in fact, emerged in a debate with the socialism of Wilhelm Weitling and Moses Hess in which he invoked egoism against socialism.[213]

For a New World

As discussed above, the anarchists stress the need to create a new social order based on social and economic equality, self-management, and individual freedom, sometimes termed "anarchist communism," libertarian socialism, or libertarian communism. The actual details of the new society are often vague, but they can certainly be distinguished from the policies of the old East bloc. Libertarian socialism would be a social order that allowed genuine individual freedom, achieved through cooperation, to exist. It would be international, not "anarchism in one country," and stateless, with production, distribution, and general administration carried out from below through self-management.

Democratic local groups at the workplace and in the neighbourhood would be the nucleus of the social movement that would create libertarian socialism. As the revolution took place, these groups would form the basis of the new society. Wherever possible, these groups would deal with local matters in their own way, democratically—for instance, to determine working hours, local parks, school festivals, and so forth.

A few anarchists after Bakunin and Kropotkin evidently believed that this required an almost total decentralisation of production and the creation of self-sufficient local economies—a position that raises many doubts. Even at a local level, total autonomy is not possible. Decisions regarding which goods to produce, for example, obviously affect consumers who are not involved in production. The more sophisticated an economy, the more every workplace forms part of a complex chain of production and distribution. Many services also cannot be produced and consumed only at a local level, such as transportation and communications. Finally, unequal resource endowments mean that it is difficult to envisage industrial production taking place on the basis of local autonomy and isolation, and points to the danger of reproducing regional and international disparities in income and living standards.

Bakunin and Kropotkin were keenly aware of these problems, and certainly did not envision an international anarchist revolution creating a world of isolated villages. Seeing the new society as making use of the most advanced technologies, and aware of the possibility that regional unevenness would provide a recipe for future conflicts, they saw the need to plan distribution and production, and co-ordinate production chains as well as large-scale public services. Free federation between local groups was seen as the key means of allowing coordination and exchange without a state or market. Councils of mandated delegates accountable to local groups would link the federation.

Bakunin stressed that "revolutionary delegations" from "all the rebel countries" would help knit together the "free federation of agricultural and industrial associations" from "the bottom up." Society would be "reorganised" "from the bottom up through the free formation and free federation of worker associations, industrial, agricultural, scientific and artistic alike," "free federations founded upon collective ownership of the land, capital, raw materials and the instruments of labour."[214] Kropotkin expected multitudes of organisations to exist, ranging from chess clubs to scientific societies, and that they would link up with one another.[215] Federation would also allow association on the basis of national and cultural interests and differences, and form part of a "future social organisation" that was "carried out from the bottom up, by free association, with unions and localities federated by communes, regions, nations, and, finally, a great universal and international federation."[216]

Federalism linking neighbourhoods and workplaces, producers with other producers as well as consumers, would allow large-scale but participatory and democratic economic planning. There would not be a state coordinating production from above through a central plan or a market coordinating production through the price system but a vast economic federation of self-managing enterprises and communities, with a supreme assembly at its head that would balance supply and demand, and direct and distribute world production on the basis of demands from below. The anarchists favoured, as Daniel Guérin astutely noted, worldwide planning based on "federalist and noncoercive centralisation."[217] For Rocker,

> What we seek is not world exploitation but a world economy in which every group of people shall find its natural place and enjoy equal rights with all others. Hence, internationalisation of natural resources and territory affording raw materials is one of the most important prerequisites for the existence of a socialistic order based on libertarian principles.... We need to call into being a new human community having its roots in equality of economic conditions and uniting all members of the great cultural community by new ties of mutual interest, disregarding the frontiers of the present states.[218]

We mentioned above Bakunin and Kropotkin's commitment to rationalism along with the use of advanced technologies in the new society. This arose partly from a broader anarchist commitment to rationalist and scientific ways of thinking. The notion—presented, for example, in Eric Hobsbawm's research on the Spanish anarchists—that the anarchist movement was millenarian and irrational is not sustainable.[219] Subsequent research has challenged Hobsbawm's analysis as flawed "on virtually every point," perhaps as a consequence of Hobsbawm's general hostility to anarchism.[220] In Spain, as elsewhere, anarchism acted as a culture of "radical popular enlightenment" that placed a "high premium on scientific knowledge and technological advance," and "expounded continually on such themes as evolution, rationalist cosmologies, and the value of technology in liberating humanity."[221] This goes back to Bakunin and his circle. Contrary to the view that he disparaged formal education and Enlightenment ideals, Bakunin was a rationalist and modernist.[222] As Bookchin described him,

> Like virtually all of the intellectuals of his day, he acknowledged the importance of science as a means of promoting eventual human betterment; hence the embattled atheism and anticlericalism that pervades all his writings. By the same token, he demanded that the scientific and technological resources of society be mobilised in support of social cooperation, freedom, and community, instead of being abused for profit, competitive advantage, and war. In this respect, Mikhail Bakunin was not behind his times, but a century or two ahead of them.[223]

The rationalist impulse in anarchism—which locates anarchism firmly within the modern world, rather than the premodern ones of moral philosophy and religion, and situates it, moreover, in the world of nineteenth-century socialism—was shared with the mutualists and Godwin, with his stress on reason and the belief that even politics could be a precise science.[224] Rationalism was, however, absent from the thinking of Tolstoy and Stirner; Stirner was a relativist for whom "truth awaits and receives everything from you, and itself is only through you; for it exists only—in your head."[225]

Crime and Social Order

Woodcock's claim that anarchists opposed majority rule and direct democracy is, when seen against this backdrop, most unconvincing. Bakunin was quite clear that "we too seek cooperation: we are even convinced that cooperation in every branch of labour and science is going to be the prevailing form of social organisation in the future."[226] Anarchism would be nothing less than the most complete realisation of *democracy*—democracy in the fields, factories, and neighbourhoods, coordinated through federal structures and councils from below upward, and based on economic and social equality. With the "abolition of the state," Bakunin commented, the "spontaneous self-organisation of popular life, for centuries paralysed and absorbed by the omnipotent power of the state, would revert to the communes"—that is, to self-governing neighbourhoods, towns, cities, and villages.[227]

An anarchist society must also include a measure of legitimate coercive power exercised against those who committed harmful acts against the commonwealth— that is, acts against the social order and the freedom of other individuals. In particular, the linkage between rights and duties had to be maintained. Given that the anarchist society would be a voluntary association, membership assumed a basic commitment to the goals and values of that society.

Those who disagreed with those values were under no obligation to remain within a society with which they were at odds; equally, that society was under no obligation to maintain such persons. To allow some to enjoy the rights and benefits of a cooperative commonwealth, while allowing these same individuals to refuse to fulfill their duties according to their abilities, was tantamount to resurrecting social and economic inequalities and exploitation—precisely the evils of class that the new world was meant to abolish. Likewise, to allow some individuals to disregard the rights and freedoms of others—even if they otherwise fulfilled their social duties— would amount to a restoration of hierarchy.

An anarchist society would be well within its rights to exercise legitimate coercive power against harmful acts—acts criminal in the manner that they are understood today, such as rape or murder, or in terms of the new morality, such as exploitation. If authority was defined as obedience to a moral principle, anarchism was not against authority; if individual freedom was defined as freedom from every restriction, anarchists were not in favour of individual freedom.[228] Bakunin and Kropotkin tended to assume that in an egalitarian and libertarian social order, based on values of equality, solidarity, and responsible individuality, crime would generally decline sharply.[229] Inequality would not exist to prompt desperate theft and acts of violence; ruthless competition would no longer exist to generate rage and violence; the envy and greed of the capitalist market would not exist to generate ruthless acquisition.

Nonetheless, some crime would still exist. An open and libertarian economic and social order would provide numerous avenues for conflict resolution in cases of minor crimes. It was also suggested that the power of public pressure would restrain people from criminal actions, and the withdrawal of cooperation would suffice to discourage the repetitions of such actions when they occurred. The existence of a popular militia and a dense network of associational life would also tend to prevent crime, as the isolation and alienation of modern society would be a thing of the past.

In more serious cases, the militia could be invoked to intervene, and some form of trial would presumably take place within a structure set up for this purpose. If the criminal was found to be mentally ill and therefore could not be held accountable for their actions, the solution would be some form of medical treatment. Otherwise, some measures would have to be taken: possibly compensation, maybe a period of isolation or exile, or perhaps permanent expulsion from the anarchist society. The use of prisons was, however, out of the question; as Kropotkin argued, they created new evils, acting as "schools of crime" and abuse that transformed their inmates into habitual offenders.[230]

Anarchism Redefined: Socialism, Class, and Democracy

Having rejected the contention that antistatism and a belief in individual freedom constitute the defining features of anarchism, we have suggested that a more adequate definition of anarchism can be derived from an examination of the intellectual and social trend that defined itself as anarchist from the 1860s onward. Given that antistatism is at best a *necessary* component of anarchist thought, but not a *sufficient* basis on which to classify a set of ideas or a particular thinker as part of the anarchist tradition, it follows that Godwin, Stirner, and Tolstoy cannot truly be considered anarchists. Thinkers and activists who follow in the footsteps of these writers cannot, in turn, be truly considered anarchists or part of the anarchist tradition, even if they may perhaps be considered libertarians.

It follows from there that commonly used categories such as "philosophical anarchism" (often used in reference to Godwin or Tucker), "individualist anarchism" (used in reference to Stirner or the mutualists), "spiritual anarchism" (used in reference to Tolstoy and his cothinkers), or "lifestyle anarchism" (usually used in reference to latter-day Stirnerites) fall away. Because the ideas designated by these names are not part of the anarchist tradition, their categorisation of variants of anarchism is misleading and arises from a misunderstanding of anarchism. Likewise, adding the rider "class struggle" or "social" to the word anarchist implies that there are anarchists who do not favour class struggle or who are individualists, neither of which is an accurate usage.

There is only one anarchist tradition, and it is rooted in the work of Bakunin and the Alliance. The practice of speaking of class struggle anarchism or social anarchism is probably sometimes necessary, but it does imply that there is a legitimate anarchist tradition that is against class struggle or is antisocial, which is incorrect. In a number of polemics, Bookchin set out to distinguish the "social anarchist" tradition from a host of individualist and irrationalist tendencies that have tried to claim the anarchist label, and provided a powerful critique of these currents. Yet Bookchin still referred to these tendencies as "lifestyle anarchism," conceding their place in a larger anarchist tradition.[231] This was a mistake.

It is our view that the term anarchism should be reserved for a particular rationalist and revolutionary form of libertarian socialism that emerged in the second half of the nineteenth century. Anarchism was against social and economic hierarchy as well as inequality—and specifically, capitalism, landlordism, and the state—and in favor of an international class struggle and revolution from below by a self-organised working class and peasantry in order to create a self-managed, socialist, and stateless social order. In this new order, individual freedom would be harmonised with communal obligations through cooperation, democratic decision making, and social and economic equality, and economic coordination would take place through federal forms. The anarchists stressed the need for revolutionary means (organisations, actions, and ideas) to prefigure the ends (an anarchist society). Anarchism is a libertarian doctrine and a form of libertarian socialism; not every libertarian or libertarian socialist viewpoint is anarchist, though.

Both the anarchist analysis and vision of a better society were underpinned by a rationalist worldview and a commitment to scientific thought, albeit mixed in with a hefty dose of ethics. Anarchism was and is a political ideology, and one that embraces rationalist methods of analysis to inform its critique, strategy, and tactics. Its large moral component, however, is also important—and cannot be scientifically proven to be correct. Just as Marx's claim to have shown exploitation through wage labour in no way proves that exploitation is wrong—that was a moral judgment, not an empirical fact—so Bakunin's and Kropotkin's class analysis did not, in fact, show that individual freedom was right or necessary.

In Conclusion: The Modernity of Anarchism

It is possible to identify libertarian and libertarian socialist tendencies throughout recorded history, analyse the ideas of each tendency, and examine their historical role. Yet anarchism, we have argued, is not a universal aspect of society or the psyche. It emerged from within the socialist and working-class movement 150 years ago, and its novelty matters. It was also very much a product of modernity, and emerged against the backdrop of the Industrial Revolution and the rise of capitalism. The ideas of anarchism themselves are still profoundly marked by the modern period and modernist thought. Its stress on individual freedom, democracy, and egalitarianism, its embrace of rationalism, science, and modern technology, its belief that history may be designed and directed by humankind, and its hope that the future can be made better than the past—in short, the idea of progress—all mark anarchism as a child of the eighteenth-century Enlightenment, like liberalism and Marxism. Premodern libertarian ideas were expressed in the language of religion and a hankering for a lost idyllic past; anarchism, like liberalism and Marxism, embraces rationalism and progress. Nothing better expresses this linkage than the notion of "scientific socialism," a term widely used by Marxists, but actually coined by Proudhon.[232]

Not only is it the case that anarchism *did not* exist in the premodern world; it is also the case that it *could not* have, for it is rooted in the social and intellectual revolutions of the modern world. And as modernity spread around the globe from the northern Atlantic region, the preconditions for anarchism spread too. By the time of Bakunin, the Alliance, and the First International, the conditions were ripe for anarchism in parts of Europe, the Americas, and Africa; within thirty years, the modernisation of Asia had opened another continent.

In the following chapters, having developed a clear understanding of anarchism, we will examine its intellectual history, the debates that took place within anarchism, the links between anarchism, syndicalism, and the IWW, and the ways in which the broad anarchist tradition dealt with questions of community organising, the unemployed, race, nationality, imperialism, and gender. Part of this involves delineating different currents within anarchism: having rejected earlier subdivisions like "philosophical anarchism," we propose new ones, like mass anarchism and insurrectionist anarchism. For now, though, we turn to the relationship between Proudhon, Marx, and anarchism.

Notes

1. Kedward, *The Anarchists*, 6.

2. See also Fleming, *The Anarchist Way to Socialism*, 20–21.

3. "N. *evildoer ... destroyer*; nihilist, anarchist ... pyromaniac ... *ruffian ... knave ... murderer*"; R. A. Dutch, *Roget's Thesaurus of English Words and Phrases*, rev. ed. (London: Longmans, Green and Co., 1962), 598.

4. Kedward, *The Anarchists*, 5–6.

5. C. Jacker, *The Black Flag of Anarchy: Antistatism in the United States* (New York: Charles Scribner's Sons, 1968), 1–2.

6. R. Hoffman, introduction to *Anarchism*, ed. R. Hoffman (New York: Atherton Press, 1970), 2, 9, 10.

7. Statz, introduction, xi–xii, xiii.

8. Perlin, *Contemporary Anarchism*, 109.

9. The roots of so-called "anarcho-capitalism" lie primarily in the Austrian school of neoclassical economics, with the work of Ludwig von Mises a major influence. Rothbard praised Mises as "the pre-eminent theorist of our time," the victor in many battles "on behalf of free markets and sound money," the writer of "the most important theoretical critique ever leveled at socialism," the ardent opponent of the revolutionary struggles in Austria in the late 1910s, mentor of the great economic liberal Frederick von Hayek, and the great exponent of the view that state welfare schemes and the regulation of the market inevitably lead to dictatorship; see M. Rothbard, *Ludwig von Mises: Scholar, Creator, Hero* (Auburn, AL: Ludwig von Mises Institute, 1988), available at http://www.mises.org/rothbard/scholarhero.pdf (accessed June 30, 2006), 4, 7, 19, 23–24, 27–31, 46–47. Also revealing of Rothbard's capitalist extremism was his critique of Milton Friedman, perhaps the single most important advocate of neoliberalism. Rothbard viewed Friedman as excessively egalitarian, because he suggested that the state should levy income tax, provide a minimal welfare system (including welfare for the disabled), maintain public parks and schools, and tackle corporate monopolies. See M. Rothbard, "Milton Friedman Unravelled," *Journal of Libertarian Studies* 16, no. 4 (2002): 37–54 (originally published in 1971).

10. Fleming, *The Anarchist Way to Socialism*, 19.

11. Ibid., 17.

12. Ibid., 19.

13. Eltzbacher, *Anarchism*, 7.

14. This term is used in works as early as E. A. Vizetelly, *The Anarchists: Their Faith and Their Record* (Edinburgh: Turnbull and Spears Printers, 1911).

15. See Eltzbacher, *Anarchism*, 184–96.

16. See W. Godwin, *Enquiry concerning Political Justice, with Selections from Godwin's Other Writings*, ed. and abridged K. Cordell Carter (1798; repr., London: Clarendon Press, 1971). It should be noted that Godwin revised this work several times—in 1793, 1796, and 1798—and this text is based on the third edition. The editor's introduction to this volume is useful, but John Clark's analysis of Godwin is indispensable; see J. P. Clark, *The Philosophical Anarchism of William Godwin* (Princeton, NJ: Princeton University Press, 1977). A fair account of Godwin is presented in Eltzbacher, *Anarchism*, chapter 3. Discussions of Godwin are a standard feature of most general histories of anarchism; see Joll, *The Anarchists*; Marshall, *Demanding the Impossible*; Woodcock, *Anarchism*.

17. Godwin, *Enquiry concerning Political Justice*, 222.

18. Ibid., 23–26, 109, 282–91, 292–95.

19. Clark, *The Philosophical Anarchism of William Godwin*, 82–85.

20. Godwin, *Enquiry concerning Political Justice*, 301–3; see also 140–41. See also Clark, *The Philosophical Anarchism of William Godwin*, 82–85.

21. See, for example, Godwin, *Enquiry concerning Political Justice*, 125, 132–33, 138–39, 262–63, 266, 290.

22. The standard edition is M. Stirner, *The Ego and His Own* (1844; repr., New York: Benjamin R. Tucker Publishers, 1907). Yet the introduction is of limited use; J. L. Walker, introduction to *The Ego and His Own*, ed. M. Stirner (New York: Benjamin R. Tucker Publishers, 1907). The introduction to the 1963 edition is essential reading; J. J. Martin, introduction to *The Ego and His Own*, ed. M. Stirner (New York: Libertarian Book Club, 1963). Besides the discussion of Stirner in Eltzbacher, *Anarchism*, chapter 4, see also the relevant sections of Joll, *The Anarchists*; Marshall, *Demanding the Impossible*; Woodcock, *Anarchism*.

23. Stirner, *The Ego and His Own*, 3, 472.

24. For a contrary view, see Eltzbacher, *Anarchism*, 67–70.

25. Stirner, *The Ego and His Own*, 421.

26. Woodcock, *Anarchism*, 91.

27. Tolstoy's output was formidable. Marshall S. Statz provides an edited version of his key work—the 1893 "The Kingdom of God Is Within You"—in M. Statz, ed., *The Essential Works of Anarchism* (New York: Bantam, 1971). Another useful starting point is J. Lavrin, *Tolstoy: An Approach* (London: Methuen and Co., 1944). See also the relevant sections of Joll, *The Anarchists*; Marshall, *Demanding the Impossible*; Woodcock, *Anarchism*.

28. Utopian socialism included authoritarians as well as libertarians. Claude Saint-Simon (1760–1825), for example, advocated a regimented and hierarchical socialism directed by an elite made up of the most talented; see R. Michels, *Political Parties: A Sociological Study of the Oligarchical Tendencies of Modern Democracy* (1915; repr., New York: Free Press, 1962), 344.

29. Proudhon was a prolific writer, and his ideas were not always consistent; it is important to note that he moved to the Right in the 1850s, returning to his original positions in the 1860s. He did not oppose collective ownership, notwithstanding a common stereotype. Key texts are excerpted in D. Guérin, ed., *No Gods, No Masters: An Anthology of Anarchism, Book One* (Oakland: AK Press, 1998). There are numerous quotations in Eltzbacher, *Anarchism*, chapter 4. A useful anthology is S. Edwards, ed., *Selected Writings of Pierre-Joseph Proudhon* (Basingstoke, UK: Macmillan, 1969). An excellent commentary on Proudhon's ideas is scattered throughout D. Guérin, *Anarchism: From Theory to Practice* (New York: Monthly Review Press, 1970). Also useful is D. W. Brogan, *Proudhon* (London: H. Hamilton, 1934). For good discussions of Proudhon, with the accent on biography, see Joll, *The Anarchists*; Woodcock, *Anarchism*.

30. This is precisely how David MacNally described Proudhon in his critique of liberal economics and contemporary market socialism; see D. MacNally, *Against the Market: Political Economy, Market Socialism, and the Marxist Critique* (London: Verso, 1993).

31. Thorpe, *"The Workers Themselves,"* 4.

32. Quoted in Guérin, *Anarchism*, 45.

33. See, inter alia, Bookchin, *The Spanish Anarchists*; J. Hart, *Anarchism and the Mexican Working Class, 1860–1931* (Austin: Texas University Press, 1978); National Confederation of Labour, *Resolution on Libertarian Communism as Adopted by the Confederacion Nacional del Trabajo, Zaragoza, 1 May 1936* (Durban: Zabalaza Books, n.d.).

34. For an introduction to Tucker, see, in particular, Paul Avrich's essays "Proudhon and America" and "Benjamin Tucker and His Daughter," both in P. Avrich, *Anarchist Portraits* (Princeton, NJ: Princeton University Press, 1988). The quote is from ibid., 140. For his key essay, see B. R. Tucker, "State Socialism and Anarchism: How Far They Agree, and Wherein They Differ," in *Selections from the Writings of Benjamin R. Tucker*, ed. B. R. Tucker (1926; repr., Millwood, New York: Kraus Reprint Company, 1973). By anarchism, Tucker meant mutualism.

35. Most English-language biographies of Bakunin are overtly hostile to their subject. Representative examples include A. Kelly, *Mikhail Bakunin: A Study in the Psychology and Politics of Utopianism* (Oxford: Clarendon Press, 1982); A. Mendel, *Michael Bakunin: Roots of Apocalypse* (New York: Praegerm, 1981). While manifestly unsympathetic and not altogether accurate in its presentation of Bakunin's views, the best biography in English is probably still E. H. Carr, *Michael Bakunin*, rev. ed. (Basingstoke, UK: Macmillan, 1975). A more balanced discussion of Bakunin's views may be found in A. W. Gouldner, "Marx's Last Battle: Bakunin and the First International," *Theory and Society* 11, no. 6 (1982): 853-84. A study that demonstrates Bakunin's abilities as a political activist is T. R. Ravindranathan, "Bakunin in Naples: An Assessment," *Journal of Modern History* 53, no. 2 (1981). A useful recent treatment is B. Morris, *Bakunin: The Philosophy of Freedom* (Montréal: Black Rose, 1996). There is also much interesting material in standard works on anarchism like Eltzbacher, *Anarchism*; Joll, *The Anarchists*; Marshall, *Demanding the Impossible*; Woodcock, *Anarchism*. See also J. Guillaume, "A Biographical Sketch [Bakunin]," in *Bakunin on Anarchy: Selected Works by the Activist-Founder of World Anarchism*, ed. S. Dolgoff (London: George Allen and Unwin, 1971).

36. For contrary views, see Carr, *Michael Bakunin*, 421–23; Joll, *The Anarchists*, 87.

37. Kropotkin has been the subject of several excellent biographies. See, in particular, M. A. Miller, *Kropotkin* (Chicago: University of Chicago Press, 1976; J. A. Rogers, "Peter Kropotkin, Scientist and Anarchist" (PhD diss., Harvard University, 1957); G. Woodcock and I. Avakumovic, *The Anarchist Prince* (London: Boardman, 1950). Also useful is C. Cahm, *Kropotkin and the Rise of Revolutionary Anarchism, 1872–1886* (Cambridge: Cambridge University Press, 1989). Again, standard works on anarchism are also useful; see Joll, *The Anarchists*; Marshall, *Demanding the Impossible*; Woodcock, *Anarchism*. For interesting discussions of Kropotkin, see Avrich, *Anarchist Portraits*; G. Purchase, *Evolution and Revolution: An Introduction to the Life and Thought of Peter Kropotkin* (Sydney, Australia: Jura Media, 1996). Some autobiographical material may be found in P. Kropotkin, *In Russian and French Prisons* (1887; repr., New York: Schocken Books, 1971); P. Kropotkin, *Memoirs of a Revolutionist* (1899; repr., New York: Dover Publications, 1980).

38. Woodcock, *Anarchism*, 203; Avrich, *Anarchist Portraits*, 69.

39. See, for example, Joll, *The Anarchists*, 151; Woodcock, *Anarchism*, 172.

40. M. Bakunin, "Statism and Anarchy," in *Bakunin on Anarchy: Selected Works by the Activist-Founder of World Anarchism*, ed. S. Dolgoff (1873; repr., London: George Allen and Unwin, 1971), 332; P. Kropotkin, "Anarchist Communism: Its Basis and Principles," in *Kropotkin's Revolutionary Pamphlets: A Collection of Writings by Peter Kropotkin*, ed. R. N. Baldwin (1887; repr., New York: Dover Publications, 1970), 46, 61; Kropotkin, "Anarchism," 285.

41. Eltzbacher, *Anarchism*, 189, 201.

42. Ibid., 189, 191.

43. Fleming, *The Anarchist Way to Socialism*, 20.

44. J. J. Martin, editor's preface to *Anarchism: Exponents of the Anarchist Philosophy*, P. Eltzbacher (London: Freedom Press, 1960), vii.

45. See Kropotkin, "Anarchism," 287.

46. Nettlau's numerous works have long been out of print. Only a few volumes of his masterwork were published in his lifetime—there were reissues in German in the 1970s by Topos Verlag, along with several others in a small print run The 1980s saw another partial printing by Verlag Detlev Auvermann KG; these editions are difficult to obtain. Currently, a new edition by the Bibliotheque Thélèm is in the works. A projected English edition, announced in the 1990s, never materialised. Nettlau's multivolume Bakunin biography was issued only once, in a run of fifty copies; see the editor's notes to Nettlau, *A Short History of Anarchism*. Nettlau's papers formed the early core of the archives of the International Institute of Social History in Amsterdam.

47. Considérant was "the actual founder of the Fourierist movement"; editor's note to Nettlau, *A Short History of Anarchism*, 374, 1–13. Regarding Stirner, Bellegarrigue, and Déjacque, see ibid., 14–98.

48. See, inter alia, M. Vallance, "Rudolf Rocker: A Biographical Sketch," *Journal of Contemporary History* 8, no. 3 (1973): 75–95.

49. Even Kautsky, the SDP's great theorist, flirted with anarchism in the 1870s; see G. P. Steenson, *Karl Kautsky, 1854–1938: Marxism in the Classical Years*, 2nd ed. (Pittsburgh, PA: University of Pittsburgh Press, 1991), 39–41.

50. R. Rocker, *Anarcho-Syndicalism* (Oakland: AK Press, 2004), also available at http://www.spunk.org/library/writers/rocker/sp001495/rocker_as1.html (accessed November 12, 2000), chapter 1.

51. G. Woodcock, *Anarchy or Chaos* (London: Freedom Press, 1944), 25–26.

52. Woodcock, *Anarchism*, 13, 15, 19; compare to D. Miller, *Anarchism* (London: J. M. Dent and Sons, 1984), 5–10.

53. Miller, *Anarchism*, 3.

54. P. Feyerabend, *Against Method: Outline of an Anarchistic Theory of Knowledge* (London: New Left Books, 1975).

55. K. Marx and F. Engels, *The Communist Manifesto* (1848; repr., Chicago: Henry Regnery Company, 1954), 56–57.

56. Lenin, "The State and Revolution," 257, 281.

57. N. Bukharin, *The ABC of Communism* (1922; repr., Ann Arbor: University of Michigan Press, 1966), 74–75.

58. Eltzbacher, *Anarchism*, 189, 201.

59. Marshall, *Demanding the Impossible*, 629.

60. Eltzbacher, *Anarchism*, 189, 194, 201.

61. Hoffman, introduction, 5; D. Novak, "The Place of Anarchism in the History of Political Thought," in *Anarchism*, ed. R. Hoffman (1958; repr., New York: Atherton Press, 1970), 22, 24–30.

62. Marshall explicitly describes Gandhi as an anarchist, but argues that he did not call for the "immediate abolition of State and government," nor did he "reject the notion of a State in a transitional period"; see Marshall, *Demanding the Impossible*, 422, 425, 442, 591–93.

63. Ibid., 3, 564–65. Marshall admits that not all of his "anarchists" favour positive freedom (that is, the freedom *to* act, which implies "equality and social justice") as well as negative freedom (that is, the freedom *from* direct external coercion, which can take place in an inegalitarian context); see ibid., 36–37.

64. A. Carter, *The Political Theory of Anarchism* (London: Routledge and Kegan Paul, 1971), 1–11, 25, 26, 63–73.

65. Thus, the section on the state draws almost entirely on Kropotkin; the section on law mainly uses Tolstoy; the part on federalism and nationality takes from Proudhon; the portion on the individual pulls from Stirner; and the part on morality again draws from Tolstoy. See ibid., 29–38, 41–46, 61–63, 89–95.

66. Fleming, *The Anarchist Way to Socialism*, 16.

67. Ibid., 17–19.

68. For example, Vizetelly, *The Anarchists*.

69. Fleming, *The Anarchist Way to Socialism*, 19.

70. Joll, *The Anarchists*, 58, 82.

71. Kedward, *The Anarchists*, 5.

72. Miller, *Anarchism*, 4, 45.

73. Woodcock, *Anarchism*, 136, 170.

74. Ibid., 155; Joll, *The Anarchists*, 84.

75. Marshall, *Demanding the Impossible*, 3–4, 264.

76. Kropotkin, "Anarchist Communism," 46.

77. P. Kropotkin, *The Place of Anarchism in Socialistic Evolution* (1886; repr., Cyrmu, Wales: Practical Parasite Publications, 1990), 5–6; Kropotkin, "Anarchism," 295.

78. Rocker, *Anarcho-Syndicalism*, chapter 1.

79. Woodcock, *Anarchy or Chaos*, 36.

80. M. A. Miller, introduction to *Selected Writings on Anarchism and Revolution: P. A. Kropotkin*, ed. M. A. Miller (Cambridge, MA: MIT Press, 1970), 6; see also J. M. Allen, "Ambivalent Social Darwinism in Korea," *International Journal of Korean History* 2 (2002): 1–24; R. Kinna, "Kropotkin's Theory of Mutual Aid in Historical Context," *International Review of Social History* 40, no. 2 (1995): 259–83.

81. Fleming, *The Anarchist Way to Socialism*, 2.

82. Woodcock, *Anarchism*, 13, 15, 19; Miller, *Anarchism*, 5–10; Marshall, *Demanding the Impossible*, 641, 653.

83. Compare to M. Molyneux, "No God, No Boss, No Husband: Anarchist Feminism in Nineteenth-Century Argentina," *Latin American Perspectives* 13, no. 1 (1986): 123.

84. Joll, *The Anarchists*, 103.

85. For some of the key documents, see Guérin, *No Gods, No Masters*, 183–202.

86. Avrich, *Anarchist Portraits*, 97.

87. Kropotkin, "Anarchist Communism," 61.

88. M. Bakunin, "Federalism, Socialism, Anti-Theologism," in *Bakunin on Anarchy: Selected Works by the Activist-Founder of World Anarchism*, ed. S. Dolgoff (1867; repr., London: George Allen and Unwin, 1971), 118.

89. Carr, *Michael Bakunin*, 434. Carr attributes this to the supposedly profound influence that Stirner had on Bakunin. There is no evidence that Stirner had any influence on Bakunin, least of all in Carr's study.

90. M. Bakunin, "God and the State," in *Bakunin on Anarchy: Selected Works by the Activist-Founder of World Anarchism*, ed. S. Dolgoff (1871; repr., London: George Allen and Unwin, 1971), 236–37.

91. M. Bakunin, "Three Lectures to Swiss Members of the International," in *Mikhail Bakunin: From out of the Dustbin: Bakunin's Basic Writings, 1869–1871*, ed. R. M. Cutler (1871; repr., Ann Arbor, MI: Ardis, 1985), 46–47.

92. P. Kropotkin, "Letter to Nettlau," March 5, 1902, in *Selected Writings on Anarchism and Revolution: P. A. Kropotkin*, ed. M. A. Miller (Cambridge, MA: MIT Press, 1970), 296–97.

93. Kropotkin, "Modern Science and Anarchism," 161–62.

94. Stirner, *The Ego and His Own*, 3, 37.

95. Bakunin, "Federalism, Socialism, Anti-Theologism," 118.

96. M. Bakunin, "Letter to *La Liberté*," in *Bakunin on Anarchy: Selected Works by the Activist-Founder of World Anarchism*, ed. S. Dolgoff (1872; repr., London: George Allen and Unwin, 1971), 289.

97. Kropotkin, "Anarchist Communism," 56, 59.

98. It is therefore incorrect to define anarchism as a philosophy that holds that every individual should be entirely free to establish one's obligations to society; given that anarchism advocated a social vision of freedom as realised through society and cooperation, it could not be in favour of absolute and unrestrained individual sovereignty. This misreading of anarchism as a doctrine of absolute autonomy is the key flaw in R. P. Wolff, *In Defence of Anarchism* (New York: Harper and Row, 1970). While an interesting treatise, it is not really a treatise on anarchism.

99. Stirner, *The Ego and His Own*, 339.

100. M. Bakunin, *The Capitalist System* (1871; repr., Champaign, IL: Libertarian Labor Review, 1993), n.p.

101. Bakunin, "God and the State," 238.

102. Bakunin, "Three Lectures to Swiss Members of the International," 46.

103. Bakunin, "Statism and Anarchy," 343.

104. Quoted in Eltzbacher, *Anarchism*, 108.

105. M. Bakunin, "Letters to a Frenchman on the Current Crisis," in *Bakunin on Anarchy: Selected Works by the Activist-Founder of World Anarchism*, ed. S. Dolgoff (1870; repr., London: George Allen and Unwin, 1971), 189.

106. Kropotkin, "Anarchist Communism," 55.

107. Bakunin, *The Capitalist System*, n.p.

108. Ibid.

109. Kropotkin, "Anarchist Communism," 71.

110. Bakunin, *The Capitalist System*, n.p.

111. Kropotkin, "Anarchist Communism," 55–56.

112. Woodcock, *Anarchism*, 13, 15, 19.

113. Miller, *Anarchism*, 5–10; Marshall, *Demanding the Impossible*, 641, 653.

114. Marshall, *Demanding the Impossible*, 229, 232.

115. Bakunin, "Letters to a Frenchman on the Current Crisis," 216–17.

116. Kropotkin, "Modern Science and Anarchism," 182–83.

117. F. Engels, "Letter to C. Cuno in Milan," January 24, 1872, in *Marx, Engels, Lenin: Anarchism and Anarcho-syndicalism*, ed. N. Y. Kolpinsky (Moscow: Progress Publishers, 1972), 71.

118. M. Bakunin, "The International and Karl Marx," in *Bakunin on Anarchy: Selected Works by the Activist-Founder of World Anarchism*, ed. S. Dolgoff (1872; repr., London: George Allen and Unwin, 1971), 318.

119. Kropotkin, "Modern Science and Anarchism," 149–50, 181.

120. Bakunin, "Federalism, Socialism, Anti-Theologism," 144.

121. Kropotkin, "Anarchist Communism," 52.

122. Kropotkin, "Modern Science and Anarchism," 165.

123. Lenin, "The State and Revolution."

124. Bakunin, "Letter to *La Liberté*," 281. See also Bakunin, "Statism and Anarchy," 330.

125. Bakunin, "Statism and Anarchy," 337.

126. Bakunin, "The Paris Commune and the Idea of the State," 269.

127. Kropotkin, "Anarchist Communism," 50.

128. Kropotkin, "Modern Science and Anarchism," 181.

129. Ibid., 170.

130. Bakunin, "Statism and Anarchy," 338.

131. M. Bakunin, "Representative Government and Universal Suffrage," in *Bakunin on Anarchy: Selected Works by the Activist-Founder of World Anarchism*, ed. S. Dolgoff (1870; repr., London: George Allen and Unwin, 1971), 220–22.

132. Bakunin, "Letters to a Frenchman on the Current Crisis," 194, 213–17.

133. Bakunin, "God and the State," 228.

134. Kropotkin, "Anarchist Communism," 49.

135. Bakunin, "Letters to a Frenchman on the Current Crisis," 193–94.

136. Bakunin, "Letter to *La Liberté*," 284.

137. Kropotkin, "Anarchist Communism," 50.

138. Bakunin, "Letter to *La Liberté*," 284.

139. Bakunin, "Letters to a Frenchman on the Current Crisis," 217.

140. Kropotkin, "Modern Science and Anarchism," 170, 186.

141. Bakunin, "Letters to a Frenchman on the Current Crisis," 185, 189.

142. Bakunin, "The International and Karl Marx," 294–95.

143. M. Bakunin, "The Policy of the International," in *Bakunin on Anarchy: Selected Works by the Activist-Founder of World Anarchism*, ed. S. Dolgoff (1869; repr., London: George Allen and Unwin, 1971), 166–67.

144. Marx and Engels, *The Communist Manifesto*, 22; K. Marx, *The Eighteenth Brumaire of Louis Bonaparte* (1852; repr., Moscow: Progress Publishers, 1983), 110–11.

145. Marx, *The Eighteenth Brumaire of Louis Bonaparte*, 110–11.

146. Steenson, *Karl Kautsky*, 102–11.

147. J. Joll, *The Second International, 1889–1914* (New York: Harper Colophon Books, 1966), 91; Steenson, *Karl Kautsky*, 3.

148. Steenson, *Karl Kautsky*, 135–36.

149. V. I. Lenin, "Two Tactics of Social-Democracy in the Democratic Revolution,"in *Selected Works in Three Volumes*, ed. V. I. Lenin (1905; repr., Moscow: Progress Publishers, 1975), 451–52.

150. See, for example, ibid., 480–83.

151. Mao Tsetung, "Report on an Investigation of the Peasant Movement in Hunan," in *Selected Readings from the Works of Mao Tsetung*, ed. Editorial Committee for Selected Readings from the Works of Mao Tsetung (1927; repr., Peking: Foreign Languages Press, 1971), 28, 30.

152. Mao, "On the People's Democratic Dictatorship," 379.

153. For Lenin's classic statement of this position, see Lenin, "Two Tactics of Social-Democracy in the Democratic Revolution."

154. Bakunin, "Letters to a Frenchman on the Current Crisis," 189, 192.

155. Ibid., 189–92, 197, 208–9.

156. Ibid., 189–92, 197, 208–9; see also Bakunin, "Statism and Anarchy," 346–50.

157. Harman, *A People's History of the World*, 615; H. Bernstein, "Farewells to the Peasantry," *Transformation: Critical Perspectives on Southern Africa*, no. 52 (2003): 3.

158. Bernstein, "Farewells to the Peasantry," 14, 16n10.

159. Bakunin, "Letters to a Frenchman on the Current Crisis," 191–92, 204.

160. Clark, *The Philosophical Anarchism of William Godwin*, 280–81, 281–82.

161. P. Avrich, "The Legacy of Bakunin," in *Bakunin on Anarchy: Selected Works by the Activist-Founder of World Anarchism*, ed. S. Dolgoff (London: George Allen and Unwin, 1971), xx–xxi; M. Statz, introduction to *Statism and Anarchy*, M. Bakunin (Cambridge: Cambridge University Press, 1990), xxxiii–xxxiv.

162. Bookchin, one of the more prominent recent writers influenced by anarchism, sought to erect a new "anarchist" strategy—freed of class struggle and hostile to the organised working class—by insisting that Bakunin distrusted the working class. See Bookchin, *The Spanish Anarchists*, 28, 304–12; M. Bookchin, *To Remember Spain: The Anarchist and Syndicalist Revolution of 1936: Essays by Murray Bookchin* (Edinburgh: AK Press, 1994), 25–26, 29–33.

163. Bookchin, *The Spanish Anarchists*, 28. See also M. Bookchin, "Deep Ecology, Anarchosyndicalism, and the Future of Anarchist Thought," in *Deep Ecology and Anarchism: A Polemic*, ed. G. Purchase, M. Bookchin, B. Morris, and R. Aitchley (London: Freedom Press, 1993), 49–50; Bookchin, *To Remember Spain*, 25–26, 29–33.

164. Bakunin, "Letters to a Frenchman on the Current Crisis," 185, 189.

165. Bakunin, "The International and Karl Marx," 294–295.

166. Bakunin, "The Policy of the International," 166–67.

167. Bakunin, "Three Lectures to Swiss Members of the International," 61–62.

168. M. Bakunin, "Geneva's Double Strike," in *Mikhail Bakunin: From out of the Dustbin: Bakunin's Basic Writings, 1869–1871*, ed. R. M. Cutler (1869?; repr., Ann Arbor, MI: Ardis, 1985), 148.

169. Ibid., 147.

170. M. Bakunin, "The Programme of the Alliance," in *Bakunin on Anarchy: Selected Works by the Activist-Founder of World Anarchism*, ed. S. Dolgoff (1871; repr., London: George Allen and Unwin, 1971), 249, 252; see also 253–54.

171. Ibid., 255.

172. Bakunin, "The Policy of the International," 174.

173. M. Bakunin, "Internationalism and the State," in *Marxism, Freedom, and the State*, ed. K. J. Kenafick (London: Freedom Press, 1990), 43.

174. Bakunin, "Letters to a Frenchman on the Current Crisis," 192.

175. Bakunin, "Federalism, Socialism, Anti-Theologism," 147.

176. M. Bakunin, "Preamble and Programme of the International Alliance of the Socialist Democracy," in *Bakunin on Anarchism*, ed. S. Dolgoff (1868; repr., Montréal: Black Rose, 1980), 427–28.

177. Bakunin, "Letter to *La Liberté*," 281.

178. M. Bakunin, *Statism and Anarchy* (1873; repr., Cambridge: Cambridge University Press, 1990), 51.

179. Bakunin, "Internationalism and the State," 43.

180. M. Forman, *Nationalism and the International Labor Movement: The Idea of the Nation in Socialist and Anarchist Theory* (University Park: Penn State University Press, 1998), 33.

181. M. Bakunin, "Manifesto of the Russian Revolutionary Association to the Oppressed Women of Russia on Women's Liberation," in *Bakunin on Anarchism*, ed. S. Dolgoff (Montréal: Black Rose, 1980), 396–98.

182. Ibid.

183. Bakunin, "Preamble and Programme of the International Alliance of the Socialist Democracy," 427.

184. Bakunin, quoted in Guérin, *Anarchism*, 68.

185. Quoted in Eltzbacher, *Anarchism*, 81.

186. Bakunin, quoted in Guérin, *Anarchism*, 68.

187. Bakunin, "Federalism, Socialism, Anti-Theologism," 99.

188. Bakunin, "Statism and Anarchy," 343.

189. S. Cipko, "Mikhail Bakunin and the National Question," *Raven* 3, no. 1 (1990): 11.

190. Bakunin, "Statism and Anarchy," 343, 339.

191. P. Kropotkin, *War!* (London: William Reeves, 1914), available at http://dwardmac.pitzer.edu/Anarchist_Archives/kropotkin/War!/war!1.html (accessed April 1, 2000).

192. Ibid.

193. R. Rocker, *Nationalism and Culture* (1937; repr., Cornucopia, WI: Michael E. Coughlin, 1978), 269, 253.

194. G. P. Maximoff, *The Programme of Anarcho-syndicalism* (1927; repr., Sydney: Monty Miller, 1985), 46, 47.

195. P. Avrich, *The Russian Anarchists* (Princeton, NJ: Princeton University Press, 1967), 139–40.

196. Avrich, *Anarchist Portraits*, 127.

197. Bakunin, "Statism and Anarchy," 341.

198. Ibid., 342–43; see also 341.

199. Rocker, *Nationalism and Culture*, 213.

200. Marshall, *Demanding the Impossible*, 256.

201. Bakunin, "Letter to *La Liberté*," 276–77

202. Kropotkin, "Modern Science and Anarchism," 188.

203. Kropotkin, "Anarchist Communism," 52.

204. Bakunin, "The Policy of the International," 166–67.

205. Bakunin, "Letters to a Frenchman on the Current Crisis," 209; see also Bakunin, "Statism and Anarchy," 335.

206. Bakunin, "The Programme of the Alliance," 249, 250–51.

207. P. Kropotkin, *The Great French Revolution, 1789–1973, volume 1*, ed. A. M. Bonanno (1909; repr., London: Elephant Editions, 1986), 22–23.

208. M. Bakunin, "The Programme of the International Brotherhood," in *Bakunin on Anarchy: Selected Works by the Activist-Founder of World Anarchism*, ed. S. Dolgoff (1869; repr., London: George Allen and Unwin, 1971), 152–54.

209. Bakunin, "Letters to a Frenchman on the Current Crisis," 190.

210. F. Engels, "On Authority," in *Marx, Engels, Lenin: Anarchism and Anarcho-syndicalism*, ed. N. Y. Kolpinsky (1873; repr., Moscow: Progress Publishers, 1972), 102–5.

211. Martin, introduction, xviii.

212. Stirner, *The Ego and His Own*, 421.

213. M. Bookchin, *Social Anarchism or Lifestyle Anarchism: An Unbridgeable Chasm* (Edinburgh: AK Press, 1995), 54.

214. M. Bakunin, "Worker Association and Self-Management," in *No Gods, No Masters: An Anthology of Anarchism, Book One*, ed. D. Guérin (January 3, 1872; repr., Edinburgh: AK Press, 1998), 182.

215. See, for example, Kropotkin, *The Conquest of Bread*, chapters 8, 9, 11

216. Bakunin, "The Paris Commune and the Idea of the State," 270.

217. Guérin, *Anarchism*, 55, 153.

218. Rocker, *Nationalism and Culture*, 527.

219. Hobsbawm, *Primitive Rebels*; see also Hobsbawm, *Revolutionaries*.

220. J. R. Mintz, *The Anarchists of Casas Vejas* (Chicago: University of Chicago Press, 1982), especially 1–9, 217ff.

221. Bookchin, *The Spanish Anarchists*, 13–14, 58.

222. Compare to Forman, *Nationalism and the International Labor Movement*, 33.

223. Bookchin, *The Spanish Anarchists*, 29–30.

224. See, for example, Godwin, *Enquiry concerning Political Justice*, 18, 68, 98, 147, 327.

225. Stirner, *The Ego and His Own*, 471–72.

226. M. Bakunin, "On Cooperation," in *No Gods, No Masters: An Anthology of Anarchism, Book One*, ed. D. Guérin (Edinburgh: AK Press, 1998), 181–82.

227. Bakunin, "Letters to a Frenchman on the Current Crisis," 207.

228. See R. B. Fowler, "The Anarchist Tradition of Political Thought," *Western Political Quarterly* 25, no. 4 (1972): 741–42. Fowler—who accepted the canon of the seven sages—nonetheless rejected the notion that anarchism could be adequately defined as an opposition to the state or the exaltation of the individual. As an alternative, he suggested that anarchism be defined as a revolt against "convention" in favour of "natural truth"; ibid., 747, 749. This approach, however, fails to come to terms with the socialist character of anarchism.

229. See, inter alia, M. Bakunin, "The Revolutionary Catechism," in *Bakunin on Anarchy: Selected Works by the Activist-Founder of World Anarchism*, ed. S. Dolgoff (1866; repr., London: George Allen and Unwin, 1971); P. Kropotkin, *Organised Vengeance Called "Justice": The Superstition of Government* (London: Freedom Press, 1902).

230. P. Kropotkin, "Prisons and Their Moral Influence on Prisoners," in *Kropotkin's Revolutionary Pamphlets: A Collection of Writings by Peter Kropotkin*, ed. R. N. Baldwin (1877; repr., New York: Dover Publications, 1970), 220–21, 235.

231. Bookchin, *Social Anarchism or Lifestyle Anarchism*.

232. S. T. Possony, introduction to *The Communist Manifesto*, ed. K. Marx and F. Engels (Chicago: Henry Regnery Company, 1954), xix.

Errico Malatesta (1853–1932)

The most prominent anarchist theorist and activist after Bakunin and Kropotkin, Malatesta's life was one of activism and exile in Africa, Latin America, and Europe. A diminutive mechanic by trade, he remains one of the clearest and most approachable of anarchist writers. He died under house arrest under the Italian Fascist regime, an unblemished and revered anarchist hero.

Ricardo Flores Magón (1874–1922) in the Los Angeles County Jail, 1916.

Mexican anarchist revolutionary, Magón was the organiser of the Mexican Liberal Party—which retained its early name despite its anarchist nature. A prolific writer in defence of radical change to Mexico's hacienda-dominated society, he was involved in a series of revolutionary uprisings, and died in exile in an American prison in 1922.

CHAPTER 3

Proudhon, Marx, and Anarchist Social Analysis

The previous chapters have introduced some of the key features of anarchist theory. In this one, we set up a dialogue between anarchism, classical Marxism, and to a lesser extent, mutualism and economic liberalism. As the other major class-based socialist ideology, classical Marxism both influenced anarchism and was the primary ideology against which anarchism defined itself. Discussing the relationship between classical Marxism and anarchism, and also comparing anarchism with economic liberalism, we are able to draw out many key features of anarchism—some of which are implicit and thus not often recognised—and also show that the differences between anarchism and Marxism go far beyond questions of the role of the state in a revolutionary strategy.

There is little doubt that anarchism is deeply imprinted with elements of classical Marxism—specifically, Marxist economics. At the same time, it generally rejects many of Marx's other ideas and incorporates many of Proudhon's views. Anarchism includes both "Proudhonian politics and Marxian economics."[1] In this respect, we can largely agree with Guérin's view that classical Marxism and anarchism belong to the same family of ideas, and drink "at the same proletarian spring."[2] The relationship between classical Marxism and the broad anarchist tradition is not necessarily as stark or polarised as sometimes assumed; the two are deeply entangled.

Nonetheless, we would suggest that the differences between classical Marxism and anarchism remain too profound to merit a "synthesis" of the two.[3] The two hold different views on the nature of history and progress, the structure of society, the role of the individual, the goals of socialism, and the definition of class itself. At the same time, anarchism differs from important elements of a Proudhonian politics. Anarchism, then, is influenced by both Proudhon and Marx, but cannot be reduced to an amalgam of the two elements.

Cooperatives, Proudhon, and Peaceful Change

While it is not possible to demonstrate any links between Godwin, Stirner, and Tolstoy and the anarchist tradition, the same cannot be said of Proudhon. The anarchists acknowledged Proudhon as a forebear and the mutualists as kindred spirits. But anarchism was not Proudhonism, for there was much in the mutualist tradition that the anarchists could not accept. Anarchism, argued Bakunin, was "Proudhonism, greatly developed and taken to its ultimate conclusion."[4] From Proudhon, the anarchists took the notion of the self-management of the means of production, the idea of free federation, a hatred of capitalism and landlordism, and a deep distrust of the state. In his "instinct" for freedom, Bakunin commented, Proudhon was the "master of us all" and immeasurably superior to Marx.[5]

Yet anarchists rejected the mutualist notion that a noncapitalist sector could gradually and peacefully overturn the existing order. Bakunin maintained that cooperatives could not compete with "Big Business and the industrial and commercial bankers who constitute a despotic, oligarchic monopoly." A noncapitalist sector could not, therefore, transform society by defeating the capitalist sector at its own game. On the contrary, the capitalist sector would conquer the noncapitalist one: economic pressures would lead cooperatives to hire wage labour, resulting in exploitation and a "bourgeois mentality."[6]

Moreover, the Proudhonist solution offered little to the majority of peasants, not to mention the working class. Most peasants lived on rented land or were deeply indebted; they were not in a position to start operating a viable noncapitalist sector, let alone one that could overturn the existing order. For the anarchists, the peasants could only secure more land through direct confrontations, certain to be dramatic and violent; defending private property or promoting market socialism would not meet their needs. For many in the working class, subsisting on wages, the dream of setting up small business—of becoming one's own boss—had a great appeal but was simply not practical, as the vast majority lacked the necessary income or the funds to invest in a People's Bank. Unions and community groups that united workers in direct struggle were more relevant and effective.

Three basic distinctions between mutualism and anarchism followed. First, anarchists rejected private property in the means of production as unable to meet the needs of the peasantry and working class, whereas mutualists supported small proprietors and envisaged private profits and private property in their market utopia. Bakunin asserted that while cooperatives provided a valuable practical experience of self-management, they were not a significant challenge to the status quo. Furthermore, the popular classes could only reach their "full potential" in a society based on *collective* ownership by "industrial and agricultural workers."[7] Thus, within the First International, the anarchists voted with the Marxists against the mutualists in debates on property rights in 1869, contributing directly to the eclipse of mutualism and the generalised acceptance of common ownership as a core demand of the popular classes.

Second, the anarchists insisted on the need for revolutionary change, while the mutualists denied it. If the growth of a noncapitalist sector could not overwhelm capitalism, other means had to be found; if neither parliament nor revolutionary dictatorship were desirable, then only organs of counterpower, direct action, radical ideas, and ultimately revolution remained. Proudhon, on the other hand, did not really like or understand large-scale industry, and was hostile to strikes, which isolated him from the emerging labour movement.[8] From his mutualist perspective, strikes were at best irrelevant and at worst a positive threat; they were not really viable means of struggle for his constituency of petty commodity producers, and if they took place within the noncapitalist, cooperative sector, they would have highly destructive consequences.

This brings us to the third major difference: the mutualist tradition was historically geared toward the needs of the small independent farmers and craftspeople. These groups were relatively common in the France of Proudhon's time. In the late nineteenth-century United States, when Tucker wrote, these groups were under great pressure from the rise of modern industry and large-scale agricultural capitalism, and it was against this background that Proudhon's ideas got a new lease on life abroad. By contrast, the anarchism of Bakunin and Kropotkin had a different class character, addressing itself to the majority of peasants and the growing working class, and proposing radical struggles. Bakunin was certainly sympathetic to small producers, but he was convinced that Proudhon's solutions were no longer viable.

In Bakunin's view, the fundamental weakness in Proudhon's work was the absence of a sufficiently rigorous analysis of capitalism, which left his strategy for social change somewhat weak. He was an "incorrigible" idealist who lacked a sufficiently "scientific" analysis of the workings of society.[9] The latter was to be found in Marx's economic analyses, and Bakunin praised Marx's economics as "an analysis so profound, so luminous, so scientific, so decisive ... so merciless an expose of the formation of bourgeois capital" that no apologist for capitalism had yet succeeded in refuting it.[10]

A Critical Appropriation of Marxist Economics

Marx's analysis of the core features of capitalism deeply impressed the early anarchists. His starting point was that production was the basis of all societies, and that it was in the organisation of production that the true character of a given society was to be found.[11] History consisted of a series of changing modes of production, each with their own internal logic. A mode of production was a specific configuration of "forces of production" (labour plus the means of production, like equipment and raw materials) and "relations of production" (the way in which people organised production), and each mode had its own peculiar dynamics and laws of motion.

A class society was one in which the means of production were owned by one class, with that class acting as the dominant force in society. Most modes of production were class systems and based on exploitation, meaning that an economic surplus, produced by the nonowning productive class, was transferred to the nonproducing class by virtue of its ownership of the means of production. Each mode of production, in turn, had internal contradictions, and these ultimately gave rise to the emergence of a new mode of production. On a general level, there was a basic contradiction between the tendency of the forces of production to expand over time and the relations of production through which the forces were deployed; on another, there was the inherent struggle between the classes. These factors would lead to the overthrow of the old mode by a new one that allowed for the further development of the forces of production.

The current mode of production, Marx argued, was capitalism. Here, the means of production were held by capitalists but worked by wage labour, production was directed toward profit, and capitalists competed by reinvesting profits to increase the means of production under their control. In all modes of production, the exploitation took place in production rather than in distribution; in the case of capitalism, workers were not exploited in the market, as Proudhon believed, but at the workplace. Workers sold their labour power or ability to work for a wage, but the value they added to goods through their labour, their actual work, was higher than the value of their wage. The workers, in other words, produced more value than they received in wages. The capitalists owned the products of the workers' labour and sold those goods for a profit, and this profit was derived from the unpaid surplus value created by the workers.

Capitalists invested much of the surplus value back into the forces of production, increasing the amount of variable capital (labour power) and constant capital (the means of production) at their disposal. Now Marx, like Proudhon, used a labour theory of value; he argued that only living labour created new value, and that value underpinned prices. All things being equal, and given the operation of a competitive market system that equalised prices for given commodities, the price of a commodity must correspond closely to the "socially necessary" or average labour time used to produce it. The cost of a Rolls-Royce was higher than that of a loaf of bread, because the socially necessary labour time involved in producing a Rolls-Royce was higher.

More specifically, Marx spoke of the exchange values of commodities, set in production by labour time, as determining prices. The use value or utility of a good could not explain prices, as use values varied widely between individuals, while many items with high use values (like water) had low prices and those with low use values (like diamonds) had high prices. It followed that there was a "law of value" operating in capitalism: given that all commodities had exchange values deriving from labour time, they must exchange in fixed ratios to one another. As capitalists competed with one another on the basis of price, lowering prices required reducing the amount of labour time necessary for the production of particular goods. This could be done by restructuring work or developing new means of production, with mechanisation providing the key means of lowering prices. Thus, capitalism demonstrated a tendency toward a "rising organic composition of capital," meaning an increase in the ratio of constant to variable capital.

It was the drive to mechanise that underpinned the astounding technological advances of the modern world, and allowed capitalism to sweep aside the peasantry and independent producers through large-scale capitalist production. These advances in the forces of production, however, did not benefit the working class. New technologies were typically used to increase exploitation (workers could produce a larger mass of surplus value for the same wage), which led to job losses, which in turn swelled the labour market and placed a downward pressure on wages. Given the limited purchasing power of the working class and the lack of overall planning in the economy, the output tended to outstrip the available markets. The immediate result was a tendency for capitalism to enter recurrent—for Marx, increasingly severe—crises, which were characterised by a sharp increase in competition between capitalists, attacks on the working class to reduce labour costs, a search for new markets, and the outright destruction of surplus productive capacity.

These developments were expressions of the contradiction between the forces of production and the relations of production in capitalism. The second contradiction in the capitalist system was the class struggle. The capitalist class, Marx and Engels maintained, would grow smaller as a result of ongoing competition, while the working class would keep expanding, as other classes were swept into its ranks by capitalism.[12] Moreover, the working class would be concentrated in large plants, become increasingly unified as mechanisation eroded divisions of skill, and become increasingly organised. Locked together in large-scale production systems, existing as "social" rather than individual labour, workers had to cooperate in defence of their interests. Their struggles would lead first to unions, then to revolutionary Marxist parties, and ultimately to the dictatorship of the proletariat. Contrary to the views of economic liberals like Smith, capitalism was not the normal and inevitable human condition but merely the most recent in a series of modes of production, and was inevitably going to be replaced by a new socialist mode.

What Marx had done, drawing on liberal economics, French socialism, and German philosophy, was to develop a new theory of capitalism—a theory of unprecedented and still-unmatched analytic power. The imprint of Marx's economic analysis can clearly be seen in the thinking of the anarchists. Bakunin's only quibble with Marx's *Capital* was that it was written in a style quite incomprehensible to the average worker, and he began a Russian translation of the book.[13] Kropotkin despised Marx, but his understanding of class struggle, exploitation, and capitalist crisis was deeply imprinted with Marxist economics.[14]

Malatesta, who complained that anarchism had been too "impregnated with Marxism," did not develop an alternative economic analysis, and implicitly used Marxist categories and models. Indeed, his close associate Carlo Cafiero (1846–1892) even published a summary of Marx's *Capital*.[15] Perhaps the most influential anarchist after Bakunin and Kropotkin, Malatesta was born to a moderately prosperous family of landowners in Italy.[16] He became involved in the Italian radical movement as a student, linked up with the anarchists of the First International and joined the Alliance, and was involved in insurrectionary activity in the 1870s, after which he became a mass anarchist. Malatesta spent much of his life in exile, returning to Italy in 1914 and again in 1919. His last years were lived out under house arrest by Benito Mussolini's fascist regime.

Marxist Economics and Anarchist Communism

The anarchists, however, did not adopt Marx's ideas unconditionally or uncritically, and developed Marxist economics in important ways. First, they tended, probably unfairly, to downplay Marx's achievements and innovations. Second, they criticised Marx's use of the labour theory of value. Third, they sought to delink Marxist economics from Marxist politics. In the sections that follow, we look at how the anarchist tradition critically appropriated Marx's economic theory as part of a process of developing its own insights into economics.[17]

Anarchists emphasised Marx's largely unacknowledged debt to earlier English and French socialists, especially Fourier, Robert Owen, and Proudhon. For Rocker, Proudhon's ideas played a key role in Marx's conversion to socialism in the early

1840s, and Proudhon's analysis was a formative influence on Marxist economic theory.[18] Rocker noted that Marx initially praised Proudhon as "the most consistent and wisest of socialist writers," and his writings as the "first resolute, ruthless, and at the same time scientific investigation of the basis of political economy, *private property*," a breakthrough that "makes a real science of political economy possible" for the first time. Proudhon, said the early Marx and Engels, was "a proletarian, an *ouvrier*," a champion of the "interest of the proletarians," the author of the first "scientific manifesto of the French proletariat."

Marx subsequently turned on Proudhon, suddenly declaring him a representative of "bourgeois socialism," and a plagiarist, whose ideas "scarcely" deserved a "mention" in a "strictly scientific history of political economy." This, Rocker argued, was unjust and hypocritical, for Marx always remained fundamentally indebted to Proudhon's ideas. Marx's concept of surplus value, "that grand 'scientific discovery' of which our Marxists are so proud," was derived directly from Proudhon's earlier use of the labour theory of value for a theory of exploitation, as well as from the insights of early English socialists. It followed that the Marxist claim to represent a scientific socialism sharply opposed to the older utopian socialism was misleading and dishonest.[19] The term scientific socialism was, indeed, actually coined by Proudhon.[20] Later anarchists have also noted that Marx was influenced by Bakunin.[21]

Rocker did not leave rest the argument at this compelling point, however, but went on to cite questionable claims that key Marxist texts were plagiarised from earlier writers. These assertions were promoted by the anarchist Varlaam Cherkezov (1846–1925). Initially involved in extremist narodnik groups in Russia, Cherkezov was prosecuted in 1871, sent to Siberia but escaped in 1876, and moved via French and Swiss anarchist circles to London, where he became a close friend of Kropotkin and Malatesta. For Cherkezov, *The Communist Manifesto* was copied from *The Manifesto of Democracy*, an 1841 work by Fourier's disciple, Considérant.[22] This contention had quite a wide circulation: for instance, in China it "quickly assumed nearly formulaic status."[23]

These charges of plagiarism are not very convincing and smack of sectarianism. Nettlau made the point that Considérant and Marx were part of the same radical culture and aware of the same "general facts," and therefore neither needed to plagiarise the other; moreover, they interpreted these general facts in quite different ways, according to their political views.[24] It is worth adding that Considérant's views were quite different from those of Marx: he stressed peaceful reforms rather than revolution, the voluntary reorganisation of the economy rather than nationalisation, and class collaboration rather than the dictatorship of the proletariat.[25]

The anarchists criticized Marx's use of the labour theory of value. For Marx, it was not possible to work out the exact contribution of each individual to production and the creation of new value but it was possible to determine the *average* value added to a given commodity. Marx believed that the law of value would operate after the "abolition of the capitalist mode of production."[26] Stalin later claimed that the law of value existed in the USSR.[27] This implied, in the first place, that some sort of nonexploitative wage system could operate under the proletarian dictatorship, with workers paid on the basis of output by the state. Second, this suggested that the distribution of consumer goods under socialism would be organised through purchases with money—that is, markets.

It is against this background that Kropotkin's notion that an anarchist society must also be a communist one—communist in the sense of distribution by need, not output—should be understood. The anarchists of the First International tended to share with classical Marxism the view that a just wage system could be applied in a postcapitalist society, based on remuneration by output. This "anarchist collectivism" (as it was later known) was partly a holdover of mutualist ideas of the workers receiving the full product of their labour and was reinforced by Marxist thinking about a postcapitalist society.

Kropotkin challenged these views in a series of works.[28] In the first place, he made an argument for the social character of production. Production was, he insisted, a collective process, based on the knowledge, experience, and resources developed in the past, and undertaken by large numbers of people in a complex division of labour in the present. Consequently, individual contributions could not be isolated or calculated, nor could the contribution of a particular group of workers, in a particular industry, to a particular good, be properly calculated. The work of the metalworker was not separate from that of the miner who retrieved the ore, the railway person who transported it, or the worker who built the railway, and so on. This also meant that no clear distinction could be made between the production of capital equipment and consumer goods.

Luigi Galleani (1861–1931), who we will discuss more in chapter 4, added the point that the value of less tangible products, such as "Pascal's theorem ... Newton's law of gravitation, or ... Marconi's wireless telegraphy," could scarcely be assessed, nor could the innovations of these men be separated from the ideas and discoveries of others.[29] Marx, then, may have been correct to contend that workers, by virtue of their position in production as social labour, needed to cooperate in order to change society, but his view that remuneration could be fairly calculated for different sections did not follow.

It is necessary at this point to discuss the question of the determination of prices under capitalism. Marx's use of the labour theory of value, his idea of exchange value, and his law of value were integral to his view that prices were objective and set by the average labour time in production. This notion was present in economic liberalism before the late nineteenth century, notably but not only in the work of Smith, where it coexisted uneasily with the perspective that prices were set by subjective factors through the "law" of supply and demand. According to this theorem, the competition of innumerable individuals within the market to maximize the consumption of goods that satisfied personal preferences set prices. A high supply and low demand led to a fall in prices, while a low supply and high demand led to a rise in prices.

Marx admitted that prices could vary somewhat according to supply and demand, but argued that prices were fundamentally set by labour time prior to sale. By the late nineteenth century—and in no small part in reaction to the way in which mutualists, Marxists, anarchists, and others were using the labour theory of value to claim class exploitation—economic liberals sought to develop an entirely subjective theory of price. The theory of marginal utility, developed from William Stanley Jevons onward, suggested that in a free market all prices, including production prices, were determined entirely by individual preferences.

Where did the anarchists fit into these debates? It is useful here to look at Kropotkin's views on wages in capitalism. For Marx, labour power was a commodity, and like any other commodity, its price was set by the labour time required in its production—the labour time required to produce and reproduce the workers who embodied labour power. For Kropotkin, however, wage rates were often quite arbitrary and were set by a wide variety of factors, including the unequal power relations between the classes, government policies, the relative profitability of particular industries, and, last but not least, the ability of skilled and professional employees to establish monopolies in particular trades.[30]

Like Smith, then, Kropotkin believed that *both* subjective utility and exchange value shaped prices, but he added that power relations also played an important role. Berkman developed the point, arguing that prices were not simply a reflection of subjective individual choices or objective exchange values.[31] Prices were affected by labour time, by levels of supply and demand, and were also manipulated by powerful monopolies and the state.[32] Born to a modest Jewish family in Lithuania, Berkman became an activist and left Russia for the United States, where he joined the anarchists.[33] In 1892, he attempted to assassinate the industrialist Henry Clay Frick and was jailed for fourteen years. After his release, he became active again, served two years for antimilitarist activities, and was deported in 1919 as part of the Red Scare—a massive crackdown on the Left starting in 1917—to Russia, where he became bitterly disillusioned with the Bolsheviks. He left in 1921 and ended up in Paris, committing suicide in 1936.

It followed from arguments like those of Kropotkin and Berkman that there was no possibility of operating a fair postcapitalist wage system. Indeed, if wages—like other prices—were partly set by power and class relations, and if—as Kropotkin believed—the dictatorship of the proletariat would be a new class system, then there was no reason to expect that the wages paid by the revolutionary state would be any more fair than those paid by openly capitalist ones. On the contrary, they would tend to form part of a larger apparatus of class.

Kropotkin's second argument against a postcapitalist wage system was centred on the issue of justice. Even if wages were a fair representation of individual contributions to production, it by no means followed that a wage system was desirable. Remuneration on the basis of output meant remuneration on the basis of occupation and ability, rather than effort or need. The output of an unskilled worker in an unskilled low-productivity job, like cleaning, was less than the output of a skilled worker in a high-productivity job, such as engineering, even if the actual effort of the engineer was lower. Further, remuneration by output provided no mechanism for linking income to needs; if the hypothetical engineer lived alone without family commitments and was healthy, and the hypothetical cleaner supported several children and had serious medical problems, the engineer would nonetheless earn a higher wage than the cleaner. Such a situation was both unjust and would "maintain all the inequalities of present society," particularly the gap between skilled and unskilled labour.[34]

Consequently, Kropotkin declared, genuinely communist distribution was necessary. Everyone should contribute to society to the best of their ability, and society should in turn provide for everyone's particular needs as far as possible. Kropotkin did not, it is worth noting, believe that people who refused to contribute to society but could do so should be rewarded; in line with the idea that rights followed from duties, he held that "everyone who cooperates in production to a certain extent has in the first place the right to live, and in the second place the right to live comfortably."[35]

This conception meant that production should not be directed toward profit, as was the case in capitalism, but toward meeting human needs: "The great harm done by bourgeois society is not that capitalists seize a large share of the profits, but that all production has taken a wrong direction, as it is not carried on with a view to securing well-being to all."[36] Goods would be distributed from a "common store," created by labour, and where a particular good was scarce, it could be rationed with priority given to those most in need. In speaking of needs, Kropotkin did not refer only to basic goods like food and shelter, for he believed needs were wide-ranging and ever changing. In his view, there was a "need for luxury," including "leisure," resources to develop "everyone's intellectual capacities," and "art, and especially ... artistic creation."[37] This followed from the anarchist stress on individual freedom and the development of individuality, and from the creed's deep faith in human creativity and learning.

Kropotkin's communist approach meant the abolition of markets as a means of both distribution and setting prices. The information contained in prices arising in markets—whether from subjective utility or objective exchange value—must always provide inadequate information for a just system of distribution and a socially desirable coordination of economic life more generally. While some recent anarchists have suggested that prices could be used to coordinate economic life in an anarchist society, they concede Kropotkin's point in stressing that such prices should reflect not only use value or exchange value but factor in the costs and benefits of particular goods to society as a whole, and should not be generated in the market but through a process of participatory planning.[38]

The importance of Kropotkin's arguments for anarchism is widely recognised, and the notion of "anarchist communism" was widely adopted in the broad anarchist tradition in place of "anarchist collectivism." Kropotkin was not the first to link anarchism and communism but he played the key role in winning the argument for communism in anarchist and syndicalist circles by the 1880s.[39] There are hints of a communist approach in some of Bakunin's works, while his close associate Guillaume was advocating communist distribution by 1876.[40] The Italians around Malatesta were also moving to adopting communism around this time, while the French anarchist Elisée Reclus (1830–1905) seems to have coined the term "anarchist communism." A geographer like Kropotkin, Reclus had been a Fourierist and was briefly involved, along with his brother Elie, in Bakunin's Brotherhood. From 1871 on, the brothers became militant anarchists. Reclus edited the journal *La Revolté* ("Revolt") and produced a stream of anarchist propaganda, enjoying at the same time a successful academic career. Like Kropotkin, he tended to the view that "anarchism was the truth" and "science would prove him right."[41]

It is important, then, to see Kropotkin's contentions about wages, prices, and markets not just as a debate among the anarchists about the operation of a tentative future society but also as part of a wider anarchist engagement with both economic liberalism and Marxist economics. This is a useful way to examine Kropotkin as well as reconsider his relevance for current debates in economics and development studies. In raising questions about the information provided by prices, Kropotkin also raised questions about neoliberalism, which draws on the marginalist tradition of price theory.

For Ludwig von Mises and Frederick von Hayek, only a price system based on a free market could generate the information needed to coordinate a modern economy, and provide scope for individual choice and freedom; the alternative was economic disaster due to the arbitrary calculations of self-interested state planners, and the continued expansion of the power of the state into public and private life.[42] What Kropotkin was pointing out, however, was that prices in capitalism provided at best incomplete and partial information that obscured the workings of capitalism, and would generate and reproduce economic and social inequalities. Ignoring the social character of the economy with their methodological individualism, economic liberals also ignored the social costs of particular choices and the question of externalities: "It remains to be seen whether a robust day-labourer does not cost more to society than a skilled artisan, when we have taken into account infant-mortality among the poor, the ravages of anaemia and premature deaths."[43] While Mises and Hayek championed the free market, and saw in competition both the expression of human nature and the means of promoting individual freedom, Kropotkin viewed cooperation rather than competition as the basis for true individuality, and demanded the subordination of the economy to the needs of society rather than the freeing of the market from social controls.

History, Progress, and the State

From Kropotkin's stress on the satisfaction of human needs as a measure of progress, it is possible to derive a different conception of what is commonly called "development." For liberal economics, development consists of the creation of a competitive market system. For economic nationalists, development consists in creating a powerful national economy, even at the cost of popular living standards and labour rights. By contrast, for Kropotkin, development is about increasing the ability of society to meet human needs as well as facilitate individual freedom and fulfilment, and neither the free market nor state power can undertake this task for the mass of the people.

Measured like this, capitalism is not necessarily a highly developed form of society; it is perhaps less developed than egalitarian tribal societies. The achievement of a powerful industrial base is meaningless in itself. Indeed, unless the majority of people benefit directly, by having their scope for individuality and ability to meet their needs increased, it may even be a retrograde move. Given the class character of capitalism, the rise of newly industrialised countries really means the rise of powerful new ruling classes; it is by no means a necessary step toward popular emancipation. That a previously oppressed country develops into a world power would, in other words, not break the cycle of class rule but simply reproduce it in new ways.

This view of historical progress also differs with that of classical Marxism, where historical progress is measured by the expansion of the forces of production. There can be little doubt that while Marx opposed capitalism, he also saw it is as a necessary evil. It was a stage of history that laid the basis for socialism through developing the forces of production to the highest pitch, while also creating the working class that could overthrow the capitalists and create a socialist society based on the abundance that an advanced economy made possible.

It was precisely on this issue that Marx distinguished his scientific socialism from both utopian socialism and the views of Bakunin, who, he claimed, "does not understand a thing about social revolution, only the political phrases about it; its economic conditions do not matter to him."[44] This was part of a larger tendency toward a teleological view of history in Marx's thought: history progressed inexorably through an ongoing expansion of the forces of production that laid the basis for a succession of increasingly advanced modes of production, culminating in socialism and then the withering away of the state, the end goal of history.

There are ambiguities and contradictions in Marx's thought, which can be interpreted as "Two Marxisms": a "Scientific Marxism" centred on a deterministic and teleological approach, and a "Critical Marxism" that stressed human agency and will.[45] The two tendencies coexist uneasily in Marx's thinking as well as in classical Marxism more generally. On the one hand, there is the Marxism of necessary stages of history and socialist predestination; on the other, there is the Marxism that sees the revolutionary party—with its ideas, tactics, will, dictatorship of the proletariat, and struggles—as the necessary bridge between capitalism and the end goal of history.[46]

However, it is significant that Marx's most voluntaristic works—dating mainly from the mid-1840s to the late 1850s—were not published in his lifetime; the public persona of Marx stressed scientific Marxism (even if his political strategy involved a fair degree of voluntarism). It is from the determinist and teleological strand of Marxism that Marx's and Kautsky's dismissal of the peasantry arises, and the view that one merit of capitalism is that it "rescued a considerable part of the population from the idiocy of rural life."[47] It is also from this strand that the idea that societies must pass through bourgeois democratic revolutions before they can consider proletarian revolutions arises.

Such determinism led classical Marxists to see particular states as "progressive," in the sense that they promoted capitalist transformation, and only some nationalities as "historic." Marx and Engels tended to cast Germany in the role of the champion of progress in Europe, and supported the liberation of so-called historic nationalities like the Poles, while rejecting the liberation of many others, like the Czechs. Their preference for Germany arguably hid an "irrational nationalism" on the part of the two men.[48] At the same time, their tendency to disparage most Slavic nationalities was probably shaped by their own Russophobia.[49] In 1849, for example, Marx and Engels brought the pro-German and anti-Slav positions together:

> It is inadmissible to grant freedom to the Czechs because then East Germany will seem like a small loaf gnawed away by rats.... The revolution

can only be safeguarded by putting into effect a decisive terror against the Slav peoples who for their perspective of their miserable "national independence" sold out democracy and the revolution.[50]

Once certain states and nationalities were seen as progressive—Engels even spoke of "counterrevolutionary nations"—it was a small step to argue that working-class politics should be aligned to particular states.[51] Discussing the impending Franco-Prussian War of 1870, Marx argued that the "French need a thrashing": if "the Prussians are victorious the centralisation of state power [will] be helpful to the centralisation of the German working class," and "German predominance will shift the centre of gravity [in] the Western European labour movements from France to Germany." German domination "on the world stage would mean likewise the dominance of our theory over that of Proudhon, etc."[52]

Accordingly, Engels condemned the leaders of German socialism for failing to vote for war credits in the *Reichstag* (parliament) at this time, as the "establishment of a united German state is necessary for the ultimate emancipation of the workers, the war must be supported."[53] In later years, it was the regimes of the East bloc and various nationalist regimes in the less industrialised countries that were identified with "progress." Marxism's formal commitment to working-class internationalism has been consistently overwhelmed by this tendency of loyalty to particular states.

It was also from the perspective of capitalism as a necessary evil that Marx considered colonialism to be progressive in some respects. If capitalism was necessary, then those societies that did not spontaneously generate capitalism could only benefit from external domination that introduced capitalism. Marx claimed that "English interference" in India had "produced the greatest, and, to speak the truth, the *only* social revolution ever heard of in Asia." Thus, "whatever may have been the crimes of England, she was the unconscious tool of history in bringing about the revolution."[54] As with the Germans and the Slavs, Marx's determinism hid a set of prejudices regarding Asian peoples as stagnant and nonhistoric.[55] Likewise, Engels declared that the colonisation of Algeria was a "fortunate fact for the progress of civilisation," and that the colonies "inhabited by a native population ... must be taken over" by the Western proletariat in the event of revolution and then "led as rapidly as possible towards independence."[56]

The Labour and Socialist International passed anticolonial resolutions at its congresses in 1900, 1904, and 1907.[57] This was partly on the basis of humanitarian concerns about colonial repression. It also reflected a changing assessment of colonialism, increasingly regarded as making little contribution to fostering the development of the forces of production. In the Comintern, this assessment was developed to its logical conclusion: imperialism was now seen as a major obstacle to the development of the forces of production. For Lenin, imperialism no longer played a progressive role in promoting capitalist development.[58] The bourgeois democratic revolutions of the colonial and semicolonial world were therefore necessarily anti-imperialist, and must struggle against both local backwardness and foreign domination.

The initial Comintern theses on the national and colonial questions instructed Communists in these countries to support "revolutionary liberation movements" that were willing to break with imperialism, stating that where capitalism was not "fully developed," the struggle was primarily against feudalism and imperialism.[59] The Comintern theses on the Eastern question, likewise, argued for "the most radical solution of the tasks of a bourgeois-democratic revolution, which aims at the conquest of political independence."[60] In this context, the bourgeois democratic revolution was also a national democratic one, as it had an anti-imperialist content.

By 1928, these ideas were explicitly formulated as the two-stage theory, which has dominated Communist parties in the less developed countries ever since. The task of the bourgeois democratic revolution was seen as so essential that both Lenin and Mao were willing to suggest that it must be led by the Communist Party where necessary.[61] A "bourgeois revolution expresses the needs of capitalist development," and is "*in the highest degree advantageous to the proletariat.*"[62]

For Mao, the "chief targets at this stage of the Chinese revolution" were not capitalism, or capitalists as such, but "imperialism and feudalism, the bourgeoisie of the imperialist countries and the landlord class of our own country" as well as "the bourgeois reactionaries who collaborate with the imperialist and feudal forces."[63] The key tasks were a "national revolution to overthrow imperialism" and a "democratic revolution to overthrow the feudal landlord oppression," by an alliance of four classes—proletariat, peasant, petty bourgeois, and national bourgeois—led by the CCP: "Our present policy is to regulate capitalism, not to destroy it."[64] This was followed in the 1950s by the period of "building socialism" and "socialist construction," mainly based on extending state control of the peasantry in order to extract surplus that would finance industrialisation.[65]

Many anarchists and syndicalists were openly sceptical of the determinist Marxist theory of history. On one level, as we have seen, this reflected a different yardstick for understanding progress and development. On another, the broad anarchist tradition was uncomfortable with Marx's view that history moved in a straight line toward a better future. Both Bakunin and Kropotkin showed more than a hint of teleological thinking, but both generally advocated a more open-ended, voluntaristic, and humanistic model of history. For Bakunin, Marx's position led him to regard the defeat of the peasant uprisings of feudal Europe as beneficial to the cause of human emancipation in general. If the "peasants are the natural representatives of reaction," and the "modern, military, bureaucratic state" that emerged from these defeats aided the "slow, but always progressive" movement of history, it followed that the "triumph of the centralised, despotic state" was "an essential condition for the coming Social Revolution."[66]

This amounted, in Bakunin's view, to supporting the defeat of popular movements and the expansion of a hostile state power. The result was the "out-and-out cult of the state" that led Marx to endorse some of the worst acts of the ruling classes. This sort of thinking led to a nationalist agenda: Marx's support for the rising Germany, regardless of its rationale, made him a de facto "German patriot" who desired the glory and power of the German state above all, a "Bismarck of socialism."[67] In contrast to Marx, Bakunin and Kropotkin regarded all states—not least modern capitalist ones—as obstacles to the liberation of the popular classes.

Scientific Marxism's claim to a special understanding of history and its vision of a single linear history were also viewed with a good deal of scepticism. For Bakunin, Marx's view of history led him to treat the horrors of the past as necessary

evils, rather than simply as evils, and to assume that the events of history were necessary for the cause of ultimate emancipation and therefore progressive. This prevented him from seeing that history did not simply move forward but often moved
backward or sideways. It was full of accidents and tragedies, and even the forces
of production did not inexorably expand over time. While the "necessity of dying
when one is bitten by a mad dog" was inevitable but hardly desirable, so too were
there many events in history that were inevitable but must still be condemned "with
all the energy of which we are capable in the interest of our social and individual
morality."[68]

Marxism's teleological view of history, Kropotkin argued, was rooted in metaphysical ideas that had no rational basis. The Marxists had failed to "free themselves
from the metaphysical fictions of old." Kropotkin insisted that "social life is incomparably more complicated, and incomparably more interesting for practical purposes" than "we should be led to believe if we judged by metaphysical formulae." He
thought it was possible to develop a single, overarching theory of society, but added
this must be through the "natural-scientific method, the method of induction and
deduction," with evidence and logic used to test different hypothesis.[69]

For Rocker, Marx remained influenced by philosophies like those of Georg
Wilhelm Friedrich Hegel that held "every social phenomenon must be regarded as
a deterministic manifestation of the naturally necessary course of events." Nevertheless, while it was possible to discover inexorable laws for the natural world that
applied with "iron necessity," society was more complicated and unpredictable, and
the direction of change was indeterminate, being the product of an incredible diversity of motives and decisions. Marx's historical "laws" were a system of "political and
social astrology" with a predictive power "of no greater significance than the claim
of those wise women who pretend to be able to read the destinies of man in teacups
or in the lines of the hand."[70]

While anarchism itself was a product of the capitalist world and the working
class it created, many anarchists and syndicalists rejected the view that capitalism
would inexorably lead to socialism. This was partly a critique of Marx's vision of
how capitalism would develop. Rocker, for instance, doubted Marx's theory of the
inevitable centralisation of capital.[71] Malatesta pointed out that small and midsize
companies were a typical, not a transitory, feature of capitalism, and formed a considerable part of the economy, even expanding in numbers alongside the growth of
large centralised firms.[72] He added that the working class itself did not necessarily
become unified by the expansion of capitalism; it remained highly internally differentiated, and it was often the workers themselves who entrenched these divisions
within their own ranks.[73]

The matter went beyond a simple empirical critique to questions of strategy.
Berkman, for one, insisted that it was a fallacy to claim that capitalism would inevitably be replaced by socialism: "If the emancipation of labour is a 'historic mission,'
then history will see to it that it is carried out no matter what we may think, feel,
or do about it. The attitude makes human effort unnecessary, superfluous; because
'what must be will be.' Such a fantastic notion is destructive to all initiative."[74]

Likewise, for Malatesta, it was not the march of history that would unite the
popular classes but the political work of revolutionaries.[75] For Rocker, the recogni-

tion of the centrality of human choice and will provided the basis for a truly revolutionary theory of history. If people could change the world by "human hand and human mind," the popular classes could prepare the "way for a reshaping of social life."[76] What was necessary was the "new faith" of which Bakunin spoke. For Berkman,

> There is no power outside of man which can free him, none which can charge him with any "mission." … It is not the "mission" but the interest of the proletariat to emancipate itself…. If labour does not consciously and actively strive for it, it will never happen.[77]

Without this new consciousness, even a terrible capitalist crisis would not necessarily be replaced by socialism; it would more likely lead to an economic reconstruction in which the popular classes were crushed, such as a totalitarian state capitalism.[78] What happened depended, ultimately, on the choices made by the popular classes.

When Marx said of Bakunin "economic conditions do not matter to him," he also remarked that "will, not economic conditions, is the foundation of his social revolution."[79] If we qualify this by adding that Bakunin had in mind *conscious* will, informed by the "new faith," Marx was perfectly correct. Bakunin was quite explicit on this issue: the anarchists do not want a revolution that was "realisable only in the remote future" but rather the "completed and real emancipation of all workers, not only in some but in all nations, 'developed' and 'undeveloped.'"[80] It was not a question of struggling against, for instance, landlordism in order to facilitate the further development of capitalism but of struggling against landlordism where necessary, and capitalism where necessary, and destroying both; it was not a question of waiting for the transformation of the peasantry into proletarians but of uniting both popular classes in an international class struggle.

There was no need for the capitalist stage to be completed or even begun. Bakunin stressed the possibility that Russian peasant villages, organised through the semidemocratic commune (the *mir* or *obschina*) could help make the revolution. Again, consistent with the emphasis on ideas as the key to changing society, he asserted that the mir itself must change if it were to play a revolutionary role; it must overcome its "shameful patriarchal regime," lack of individual freedom, "cult of the Tsar," isolation from other villages, and the influence of rich landlords on the village. This required that the "most enlightened peasants" take the lead in remaking the mir, linking with the working class, and uniting the villages. Radical intellectuals could play a part too, but only if they went to the people to "share their life, their poverty, their cause, and their desperate revolt."[81]

The theme that peasant cultural traditions could facilitate revolution, if suitably reinvented, appears repeatedly in anarchist writings. It was stressed, for example, by Flores Magón, looking at Mexican peasant communities, and has appeared more recently in the writings of Nigerian anarchists.[82] Born to a poor mestizo family in 1874, Flores Magón was initially a radical liberal (in the Latin American sense of a progressive democrat) who aimed at political reforms.[83] He was involved in university protests against the dictator Porfirio Díaz, edited *El Demócrata* ("The Democrat") and then *Regeneración* ("Regeneration") with his brother Jesús, and worked from exile in the United States starting in 1904. He founded the Mexican

Liberal Party (PLM), which organised armed uprisings in 1906 and 1908 as well as unions and strikes, became an anarchist and made the PLM into a largely anarchist body, and was arrested in 1912. Sentenced to twenty years in 1918, he died in Leavenworth Prison, Kansas, in 1922.

Kropotkin, Berkman, and Rocker developed another argument against the need for a capitalist stage.[84] Capitalism continually created obstacles to the realisation of human creativity and productivity through alienating work, low wages, unequal education, the use of new technologies to maximise profits and cut labour costs, economic crises, and unequal economic development within and between countries. This crippled the creativity and capacities of the popular classes.

An anarchist society, on the other hand, would achieve great advances in technology and scientific knowledge as labour was emancipated, work restructured, and a "general scientific education" was provided to all, "especially the learning of the scientific method, the habit of correct thinking, the ability to generalise from facts and make more or less correct deductions."[85] This would provide the basis for an emancipatory technology and a prosperous society, created by the popular classes rather than inherited from the old ruling class. It was not necessary to wait for capitalism to create the material basis for freedom; freedom would create its own material basis.

The Vanguard and the State

In claiming that his theory was scientific, Marx was no different from, say, Kropotkin or Reclus, who saw their own theories as scientific. And both classical Marxists and anarchists were really developing social scientific theories in that they sought to find explanatory models of society that were empirically verifiable and logically consistent. Claims to scientific status are the common currency of modern ideologies. What classical Marxism also claimed, however, was that its theory was an "extraordinary and very superior theory of knowledge" that originated among middle-class intellectuals, but was able to transcend its social origins, and that must be embodied in the revolutionary party, with the sole right to lead the masses.[86]

Classical Marxism purported to alone understand the movement of history and express the fundamental interests of the proletariat; it was, in fact, the only legitimate ideology of the working class. The Communists

> do not set up any sectarian principles of their own, by which to shape and mould the proletarian movement [but instead] always and everywhere represent the interests of the movement as a whole. The Communists, therefore, are on the one hand, practically, the most advanced and resolute section of the working-class parties of every country, that section which pushes forward all others; on the other hand, theoretically, they have over the great mass of the proletariat the advantage of clearly understanding the lines of march, the conditions, and the ultimate general results of the proletarian movement.[87]

It was the Marxist character of the revolutionary party—bearing in it the "true" destiny of the working class—that entitled it alone to lead the working class to socialism via the dictatorship of the proletariat. For Lenin, there could "be no talk of an independent ideology formulated by the working masses themselves in the process of their movement, the only choice is—either bourgeois or socialist ideology."[88] By itself, the working class could only generate an economistic consciousness, and this was a bourgeois consciousness. Citing Kautsky, Lenin declared that the radical intellectuals must bring "socialist ideology" to the working class from without. Even if—as Lenin was well aware—the Bolsheviks were disproportionately drawn from the middle class, they alone truly understood and represented proletarian interests.

Even on this level, the argument for the revolutionary party did not necessarily entail an authoritarian relationship between party and class. It was when the claim to a unique truth was welded to the strategy of the dictatorship of the proletariat that the transition to a claim to *rule* was made and the formula for a one-party dictatorship through an authoritarian state was written. On the one hand, the dictatorship of the proletariat was a "centralised organisation of force, of violence," and "undivided power." On the other, it was the revolutionary party that alone represented the proletariat, from which it followed that a proletarian dictatorship was equivalent to—and indeed required—party dictatorship:

> By educating the workers' party, Marxism educates the vanguard of the proletariat, capable of assuming power and *leading the whole people* to socialism, of directing and organising the new system, of being the teacher, the guide, the leader of all the working and exploited people in organising their social life without the bourgeoisie and against the bourgeoisie.[89]

The "revolutionary dictatorship of a proletarian party" was an "objective necessity" due to "the heterogeneity of the revolutionary class."[90] And anyone who refuses to recognise that the "leadership of the Communist Party and the state power of the people's dictatorship" are conditions for revolutionary change "is no communist."[91] "Only he is a Marxist who extends the recognition of the class struggle to the recognition of the dictatorship of the proletariat."[92]

The working class as a whole could not rule since it was infused with "bourgeois ideology" and was politically heterogeneous. Every view that was not truly Marxist was antiproletarian and counterrevolutionary by definition. In Russia, the Bolsheviks were only one wing of a deeply Russian Social Democratic Labour Party (RSDRP); their main rivals were the Mensheviks. Yet, for Lenin, the Bolsheviks alone were revolutionary and proletarian; even the Mensheviks were "henchmen and hangers-on" of the capitalists, while "anarchism and anarcho-syndicalism are *bourgeois* trends ... irreconcilably opposed ... to socialism."[93]

For Bakunin, this linking of a claim to truth and a claim to rule was a recipe for an authoritarian regime that would enslave the popular classes and create a new ruling class. On the one hand, as we have seen, Bakunin viewed the state as a centralised instrument wielded by a ruling minority, and he did not believe that even the most democratic dictatorship of the proletariat could lead to popular freedom:

> What does it mean that the proletariat will be elevated to a ruling class? Is it possible for the whole proletariat to stand at the head of the government? There are nearly forty million Germans. Can all forty million be members of the government? In such a case there will be no government, no state, but, if there is to be a state there will be those who are ruled and those that are slaves.[94]

If the proletarian dictatorship was "really of the people" and the whole proletariat was "elevated to a ruling class," "why eliminate it" by having the state wither away?[95] If the dictatorship was not "of the people," why claim that it was really the "proletariat ... elevated to a ruling class" rather than a regime dominating the proletariat?

On the other hand, Bakunin argued, the dictatorship of the proletariat would really be the dictatorship of the Communists: "Mr Marx and his friends" would "liberate" the masses in "their own way," establishing a "despotic control" over the populace, which would be a "regimented herd."[96] The strategy for socialism through a proletarian dictatorship was, in short, the road to a dictatorship *over* the proletariat. Authoritarian methods could not create libertarian outcomes; to "*impose* freedom and equality obliterates both."[97]

A "dictatorship has no objective other than self-preservation," wrote Bakunin, and "slavery is all that it can generate and instil in the people who suffer from it."[98] The party and the state would develop into a new class system—the "new privileged political-scientific class," the "state engineers," who would hold power.[99] The revolutionary state would also have to compete with other states to survive in the international state system; given the Marxist sympathy for capitalism's civilising mission, it might realistically be expected to embark on wars and conquests, becoming a new imperial power.[100]

In the wake of the Russian Revolution, these themes were further developed in the broad anarchist tradition. For Berkman, the "Bolshevik idea was a dictatorship" and "that dictatorship to be in the hands of *their* political Party ... because their Party, they said, represented the best and foremost elements, the advance guard of the working class, and their Party should therefore be dictator in the name of the proletariat."[101] For Maximoff, Lenin's theory of the vanguard party was an "altogether reactionary" recipe for dictatorship, rooted in the writings of Marx and Engels:

> The Marxian "dictatorship of the proletariat" connotes the dictatorship
> of the vanguard of the working class ... the "dictatorship of the prole-
> tariat" is in the last analysis, the dictatorship of the party, and by the same
> logic, the adversaries and enemies of this dictatorship inevitably are ...
> all those who do not belong to this ruling party. And since the state of the
> transitional period is also the party, and since this state must ruthlessly
> suppress its adversaries, it follows logically that terror has to be applied
> against all, save a very small handful of the "vanguard of the proletariat"
> organised into a party.[102]

Moreover, Lenin advocated a highly centralised party, based on a "stable organisation of leaders," and rejected the "absurdity" of a "primitive" conception of democracy as participatory.[103] Since the party is organised around subordination to the leaders, who "get control of the party apparatus," "we have the dictatorship of the leaders within the party, and the 'dictatorship of the proletariat' becomes the dictatorship of the leaders," and ultimately, "one single leader."[104]

State Capitalism and Libertarian Socialism

As we have noted in the previous chapter, Bakunin and Kropotkin went on to argue that Marxist regimes would not simply be dictatorships but also class systems. The state was necessarily an instrument for the rule of a (class) minority over a (class) majority, and a party dictatorship must therefore be part of an apparatus of class rule. This was particularly true of the dictatorship of the proletariat, for it involved the centralisation of the means of production in the hands of the state and thus the party. For Marx and Engels, the revolutionary state must "centralise all instruments of production" and "increase the total of productive forces as rapidly as possible." While the measures could differ between countries, there were "generally applicable" measures:

> 1. Abolition of private property in land and application of rents of land to public purposes.

> 2. A heavy progressive or graduated income tax.

> ...

> 5. Centralisation of credit in the hands of the state, by means of a national bank with state capital and an exclusive monopoly.

> 6. Centralisation of all means of communication and transport in the hands of the state.

> 7. Extension of factories and instruments of production owned by the state; the bringing into cultivation of wastelands, and the improvement of the soil generally in accordance with a common plan.

> 8. Equal liability of all to labour. Establishment of industrial armies, especially for agriculture.[105]

In placing both the means of production and labour under direct state control, Bakunin contended, the revolutionary regime would be "the only banker, capitalist, organiser, and director of all national labour, and the distributor of its products."[106] For Kropotkin, it would be "centralised state-capitalism," "preached under the name of collectivism."[107]

Before 1917, of course, there were no such regimes and hence no way to test this hypothesis. After the Russian Revolution, a whole score of Marxist regimes were established. The death of Lenin in 1924 created a leadership crisis in the Bolshevik Party, fought out between a majority centred on Stalin and a Trotsky faction. In 1929, Trotsky was expelled from the USSR and later assassinated in Mexico under Stalin's orders. Classical Marxism, by then largely embodied in Leninism, was split into the Stalinist mainstream, aligned with the USSR and including all the major Communist parties, and a tiny but vocal Trotskyist current. The differences between the two should not be overstated: both embraced classical Marxism and its theories, both saw the USSR as postcapitalist and progressive, and both envisaged revolution by stages in less developed countries.[108] It was, contrary to Trotsky's prognosis that "Stalinism" was counterrevolutionary and unstable, the "Stalinists" who established every subsequent Marxist regime, starting with Eastern Europe, then East Asia, and then parts of Africa, Latin America, and the Middle East.

There was some initial confusion among anarchists and syndicalists regarding the USSR and the Bolsheviks, who seemed far to the left of the old Labour and Socialist International, raised slogans that seemed quite libertarian, and sought to draw the syndicalist unions into a special wing of the Comintern: the Red International of Labour Unions, or "Profintern." The soviets that arose in the 1917 revolution, and from which the USSR derived its name, were also initially democratic and self-managed popular councils, and gave Lenin by association a libertarian aura. Early news reports added to the confusion. Morgan Philips Price, a special correspondent for the *Manchester Guardian*, alleged for example that the "inner character of the Bolshevik movement" was "based on the theory of anarchy and syndicalism preached during the last century by Bakunin"; "It is not Socialism at all but Syndicalism."[109]

It is not surprising, then, that anarchists and syndicalists founded many of the Communist parties outside Russia—often on an openly libertarian and anti-statist platform—and that syndicalists attended the early Profintern meetings. Yet most anarchists and syndicalists came to the conclusion that the Bolshevik regime bore out Bakunin's and Kropotkin's predictions about the character of a revolutionary Marxist regime, pointing to the repression of Russian and Ukrainian anarchists along with the subordination of the soviets and the popular classes to the new state. Berkman's Russian diary eloquently expresses this viewpoint:

> One by one the embers of hope have died out. Terror and despotism have crushed the life born in October 1917. The slogans of the Revolution are foresworn, its ideals stifled in the blood of the people. The breath of yesterday is dooming millions to death: the shadow of today hangs like a black pall over the country. Dictatorship is trampling the masses under foot. The Revolution is dead; its spirit cries in the wilderness.[110]

Goldman held the same position.[111] The Bolshevik state was an "air-tight dictatorship," in which "every channel of human contact is closed ... every thought is thrown back on itself and expression stifled," a "dictatorship" that "paralysed the initiative of both the city proletariat and the peasantry."[112] The "dictatorship of the proletariat had been turned into a devastating dictatorship of the Communist Party," characterised by popular "unrest and dissatisfaction" with the "different rations and discriminations" meted out by the party. Born in a Jewish ghetto in Russia, Goldman immigrated to the United States, where she worked in various jobs, including as a seamstress and nurse.[113] Becoming an anarchist and Berkman's lover, she helped plan the attack on Frick, published *Mother Earth* from 1906 on, and was a tireless agitator and speaker. In 1910 alone, Goldman gave 120 talks in 37 cities in 25 states in the United States to 25,000 people.[114] Jailed in 1917, and described by authorities as "one of the most dangerous women in America," she was deported to Russia in 1919, campaigned against the Bolsheviks in the 1920s, joined the Spanish Revolution of 1936–1939, and died in 1940.

For Maximoff, too, the USSR was a class society. He described it as similar to the ancient slave-based societies, with a "slaveholding class" centred on a small "oligarchy," characterised by "socialistic Caesarism based upon the bureaucracy—the new class which sprang from the Marxist State."[115] The "small class of the bureaucracy" exploited the "rest of the population ... workers, forced to give their labour energy to the State Trust ... to create the power of this Trust, at the same time increasing the economic standards of the administrative class." It "imitated" the bourgeoisie, but was not capitalist.[116] Its "principal economic peculiarity ... is production for use, rather than exchange," with distribution organised by the bureaucracy rather than the market, with all resources, including "the individual himself," concentrated in the hands of the state.[117]

It was not clear from Maximoff's initial analysis what dynamics shaped the mode of the production in the USSR. He argued that the system operated to increase the power and wealth of the ruling class, but this was vague. For anarchists, all class systems operate to the advantage of the ruling class.[118] The same problem can be found in other anarchist texts of the time. Thus, Kubo Yuzuru (1903–1961), a Japanese militant from the syndicalist Libertarian Federal Council of Labour Unions of Japan (usually abbreviated as Nihon Jikyo), asserted that "Marxist class struggle does not bring an end to the strife or the contradiction of classes, but reverses the position of the opposed classes.... Their goal is to replace one ruling class with another."[119] Neither Maximoff nor Kubo explain why the USSR's industrial base grew so rapidly under Stalin and his successors, or why it became an expansionist power starting in the 1930s.

Maximoff's and Kubo's approach nonetheless had the great merit of insisting that the USSR had a class system, and was more convincing than the notion, propounded by the elderly Kropotkin, that the Bolshevik regime was a system of "state communism."[120] This formulation was unclear on the issue of whether the USSR was actually a class system and suggested, unlike Maximoff's analysis, that distribution was based on need. If the USSR was communist—even state communist—why was the "devastating dictatorship of the Communist Party" associated with "different rations and discriminations," as Goldman had reported?[121] If there were different rations and discriminations, who—or rather, which class—made the decisions?

An alternative anarchist and syndicalist analysis used the idea of state capitalism, and focused on the notion that the Soviet state acted as a single capitalist conglomerate, exploiting labour and realising the surplus through the sale of commodities on behalf of a ruling class centred on the state managers who controlled the means of production. While council communists and a section of the Trotskyists also developed theories of the USSR as state capitalist, the anarchist analysis seems to have been the first of its type by socialists. The state capitalist theory was Maximoff's initial line of reasoning. Writing in 1918, he argued,

> Instead of hundreds of thousands of property owners there is now a single owner served by a whole bureaucratic system and a new "statised" morality. The proletariat is gradually being enserfed by the state. The people are being transformed into servants over whom there had risen a new class of administrators ... if the elements of class inequality are as yet indistinct, it is only a matter of time before privileges will pass to the administration.... Thus we are presently moving not towards socialism but towards state capitalism.... The single owner and state capitalism form a new dam before the waves of our social revolution.[122]

Berkman, too, described the USSR as "a country partly State capitalistic and partly privately capitalistic," and claimed that the state, headed by a "new class," had become the employer instead of the individual capitalist of the past.[123]

"Voline" (1882–1945) had a similar analysis. Voline was the pseudonym of Vsevolod Eichenbaum, who was born in 1882 to a Russian Jewish professional family. A law student radicalised by the 1905 Russian uprising, he forced into exile by a state tribunal. In particular, he was linked to the Socialist Revolutionary Party (SR) formed in 1901. The SRs, who were divided into the Right SRs, the Left SRs, and SR Maximalists (whose views were often close to anarchism), evolved from the nineteenth-century narodniks and were by far the largest Russian revolutionary party. Voline moved to anarchism, left his exile in France for the United States in 1915 to avoid internment for antiwar activities, and returned to Russia in 1917.[124] Actively involved in the newspaper *Golos Truda*, he went to the Ukraine, where he helped found the regional anarchist federation Nabat ("Alarm Confederation of Anarchist Organisations") and actively participated in the Ukrainian Revolution of 1918–1921, an event discussed in more detail in chapters 9 and 10. When the Bolsheviks crushed the Ukrainian anarchists, Voline went into exile, mainly in France, where he lived until his death in 1945.

Voline's *The Unknown Revolution, 1917–1921*, is the definitive anarchist study of the Russian and Ukrainian Revolutions. Its core argument is that there was an "explicit and irreconcilable contradiction between the true Revolution," based on the "vast and free creative movement of the labouring masses," and "the theory and practice of authoritarianism and statism," exemplified by the Bolsheviks.[125] The "*government nationalised and monopolised everything, including speech and thought.*" The Bolshevik state became the universal landlord, with the peasants "veritable serfs," and also expropriated "the works, factories, [and] mines," becoming the "sole initiator, organiser, and animator of the whole life of the country."[126] It enforced its power through a centralised administration and network of police terror. Its system was "totalitarian" and "integral state capitalism":

> State-capitalism: such is the economic, financial, social and political system of the USSR, with all of its logical consequences and manifestations in all spheres of life—material, moral, and spiritual. The correct designation of this state should ... be ... USCR, meaning Union of State Capitalist Republics.... This is the most important thing. It must be understood before all else. The rest follows.[127]

The situation of the Russian working class was essentially the same as that of the workers in other capitalist countries, except that there was only one employer, the party-state, in whose collective hands all the means of production were concentrated, to the benefit of the "state bourgeoisie."[128] The peasantry fared even worse: having initially taken over the great estates in 1917, it was terrorised by the Bolsheviks beginning in 1918, lost control of the land, and by the 1930s was transformed into a class of unfree wage labourers on giant state "collective" farms.

Neither Maximoff nor Voline had much reason to regard the Bolshevik regime with sympathy. *Golos Truda* was suppressed, and both Maximoff and Voline received death sentences. In 1921, both men were in jail, went on a hunger strike, and were only released after the intercession of syndicalists attending Profintern meetings. Such experiences obviously biased the two against Bolshevism, but cannot be lightly dismissed, and form part of their case against the USSR and its rulers. Rocker reached the same conclusions independently:

> That which today is called by this name [socialism] in Russia—and unthinking people abroad are repeating it mechanically—is in reality only the last word of modern monopoly capitalism which uses the economic

dictatorship of the trusts and cartels for the purpose of eliminating any undesirable competition and reducing the entire economic life to certain definite norms. The last link of such a development is not socialism but state capitalism with all its inevitable accompaniments of a new economic feudalism and a new serfdom; and that is the system which today is actually operating in Russia.[129]

There are obvious Marxist objections to the anarchist theory of state capitalism. One is that the law of value did not operate properly in the USSR, partly because the state as sole proprietor did not operate a competitive internal market. As we have seen, however, the broad anarchist tradition does not see the law of value as a central feature of capitalism, and does not see centralised price setting as a particular objection to a theory of state capitalism.

A related objection is the view that competition did not exist within the Soviet economy, as it was centrally planned by the state. Yet it could be argued that as competition under capitalism does not take place *within* firms, and the "USCR" was a single giant firm, competition would rather take place at the international level with other capitalist firms. This suggests that the twentieth-century competition between the United States and the USSR was not a rivalry between two radically different systems but a form of *intercapitalist* competition. A third Marxist objection to the state capitalist thesis centres on the question of the ownership of the means of production. This is a complicated issue, but it is most revealing about the different ways in which classical Marxists and the broad anarchist tradition understood class itself, and will be discussed below in some depth.

For now, it is worth noting that the anarchists and syndicalists contended that the evolution of the USSR into a class system and ruthless dictatorship was not a deviation from classical Marxism but its logical conclusion. Stalin did not "fall from the moon," for all of the key features later called Stalinist—repression, labour camps, the suppression of dissent, the crushing of unions and the peasantry, and an official dogma enforced by the state—were created from 1917 onward, when Lenin and Trotsky held sway.[130] If the system was state capitalism, it also followed that the broad anarchist tradition should not support either of the sides in the post-1945 Cold War rivalry between the West and the East, for the two sides were rival *capitalist* blocs pursuing ruling class agendas. There was nothing progressive or socialist about the East bloc, and its collapse in many regions in 1989–1991 was *not* a defeat for the popular classes or socialism but a moment in the development of class society. Indeed, inasmuch as class struggle played a critical role in this collapse and opened some democratic space, the crisis of the East bloc was a popular *victory*.

Economic Determinism and the Broad Anarchist Tradition

Earlier, we noted that the "public" Marx stressed the scientific Marxism dimension of his thought. In this persona, Marx presented the "social world as imposing itself on persons, rather than being a fluid medium open to human intervention," and saw capitalism as a "stage in a social evolution *destined* to give rise to another, higher society—socialism."[131] This outlook was at odds with the strand of critical Marxism in Marx's thought, and a number of Marxists have developed Marx's theories along more humanistic lines. Nonetheless, it is undeniable that Marx held many

avowedly deterministic views, and he took his public stand against the utopian socialists and the anarchists on precisely this basis.

More specifically, Marx saw history as primarily driven by economic developments. The relations and forces of production, on the one hand, were the base
on which a superstructure of culture, law, philosophy, and politics—including the
state—arose, with the superstructure viewed as determined by the needs of the base
and functional to its reproduction. On the other hand, Marx tended to assign primacy to the forces of production over the relations of production, presenting the
inexorable expansion of the forces of production as the primary mover in human
history, the factor that necessitated ongoing revolutions in the relations of production, with new relations of production selected by their ability to facilitate the further expansion of the forces of production. Thus,

> At a certain stage of development, the material productive forces of soci-
> ety come into conflict with the existing relations of production, or—this
> merely expresses the same thing in legal terms—with the property rela-
> tions within the framework of which they have operated hitherto. From
> forms of development of the productive forces these relations turn into
> their fetters. Then begins an era of social revolution. The changes in the
> economic foundation lead sooner or later to the transformation of the
> whole immense superstructure.[132]

Likewise, for Engels,

> *all* past history ... was the history of class struggles; ... these warring
> classes of society are always the product of the modes of production and
> of exchange—in a word, of the *economic* conditions of their time; that
> the economic structure of society always furnishes the real basis, start-
> ing from which we can alone work out the ultimate explanation of the
> whole superstructure of juridical and political institutions as well as of
> the religious, philosophical and other ideas of a given historical period
> ... the final causes of all social changes are to be sought ... in changes
> in the modes of production and exchange. They are to be sought, not in
> the *philosophy*, but in the *economics*, of each particular epoch. All moral
> theories are the *product*, in the last analysis, of the *economic stage* which
> society reached at that particular epoch.[133]

The primacy of the "economic structure of society" as the "real basis" of society resounds throughout classical Marxism, and may be seen, inter alia, in Marx's
definition of class as the (non)ownership of the means of *production*, description
of class systems as relations of *production* that arise from a particular development
of the forces of *production*, view of the state as the instrument of the *economically*
dominant class, hypothesis that the evolution of the *productive* forces lays the basis
for socialism, and criticism of Bakunin for ignoring the *economic* conditions for
social revolution. Marx called his model the "materialist" conception of history.

Both Marx and Engels qualified their conception somewhat, cautioning
against a crude reading of the superstructure from the base—Engels speaks of the
base as the "ultimate explanation" of the superstructure, the site of the "final causes"
in the "last analysis"—but this does not fundamentally break with the economic
determinism of the overall model. It opens the space to admit the possibility of
some autonomous development in the superstructure, but does not admit of the

possibility that the superstructure can have fundamental and independent effects on the base, which remains the site of "final causes" and the "real basis" of society. The assertion that the base must be the "ultimate explanation" is exempted from verification, providing a "real" cause that is freed from the very scientific methodology on which Marx prided himself, and on which basis Marx declared his theory as uniquely suited to represent the working class.

Marx's "materialist" conception of history is a profound and immensely compelling explanatory framework, capable of generating stunning insights. It is not surprising that the broad anarchist tradition responded to the doctrine in a range of ways. A section of the tradition embraced the model uncritically. IWW militants Haywood and Frank Bohm, for example, believed the "great facts of history ... were created by a deeper social force ... the economic or material force."[134] Born in 1869 in the United States, Haywood worked from his youth, was radicalised by the execution of the Chicago martyrs, became a leading figure in the militant Western Federation of Miners, and helped form the IWW in 1905.[135] He served the Wobblies in a number of leading roles, even after the miners withdrew from the IWW. His views shifted toward syndicalism, and in 1913 he was among the syndicalists expelled from the Socialist Party of America (SPA) and "could not have cared less."[136] In 1917, the U.S. federal government raided the IWW as part of the Red Scare, and Haywood was prosecuted. Found guilty, he fled to the USSR in 1921. In his last years he helped organise an unusual (and state-sanctioned) experiment in self-management in the Urals and Siberia called the Autonomous Industrial Colony. He died in 1928 and the Colony was closed by Stalin that year.

An alternative approach in the broad anarchist tradition is to formally adopt the materialist conception of history, but to use it in a critical and nuanced manner. The contemporary Italian Platfomist group, the Federazione dei Comunisti Anarchici (FdCA), for example, is a "firm" supporter of "historical materialism" yet rejects teleological views of history, and denies the notion that any clear distinction can be drawn between the base and the superstructure.[137] This is an enormous modification of the theory and implicitly breaks with the materialist conception of the primacy of the economic factor.

This is also close to the approach adopted by Bakunin, Kropotkin, and others who maintained that economic factors were central but not necessarily primary. Economic factors shaped society in a range of profound ways, but cannot be taken as primary and determinant in every situation. Bakunin famously declared himself a "materialist," yet went on to argue that Marx ignored "other factors in history, such as the ever-present reaction of political, juridical and religious institutions on the economic situation."[138]

Such "factors" were shaped by the "economic situation," but also had independent effects on the economy. For instance, in Bakunin's view, political cultures played an important role: "Even apart from and independent of the economic conditions in each country," the "temperament and particular character of each race and each people," arising from particular historical and social conditions, affected the "intensity of the sprit of revolt."[139] Bakunin also alluded to historical events that had no economic basis and undermined the forces of production. He cited the destruction of the libraries of antiquity by the early Christians, which did not follow from economic causes and was economically retrogressive in its effects.[140] Moreover, Bakunin noted, the classical Marxist strategy of a revolutionary state that acted as midwife to a new mode of production was inconsistent with Marx's own materialist theory of history, for it meant that the superstructure, which Marx treated as a reflection of the base, could revolutionise the base and fundamentally change society.[141]

Rocker acknowledged that "economic conditions and the special forms of social production" had played a key part in the "evolution of humanity," and added that the recognition of the "influence and significance of economic conditions on the structure of social life" lay at the heart of socialism. Marx, however, was incorrect in suggesting that "every historical event" could be traced to and explained on the basis of "the prevailing conditions of production," or that as a result, there were universal laws that shaped society and could be used to predict future events.[142]

Many "thousands of events in history ... cannot be explained by purely economic reasons, or by them alone," observed Rocker, and this directed attention to factors such as the will to power, culture, and competition between states. The destruction of heresies by the medieval Catholic Church in Europe, for example, was an attempt at "the unification of faith" that was rooted in the church's "efforts at political power."[143] The state was no mere puppet of economic forces, but could and did act in ways contrary to the development of the forces of production; even where it promoted the forces of production, it did not follow that this was done at the behest of those forces.

The long-term economic decline of Christian Spain from the sixteenth century onward, starting with the expulsion of the Moors and the Jews, was one example.[144] The rulers of the state were driven in this instance by religious fanaticism, a desire to consolidate power, and the imperatives of the alliance of state and church. The ruling class was also often concerned with a drive to maintain and expand state power, as was the case in the First World War, where the struggle for dominance in Europe between the great powers was as important as economic gain.[145] It was also too crude to discern in the motivations of capitalists nothing but a quest for economic aggrandisement. The "morbid desire to make millions of men submissive to a definite will," declared Rocker, "is frequently more evident in the typical representatives of modern capitalism than are purely economic considerations or the prospect of greater material profit," and the "possession of great wealth" is itself often pursued primarily as a means to access "enormous power."[146]

The Anarchist Understanding of Class

Both classical Marxism and the broad anarchist tradition were models in which class was absolutely central. It would be a serious mistake, however, to assume that their understandings of class were the same. For Marx and Engels, as we have seen, class was a relation of production and premised on the ownership of the means of production: "By bourgeoisie is meant the class of modern Capitalists, owners of the means of social production and employers of wage-labour"; and "by proletariat, the class of modern wage-labourers who, having no means of production of their own, are reduced to selling their labour-power in order to live."[147] In this sense, the state was an instrument of class power, but only in the sense that it was an instrument of an *economically* dominant class; it was a superstructure that arose from an *economic* base and thus reflected the imperatives of that base.

It is, on the other hand, only possible to understand the anarchist and syndicalist claim that a state must generate a new ruling class, and the contention that state managers are themselves part of a ruling class, by recognising that the broad anarchist tradition sees class as premised on the control of a range of resources and *not* only on economic ownership. We have touched on this issue in the previous chapter, where we saw that Bakunin spoke of the Serbian patriots becoming a ruling class in a country that had "no nobles, no big landowners, no industrialists and no very wealthy merchants" at independence.[148] His view that the patriots who controlled the newly independent state were a "new bureaucratic aristocracy" cannot be understood unless it is noted that class, in Bakunin's thinking, is not just about the relations of production but also the *relations of domination*, not just about the ownership of the means of production but also about the ownership of the means of *coercion*—the capacity to physically enforce decisions—and the means of *administration*—the instruments that govern society.

Viewed in this way, the unequal ownership of the means of production is a necessary but not sufficient description of a class system. In the first place, the ownership of the means of production can only be used for exploitation if buttressed by relations of domination between the classes. If, as Marx argued, workers sell their labour power for less than the value of their actual labour, then the process of exploitation requires the deployment of both coercive and administrative resources to ensure that more work is done than is remunerated. For Bakunin, the "merchandise" that the worker "sold to his employer" is "his labour, his personal services, the productive forces of his body, mind, and spirit that are found in him and are inseparable from his person—it is therefore himself." To force this self to work for another, to another's benefit, requires that "the employer ... watch over him, either directly or by means of overseers; every day during working hours and under controlled conditions, the employer will be the owner of his actions and movements."[149]

Even in the workplace, then, where the relations of production are central, they are necessarily intertwined with the relations of domination, and the processes of exploitation and domination are interlinked. Nevertheless, given the rejection of economic determinism it is not possible to assert the primacy of one over the other. If the state is the ultimate guarantor of domination in the workplace, it also exercises domination outside the workplace, and not simply for the purposes of ensuring exploitation: the state controls persons and territories by virtue of the concentration of many of the means of coercion and administration in its hands in order to effect its rule. In the case of postindependence Serbia, the relations of domination preceded the creation of the relations of production enabling exploitation; in turn, the exploitation that arose helped to reinforce the domination. The "State ... and capitalism are inseparable concepts," said Kropotkin, "bound together ... by the bond of cause and effect, effect and cause."[150]

From a strict Marxist perspective, the president of a country must be regarded as a waged worker, sharing the same position as the working class more generally; from an anarchist perspective, a president is by definition part of the ruling class, and if great wealth is a means to obtain state power, state power is also a means to obtain great wealth. Here, presidents, kings, generals, members of parliament, mayors, directors of government departments, and heads of state companies are as much a part of the ruling class as are mining magnates or factory owners.

It follows that when Bakunin or Kropotkin speak of the *ruling class*, they do not simply mean the bourgeoisie, the *capitalists*, like Marx, but include also landlords and state managers. This class has common interests, although it is not necessarily a monolithic group with a single mind. While the relations of production and the relations of domination are deeply intertwined, and form different and mutually reinforcing elements of a single class system, they can also contradict one another. For example, the state might seek a war that disrupts the process of exploitation; likewise, the need to legitimise the larger class system and thereby aid in the reproduction of the relations of domination might lead to reforms that place limits on the rate of exploitation.

It is also possible to discern a somewhat wider understanding of the relations of production in the broad anarchist tradition than in the cruder forms of classical Marxism. This understanding is revealed by revisiting the issue of state capitalism. The exiled Trotsky insisted that the USSR was a proletarian dictatorship because the means of production were not "privately" held in the form of inheritable property.[151] He believed that the victory of Stalin represented the victory of a "bureaucracy" that was not yet a class, and whose rise signified the degeneration of the USSR, but was not a break with its fundamentally postcapitalist character. Just as a union bureaucracy distorts a union yet leaves the union basically proletarian in character, the Stalinist bureaucracy distorted the USSR, yet left it a (degenerated) workers' state.

Leaving aside Trotsky's view that the negative features of the USSR arose with Stalin and his conceit that he had not been part of the ruling bureaucracy, there is an important point here. This is the narrow conception of ownership of the means of production that allows Trotsky to claim that a company director who does not own shares is not really a capitalist and that "nationalized" state property is by definition not "private" property. In arguing that the USSR was state capitalist, the anarchists revealed a differing perspective on the issue: there was "a single owner served by a whole bureaucratic system and a new 'statised' morality" operating a system of state capitalism; a "new class" had replaced the individual capitalist of the past; the state was the owner of "the works, factories, [and] mines," operating an "integral state capitalism"; and it was the "last word of modern monopoly capitalism which uses the economic dictatorship of the trusts and cartels for the purpose of eliminating any undesirable competition."[152]

These contentions only make sense if the broad anarchist tradition posits a somewhat broader understanding of ownership than that of Trotsky. A ruling class can own property collectively through a state and deprive another class of ownership. This is legal ownership—inasmuch as appointment to posts, the rights and powers that accompanied particular offices, and the procedures governing decisions are legally defined—but it is not the individualised legal ownership that Trotsky had in mind. It is institutional ownership, in which a ruling class collectively holds the means of production through the state apparatus, rather than through stock certificates. At the same time, ownership involves more than simply a right to allocate existing property to one's heirs. It also entails *control* over the uses to which the means of production are put—that is, decisive power over fundamental decisions regarding major investments and day-to-day utilisation. In state capitalism, then, exploitation and domination are even more closely linked than in private capitalism, concentrating class rule to an extraordinary extent, accounting for Bakunin's and Kropotkin's use of images like "barracks" and "autocracy," respectively, to describe such regimes.[153]

Finally, it is necessary to examine the question of why *class* is regarded as central to the anarchists and syndicalists. There are innumerable forms of hierarchy and inequality in society, after all, and the victims in every case have an interest in changing the social relations that oppress them. Moreover, anarchists are committed to the removal of all forms of economic and social inequality, and regard their revolution as emancipating all humanity. Why, then, do anarchists and syndicalists advocate a class-based strategy for social change, and link women's emancipation and national liberation to a class framework, rather than favour a decentralised multiplicity of emancipatory struggles, or subordinate class issues to feminist or anti-imperialist concerns?

The answer lies in the unique character of class inequality. Only class, of all the social relations, involves both domination *and* exploitation; *only* the popular classes are exploited, and *only* exploited classes are able to create a society without exploitation, for they alone do not have a vested interest in exploitation. If exploitation is an integral feature of modern society and human freedom requires the abolition of exploitation, then class struggle alone can emancipate humanity. Viewed from this perspective, forms of oppression that are not strictly reducible to class—such as gender and race—must be addressed within a class framework, for this provides the only basis for general emancipation; conversely, it is only through opposing divisions in the working class—divisions that are based on prejudice and unfair discrimination—that the class revolution, which can alone emancipate humanity, is possible. As Bakunin put it, "You are working for humanity…. The working class [and peasantry] has today become the sole representative of the great and sacred cause of humanity. The future now belongs to the workers: those in the fields and those in the factories and cities."[154]

These points bring us back to the broad anarchist tradition's advocacy of counterpower and counterculture. While social structure is important, agency is vital, and the anarchists and syndicalists stress the centrality of self-organisation and ideas in shaping society. If one's class position generates basic sets of class interests shaped by one's position in the larger system of class rule—and provides the broad parameters of individual consciousness and choice—real living individuals interpret those interests and organise their actions in a wide range of ways, even ways that contradict their basic class interests.

If there is a degree of correspondence between social position and individual outlook, then there is also space for contradictions between the two. Bakunin, for instance, held that the difference between the irrational prejudices of the popular classes and the ruling classes was that "the masses' prejudices are based only on their ignorance, and totally oppose their very interest, while the bourgeoisie's are based precisely on its class interests and resist counteraction by bourgeois science itself."[155]

Here we have claims that ideas have their own irreducible logic, that it cannot be assumed that classes always act in a unified manner, and that popular class unity is in large part the product of the battle of ideas, rather than the inexorable outcome of capitalist development.

Thus, for Rocker, class divisions and class interests are facts. Every "larger country contains many distinctions of a climatic, cultural, economic and general social nature," "between its great cities, its highly developed industrial regions, its out-of-the-world villages and mountain valleys to which hardly a glimmer of modern life has penetrated." This corresponds in part to class, for the "differences of economic interest and intellectual effort within the nation have naturally developed special habits and modes of living among the members of the different social classes," and "every stratum of society develops its special habits of life into which a stranger penetrates with difficulty."[156]

What "national customs and morals," Rocker asks, can be shared by a "modern industrial magnate and a common labourer," by "a society lady surrounded by every luxury and a cottage housewife in the Silesian mountains," by "one of the members of Berlin's 'millionaire quarter' and a Ruhr miner"? The classes have almost no points of "intellectual contact": workers find it difficult to understand that there is a "purely human" dimension to the capitalist, while the capitalist sees the worker as a "total stranger," often with "openly displayed contempt."[157]

Yet there are also deep divisions between the worker and peasant, a "sharp antagonism of town and country," and a gulf between the "intellectual leaders of the nation and the great masses of the working people," affecting even those intellectuals involved in the popular movements.[158] There are also many divisions within each class, and a wide range of possible views; a worker in exactly the same objective circumstances might be a Christian, a Muslim, or a Jew.[159] Likewise, while the "mental attitude" of command and the "brutal spirit of mastery" shapes many capitalists, others support reform movements that are "by no means determined" by their economic interests, such as the abolition of monarchy and the power of the church.[160]

If these variations cannot be explained simply by reference to class position, ideas must be independent variables, even if it is arguable that the class system sets the broad *boundaries* of subjectivity. It follows that the ruling classes are not a monolithic entity with a single mind, or necessarily understand perfectly their own interests or act in a rational manner to secure those interests in the most effective manner. It is possible for the rich and powerful to fall out among themselves over issues of nationality, politics, or the question of future reform as well as to fight civil wars, and it is equally possible for them to make serious mistakes. There is no reason to regard the popular classes as different from the ruling ones in any of these respects.

Thus, anarchists like Bakunin and Rocker lay the basis for the rejection of functionalist reasoning, which when coupled with a crude class analysis, posits that classes always act in accord with their own best interests and infers that their actions are always somehow functional to those interests. This is a form of circular reasoning—if capitalists, for example, always act in their own best interests, it is difficult to find an action that cannot be construed as functional to their ultimate interests—and follows from a structuralist view of the class system as an automated social machine, rather than as a society of people with all their biases, complexities, and shortcomings.

In Conclusion: Toward an Anarchist Social Analysis

In *Anarchist Communism*, Kropotkin stressed the anarchist commitment to careful social analysis; the "method followed by the anarchist thinker," he argued, "entirely differs from that followed by the utopists," for it "does not resort to metaphysical conceptions" but "studies human society as it is now and as it was in the past."[161] Anarchists should develop a nuanced and careful social analysis, one that is empirically verifiable and theoretically logical, and that can provide a basis for social transformation.

How well do the anarchists and syndicalists fare? In this chapter, we have suggested that the broad anarchist tradition was profoundly influenced by both Proudhon and Marx (see figure 3.1), but did its best to eschew determinism, teleological views of history, economic reductionism, and functionalism. The key elements of an anarchist social analysis have emerged in schematic form. Anarchist analysis, in its most sophisticated form, centres on the notion that class is a principal feature of modern society and thus that class analysis must be key to understanding society. At the same time, it takes ideas, motives, and actions seriously, and avoids monistic models of society.

In rejecting economic determinism and stressing the importance of subjectivity, though, this analysis does not replace one form of determinism with another. Reacting against Marxism, for example, postmodernists adopted an idealist form of determinism, in which reality consists of discourses and texts that determine the social world but cannot be scientifically tested, for every person is trapped within a discourse and must therefore reproduce the discourse in the process of research and analysis. Postmodernists are, like Stirner, relativists for whom truth is a matter of opinion, and the most widely accepted truth is that imposed by the most powerful people. This is not the route anarchism takes.

Without necessarily going as far as Kropotkin, whose later writings optimistically claimed society could be analysed with the precision of the "exact natural sciences," anarchism maintains that the validity of theories can be tested against a reality external to the subject.[162] A fairly sophisticated social analysis that does not reduce the social world to class, or class to economics, and that avoids structuralism as well as idealism yet still takes class as central, is present in anarchist thought.

It follows from these points that anarchists and syndicalists cannot take refuge in the faith that history will automatically generate a revolution. The transition from a class-in-itself—existing objectively, with its own interests, but disorganised—to a class-for-itself—organised to pursue its own agenda and aims—requires activism and ideological work. In his discussion of anarchism, Berkman stressed that no fundamental social change can ever take place until the working masses themselves rejected the "present institutions" that oppressed them—that is, until they changed their minds.[163] This change requires recognition of Berkman's key point that "the Idea is the Thing." The *possibility* of a revolutionary class struggle arises from the character of modern society, in other words, but a revolutionary popular movement has to be *politically* constituted.

Figure 3.1
The Anarchist Tradition

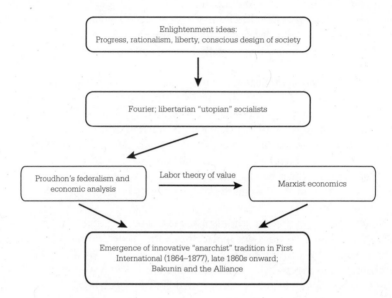

Notes

1. K. J. Kenafick, "The Life of Bakunin," in *Marxism, Freedom, and the State*, ed. K. J. Kenafick (London: Freedom Press, 1990), 15.

2. Guérin, "Marxism and Anarchism," 118–19.

3. For a contrary view, see ibid., 124–25.

4. Bakunin, "The Paris Commune and the Idea of the State," 263.

5. Ibid., 263.

6. M. Bakunin, "On the Cooperative Movement," in *Bakunin on Anarchism*, ed. S. Dolgoff (Montréal: Black Rose, 1980), 399.

7. Ibid., 399.

8. See, especially, Brogan, *Proudhon*, chapters 4 and 5.

9. Bakunin, quoted in Guillaume, "A Biographical Sketch [Bakunin]," 26.

10. Bakunin, *The Capitalist System*, n.p.

11. While there are numerous general guides to Marxist theory, including his theory of capital-ism, the following ones are highly recommended: B. Fine, *Marx's "Capital"* (London: Macmillan, 1975); A. Giddens, *Capitalism and Modern Social Theory: An Analysis of the Writings of Marx, Durkheim, and Max Weber* (Cambridge: Cambridge University Press, 1971); D. McLellan, *Karl Marx: His Life and Thought* (New York: HarperCollins, 1976); R. Miliband, *Marxism and Politics* (Oxford: Oxford University Press, 1977). The reader who wishes to tackle Marx's own texts on economics is advised to start with his *Value, Price, and Profit*, before moving to volume 1 of his masterwork, *Capital: A Critique of Political Economy*. See K. Marx, *Value, Price, and Profit: Addressed to Working Men* (1865; repr., Chicago: Charles H. Kerr, n.d.); K. Marx, *Capital: A Critique of Political Economy* (1867; repr., London: Penguin, 1976).

12. Engels, *The Communist Manifesto*, 15–38.

13. Bakunin, *The Capitalist System*, n.p., note 2.

14. See, for example, P. Kropotkin, *The Conquest of Bread* (1892; repr., London: Elephant Editions, 1990), 168.

15. Quoted in Guérin, "Marxism and Anarchism," 117, 118.

16. See, inter alia, V. Richards, "Notes for a Biography," in *Errico Malatesta: His Life and Ideas*, ed. V. Richards (London: Freedom Press, 1965).

17. In an important article, Rob Knowles has drawn attention to the way in which anarchism has been marginalised in accounts of the history of economic thought and economics; R. Knowles, "Political Economy from Below: Communitarian Anarchism as a Neglected Discourse in Histories of Economic Thought," *History of Economics Review*, no. 31 (2000): 30-47. We hope our discussion can make some contribution to rectifying this situation.

18. R. Rocker, "Marxism and Anarchism," in *The Poverty of Statism: Anarchism versus Marxism*, ed. A. Meltzer (1920; repr., Orkney, Scotland: Cienfuegos Press, 1981), 79–83. The following Marx and Engels quotes are from Rocker.

19. Ibid., 76–83. The Marx quotes are from Rocker. See also Nettlau, *A Short History of Anarchism*, 246–47.

20. Possony, introduction, xix.

21. Guérin, "Marxism and Anarchism," 119.

22. Nettlau, *A Short History of Anarchism*, 76–77; see also Nettlau, *A Short History of Anarchism*, 246–47.

23. Dirlik, *Anarchism in the Chinese Revolution*, 227.

24. Nettlau, *A Short History of Anarchism*, 246–47.

25. Ibid., xxxvi–xxxviii.

26. See Marx, *Capital*, especially chapter 49. In Marx's comments on *The Gotha Programme*, the same idea can be found: "He [the worker] receives from the community a check showing that he has done so much labour ... and with this check he draws from the common store as much of the means of consumption as costs an equal amount of labour ... there prevails the same principle that today regulates the exchange of commodities"; Marx, *The Gotha Programme*, 28–29.

27. See J. Stalin, *Economic Problems of Socialism in the USSR* (1951; repr., Beijing: Foreign Languages Press, 1972), especially chapters 3 and 7.

28. See, for instance, Kropotkin, "Anarchist Communism," 57–62; Kropotkin, *The Conquest of Bread*, 45–49, 159–73; Kropotkin, "Modern Science and Anarchism," 169–74.

29. L. Galleani, *The End of Anarchism?* (1925; repr., Orkney, Scotland: Cienfuegos Press, 1982), 19–20, 42.

30. Kropotkin, *The Conquest of Bread*, 165–66.

31. *Now and Then: The ABC of Communist Anarchism* was published as a single volume in 1929 in the United States by the Vanguard Press, but is currently generally available as two separate

books: A. Berkman, *The ABC of Anarchism*, 3rd ed. (1929; repr., London: Freedom Press, 1964); A. Berkman, *What Is Communist Anarchism?* (1929; repr., London: Pheonix Press, 1989).

32. Berkman, *The ABC of Anarchism*, 18–21, 68–70; see also Berkman, *What Is Communist Anarchism?* 5–8.

33. Avrich, *Anarchist Portraits*, chapter 14.

34. Kropotkin, *The Conquest of Bread*, 164.

35. Quoted in Eltzbacher, *Anarchism*, 114.

36. Kropotkin, *The Conquest of Bread*, 101.

37. Ibid., 108–10.

38. For instance, the recent anarchist "participatory economics" model suggests the use of prices to assess the costs and benefits of different choices, but argues that these prices must take account of efforts, externalities, and social costs; M. Albert, *Parecon: Life after Capitalism* (London: Verso, 2003).

39. A. Pengam, "Anarcho-Communism," in *Non-Market Socialism in the Nineteenth and Twentieth Centuries*, ed. M. Rubel and J. Crump (Basingstoke, UK: Macmillan, 1987), 67–70.

40. See J. Guillaume, "On Building the New Social Order," in *Bakunin on Anarchy: Selected Works by the Activist-Founder of World Anarchism*, ed. S. Dolgoff (1876; repr., London: George Allen and Unwin, 1971).

41. Fleming, *The Anarchist Way to Socialism*, 166.

42. Mises, *Socialism*; Hayek, *The Road to Serfdom*.

43. Kropotkin, *The Conquest of Bread*, 164.

44. A. W. Gouldner, *The Two Marxisms: Contradictions and Anomalies in the Development of Theory* (Houndmills, UK: Macmillan, 1980), 11:69.

45. Ibid., 33–88. These should not be misunderstood as equivalent to classical Marxism and libertarian Marxism, respectively; council communism is often infused with determinism and teleology, while Lenin's stress on the vanguard party as the critical agent of change was profoundly voluntaristic, as was the Maoist stress on the "people's army."

46. We would like to thank Bert Altena for his comments on this section.

47. Engels, *The Communist Manifesto*, 22.

48. A. M. Bonanno, *Anarchism and the National Liberation Struggle*, 2nd ed. (London: Bratach Dubh, 1976), 13.

49. On Marx's "Russophobia," see McLellan, *Karl Marx*, 202–3, 261–62, 288, 362, 377, 389, 438–39.

50. Quoted in Bonanno, *Anarchism and the National Liberation Struggle*, 1315.

51. Forman, *Nationalism and the International Labor Movement*, 58.

52. Karl Marx, letter to Friedrich Engels, July 20, 1870, quoted in Rocker, "Marxism and Anarchism," 85. Also quoted in Rocker, *Nationalism and Culture*, 234–35; F. Mehring, *Karl Marx: The Story of His Life* (1936; repr., London: George Allen and Unwin, 1951), 438.

53. Mehring, *Karl Marx*, 438–41.

54. Quoted in B. Warren, *Imperialism: Pioneer of Capitalism* (London: Verso, 1980), 40–41.

55. S. Seth, *Marxist Theory and Nationalist Politics: The Case of India* (New Delhi: Sage, 1995), chapters 1 and 2.

56. Quoted in Warren, *Imperialism*, 44.

57. Steenson, *Karl Kautsky*, 72–75, 174–79, 192–93.

58. Warren, *Imperialism*, chapter 3. Warren was, however, incorrect to suggest that Lenin believed that the historical role of capitalism as a whole was ended; while Lenin saw capitalism in the West as entering into a state of decay, his formulations continued to see the "national bourgeoisie" of the colonial and semicolonial world as a progressive force.

59. Comintern, "Theses on the National and Colonial Question Adopted by the Second Comintern Congress," in *The Communist International, 1919–1943: Documents*, ed. J. Degras (1920; repr., London: Frank Cass and Co., 1971), 141, 143–44.

60. Comintern, "Theses on the Eastern Question Adopted by the Fourth Comintern Congress," in *The Communist International, 1919–1943: Documents*, ed. J. Degras (1922; repr., London: Frank Cass and Co., 1971), 389.

61. See, for example, Lenin, "Two Tactics of Social-Democracy in the Democratic Revolution," 429–61; Mao Tse-tung, "The Chinese Revolution and the Chinese Communist Party," in *Revolutionary Thought in the Twentieth Century*, ed. B. Turok (1939; repr., Johannesburg: Institute for African Alternatives, 1990), 77–79.

62. Lenin, "Two Tactics of Social-Democracy in the Democratic Revolution," 451–52.

63. Mao, "The Chinese Revolution and the Chinese Communist Party," 77–79 (emphasis added).

64. Mao, "On the People's Democratic Dictatorship," 372, 379, 384.

65. Mao Tse-tung, "On the Correct Handling of Contradictions among the People," in *Selected Readings from the Works of Mao Tsetung*, ed. Editorial Committee for Selected Readings from the Works of Mao Tsetung (1957; repr., Peking: Foreign Languages Press, 1971), 433–34, 444–45.

66. Bakunin, "The International and Karl Marx," 309–10.

67. Ibid., 314–16.

68. Ibid., 311.

69. Kropotkin, "Modern Science and Anarchism," 150–54.

70. Rocker, *Nationalism and Culture*, 23–28; see also 520–22.

71. Rocker, "Marxism and Anarchism," 75.

72. See, for example, E. Malatesta, *Fra Contadini: A Dialogue on Anarchy* (1883; repr., London: Bratach Dubh, 1981), 40n2.

73. E. Malatesta, "Syndicalism: An Anarchist Critique [*sic*]," in *The Anarchist Reader*, ed. G. Woodcock (1907; repr., Glasgow: Fontana/Collins, 1977), 221–22; E. Malatesta, in *Errico Malatesta: His Life and Ideas*, ed. V. Richards (London: Freedom Press, 1965), 199–201.

74. Berkman, *The ABC of Anarchism*, 44.

75. Malatesta in Richards, *Errico Malatesta*, 118.

76. Rocker, *Nationalism and Culture*, 27, 32–37, 40–41.

77. Berkman, *The ABC of Anarchism*, 44.

78. Rocker, *Nationalism and Culture*, 32–35, 522.

79. Quoted in Gouldner, *The Two Marxisms*, 69.

80. Bakunin, "Letter to *La Liberté*," 284.

81. See Bakunin, "Statism and Anarchy," 346–50.

82. See, for example, R. Flores Magón, "*Sin Jefes*" ["Without Bosses"], *Regeneración*, March 21, 1914; S. Mbah and I. E. Igariwey, *African Anarchism: The History of a Movement* (Tucson, AZ: See Sharp Press, 1997).

83. Flores Magón has received increasing scholarly attention. Useful sources include Avrich, *Anarchist Portraits*, chapter 15; Hart, *Anarchism and the Mexican Working Class*; C. M. MacLachlan, *Anarchism and the Mexican Revolution: The Political Trials of Ricardo Flores Magón in the United States* (Berkeley: University of California Press, 1991); D. Poole, ed., *Land and Liberty: Anarchist Influences in the Mexican Revolution: Ricardo Flores Magón* (Orkney, Scotland: Cienfuegos Press, 1977).

84. Berkman, *The ABC of Anarchism*, 21–25, 74–80. See, for example, Rocker, *Nationalism and Culture*, 525–27, 550–51.

85. Bakunin, "Statism and Anarchy," 327.

86. Gouldner, *The Two Marxisms*, 57–58.

87. Engels, *The Communist Manifesto*, 40.

88. V. I. Lenin, "What Is to Be Done? Burning Questions of Our Movement," in *Selected Works in Three Volumes*, ed. V. I. Lenin (1902; repr., Moscow: Progress Publishers, 1975), volume 1, 121–22.

89. Lenin, "The State and Revolution," 255.

90. Trotsky, *Writings of Leon Trotsky*, 513–14.

91. Mao, "On the People's Democratic Dictatorship," 371.

92. Lenin, "The State and Revolution," 261–62.

93. V. I. Lenin, "The Immediate Tasks of the Soviet Government," in *Selected Works in Three Volumes*, ed. V. I. Lenin (1918; repr., Moscow: Progress Publishers, 1975), volume 2, 599.

94. Bakunin, "Statism and Anarchy," 330.

95. Ibid., 331–32.

96. Ibid.

97. Bakunin, "Letters to a Frenchman on the Current Crisis," 193–94.

98. Ibid., 204.

99. Bakunin, "Statism and Anarchy," 331–33.

100. Ibid., 339.

101. Berkman, *What Is Communist Anarchism?* 98; see also 105–7, 111.

102. G. P. Maximoff, *The Guillotine at Work: Twenty Years of Terror in Russia: The Leninist Counter Revolution* (1940; repr., Orkney, Scotland: Cienfuegos Press, 1979), 19–20, 257; see also 35–47, 322–26, 330, 333–34.

103. Lenin, "What Is to Be Done?," 151–52, 178, 182, 187–89, 197–202, 207.

104. Maximoff, *The Guillotine at Work*, 257.

105. Engels, *The Communist Manifesto*, 55–56.

106. Bakunin, "Letters to a Frenchman on the Current Crisis," 217.

107. Kropotkin, "Modern Science and Anarchism," 170, 186.

108. The two-stage formulation of Stalin and Mao found its echo in Trotsky's "permanent revolution" thesis: under the conditions of late development, the bourgeoisie was supposedly too weak to carry out bourgeois democratic tasks, which then fell to the revolutionary party. Trotsky envisaged a rapid move from one stage to another in some cases, where the democratic revolution develops quickly into the socialist one, becoming a "permanent revolution." There is no break with stage theory here, simply a compression of the time frame.

109. M. P. Philips, "The Russian Class Struggle: Bolshevik Syndicalism Leading," in *Dispatches from the Revolution: Russia, 1916–1918: Morgan Price Philips*, ed. T. Rose (December 5, 1917; repr., London: Pluto Press, 1997), 105.

110. A. Berkman, *The Bolshevik Myth (Diary, 1920–1922), including the "Anti-Climax"* (1925; repr., London: Pluto Press, 1989), 319.

111. See E. Goldman, *My Disillusionment in Russia* (New York: Doubleday, Page and Company, 1923); E. Goldman, "The Failure of the Russian Revolution," in *The Anarchist Reader*, ed. G. Woodcock (1924; repr., Glasgow: Fontana/Collins, 1977).

112. E. Goldman, *Trotsky Protests Too Much* (Glasgow: Anarchist Communist Federation, 1938), available at http://sunsite.berkeley.edu/Goldman/Writings/Essays/trotsky.html (accessed February 19, 2004).

113. See E. Goldman, *Living My Life*, 2 vols. (1931; repr., London: Pluto Press, 1988). See also R. Drinnon, *Rebel in Paradise: A Biography of Emma Goldman* (Chicago: University of Chicago Press, 1961); A. Wexler, *Emma Goldman: An Intimate Life* (New York: Pantheon Books, 1984).

114. Marshall, *Demanding the Impossible*, 399.

115. Maximoff, *The Guillotine at Work*, 256; see also 41–43, 321.

116. Ibid., 326. At one point Maximoff even spoke of a "soviet bourgeoisie"; ibid., 327.

117. Maximoff, *The Programme of Anarcho-syndicalism*, 11–12.

118. Ibid., 11–12.

119. Kubo Yuzuru, "On Class Struggle and the Daily Struggle," in *Anarchism: A Documentary History of Libertarian Ideas, Volume 1: From Anarchy to Anarchism, 300 CE to 1939*, ed. R. Graham (1928; repr., Montréal: Black Rose, 2005), 380.

120. P. Kropotkin, "Letter to the Workers of Western Europe," in *Kropotkin's Revolutionary Pamphlets: A Collection of Writings by Peter Kropotkin*, ed. R. N. Baldwin (April 28, 1919; repr., New York: Dover Publications, 1970), 252ff.

121. Goldman, *Trotsky Protests Too Much*.

122. M. Sergven [G. P. Maximoff], "Paths of Revolution," in *The Anarchists in the Russian Revolution*, ed. P. Avrich (September 16, 1918; repr., London: Thames and Hudson, 1973), 122–25.

123. Berkman, *What Is Communist Anarchism?* 111–12.

124. See Avrich, *The Russian Anarchists*, 137–38; Avrich, *Anarchist Portraits*, chapter 8.

125. Voline, *The Unknown Revolution, 1917–1921* (1947; repr., Montréal: Black Rose, 1990), 247–48; see also 157–58, 188–93, 209–17, 249–56, 356–58, 381–89, 418–20, 423–25, 430–32.

126. Ibid., 255–56.

127. Ibid., 358.

128. On the workers and peasants, see ibid., 359–75. On the ruling class, see ibid., 377–85, 395–98, 410–15.

129. Rocker, *Nationalism and Culture*, 546.

130. Voline, *The Unknown Revolution*, 351.

131. Gouldner, *The Two Marxisms*, 32, 41.

132. K. Marx, *A Contribution to the Critique of Political Economy* (1859; repr., London: Lawrence and Wishart, 1971), 20–21.

133. F. Engels, *Socialism: Utopian and Scientific* (1883; repr., Chicago: Charles H. Kerr, 1917), 90–91, 94–95.

134. W. D. Haywood and F. Bohm, *Industrial Socialism* (Chicago: Charles H. Kerr, 1911), 56. For other examples, see, inter alia, A. E. Woodruff, *The Advancing Proletariat: A Study of the Movement of the Working Class from Wage Slavery to Freedom* (Chicago: IWW Publishing Bureau, 1919); Industrial Workers of the World, *The IWW: What It Is and What It Is Not* (Chicago: IWW Publishing Bureau, 1928). For a De Leonist example, see Socialist Labour Party [Daniel De Leon], *The Socialist Labour Party: Its Aims and Methods* (Edinburgh: Socialist Labour Press, 1908.

135. See M. Dubofsky, *"Big Bill" Haywood* (Manchester: Manchester University Press, 1987).

136. Ibid., 60.

137. S. Craparo, *Anarchist Communists: A Question of Class*, Studies for a Libertarian Alternative Series (Fano, Italy: Federazione dei Comunisti Anarchici, 2005), 90–96.

138. Bakunin, "God and the State"; Bakunin, "Letter to *La Liberté*," 281–82.

139. Ibid., 282–83.

140. Bakunin, "The International and Karl Marx," 310–11.

141. Bakunin, "Letter to *La Liberté*," 281–82.

142. Rocker, *Nationalism and Culture*, 23–31.

143. Ibid., 28, 28–29.

144. Ibid., 29–31.

145. Ibid., 35–40.

146. Ibid., 40–41.

147. Marx and Engels, *The Communist Manifesto*, 13n1.

148. Bakunin, "Statism and Anarchy," 343.

149. Bakunin, *The Capitalist System*, n.p.

150. Kropotkin, "Modern Science and Anarchism," 181.

151. L. Trotsky, *The Revolution Betrayed* (London: New Park, 1967), 254.

152. Sergven [Maximoff], "Paths of Revolution," 122–25; Berkman, *What Is Communist Anarchism?* 111–12; Voline, *The Unknown Revolution*, 358; Rocker, *Nationalism and Culture*, 546.

153. Bakunin, "Letter to *La Liberté*," 284; Kropotkin, "Anarchist Communism," 50.

154. Bakunin, "Three Lectures to Swiss Members of the International," 62.

155. Bakunin, "The Policy of the International," 100–1.

156. Rocker, *Nationalism and Culture*, 270–72; see also 260.

157. Ibid., 270–72; see also 260.

158. Ibid.

159. Ibid., 25.

160. Ibid., 32, 40–41.

161. Kropotkin, "Anarchist Communism," 47.

162. Kropotkin, "Modern Science and Anarchism," 150.

163. Berkman, *The ABC of Anarchism*, 35–39.

2
STRATEGY AND TACTICS

A mass rally by African workers in Johannesburg, South Africa, in June 1918.

Addressed by speakers from two local syndicalist groups, the Industrial Workers of Africa and the International Socialist League, in conjunction with the Transvaal Native Congress, the rally helped lead to the abortive general strike of 1 July 1918. Shortly afterward, South Africa underwent a spurt of syndicalist organising that saw the creation of the Indian Workers Industrial Union and the Industrial Workers of Africa—the impact of which would be felt as far away as Northern Rhodesia (Zambia).

Luigi Galleani (1861–1931) in Italy following his deportation from the United States.

Leading theorist of insurrectionist anarchism, Galleani believed all reforms including trade union and community organising were futile, and that "propaganda by the deed"—violent actions including assassination—was necessary to awaken the popular classes to the social revolution. This purist, catalytic position was rejected by the mass anarchists.

CHAPTER 4

Roads to Revolution: Mass Anarchism versus Insurrectionist Anarchism

The broad anarchist position and its relationship to other socialist traditions have been outlined in previous chapters. It will also be recalled, of course, that we have dispensed with the commonly used categorisations of different types of anarchism, such as the notions of "philosophical anarchism," "individualist anarchism," and "spiritual anarchism," stressing that anarchism is a coherent intellectual and political current dating back to the 1860s and the First International, and part of the labour and left tradition.

It is at the level of *strategy*, we would suggest, that distinctions between the types of anarchism should be drawn. In chapter 2, we identified the principles that frame anarchist strategy, but noted that this foundation still allows a range of strategic choices. Within these principles, there are different possibilities for strategy, and it is possible to identify two main anarchist ones.

The first strategy, insurrectionist anarchism, argues that reforms are illusory and organised mass movements are incompatible with anarchism, and emphasises armed action—propaganda by the deed—against the ruling class and its institutions as the primary means of evoking a spontaneous revolutionary upsurge. It is this strand of anarchism that has been imprinted on the public mind, not least as a result of the spectacular wave of assassinations carried out by insurrectionist anarchists in the late nineteenth and early twentieth centuries. "Placid and carefree sleeps the bourgeoisie, but the day of shuddering and fear, of ferocious tempests, of bloody revenge is approaching," declared an insurrectionist manifesto. "The savage, blinding light of explosions begins to light up its dreams, property trembles and cracks under the deafening blows of dynamite, the palaces of stone crack open, providing a breach through which will pour the wave of the poor and the starving"; here "is the hour of revenge, the bombs have sounded the charge—by Dynamite to Anarchy!"[1] The insurrectionist anarchists were generally people of action; their analysis left little space for possibilist action, but opened the door to dramatic and usually violent actions designed to rouse the masses from their slumber, including bank robberies to raise funds ("expropriation") as well as retributive assassinations and bombings.

The second strategy—what we refer to, for lack of a better term, as mass anarchism—is rather different. This stresses the view that only mass movements can create a revolutionary change in society, that such movements are typically built through struggles around immediate issues and reforms (whether around wages, police brutality, or high prices, and so on), and that anarchists must participate in such movements to radicalise and transform them into levers of revolutionary change.

Insurrectionist anarchism disparages such struggles as futile and as perpetuating the current social order. Mass anarchism, however, underscores the importance of daily struggles, even around limited goals, as a means of strengthening popular movements, raising popular consciousness, and improving popular conditions; it is only thus that a genuine social revolution by the popular classes can be made possible. What is crucial is that reforms are won *from below*, rather than doled out from above, which can only lead to mass passivity as well as measures that undermine popular autonomy and struggle. As Malatesta put it, "It is not all that important that the workers should want more or less; what is important is that they should try to get what they want, by their own efforts, by their *direct action* against the capitalists and the government." A "small improvement achieved by one's own effort" is worth more than a "large-scale reform" granted from above.[2]

It can be fairly said that while insurrectionist anarchism is impossibilist, in that it views reforms, however won, as futile, mass anarchism is *possibilist*, believing that it is both possible and desirable to force concessions from the ruling classes. Most mass anarchists embraced syndicalism, with its view that union struggles could play a central role in destroying capitalism, landlordism, and the state. Contrary to the notion that the "record of the anarchosyndicalist movement has been one of the most abysmal in the history of anarchism generally," it was above all through syndicalism that anarchism had its greatest influence.[3]

Other mass anarchists were antisyndicalists of two types: those who rejected workplace activity, emphasising community activity instead, and those who favoured workplace activity independent of the unions, which included a substantial body whose approach converged with the rank-and-file version of syndicalism, including work within orthodox unions. Unlike insurrectionist anarchists, these antisyndicalists emphasised the importance of mass struggles, whether carried out in communities or at work, and were possibilists.

Anarchist Communism versus Anarcho-syndicalism?

We will explore the relationship between anarchism and syndicalism in more depth in subsequent chapters. First, though, we need to consider an alternative way of categorising the types of anarchism on the basis of the strategy that commonly appears in the literature. This is the idea that it is possible to organise the history of the broad anarchist tradition around a contrast between "anarchist communism … perhaps the most influential anarchist doctrine," and "another doctrine of comparable significance, anarcho-syndicalism."[4] We do not find this useful or accurate. The vast majority of people described in the literature as "anarchist communists" or "anarcho-communists" championed syndicalism, and the majority of syndicalists endorsed anarchist communism: a stateless socialist society based on distribution according to need. There were national and local contexts in which the "anarcho-communist" label was used to distinguish particular positions among the anarchists and syndicalists, but there was no general distinction between "anarchist communists" and anarcho-syndicalists.

One of the basic problems with this purported distinction is that it is applied in an inconsistent and often incompatible manner. Paul Avrich, when exploring Russian anarchism, talked of an "Anarchist-Communism" that, inspired by Bakunin and Kropotkin, wanted a "free federation of communities," looked back to a preindustrial Russia, had "little use for large-scale industry or bureaucratic labour organisations," and embraced "expropriation" and armed actions. The Russian anarcho-syndicalists, however, embraced modern industry, "technological progress," and the "cult of the machine," and stressed workplace struggle, "a decentralised society of labour organisations," and self-management.[5]

Bookchin distinguished between the Spanish anarcho-syndicalists, who controlled the labour movement, and the "anarchist communists." The latter supposedly viewed syndicalists of all types "with disdain," and as "deserters to reformism."[6] The "anarcho-communists" were radicals who wanted to form "an authentically revolutionary movement, however small its size and influence," while the anarcho-syndicalists were pragmatic unionists.[7] Many key "anarchist theorists," he claimed, distrusted syndicalism as a "change in focus from the commune to the trade union, from all the oppressed to the industrial proletariat, from the streets to the factories, and, in emphasis at least, from insurrection to the general strike," according to Bookchin.[8] Almost all the major "anarchist communists," including Goldman, Kropotkin, Malatesta, and Reclus, "initially opposed" syndicalism. If Avrich spoke of a distinction centred on technology, Bookchin posed it as a difference over the "authentic locus" of struggle.[9]

A third variant of the supposed distinction is provided by writers who define "anarcho-communism" primarily as a model of postcapitalist society, aimed at "ending exchange value" and "making this the immediate content of the revolutionary process."[10] Here, "anarcho-communism" is distinguished from the "anarchist collectivism" of Bakunin, and is presented as opposed to the "official workers' movement" and struggles that "put forward wage or other claims, or which were organised by trade unions," thereby reproducing the wage system.[11]

By this account, "anarcho-communism" subsequently splintered into those who favoured unions, like Kropotkin, and those who did not, and it withered away by the 1930s, despite attempts at "practical" activity by Flores Magón, the Russians, and Hatta Shūzō (1886–1934) in Japan.[12] Born to an impoverished merchant family in the port town of Tsu, Hatta left school early and eventually trained as a Presbyterian minister.[13] He became sympathetic to anarchism and held a memorial meeting for the murdered anarchist Ōsugi. Ōsugi was the key figure in Japanese anarchism after the death of Kōtoku; the son of an army officer and an accomplished linguist, he was an ardent syndicalist who played an important part in anarchist union work in Japan in the 1910s.[14] Hatta's increasing politicisation and scandalous personal life saw him leave the clergy, and from there he went to live in Tokyo and dedicated himself to anarchism. An excellent orator, he also translated key anarchist works and wrote widely on anarchist theory, dying in 1934 of alcoholism and poverty.

Hatta elaborated his anarchist communism into a doctrine of "pure anarchism" that opposed syndicalism as reformist, hierarchical, and narrow, and wanted an anarchist society based on self-sufficient villages. Here, "anarcho-communism" is defined as a revolutionary objective.

The more contemporary anarchist movement provides a final variant of the distinction, in that contemporary advocates of organisational dualism use the term "anarchist communist" to distinguish their views. The Workers Solidarity Movement (WSM) of Ireland argues that syndicalism ignores the need for a specific political group to champion anarchism: "They see the biggest problem in the structure of the existing unions rather than in the ideas that tie workers to authoritarian, capitalist views of the world."[15] "We will not liquidate our specific politics and organisation into the a-politicism of syndicalism," but will organise on Platformist lines.[16] The WSM calls for a style of unionism that is "essentially the same" as that of syndicalism, but does not regard itself as syndicalist. The FdCA of Italy contends that the "feature which best distinguishes Anarchist Communism from all other schools of thought within anarchism is ... 'organisational dualism.'"[17] Here, "anarchist communism" is identified with Bakunin and the Alliance as well as organisational dualism, and Kropotkin is sometimes excluded.[18]

The problems with drawing a sharp distinction between "anarcho-communism" and anarcho-syndicalism should be clear from the above discussion. At the very least, these writers are talking about quite different tendencies when they refer to "anarcho-communism," and this alone suggests that the notion of a universal distinction between "anarcho-communists" and anarcho-syndicalists is not convincing. Kropotkin, for instance, produced a paper called *Kleb i Volya* (Bread and Liberty) for Russian distribution in order to combat the "Anarchist Communist" tendency by promoting syndicalism.[19] He believed that revolutionary unions were "absolutely necessary."[20] Other major anarchist theorists, identified as "anarchist communists," also embraced syndicalism. Malatesta described the unions as "the best of all means" and "the greatest force for social transformation," and saw the general strike as the "starting" point of the revolution.[21] He pioneered anarchist unionism in Argentina.[22] Berkman was an unqualified supporter of syndicalism, claiming that the revolution "lies in the hands" of "the industrial worker ... the farm labourer," and the "intellectual proletariat" through a "real labour union" and the "General Strike."[23] Goldman held that "syndicalism is, in essence, the economic expression of Anarchism."[24] The choice was "between an Industrial State and anarcho-syndicalism," she noted.[25] Flores Magón was greatly admired by the Mexican syndicalist union, the CGT, formed in 1921, and the PLM was active in the labour movement.[26]

Shifu of China, "an anarchist-communist, a self-acknowledged disciple of Kropotkin," and founder of the Society of Anarchist-Communist Comrades, was the pioneer of Chinese syndicalism.[27] Born in 1884 to the educated class and radicalised in Japan, Shifu joined Sun Yat-Sen's republican movement, was jailed, and became an anarchist soon after the May 1911 republican uprising. He formed groups in

Canton (now Guangzhou) and published *Hui-Ming-lu* ("The Voice of the People"). Shifu died of tuberculosis in 1915.[28]

Most anarcho-syndicalists explicitly defined their goal as an anarchist and communist society, raising further questions about the usefulness of the distinction. The Russian anarcho-syndicalists declared their aim "the full realisation of the Anarchist-Communist ideal" of distribution according to needs.[29] The Mexican CGT adopted the goal of anarchist communism.[30] The syndicalist Argentine Regional Workers' Federation (FORA), formed in 1901 and captured by anarchists in 1904, declared that it advocated the "economic and philosophical principles of anarchist-communism."[31] FORA played a central role in the formation in 1929 of the American Continental Workingmen's Association (ACAT) within the IWA, which declared, "It recommends communism."[32] The IWA also advocated a "free communist future."[33]

The Bulgarian Anarchist Communist Federation (FAKB), which was formed in 1919, worked closely with the country's Anarcho-Syndicalist National Confederation of Labour. The British syndicalist Tom Brown, a former CPGB member active from the 1930s, argued that "as to distribution, the Syndicalist method of distribution is free; a system of common ownership and Workers' Control must have a system of free and common distribution to supplement it."[34] Even Bookchin admits that the Spanish CNT "unequivocally declared its belief in *comunismo anarquico*."[35] Hatta and his so-called "pure anarchists" found their main support within the National Libertarian Federation of Labour Unions (usually abbreviated as Zenkoku Jiren); formed as a syndicalist union federation in 1926, the Zenkoku Jiren split in 1928 when anarcho-syndicalists walked out to form the Nihon Jikyo. The Zenkoku Jiren was not a syndicalist federation but its daily activities included union work and strikes, and it had an ability to "enthuse significant numbers of rank and file unionists."[36] Hatta's own view that the unions should "advance with the method and in the spirit of anarchism" served as a caution against setting up too sharp a distinction between "pure anarchism" and syndicalism.[37]

Nor were the key texts of Platformism hostile to syndicalism. The *Platform* itself, for example, stated that the "tendency to oppose" communist anarchism to syndicalism is "artificial, and devoid of all foundation and meaning."[38] The task of anarchists was to promote anarchism in an organised and systematic manner in the syndicalist unions as well as elsewhere, and to do so through an anarchist political group. In 1938, the Friends of Durruti (AD), a radical group in the Spanish anarchist movement, produced *Towards a Fresh Revolution*, regarded as the second core text of Platformism. The AD called for a "Revolutionary Junta" or "National Defence Council" to coordinate the revolution, which would be "elected by democratic vote in the union organisations," leaving the "economic affairs ... the exclusive preserve of the unions," and "the trade union assemblies will exercise control over the Junta's activities."[39] The Platformist advocacy of the need for a specific anarchist political group differentiates Platformism from some syndicalist positions, but there is no reason to set up an artificial divide between platformism and syndicalism—this is a matter to which we will return in chapter 8.

The Insurrectionist Tradition

It follows from our discussion that a new typology, which can be generally applied and can provide a guide in understanding the differences within the broad anarchist tradition, needs to be developed. We suggest that a more useful distinction can be drawn between insurrectionist anarchism and mass anarchism. The insurrectionist approach to anarchism has played a persistent, prominent, but decidedly minority part within the overall anarchist movement for most of its history. It bears examining before turning to the mass anarchist tradition for several reasons: first, because the insurrectionist tradition is a fair approximation of what many people have in mind when they think of anarchism; second, because it is a fairly monolithic approach and can therefore be dealt with relatively easily; and third, because the insurrectionist anarchist tradition offers a useful set of contrasts with the mass anarchist approach.

Galleani was one of the most articulate spokespeople for the insurrectionist tradition. Born in Italy, he initially studied law in Turin, but rejected it when he adopted anarchism.[40] He subsequently fled Italy, and was expelled from France and then Switzerland; returning to Italy he was soon jailed on charges of conspiracy on the island of Pantelleria, off the coast of Sicily, in 1898. Galleani escaped in 1900, spending nearly a year in Egypt until, threatened with extradition, he fled to the United States.

There Galleani settled in Paterson, New Jersey. Unable to speak English properly, his activities were focused on the Italian immigrant community, where insurrectionist views already had some influence. He assumed editorship of *La Questione Sociale* ("The Social Question"), perhaps the leading Italian anarchist periodical in the United States, fled to Canada after being charged with instigating riots in 1902, returned to Barre, Vermont, to found *Cronaca Sovversiva* ("Subversive Chronicles") in 1903, and relocated to Lynn, Massachusetts in 1912. In 1919, Galleani and a number of his supporters were deported as part of the general crackdown by the U.S. government on the Left from 1919 to 1920; he was forced to leave his wife and children behind. In Italy, he suffered continual harassment under the Mussolini regime, including repeated jailing and around-the-clock police surveillance, dying in 1931 in a small village.

Cronaca Sovversiva, which lasted until 1918 in the United States, and was revived briefly in Italy in 1920, was distributed among Italian speakers worldwide, including Australia, Latin America, and North Africa. It advocated violent retribution against the forces of capitalism and the state, and praised and venerated the anarchists who took the road of armed action—perspectives fervently adopted by Galleanist groups. One adherent, Gaetano Bresci, a silk weaver from Paterson, sailed to Italy, where he then assassinated King Umberto I in 1900; Galleanists were involved in attempts on the lives of industrialist John D. Rockefeller and other capitalists as well as Attorney General A. Mitchell Palmer and others, attacks on police stations, a wave of bombings in 1919, and in 1920, the Galleanist Mario Buda bombed Wall Street, leaving thirty dead and over two hundred seriously injured.

The famous anarchist militants Nicola Sacco (1891–1927), a shoemaker, and Bartolomeo Vanzetti (1888–1927), a fishmonger, were both ardent Galleanists. Arrested in 1919 for involvement in two violent robberies and tried on flimsy evidence by a hostile court, the two men became the centre of an international campaign involving millions, but were executed in 1927. It is understandable that much of the defence campaign tried to present the two as peaceful victims, yet it should be noted that "they belonged to a branch of the anarchist movement which preached insurrectionary violence and armed retaliation, including the use of dynamite and assassination."[41] This is not to cast aspersions on their characters but to acknowledge their militancy and fervent commitment to the cause in which they believed, to see them as they saw themselves, as class warriors.

Fundamentally, the insurrectionist anarchist tradition tended to dismiss any pursuit of immediate and partial gains by the working class and peasantry as futile. According to Galleani, the "anarchists believe that no effective conquest in the economic field is possible so long as the means of production remain the personal property of the capitalists."[42] Galleani made recourse to a version of the "iron law of wages" argument common among many pre-Marxist socialists: any wage gains and reductions in working hours will necessarily result in an increase in the cost of living as the capitalists strive to recoup their losses. Therefore, "every conquest of such improvements is deceitful and inconsistent." Reforms can only benefit workers for a "short time," before the "high cost of living ... has re-established equilibrium to the exclusive advantage of the ... capitalist."[43]

The anarchists, in Galleani's view, thus had no interest in promoting reforms and struggles for immediate gains; their aim was to promote the spirit of individual and collective revolt. They favoured the widespread adoption of "tactics of corrosion and continuous attack" through direct action by the working class. While these tactics might result in some reforms, this was merely incidental: the real aim was to foster an ever-increasing proletarian revolt against existing institutions, resulting in the forcible expropriation of the ruling class in the "violent social revolution." Galleani insisted that reforms are cunning attempts by the ruling class to sanitise its rule, for the "purpose of saving its bankrupt privileges." These attempts arise inevitably from the "violent pressure of the masses," but tend to create a "dangerous mirage" of illusions about the kindliness of the ruling class that must be discredited.[44]

Given such perspectives, Galleani predictably viewed union work with suspicion. The "anarchist movement and the labour movement follow two parallel lines," he argued, and "it has been geometrically proven that parallels never meet."[45] In general, unions were a positive danger to anarchist action; this rejection applied equally and explicitly to anarcho-syndicalist and revolutionary syndicalist unions. Unions existed primarily to win demands for "immediate and partial improvements," and in doing so, inevitably consented to "the existing economic system in all its manifestations and relations."[46]

It also meant accommodating the reformist "crowd" that comprised the majority of the working class. No anarchist, asserted Galleani, could assume a position of responsibility in a union organisation. Anarchists must participate in unions only from a position of permanent opposition to their operations, programmes, and actions, "continually demonstrating" the "futility" of union work and its disappointing results: "correct and integral emancipation" required revolution. Revolution might, Galleani conceded, involve a general strike as part—but only part—of the broader popular insurrection.[47] Yet it seems clear enough that this would take place *despite* the unions, not through them, and it would not follow from the patient construction of a syndicalist labour movement.

Over time, the insurrectionist distrust of unions that may be found in Galleani has evolved into a perspective of active hostility, according to which unions are regarded as bureaucratic bodies that always and everywhere sabotage working-class struggles, and that always and everywhere actively connive with capitalism and the state to prevent working-class struggles. Contemporary Italian insurrectionist anarchist Alfredo Bonanno represents the latter view in his 1975 *Critique of Syndicalist Methods*. He contended that all union struggles were futile, for even "in the best of cases everything concluded in a deal perked up with a few mere trifles and concessions that soon disappeared through increases in consumer prices," that even the best union always disempowers the workers who make up its members, and that over time the unions have adopted the role of "guarantor and collaborator" with capitalism. This meant that the struggle had to be outside the unions, as "direct action by grassroots nuclei at the level of production is impossible within the dimension of trades union or syndical[ist] organisations," according to Bonanno.[48]

Once arguments are made that struggles for immediate gains are futile, participation in unions is possible only on the condition that it is resolutely opposed to actual union work, and that formal organisations as such are a brake on freedom, initiative, and revolt, there are few fields left for anarchist activity. One is the production of abstract propaganda for anarchism. But for many others, another path presented itself: the act of rebellion, often violent, by anarchist individuals and groups, known as "propaganda by the deed," as opposed to the "propaganda by the word" of writings and speeches. Initially, the phrase "propaganda by the deed" referred to any attempt to demonstrate, in practice, the possibility and desirability of revolution. Since the mid-1880s, however, propaganda by the deed had come to be identified almost exclusively with acts of individual terrorism and assassination, or *attentats*, carried out by anarchists.

Some basic ideas underlay propaganda by the deed: the need to wreak vengeance on particularly reprehensible members of the ruling class, the belief that these actions undermined authority and expressed the individual, and the hope that such acts would inspire the working class and peasantry with the spirit of revolt to undertake similar acts of insurrection and disobedience, coalescing into a general insurrection and revolution. Propaganda by the deed could also encompass expropriations of funds and resources from the ruling class in order to subsidize the revolutionary cause; it could not, though, involve struggles for reforms or actions that could be seen as in any way compromising with the present social order.

In Galleani's vision, propaganda by the deed plays an absolutely central role. It arises from the intolerable conditions of modern society: the "awful responsibility for the rebellious act" must be "thrown back in the face of the exploiters who squeeze out the last drop of sweat and blood from the common people, back into the face of the cops holding the bag open for the crooks," and "the judiciary winking indulgently and conniving impunity for oppressors, exploiters, corrupters."[49] It is not, in short, the individual rebellion that is immoral but the society that produced it. Such revolts are inevitable—"Of what value is repudiation?"—and justified—"the bourgeoisie and its misfortunes do not move us one bit." The "individual act of rebellion" cannot be separated from the revolutionary process of which it is the initial phase: the "Ideal ... is embodied in the martyrdom of its first heralds and sustained by the blood of its believers." The individual revolt and sacrifice is the necessary and inevitable intermediary between the original ideal and the insurrectionary movement that culminates in revolution. The "sacrifice" is "raised as a sacred standard," inspiring further revolts until eventually there "are no jails big enough to sustain the expanding insurrection" and the torrent of revolution, "the final desperate conquest," overwhelms all.[50]

Insurrectionist anarchism and propaganda by the deed had not really existed in the period of the First International, and did not form part of Bakunin's thought. It was after the dissolution of the anarchist First International in 1877 that these ideas came to the fore, enjoying a brief period of dominance in the 1880s. The shift toward violent acts of insurrection was not, it must be stressed, confined to the anarchists of the time. A section of the Russian narodnik movement in the 1870s adopted assassination and robbery for the cause as central planks of its strategy, leading to the assassination of Czar Alexander II in 1881 by Ignatei Grinevitski.[51] This approach was popularised and dramatised in Western Europe in books such as Stepniak's 1883 *Underground Russia*. Stepniak was the pseudonym of the Russian anarchist Sergei Kravchinski (1852–1895), who was involved in the assassination of General Nikolai Mezentsev, the czar's police chief. Terrorism of this sort would remain a defining feature of the narodniks' successors, the SRs, although most SRs were not anarchists.

Within the Marxist SDP of Germany, an extremist faction coalesced around the former SDP parliamentary deputy Johann Most (1846–1906), attracting even the young Kautsky, later a bastion of Marxist orthodoxy. Born in Bavaria, Most apprenticed as a bookbinder, associated with the First International in the late 1860s, and as a tireless and powerful agitator, helped organise the SDP. He was jailed repeatedly, elected to the German Reichstag twice, and driven out of Germany in 1878. Even before adopting anarchism, Most advocated armed action; it was only in 1880 that he moved toward insurrectionist anarchism in his London-based *Freiheit* ("Freedom"); he was then expelled from the SDP. An article titled "At Last!"—celebrating Alexander II's assassination and advocating similar actions—led to eighteen months of hard labour, following which Most moved to the United States, relocating *Freiheit* to New York.[52]

There, he played a central role in founding the U.S. anarchist group the International Working People's Association in 1883 (IWPA, not to be confused with the First International or the syndicalist international formed in 1922), and continued to advocate insurrectionist positions well into the 1880s. Insurrectionist anarchism had an ongoing influence on the IWPA. Most, for example, issued a manual on *The Science of Revolutionary Warfare*, which contained details of preparing and using explosives, and the IWPA issued his bloodthirsty pamphlet *The Beast of Property*, which called for "massacres of the people's enemies."[53] The IWPA, however, was increasingly, and predominantly, influenced by syndicalism and the notion that the union was the vehicle of class struggle, a weapon for revolution, and "the embryonic group of the future 'free society,'" "the autonomous commune in the process of incubation."[54] The IWPA took over the Federative Union of Metal Workers of America, and in 1884 its Chicago section formed the Central Labour Union (CLU), the largest union centre in the city. Many IWPA publications also showed a definite fascination with insurrectionism, even though, as we shall see, the general thrust of the organisation was toward mass anarchism and particularly syndicalism.

Within Italy, shifts to insurrectionism were also afoot. In 1877, the young Malatesta and an armed group of about twenty-five other anarchists attempted to spark a rural uprising, meeting with little success; Stepniak had been involved in the preparations for the planned uprising. A second key moment in the anarchist shift to propaganda by the deed was the founding of the Anti-Authoritarian International—better known as the Black International—in London on July 14, 1881, at an International Social-Revolutionary Congress organised by prominent figures such as Kropotkin, Most, and Malatesta. Unlike the First International, which was characterised by political diversity and a focus on the immediate struggles of the working class, the Black International was to be "anarchist, communist, anti-religious, anti-parliamentary, and revolutionary, all at the same time."[55] It proved particularly attractive to insurrectionist anarchists, and its manifesto declared, "A deed performed against the existing institutions appeals to the masses much more than thousands of leaflets and torrents of words."[56]

While its largest affiliates—the IWPA in the United States, and the Mexican Workers' General Congress (CGOM) formed in 1876—were heavily influenced by syndicalism, the Black International is best known for its role in popularising propaganda by the deed. Many anarchists switched over to the new approach, if only for a time. Kropotkin proclaimed in 1880, "Permanent revolt in speech, writing, by the dagger and the gun, or by dynamite," and added, "Anything suits us that is alien to legality."[57] The young Berkman, influenced by Most and aided by Goldman, was jailed in 1892 in the United States for fifteen years after he attempted to assassinate strikebreaking industrialist Henry Clay Frick, who was responsible for the deaths of several strikers at the Homestead steel mills. Malatesta helped pioneer the basic ideas of the propaganda by the deed approach, although he disapproved of its evolution into mere assassination.

The period of insurrectionist hegemony in the anarchist movement was over by the 1890s, but not before anarchism had become widely associated with terrorism; a wave of attempted and successful assassinations of heads of state and bombings also continued into the twentieth century. The ideas of this tradition would be preserved by the Galleanists, elements linked to the Tierra y Libertad ("Land and Liberty") faction in Spain, the La Battaglia ("The Battle") group in Brazil, the "anti-organisationalists" in Argentina associated with *La Antorcha* ("The Torch"), and the Culmine group, and lingered in East Asia as well. The goals and methods of Shifu's Society of Anarchist-Communist Comrades, formed in China in 1914, included mass actions like strikes but left the door open to "disturbances, including assassination, violence and the like" in its tactical repertoire.[58]

Mass Anarchism, Possibilism, and Syndicalism

By the late 1880s, there was a widespread reaction against propaganda by the deed in anarchist circles, and many of those who had advocated it in the past, including Berkman, Goldman, Kropotkin, Malatesta, and Most, began to point to its disadvantages. For most anarchists, propaganda by the deed had proved ineffective and an outright danger to anarchism. It brought down immense repression, thereby crippling attempts at forming an anarchist mass movement. Insurrectionism did not demonstrably weaken capitalism and the state either. As Malatesta commented, "We know that *these attentats*, with the people insufficiently prepared for them, *are sterile*, and often, by provoking reactions which one is unable to control, produce much sorrow, *and harm the very cause they were intended to serve.*" What was essential and useful was "*not just to kill a king*, the man, *but to kill all kings*—those of the Courts, of parliaments and of the factories *in the hearts and minds of the people*; that is, to *uproot faith* in the *principle of authority* to which most people owe allegiance."[59] Kropotkin had been sympathetic to the syndicalism of the First International, but fairly hostile to the unions in the period of the Black International.[60] By the 1890s, however, he was calling for a return to the syndicalism of Bakunin and the First International, although "ten times stronger": "Monster unions embracing millions of proletarians."[61] By the late 1880s, Michel (of whom, more later) saw in the revolutionary general strike the road to revolution, even if she retained some sympathy for propaganda by the deed.[62]

The very nature of the insurrectional act was increasingly seen as elitist; rather than inspiring the working class and peasantry to action, at best it reinforced the passive reliance of the masses on leaders and saviors from above, substituting a self-elected vanguard for the popular classes. This was mirrored by the dismissal of immediate concerns, such as higher wages. Anarchism became the creed of a select elite, untroubled by the daily concerns of the popular classes, dismissive of unions, and in practice, destructive of popular movements. Propaganda by the deed did little to spread the anarchist idea, unless it was to link anarchism in the public mind with violence and bombings, and divorce anarchism from the masses. By the 1890s, insurrectionist anarchism was very much a minority current.

These criticisms drew on the traditions of the First International anarchists, who had embraced what we term mass anarchism. For Bakunin and the Alliance, the key strategy was to implant anarchism *within* popular social movements in order to radicalise them, spread anarchist ideas and aims, and foster a culture of self-management and direct action, with the hope that such movements would help with the social revolution. In their time, of course, it was the First International itself that they wished to influence. Integral to this outlook was the possibilist view that real reforms *could* be won from below, and that these reforms, rather than cripple popular social movements, could, if won *from below*, aid them, increasing the confidence of the masses and improving the conditions of their lives.

Syndicalism: Prefiguring the Future in the Present

The syndicalist idea was an excellent expression of this general outlook, and quite different from the impossibilist approach, which distrusted immediate gains, large-scale organisation, and political programmes, with a general hostility toward unions and dreams of sparking revolt from outside the workers' movements. It was, indeed, within the First International that syndicalist ideas first emerged—as reflected in Bakunin's writings.[63] Most anarchists of this era, including Bakunin, embraced syndicalism—an issue to which we will return in chapter 5.

The syndicalist position that existed within mass anarchism centred on two positions: the view that reforms and immediate gains were positive conquests for the popular classes, and played a central role in improving the lives of ordinary people, building mass organisations, and developing the confidence of the popular classes in their abilities; and the notion that the unions could take the lead in the struggle for revolution and form the nucleus of the new society. In criticising insurrectionist anarchism, then, anarchists like Kropotkin returned to the view that it was necessary to form "revolutionary" unions, a *revolutionary workers' movement* … the milieu which, alone, will take arms and make the revolution."[64]

It is thus not surprising that the majority of the mass anarchists placed great stress on the view that unions could potentially be central components of the revolutionary overthrow of capitalism. It must be noted that not all mass anarchists accepted syndicalism, although the vast majority certainly did. Some, like Bakunin, were unreserved syndicalists. Others, like Kropotkin, saw syndicalism as essential but had some doubts about the "embryo hypothesis," that the syndicalist unions were the kernel of the new society. There were also the antisyndicalist mass anarchists: some accepted workplace struggles but rejected unions as such; some, like Hatta, worked with unions but did not see them as potentially revolutionary; and some rejected the workplace as a site of struggle as such.[65] By contrast, the insurrectionist approach stressed that reforms were illusory, movements like unions were the bulwarks of the existing order, and formal organisations were authoritarian. Insurrectionist anarchism consequently stressed armed action—propaganda by the deed—as *the* means of evoking a spontaneous revolutionary upsurge, in conjunction with ordinary propaganda of the word, which emphasised the need for revolution.

For those anarchists who actively embraced syndicalism, wide vistas were opened. The young French activist Pelloutier provided an excellent statement of the case for mass anarchism of the syndicalist type in an 1895 polemic, "Anarchism and the Workers' Union." Born in 1867 to a professional family, Pelloutier embarked at an early age on a career in journalism and became involved in the French union movement in the early 1890s, initially as a Marxist, but from 1893 onward as an anarchist. In 1895, he was appointed secretary of the federation of the Bourses du Travail, which were local labour centres that initially served as hiring halls and labour exchanges, but developed into places for union organising. Pelloutier sought to use them as centres for anarchist education and worker mobilisation, and transform them into the cells of a revolutionary unionism. He died in 1901 of tuberculosis, by which time his "dedication, his mixture of practical gifts with moral enthusiasm," and "his devotion to the ideal of education and self-improvement among the workers" had "made him a legendary figure."[66]

Pelloutier's polemic argued that anarchists must enter the unions to promote both workers' struggles and spread anarchist ideas, and thereby detach the working class from the parties of political socialism. He took a swipe at propaganda by the deed, noting that many workers had become "loath to confess their libertarian socialism" because "as they see it, anarchy boils down to the individual recourse to dynamite." Even those who "venerate Ravachol," a famed French anarchist bomber, did not dare declare themselves anarchists for fear that they "might appear to be turning away from working towards collective rebellion and opting for isolated rebellion in its place." The anarchist doctrine, maintained Pelloutier, could therefore only "make headway" if it managed without the "individual dynamiter."[67]

Anarchists should drop their "lingering mistrust" of collective organisation and join the unions, where some anarchists had already gained a "moral authority" for their work, and where "libertarian propaganda" was gaining ground. According to Pelloutier, the workers were losing faith in the state and its labour reforms, and along with these, their faith in the socialist parties, which faced "ruination" from their association with the failed reforms and for the divisions that their sectarian infighting had caused in the unions. Anarchists must enter the unions and show the workers what their organisations might become. The union, Pelloutier declared, "governing itself on anarchic lines," disdaining elections, and relying on economic action, could be "simultaneously revolutionary and libertarian," and with the outbreak of revolution, could suppress the state and provide an organisation that could govern production: "Would this not amount to the 'free association of free producers?'" In his view, it was up to the anarchists "to commit all of their efforts" to this goal.[68]

The basic idea was that unions had the potential to perform a dual role: defending and improving workers' rights, incomes, and conditions in the present day; and acting as the key instrument in the destruction of the old order as well as the basic framework for worker self-management of the means of production in the new one. The classic statement of this approach is provided by Rocker's *Anarcho-Syndicalism*:

> The trade union ... is the unified organisation of labour and has for its purpose the defence of the interests of the producers within existing society and the preparing for and the practical carrying out of the reconstruction of social life after the pattern of Socialism. It has, therefore, a double purpose:
>
> 1. As the fighting organisation of the workers against the employers to enforce the demands of the workers for the safeguarding and raising of their standard of living;
>
> 2. As the school for the intellectual training of the workers to make them acquainted with the technical management of production and economic life in general, so that when a revolutionary situation arises they will be capable of taking the socio-economic organism into their own hands and remaking it according to Socialist principles.[69]

When the time was ripe, the revolutionary union movement would launch a revolutionary general strike (or in the De Leonist phrase, a "general lockout of the capitalist class").[70] Rather than picket outside the workplace gates, stay at home, or attend marches, the workers would *occupy* the factories, mines, farms, offices, and so forth, and place them under self-management. The revolutionary occupation undertaken, the union structure would provide the model through which self-management was exercised, with local assemblies, mandated committees, and coordination between and within industries through the larger union federation.

With the means of production under workers' self-management, the working class would now literally rule society; the workers, "when they are powerful enough," would "*shut the factories against the present employers* and commence production for *use*."[71] The unions themselves, Rocker stressed, would provide the basis for "taking over the management of all plants by the producers themselves." The "socialist economic order" would thus not "be created by the decrees and statutes of any government" but only "by the unqualified collaboration of the workers, technicians and peasants to carry on production and distribution by their own administration in the interest of the community and on the basis of mutual agreements."[72]

The IWA, in line with this sort of thinking, defined its tasks as twofold: "the daily revolutionary struggle," and the "assumption of the administration of every individual operation by the producers themselves."[73] The IWA's Latin American umbrella body, ACAT, likewise, staked "all its hopes on organising labour" to "assume possession of the means of production, distribution and transport."[74] The Uruguayan Regional Workers' Federation (FORU), formed in 1905, argued that "all its efforts should be geared towards bringing about the complete emancipation of the proletariat" through a universal union federation.[75]

The same idea was central to the IWW as well, including its De Leonist wing. William Trautmann, a founder of the IWW—and in the 1910s a De Leonist—expressed the idea succinctly. The One Big Union would organise the workers with the ultimate purpose that every worker have equal rights and duties in managing industry: "With the construction of the industrial organisation perfected for their [sic] future functions in a workers' republic the political state will collapse completely, and in its place will be ushered in the industrial-political administration for a further advanced social system."[76]

In other words, syndicalism envisages the revolutionary union *prefiguring* the organs of the postcapitalist society. "Our class struggle," wrote Kubo, "is to achieve the radical transformation of economic and political institutions by means of the workers' organisations based on the ideal of free federation."[77] Not every anarchist who supported syndicalism was entirely comfortable with this specific aspect of its strategy. Kropotkin championed syndicalism, but unlike Bakunin, had reservations that the union structure would necessarily form an adequate basis for a postcapitalist society, i.e. with the embryo hypothesis.[78]

Obviously the syndicalist approach implied anarchist involvement in the immediate struggles of the working class. As Rocker argued, the work of a "fighting organisation of the workers against the employers" aimed at "safeguarding and raising" workers' "standard of living."[79] In order for an anarchist union to survive, it *had* to engage with day-to-day struggles for reforms, yet know that none of these minor reforms, however bitterly won, meant that capitalism had been overthrown.

Anarchists who supported union work explicitly denied that this involvement in winning immediate gains was in any sense harmful to the prospects for making a revolution. Rocker stressed that if workers were unable to fight for minor reforms that improved their everyday lives—such as higher wages or shorter hours—then they were certainly highly unlikely to undertake the revolutionary reconstruction of the world.[80] On the other hand, in Rocker's view, basic material improvements laid the basis for ever-greater aspirations by the workers:

> It may also be taken as true that as long as the worker has to sell hands and brain to an employer, he will in the long run never earn more than is required to provide the most indispensable necessities of life. But these necessities of life are not always the same, but are constantly changing with the demands which the worker makes on life....
>
> By the intellectual elaboration of their life experiences there are developed in individuals new needs and the urge for different fields of intellectual life....
>
> True intellectual culture and the demand for higher interests in life does not become possible until man has achieved a certain material standard of living, which makes him capable of these.... [M]en who are constantly threatened by direst misery can hardly have much understanding of the higher cultural values. Only after the workers, by decades of struggle, had conquered for themselves a better standard of living could there be any talk of intellectual and cultural development among them.[81]

For Kubo, likewise, "raising wages and improving working conditions are not our goals *per se*" but a "means" to "rouse direct action and cultivate a bud of anarchism through daily struggle, which I believe will be the preparation for revolution."[82] Rather than the insurrectionist anarchist notion that immediate gains were "mere trifles and concessions that soon disappeared," syndicalists argued that such gains, which improved conditions, raised aspirations, and created the space for the rise of a large anarchist movement.

These sorts of ideas were subsequently adopted by the mainstream French unions. Beginning in 1890, mass anarchists had entered into the two main components of the French union movement: the federation of Bourses du Travail, and the National Federation of Unions. Besides Pelloutier, mention must be made of Emile Pouget (1860–1931), an anarchist shop worker who was jailed for three years after leading a demonstration of the unemployed in 1883 with Michel. An excellent radical journalist, Pouget played a key role in the rise of French syndicalism, wrote many of its classic texts, and served as assistant secretary of the CGT from 1900 to 1908, retiring from political activism in 1914.[83] In 1895, the National Federation of Unions was renamed the CGT, and declared itself independent of all political parties; that same year, Pelloutier became secretary of the Federation of Chambers of Labour. In 1902, the CGT and the Federation of Chambers of Labour merged into one CGT, with Pouget as assistant secretary and head of the national union sections. In 1906, the French CGT adopted the famous *Charter of Amiens*:

> The Confederal Congress of Amiens confirms article 2 of the constitution of the CGT constitution. The CGT unites, outside all political schools, all workers conscious of the struggle to be waged for the disappearance of the wage-earning and employing classes....
>
> The Congress considers this declaration to be a recognition of the class struggle which, on the economic plane, puts the workers in revolt against all forms of exploitation and oppression, material as well as moral, exercised by the capitalist against the working class;
>
> The Congress clarifies this theoretical affirmation by the following points: In its day-to-day efforts, syndicalism seeks the coordination of

workers' efforts, the increase of workers' well-being by the achievement of immediate improvements.... But this task is only one aspect of the work of syndicalism: it prepares for complete emancipation, which can be realized only by expropriating the capitalist class; it sanctions the general strike as its means of action and it maintains that the trade union, today an organisation of resistance, will in the future be the organisation of production and distribution, the basis of social reorganisation.[84]

Against Economism: Direct Action versus "Political Action"

Winning immediate gains was, in short, vital to sustaining a popular social movement. Anarchists who favoured the creation of a revolutionary union movement stressed that the manner in which immediate gains were won and the way in which the unions operated were both of great importance in building revolutionary momentum. They emphasised the use of direct action, ongoing political education, and the creation of a radically democratic, decentralised, and participatory form of unionism as vital components of a union movement able to overthrow capitalism and the state. If insurrectionist anarchists saw struggles for immediate gains as futile and such reforms as poison to the revolution, mass anarchists regarded small victories as the sustenance of a revolutionary movement and in no way preventing the final revolutionary struggle.

What was crucial was the *manner* in which the immediate improvements were won. Emphasis was placed on the use of direct action in working-class struggles. For Rocker, direct action meant "every form of immediate warfare by the workers against their economic and political oppressors," including strikes, workplace sabotage, boycotts, antimilitarist activity, and the "armed resistance of the people."[85] For syndicalists, this could take place *within and through* unions.

Mass anarchists, including syndicalists, regarded direct action as the most *effective* method of combating employers and the state. Direct action was contrasted favourably with "political action," which was defined as the strategy of using political parties and the state apparatus to emancipate labour. "Political action," in this sense, was not the same as *political struggle*, and the rejection of political action did not therefore imply any rejection of political struggles more broadly. As we discuss elsewhere in this volume, political struggles—around state policy as well as civil and political freedoms—were absolutely central to the syndicalist project; however, political action, understood as *using* the state machinery, was not; this point applies to the De Leonist tradition as well.

Direct action was also regarded as essential to the process of creating a revolutionary working-class movement and counterculture. For syndicalists, as Wayne Thorpe notes, unions mobilised workers as a class at the point of production on the basis of their class interests, and against capitalism and the state, while political parties (even those of the Left) were typically multiclass institutions led by outsiders, and generally used workers as passive voters in a futile quest to use the capitalist government for socialist transformation.[86] Socialist parties were not only "unnecessary for the emancipation of the proletariat" but "a positive hindrance to it."[87] Rather, it was through union struggles against *both* capitalists and the state that workers could be drawn into anarchism, and consequently, as Kubo wrote, "We urge grabbing every chance and utilising any moment ... to shake the foundations of society."[88]

This argument is also lucidly presented in *Syndicalism*, written in 1912 by Earl C. Ford (n.d.) and William Z. Foster (1881–1961) of the Syndicalist League of North America (SLNA).[89] Foster (the main author) was born to a poor immigrant family in a Philadelphia slum.[90] He left school at a young age to seek employment, and worked at jobs ranging from a deep-sea sailor to a miner to a locomotive fire-fighter. Disillusioned with the SP and influenced by the veteran anarchist Jay Fox, who published the *Agitator*, he joined the IWW in 1909, travelled around Europe from 1910 to 1911 to learn from its labour movements, and spent much of his time with militants of the French CGT. On his return, Foster wrote *Syndicalism*, formed the SLNA in 1912, and left the IWW a year later to try and conquer the moderate American Federation of Labour (AFL) from within. The SLNA lasted until 1914, grew to about two thousand members, and had a substantial influence in Chicago, Kansas City, and Saint Louis. Former SLNA members played a central role in strikes and union drives in later years, most notably the great 1919 Chicago steel strike. Foster himself, however, was later won over to Bolshevism, joined the Communist Party of the United States (CPUSA), and served as the party's national chair from 1932 to 1957.[91]

According to Ford and Foster, "Working class political parties" (meaning here parties aiming to "capture the State"), "in spite of the great efforts spent on them, have proven distinct failures, while on the other hand, labour unions, though of-ten despised and considered as interlopers by revolutionists, have been pronounced successes." This was largely because the parties were "composed of individuals of all classes," controlled by the "non-working class elements" and caught up in the state machinery, which was inherently anti-working class.[92]

For Ford and Foster, political action—in the sense of participation in the state machinery through such means as elections—was "merely an expression of pub-lic sentiment," but direct action by the working class was a "demonstration of real power." It had the great merit of bringing the masses of the working class into ac-tion: "It is evident that if the workers are to become free it must be through their own efforts and directly against those of the capitalists."[93] Direct action, as Rocker contended, would win "substantial concessions," unlike electioneering, which had "achieved practically nothing for the working class" in either economic or politi-cal terms. It was far better to struggle outside of and against the state, than try to capture it. Even positive reforms by the state were often "caused by the influence of direct action tactics"; for Rocker, this was not an argument for "political action" but "simply a registration of direct action," and proof of its superiority. Syndicalists have "proven time and again that they can solve the many so-called political ques-tions by direct action," including "old age pensions, minimum wages, militarism, international relations, child labour, sanitation of workshops, mines, etc., and many other questions."[94]

Rocker also complained bitterly about the view that syndicalists were econo-mistic, that is, narrowly concerned with wages and working conditions:

> It has often been charged against Anarcho-syndicalism that it has no interest in the political structure of the different countries, and conse-

quently no interest in the political struggles of the time, and confines its activities to the fight for purely economic demands. This idea is altogether erroneous and springs either from outright ignorance or wilful distortion of the facts....

For just as the worker cannot be indifferent to the economic conditions of his life in existing society, so he cannot remain indifferent to the political structure of his country. Both in the struggle for his daily bread and for every kind of propaganda looking toward his social liberation he needs political rights and liberties, and he must fight for these himself in every situation where they are denied him, and must defend them with all his strength whenever the attempt is made to wrest them from him.[95]

What distinguished the syndicalist position on the struggle for political rights from that of the political parties "was the form of this struggle" for political rights and "the aims which it has in view." Fundamentally, contended Rocker, the "peoples owe all the political rights and privileges" that they enjoy "not to the good will of their governments, but to their own strength." As he emphasised, "*What is important is not that governments have decided to concede certain rights to the people, but the reason why they have had to do this.*"[96] It was popular struggle, rather than the goodwill of the powerful or the skillful interventions of the left-wing politicians, that secured the rights and privileges in the first place. The best vehicle for both the economic and political struggles of the modern working class was the union, and specifically, the syndicalist union:

The lance head of the labour movement is ... not the political party but the trade union, toughened by daily combat and permeated by Socialist spirit. Only in the realm of the economy are the workers able to display their full social strength, for it is their activity as producers which holds together the whole social structure, and guarantees the existence of society at all. In any other field they are fighting on alien soil.... This direct and unceasing warfare with the supporters of the present system develops at the same time ethical concepts without which any social transformation is impossible: vital solidarity with their fellows-in-destiny and moral responsibility for their own actions.[97]

For the International Socialist League—established in 1915 in Johannesburg, and the single most important syndicalist formation in South Africa—the One Big Union would champion *both* economic and political freedom:

The workers' only weapon are [*sic*] their labour.... All ... activities should have this one design, how to give the workers greater control of industry.... With greater and greater insistence comes ... the need for men to forego the cushion and slipper of parliamentary ease, and recognise the Industrial Union as the root of all the activities of Labour, whether political, social or otherwise.[98]

South African capitalism used a wide range of coercive measures against the Africans who formed the majority of the local working class: an internal passport system, racial segregation along with other discriminatory laws and practices, housing for migrant workers in closely controlled compounds, and a system of contracts that effectively indentured Africans. The International Socialist League saw direct action through One Big Union as the key to defeating this system of national oppression, advising mass action and resistance: "Once organised, these workers can

bust-up any tyrannical law. Unorganised, these laws are iron bands. Organise industrially, they become worth no more than the paper rags they are written on."[99]

For Pouget of the French CGT, likewise, "political changes are merely a consequence of amendments made to the system of production," the method of attack
was "direct action," "the symbol of syndicalism in action," part of the "combined
battle against exploitation and oppression" by the working class "in its relentless attack upon capitalism."[100] For Berkman, revolutionary unions must

> relate not only to the daily battle for material betterment, but equally so
> to everything pertaining to the worker and his existence, and particu-
> larly to matters where justice and liberty are involved.... It is one of the
> most inspiring things to see the masses roused on behalf of social justice,
> whomever the case at issue may concern. For, it is the concern of all of us,
> in the truest and deepest sense. The more labour becomes enlightened
> and aware of its larger interests, the broader and more universal grow its
> sympathies, the more world-wide its defence of justice and liberty ... the
> tremendous power of the proletariat ... has ... on numerous occasions
> ... prevented planned legal outrages.[101]

In short, while classical Marxism tended to pose a strict dichotomy between
a "political field" (centred on the state, and engaged by the revolutionary party
through political action) and an "economic field" (dealing with wages and working
conditions, and relegated to the unions, but led by the party) the syndicalists saw
the revolutionary union as *simultaneously* undertaking both political and economic
functions. Some, like De Leon, still used the language of two fields—his "Socialist
Industrial Unionism" would organise on both fields, and even make a limited use
of electoral activity—but stressed the centrality of the One Big Union in developing a revolutionary movement and shaping both fields: "the political movement is
absolutely the reflex of the economic organisation."[102] Others rejected the very concept of a political field, some doing so explicitly.[103] And others, like the U.S. IWW,
rejected the concept implicitly:

> The IWW is not anti-political. Nor is it non-political. It is ultra-political.
> Its industrial activities have affected the political institutions of the coun-
> try in a manner favourable to labour.... Following the Wheatland strike,
> the housing commission of California used its authority to clean up la-
> bour conditions on all the ranches in the state.... The political results of
> the IWW are undoubtedly many, and to its credit.[104]

What all of these approaches shared was the view that the revolutionary union
transcended any attempt to develop a socialist strategy based on the identification
of two distinct fields of working-class activity, and the notion that politics should be
left to a party, with the union confining itself to economistic concerns. As the Italian
syndicalist Enrico Leone commented in 1906,

> Syndicalism is to put an end to the dualism of the labour movement by
> substituting for the party, whose functions are politico-electoral, and for
> the trade union, whose functions are economic, a completer organism
> which shall represent a synthesis of the political and the economic func-
> tion.[105]

The view that syndicalism was a form of "'left' economism" without a revolutionary strategy, that it lacked a serious analysis of the state which appreciated

"the need for politics" and "the role of the state in maintaining the domination of capital,"[106] and that it was also unable "to adequately confront the issue of state power"[107] is simply not defensible.

Anarcho-syndicalism, Revolutionary Syndicalism, and De Leonism

We have spoken so far of both anarcho-syndicalism and revolutionary syndicalism. These share the same basic strategy: using union activities as a basis for revolution. What these approaches have in common, and what distinguishes them from other militant forms of unionism, is a stress on the workers' self-management of the means of production, a position of antistatism as well as a hostility toward political parties and parliament, and a commitment to a social revolution in which unions play the key role and the union structures provide the basis for postcapitalist self-management. At this level, the terms anarcho-syndicalism and revolutionary syndicalism may be used interchangeably.

It should also be noted, however, that there is a basis for retaining a distinction between the two terms. While fundamentally the same, the terms are useful as indicators of two main *variants* of the revolutionary and libertarian union approach. This basic distinction is generally implicit in anarchist writings, but should be set out clearly.

Anarcho-syndicalism is a term best reserved for the revolutionary unionism that is openly and consciously anarchist in origins, orientation, and aims. The classical example would be Spain's CNT, which traced its roots back to the anarchist Spanish section of the First International—the Spanish Regional Workers' Federation (FORE)—and the ideas of Bakunin. In a situation where anarchists were deeply implanted in the working class and peasantry, and where there was no force that could seriously challenge the anarchist grip on the CNT from within, the union had no problem in declaring itself anarchist and identifying explicitly with the anarchist tradition. Thus, in the 1936 Spanish Revolution, the main CNT military base in Barcelona was named the Bakunin Barracks.

Revolutionary syndicalism, on the other hand, is a term best reserved for the syndicalist variant that for a range of reasons, did not explicitly link to the anarchist tradition, and was unaware of, ignored, or downplayed its anarchist ancestry. It is typical of revolutionary syndicalist currents to deny any alignment to particular political groupings or philosophies— to claim to be "apolitical," notwithstanding the radical politics that they embody. The French CGT after 1895 is a classic example of a revolutionary union that downplayed its links to anarchism. The CGT's leaders claimed that the federation was "outside of all political schools" at the very time that they declared that the federation united all workers "conscious of the struggle to be waged for the disappearance of the wage-earning and employing classes" by "expropriating the capitalist class"—a position that can scarcely be regarded as apolitical.[108]

Like Bakunin's envisaged "antipolitical" First International, which would recruit on the basis of a "realistic understanding" of the workers' "daily concerns," revolutionary syndicalist unions like the French CGT presented themselves as apolitical or antipolitical, and thus independent of all political parties.[109] This had the advantage of opening the unions to workers who would never even consider joining a socialist party. In addition, the claim of neutrality helped prevent political party affiliations from dividing the membership of revolutionary syndicalist unions, and defended these unions from capture by socialist parties and factions.[110]

The IWW is a slightly different case, largely characterised by a general ignorance of the anarchist roots of its syndicalist approach. Indeed, it is not at all uncommon to find IWW literature that describes the union's views as Marxist or "Marxian." This tendency was particularly marked in the Detroit IWW, the De Leonists. The De Leonists argued that only "trade union action could transfer property from individual to social ownership."[111] In their view, the *Industrial Unions will furnish the administrative machinery for directing industry in the socialist commonwealth*" after the "general lock out of the capitalist class" and the "razing" of the state to the ground.[112] However much De Leon believed he worked "with Marx for text," called his doctrine "Socialist Industrial Unionism" rather than syndicalism, and remained overtly hostile to anarchism because of the propaganda by the deed, his basic approach was syndicalist.[113] In short, De Leon has a better claim to inclusion in an anarchist canon than, say, Godwin, Stirner, or Tolstoy.

In Conclusion: Building Tomorrow Today

In this chapter, we have argued that the main division within the broad anarchist tradition was not between "anarcho-communism" and anarcho-syndicalism but between insurrectionist anarchism and mass anarchism, with the latter category including syndicalism. It is important to stress at this point that the difference between the two does *not* centre around the issue of violence as such: mass anarchist formations like the Spanish CNT, for example, operated armed reprisal squads in the 1920s and organised an armed militia in the 1930s. The difference is the role that violence plays in the strategy: for insurrectionist anarchism, propaganda by the deed, carried out by conscious anarchists, is seen as a means of *generating* a mass movement; for mass anarchism, violence operates as a means of self-defence for an *existing* mass movement. For syndicalism, the immediate struggle prefigures the revolutionary struggle and the union prefigures the society of tomorrow; we have here an organ of revolutionary counterpower emerging from the daily struggle.

We have also emphasised the essential identity of anarcho-syndicalism, revolutionary syndicalism, and De Leonism, suggesting that the differences between these types of syndicalism are secondary. For now, for the purposes of clarity, let us note that we use the term syndicalism without any prefixes or qualifications, referring to all varieties of syndicalism. We have posited that a self-identification with the anarchist tradition is not a necessary condition for inclusion in the broad anarchist tradition. We understand the broad anarchist tradition as including insurrectionist and mass anarchism, and *all* varieties of syndicalism.

It is, in short, quite possible for people to accept and act on the basic ideas of Bakunin in the absence of any conscious link to the anarchist tradition; it is equally possible for a self-described Marxist to be part of the broad anarchist tradition, and for a self-identified anarchist to be outside that tradition. What is critical is that the basic ideas are derived from anarchism, with anarchism understood—as we have contended at some length—as a revolutionary form of libertarian socialism that harkens back to the First International, Bakunin, and the Alliance. These points do require some more substantiation, and it is to this task that we turn in the following chapter, which deals with various issues that arise, such as the origins of syndicalism, its history before the French CGT, the relationship between anarchism, syndicalism, and the IWW, and the ideas of De Leonism.

Notes

1. Quoted in C. Harper, *Anarchy: A Graphic Guide* (London: Camden Press, 1987), 65.
2. Malatesta in Richards, *Errico Malatesta*, 126.
3. Bookchin, "Deep Ecology, Anarchosyndicalism, and the Future of Anarchist Thought," 50.
4. Graham, preface, xiii; see also Pengam, "Anarcho-Communism," 60, 75–76.
5. P. Avrich, introduction to *The Anarchists in the Russian Revolution*, ed. P. Avrich (London: Thames and Hudson, 1973), 10–12.
6. Bookchin, *The Spanish Anarchists*, 145–46.
7. Bookchin, *To Remember Spain*, 21–22.
8. Bookchin, *The Spanish Anarchists*, 137; Bookchin, *To Remember Spain*, 20–21.
9. Bookchin, "Deep Ecology, Anarchosyndicalism, and the Future of Anarchist Thought," 51.
10. Pengam, "Anarcho-Communism," 60; see also J. Crump, *Hatta Shuzo and Pure Anarchism in Interwar Japan* (New York: St. Martin's Press, 1993), chapter 2.
11. Pengam, "Anarcho-Communism," 74–75.
12. Crump, *Hatta Shuzo and Pure Anarchism in Interwar Japan*.
13. Ibid.
14. Ibid., chapter 2.
15. Workers Solidarity Movement, *Position Paper: The Trade Unions* (Dublin: Workers Solidarity Movement, 2005), sections 5.1, 5.9.
16. N. Makhno, et. al., *The Organisational Platform of the Libertarian Communists*.
17. Craparo, *Anarchist Communists*, 65.
18. "The Kropotkinist Anarcho-Communists (not for nothing known as anti-organisationalists) believe that any work among the masses apart from pure and simple propaganda of the 'right' ideas, is useless. This is the origin of their lack of interest in the daily struggles of the working class which are seen as pointless and counterproductive"; ibid., 65.
19. Avrich, *The Russian Anarchists*, 54, 61, 63, 84, 107; see also Avrich, *Anarchist Portraits*, 68.
20. Quoted in Crump, *Hatta Shuzo and Pure Anarchism in Interwar Japan*, 10. It is no illusion to speak of a syndicalist Kropotkin, contrary to Pengam, "Anarcho-Communism," 249.
21. Malatesta, "Syndicalism," 220–25 .
22. See R. Munck, *Argentina: From Anarchism to Peronism: Workers, Unions, and Politics, 1855–1985* (London: Zed Books, 1987); R. A. Yoast, "The Development of Argentine Anarchism: A Socio-ideological Analysis" (PhD diss., University of Wisconsin at Madison, 1975), 155–56.
23. Berkman, *The ABC of Anarchism*, 46–49, 53–62.
24. E. Goldman, *Syndicalism: The Modern Menace to Capitalism* (New York: Mother Earth Publishing Association, 1913), 7.
25. Goldman, "The Failure of the Russian Revolution," 155.
26. Hart, *Anarchism and the Mexican Working Class*, 161–62.
27. On his pioneering role, see Dirlik, *Anarchism in the Chinese Revolution*, 128. "Our principles are communism, anti-militarism, syndicalism, anti-religion, anti-family, vegetarianism, an

international language and universal harmony"; quoted in Marshall, *Demanding the Impossible*, 521.

28. See Dirlik, *Anarchism in the Chinese Revolution*, 124–33.

29. Petrograd Union of Anarcho-syndicalist Propaganda, "Declaration of the Petrograd Union of Anarcho-syndicalist Propaganda," in *The Anarchists in the Russian Revolution*, ed. P. Avrich (June 4, 1917; repr., London: Thames and Hudson, 1973), 71; see also I. Makalsky, "To the Worker," in *The Anarchists in the Russian Revolution*, ed. P. Avrich (December 19, 1917; repr., London: Thames and Hudson, 1973), 78.

30. Hart, *Anarchism and the Mexican Working Class*, 161–62, 174–76.

31. Quoted in R. Graham, ed., *Anarchism: A Documentary History of Libertarian Ideas, Volume 1: From Anarchy to Anarchism, 300 CE to 1939* (Montréal: Black Rose, 2005), 199; and Marshall, *Demanding the Impossible*, 505.

32. American Continental Workers' Association, "American Continental Workers' Association," in *Anarchism: A Documentary History of Libertarian Ideas, Volume 1: From Anarchy to Anarchism, 300 CE to 1939*, ed. R. Graham (1929; repr., Montréal: Black Rose, 2005), 331.

33. Thorpe, *"The Workers Themselves,"* 324, appendix D.

34. T. Brown, *The Social General Strike* (Durban: Zabalaza Books, n.d.), 9.

35. Bookchin, *The Spanish Anarchists*, 182, 289–96; see also National Confederation of Labour, *Resolution on Libertarian Communism as adopted by the Confederacion Nacional del Trabajo, Zaragoza, 1 May 1936*.

36. Crump, *Hatta Shuzo and Pure Anarchism in Interwar Japan*, 87–91.

37. Hatta Shuzo, "On Syndicalism," in *Anarchism: A Documentary History of Libertarian Ideas, Volume 1: From Anarchy to Anarchism, 300 CE to 1939*, ed. R. Graham (1927; repr., Montréal: Black Rose, 2005), 378.

38. N. Makhno, et. al., *The Organisational Platform of the Libertarian Communists*, 6–7.

39. The Friends of Durruti, *Towards a Fresh Revolution* (1938; repr., Durban: Zabalaza Books, 1978), 25.

40. See G. W. Carey, "The Vessel, the Deed, and the Idea: Anarchists in Paterson, 1895–1908," *Antipode: A Radical Journal of Geography* 10, no. 3 and 11, no. 1 (1979); Introduction to Galleani, *The End of Anarchism?*

41. P. Avrich, *Sacco and Vanzetti: The Anarchist Background* (Princeton, NJ: Princeton University Press, 1991), 56–57; see also Avrich, *Anarchist Portraits*, chapter 12.

42. Galleani, *The End of Anarchism?* 11.

43. Ibid., 11–13.

44. Ibid., 11.

45. Ibid., 47.

46. Ibid., 49.

47. Ibid., 49, 11.

48. A. M. Bonanno, *A Critique of Syndicalist Methods*, 1975, available at http://www.geocities.com/kk_abacus/ioaa/critsynd.html (accessed March 25, 2005).

49. Galleani, *The End of Anarchism?* 55.

50. Ibid., 51–53, 57.

51. For a fascinating account of the narodniks, see D. Foot, *Red Prelude: A Life of A. I. Zhelyabov* (London: Cresset Press, 1968).

52. See P. Avrich, *The Haymarket Tragedy* (Princeton, NJ: Princeton University Press, 1984).

53. J. Most, *The Beast of Property*, IWPA, Group New Haven, reprinted in J. J. Most, *Revolutionare Kriegswissenschaft, Together with the Beast of Property* (New York: Kraus Reprint Co., 1983), 12.

54. See Avrich, *The Haymarket Tragedy*, 73–75. Also important is J. Bekken, "The First Daily Anarchist Newspaper: The *Chicagoer Arbeiter-Zeitung*," *Anarchist Studies*, no. 3 (1995): 13–14.

55. Guérin, *Anarchism*, 74.

56. Quoted in Bookchin, *The Spanish Anarchists*, 115.

57. Quoted in Guérin, *Anarchism*, 74, 78.

58. Graham, *Anarchism*, 351.

59. Quoted in Carey, "The Vessel, the Deed, and the Idea," 52.

60. Cahm, *Kropotkin and the Rise of Revolutionary Anarchism*, 231–69.

61. Quoted in Guérin, *Anarchism*, 78.

62. B. Lowry and E. E. Gunter, epilogue to *The Red Virgin: Memoirs of Louise Michel*, ed. B. Lowry and E. E. Gunter (Tuscaloosa: University of Alabama Press, 1981), 199.

63. Notably in Bakunin, "The Policy of the International"; Bakunin, "The Programme of the Alliance."

64. Kropotkin, "Letter to Nettlau," 304–5.

65. For these people, the union struggle "for everyday interests" was "petty, worthless and even harmful ... a penny-wise policy which serves only to deflect the attention of the workers from their main task, the destruction of capital and the state"; G. P. Maximoff, *Constructive Anarchism* (1930; repr., Sydney: Monty Miller, 1988), 6.

66. Joll, *The Anarchists*, 200.

67. F. Pelloutier, "Anarchism and the Workers' Union," in *No Gods, No Masters: An Anthology of Anarchism, Book Two*, ed. D. Guérin (1895; repr., Edinburgh: AK Press, 1998), 51–57.

68. Ibid., 52–56.

69. R. Rocker, *Anarcho-Syndicalism* (Oakland: AK Press, 2004), chapter 4, also available at http://www.spunk.org/library/writers/rocker/sp001495/rocker_as4.html (accessed November 12, 2000).

70. D. De Leon, *The Preamble of the Industrial Workers of the World, Address Delivered at Union Temple, Minneapolis, Minnesota, July 10, 1905* (1905; repr., Edinburgh: Socialist Labour Press, n.d.), 23–24, 25, 27–28.

71. W. E. Trautmann, *One Great Union* (Detroit: Literature Bureau of the Workers' International Industrial Union, 1915), 32.

72. Rocker, *Anarcho-Syndicalism*, chapter 4.

73. Thorpe, *"The Workers Themselves,"* 323, appendix D.

74. American Continental Workers' Association, "American Continental Workers' Association," 331–32.

75. Uruguayan Regional Workers' Federation, "Declarations from the Third Congress," in *Anarchism: A Documentary History of Libertarian Ideas, Volume 1: From Anarchy to Anarchism, 300 CE to 1939*, ed. R. Graham (1911; repr., Montréal: Black Rose, 2005), 200–1.

76. Trautmann, *One Great Union*, 8.

77. Kubo, "On Class Struggle and the Daily Struggle," 380.

78. Nettlau, *A Short History of Anarchism*, 277–78.

79. Rocker, *Anarcho-Syndicalism*, chapter 4.

80. See also Maximoff, *Constructive Anarchism*, 6.

81. R. Rocker, *Anarcho-Syndicalism* (Oakland: AK Press, 2004), chapter 5, also available at http://www.spunk.org/library/writers/rocker/sp001495/rocker_as5.html (accessed November 12, 2000).

82. Kubo, "On Class Struggle and the Daily Struggle," 380–81.

83. G. Brown, introduction to *How We Shall Bring about the Revolution: Syndicalism and the Co-operative Commonwealth*, ed. E. Pataud and E. Pouget (London: Pluto Press, 1990), xiii–xvi.

84. Thorpe, *"The Workers Themselves,"* 319–20, appendix A.

85. Rocker, *Anarcho-Syndicalism*, chapter 5.

86. See Thorpe, *"The Workers Themselves,"* chapter 1.

87. Brown, introduction, xvi.

88. Kubo, "On Class Struggle and the Daily Struggle," 381.

89. E. C. Ford and W. Z. Foster, *Syndicalism*, facsimile copy (1912; repr., Chicago: Charles H. Kerr, 1990).

90. See J. R. Barrett, "Introduction to the 1990 Edition," in *Syndicalism*, by E. C. Ford and W. Z. Foster, facsimile copy (Chicago: Charles H. Kerr, 1990); E. P. Johanningsmeier, "William Z. Foster and the Syndicalist League of North America," *Labour History* 30, no. 3 (1985); A. Zipser, *Working Class Giant: The Life of William Z. Foster* (New York: International Publishers, 1981).

91. See W. Z. Foster, *From Bryan to Stalin* (London: Lawrence and Wishart, 1936).

92. Ford and Foster, *Syndicalism*, 4, 21–22, 26.

93. Ibid., 20, 3.

94. Rocker, *Anarcho-Syndicalism*, chapter 5.

95. Ibid.

96. Ibid.

97. Ibid.

98. "What's Wrong with Ireland," *The International*, May 5, 1916.

99. "The Pass Laws: Organise for Their Abolition," *The International*, October 19, 1917.

100. E. Pouget, *Direct Action* (London: Fresnes-Antony Group of the French Anarchist Federation, n.d.), n.p. (English translation by the Kate Sharpley Library).

101. Berkman, *The ABC of Anarchism*, 55–56.

102. De Leon, *The Preamble of the Industrial Workers of the World*, 21, 23–24, 25, 27–28. .

103. Notably Ford and Foster, *Syndicalism*.

104. Industrial Workers of the World, *The IWW in Theory and Practice*, 5th rev. and abridged ed. (Chicago: IWW Publishing Bureau, 1937), available at http://www.workerseducation.org/crutch/pamphlets/ebert/ebert_5th.html (accessed July 20, 2004).

105. As summarised in Michels, *Political Parties*, 317.

106. Holton, "Syndicalist Theories of the State," 5; J. Hinton, *The First Shop Stewards Movement* (London: George Allen and Unwin, 1973), 276, 280.

107. R. V. Lambert, "Political Unionism in South Africa: The South African Congress of Trade Unions, 1955–1965" (PhD diss., University of the Witwatersrand, 1988), 45.

108. Thorpe, "*The Workers Themselves*," 319, appendix A.

109. Bakunin, "The Programme of the Alliance," 250.

110. Thorpe, "*The Workers Themselves*," 18–19.

111. D. K. McKee, "The Influence of Syndicalism upon Daniel De Leon," *Historian*, no. 20 (1958): 277.

112. Socialist Labour Party [De Leon], *The Socialist Labour Party*, 23; De Leon, *The Preamble of the Industrial Workers of the World*, 23, 27.

113. See, for example, D. De Leon, "With Marx for Text," *Daily People*, June 29, 1907; D. De Leon, "Syndicalism," *Daily People*, August 3, 1909. Kropotkin was extremely hostile to De Leon for his intemperate attacks on anarchism; see Avrich, *Anarchist Portraits*, 98.

The key figures associated with the Japanese anarcho-syndicalist journal *Rōdō Undō* ("Labour Movement") in February 1921.

From left to right: Nakamura Gen'ichi, Kondō Kenji, Takeuchi Ichirō, Iwasa Sakutarō, Takatju Seidō, Itō Noe (1895–1923), Ōsugi Sakae (1885–1923), and Kondō Eizō. Itō and Ōsugi were murdered by military police in 1923. Small but trenchantly militant, the Japanese anarchist movement waged war on the strictures of Japanese traditions from geishas to the "divine" emperor, later clashing head-on with the militarist state. *Picture courtesy of the Centre for International Research on Anarchism.*

Mexico City: a scene from the 1916 general strike by the anarcho-syndicalist House of the Workers of the World.

"No era in the history of labour in the western hemisphere has witnessed the working-class belligerence" that la Casa's members "demonstrated in 1915 and 1916" (Hart 1991: 197). The organisation's strength peaked in this mid-revolutionary year, but it made a severe error of judgment in using its "Red Battalions" to fight what should have been a natural ally, the anarchist-influenced rural Zapatista guerrillas. *Picture courtesy of University of Texas Press.*

CHAPTER 5

Anarchism, Syndicalism, the IWW, and Labour

This book has consistently linked anarchism to syndicalism, and grouped the varieties of anarchism, including syndicalism, into the broad anarchist tradition. We have also stated that syndicalists who identified themselves as Marxists, like Connolly and De Leon, should be considered part of the broad anarchist tradition, while figures like Godwin, Proudhon, and Tolstoy should be excluded from that tradition. In this chapter, we develop these arguments more fully, focusing on broad strategic distinctions; we also deal with the various issues that arise, such as the origins of syndicalism, its early history, the relationship between anarchism, syndicalism, and the IWW, and the De Leonist tradition.

Bakunin, Sorel, and the Origins of Syndicalism

Most immediately, it is necessary to confront a number of traditional arguments that deny a connection between anarchism and syndicalism, and in some instances, even suggest an opposition between the two currents. Such assertions may be classified into two groups: that which maintains anarchism and syndicalism were based on conflicting principles; and that which identifies the roots of revolutionary syndicalism as lying outside anarchism—specifically either the late nineteenth-century "Revolt against Reason," or classical Marxism.

The first set of claims is represented by the perspective that although "some syndicalist viewpoints share a superficial similarity with anarchism, particularly its hostility to politics and political action," "syndicalism is not truly a form of anarchism."[1] According to this, by "accepting the need for mass, collective action and decision-making, syndicalism is much superior to classical anarchism." A variant of this argument, often made in reference to Italian syndicalism, suggests that anarchism and syndicalism were rival movements that "agreed on tactics but not on principles," or were different, albeit overlapping, tendencies.[2] For Miller, syndicalism was "far from being an anarchist invention," although its stress on class struggle, direct action, and self-management helped make it attractive to the anarchists.[3] Another writer points out that while there were similarities between anarchism and syndicalism, the "anarchist movement continued in existence parallel to syndicalism and there was considerable interchange between the two."[4]

This contention is commonly linked to the view that attributes the origins of the syndicalist conception to Sorel, a retired French engineer and former Marxist, and consequently, to his admirers, like Antonio Labriola in Italy.[5] According to Louis Levine, this claim was first developed in Werner Sombart's *Socialism and the Social Movement*, which appeared in English translation in 1909, and then "made its way into other writings on revolutionary syndicalism."[6] Nearly a century later, this idea remains pervasive. Joll described Sorel as "the theorist of anarcho-syndicalism," while Kieran Allen alleged that the French CGT was "committed to the ideas of Georges Sorel."[7] According to Darrow Schechter, Sorel was "the leading theorist of Revolutionary Syndicalism," and he therefore speaks of syndicalism's "synthesis of Marx and Sorel"—a view shared by Charles Bertrand, who maintains that the syndicalists "attempted to reconcile the positions of Karl Marx and Georges Sorel."[8] Jeremy Jennings refers to Sorel as "syndicalism's foremost theoretician,," and to his paper, *Le Mouvement socialiste*, as "the syndicalist movement's principal journal."[9]

Sorel's ideas were not always consistent (according to Jennings, the key feature of Sorel's thought was precisely its "disunity" and "pluralism").[10] Sorel was also very much a representative of a particular mood among radical Western intellectuals in the late nineteenth and early twentieth centuries—a mood that has been called the "Revolt against Reason."[11] This stressed feeling over thought, action over theory, will over reason, and youth over civilisation. It is from this perspective that Sorel's characteristic opposition to rationalism and parliamentary democracy, and his belief in the regenerative power of myth and violence, must be understood. Sorel thought that Europe was in a state of decadence, and that the bourgeoisie was incapable of carrying out the historic mission ascribed to it by Marx: the development of an advanced industrial basis for a future socialist society. There is no doubt that Sorel gravitated toward the French CGT when it adopted a syndicalist platform; he believed that the general strike of the syndicalists was a heroic (if irrational) myth that would galvanise the working class into violent action and thereby regenerate Europe.[12]

By linking syndicalism to the Revolt against Reason, this identification of Sorel with syndicalism has significant implications. For Bertrand, the syndicalists "failed to produce a coherent ideology ... the only identifiable common principle ... became a belief in the efficacy of violence and direct action."[13] According to Emmet O'Connor, syndicalism was less a strategy than a mood, an "exaltation of will over reason," an "anti-intellectual and anti-rational" trend in the labour movement that infused an "irrational impulse ... into industrial unrest."[14] Further, given that the sentiments of the Revolt against Reason later found their key expression in Italian fascism, and given that Sorel later associated with the far Right, while Labriola became an outright fascist, the identification of syndicalism and Sorel lends itself to the thesis that syndicalism had close links to Italian fascism—a claim that will be dealt with separately below.

The notion that Sorel was the "leading theorist" of syndicalism was assiduously promoted by the man himself, but is nonetheless quite baseless.[15] Sorel was essentially a commentator on the syndicalist movement from outside, one who, moreover, tended to see his own convictions—such as an opposition to rationalism, a hostility toward democracy, and the belief in the power of myth and violence—in the CGT. His actual influence on the syndicalist movement was negligible. As far back as 1914, Levine argued that the notion that Sorel was the leader of syndicalism "is a 'myth' and should be discarded," noting that Sorel and his circle did not develop the basic ideas of syndicalism or act as spokespersons for the CGT; they were "no more than a group of writers ... watching the syndicalist movement from the outside ... stimulated by it," but whose ideas were often at odds with those of the syndicalists.[16]

The syndicalists agreed. Sorel and his followers, argued Rocker, "never belonged to the movement itself, nor had they any mentionable influence on its internal development."[17] Syndicalism "existed and lived among the workers long before" Sorel and others wrote about it," Goldman observed.[18] Her point is important. Sorel's interest in syndicalism in the early twentieth century came nearly ten years *after* the start of the rise of French syndicalism and therefore he can hardly be described as the movement's "theorist." The key biography of Sorel supports these claims: Sorel's outline of syndicalist doctrine was unoriginal, his reflections on syndicalism were a "response" to an existing movement, his influence was "negligible," and his support for syndicalism lasted only from around 1905 to 1909, at which time he moved to the far Right.[19] It is, moreover, "impossible to show a direct link between the militants of the French labour movement and the philosophers of the Revolt against Reason": "Sorel had no contact with the labour movement," never set foot in the CGT offices, "played no part, however small, in its affairs," and had "fundamental differences" with the CGT unionists.[20]

"Sorel speculated on the syndicalist movement from outside, elaborating ideas that syndicalist militants would not have endorsed even had they been fully familiar with them."[21] Sorel had no "appreciable attention in France, let alone a following."[22] It would have been difficult to find syndicalist militants who preferred to "regenerate decadent bourgeois society" rather than destroy it, or who regarded the general strike as nothing but a heroic myth. He "had no direct connection with the syndicalist movement, whose ideas were evolved independently of and, indeed, before the appearance of Sorel, and the real syndicalists certainly did not support his mythical interpretation of syndicalism."[23] Despite suggesting that Sorel was the "theorist" of syndicalism, even Joll admitted that "Sorel was not ... launching a new strategy for the working classes ... but rather trying to fit what they were already doing into his own highly personal, subjective and romantic view of society." [24] Sorel was indeed far closer to the extreme Right than to the syndicalists. To these points it might be added that the Revolt against Reason was largely confined to academic and artistic circles, and had a negligible impact on the broad socialist movement, and even less on organised labour.

The distance between Sorel, Labriola, and the Revolt against Reason, on the one hand, and syndicalism, on the other, removes much of the basis for claims that there was some sort of special affinity between fascism and syndicalism. Nevertheless, because of the assertions positing such a connection—which are made mainly by reference to Italy and the archetypal fascist movement of Mussolini—it is necessary to sketch out some historical background. A syndicalist current emerged in the Italian Socialist Party (PSI) and its affiliated General Confederation of Labour (CGL, later the Italian General Confederation of Labour, CGIL) in the early twentieth century. It formed a National Resistance Committee in 1907, which was expelled in 1908. Placed under severe pressure in the CGL, the syndicalists broke away en bloc to form the Italian Syndicalist Union (USI) in 1912. When the First World War started, it became clear that a militantly nationalist and militarist faction had emerged in the USI, which adopted a prowar position; associated with Labriola, this minority was driven out by the USI, formed the Italian Labour Union (UIL) in 1915, and eventually linked up with Mussolini, who represented a similar breakaway from the PSI.

These developments have suggested to some writers that there was a close connection between syndicalism and fascism. Bertrand identifies Italian syndicalism with the UIL (as opposed to the USI, which he describes as anarchist).[25] Likewise, O'Connor alleges that Italian syndicalism laid "a theoretical basis for post-war fascism," drawing on the work of A. James Gregor, and David Roberts, who stress the UIL link to the later Fascist movement and the influence of Sorel on Mussolini.[26] Another writer on Italian anarchism maintains that there were "syndicalist intellectuals" influenced by Sorel and his cothinkers who "helped to generate, or sympathetically endorsed" the emerging Fascist movement, sharing its "populist and republican rhetoric."[27]

Such arguments are not convincing. The critical point is that the UIL group had broken with the basic politics of syndicalism with its embrace of nationalism and militarism. Moreover, the prowar section of the USI was a minority, and was roundly defeated and expelled at a special USI congress in September 1914, in line with the victorious antiwar resolution put forward by Armando Borghi.[28] Born in Castel Bolognese, he became an anarchist militant at age sixteen, moved to Bologna in 1900, was arrested repeatedly for antimilitarist and anarchist work as well as propaganda, and edited *L'Aurora* ("The Dawn").[29] In 1907, he became a union activist, was part of this syndicalist current in the CGL and PSI, went into exile in 1911, and returned in 1912, joining the USI. Active in antimilitarist work and the Red Week of 1914, a popular uprising, he led the struggle against the UIL tendency, became the USI secretary, and directed the union paper *Guerra di classe* ("Class War"). In 1920, he visited the USSR (missing the 1920 Italian factory occupation movement) and was singularly unimpressed by Lenin. Jailed with Malatesta and others later that year, he left Italy with the Fascist takeover in 1922 for France and then the United States, returning in the 1940s and 1950s to Italy, where he helped produce the revived *Umanita Nova* ("New Humanity"). He died in 1968.

It was people of the calibre and convictions of Borghi, not nationalists like Labriola, who represented Italian syndicalism. Furthermore, rather than enjoying close link with Fascists, the "anarchists probably suffered greater violence proportionate to their numbers than other political opponents of fascism," and Fascist squads played a central role in the destruction of the syndicalist unions in Italy.[30] "It is no coincidence," notes a recent study, "that the strongest working class resistance to Fascism was in ... towns or cities in which there was a strong anarchist, syndicalist or anarcho-syndicalist tradition."[31] In 1922, the USI helped organise a general strike to try to halt the Fascist takeover in Italy and was involved in great street battles against fascist paramilitaries in Parma in August that year. Banned in 1926, the underground USI and other anarchist groups, such as the Galleanists, continued to wage a bitter struggle against the dictatorship.

The First International and the First Syndicalists

Where, then, did syndicalist ideas emerge? The evidence supports an alternative argument: that the syndicalist conception arose within the anarchist movement in the first days of the First International. According to Levine, the "anarchists entering the syndicates" in France "largely contributed to the revolutionary turn which the syndicates took," and their "main ideas" may "all be found" in the First International, "especially in the writings of the Bakounist [*sic*] or federalist wing"; syndicalism was not really a "new theory" but "a return to the old theories."[32] For Lewis Lorwin, similarly, the "first anticipations of syndicalist ideas may be found in the discussions and resolutions of the First International between 1868 and 1872 and especially in those of its Bakuninist sections between 1872 and 1876."[33] Joll admits that syndicalist ideas were, "in a sense," a return to Bakunin and the anarchists of the First International.[34]

Reviewing the literature, Thorpe holds that the syndicalists were "the anarchist current within the workers' movement," representing "the non-political tradition of socialism deriving from the libertarian wing of the First International" and the writings of Bakunin.[35] In his excellent study of the IWW, Sal Salerno likewise notes that "the libertarian wing of the First International" launched modern syndicalism.[36] Obviously syndicalism cannot be conflated with anarchism—not all anarchists accepted it, and some syndicalists rejected the anarchist label—but syndicalism must be regarded as the progeny of anarchism, as an anarchist *strategy or variant* rather than an alternative to anarchism.

The view that anarchism and syndicalism were integrally linked was commonplace in the anarchist literature of the "glorious period," the movement's peak from the mid-1890s to the mid-1920s. Guillaume commented: "What is the CGT if not the continuation of the First International?"[37] Goldman argued that the First International saw "Bakunin and the Latin workers forging ahead along industrial and Syndicalist lines": "Syndicalism is, in essence, the economic expression of Anarchism."[38] Kropotkin maintained that the "current opinions of the French syndicalists are organically linked with the early ideas formed by the left wing of the International," and that syndicalism's "theoretical assumptions are based on the teachings of Libertarian or Anarchist Socialism."[39] Malatesta believed that syndicalism was "already glimpsed and followed, in the International, by the first of the anarchists."[40] Maximoff stated that the views "basic to French Revolutionary Syndicalism, and which have since been stressed continually by those Anarchists who now call themselves Anarcho-Syndicalists," went back to the First International.[41] For Rocker, "Anarcho-Syndicalism is a direct continuation of those social aspirations which took shape in the bosom of the First International, and which were best understood and most strongly held by the libertarian wing of the great workers' alliance."[42]

If many syndicalists viewed "themselves as the descendants" of the anarchist wing of the First International, it is also notable that both Marx and Engels consistently identified anarchism with syndicalism.[43] Marx, for example, complained that anarchists contended that workers "must ... organise themselves by trades-unions" to "supplant the existing states," while Engels lamented the "Bakuninist" conception that the "general strike is the lever employed by which the social revolution is started"; "One fine morning all the workers of all the industries of a country, or even of the whole world, stop work," added Engels, to "pull down the entire old society."[44]

There was certainly ample support for this view in the works of Bakunin and the Alliance.[45] For instance, the Jura section of the First International, an anarchist stronghold, maintained that "the future Europe would be a simple federation of labour unions without any distinction according to nationality," while the Romande Federation, based in Francophone Switzerland, described "federated unions as the only weapon capable of assuring the success of the social revolution."[46] While Marx hoped to see the First International become an international grouping of political parties aiming at state power, Bakunin tended to regard the organisation as the nucleus of an international union federation, an "organisation of professions and trades" that should strive for the "immediate aim—reduction of working hours and higher wages," prepare "for strikes," raise "strike funds," and unify "workers into one organisation."[47] These unions must be democratic, participatory, and accountable to the membership to prevent hierarchies from emerging, and to promote the self-activity of the rank-and-file; "the absence of opposition and control and of continuous vigilance" by members becomes a "source of depravity for all individuals vested with social power."[48]

For Bakunin, the experience of practical solidarity and immediate struggles, in tandem with the work of the Alliance in promoting the "new faith" of anarchism, would see the First International forge the powerful "ties of economic solidarity and fraternal sentiment" between the "workers in all occupations in all lands." The First International should also provide the basis to "erect upon the ruins of the old world the free federation of workers' associations." Its structures, organised along the lines of trades and professions, crossing national borders, and coordinated through "Chambers of Labour," would supply the lever for social revolution along with the basic infrastructure of a self-managed and stateless socialist order:

> The organisation of the trade sections and their representation in the Chambers of Labour creates a great academy in which all the workers can and must study economic science; these sections also bear in themselves the living seeds of the new society which is to replace the old world. They are creating not only the ideas, but the facts of the future itself.[49]

When the "revolution, ripened by the force of events, breaks out, there will be a real force ready which knows what to do and is capable of guiding the revolution in the direction marked out for it by the aspirations of the people: a serious international organisation of workers' associations of all lands capable of replacing this departing world of *states*."[50] Bakunin did not himself seem to have raised the idea of the revolutionary general strike at this time, but the notion was current in anarchist circles. The first properly constituted congress of the anarchist wing of the First International, held in Geneva in 1873, suggested a focus on "international trade union organisation" and "active socialist propaganda," and delegates raised the view that a general strike was the key to social revolution.[51] It is not surprising, then, that the syndicalist IWA formed in 1922 adopted as its name the International Working-men's Association—the name of the old First International—for they considered themselves the real heirs of that venerated body.[52]

The First Wave: Syndicalism before the French CGT

To summarise, one of the main differences between Marx and Bakunin was on the union question: Marx saw unions as (at most) a school of struggle that could contribute to the formation of a revolutionary political party, while Bakunin adopted a syndicalist position.[53] Now if syndicalism existed as a key element of anarchism from its origins, two points follow. First, syndicalism is *part of* anarchism. Second, syndicalism *preceded* the formation of the French CGT. The latter point contradicts both the notion that Sorel was the theorist of syndicalism and the view that syndicalism first "arose in France as a revolt against political Socialism" in the 1890s, as a result of a rapprochement between "various groups" on the Left.[54] Obviously the French example is absolutely central: the term "revolutionary syndicalism" is, after all, an Anglicisation of *syndicalisme révolutionnaire*, literally "revolutionary union-ism," and only appears from the 1890s against the backdrop of the rise of the CGT.

The notion that syndicalism "was born in France" in the late nineteenth century is mistaken, however.[55] The doctrine of syndicalism, as we have argued, can be traced back to the days of the anarchist wing of the First International. To this should be added that there was a significant wave of syndicalist unionism in the 1870s and 1880s. In 1870, the anarchists of the Alliance formed the FORE in Spain, which was to become the largest single section of the First International. At its 1872 congress, delegates represented 20,000 Spanish workers in 236 local federations and perhaps 600 union trade sections, and in 1873, the membership reached 60,000.[56] "Whether or not one uses the term, the fundamental structure of anarchism" in Spain and elsewhere was "always syndicalist."[57]

The FORE structure adopted in 1871 anticipated in "many respects the syndicalist form of organisation later adopted by the French CGT," and a vision of syndicalist revolution was widely held by 1873—the year that the anarchists helped organise a general strike in Alcoy and Barcelona, and were driven underground.[58] These early Spanish anarchists saw the unions as "an arm of war" under capitalism and a "structure for the peace that would follow," with revolutionary unionism "a basic article in the credo of the Spanish Internationalists" that preceded the CGT example by decades.[59] Like Bakunin, the founders of Spanish anarchism believed revolutionary "labour organisations" would "destroy the bourgeois state": "the Federation would rule."[60]

The successors of FORE, such as the Spanish Regional Labourers' Federation (FTRE) formed in 1881 and claiming to have seventy thousand members a year later, and the Pact of Union and Solidarity, launched in 1891, revived this approach and anticipated the better-known syndicalist unions of twentieth-century Spain like the CNT.[61] The FORE model was also adopted in Cuba, where anarchists took control of the labour movement from around 1884. Following an early success with the 1883 Artisans' Central Council in Havana, the anarchists formed a Workers' Circle among cigar makers, printers, and tailors in 1885, a Tobacco Workers' Federation in 1886, the Workers' Alliance in 1887 or 1888, and then the Federation of Cuban Workers, followed by the anarchist Cuban Labour Confederation (CTC) in 1895.[62]

The Cuban movement organised among both white workers and newly emancipated black slaves (abolition took place only in 1886), and also established affiliates in Cuban communities in the United States.[63] A key figure was Enrique Roig de San Martín.[64] Born in Havana, he wrote in *El Obrero* ("The Worker"), the first Cuban anarchist newspaper, *El Boletín del Gremio de Obreros* ("Workers' Guild Bulletin"), and founded, in 1887, *El Productor* ("The Producer"), a popular anarchist paper. Roig de San Martín helped found the Workers' Alliance and was active in the Cuban labour movement. He died in 1889 at the age of forty-six in a diabetic coma, a few days after being released from a jail term.

The 1880s also saw a parallel development in the United States, where an anarchist network of "considerable proportions" emerged in the early 1880s.[65] Organised through the IWPA in Pittsburgh in 1883, these anarchists endorsed a syndicalist approach, according to which the union was the vehicle of class struggle, a weapon for revolution, and "the embryonic group of the future 'free society,'" "the autonomous commune in the process of incubation."[66] The person who formulated this thesis was Albert Parsons. Born in Montgomery, Alabama, he served in the Confederate Army, like many young white men of his generation, during the American Civil War (1861–1865). After the war, he became a firm opponent of slavery, and one of the "Radical Republicans" who tried to use postwar Reconstruction and abolition to enfranchise blacks and redistribute land. Subject to numerous attacks from the groups that would coalesce as the Ku Klux Klan, and married to Lucy Parsons, who will be discussed more in chapter 10, he moved to Chicago, helped found the IWPA, and became a leading anarchist orator as well as the editor of the anarchist paper the *Alarm*.

From its Chicago stronghold, the IWPA took over the Federative Union of Metal Workers of America and founded the syndicalist CLU in 1884; by 1886, the CLU was Chicago's biggest union federation, counting among its twenty-four affiliates the city's eleven largest unions. That year it was able to mobilise eighty thousand marchers on May 1 as part of the U.S.-wide strike for the eight-hour day, in which the anarchists played an important role. This movement was crippled by the Haymarket Affair, which saw eight Chicago IWPA militants arrested in 1887 for a supposed bomb plot; five, among them Albert Parsons and August Spies (1855–1887), were sentenced to death, and three got life imprisonment.[67]

November 11, the day of the executions, was long commemorated by the anarchist movement. Another IWPA legacy was May Day, which was chosen as an international day of labour unity and action to commemorate the martyred Haymarket anarchists and their role in the struggle for the eight-hour day.[68] The IWPA's syndicalism would later be known as the "Chicago Idea," and would profoundly influence subsequent generations of radicals in the United States. Foster of the SLNA, for instance, would later recall that his circle, which defined syndicalism as "anarchism made practical," "consciously defined itself the continuer of the traditions of the great struggle of '86, led by the Anarcho-Syndicalists, Parsons, Spies, *et al*, and we were in constant contact with many of the veterans of that heroic fight."[69] He was heavily influenced by Jay Fox, an anarchist whose "theories in 1911 were a curious amalgam of the old anarchist 'Chicago Idea' and Social Darwinism."[70] The Haymarket case and the Chicago Idea also had an important influence on the founders of the IWW, many of whom (their number included Lucy Parsons) consciously linked the new union to the efforts of the Chicago martyrs.[71]

There are indications of similar developments elsewhere. In Mexico, the early labour movement was heavily influenced by Fourier and Proudhon, and orientated toward forming cooperatives, mutual aid groups, and proto-union "resistance societies."[72] This libertarian orientation, the rise of the First International, and ongoing links with Spain through immigration and language contributed to the rise of a distinctly anarchist current in the country. A clandestine anarchist political group, La Social, dated back to 1865, reconvened in 1871, and reorganised in 1876.[73] A key figure was Francisco Zalacosta (1844–1880), the son of an officer in the Liberal forces that entered Mexico City in 1854. The ward of a wealthy family in the city, he was exposed to anarchist ideas, became active in La Social, and edited its paper, *La Internacional* ("The International"). He was also active in the early labour group Círculo Proletario ("Workers' Circle"), which was formed in 1869 and organised urban workers, and in 1878 played a leading role in a peasant uprising in Chalco. Following an eighteen-month campaign, in which haciendas were attacked and their land given to peasants, Zalacosta was captured and executed.

The Círculo Proletario, inspired by news of the First International, helped convene a Workers Grand Circle (CGO); anarchists soon became prominent, with La Social sending representatives. The CGO was mainly made up of resistance societies. It supported strikes, and favoured a "political boycott and the refusal to recognise governments larger than the local community, or *municipio libre*," and insisted that workers must emancipate themselves, "using as their ultimate weapon the social revolution."[74] In practice, though, the anarchist minority was heavily focused on forming cooperatives. By 1874, the CGO had around 8,000 members, but the anarchists felt that the time had come for a proper union body; this was duly established in 1876 as the CGOM, which claimed to have 50,236 members by 1882.[75] Its manifesto called for "emancipating the workers from the capitalist yoke," and La Social aimed to develop the body into something "similar in nature" to the twentieth-century Spanish CNT.[76] La Social was represented at the 1877 congress of the anarchist First International, and the CGOM joined the Black International.

These early syndicalist initiatives were overshadowed by the rise of insurrectionist anarchism. By the late 1880s, however, as we have indicated in the previous chapter, there was a major swing back to mass anarchism. Malatesta quietly moved away from propaganda by the deed, and Kropotkin, who had initially been sympathetic to insurrectionism, now declared, "We have to be with the people, which is no longer calling for isolated acts, but for men of action in its own ranks."[77] He reminded his comrades of the centrality of "the economic struggle of labour against capital," noting that "since the times of the International ... the anarchists have always advised taking an active part in those workers' organisations which carry on the *direct* struggle of labour against capital and its protector—the State."[78] Even Most, previously a firebrand insurrectionist, shifted his stance in the 1890s, promoting syndicalism to German and Russian immigrants in the United States as "the most practical form of organisation for the realisation of anarchist-communism."[79]

Developments in France played a particularly important role in the revitalisation of syndicalism. The general decline in anarchism in the 1880s in many countries—in large part due to the isolation attendant on the rise of insurrectionist anarchism—was rapidly reversed in the 1890s by the situation in France, where "the Anarchists, beginning with their famous 'raid' on the unions in the nineties had defeated the reformist Socialists and captured almost the entire French union movement."[80]

The French breakthrough attracted worldwide attention (unlike, for example, the concurrent successes of syndicalism in Cuba and Spain), and in this sense it is not without justice that Rocker could argue that the "modern Anarcho-syndicalist movement in Europe ... owes its origin to the rise of revolutionary Syndicalism in France, with its field of influence in the CGT."[81] It opened up the glorious period of anarchism and syndicalism, from the mid-1890s to the mid-1920s.[82] In this period, it was above all in the union movement that anarchism advanced. Rather than "the record of the anarchosyndicalist movement" being "one of the most abysmal in the history of anarchism generally," as Bookchin states, it was precisely through the new wave of syndicalism that anarchism was reborn as a mass movement.[83] Indeed, it was through syndicalism that anarchism became "an effective and formidable force in practical politics."[84] The Marxist historian Eric Hobsbawm, by no means an admirer of anarchism and syndicalism, would later admit that

> in 1905–1914, the marxist left had in most countries been on the fringe of the revolutionary movement, the main body of marxists had been identified with a *de facto* non-revolutionary social democracy, while the bulk of the revolutionary left was anarcho-syndicalist, or at least much closer to the ideas and the mood of anarcho-syndicalism than to that of classical marxism.[85]

In the glorious period, and after, anarchists and syndicalists established or influenced unions in countries as varied as Argentina, Australia, Bolivia, Brazil, Bulgaria, Canada, Chile, China, Colombia, Costa Rica, Cuba, Ecuador, Egypt, El Salvador, France, Germany, Guatemala, Ireland, Italy, Japan, Mexico, the Netherlands, New Zealand, Paraguay, Peru, Poland, Portugal, South Africa, Spain, Sweden, the United States, Uruguay, and Venezuela.

In summary, syndicalism preceded the French CGT by more than two decades, and was intrinsically linked to the anarchist movement from the start. The syndicalist conception was not invented in France in the 1890s and then exported elsewhere; instead, what happened in France in the 1890s was a *revival* of the mass anarchist tradition, a return to the policies of Bakunin, not their supersession by a new current. The politics of the French CGT itself must be situated within the broad anarchist tradition and its history, and the entry of the anarchists into the French unions must be seen as the consequence of an *internal* strategic debate within the broad anarchist tradition. The conquest of the CGT played a decisive role in the decline of insurrectionist anarchism, but this role was demonstrative and inspirational, rather than innovative. The point is that there was in fact a wave of early syndicalist organizing, in the 1870s and 1880s, preceding the better known wave starting in the 1890s.

The IWW and Syndicalism

We have consistently identified the IWW with syndicalism and therefore as part of the broad anarchist tradition. There are, however, two traditions in the literature that would reject this assertion: the argument that maintains that the IWW was more Marxist than syndicalist in character, and the view that sees the IWW as developing independently of and separate to syndicalism. We suggest neither of these approaches is convincing.

The view that the IWW was Marxist rather than anarchist takes various forms. In some cases, the IWW is presented as "a curious blend of Marxism, syndicalism and anarchism" that "contained too many Marxist elements to be truly libertarian."[86] The "central idea of the One Big Union" has, for example, been seen as "fundamentally opposed to the anarchists' passionately held ideals of localism and decentralisation."[87] Alternatively, it has been suggested that the IWW was "by no means committed to anarchism," and that major IWW leaders were never anarchists.[88] A more far-reaching version of this line maintains that the IWW was "classically Marxist" in outlook and "owed its greatest philosophical debt to Marx."[89] Whereas European syndicalists were influenced by anarchism, the IWW had "strongly defined Marxist views, which were impressed on it more particularly by Daniel De Leon."[90] Thus, the IWW expected an "understanding of Marxism to catalyse the experience of workers," and its "particular novelty" was really "the temper with which it expounded Marxism."[91]

The notion that the IWW was classically Marxist and distinguished from other Marxists chiefly by its "temper" is obviously not easily reconciled with Marx and Engels' view that the "constitution of the proletariat into a political party is indispensable," and that the "conquest of political power" is the "great task of the proletariat."[92] It is difficult to imagine Marx endorsing the IWW's *Preamble* of 1908:

> The working class and the employing class have nothing in common.... Between these two classes a struggle must go on until the workers of the world organise as a class, take possession of the earth and the machinery of production and abolish the wage system....
>
> It is the historic mission of the working class to do away with capitalism. The army of production must be organised, not only for every-day struggle with capitalists, but also to carry on production when capitalism shall have been overthrown. By organising industrially we are forming the structure of the new society within the shell of the old.[93]

This is a characteristically syndicalist outlook, and its substance is not changed by the fact that the IWW was influenced by Marxist economics: there was nothing unusual about this.[94] Arguments that the IWW differed from anarchism in that it favoured mass struggles, and differed from syndicalism in that it advocated political education and opposed craft unionism, are based on something of a misunderstanding of anarchism and syndicalism, as is the notion that One Big Union is incompatible with anarchism.[95] In stressing industrial rather than craft unions, the IWW differed with many in the French CGT, but craft unionism was not a syndicalist principle; the Spanish CNT, for example, sought to organise industrial unions.

The view that the IWW developed independently of syndicalism usually makes the case that the IWW was purely the product of U.S. circumstances—specifically the bitter class struggles on the frontier. This stance emerged in the 1920s in U.S. scholarship, has been restated in recent years, and maintains that the IWW developed parallel to and independently of syndicalism elsewhere.[96] This perspective can be found in standard histories of anarchism, which claim the IWW "drew so much of its vigour and methods from the hard traditions of the American frontier" as well as in anarchist accounts that see the IWW as "wholly the outgrowth of American conditions."[97]

This "frontier origins thesis" is partly the result of a methodological nationalism that presents U.S. culture as free of foreign influences, and also arises from attempts by sympathisers to stress the U.S. credentials of the IWW.[98] The IWW itself sometimes stressed its U.S. character and roots.[99] Yet it is difficult to defend the view that the IWW developed separately to syndicalism elsewhere or was really a product of U.S. frontier conditions. The IWW was demonstrably influenced by both U.S. and immigrant anarchist and syndicalist traditions going back as far as the IWPA, was directly shaped by the French CGT, and expressed its identity with syndicalism elsewhere in many ways.[100]

The ideas of the IWW were also clearly syndicalist in character. Political socialism was "completely absent" in IWW thinking, and the IWW had "no conception of the dictatorship of the proletariat."[101] "There will be no such thing as the State or States ... industries will take the place of what are now existing States."[102] It aimed to form a union movement that would "serve as a militant organ in the daily struggle with the employing class" and ultimately "a means of taking over the industry by the workers and ... function as a productive or distributive organ."[103] The IWW's "refusal to ally itself with parliamentary socialism, its repudiation of leaders or apotheosis of the collective membership, and its counter-emphasis on drawing from a proletarian culture of struggle as a means of building a movement aimed at social transformation, defines its indigenous anti-political philosophy as well as its major link to European anarcho-syndicalism."[104]

"There is no doubt that all the main ideas of modern revolutionary unionism ... exhibited by the IWW may be found in the old International Workingmen's Association."[105] There is "no escaping the similarities between the principles of the IWW and the sort of Syndicalism which was ... sweeping ... the European labour movement."[106] The "basic nature of the IWW was that of a syndicalist organisation"; there was "no difference on most fundamental issues" between the French CGT and the U.S. IWW, and virtually "every scholar who has dealt extensively with the IWW has considered it as a form of syndicalism."[107] There is, in short, very little basis to present the IWW as Marxist, rather than syndicalist, or to suggest that the IWW was not basically syndicalist.

De Leon and Connolly

The question of Marxism and the IWW does bear more examination, though. There is no doubt that many prominent IWW figures like Haywood and Trautmann admired Marx, identified as Marxian socialists, accepted Marx's economic determinism to an extent unmatched by most other anarchists and syndicalists, and sometimes denounced anarchism.[108] At the same time, they advocated a "government" of "Industrial Socialism" through One Big Union rather than a "political state."[109] This is not a serious objection to the IWW being included within the broad anarchist tradition. As we have argued, self-identification as a Marxist or an anarchist is less important than the *content* of the ideas adopted, and the ideas of the IWW are certainly within the ambit of the broad anarchist tradition. It was not necessary that every IWW leader declare themselves an anarchist; their syndicalism was anarchist in itself, for syndicalism was a type of anarchism.

It may yet be necessary to explain why we have described De Leonism as a form of syndicalism. De Leon was born in Curaçao and educated in Europe, moving in 1874 to the United States, where he studied at Columbia University. In 1890, he joined the Socialist Labour Party (SLP) and edited its paper, *The People*. The SLP, formed in 1876 by classical Marxists associated with the First International, developed a significant anarchist section that included Albert Parsons and broke away to form the IWPA.[110] The remaining SLP adopted the view that a working-class majority would "sweep presidential and congressional elections, and then utilise its governmental majority to legislate into existence public ownership," and joined the Labour and Socialist International.[111] Under De Leon, it developed a reputation for purism and sectarianism, organisational authoritarianism, and nasty polemics; increasingly influenced by the iron law of wages idea, it began to reject struggles for reforms and became a vehicle of "revolutionary authoritarianism" by the early twentieth century.[112] Driven out of the established unions, the SLP formed an unsuccessful Socialist Trade and Labour Alliance in 1895, and was soon overshadowed by the newly launched SPA.

It was from these unlikely beginnings that the SLP evolved into a syndicalist party. For reasons that are not entirely clear, around 1904 the "heart" of De Leon's "revolutionary theory" was undergoing "dramatic and thoroughgoing alterations" toward revolutionary syndicalism.[113] The SLP was one of the founders of the IWW, and by the close of the founding conference, De Leon had completed his metamorphosis. He now believed that only "trade union action could transfer property from individual to social ownership."[114] For De Leon, henceforth, a parliamentary road to socialism was a "gigantic Utopia," because the working class could not use a state "built up in the course of centuries of class rule for the purpose of protecting and maintaining the domination of the particular class which happens to be on top" to overthrow class society.[115]

It could only emancipate itself through "Industrial Unionism, an economic weapon, against which all the resources of capital ... will be ineffective and impotent."[116] The *"Industrial Unions will furnish the administrative machinery for directing industry in the socialist commonwealth"* after the "general lockout of the capitalist class" and the "razing" of the state to the ground.[117] Self-management in industry would be impossible under the state, whose electoral districts were based on regional demarcations; only along industrial lines could workers organise direct and democratic control over the different sectors of the economy.[118] While De Leon continued to insist that he was a good Marxist and certainly no anarchist or syndicalist, his new approach "ran directly counter to the thought of Marx and Engels."[119] The following quote serves as ample illustration:

> The overthrow of class rule means the overthrow of the political State, and its substitution with the Industrial Social Order, under which the necessaries for production are collectively owned and operated by and for the people.... Industrial Unionism casts the nation in the mould of useful occupations, and transforms the nation's government into the representations from these.... Industrial Unionism is the Socialist Republic in the making ... the Industrial Union is at once the battering ram with which to pound down the fortress of Capitalism, and the successor of the capitalist social structure itself.[120]

De Leon did not, however, repudiate all electoral activity. In his view, "Socialist Industrial Unionism" must organise on the "economic field" as well as the "political field." By the political field, he meant not only elections but also the realm of ideas. The aim was partly to spread propaganda to build One Big Union.[121] Conversely, the growth of One Big Union would see increasing electoral power for the SLP: De Leon asserted that "the political movement is absolutely the reflex of the economic organisation." In addition he suggested—and this was something few other syndicalists would accept—that a socialist majority in parliament (a consequence of One Big Union) could aid the "general lockout of the capitalist class" by paralysing the state. The state was to be "taken" only "for the purpose of *abolishing it*," and the representatives of the working class would "*adjourn themselves on the spot*."[122] In other words, elections were *secondary*, a tactic subordinated to the strategy of revolutionary industrial unionism.[123]

This view, which was not so different from that supported at times by figures like Haywood, proved highly controversial, and coupled with suspicions regarding the SLP, led to a serious schism in the IWW.[124] At the fourth annual IWW convention in 1908, the union's "anti-political" majority, centred on Vincent St. John and Haywood, argued that participation in elections was futile, created illusions in the capitalist state, divided workers into different political parties, and in any case was irrelevant to a large part of the working class that the One Big Union sought to organise: blacks, immigrants, women, and children.[125]

Charging that the convention was rigged, De Leon and the SLP withdrew, and the union split into the "Detroit IWW," headed by the De Leonists, and the "Chicago IWW" majority, opposed to electioneering. Because the De Leonist faction was a distinct minority in the United States, and because it changed its name to the Workers' International Industrial Union in 1915, we will, except where stated otherwise, use the phrase "U.S. IWW" to refer to the Chicago IWW. The De Leonists adopted the IWW's original 1905 *Preamble*, which had a clause stating that the working class must "come together on the political, as well as on the industrial field."[126] The Chicago IWW, however, revised the *Preamble* in 1908 to remove all references to the political field.

The split was replicated in movements inspired by the IWW across the English-speaking world, although the balance of influence between the Chicago IWW and the SLP did not always follow the U.S. pattern: in Australia, the SLP was routed by Chicago IWW adherents; in Britain, the SLP tradition was, however, the most influential; both traditions were represented in South Africa, but the SLP approach tended to predominate. Many overseas SLP groups were notably less sectarian and dogmatic than the SLP in the United States, and less committed to the principle of "dual unionism"—that is, the idea that new separate revolutionary unions must be formed outside the existing unions. In Scotland, for example, De Leonists played a crucial part in the radical shop stewards' movement that began in the industrial Clydeside area in 1915; faced with the new development and its own leading role in it, the SLP "abandoned dual unionism."[127] In South Africa, adherents of both IWW tendencies worked together to form some of the first unions among workers of colour.

In Ireland, De Leonist ideas had a significant influence on the legendary activist Connolly. Born in the slum of Cowgate in Edinburgh, Connolly was active in a number of socialist groups before moving to Ireland in 1896. In 1902, he went to the United States to help an SLP election campaign; in 1903, he worked briefly as an organiser for the SLP in Scotland; from 1903 to 1908, he lived in the United States as an SLP and IWW activist, and clashed with De Leon over the iron law of wages, marriage, and religion.[128] Returning to Ireland, Connolly was active in labour and the Left. He was executed in 1916 for his role in the Easter Uprising, an unsuccessful insurrection against Britain, headed by Irish nationalists.

In Ireland, Connolly worked with James "Big Jim" Larkin to unite workers across sectarian lines in the Irish Transport and General Workers Union (ITGWU), formed in 1908. This was not a syndicalist union, although it had syndicalist elements.[129] Both men hoped it could become the nucleus of a revolutionary One Big Union.[130] Larkin, born in the slums of Liverpool to a poor family, became an organiser for the National Dock Labourers' Union in Britain and Ireland, was expelled from the union for his role in unofficial strikes, and then helped found the ITGWU. Working from Dublin, he founded the *Irish Worker*, and with Connolly, formed the Independent Irish Labour Party in 1912, following which the ITGWU was involved in the Dublin Lockout from 1913 to 1914. Larkin later left for the United States, where he was involved with the IWW and SPA, became a supporter of Bolshevism, and was jailed and then deported in the Red Scare of the late 1910s. On his return, he formed the Irish Worker League (linked to the Comintern), was involved in elections, broke with the USSR in the 1930s, and then rejoined the Labour Party, dying in 1947.

Like De Leon, Connolly stressed the primacy of revolutionary industrial unions and their role as the "framework of the society of the future," rejected the "bureaucratic state," and maintained that "the political, territorial state of capitalist society will have no place or function under Socialism":

> In the light of this principle of Industrial Unionism every fresh shop or factory organised under its banner is a fort wrenched from the control of the capitalist class and manned with soldiers of the Revolution to be held by them for the workers. On the day that the political and economic forces of labour finally break with capitalist society and declare the Workers' Republic these shops and factories so manned by Industrial Unionists will then be taken charge of by the workers there employed, and force and effectiveness thus given to that proclamation. Then and thus the new society will spring into existence ready equipped to perform all the useful functions of its predecessor.[131]

In other words, "they who are building up industrial organisations for the practical purposes of to-day are at the same time preparing the framework of the society of the future ... the principle of democratic control will operate through the workers correctly organised in ... Industrial Unions." Like De Leon, Connolly favoured participation in elections, as the "perfected" industrial organisation should organise a Socialist Party as a "political weapon" wielded by the "Industrially Organised Working Class." Yet "the fight for the conquest of the political state is not the battle, it is only the echo of the battle," and the state must be abolished on the day of the revolution.[132]

In closing the discussion on the IWW, there are several points worth highlighting. The IWW should be considered a syndicalist movement, and more precisely, as a revolutionary syndicalist movement. Furthermore, figures like Haywood, De Leon, and Connolly should be included in the broad anarchist tradition, of which they form an integral part, unlike, for instance, Godwin or Stirner. The view that Connolly was "the founder of Marxism in Ireland" and worked within the "framework of the Marxism of the Second International" is misleading.[133] Whether he is called a "Marxian-syndicalist" or a Marxist-De Leonist, he was a syndicalist for much of his active political life.[134]

There are obvious problems with De Leonism. One is a failure to consider the possibility that a steady series of SLP electoral victories would be accompanied by an equally steady incorporation of the SLP into the state apparatus, changing the revolutionary character of the party. De Leonism did not propose any systematic safeguards against this eventuality. More seriously, the view that the capitalist state could simply be closed down by a parliamentary decision assumes that parliament may act as it wishes, when there is a great deal of evidence that the state bureaucracy and military are quite capable of subverting parliamentary decisions. De Leonism does not really address this problem, unlike other types of syndicalism. We will look at rank-and-file syndicalism in chapter 7.

The "Glorious Period" of the mid-1890s to mid-1920s

It is a fairly commonly held view that the zenith of syndicalism was in the period before the outbreak of the First World War in August 1914. Kedward, for example, spoke of the "great age of the anarchists in Europe and America ... between 1880 and 1914," while Joll argued that anarchist and syndicalist ideas were "widespread" before 1914 but declined thereafter.[135] Hobsbawm claimed that anarchism and syndicalism were major forces from 1905 to 1914, but from 1917 on, "Marxism was ... identified with actively revolutionary movements," and "anarchism and anarcho-syndicalism entered upon a dramatic and uninterrupted decline."[136]

The notion that syndicalism declined after 1914 is misleading. It is true that the French CGT underwent a severe internal crisis with the outbreak of the war and—alone of all the syndicalist unions—declared its support of the war effort, even joining a "Sacred Union" with employers, politicians, and the state for the duration of the war. No longer syndicalist, it fractured, eventually coming under the control of the Communist Party of France (PCF). It is also true that Kropotkin and a number of other prominent anarchists like Jean Grave (1854–1939) and Cherkezov came out in support of the Allied side. Even though "the anarchist movement as a whole opposed the war," the prowar stance of such leading anarchists certainly disrupted it.[137]

On the whole, however, syndicalist unions generally peaked *during and after* the war, a number expanded in the 1920s and 1930s, and several continued to operate after the Second World War as well. The membership in the U.S. IWW rose rapidly from less than 10,000 in 1910, to 14,000 in 1913, to 30,000 by 1915, and 100,000 by 1917.[138] Disrupted by the Red Scare of the late 1910s, it nonetheless retained 35,000 members in 1919, and seems to have continued to grow until 1924, when a serious split took place.[139] In Australia, the peak of the IWW influence was in the 1910s.

In Scotland, the SLP exerted its greatest influence through the Shop Stewards and Workers' Committee Movement, a key example of the rank-and-file version of syndicalism that emerged in 1915.[140] "The *ultimate aim* of the Clyde Workers' Committee," wrote Willie Gallacher (1881–1965), its chair and a De Leonist, in January 1916, "is to weld these [existing] unions into one powerful organisation that will place the workers in complete control of the industry."[141] Born in Paisley and trained as a fitter, Gallacher was converted to socialism by the Marxist John MacLean and became a syndicalist.[142] In 1916, the SLP's Glasgow offices and press were raided, and Gallacher and John Muir, editor of the Clyde Workers' Committee's paper, the *Worker*, were jailed. After the war Gallacher was active in strikes and arrested, and helped found the CPGB. In the United States, meanwhile, Foster and the SLNA— and its successors after 1914 like the Trade Union Education League—played an important role in the AFL, and were prominent in the mass steel strike of 1919.[143]

The Italian USI surged from 80,000 members in 1912 to 800,000 in 1920.[144] The Spanish CNT shot up from 100,000 members in 1914 to 700,000 in 1919.[145] In Portugal, the anarchists were involved in forming the National Labour Union (UON) in 1914; conquered by the anarchists and reorganised as the syndicalist CGT in 1919, it was the only national union centre in Portugal and reached a peak of 90,000 members in 1922.[146] In relative terms, assessed against the size of the working class and the structure of the union movement, the Portuguese CGT was considerably larger than the USI in Italy, representing perhaps 40 percent of organised labour at its peak, and the CNT in Spain, representing around 50 percent of organised labour, for it faced no rival union centres. In Germany, in "the immediate postwar period" the syndicalist Free Association of German Trade Unions, or FVdG, "expanded at a rate six times greater than any other labour organisation in the country."[147] It was restructured in 1919 as the Free Workers' Union of Germany (FAUD), which claimed 120,000 members in 1922.[148]

In South Africa, the broad anarchist tradition can be traced back to the pioneering work in the 1880s of Henry Glasse, an anarchist linked to the Freedom Press group in London. Yet it was only in the 1910s that anarchists and syndicalists became a significant force, establishing a number of syndicalist unions among workers of colour from 1917 onward. These included the Clothing Workers' Industrial Union, the Horse Drivers' Union, the Industrial Workers of Africa, the Indian Workers' Industrial Union, and the Sweet and Jam Workers' Industrial Union.[149] The Industrial Workers of Africa was based in Cape Town and Johannesburg, and is particularly notable as the first union for African workers in southern Africa. The International Socialist League played an important role in these developments; the group was heavily influenced by De Leonism and rank-and-file syndicalism, and was mainly active in Durban, Johannesburg, and Kimberley. In Cape Town, though, it was the Industrial Socialist League—a separate group, close to the views of the Chicago IWW—that formed the Sweet and Jam Workers' Industrial Union.

Two of the key figures in the South African movement were the African militant Thomas William "T. W." Thibedi (his dates of birth and death are unknown) and the Scottish immigrant Andrew B. Dunbar (1879–1964). Thibedi, the son of a Wesleyan minister, resided in the multiracial slums of Johannesburg. He joined the International Socialist League and played a crucial part in the Industrial Workers of Africa in Johannesburg, and was active in the left wing of the African nationalist group, the Transvaal Native Congress. Like many other local syndicalists, he was a founding member of the Communist Party of South Africa (CPSA) in 1921. Subsequently head of the Federation of Non-European Trade Unions sponsored by the CPSA, Thibedi was expelled from both the union and the party during the purges of the late 1920s. He rejoined the CPSA in 1935 and flirted with Trotskyism in the 1940s.

Dunbar was a Scottish blacksmith who immigrated in 1906 to South Africa, where he joined the labour movement. He was the general secretary of the South African IWW formed in 1910, a founding member of the International Socialist League, and active in launching the Industrial Workers of Africa, later switching over to the syndicalist Industrial Socialist League. In October 1920, the Industrial Socialist League reorganised as Africa's first Communist Party, on a largely revolutionary syndicalist platform, and with Dunbar as general secretary. This party merged into what became the CPSA, where Dunbar headed a syndicalist faction. Dunbar seems to have been expelled from the CPSA and later withdrew from political activism. In Australia, too, IWW ideas continued to influence the early Communist Party of Australia (CPA), and it was only in the late 1930s that the CPA "succeeded in laying to rest the ghost of the IWW that had haunted it in its formative era."[150]

In Argentina, the FORA federation had split into two in 1914: the FORA of the fifth congress (FORA-V) and the FORA of the ninth congress (FORA-IX). Nonetheless, both sections grew rapidly, with FORA-IX increasing from 20,000 in 1915 to 70,000 in 1920, while FORA-V claimed 180,000 members in 1920 and 200,000 by 1922.[151] (In the meantime, the moderate socialist General Union of Labour, or UGT, had developed into a third syndicalist union centre, the Argentine Regional Workers' Confederation, or CORA, and merged into FORA, which precipitated the breakaway of FORA-V). In Mexico, the first countrywide syndicalist federation since the days of the old CGOM was formed in 1912; this was the House of the Workers of the World (COM), reorganised as the Mexican Regional Workers' Federation (FORM) in 1916. The COM/FORM saw its membership rise to 50,000 in 1915 and then to around 150,000 the following year.[152]

Disrupted in the late 1910s, Mexican anarcho-syndicalism revived with the formation of the CGT in 1921, which had a core membership of 40,000 in the 1920s and peaked at 80,000 in 1928–1929.[153] The IWW, which had a local presence since around 1912, also established a Mexican IWW federation in 1919.[154] The Communist Party of Mexico (CPM) was founded in the same year, but was heavily influenced by anarchism in the 1920s, despite being repudiated by the CGT in 1921. This influence was unsurprising given the enormous influence of anarchism and syndicalism—an influence that extended deeply into the Socialist Workers' Party, the body that initiated the CPM.[155]

Meanwhile, it was only in the late 1910s that the syndicalists, who already dominated labour in Argentina, Brazil, Mexico, Uruguay, and elsewhere, made their greatest breakthroughs other parts of Latin America. In 1912, anarcho-syndicalists formed the Chilean Regional Workers' Federation (FORCh), and in 1917, they captured the Grand Workers' Federation of Chile, the main labour formation, reorganising it as the Chilean Workers' Federation.[156] In 1918, the Chilean IWW was formed, growing from 200 to 9,000 to 25,000 members by the early 1920s.[157] In Peru, anarchists organised the syndicalist Peruvian Regional Workers' Federation (FORPe) in 1919.[158] In Cuba, syndicalism revived in the 1910s, and 1921 saw the formation of the syndicalist Havana Workers' Federation (FOH), followed by a countrywide federation, the Cuban Workers' National Confederation (CNOC) in 1925, which grew to 200,000 workers.[159] In Bolivia, the first syndicalist federation, the Local Workers' Federation (FOL), was only formed in 1927. It was in fact a national federation and the most important union body in the country; the term "local" was used to signify that the union was the local branch of the IWA and the ACAT.[160]

Anarchism and syndicalism only spread to East Asia in the early twentieth century and peaked in the 1920s. The first anarchist and syndicalist influences emerged in the Philippines, where a critical role was played by Isabelo de los Reyes (1864–1938).[161] Born to a poor Ilocano family in the small coastal town of Vigan on the northern island of Luzon, his mother a famous poet, de los Reyes was raised by wealthy relatives, ran away to study at a university in Manila, and published the paper *El Ilocano* ("The Ilocano") and several anthropological studies. In the crackdown after the failed 1896 Philippine Revolt, de los Reyes was sent to the notorious Montjuich prison in Barcelona, Spain, where he was exposed to anarchism. On his return, armed with works by Charles Darwin, Kropotkin, Malatesta, Marx, and Proudhon, he threw himself into union work, and although he was a small capitalist, used syndicalist ideas from Spain:

> His success with organised strikes encouraged other sectors to follow suit and the union became quite quickly a Barcelona-style free-wheeling central—a Unión Obrera Democratica ["Democratic Workers' Union,"]— that would have delighted Tárrida [del Mármol, a famed Cuban anarchist] of *anarquismo sin adjectives* ["anarchism without adjectives"]. The American rulers watched in disbelief and alarm, a huge wave of strikes in Manila and its surroundings, many of them successful because they were unexpected by capitalists and administrators alike.[162]

The colonial authorities arrested him in 1902 for "labour conspiracy," but he was released after four months when it became clear that much of the prosecution's evidence was fabricated, and his position in the Unión Obrera Democratica was eventually taken over by Hermenegildo Cruz. Cruz was a self-educated worker influenced by anarchism who translated Reclus into Tagalog. For his part, de los Reyes became a politician. He was crippled by a stroke in 1929 and died in 1938. The

Unión Obrera Democratica collapsed in 1903, but it was important: it was a pioneer of the Filipino labour movement and the Left, as well as the more substantial syndicalist currents elsewhere in East Asia.[163]

In China, Shifu championed syndicalism, and his circles pioneered unionism. By 1917, anarchists and syndicalists had founded the first modern labour unions in China, organising at least forty unions in the Canton area by 1921.[164] Chinese anarchists faced a number of challenges in union work: besides the various union initiatives of the nationalist Guomindang, there was also the rise of the CCP starting in 1920. The CCP managed to attract to its ranks a number of Chinese anarchists and anarchist sympathisers—among them the young Mao—and soon assumed a key role in the labour movement in Peking (now Beijing), Shanghai, and Wuhan.[165] In some cases—like the Beijing Communist nucleus, to which anarchists were initially admitted, even editing the group's journal—anarchists were part of the early Communist movement.[166] Meanwhile, in central China, the anarchists Huang Ai and Pang Renquan formed a syndicalist Hunan Workers' Association (*Hunan laogonghui*) in the provincial capital Changsha in 1921.[167] This may have had up to 5,000 members. Nonetheless, "anarchist domination of the existing labour movement" continued in Canton and Changsha, despite CCP advances, into the mid-1920s.[168] Anarchists also played a significant role in the Shanghai Federation of Syndicates (*Shanghai gongtuan lianhe hui*). In 1927, Canton anarchists formed the Federation of Revolutionary Workers (*Geming gongren lainhehui*), which aimed at forming a revolutionary union; it was one of many syndicalist groups formed in the 1910s and 1920s.[169]

Kōtuku was an early Japanese proponent of syndicalism.[170] Born in Nakamura, he moved to Tokyo, where he became a journalist in 1893, founded the Social Democratic Party in 1901, translated *The Communist Manifesto*, and was jailed in 1905 for his outspoken opposition to Japanese imperialism. In jail, he read Kropotkin, became an anarchist and a syndicalist, translated Kropotkin's *Conquest of Bread*, and launched the anarchist *Heimin Shimbum* ("Common People's Newspaper"). In 1911, twenty-six anarchists—some influenced by insurrectionism—were convicted of plotting to assassinate the emperor. Kōtuku, who was not involved in the High Treason Incident, was caught up in the repression anyway, and was one of twelve anarchists hanged in January.

Japanese syndicalism grew in the following years, however, particularly in the late 1910s. By 1916, there was a syndicalist Sincere Friends' Society (Shinyūkai) printers' union, the Labour Movement (Rōdō Undō) circle, and the Righteous Progress Society (Seishinkai) newspaper workers' union formed in 1919.[171] Anarchists were also active in the Yūaikai, a moderate union that developed into the Japanese Federation of Labour (Nihon Rōdō Sōdōmei, often abbreviated to Sōdōmei) in 1921, and there was an attempt to merge the Sōdōmei, Shinyūkai, and Seishinkai. Worsening relations between moderates and anarchists saw cooperation break down. The first anarcho-syndicalist union federation was only formed in 1926, the Zenkoku Jiren, which soon claimed 15,000 members.[172] Internal conflicts between syndicalists and "pure anarchists" saw a split in 1928 when syndicalists left to form the Nihon Jikyo. Both federations peaked in 1931, the Zenkoku Jiren with 16,300 members, and the Nihon Jikyo with 3,000 members..[173] The two federations were reunited in 1934—partly because many pure anarchists came back to a syndicalist position—but Japan was then evolving into a semifascist state, and anarchism was crushed soon afterward. There were also unions among the Koreans in Japan: such as the Black Labour Association (Kokurōkai), founded in 1923; the Dong Heong labour union, founded in 1926; and the Korea Free Labour Union, founded in 1927.

It should be clear from the above account that syndicalism was by no means a spent force by 1914; many of the most important developments of the glorious period took place after this time. Nor did Bolshevism suddenly replace syndicalism after 1917. The international revolutionary turmoil of 1916–1923 certainly fostered the rise of Communist parties linked to the Comintern, but the anarchists and syndicalists were also major beneficiaries of the worldwide climate of radicalism. Syndicalism grew rapidly in this period, and many of the new Communist parties were founded by and remained for years deeply influenced by anarchists and syndicalists.

The glorious period came to a close in the mid-1920s. Anarchism and syndicalism fell back in the face of rival movements like Bolshevism, fascism and radical nationalism, and the authoritarian regimes with which such movements were closely associated; the early globalisation of the late nineteenth and early twentieth centuries was coming to a close with the rise of closed economies, a stricter immigration regime, and the consolidation of nation states with their attempts to incorporate the working class into a more "national" community.

Even so, it is possible to speak of a third wave of anarchist and syndicalist organising and influence starting in the late 1920s. The Korean, Malaysian, and Vietnamese anarchist movements only really started in the late 1910s, growing in the 1920s and 1930s. Movements in Bulgaria and Poland also expanded in the 1920s and 1930s, remaining substantial in the 1940s. Important syndicalist unions grew and peaked after the mid-1920s, including the Bolivian FOL, the Cuban CNOC, the Mexican CGT, and the Japanese Zenkoku Jiren and Nihon Jikyo; in Spain the CNT grew massively, peaking in the late 1930s with nearly two million members. In volume 2 we will look at further waves of anarchist and syndicalist activism in the second half of the twentieth century, which were closely linked to international high points of social struggles like 1945, 1956, 1968, and 1989. There has been sustained growth from the 1990s onwards, including entirely new movements in parts of Africa and Asia.

A final point is this: there were different models of syndicalist organisation, but the two main ones appear to have been the Spanish FORE, the French CGT, and the U.S. IWW. Besides the prevalence of CGTs, CNTs, and IWWs, there is also the striking pattern of union names in Latin America: the FORA in Argentina, the FORCh in Chile, the FORM in Mexico, the FORP in Peru, the Paraguayan Regional Workers' Federation (FORPa, formed in 1906), the FORU and the Venezuelan Regional Workers' Federation (FORV, circa 1940); the syndicalist Confederation of Brazilian Workers (COB) also referred to itself as the Brazilian Regional Workers' Federation (FORB).

In Conclusion: Syndicalism and the Broad Anarchist Tradition

At this point, we are able to summarise and outline a broad typology of anarchism and syndicalism. First, anarchism is a revolutionary, internationalist, class struggle form of libertarian socialism, and it first emerged in the First International. Second, there were two main currents in anarchism, defined by their strategic orientation: insurrectionist and mass anarchism. Bookchin, it will be recalled, used the term "lifestyle anarchism" to refer to a range of Stirnerite currents and eccentric groupings that claim the anarchist label, and distinguished this from the "social anarchism" of Bakunin, Kropotkin, and so forth.[174] We suggest, on the contrary, that it is incorrect to label these sects anarchist at all; they have no place in the anarchist tradition, for they are not anarchist.

Syndicalism was a form of mass anarchism that exemplified the view that the means must prefigure the ends and that daily struggles could generate revolutionary counterpower, and the great majority of anarchists embraced it. There were also antisyndicalist mass anarchists, including both opponents and supporters of workplace activity. Third, there were two main forms of syndicalism: anarcho-syndicalism and revolutionary syndicalism; De Leonism was a form of revolutionary syndicalism. There was also rank-and-file syndicalism: this could be either anarcho-syndicalist (the version associated with Maximoff, the Union of Anarcho-syndicalist Propaganda, and the Confederation of Russian Anarcho-syndicalists) or revolutionary syndicalist (the Shop Stewards and Workers' Committee Movement in Britain). Syndicalism was a mass anarchist strategy and should be understood as such, regardless of whether its proponents are aware of its anarchist genealogy. We use the term "syndicalism," without prefixes or qualifications, to refer to all of these types.

All of these variants of anarchism can be grouped together as the "broad anarchist tradition," which therefore excludes figures like Godwin, Stirner, Proudhon, and Tolstoy, while it includes figures like Bakunin, Kropotkin, Flores Magón, Makhno, Rocker, Shifu, Shin, Connolly, De Leon, and Haywood. We summarise our position in figures 5.1 and 5.2. Having established our general interpretation of the anarchist idea and movement, we can now turn to some of the key debates over tactics that have taken place in the broad anarchist tradition.

Figure 5.1
The Broad Anarchist Tradition

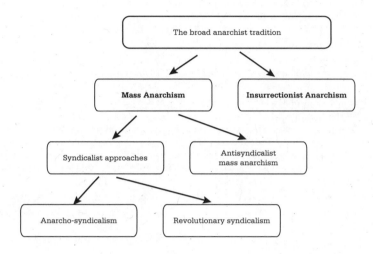

Figure 5.2
Anarchism and Syndicalism

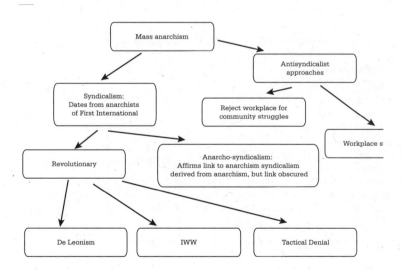

Notes

1. D. McNally, *Socialism from Below*, 2nd ed. (Chicago: International Socialist Organisation, 1984), part 3.

2. C. L. Bertrand, "Revolutionary Syndicalism in Italy," in *Revolutionary Syndicalism: An International Perspective*, ed. W. Thorpe and M. van der Linden (Otterup, Denmark: Scolar Press, 1990), 145; C. Levy, "Italian Anarchism, 1870–1926," in *For Anarchism: History, Theory, and Practice*, ed. D. Goodway (London: Routledge, 1989), 51–54.

3. Miller, *Anarchism*, 124.

4. F. F. Ridley, *Revolutionary Syndicalism in France: The Direct Action of Its Time* (Cambridge: Cambridge University Press, 1970), 41–44.

5. The standard study of Sorel is J. R. Jennings, *Georges Sorel: The Character and Development of His Thought* (Basingstoke, UK: Macmillan, 1985). Sorel's views, in fact, underwent continual change and "cannot be categorised," for "Marxism, syndicalism, royalism, fascism, bolshevism excited him one after the other"; see Jennings, *Georges Sorel*, vii. A good discussion of Sorel is also provided in Joll, *The Anarchists*, 206–12. The book usually identified with Sorel's "syndicalism" is his meandering *Reflections on Violence*, which came out in 1912, and in English translation soon after; G. Sorel, *Reflections on Violence* (1912; repr., London: Allen and Unwin, 1915).

6. L. Levine, *Syndicalism in France*, 2nd ed. (New York: Columbia University Press, 1914), 155.

7. Joll, *The Anarchists*, 207; K. Allen, *The Politics of James Connolly* (London: Pluto Press, 1987), 68.

8. Schechter, *Radical Theories*, 28, 35; Bertrand, "Revolutionary Syndicalism in Italy," 139.

9. Jennings, "The CGT and the Couriau Affair," 326, 328.

10. Jennings, *Georges Sorel*, 5, 7.

11. I. L. Horowitz, *Radicalism and the Revolt against Reason: The Social Theories of Georges Sorel* (London: Humanities Press, 1961).

12. See Jennings, *Georges Sorel*, 12–122, 134–36; see also Thorpe, *"The Workers Themselves,"* 282n41.

13. Bertrand, "Revolutionary Syndicalism in Italy," 139.

14. E. O'Connor, *Syndicalism in Ireland, 1917–1923* (Cork: Cork University Press, 1988), 6–8.

15. Sorel "prided himself on writing 'the principal document of syndicalist literature [*sic*],'" *Reflections on Violence*; see Jennings, *Georges Sorel*, 146.

16. Levine, *Syndicalism in France*, 153.

17. Rocker, *Anarcho-Syndicalism*, chapter 6.

18. E. Goldman, *Syndicalism: The Modern Menace to Capitalism* (New York: Mother Earth Publishing Association, 1913), 4

19. See Jennings, *Georges Sorel*, 118, 120, 143–46; Levine, *Syndicalism in France*, 158–61. While Jennings provides a good account of Sorel's views, he does not, unlike Levine, draw sufficient attention to the gulf between many of these ideas and those of the syndicalists. For example, Sorel's belief that capitalism needed to be "regenerated" or that the general strike was a "myth" would have been anathema to the syndicalists; compare to Levine, *Syndicalism in France*, 157–59. It is generous of Jennings to describe Sorel's "actual involvement" in the CGT as "minimal."

20. Ridley, *Revolutionary Syndicalism in France*, 38–44, 192, 249, 250–51.

21. Thorpe, *"The Workers Themselves,"* 282n40.

22. J.J. Roth, *Sorel and the Sorelians*, quoted in Thorpe, *"The Workers Themselves,"* 282n40.

23. Woodcock, *Anarchy or Chaos*, 61.

24. Joll, *The Anarchists*, 211–12.

25. Bertrand, "Revolutionary Syndicalism in Italy," 144–50.

26. O'Connor, *Syndicalism in Ireland*, 6–7; A. J. Gregor, *Young Mussolini and the Intellectual Origins of Fascism* (Berkeley: University of California Press, 1979); D. Roberts, *The Syndicalist Tradition and Italian Fascism* (Chapel Hill: University of North Carolina Press, 1979).

27. Levy, "Italian Anarchism," 53.

28. M. Colombo, "Armando Borghi," *Le Monde Libertaire*, November 10, 1988.

29. Ibid.

30. Levy, "Italian Anarchism," 73–74.

31. T. Abse, "The Rise of Fascism in an Industrial City," in *Rethinking Italian Fascism: Capitalism, Populism, and Culture*, ed. D. Forgacs (London: Lawrence and Wishart, 1986), 54; also of interest is "Italian Syndicalism and Fascism," *Black Flag: For Anarchist Resistance*, no. 217 (1999): 29. We would like to thank Iain McKay for drawing the Abse piece to our attention.

32. Levine, *Syndicalism in France*, 160–61.

33. L. Lorwin, "Syndicalism," in *Encyclopaedia of the Social Sciences* (New York: Macmillan, 1959), 497.

34. Joll, *The Anarchists*, 195–96.

35. Thorpe, *"The Workers Themselves,"* xiii–xiv.

36. Salerno, *Red November, Black November*, 52.

37. Quoted in Ibid., 52.

38. E. Goldman, *Syndicalism*, 5, 7.

39. Kropotkin, quoted in Nettlau, *A Short History of Anarchism*, 279.

40. Malatesta, "Syndicalism," 220.

41. Maximoff, *Constructive Anarchism*, 7.

42. Rocker, *Anarcho-Syndicalism*, chapter 4.

43. Thorpe, *"The Workers Themselves,"* xiii–xiv.

44. K. Marx, "Letter to Paul Lafargue in Paris," April 19, 1870, in *Marx, Engels, Lenin: Anarchism and Anarcho-syndicalism*, ed. N. Y. Kolpinsky (Moscow: Progress Publishers, 1972), 46; F. Engels, "The Bakuninists at Work: An Account of the Spanish Revolt in the Summer of 1873," in *Marx, Engels, Lenin: Anarchism and Anarcho-syndicalism*, ed. N. Y. Kolpinsky (1873; repr., Moscow: Progress Publishers, 1972), 132–33.

45. See also Cahm, *Kropotkin and the Rise of Revolutionary Anarchism*, chapter 9.

46. Quoted in Maximoff, *Constructive Anarchism*, 7.

47. Bakunin, "The Programme of the Alliance," 255; Bakunin, "The Policy of the International," 173.

48. Bakunin, "The Programme of the Alliance," 245.

49. Ibid., 249, 252, 255; see also 253–54.

50. Bakunin, "The Policy of the International," 174.

51. See Stekloff, *History of the First International*, 287–92; Woodcock, *Anarchism*, 232–34. The quotes are from Stekloff.

52. See Thorpe, *"The Workers Themselves,"* 253–54.

53. The best analysis of classical Marxism and the trade unions remains R. Hyman, *Marxism and the Sociology of Trade Unionism* (London: Pluto Press, 1971). As Hyman notes, even at their most "optimistic," Marx and Engels argued that unions were basically defensive bodies, which provided some immediate protection for workers. The real significance of unions was their potential to lay the basis for workers to "adopt political forms of action," helping to create the political party that alone could "challenge directly the whole structure of class domination." Even this "optimism" was "by no means unqualified"; see ibid., 4–20, 37–43.

54. B. Russell, *Roads to Freedom* (1920; repr., London: Routledge, 1993), 59, 62. Also compare to Ridley, *Revolutionary Syndicalism in France*, 1.

55. Schechter, *Radical Theories*, 24.

56. Bookchin, *The Spanish Anarchists*, 51, 54–55, 76–77, 87; see also M. Molnár and J. Pekmez, "Rural Anarchism in Spain and the 1873 Cantonalist Revolution," in *Rural Protest: Peasant Movements and Social Change*, ed. H. A. Landsberger (London: Macmillan, 1974), 167.

57. T. Kaplan, *Anarchists of Andalusia, 1868–1903* (Princeton, NJ: Princeton University Press, 1977), 136.

58. Bookchin, *The Spanish Anarchists*, 51–55, 132, 135–37.

59. J. Amsden, *Collective Bargaining and Class Conflict in Spain* (London: Weidenfeld and Nicholson, 1972), 14.

60. Maura, "The Spanish Case," 66–67.

61. On the FTRE, see Rocker, *Anarcho-Syndicalism*, chapter 6.

62. J. Casanovas, "Slavery, the Labour Movement, and Spanish Colonialism in Cuba, 1850–1890," *International Review of Social History* 40 (1995); J. Casanovas, "Labor and Colonialism in Cuba in the Second Half of the Nineteenth-Century" (PhD diss., State University of New York, 1994), especially chapters 6–9.

63. Casanovas, "Labour and Colonialism in Cuba in the Second Half of the Nineteenth-Century," 8, 300–2, 330–32, 336–41, 366–67.

64. F. Fernandez, *Cuban Anarchism: The History of a Movement* (Tucson, AZ: See Sharp Press, 2001), chapter 1, available at http://www.illegalvoices.org/bookshelf/cuban_anarchism/chapter_1_colonialsm_and_separatism_1865-1898_.html (accessed June 27, 2006).

65. Avrich, *The Haymarket Tragedy*, 51, 55.

66. See ibid., 73–75; Bekken, "The First Daily Anarchist Newspaper," 13–14.

67. For what has become the standard history, see Avrich, *The Haymarket Tragedy*. The final speeches of the Haymarket anarchists and related materials are collected in Fischer, "Adolph Fischer"; this was prepared during the trial by the imprisoned Albert Parsons, and published after his execution by his wife, Lucy Parsons, herself an anarchist. A range of primary materials and commentary may be found in D. Roediger and F. Rosemont, eds., *Haymarket Scrapbook* (Chicago: Charles H. Kerr Publishing Company, 1986). Also of interest is Bekken, "The First Daily Anarchist Newspaper"; B. C. Nelson, *Beyond the Martyrs: A Social History of Chicago's Anarchists, 1870–1900* (New Brunswick, NJ: Rutgers University Press, 1988).

68. J. Quail, *The Slow Burning Fuse: The Lost History of the British Anarchists* (London: Paladin, 1978), 90.

69. Foster, *From Bryan to Stalin*, 63.

70. Johanningsmeier, "William Z. Foster and the Syndicalist League of North America," 333.

71. See S. Salerno, "The Impact of Anarchism on the Founding of the IWW: The Anarchism of Thomas J. Hagerty," in *Haymarket Scrapbook*, ed. D. Roediger and F. Rosemont (Chicago: Charles H. Kerr Publishing Company, 1986), 189–91; Salerno, *Red November, Black November*, chapter 3.

72. Hart, *Anarchism and the Mexican Working Class*, 19–49.

73. Ibid., 29, 47, 54.

74. Ibid., 48.

75. Ibid., 50–54, 59.

76. Ibid., 48, 58.

77. Quoted in Guérin, *Anarchism*, 78.

78. Kropotkin, "Modern Science and Anarchism," 165, 171.

79. Quoted in Salerno, *Red November, Black November*, 53.

80. Foster, *From Bryan to Stalin*, 49.

81. Rocker, *Anarcho-Syndicalism*, chapter 6.

82. Beyer-Arnesen, "Anarcho-syndicalism," 20.

83. Bookchin, "Deep Ecology, Anarchosyndicalism, and the Future of Anarchist Thought," 50.

84. Joll, *The Anarchists*, 205.

85. Hobsbawm, *Revolutionaries*, 72–73. The odd spelling of "marxism" is from Hobsbawm's text.

86. Marshall, *Demanding the Impossible*, 500–1; Woodcock, *Anarchism*, 440.

87. Woodcock, *Anarchism*, 440.

88. Bookchin, "Deep Ecology, Anarchosyndicalism, and the Future of Anarchist Thought," 50–51.

89. V. Burgmann, *Revolutionary Industrial Unionism: The IWW in Australia* (Cambridge: Cambridge University Press, 1995), 42–47.

90. Rocker, *Anarcho-Syndicalism*, chapter 6.

91. Burgmann, *Revolutionary Industrial Unionism*, 42.

92. K. Marx and F. Engels, "From the Resolutions of the General Congress Held in the Hague," in *Marx, Engels, Lenin: Anarchism and Anarcho-syndicalism*, ed. N. Y. Kolpinsky (1872; repr., Moscow: Progress Publishers, 1972), 85.

93. Reproduced in Dubofsky, *"Big Bill" Haywood*, 159–60, appendix 2.

94. The *Preamble* includes the phrase "Instead of the conservative motto, 'A fair day's wage for a fair day's work', we must inscribe on our banner the revolutionary watchword, 'Abolition of the wage system.'" This is a quote from Marx, *Value, Price and Profit*, 126–27.

95. Burgmann, *Revolutionary Industrial Unionism*, 42–47.

96. See, for example, Dubofsky, *We Shall Be All*, 5, 19–35, 73, 76–77; Dubofsky, *"Big Bill" Haywood*.

97. Woodcock, *Anarchism*, 440; Rocker, *Anarcho-Syndicalism*, chapter 6.

98. Salerno, *Red November, Black November*, 3–5.

99. For instance, see Industrial Workers of the World, *The IWW in Theory and Practice*.

100. Salerno, "The Impact of Anarchism on the Founding of the IWW"; Salerno, *Red November, Black November*, especially 69–90.

101. P. S. Foner, *The Industrial Workers of the World, 1905–17* (New York: International Publishers, 1965), 143.

102. Dubofsky, *"Big Bill" Haywood*, 66.

103. Industrial Workers of the World, *What Is the IWW? A Candid Statement of Its Principles, Objects, and Methods*, 2nd ed. (Cleveland, OH: IWW Publishing Bureau, 1924), available at http://www.workerseducation.org/crutch/pamphlets/whatistheiww.html (accessed June 15, 2004).

104. Salerno, *Red November, Black November*, 115.

105. P. Brissenden, *The IWW: A Study in American Syndicalism* (New York: Columbia University Press, 1920), 46.

106. Dubofsky, *"Big Bill" Haywood*, 67–68.

107. Foner, *The Industrial Workers of the World*, 158–59; for an outline of the IWW's ideology, see also, in particular, 123–71.

108. Justus Ebert, an IWW writer, was angered by the view that the IWW was syndicalist. "Furious … he defended Marxism and the conduct of the German Social Democratic Party and repeated all the slanderous attacks in the integrity and the ideology of Bakunin and the libertarian wing of the First International"; see S. Dolgoff, *Fragments: A Memoir* (London: Refract Publications, 1986), 134.

109. See, for example, Haywood and Bohm, *Industrial Socialism*, 4, 40, 44, 50–52, 55–56, 58, 62.

110. Avrich, *The Haymarket Tragedy*, 23–24, 40–41, 51–55.

111. See McKee, "The Influence of Syndicalism upon Daniel De Leon," 276.

112. B. K. Johnpoll and L. Johnpoll, *The Impossible Dream: The Rise and Decline of the American Left* (Westport, CT: Greenwood Press, 1981), 249, 252, 259, 262–63, 267.

113. McKee, "The Influence of Syndicalism upon Daniel De Leon," 276–77. See also R. J. Holton, *British Syndicalism: Myths and Realities* (London: Pluto Press, 1976), 2; D. K. McKee, "Daniel De Leon: A Reappraisal," *Labour History*, no. 1 (1960); Tasuro Nomura, "Partisan Politics in and around the I.W.W: The Earliest Phase," *Journal of the Faculty of Foreign Studies*, no. 1 (1977): 98, 105–8, 111–13, 118–20; L. G. Seretan, *Daniel De Leon: The Odyssey of an American Marxist* (Cambridge, MA: Harvard University Press, 1979), 177–79, 184–86

114. McKee, "The Influence of Syndicalism upon Daniel De Leon," 277.

115 Socialist Labour Party [De Leon], *The Socialist Labour Party*, 18; see also De Leon, *The Preamble of the Industrial Workers of the World*, 23.

116. Socialist Labour Party [De Leon], *The Socialist Labour Party*, 21.

117. Ibid., 23; De Leon, *The Preamble of the Industrial Workers of the World*, 23, 27.

118. De Leon, *The Preamble of the Industrial Workers of the World*, 24.

119. See, for example, De Leon, "With Marx for Text"; De Leon, "Syndicalism"; McKee, "The Influence of Syndicalism upon Daniel De Leon," 278.

120. D. De Leon, "Industrial Unionism," *Daily People*, January 20, 1913.

121. De Leon specifically denounced the inclusion of any reforms in the SLP's electoral platform; see, for example, D. De Leon, "Getting Something Now," *Daily People*, September 6, 1910.

122. De Leon, *The Preamble of the Industrial Workers of the World*, 21, 23–24, 25, 27–28.

123. "Another brand of syndicalism ... the Socialist Labour Party ... believed in a certain amount of political action, but only as a subsidiary to industrial action"; N. Milton, introduction to *John MacLean: In the Rapids of Revolution: Essays, Articles, and Letters*, ed. N. Milton (London: Allison and Busby, 1978), 13.

124. See, for example, Haywood and Bohm, *Industrial Socialism*.

125. Foner, *The Industrial Workers of the World*, 167–71.

126. Dubofsky, *"Big Bill" Haywood*, 159–60, appendix 2.

127. Hinton, *The First Shop Stewards Movement*, 283.

128. See Allen, *The Politics of James Connolly*, 59–64.

129. We would like to thank Alan MacSimoin for his comments on this issue; correspondence with Alan MacSimoin, December 3, 1998.

130. Holton, *British Syndicalism*.

131. J. Connolly, *Socialism Made Easy* (Chicago: Charles H. Kerr, 1909), 48.

132. Ibid., 43, 46, 56–59.

133. C. Kostick, *Revolution in Ireland: Popular Militancy, 1917 to 1923* (London: Pluto Press, 1996), 15; for a contrary view, see Allen, *The Politics of James Connolly*, ix–xviii, 125.

134. Compare to O. D. Edwards and B. Ransome, introduction to *James Connolly: Selected Political Writings*, ed. O. D. Edwards and B. Ransome (London: Jonathan Cape, 1973), 25, 27; B. Ransome, *Connolly's Marxism* (London: Pluto Press, 1980), 40. Since writing these lines we have come across B. Anderson, *James Connolly and the Irish Left* (Dublin: Irish Academic Press, 1994). This makes the case for Connolly's syndicalism, but still calls Connolly a Marxist.

135. Kedward, *The Anarchists*, 5; Joll, *The Anarchists*, 223.

136. Hobsbawm, *Revolutionaries*, 72–73.

137. Woodcock, *Anarchism*, 202.

138. Dubofsky, *"Big Bill" Haywood*, 81, 95.

139. F. Thompson with P. Murfin, *The IWW: Its First Seventy Years, 1905–1975* (Chicago: IWW, 1976), 129, 150.

140. For a partial overview, see Hinton, *The First Shop Stewards Movement*.

141. Cited in ibid., 129.

142. MacLean regarded his former student as "an openly avowed anarchist"; J. MacLean, "A Scottish Communist Party," in *John MacLean: In the Rapids of Revolution: Essays, Articles, and Letters*,

ed. N. Milton (December 1920; repr., London: Allison and Busby, 1978), 225. Gallacher wrote an autobiography of his early years as an activist in which he greatly downplayed his role in the SLP; W. Gallacher, *Revolt on the Clyde*, 4th ed. (1936; repr., London: Lawrence and Wishart, 1978).

143. The Trade Union Educational League was initially syndicalist, but shifted to Communism along with Foster in the 1920s; see, for example, W. Z. Foster, *The Railroaders' Next Step*, Labor Herald pamphlets, no. 1 (Chicago: Trade Union Educational League, 1921).

144. G. Williams, *A Proletarian Order: Antonio Gramsci, Factory Councils and the Origins of Italian Communism, 1911–21* (London: Pluto Press, 1975), 194–95.

145. Woodcock, *Anarchism*, 352.

146. B. Bayerlein and M. van der Linden, "Revolutionary Syndicalism in Portugal," in *Revolutionary Syndicalism: An International Perspective*, ed. M. van der Linden and W. Thorpe (Otterup, Denmark: Scolar, 1990), 160–64.

147 W. Thorpe, "Keeping the Faith: The German Syndicalists in the First World War," *Central European History* 33, no. 2 (2000): 195.

148. Rocker, *Anarcho-Syndicalism*, chapter 6.

149. See, inter alia, L. J. W. van der Walt, "'The Industrial Union Is the Embryo of the Socialist Commonwealth': The International Socialist League and Revolutionary Syndicalism in South Africa, 1915–1919," *Comparative Studies of South Asia, Africa, and the Middle East* 19, no. 1 (1999); L. J. W. van der Walt, "Bakunin's Heirs in South Africa: Race, Class, and Revolutionary Syndicalism from the IWW to the International Socialist League," *Politikon* 30, no. 1 (2004); L. J. W. van der Walt, "Anarchism and Syndicalism in South Africa, 1904–1921: Rethinking the History of Labour and the Left" (PhD diss., University of the Witwatersrand, 2007).

150. Burgmann, *Revolutionary Industrial Unionism*, 266.

151 Munck, *Argentina*, 82, 87–88; Rocker, *Anarcho-Syndicalism*, chapter 6.

152. J. Hart, "Revolutionary Syndicalism in Mexico," in *Revolutonary Syndicalism: An International Perspective*, ed. W. Thorpe and M. van der Linden (Otterup, Denmark: Scolar Press, 1990), 194, 197.

153. Hart, *Anarchism and the Mexican Working Class*, 156; Hart, "Revolutionary Syndicalism in Mexico," 200–1.

154. Thompson with Murfin, *The IWW*, 50.

155. B. Carr, "Marxism and Anarchism in the Formation of the Mexican Communist Party, 1910–19," *Hispanic American Historical Review* 63, no. 2 (1983

156. See P. De Shazo, *Urban Workers and Labor Unions in Chile, 1902-1927* (Madison: University of Wisconsin Press, 1983).

157. Anonymous, *Chile: The IWW and FORC* (Sydney: Rebel Worker, n.d.), 4.

158. S. J. Hirsch, "The Anarcho-Syndicalist Roots of a Multi-Class Alliance: Organised Labor and the Peruvian Aprista Party, 1900–1933" (PhD diss., George Washington University, 1997).

159. See Fernandez, *Cuban Anarchism*, chapter 2, available at http://illvox.org/2007/06/23/chapter-two-intervention-and-the-republic (accessed November 22, 2008); Shaffer, "Purifying the Environment for the Coming New Dawn."

160. D. Gallin and P. Horn, *Organising Informal Women Workers*, available at http://www.street-net.org.za/english/GallinHornpaper.htm (accessed September 2006).

161. See B. Anderson, *Under Three Flags: Anarchism and the Anti-colonial Imagination* (London: Verso, 2006).

162. Ibid., 228.

163. Ibid., 229.

164. Dirlik, *Anarchism in the Chinese Revolution*, 15, 27, 170.

165. "In 1919 and 1920, Mao leaned toward anarchism rather than socialism. Only in January 1921 did he at last draw the explicit conclusion that anarchism would not work, and that Russia's proletarian dictatorship represented the model which must be followed"; S. R. Schram, "General

Introduction: Mao Zedong and the Chinese Revolution, 1912–1949," in *Mao's Road to Power: Revolutionary Writings, 1912–1949*, ed. S. R. Schram (New York: M. E. Sharpe, 1992), xvi. See A. Dirlik, *The Origins of Chinese Communism* (Oxford: Oxford University Press, 1989), 178–79; E. J. Perry, *Shanghai on Strike: The Politics of Chinese Labor* (Stanford, CA: Stanford University Press, 1993), particularly chapters 4 and 5.

166. Dirlik, *The Origins of Chinese Communism*, 217–19.

167. Nohara Shirō, "Anarchists and the May 4 Movement in China," *Libero International*, no. 1 (January 1975). Available online at http://www.negations.net/libero/number1@andmay4.htm (accessed December 1, 2006).

168. Dirlik, *The Origins of Chinese Communism*, 214–15.

169. Dirlik, *Anarchism in the Chinese Revolution*, 290.

170. See, inter alia, Crump, *Hatta Shuzo and Pure Anarchism in Interwar Japan*, chapter 2.

171. See, inter alia, ibid., chapter 2.

172. Ibid., 78.

173. Ibid., 92, 97.

174. Bookchin, *Social Anarchism or Lifestyle Anarchism*.

Tenants' rally in Lisbon, Portugal 1921.

Rent strikes and community organising were an important part of anarchist and syndicalist activity: as part of the project of building counterpower, mass anarchists built dense and overlapping networks of popular, associational life. These included theatre troupes, neighbourhood committees, workers' night-schools, and even popular universities in countries as diverse as Egypt, Peru, Cuba, and China. *Picture courtesy of João Freire.*

The Barcelona trams under self-management in 1936.

The trams were among the thousands of industries and farms placed under worker and peasant self-management during the Spanish Revolution (1936–1939), in which the anarchists and syndicalists played a central role. The explosion of creative energy unleashed by the Spanish worker's control of their own lives was evocatively captured in George Orwell's *Homage to Catalonia* (1938).

CHAPTER 6

Ideas, Structure, and Armed Action: Unions, Politics, and the Revolution

Both insurrectionist and mass anarchism are faced with a series of difficult challenges. In this chapter, we explore syndicalism in more depth, addressing ourselves to several critical issues: how can a syndicalist union avoid evolving into orthodox unionism, which focuses solely on immediate issues, and typically develops large and moderate bureaucracies? If anarchism is about the emancipation of the popular classes as a whole, how can syndicalism address the needs of those sectors of the working class and peasantry that are outside wage labour? Finally, assuming a revolutionary general strike takes place, can syndicalism effectively deal with the threat of armed counterrevolution?

We argue that syndicalism stressed a combination of radically democratic unionism and political education, welded together by direct action, as the means to develop a style of unionism that was insurgent and revolutionary. We also contend that historically, syndicalism sought to organise beyond the workplace, promote the struggles of the unemployed, working-class communities, women, and youth, and link with the peasantry. And we suggest that while many syndicalists underestimated the dangers of armed counterrevolution, there was a substantial current that aimed at armed self-defence, the destruction of the state apparatus, and the formation of a "libertarian social power" or "libertarian polity."[1] In general, syndicalism emphasised the need for both counterpower and revolutionary counterculture as well as alliances and struggles beyond the workplace. It should not be interpreted as a form of economistic or workerist unionism.

Union Activism, Anarchist Ideology, and Union Bureaucracy

Many important questions about syndicalism were raised at an international anarchist conference held in 1907 in Amsterdam and attended by about a thousand people, with eighty delegates present. Those in attendance were drawn from most of the European and Latin American countries as well as Japan and the United States. The meeting, which took place in the context of the rise of the French CGT and a second wave of syndicalism, was one of a series of ongoing attempts to form an anarchist international after the demise of the Black International. Central to the conference was the question of resurgent syndicalism.[2]

Perhaps unsurprisingly, the Amsterdam Congress endorsed syndicalism, provided the space for participants from eight countries to hold meetings to set up a syndicalist network, and established the multilingual *Bulletin International du Movement Syndicaliste* ("Bulletin of the International Syndicalist Movement").[3] This weekly was distributed and reprinted worldwide, and appeared with a great deal of regularity until mid-1914; edited by Christian Cornilessen (1864–1942), the bulletin was funded by the Dutch, German, French, Swedish, and Bohemian (Czech) syndicalists, with occasional aid from the U.S. IWW. Cornilessen trained as a schoolteacher in the Netherlands, and was initially a Marxist but moved toward syndicalism. He linked up with the radicals in the Social Democratic Union, among them Domela Nieuwenhuis, who were moving to anarchism.[4] Cornilessen was an important figure in the National Labour Secretariat (NAS), founded in 1893—the Netherlands largest union centre, which adopted a syndicalist platform in 1901—until he moved to France, where he immersed himself in the CGT. He remained active in the postwar period and also produced a number of works on socialist economic theory.

Pierre Monatte (1881–1960), representing the French CGT, and Amèdèe Dunois, a Swiss, defended syndicalism at the congress, presenting it as taking anarchism out of the "ivory tower of philosophic speculation" into the "school of will, of energy, and of fertile thinking."[5] The son of a blacksmith and employed as a proofreader, Monatte was the editor of *La Vie Ouvrière* ("Workers' Life") and later active in the PCF. Expelled in 1924 for opposing Comintern policies and authoritarianism, he returned to syndicalism, founding *La Révolution Prolétarienne* ("Workers' Revolution"). He remained active for many years, dying in 1960.

Malatesta responded to Monatte's input with an address that is of great interest as it raises questions about the adequacy of syndicalism, or at least about the views of many syndicalists. Before going into these questions, it is worth noting that Malatesta was by no means the staunch opponent of syndicalism that he appears in the literature.[6] As of the 1890s, Malatesta supported syndicalism, arguing that unions were of "vital importance," the "most powerful force for social transformation," "must play a most useful, and perhaps necessary, role in the transition from present society," and could serve as "the first necessary nucleus for the continuation of social life and the reorganisation of production without the bosses and parasites."[7] Unions were powerful forces for change, helped awaken workers to the class struggle, raised proletarian aspirations, won real improvements, and provided lessons in solidarity.[8] It is against this backdrop that we can understand why Malatesta sought to "give the libertarian movement more organisational coherency through the creation of anarchist trade unions" when he stayed in Argentina in the 1890s.[9]

Malatesta's response to Monatte started, perhaps unsurprisingly, by stressing the anarchist roots of syndicalism, and advocating "the most active participation" in the unions for propaganda and mass organising. Syndicalism was, Malatesta stated, an "excellent means of action," the unions were "doubtless the best of all the means" for revolution, and the general strike was an "excellent means for starting" a revolution.[10] Yet Malatesta rejected the view (which he believed some syndicalists held) that unions would automatically act in a revolutionary manner. According to this line of reasoning, unions that were free of political parties, were run democratically, and adopted direct action would simply plunge down the road to the revolutionary general strike. Every union action, then, was a step toward the revolution.

For Malatesta, however, union work was only *potentially* revolutionary. It would be a "great and fatal illusion to believe" that the union movement will "by its very nature, lead to ... revolution."[11] Under normal circumstances, unions tended to look after the immediate material interests of workers and foster a conservative spirit. This was, Malatesta claimed elsewhere, a "natural tendency," for unions' normal operations were "reformist" and about compromise.[12] Moreover, unions were prone to develop layers of paid officials, whose personal interests lay in social peace and steady incomes from the unions—in current parlance, union bureaucracies.[13] Therefore, unions were not a "sufficient means" for revolution, for their normal state was that of a "legalitarian and even conservative movement with no other accessible end but the amelioration of the conditions of work." The union "in itself" could not be a "revolutionary ... negation of ... present society."[14]

In addition, Malatesta was concerned about the prospect of syndicalism becoming a narrow workerism that was sectional and ignored the popular sectors outside of wage labour. Capitalism pitted people against each other, and the working class was deeply divided "between employed and unemployed, between men and women, between native and foreign workers in their midst, between workers who use a public service and those who work in that service, between those who have a trade and those who want to learn it" as well as between countries, industries, nationalities, occupations, and races. Unions easily devolved into championing the narrow interests of particular sections of workers, striving to turn their members into "the aristocrats of the factory" while waging war on the "non-organised workers ... [the] proletariat in rags." How would syndicalism deal with the "ever growing unemployed proletariat" and the peasantry? It was in this sense, from a broad view of class politics, that Malatesta argued the revolution was not the task of a "single class" but of all "enslaved humanity," which was enslaved "from the triple viewpoint, economic, political and moral."[15]

Finally, Malatesta's address raised questions about the revolutionary process. He rejected the view, which he believed was held by some syndicalists, that capitalism and the state could be peacefully toppled by a general strike, making "armed insurrection unnecessary." More specifically, he rejected the notion that a universal cessation of work would force the abdication of the ruling class, which "dying of hunger, will be obliged to surrender"; the rich and powerful controlled the stores, and would more likely starve the working class out than the reverse.[16]

Mass Anarchism, Radical Counterculture, and Syndicalism

How effectively did syndicalism address these concerns? The record suggests that—like Malatesta, who stressed the need for propaganda to "awaken" the unions and the workers to a "shared ideal," and "taking over the direction of production"—syndicalists generally maintained that misery alone was not revolutionary.[17] To change the world a "new social philosophy," a "new faith" in the possibility of a new social order and the ability of ordinary people to create a new society, were all need-ed.[18] Maximoff argued that syndicalists must respond to "all burning questions of the day," but "relate them to the final goal and utilise every opportunity for agitation, propaganda and the organisation of the exploited classes."[19] Likewise for Kubo, "We should seize every opportunity in economic and political struggles so that anarchist thought may prevail."[20] Goldman, another syndicalist, maintained that a "*funda-mental transvaluation of values*" and the removal of the principle of hierarchy were the very bases of revolutionary change in society.[21]

Rocker believed that union struggle itself played something of an educational role: it was "as a producer and creator of social wealth" that the worker becomes "aware of his strength." Workers realised their real power in society, their role as a productive but exploited class, gained a glimmer of their potential to remake the world, and learned the importance of solidarity and direct action. He therefore highlighted the "general cultural significance of the labour struggle." The union was a "practical school, a university of experience, from which they draw instruction and enlightenment in richest measure." The workers learn from and are radicalised by their experiences in struggles, and develop a powerful solidarity among them-selves—a "feeling of mutual helpfulness" under difficult conditions that matures into a "vital consciousness of a community of fate," and then into a "new sense of right." Yet this alone could *not* lead to a revolutionary movement. It was absolutely critical that there was ongoing "educational work" "directed toward the develop-ment of independent thought and action." This involved, as Rocker saw it, "the effort to make clear to the workers the intrinsic connections among social problems," and "by technical instruction and the development of their administrative capacities to prepare them for their role of re-shapers of economic life."[22]

There is no real difference between such views and those of Malatesta. All share the position that changing hearts and minds is central to the revolutionary project as well as the creation of counterpower. The stress that syndicalists routinely placed on winning the battle of ideas directs attention to an important feature of the mass anarchist tradition more generally. This is the project of creating a revolution-ary counterculture within the popular classes. According to Rocker, in the same way that the "educational work" of the anarcho-syndicalists was partly "directed toward the development of independent thought and action," they were opposed to the "centralising tendencies ... so characteristic of political labour parties."[23] For Malatesta,

> We who do not seek power, only want the consciences of men; only those who wish to dominate prefer sheep, the better to lead them. We prefer intelligent workers, even if they are our opponents, to anarchists who are such only in order to follow us like sheep. We want freedom for ev-erybody; we want the masses to make the revolution for the masses. The person who thinks with his own brain is to be preferred to the one who blindly approves everything.... Better an error consciously committed and in good faith, than a good action performed in a servile manner.[24]

It was characteristic of syndicalist unions that they put a great deal of effort into political education and the development of a radical popular counterculture. The first anarchist daily newspaper in the world seems to have been the *Chicago-*

er Arbeiter-Zeitung ("Chicago Worker News"): started as a Marxist paper in 1877, it came under anarchist IWPA control and was edited by the Haymarket martyr Spies—a unionist and former SLP member—from 1884 to 1886.[25] The paper was part of a powerful anarchist counterculture that was active in unionism, held innumerable plays, picnics, dances, and rallies, published many journals in multiple languages for a multiethnic working class, and even paraded armed detachments. This was a "distinctively working-class, revolutionary culture."[26] It was a "rich libertarian counter-culture deeply rooted in the working classes and totally at odds with the values of the prevailing system."[27]

Spanish syndicalist unions were equally immersed in a rich and dense network of anarchist community centres, schools, and libraries—the *ateneus libertarias* ("libertarian athenaeums") that existed in every district and village of anarchist strength—and a vast anarchist press.[28] The CNT alone published scores of newspapers by 1936, including the largest dailies in Spain.[29] The notion that, since syndicalist unions generally admit workers regardless of their politics, syndicalists must therefore believe that the unions' democratic structures will suffice to make workers into revolutionaries, and therefore, for example, even that the great majority of CNT members were not really anarchists, is not very convincing.[30] The Chambers of Labour in Italy—initially municipal bodies designed to promote conciliation and act as labour exchanges, they become self-managed workers' centres—provided a major conduit of anarchist and syndicalist influence.[31] In France, the Bourses du Travail were specifically used by activists like Pelloutier as centres of radical and libertarian counterculture.[32]

The U.S. IWW, to offer another example, published thousands of pamphlets and dozens of periodicals, and also operated countless local halls where workers could read books on a wide range of subjects.[33] It "staged hundreds of Sunday Educational meetings and open forums, held classes, toured speakers who addressed street-corner meetings and indoor mass meetings all over the country, opened union halls where workers could get their latest Wobbly literature, [and] held 'bull sessions' on such subjects as 'Improved Machinery and Unemployment,' 'Industrial versus Craft Unionism,' 'The General Strike,' etc."[34] As Salerno reminds us, it is a mistake to assess the IWW purely in terms of numbers and the strength of formal union structures; the union local, which grouped workers from a range of industries and operated union halls, was probably the most important structure, and the nexus of a radical proletarian counterculture that had an impact far beyond the confines of the formal union.[35]

For the broad anarchist tradition, revolution could not be imposed or delegated; it was, literally, the task of the popular classes and required that a substantial number of people accepted its necessity. Rejecting authoritarian models like Leninism, syndicalist unions sought to minimise the gulf between the conscious anarchist and syndicalist minority and the masses of the people by winning over as many people as possible to their views, and by promoting the practices of self-organisation and direct action. Even if propaganda by the deed was elitist in practice, its basic aim remained *propaganda*. The emphasis placed on popular education by syndicalist unions, then, should be seen as typical of anarchism more generally, and syndicalist efforts should be seen as part of the larger project of forming a revolutionary counterculture as a piece of the project of building counterpower.

Anarchist Schools and Syndicalist Education

Anarchist schools, centres, media, and theatre played a central role in this drive, and should be seen as key institutions in the broad anarchist tradition. Their influence is less easily estimated than that of the other major anarchist institution, the syndicalist union, but it cannot be understated. On one level, anarchist schools were an attempt to promote more libertarian methods of education along with a democratic and participatory pedagogy. Both Bakunin and Kropotkin advocated an "integral education" that covered the humanities, the natural sciences, and manual and mental skills.[36] On another level, anarchist schools were an attempt to overcome the inequalities in education arising from an inequitable social and economic order, and provide popular education.

In both cases, however, anarchist schools offered a critical worldview that rejected the ideology promoted in the education supplied by the church and state—a worldview that stressed class identity, a rejection of the status quo, and the necessity for fundamental social change. The Spanish anarchist Francisco Ferrer i Guàrdia (1859–1909), who opened the Modern School in 1901, became closely identified with anarchist schooling. Harassed by the authorities on several occasions, he was falsely charged with inciting the 1909 general strike and popular revolt in Spain against conscription for the colonial war in Morocco, known as the *Semana Trágica* or "Tragic Week." Despite massive international protests, Ferrer was executed. While his pedagogy may have had its limitations, it is undeniable that his death popularised libertarian educational methods and anarchist schools.[37]

Well before Ferrer, anarchist and syndicalist centres and schools consistently played a central role in the movement. An early example was La Escuela del Rayo y del Socialismo ("The School of the Ray of Socialism") in Chalco, Mexico. This school was established in 1865 by Plotino Rhodokanaty (1824–?), a Greek immigrant influenced by Fourier and Proudhon, and a founder of La Social; Zalacosta was also actively involved.[38] Its most notable graduate was the anarchist peasant militant Julio Chávez López (1845–1869).[39] The twentieth-century Mexican militants of the COM operated "Rational Schools" in which members of the anarchist group Luz ("Light," of which more later) ran courses in political ideology, and their efforts contrasted favourably with "the Mexican government's miserable failure to provide public services in the field of education."[40] In Egypt, an "anarchist nucleus" that included Galleani founded the Free Popular University in Alexandria; there was also an attempt to form a second university in Cairo.[41] The university drew in European as well as Egyptian and Syrian workers, and was intended to promote anarchism.

In Cuba, the anarchists quickly seized on the *lectura*—a tradition in which a worker read aloud to fellow workers during working hours that emerged in the 1860s—to promote their ideas. In the 1880s, the Workers' Circle—the *de facto* federation of unions in Havana—operated an educational centre, with a library and schools for children and workers. These challenged for the first time "the racially segregated and non-laicist [clerical] municipal and religious school system in Cuba," and had a "strong prolabour character."[42] In the twentieth century, Cuban anarchists continued to promote a revolutionary popular counterculture that reshaped every aspect of people's daily lives.[43] Its institutions included the anarchist press, rational schools, popular theatre, and cultural events; attended by the whole family, and featuring revolutionary songs as well as recitations of anarchist poetry by children, they provided an alternative to the official rituals of nationalism and religion.

In early twentieth-century Brazil, the anarchists alone "offered the transplanted, alienated and oppressed workers a sense of their own decency and dignity," with "free schools, people's universities, social drama groups," and "intense educational, sociological, broadly libertarian propaganda."[44] In the United States, a number of anarchist Modern Schools were established in the twentieth century, starting with the Ferrer Centre in New York City in 1911, which was formed by Berkman, De Cleyre, Goldman, and others, and anarchists were involved with other socialists in the Socialist Sunday School movement.[45]

During the Ukrainian Revolution, the anarchists aimed to establish rational schools, but their efforts were hampered by the ongoing war.[46] In Peru, Manuel González Prada (1844–1918, of whom more later) established the National Library in 1912. In China, anarchists formed several similar bodies, such as the Labour Movement Training Institute and the National Labour University, both established in 1927.[47] In France, Sebastian Faure (1858–1942) ran a libertarian school called La Ruche ("The Beehive"). Born to a middle-class Catholic family, and initially identifying as a political socialist, Faure became an anarchist in 1888. He was arrested many times, was closely associated with Michel, was active in antimilitarism, and starting in 1926, prepared the *Encyclopedie Anarchiste* ("Anarchist Encyclopaedia"). He also published *Le Libertaire* ("The Libertarian") beginning in 1889, which survives today as *Le Monde Libertaire* ("The Libertarian World").

While Nettlau suggested that projects of popular education through schools, theatres, and workers' centres "brought little added energy and little new force to anarchist ideas," it would seem that such initiatives were absolutely critical to the strength of anarchism and syndicalism as well as the project of counterpower.[48] The view that a revolutionary movement must aim to establish an ideological counter-hegemony as part of the class struggle is often attributed to Antonio Gramsci, a founder of the Italian Communist Party (PCI). Such ideas, however, were common currency in the broad anarchist tradition many decades before Gramsci wrote, as anarchists and syndicalists struggled to create an "oppositional counter-public" that could change the world.[49]

Democracy and Direct Action

In 1907, Malatesta had also suggested that unions must "advocate and practice direct action, decentralisation, autonomy and individual initiative" if they were not to degenerate."[50] This was precisely what syndicalists did, aiming at a militant—and radically democratic—union movement that embraced workers in different industries, in different occupations and grades within the same industry, and regardless of divisions of sex, race, and nationality. The ideal syndicalist union structure was a dual federation: there were specific unions for each sector of the economy, and all were brought together into a federation; at the same time, the different unions were interlinked through horizontal federations at the local level that brought together workers from different industries in the same locality. This structure can be traced back to the FORE in Spain.[51]

In Rocker's view, the problem with centralist styles of organising was that they concentrated power in the hands of a few, were attended by "barren official routine," "crushe[d] individual conviction, kill[ed] all personal initiative by lifeless discipline and bureaucratic ossification, and permit[ted] no independent action." So, syndicalists favoured instead federalism, "free combination from below upward," and the "right of self-determination of every member." This developed among the workers an "irresistible spirit of solidarity" and "tenacious belligerence."[52] Likewise, Ford and Foster stressed the "fundamental principle" that the "unions be decentralised and ... the workers alone have the power to decide."[53]

To avoid the problem of union bureaucracy, syndicalists emphasised a union structure that ensured that initiative and decision making reside at the local level, with local sections united through delegate structures both within and between industries. Union affairs would be run in a highly decentralised manner: the basic unit of decision making would be a workers' assembly within a given workplace—or several assemblies, if the workplace was large—that would elect a committee of mandated delegates to coordinate activity, enter negotiations, and communicate with other workplaces. The different workplaces would be federated through these committees, and the growth of a full-time union leadership, or "bureaucracy," would be avoided as far as possible. Whenever possible, delegates were to perform their duties while continuing to work at their own jobs.

The "decentralised form of the unions," asserted Ford and Foster, helped remove the "very foundation of labour fakerism, viz., delegated power."[54] The IWW, for its part, developed the slogan "We are all leaders," and placed strict limits on the power and income of paid union officials; an extremist "decentraliser" faction in its ranks even wanted to abolish the national office bearers' committee, and replace union congresses with referenda and local initiatives, opposing any delegation of tasks.[55]

An Iron Law of Oligarchy?

It is, though, inevitable that a large and successful syndicalist union would have at least some paid officials; these could include paid organisers, editors of the union press, and record keepers. Must this lead, like Robert Michels famously argued, to the operation of an unstoppable "iron law of oligarchy" in which a large organisation inevitably generates a specialised layer of leadership, which equally inevitably, uses the mass organisation for its own ends?[56] Michels praised anarchism as the first current to directly address questions of hierarchy and oligarchy, and believed the major anarchist figures, like Kropotkin and Malatesta, were "as a rule morally superior to the leaders of the organised parties working in the political field." He also suggested that syndicalism had, with a "genuinely scientific scepticism ... stripped away the veils which conceal the power exercised by the democracy in the state ... in acute opposition with the needs of the working class."[57]

Nonetheless, Michels held that an iron law of oligarchy applied to "all organisations as such without exception," and that syndicalist unions had an "oligarchical character" and were themselves an "organised elite" that dominated the unorganised workers.[58] Indeed, Michels's thesis can be considered "above all, a polemical attack on syndicalism" and the possibilities of democracy in radical mass movements.[59] (It is not insignificant that Michels was a former member of the German SDP and the Italian PSI with a strong leaning toward syndicalism; he became disillusioned with the Left, adopted the elitist view that the masses could not rule society, and ended up an apologist for fascism.)[60]

The close linkage between the iron law of oligarchy thesis and fascist conclusions immediately raises concerns about his analysis. There are, however, more basic problems with his claims. In the first place, his thesis is excessively deterministic and teleological in character; it does not take adequate account of the possibility that if a mass democratic organisation might develop oligarchic tendencies, an oligarchic organisation may also, under some circumstances, develop into a more democratic one, in part due to changing external conditions—something that Michels ignored.[61] Moreover, by focusing on the role of leaders, Michels took inadequate account of the ways in which democratic and decentralised structures, plus a strongly democratic culture among the rank and file, act as checks on oligarchic tendencies. He ignored, as a result, cases in which unions and other organisations have been able to avoid the development and domination of entrenched oligarchies.[62] He also missed the role of the rank and file's politics in developing democratic unions.[63]

It makes more sense, then, to recognise that while a tendency toward oligarchy exists in mass organisations, there is also a tendency toward democracy. The syndicalists certainly believed that both were possibilities, and their proposals for a radically democratic style of unionism—and their emphasis on political education, to be discussed below—were seen as safeguards against the emergence of a centralised and conservative leadership. Moreover, syndicalists developed a number of mechanisms for limiting the ability of paid officials in the syndicalist unions to usurp power. If oligarchy and democracy were both tendencies in unionism, syndicalist unionism sought by every means to ensure that it was democracy that would prevail.

The Spanish CNT sought to minimise the number of paid officials and their power by stressing that union work should, whenever possible, be undertaken by unpaid volunteers, that the union structure must keep power in the hands of ordinary members, and that anyone holding office, paid or not, must be directly accountable and operate within strict mandates. Ford and Foster proposed a number of other means to avoid developing a layer of "labour fakers," or treacherous and self-interested union leaders. The union treasury should be kept as small as possible, and avoid accumulating large strike and benefit funds. Any paid positions must be kept as unattractive as possible through low salaries as well as the dangers invariably associated with such posts in revolutionary unions. Only the "best and most courageous" workers would therefore consider such posts; any emergent labour fakers would be given "short shrift."[64]

Alliances and the Struggle outside the Workplace

The question of how a syndicalist union movement should relate to sections of the popular classes outside direct wage labour had also been raised by Malatesta, whose remedy was that "we must remain anarchists, in all the strength and breadth of that definition," and promote the anarchist idea on the land, in the barracks, and in the schools as well as in the factories, and mobilise all "enslaved humanity."[65]

Now, at the heart of syndicalism lies the premise that revolutionary unions are the *decisive* and *irreplaceable* organs of popular counterpower: only such bodies can provide the means for the expropriation of the means of production worked by waged labour. This is not a role that anarchist or syndicalist political groups, community bodies, movements of the unemployed, and youth and women's groups can undertake. The only possible qualification to this claim is that the peasantry, which cannot be organised in the same manner and with the same immediate objectives as the working class, may require different structures for the development of counterpower and revolutionary expropriation. The situation is different for waged farmworkers, who can be organised in the same manner as urban industrial workers. Even so, syndicalists rarely ignored other popular constituencies.

How could a syndicalist union movement relate to other sectors of the popular classes? The answer in the case of unorganised workers is fairly simple: the unorganised are organised into the syndicalist union; this is the express aspiration of syndicalist unions. The situation of the peasantry is also relatively straightforward. The syndicalist union could establish a peasant department, as was done by the French CGT in 1902, or form alliances with peasant movements; the Zenkoku Jiren in Japan, for example, argued for a united revolutionary movement of workers and tenant farmers "on the common basis of class struggle," and was involved in a number of efforts to organise the peasantry, who occupied a central place in Hatta's thought.[66]

What of the unemployed, the working-class neighbourhood, and those in groups made up of working-class students, youth, housewives, and women? There are several options: to ignore these groups, assuming their interests are represented by the syndicalist unions; incorporate these groups into the syndicalist unions; or ally with and otherwise promote specific organisations for these groups. Some syndicalists adopted the first approach; most opted for the latter two.

The Portuguese CGT adopted the position of incorporating nonworker groups, and included in its ranks tenants' associations and cooperatives as well as sections for artists and academics.[67] The Central Workers' Organisation of Sweden (SAC, formed in 1910), established a Syndicalist Youth Federation (SUF); the SAC currently allows the unemployed, students, and pensioners to enroll. Other unions went the alliance route. The U.S. IWPA, and later the U.S. and Canadian IWWs, agitated among the unemployed, organising demonstrations demanding relief and a shorter working day, with no loss of pay.[68] The U.S. IWW, addressing the unemployed, put it this way:

> Nobody can save you except yourself. The jobless have to get together, somehow, and make so much noise in the world as to attract attention. Only by making a public scandal in every city and town will you break the silence of the press and receive notice. Only fear of a general social

conflagration will make the employers of labour, private or governmental, get together and devise ways and means. As long as you are contented to rot to death in silence, you will be allowed to do so.

If you are still able to stand on your legs for hunger, get up big meetings and demonstrations, without getting in collision with "law and order." Not a drop of blood should be allowed to flow.... Adopt resolutions demanding work or relief. Present them in person to the authorities and the press. All this will take time and some money. Time you have plenty. Money you will get from the employed if you show you are in earnest.... Such measures may not bring you relief in 24 hours, but they are bound to bring some results sooner or later. They are apt to bring some artificial life into capitalism for a while by creating pressure in the proper place.

But then, when you do get a job, then is your chance to take steps that it shall not happen again. Organize industrially in such great numbers that you are able, with your organised might, to cut down the workday to the required number of hours to provide employment for the jobless. That will possibly tide us over until we are able to take complete control and put an end to unemployment forever.[69]

The Spanish case is also worth examining. The Spanish anarchists and syndicalists developed an expansive understanding of the general strike: it was a means of struggle that could draw in nonworkers. In the 1880s, the Spanish movement was wracked with debates between those who tended to ignore "enslaved humanity" outside the unions and wage labour, and those who argued for a broader approach. The debate was partly played out in the language of "collectivism" (identified with the narrowly workerist approach) and "communism" (identified with those who favoured larger communal mobilisations) as well as through a clash between syndicalist and insurrectionist approaches. Eventually,

the conflicts of the eighties were resolved through the evolution of a new theory, a compromise between anarcho-communism and anarcho-collectivism, known later as anarcho-syndicalism. It attempted to combine union strength with community organisation ... placing increased stress on workers' centres, cooperatives, mutual aid associations, and women's sections....

The tactics that united workers and the jobless were mass demonstrations and boycotts, many of which were organised through mutual aid associations, cooperatives, and workers' circles.... The Pact's main activity was to unite all the oppressed, whether or not they were employed, around May Day demonstrations calling for the eight hour day.... The general strike as developed in Andalusia was a tactic that relied on community support of organised workers [in the context of mass unemployment].... The general strike, really a mass mobilisation of the community, could take advantage of the weight of numbers ... [and] enabled militant unions and equally militant community people to march together against an oppressive system.[70]

In the twentieth century, the CNT developed an even more comprehensive approach, both forming alliances with anarchist groups outside the workplace and initiating actions in working-class communities. The CNT fostered and developed a working relationship with a range of anarchist working-class social movements outside the unions. The Libertarian Youth Federation of Iberia (FIJL) held its first national congress in 1932; originally intended to have a Portuguese section, it was really a Spanish formation.[71] There was also the Libertarian Youth of Catalonia, which used Catalan instead of Castilan as its lingua franca. A unified youth congress in 1937 claimed to represent over 80,000 members.[72] Another important group was the anarchist Mujeres Libres ("Free Women"), by far the largest left-wing women's group in the country, with over 20,000 members. Formed in 1936, it focused its activities on consciousness-raising and organising working-class and peasant women, and played an active role in the Spanish Revolution.[73] We will examine this group in more depth in chapter 10.

The CNT also played a leading role in community struggles, particularly around rent and housing. Having already developed a mass base in the workplace, the federation's militants began to pay increasing attention to the need to "combat exploitation in the field of consumption."[74] In 1931, its Construction Union initiated a dramatic rent strike across Barcelona, calling for a 40 percent decrease in rents, demanding better housing, and organising groups to forcibly prevent evictions.[75] By August 1931, perhaps 100,000 people were involved in Barcelona alone, and the movement spread into the surrounding towns. It also sought to mobilise the unemployed to demand work and secure waivers of rent. In the following year, the CNT in Gijon organised a community Union for the Defence of Public Interests; based on neighbourhood committees, and using direct action, it aimed to enforce a new law protecting renters introduced by the new republic.[76]

Rent strikes were a major feature of anarchist and syndicalist activity elsewhere as well. British anarchists organised a "No Rent" campaign in 1891, while the syndicalist Clyde Workers' Committee was involved in a major rent strike in Glasgow in 1915.[77] Anarchists organised rent strikes in Havana, Cuba, in 1899 and 1900.[78] In the Mexican city of Veracruz in 1922 anarchists and members of the CPM, which was still markedly influenced by anarchism, formed a Revolutionary Syndicate of Tenants that brought 30,000 people—more than two-thirds of the total population—out on a rent strike.[79] This inspired similar protests in other cities in the state of Veracruz like Orizaba, Córdoba, and Jalapa, full-scale rent strikes in Mexico City and Guadalajara, and efforts at tenant organising in Mérida, Puebla, San luis Potosí, Mazatlán, Monterrey, Tampico, Aguascalientes, Torreón, and Ciudad Juárez.[80]

In Chile in 1921, the Libertarian Women's Union organised a Committee for Lower Rents and Clean Housing, and anarchists were active in rent strikes in 1922 and 1925; they were also involved in the Tenants' League that was formed in Panama City in 1925 and organised a rent strike later that year.[81] Anarchists and syndicalists organised rent strikes in Buenos Aires in 1907, drawing in perhaps 140,000 people, and again in 1912, with the latter movement spreading to Córdoba, Entre Rios, and Santa Fé.[82] Another anarchist-led rent strike took place in 1920 in Peru, where the anarchists also worked with a section of the university student movement.[83] There was also an anarchist-led rent strike in Portugal in 1921.

The notion that syndicalism cannot organise outside the workplace or must necessarily ignore people outside of wage labour is thus flawed. Malatesta was correct in pointing to the danger of a narrow unionism, but the actual history of syndicalism demonstrates that it managed to avoid developing into a narrow workerism. Consequently, we would contend, it is important not to assume that syndicalist movements should be understood simply as *union* movements. Typically embedded within dense networks of peasant and working-class associational life, and central to revolutionary popular countercultures, syndicalism should be seen as a component of a larger anarchist social movement. Care should be taken not to set up an artificial divide between syndicalist unions and the larger anarchist movements of which they formed an integral part.

Defending the Revolution

As we have seen, Malatesta worried that syndicalists did not adequately address the question of defending a revolution against a counterrevolution. Engels had some interesting points as well:

> In the Bakuninist programme a general strike is the lever employed by which the social revolution is started. One fine morning, all the workers in all the industries of a country, or even of the whole world, stop work, thus forcing the propertied classes either humbly to submit within four weeks at the most, or to attack the workers, who would then have the right to defend themselves and use this opportunity to pull down the entire society.[84]

In his view, this was nonsensical. It was necessary to have a sufficiently "well-formed organisation of the working class" with "plentiful funds" to carry out such a strike without the working class succumbing to starvation, and the state was unlikely to allow such a development. Furthermore, Engels asserted, it was more likely that "political events and oppressive acts by the ruling classes" would precipitate a revolution well before such an organisation could be formed, thereby rendering the syndicalist union redundant.[85]

Engels's argument helped lay the basis for a second Marxist argument against syndicalism, which was the claim that Marxists, and scholars influenced by Marxism, have subsequently maintained: syndicalism was a form of "'left' economism" without a revolutionary strategy and serious analysis of the state.[86] James Hinton, writing from a classical Marxist position, alleged that syndicalism failed to appreciate "the need for politics" and was characterised by a "neglect of the role of the state in maintaining the domination of capital."[87] The Marxist sociologist Richard Hyman likewise suggested that syndicalists ignored the role of the state in society.[88]

In an otherwise excellent study of South African unions, Rob Lambert charged that the syndicalists had an "inability to adequately confront the issue of state power." The syndicalists emphasised their "social distance" from the state, but "failed to come to terms with the manner in which state power, located in a variety of institutions, reproduced capitalist social relations."[89] Such criticisms were and are routinely leveled by Leninists, who contended that the failure of syndicalist unions to make successful revolutions stemmed from their supposed tendency to ignore the state and, of course, the supposed need for the dictatorship of the proletariat.

There are several slightly different sets of criticisms in these points: the charge that syndicalists lacked an analysis of the state and ignored politics, the charge that syndicalists aimed to "starve out" the ruling class without necessarily assuming control of production, the charge that syndicalists ignored the need for the armed defence of the revolution, and the related charge that syndicalists took insufficient account of the need for a systematic and sustained destruction of the capitalist state.

The first of these can be dealt with fairly quickly. The notion that syndicalists simply lacked an analysis of the state and its role in relation to capitalism cannot stand up to scrutiny. As we have seen in chapter 4, syndicalists did not reject political issues; instead, they saw the union as the key to fighting *both* economic and political issues through a unified movement that would "represent a synthesis of the political and of the economic function."[90] Moreover, it was precisely *because* of a clear and specific analysis of the state's role in maintaining capitalism that syndicalists repudiated the use of state power ("political action") in changing society, and stressed instead the centrality of working-class self-activity outside of and against the state machinery.

Indeed, "syndicalist non-politicism was not neutrality at all. It meant above all anti-electoralism and anti-parliamentarism," for whereas the "political socialists believed the state merely to be in the wrong hands ... fully developed syndicalist ideology" was characterised by "anti-statism."[91] The position of the IWW, for instance, "was indeed a highly political rejection of state-based means for achieving socialism, an implacable anti-parliamentary posture, an expression of unmitigated contempt for ... reformist parties, and also about the aims and ambitions of revolutionary political parties."[92]

In addition, syndicalist movements developed sophisticated analyses of the evolving role and functions of the state, including in the promotion of capitalist ideology and nationalism, the rise of state welfare systems, and the impact of growing state regulation of the economy.[93] The notion that syndicalists simply ignored the state is, in the final analysis, a serious caricature created by classical Marxist writers. It is most unfortunate that many scholars have relied on these writings, rather than basic syndicalist texts, in their analysis of syndicalism.

The charges that syndicalists aimed to starve out the ruling class without necessarily assuming control of production, and also ignored the need for the armed defence of the revolution, are interlinked. Here it is critical not to homogenise syndicalism but to recognise the diversity of syndicalist positions. What almost all syndicalists shared was the view that the revolutionary general strike involved a revolutionary expropriation of the means of production through workplace occupations. Where syndicalists really differed amongst themselves, however, was on the question of revolutionary violence.

Malatesta himself always argued for armed self-defence. A revolutionary strike meant a clash with the forces of the state, and "then the matter cannot help resolving itself into shooting and bombs." The notion of a peaceful revolution was a "pure utopia," for the revolution must inevitably be resolved through "main force" with "victory ... to the strongest." A revolutionary general strike must involve the workers occupying the workplaces and continuing production "for their own benefit," but this must be backed up by force of arms.[94]

Yet there can be no doubt that a section of syndicalists believed in the possibility of a peaceful revolution through the general strike and ignored the possibility of violent conflict with the ruling class, and thus the question of armed self-defence. One example is the German syndicalist Siegfried Nacht (1878–1956, better known by the pseudonym Arnold Roller), who argued in the pamphlet *The Social General Strike* that the general strike had replaced the "battle on the barricades."[95] On more than one occasion, U.S. IWW figures hit a similar note, like Haywood who spoke confidently of a "bloodless revolution": "Our dynamite is mental and our force is organisation at the point of production." He added, "When we strike now, we strike with our hands in our pockets."[96]

The IWW activist Ralph Chaplin (1887–1961) provides another example. Chaplin wrote the popular union anthem "Solidarity Forever," was editor of the IWW's *Industrial Worker* in the 1930s, and is generally regarded as the originator of the black cat image widely used in anarchist and syndicalist propaganda. In his pamphlet *The General Strike*, Chaplin stated that the use of weapons was futile, and that a "well co-ordinated lockout of the Captains of Finance by both workers and technicians" would "put an end to the profit system but leave the production and transportation of goods unimpaired." He noted that "this, coupled with the program of picketing the industries by the unemployed, is what the IWW has in mind in advocating the General Strike" and anything else was simply "adding confusion onto confusion."[97] While Chaplin was probably correct that an armed insurrection alone was unlikely to defeat a modern state, he did not consider the possibility that armed self-defence might be needed to supplement a revolutionary strike, in order to defend against a military reconquest of industry by the ruling class.

Another important syndicalist current that simply failed to address the question of armed self-defence was De Leonism, with its view that the state would be paralysed and dissolved during the "general lockout" by the electoral victory of the SLP (backed by the One Big Union). Part of the problem is that it is exceedingly unlikely that a shutting out of the capitalist class and the electoral victory of the party of the One Big Union would so perfectly coincide, particularly given that elections to the state are only held periodically.

A general lockout might precede an electoral victory, in which case the SLP would be unable to prevent state repression. Alternatively, the electoral victory might take place before the unions were ready to make the revolution, in which case the SLP would find itself at the head of a capitalist government without the unions in place to institute barriers to capitalism. De Leon would doubtless have dismissed this potentiality, as he envisaged a slow and steady growth of the One Big Union, which he believed would result in the rise of the SLP. "The political movement is absolutely the reflex of the economic organisation," he wrote.[98] Nonetheless, even he feared that if the workers' representatives in parliament failed to "adjourn themselves on the spot," they would "usurp" power to create "a commonwealth of well-fed slaves" ruled by "a parliamentary oligarchy with an army of officials at its back, possessing powers infinitely greater than those possessed by our present political rulers."[99]

Malatesta, then, was to some extent justified in speaking of syndicalists who ignored the real prospect of armed counterrevolution against revolutionary uprisings. But it would be wrong to apply this charge to all syndicalists; many, on the contrary, advocated at least some measure of armed self-defence in a revolution. Spies of the IWPA thought that the workers "should arm themselves," for "the better they are armed, the easier the struggle will be ended."[100] He was one of a significant number of IWPA militants involved in organising the Lehr und Wehr Verein ("Instruction and Protection Society," or LWV); this militia, first formed in 1875, was branded illegal as of 1881, but continued to operate underground and appeared at IWPA meetings. The Haymarket martyr Adolph Fischer went to the gallows wearing a belt buckle featuring the letters LWV.[101] The Lehr und Wehr Verein was one of a number of armed groups linked to the IWPA across the United States; at least two CLU affiliates also organised militias.[102]

The revolutionary novel *How We Shall Bring About the Revolution: Syndicalism and the Cooperative Commonwealth* provides an insight into the views of the French syndicalists on the issue of defending the revolution. Published in 1909, and available in an English edition—translated by the anarchists Fred Charles and Charlotte Charles, with prefaces by Kropotkin and the British syndicalist Tom Mann (1856–1941)—the book was written by Pouget and Emile Pataud, a syndicalist electrician, strike leader, and firebrand speaker.

The story starts with violent clashes between police and strikers that quickly builds up to a general strike of insurrectionary proportions, headed by the CGT. The state finds its forces increasingly unreliable as police officers, municipal guards, and soldiers begin to switch sides; strikers in the transport sector hamper the use of military reinforcements from elsewhere in France and the colonies. The strikers raid arms depots, and a popular militia is formed. By this stage, cooperative societies and unions have started to take control of distribution. A tense showdown between the militia and the remaining government troops in Paris is averted as the soldiers mutiny and stretch "out their hands to the people": "instead of a scene of horrible carnage, there were embraces—shouts of joy." The "human flood" of "strikers, interspersed with soldiers," places state buildings under armed guard, conquers the remaining barracks, and dissolves parliament; the same development is repeated elsewhere.[103]

By the evening the unions—the "heart and soul" of the mass movement—and the general strike move toward "social reconstruction."[104] Classical Marxists are sidelined; reactionaries and pogromists are dealt with in a rough fashion. The banks are seized, and the media and production is reorganised by the unions, working alongside neighbourhood and village groups. In the countryside, the peasants—who had joined the strike from the start through the CGT's Peasant Unions, and who are increasingly armed—have already begun to expropriate the large farms and plantations, and abolish rent, mortgages, and taxes. The new society is decentralised and federalist, and promotes individual freedom; it has no standing army, and no barracks, prisons, or police stations; popular courts are established; production is coordinated and planned through democratic union congresses; and distribution is organised on primarily communist principles.

The CGT's Confederal Committee refuses diplomatic relations with foreign states, but establishes them with the popular classes abroad, advocating "international solidarity between the peoples," and the revolution starts to spread. A well-armed popular militia, structured around the unions and organised on a volunteer basis, is formed "in order not to be taken unawares in the case of any reactionary conspiracy." The "people had always detested military servitude" and "wars between nations," but this "had never meant for them the resignation and non-resistance preached by Tolstoi [*sic*]." It is just as well that "Trade Union France" is "bristling" with arms and "syndicalist battalions," because a counterrevolutionary force is organised by the remainder of the French ruling class, backed by an invasion from abroad. With an army, an air force, and "terrible" chemical weapons and explosives at which even the old ruling class had baulked, the revolutionary forces wage a "struggle relentless and without pity," "tearing to shreds, without hesitation, the rules of the game of war." The counterrevolution is crushed in a "hurricane of death and fire."[105]

Granted, the novel probably simplifies the problems facing a revolution and makes the assumption that "the revolutionary forces possessed an exclusive monopoly of scientific weaponry."[106] The key point, however, is that it can scarcely be regarded as demonstrating a "neglect of the role of the state in maintaining the domination of capital" or a refusal to face the possibility of armed counterrevolution. Other syndicalists commonly held such views. The IWPA argued forthrightly that the ruling class would not "resign their privileges voluntarily" and that there "remains but one recourse—FORCE!"[107]

Ford and Foster likewise argued that syndicalism wages a "life and death struggle with an absolutely lawless and unscrupulous enemy," and must "wrest ... by force" the means of production in a "revolution by the general strike," and link up with the small farmers in the countryside. This would "probably" be "accompanied by violence," and the armed forces of the state, dispersed to expel workers from the occupied workplaces, would have to be "overwhelmed and disarmed." Ford and Foster also projected a split in the military: "As they are mostly workingmen and in sympathy with the general strike," they could be "induced to join the ranks of their striking fellow workers." The groundwork for this would be ongoing antimilitarist work encouraging the "working class soldiers not to shoot their brothers and sisters ... but, if need be, to shoot their own officers and to desert the army when the crucial moment arrives."[108]

Similarly, for Maximoff, the initial period of the revolution would bring "the huge masses of the people into action" and paralyse the old order. This period must be used to establish a revolutionary economic order and "lay immediately the foundations for ... organised military defence" before the "terrified elements of the old regime rally ... and reassemble their forces." Revolutionary armed forces, structured along the lines of a general militia, with an elected staff of officers, and "utilising military science and all methods of modern war technique," must be established.[109]

For his part, Berkman maintained that there was no prospect of a mere armed uprising defeating the "armoured tanks, poison gas, and military planes" of the ruling class. It was necessary for workers to exercise their power "in the shop, in the mine and factory" through a revolutionary general strike. This would strike the decisive blow at the ruling class and disperse the armed forces. Yet it had to be supplemented with "armed force," based on a popular and democratic militia of "armed workers and peasants," to be deployed at the workbench" or on the battlefield, "according to need."[110] Tom Brown believed that the "workers' Syndicates would establish Workers' Militias ... and whatever other means of workers' defence were necessary.... The armed Syndicates would be a general force—a people in arms."[111]

Rocker distinguished between ordinary general strikes, for economic and political demands, and the "social general strike" against the capitalist system. All general strikes cripple the ruling classes, and scatter and weaken the army, allowing it to be subverted by the workers, observed Rocker. The social general strike, however, supplements the paralysing effects of a general strike with a deliberate programme of "collectivising of the land and the taking over of the plants by the workers' and peasants' syndicates," which must be combined with the "armed resistance of the people for the protection of life and liberty." He also noted the following:

> The ridiculous claim, which is so often attributed to the Anarcho-syndicalists, that it is only necessary to proclaim a general strike in order to achieve a Socialist society in a few days, is, of course, just a silly invention of evil-minded opponents bent on discrediting an idea which they cannot attack by any other means.[112]

The founding document of the IWA, the "Declaration of the Principles of Revolutionary Syndicalism," explicitly stated that syndicalists recognised "violence as a means of defence against the violent methods of the ruling classes in the struggle for the possession of the factories and the fields by the revolutionary people." The "defence of the revolution" must "be entrusted to the masses themselves and their economic organisations." While "syndicalists are the enemies of all organised violence in the hands of any revolutionary government, they do fail to recognise that the decisive struggles between the capitalist present and the free communist future will not occur without conflict."[113]

There is no doubt then that many syndicalists—with important exceptions like the De Leonists—envisaged the need for an armed defence of the revolution, stressed that it should be organised through a militia, democratic in character and popular by nature, rather than a traditional hierarchical military, and also saw the subversion of the state military machinery as part of the armed phase of the revolution. This approach poses an alternative to the proletarian dictatorship: rather than the struggle against counterrevolution being waged through a new state machinery, headed by a vanguard party, it would be organised through radically democratic unions and other working-class organisations.

The Question of Power and the Spanish Revolution

Nevertheless, even where syndicalists argued for armed self-defence, they still did not always take adequate account of the likelihood of *sustained* armed resistance by the old ruling class, or recognise that their revolution could only be secured by a systematic destruction of the capitalist state. The probability that the old state machinery and ruling class would prove resilient even after the means of production were expropriated was not always faced. The weakness of the De Leonists in this respect has been noted above, but De Leon's view that "the political movement is absolutely the reflex of the economic organisation" had parallels elsewhere.[114] In September 1936, mere months after the outbreak of revolution in Spain, for instance, the CNT–Federación Anarquista Ibérica (FAI) *Information Bulletin* could confidently predict the "liquidation of the bourgeois State, weakened by suffocation ... the result of economic expropriation."[115] (The Spanish Revolution started as a revolt against an attempted military coup by General Francisco Franco, but quickly escalated, as the CNT structures—sometimes in conjunction with workers from the large but moderate socialist General Workers Union, or UGT—placed hundreds of workplaces under self-management, farmworkers and peasants seized land, and a popular militia of over a hundred thousand was formed.)

The problem with the "suffocation" position, though, is that the resources of the modern state are not simply economic. As Bakunin and many others had long pointed out, the state was itself a significant body for the reproduction of a class system, and its power was partly based on its control of the means of *administration* and *coercion*. It follows that "economic expropriation" alone cannot ensure the "liquidation" of the state. Rather, this task requires the thorough dismantling of state departments, the dissolution of the armed forces and expropriation of state resources, and a comprehensive shift in power to the popular classes (at the very least along the lines suggested by Pouget and Pataud), which in turn requires a coordinated military defence.

The Friends of Durruti (again, AD), a radical group in the Spanish anarchist movement, charted an alternative position. Named after the famed anarchist militant and martyr Buenaventura Durruti (1896–1936), who we will discuss later, this group of CNT and FAI militants suggested the formation of a "Revolutionary Junta" or "National Defence Council" in a revolution to destroy the state apparatus and coordinate

a) The management of the war

b) The supervision of revolutionary order

c) International affairs

d) Revolutionary propaganda[116]

Like the term "soviet," "Junta" has subsequently acquired connotations of authoritarianism and militarism at odds with its original meaning; the AD was simply advocating a democratic and mandated coordinating body based in the mass organisations of the popular classes. Other AD proposals included the seizure of all state arms and financial reserves, thoroughgoing economic transformation, the restructuring of the armed forces, armed self-defence, working-class solidarity and a pact with the UGT, and noncollaboration with foreign and local capitalist forces.

Such views may be counterposed to the actions of the CNT at the time: asserting that the fight against fascist forces required maximum antifascist unity, the CNT joined an antifascist Popular Front government in September 1936. The abysmal and tragic failure of this tactic is something we will examine in volume 2. The move was controversial from the start, and was rejected by significant sectors of the militias, the anarchist youth, the CNT, and the FAI.

The proposals of the AD, compiled in 1938 as *Towards a Fresh Revolution*, have led some to suggest that the group had rejected the broad anarchist tradition.[117] Trotskyist writer Felix Morrow, for example, contended that the AD was "a conscious break with the anti-statism of traditional anarchism" because it "explicitly declared the need for democratic organs of power, juntas or soviets, in the overthrow of capitalism."[118] By contrast, Morrow alleged, class collaboration "lies concealed in the heart of anarchist philosophy" (anarchists, he claimed, believe revolution requires that capitalists embrace anarchism, thereby leading anarchists to embrace an ostensibly friendly state), which also supposedly "calls upon the workers to turn their backs on the state and seek control of the factories as the real source of power," assuming that the state will simply collapse as a result.[119]

Morrow's view that anarchism advocates class collaboration and statism is difficult to take seriously. The broad anarchist tradition does not base itself on the belief that the revolution requires a change of heart on the part of the ruling class. His second claim—which evidently goes back to Engels's polemic against Spanish anarchism—is more compelling, if only because it is given some support by the "suffocation thesis" presented in the CNT and FAI press.

Some anarchists also suggest that, while anarchism as such certainly has a genuinely revolutionary potential, syndicalism inevitably embraces the suffocation thesis. Syndicalism is "a-political, arguing all that is necessary to make the revolution is for the workers to seize the factories and the land," and then "the state and all the other institutions of the ruling class will come toppling down."[120] While there are significant differences between Morrow's analysis and this view, they share the proposition that the CNT's entry into the Popular Front was not simply a questionable strategic decision, but followed from the very nature of syndicalism.

There are, however, serious problems with this reasoning. As we have seen, many syndicalists argued for armed action against counterrevolution. A National Defence Council of the sort proposed by the AD was indeed very much in line with Bakunin's proposal for "permanent barricades," and "federating the fighting battalions" to create "district by district" a "common and coordinated defence against internal and external enemies."[121] Such a structure had even been created in December 1933, when the National Revolutionary Council was formed to head a revolutionary uprising, including in its number Durruti. It was the logical outcome of the position that the popular militia must be linked to the organs of popular counterpower, clearly present in Pouget and Pataud's account, where the CGT Confederal Committee, based on delegate structures and radical democracy, connects the unions and the militia. This amounts to no less than taking power in society and exercising it through an armed federation; it also involves forcing the ruling class to surrender to an anarchist society.

The Spanish anarchists actually held the view that the revolution must "annihilate the power of the state" through class struggle and "superior firing power"— since the days of FORE.[122] At its Zaragoza congress in May 1936, the CNT argued for "necessary steps" to defend against "the perils of foreign invasion ... or against counter-revolution at home." The best defence of the revolution was the "people armed," a militia of "confederal defence cadres" ready for "large-scale battles," and armed with "modern military techniques," planes, tanks, armoured vehicles, machine guns, and antiaircraft cannon, with the militia "effectively organised nationwide."[123]

The entry of the CNT into the Popular Front, then, was not the inevitable result of a concealed anarchist policy of class collaboration, nor was it the result of an intrinsic link between syndicalism and the suffocation thesis. It was a strategic mistake that led the Spanish anarchists to "throw overboard all their principles," and start to "dismantle its autonomous and revolutionary power apparatus."[124] It was against this tactic and the retreats it implied that the AD—along with others, like the FIJL—revolted. In this sense, the AD by no means represented "a conscious break with the anti-statism of traditional anarchism" by calling for "democratic organs of power, juntas or soviets, in the overthrow of capitalism," but rather a *reaffirmation* of the traditional perspectives of anarchism.[125] This can be seen, for instance, in the group's proposals around the elected Junta or National Defence Council:

> This body will be organised as follows: members of the revolutionary Junta will be elected by democratic vote in the union organisations. Account is to be taken of the number of comrades away at the front; these comrades must have the right to representation. The Junta will steer clear of economic affairs, which are the exclusive preserve of the unions ... the trade union assemblies will exercise control over the Junta's activities.... The Municipality [i.e., the commune] shall take charge of those functions of society that fall outside the preserve of the unions.[126]

This is a standard syndicalist position, and it was also the CNT position, adopted at the Zaragoza congress, actively defended by Durruti at a major CNT plenum in August 1936, reaffirmed as late as September 1936, and actually applied in part of Spain that year through through structures called the Council of Aragon and the Council of Valencia.[127] It was among the principles thrown overboard with the entry into the Popular Front.

There are, however, two important points made by the AD that mark it as profoundly innovative in the context of Spanish anarchism and worthy of the closest consideration by the broad anarchist tradition more generally. First, the AD recognised that the state would prove resilient even in the face of a revolutionary general strike and a popular militia, and that a revolutionary uprising could easily turn into a *protracted* civil war. This, arguably, the CNT and its counterparts elsewhere failed to adequately grasp. Second, it argued that the tendency of traditional anarchism and syndicalism to gloss over such issues, or invoke a suffocation thesis, meant that it failed to give serious thought to the tactics required in such a situation:

> What happened was what had to happen. The CNT was utterly devoid of revolutionary theory. We did not have a concrete programme. We had no idea where we were going. We had lyricism aplenty; but when all is said and done, we did not know what to do with our masses of workers or how to give substance to the popular effusion that erupted inside our organisations. By not knowing what to do, we handed the revolution on a platter to the bourgeoisie and the Marxists who support the farce of yesteryear. What is worse, we allowed the bourgeoisie a breathing space; to return, to re-form and to behave as would a conqueror. The CNT did not know how to live up to its role. It did not want to push ahead with the revolution with all its consequences.[128]

This opinion has been confirmed, inter alia, by the CNT's official historian and veteran activist José Peirats Valls (1908–1989), who joined the CNT aged fourteen and was an active militant for sixty years. He would write later that

> in their writings, many anarchists conceived of a miraculous solution to the problem. We fell easily into this trap in Spain. We believed that "once the dog is dead the rabies is over." We proclaimed a full-blown revolution without worrying about the many complex problems that a revolution

brings with it.... [T]o the Iberian anarchists of my generation the notion that there is an inevitable reaction to any revolution was unthinkable, or unimportant. Some Spanish comrades still lament that our revolution had to be accompanied by a civil war. But when has there been a revolution without a civil war? Is not a revolution a civil war by its very nature? And yet we were caught unprepared when our revolution inevitably provoked a civil war.[129]

It was precisely this lack of a clear plan, he maintained, that the led the CNT and the FAI to join the Popular Front when faced with Franco : it was this great flaw that the AD recognised and tried to correct.

In Conclusion: Anarchism, Syndicalism, and Counterpower

In a previous chapter, we disputed the view that the history of the broad anarchist tradition can be understood as divided into separate "anarcho-communist" and syndicalist currents, and some of the material that we have presented here confirms that analysis. For one, Malatesta should be seen as a supporter of syndicalism, if not an outright syndicalist, rather than representative of an antisyndicalist "anarcho-communist" position. Earlier, we argued that the foundational text in Platformism, the *Platform*, accepted syndicalism; we reiterate here that the same is true of the AD's *Towards a Fresh Revolution*, usually regarded as the second most significant Platformist document.

More important, we have pointed out that syndicalist movements should be understood as *part of* a larger anarchist social movement; typically embedded within dense networks of peasant and working-class associational life, and central to revolutionary popular countercultures, syndicalist unions should not be arbitrarily divided from the larger revolutionary movement of which they formed an integral part. We cannot agree with Bookchin when he described syndicalism as a narrowing of anarchism, and a "change in focus from the commune to the trade union, from all the oppressed to the industrial proletariat, from the streets to the factories, and, in emphasis at least, from insurrection to the general strike."[130] Syndicalism focuses on class struggle, but does not narrow it unduly.

While syndicalism certainly stressed the view—which was widely held in the broad anarchist tradition—that revolutionary workplace struggle was the essential lever for revolutionary change, and regarded revolutionary unions as decisive and irreplaceable organs of counterpower, it cannot reasonably be portrayed as a form of economism or workerism. These are perhaps the least appropriate terms to use to describe a revolutionary labour tradition premised on the necessity of a "fundamental transvaluation of values" and self-organised, antistatist struggle.[131]

In rejecting the insurrectionist anarchist position that unions were always and everywhere nonrevolutionary, syndicalists did not take the antithetical position that unions were always and everywhere revolutionary. Unions could only be revolutionary and make a revolution in *particular* circumstances: when they were infused with revolutionary and libertarian ideas, when they were based on direct action and self-activity, when they were radically democratic and participatory, and when they aimed at and prepared for revolution. This chapter rejects the notion that syndicalists believe that unions spontaneously generate revolutionary consciousness. It also disputes the assertion that syndicalists ignore political issues as well as the state.

Syndicalism is profoundly political, and takes the state very seriously indeed. Taken to its logical conclusion (and of course, there might be some who shy away from this conclusion), *all* mass anarchism amounts to a project of *taking power* in society and creating a coordinated system of stateless governance; this is especially true of syndicalism. Syndicalists have given the new order many names: a "libertarian social power," a "union governing power," a "libertarian polity," an "Industrial Social Order," a "Workers' Republic," and an "industrial government, a shop government."[132] It is based on structures of self-management, and is "carried out from the bottom up, by free association, with unions and localities federated by communes, regions, nations, and, finally, a great universal and international federation," allowing a "federalist and noncoercive centralisation" that is ultimately expressed in a body that might be called a confederal committee (or for those who accept that this order must also involve armed self-defence, a Revolutionary Junta or Defence Council).[133]

This polity is not, however, a state—at least as the state is understood in the broad anarchist tradition—for control is exercised from the bottom up, and linked by delegates and mandates, rather than hierarchically imposed by officials, and class no longer exists. It would take over some functions currently run by the state—such as organising public services—but it would not itself be a state. It differs from the Marxist dictatorship of the proletariat precisely in its radically democratic character and classlessness. In aiming to move from oppositional *counterpower* to a hegemonic libertarian *social power*, syndicalists also differ profoundly with autonomist Marxists like John Holloway who advocate changing the world without taking power.[134]

Auxiliary to this project is the fact that at least one sector of society—the ruling class—*will* be forcibly suppressed and coerced into the anarchist society. For some, like the De Leonists, this might be done peacefully through expropriation and the dissolution of the state; for most syndicalists, it will also involve the use of violence. Yet from the perspective of the broad anarchist tradition, the forceful overthrow of the ruling class is not in contradiction with the antiauthoritarian principle. It is force used to remove the existing coercion of the capitalist system and can be seen as an act of legitimate self-defence by the popular classes. To allow the ruling class to retain its privileges until it is willing to concede to anarchism, on the grounds that everyone must enter anarchism voluntarily, is to provide that class with a permanent veto on the emancipation of the great majority of humanity. Unlike utopian socialism, anarchism does not premise its strategy on the moral conversion of the ruling class it invokes legitimate coercive power derived from collective and democratic decision making..

Where differences do arise among syndicalists is on the question of whether force must supplement the general strike in the destruction of the state and the overthrow of the ruling class. The great majority of syndicalists believed that a revolution would need to be defended against a counterrevolution by the force of arms, with a popular militia—linked to the unions and supplied with the best weaponry— playing the main role. This coordinated military defence would complement the creation of a planned and self-managed economy, and would therefore be part of the libertarian polity.

Given that the majority of syndicalists thought that armed force would be necessary, that syndicalism was embraced by the majority of mass anarchists, and that mass anarchism was the predominant form of anarchism, the need for an armed defence of the revolution can reasonably be regarded as representative of the view of the great majority in the broad anarchist tradition on this question. Pacifist ideas have had some influence on a section of mass anarchists, a notable example being Bart de Ligt (1883–1938), a Dutch anarchist. For the pacifists, violence in any form is both unnecessary for the revolution as well as counterrevolutionary in itself in that it must supposedly generate a new system of inequality and domination. But pacificism was always marginal.

The use of force, even force without violence, in the revolution has a class character. Engels claimed that anarchists were hypocritical for opposing "authority" when a "revolution is certainly the most authoritarian thing there is; it is an act whereby one part of the population imposes its will upon the other part."[135] But this formulation, which conflates the use of force to defend exploitation and domination with the actions of popular resistance and self-emancipation, amounts to treating murder and self-defence as identical. Even a pacifist strategy implies some measure of coercion, however peaceful, to impose the will of the popular classes on the ruling classes. Many anarchist and syndicalist actions—propaganda, boycotts, protests, strikes, and union organising—are peaceful, yet they are nonetheless coercive.

Many mass anarchists clearly believed that violence was regrettably necessary for a revolution, but would probably have agreed with Malatesta that "violence is justifiable only when it is necessary to defend oneself and others against violence. It is where necessity ends that crime begins."[136] This should not imply a reign of reprisals against the former rulers or the use of terror as a revolutionary weapon. As Bakunin put it, "Bloody revolutions are often necessary, thanks to human stupidity; yet they are always an evil, a monstrous evil and a great disaster, not only with regard to the victims, but also for the sake of the purity and perfection of the purpose in whose name they take place."[137] For Malatesta, "To condone ferocious anti-human feelings and raise them to the level of principle," advocating them "as a tactic for a movement ... is both evil and counter-revolutionary."[138]

Notes

1. A. Guillen, *Anarchist Economics: The Economics of the Spanish Libertarian Collectives, 1936–39* (Durban: Zabalaza Books, 1992), 17; T. Wetzel, *Looking Back after 70 Years: Workers Power and the Spanish Revolution*, available at http://www.workersolidarity.org/Spanishrevolution.html#power (accessed June 15, 2005).

2. We would specifically like to thank Bert Altena for his comments on this section.

3. Thorpe, *"The Workers Themselves,"* 31.

4. A. Lehning, "Cornilessen, Christian," in *Biografisch Woordenboek van het Socialisme en de Arbeidersbeweging in Nederland* (Amsterdam: International Institute of Social History, 1987), 35–39.

5. P. Monatte, "Syndicalism: An Advocacy," in *The Anarchist Reader*, ed. G. Woodcock (1907; repr., Glasgow: Fontana/Collins, 1977), 218–19.

6.   Malatesta is commonly presented as hostile to syndicalism. Bookchin states that Malatesta was "uncomfortable with syndicalist doctrines" and developed a "fundamental criticism of syndicalism"; Joll writes that Malatesta saw syndicalism as a rival "new movement" and "not only attacked some of the basic conceptions of the syndicalists; he also attacked their tactical methods"; Kedward claims that Malatesta "put the case" against syndicalism as "inevitably conservative, working within the established economic system for legal ends"; Woodcock labels Malatesta's input at the Amsterdam meeting "Syndicalism: an anarchist critique" (see Malatesta, "Syndicalism"); and Graham adds that Malatesta had a "broader conception of anarchism ... not exclusively working class." See Bookchin, *The Spanish Anarchists*, 137; Bookchin, "Deep Ecology, Anarchosyndicalism, and the Future of Anarchist Thought," 50; Joll, *The Anarchists*, 205; Kedward, *The Anarchists*, 65; Graham, *Anarchism*, 206, 328.

7.   See Malatesta in Richards, *Errico Malatesta*, 113, 115, 120–21, 126; Malatesta, "Syndicalism," 223; E. Malatesta, "Anarchism and Syndicalism," in *The Anarchist Revolution: Polemical Writings, 1924–1931: Errico Malatesta*, ed. V. Richards (April-May 1925; repr., London: Freedom Press, 1995), 23; E. Malatesta, "A Project of Anarchist Organisation," in *The Anarchist Revolution: Polemical Writings, 1924–1931: Errico Malatesta*, ed. V. Richards (October 1927; repr., London: Freedom Press, 1995), 94.

8.   Malatesta in Richards, *Errico Malatesta*, 113.

9.   Yoast, "The Development of Argentine Anarchism," 149.

10.   Malatesta, "Syndicalism," 220–23, 225.

11.   Malatesta in Richards, *Errico Malatesta*, 113

12.   Malatesta in Richards, *Errico Malatesta*, 114–115, 117, 119, 123–24

13.   Malatesta, "Syndicalism," 223; see also Malatesta in Richards, *Errico Malatesta*, 129.

14.   Malatesta, "Syndicalism," 221–22.

15.   Malatesta in Richards, *Errico Malatesta*, 118–21; Malatesta, "Syndicalism," 225.

16.   Malatesta, "Syndicalism," 223.

17.   Malatesta in Richards, *Errico Malatesta*, 113–18, 125–26, 129–30; Malatesta, "Syndicalism," 221–23.

18.   Bakunin, "The Programme of the Alliance," 249, 250–51.

19.   Maximoff, *The Programme of Anarcho-syndicalism*, 58.

20.   Kubo, "On Class Struggle and the Daily Struggle," 381.

21.   Goldman, "The Failure of the Russian Revolution," 159.

22.   Rocker, *Anarcho-Syndicalism*, chapters 4 and 5.

23.   Ibid., chapter 4.

24.   Malatesta in Richards, *Errico Malatesta*, 115.

25.   See Bekken, "The First Daily Anarchist Newspaper."

26.   Ibid., 5.

27.   Avrich, *The Haymarket Tragedy*, 131; see also Nelson, *Beyond the Martyrs*.

28.   M. A. Ackelsberg, "Revolution and Community: Mobilization, De-politicisation, and Perceptions of Change in Civil War Spain," in *Women Living Change*, ed. S. C. Bourque and D. R. Divine (Philadelphia: Temple University Press, 1985); R. Hadfield, "Politics and Protest in the Spanish Anarchist Movement: Libertarian Women in Early Twentieth-Century Barcelona," *University of Sussex Journal of Contemporary History*, no. 3 (2001).

29.   Rocker, *Anarcho-Syndicalism*, chapter 6.

30.   V. Richards, *Lessons of the Spanish Revolution*, rev. ed. (London: Freedom Press, 1983), 198–99, 206.

31.   Levy, "Italian Anarchism," 48–49.

32.   A. B. Spitzer, "Anarchy and Culture: Fernand Pelloutier and the Dilemma of Revolutionary Syndicalism," *International Review of Social History* 8 (1963).

33.   Foner, *The Industrial Workers of the World*, 146–51.

34. Ibid., 149.

35. Salerno, *Red November, Black November*, 6ff.

36. Avrich, *Anarchist Portraits*, 65.

37. On its limitations, see, for example, Bookchin, *The Spanish Anarchists*, 129–32.

38. On Rhodokanaty, see anonymous, *Plotino Rhodakanaty: The Actions of a Greek Anarchist in Mexico* (East Brunswick, NJ: No God, No Master Anarchist Pamphlets, n.d.); Hart, *Anarchism and the Mexican Working Class*.

39. Hart, *Anarchism and the Mexican Working Class*, 32–42.

40. Ibid., 113–15. In 1911, 84 percent of the population was illiterate; J. D. Cockcroft, *Mexico: Class Formation, Capital Accumulation, and the State* (New York: Monthly Review Press, 1968), 88.

41. A. Gorman, "Anarchists in Education: The Free Popular University in Egypt (1901)," *Middle Eastern Studies* 41, no. 3 (2005): 306–7, 311–12.

42. Casanovas, "Labour and Colonialism in Cuba in the Second Half of the Nineteenth-Century," 303–5.

43. Shaffer, "Purifying the Environment for the Coming New Dawn."

44. E. A. Gordon, "Anarchism in Brazil: Theory and Practice, 1890–1920" (PhD diss., Tulane University, 1978), 176; R. Ramos, E. Rodrigues, and A. Samis, *Against All Tyranny! Essays on Anarchism in Brazil* (London: Kate Sharpley Library, 2003), 4.

45. P. Avrich, *The Modern School Movement: Anarchism and Education in the United States* (Princeton, NJ: Princeton University Press, 1980); K. Teitelbaum and W. J. Reese, "American Socialist Pedagogy and Experimentation in the Progressive Era: The Socialist Sunday School," *History of Education Quarterly* 23, no. 4 (1983).

46. Avrich, *Anarchist Portraits*, 121; see also M. Malet, *Nestor Makhno in the Russian Civil War* (London: London School of Economics and Political Science, 1982).

47. Dirlik, *Anarchism in the Chinese Revolution*, 262–69, 290.

48. Nettlau, *A Short History of Anarchism*, 289.

49. On the idea of an "oppositional counter-public" see F. Shor, "Left Labor Agitators in the Pacific Rim in the Early Twentieth Century," *International Labor and Working Class History*, no. 67 (2005): 150.

50. Malatesta, "Syndicalism," 221–22; also Malatesta in Richards, *Errico Malatesta*, 125.

51. See, for example, Molnár and Pekmez, "Rural Anarchism in Spain and the 1873 Cantonalist Revolution," 171–72.

52. Rocker, *Anarcho-Syndicalism*, chapter 4.

53. Ford and Foster, *Syndicalism*, 38.

54. Ibid., 39–40.

55. See Foner, *The Industrial Workers of the World*, 144–46.

56. Michels, *Political Parties*.

57. Ibid., 318, 325–26.

58. Ibid., 318–19, 322–23.

59. P. J. Cook, "Robert Michels's *Political Parties* in Perspective," *Journal of Politics* 33, no. 3 (1971): 775–76, 781–83, 785–86, 789.

60. Ibid., 776–79.

61. For example, a number of contemporary U.S. unions, long considered exemplars of a bureaucratic and moderate style of unionism, have recently been increasingly revitalised by a crisis in the old leadership, the rise of new layers of activists, and pressure from other unions to act in a more innovative manner. As new members were recruited, and new organising and resistance tactics were adopted, including political education, the process of revitalisation gained momentum. Significantly, some of the impetus for change came from the union bureaucracy, raising questions about the link that Michels postulated between oligarchy and conservatism. See K. Voss

and R. Sherman, "Breaking the Iron Law of Oligarchy: Union Revitalization in the American Labor Movement," *American Journal of Sociology* 106, no. 2 (2000).

62.   A classic study that made this point was S. M. Lipset, *Union Democracy: The Internal Politics of the International Typographical Union* (Glencoe, IL: Free Press, 1956), which argued that a decentralised and democratic structure, a commitment to local autonomy and democracy, and competition between different factions provided major obstacles to the emergence of oligarchy.

63.   Union education, plus the existing cultural and political traditions of union members, play a fundamental role in the emergence of democratic unionism; S. M. Buhlungu, "Democracy and Modernisation in the Making of the South African Trade Union Movement: The Dilemma of Leadership, 1973–2000" (PhD diss., University of the Witwatersrand, 2000).

64.   Ford and Foster, *Syndicalism*, 39–40.

65.   Malatesta in Richards, *Errico Malatesta*, 124–25; 125; Malatesta, "Syndicalism," 221, 225.

66.   Quoted in Graham, *Anarchism*, 376, editor's notes.

67.   Bayerlein and Van der Linden, "Revolutionary Syndicalism in Portugal," 160–64.

68.   See, for example, Avrich, *The Haymarket Tragedy*; Foner, *The Industrial Workers of the World*, chapter 19.

69.   Industrial Workers of the World, *What Is the IWW?*

70.   T. Kaplan, "Other Scenarios: Women and Spanish Anarchism," in *Becoming Visible: Women in European History*, ed. R. Bridenthal and C. Koonz (Boston: Houghton Mifflin Co., 1977), 166.

71.   José Peirats, *Anarchists in the Spanish Revolution* (1964; repr., London: Freedom Press, 1990), 264–65.

72.   Ibid., 268.

73.   There is a fairly wide literature on this group; see, inter alia, Ackelsberg, "Revolution and Community"; M. A. Ackelsberg, "'Separate and Equal'? Mujeres Libres and Anarchist Strategy for Women's Emancipation," *Feminist Studies* 11, no. 1 (1985); M. A. Ackelsberg, "Models of Revolution: Rural Women and Anarchist Collectivisation in Spain," *Journal of Peasant Studies* 20, no. 3 (1993); M. A. Ackelsberg, *Free Women of Spain: Anarchism and the Struggle for the Emancipation of Women*, rev. ed. (Oakland: AK Press, 2005); P. Carpena, "Spain 1936: Free Women, a Feminist, Proletarian, and Anarchist Movement," in *Women of the Mediterranean*, ed. by M. Gadant (London: Zed Books, 1986); Kaplan, "Other Scenarios"; M. Nash, "*Mujeres Libres*: Anarchist Women in the Spanish Civil War," *Antipode: A Radical Journal of Geography* 10–11, nos. 3 and 1 (1979).

74.   Quoted in N. Rider, "The Practice of Direct Action: The Barcelona Rent Strike of 1931," in *For Anarchism: History, Theory, and Practice*, ed. D. Goodway (London: Routledge, 1989), 88.

75.   Ibid., 87–101.

76.   For a fascinating account, see P. B. Radcliff, *From Mobilization to Civil War: The Politics of Polarization in the Spanish City of Gijon, 1900–1937* (Cambridge: Cambridge University Press, 1996).

77.   See Gallacher, *Revolt on the Clyde*; Quail, *The Slow Burning Fuse*; Hinton, *The First Shop Stewards Movement*.

78.   Shaffer, "Purifying the Environment for the Coming New Dawn."

79.   A. G. Wood, "Postrevolutionary Pioneer: Anarchist María Luisa Marín and the Veracruz Renters' Movement," *A Contracorriente* 2, no. 3 (2005).

80.   Ibid., 3–6, 13–35.

81.   A. Wood and J. A. Baer, "Strength in Numbers: Urban Rent Strikes and Political Transformation in the Americas, 1904–1925," *Journal of Urban History* 32, no. 6 (2006): 869, 874–75.

82.   J. A. Baer, "Tenant Mobilization and the 1907 Rent Strike in Buenos Aires," *Americas* 49, no. 3 (1993); Yoast, "The Development of Argentine Anarchism."

83.   Hirsch, "The Anarcho-Syndicalist Roots of a Multi-Class Alliance."

84.   Engels, "The Bakuninists at Work," 132–33.

85.   Ibid.

86. Holton, "Syndicalist Theories of the State," 5.

87. Hinton, *The First Shop Stewards Movement*, 276, 280.

88. Hyman, *Marxism and the Sociology of Trade Unionism*, 43.

89. Lambert, "Political Unionism in South Africa," 45.

90. Enrico Leone, as summarised in Michels, *Political Parties*, 317.

91. Thorpe, *"The Workers Themselves,"* 18–19.

92. Burgmann, *Revolutionary Industrial Unionism*, 53.

93. Holton, "Syndicalist Theories of the State."

94. Malatesta, "Syndicalism," 224.

95. See Richards, "Notes for a Biography," 283–84.

96. Quoted in Dubofsky, *"Big Bill" Haywood*, 65.

97. R. Chaplin, *The General Strike* (1933; repr., Chicago: IWW, 1985), n.p.

98. De Leon, *The Preamble of the Industrial Workers of the World*, 21.

99. Ibid., 23–24; Socialist Labour Party [De Leon], *The Socialist Labour Party*, 20.

100. Quoted in Bekken, "The First Daily Anarchist Newspaper," 13.

101. Roediger and Rosemont, *Haymarket Scrapbook*, 86.

102. Avrich, *The Haymarket Tragedy*, 160–63.

103. E. Pataud and E. Pouget, *How We Shall Bring about the Revolution: Syndicalism and the Cooperative Commonwealth* (1909; repr., London: Pluto Press, 1990), 75–84, 90–102.

104. Ibid., 83–84.

105. Ibid., 154–55, 156, 158, 159–65.

106. Holton, "Syndicalist Theories of the State," 11.

107. International Working People's Association, "The Pittsburgh Proclamation," in *Anarchism: A Documentary History of Libertarian Ideas, Volume 1: From Anarchy to Anarchism, 300 CE to 1939*, ed. R. Graham (1883; repr., Montréal: Black Rose, 2005), 192.

108. Ford and Foster, *Syndicalism*, 9–13, 29–30.

109. Maximoff, *The Programme of Anarcho-syndicalism*, 49–52.

110. Berkman, *The ABC of Anarchism*.

111. Brown, *The Social General Strike*, 10.

112. Rocker, *Anarcho-Syndicalism*, chapter 5.

113. Thorpe, *"The Workers Themselves,"* 324, appendix D.

114. De Leon, *The Preamble of the Industrial Workers of the World*, 21.

115. Quoted in Richards, *Lessons of the Spanish Revolution*, 71.

116. Friends of Durruti, *Towards a Fresh Revolution*, 25.

117. Ibid.

118. F. Morrow, *Revolution and Counter Revolution in Spain* (1938; repr., New Park Publications Ltd., London 1963), chapter 17, available at http://www.marxists.org/archive/morrow-felix/1938/revolution-spain/ch17.htm (accessed June 30, 2006).

119. Ibid., chapter 5, available at http://www.spunk.org/library/writers/rocker/sp001495/rocker_as5.html (accessed June 30, 2006).

120. Workers Solidarity Movement, *Position Paper*, section 5.2.

121. Bakunin, "The Programme of the International Brotherhood," 152–54; Bakunin, "Letters to a Frenchman on the Current Crisis," 190.

122. Maura, "The Spanish Case," 66, 68, 72, 80–83.

123. National Confederation of Labour, *Resolution on Libertarian Communism as Adopted by the Confederacion Nacional del Trabajo, Zaragoza*, 10–11.

124. Richards, *Lessons of the Spanish Revolution*, 83; A. Bar, "The CNT: The Glory and Tragedy of Spanish Anarchosyndicalism," in *Revolutionary Syndicalism: An International Perspective*, ed. M. van der Linden and W. Thorpe (Otterup, Denmark: Scolar, 1990), 131.

125. Morrow, *Revolution and Counter Revolution in Spain*, chapter 17. The Marxist author of the major English-language study of the AD notes that "its ideology and watchwords were quintessentially in the CNT idiom: it cannot be said that they displayed a Marxist ideology at any time." Rather than seeking to revise anarchism, the group was "against the abandonment of revolutionary objectives and of anarchism's fundamental and quintessential ideological principles, which the CNT-FAI leaders had thrown over." See A. Guillamón, *The Friends of Durruti Group, 1937-1939* (Oakland: AK Press, 1996), 61, 95, 107.

126. Friends of Durruti, *Towards a Fresh Revolution*, 24–25.

127. A. Paz, *Durruti: The People Armed* (Montréal: Black Rose, 1987), 247. An important review of the debate over taking power or joining the Popular Front is provided by Wetzel, *Looking Back after 70 Years*. The earlier version of this piece, which has some substantial differences, is also worth consulting: T. Wetzel, *Workers' Power and the Spanish Revolution*, available at http://www.uncanny.net/~wsa/spain.html (accessed September 10, 2004).

128. Friends of Durruti, *Towards a Fresh Revolution*, 12.

129. Peirats, *Anarchists in the Spanish Revolution*, 13–14.

130. Bookchin, *The Spanish Anarchists*, 137; Bookchin, *To Remember Spain*, 20–21.

131. Goldman, "The Failure of the Russian Revolution," 159.

132. For these terms, see works like Guillen, *Anarchist Economics*, 17; Wetzel, *Workers' Power and the Spanish Revolution*; Wetzel, *Looking Back after 70 Years*; De Leon, "Industrial Unionism"; Connolly, *Socialism Made Easy*, 48; Haywood and Bohm, *Industrial Socialism*, 49.

133. Bakunin, "The Paris Commune and the Idea of the State," 270; Guérin, *Anarchism*, 55, 153.

134. Holloway rejects both the parliamentary road to power and the dictatorship of the proletariat, and advocates a system with a "commune of communes or council of councils," but rejects the idea of destroying the state or making a revolution; see J. Holloway, *Change the World without Taking Power: The Meaning of Revolution for Today*, rev. ed. (London: Pluto Press, 2005), 241. How exactly his "commune of communes" would abolish capitalism and state power remains rather vague.

135. Engels, "On Authority," 102–5.

136. Malatesta in Richards, *Errico Malatesta*, 55.

137. Quoted in Eltzbacher, *Anarchism*, 89.

Alexander Berkman (1870–1936) addresses a rally of the Industrial Workers of the World in New York in 1914.

The revolutionary syndicalist IWW (nick-named the "Wobblies"), part of the broad anarchist tradition, started in the United States in 1905 and soon spread across the world, organising militant IWW trade unions as far afield as Australia, Siberia, South Africa, and Chile, and with its propaganda finding an audience in places such as Punjab, Fiji, Cuba, New Zealand, Mexico, and Hong Kong. The IWW stressed "dual unionism."

Railway workers of the General Confederation of Labour of France on strike in 1910.

The French CGT played a critical role in the second wave of syndicalism from the 1890s onwards, and stressed the importance of "boring-from-within" the orthodox unions. The CGT's 1906 *Charter of Amiens* was, alongside the IWW's 1905 Preamble, the most influential syndicalist document of the era, inspiring the establishment of anarcho-syndicalist organisations across Europe and Latin America. *Picture courtesy of the Centre for International Research on Anarchism.*

CHAPTER 7

Dual Unionism, Reforms, and Other Tactical Debates

In this chapter and the one that follows, we will shift our analysis toward an examination of anarchist tactics, asking, What were the different positions adopted in pursuit of long-term anarchist strategies?

This chapter will explore two main sets of tactical issues. The first deals with the tactical issues posed by the activities of the state machinery, and how the movement responded to questions of warfare, labour law, and state welfare systems. How can the military operations of the state be opposed? Should anarchists and syndicalists participate in statutory industrial relations systems? Should anarchists and syndicalists support state welfare systems?

The second set of tactical issues deals with how anarchists and syndicalists should relate to the union movement. The adoption of a syndicalist strategy, for instance, begs the question of what immediate steps are to be taken in order to realise the project of building a revolutionary labour movement. In particular, it raises tactical concerns about how to relate to existing, orthodox unions. Should such unions be captured (by "boring from within"), or should new syndicalist unions be formed outside the existing unions ("dual unionism")? Or should anarchists and syndicalists work within existing unions in order to promote oppositional rank-and-file movements independent of the formal union structure?

The Antimilitarist Tradition and Popular Revolt

The broad anarchist tradition's fervent opposition to state wars and imperialism was an important expression of its antistatism. Anarchist and syndicalist antimilitarism was not just about opposition to the use of force to uphold the state but also a rejection of the *class* character of the modern military. Anarchist and syndicalist opposition to war did not derive so much from pacifism—an opposition to violence in any form—but from a class analysis. The modern military served, on the one hand, as the weapon of last resort in the maintenance of the class system; on the other hand, wars by the state were waged only to benefit the interests of the ruling classes, and offered nothing to the popular classes but conscription, regimentation, injury, and death.

Arising from competition in the state system along with the drive for new markets as well as sources of labour and raw materials—at its most sophisticated, the broad anarchist tradition avoided the crude economic explanations of Marxism—these wars pitted sailors and soldiers, drawn overwhelmingly from the popular classes, against one another to serve ends not their own. The socialising role of the military, and the role of nationalism in fostering war and dividing the international popular classes, was duly noted by Kropotkin:

> Childhood itself has not been spared; schoolboys are swept into the ranks, to be trained up in hatred of the Prussian, the English or the Slav; drilled in blind obedience to the government of the moment, whatever the colour of its flag, and when they come to the years of manhood to be laden like pack-horses with cartridges, provisions and the rest of it; to have a rifle thrust into their hands and be taught to charge at the bugle call and slaughter one another right and left like wild beasts, without asking themselves why or for what purpose.[1]

It was, Maximoff argued, the "criminally mercenary interests" of rival ruling classes that impel them to "sow hatred and hostility between nations."[2]

Antimilitarism was a central theme in the revolutionary popular counterculture promoted by the broad anarchist tradition. There was little debate among the anarchists and syndicalists in the glorious period about the necessity of antimilitarism; current anarchism is also strongly associated with opposition to the wars of the late twentieth and early twenty-first centuries. The "military spirit is the most merciless, heartless and brutal in existence," said Goldman, and militarism must be halted by "human brotherhood and solidarity," which alone could "clear the horizon from the terrible red streak of war and destruction."[3]

If wars "are only waged in the interest of the ruling classes," observed Rocker, then "any means is justifiable that can prevent the organised murder of peoples." These include strikes, boycotts of military production, the disruption of military facilities and transport, and the subversion of the armed forces themselves:

> As outspoken opponents of all nationalist ambitions the revolutionary Syndicalists ... have always devoted a very considerable part of their activity to anti-militarist propaganda, seeking to hold the workers in soldiers' coats loyal to their class and to prevent their turning their weapons against their brethren in time of a strike. This has cost them great sacrifices; but they have never ceased their efforts, because they know that they can regain their efforts only by incessant warfare against the dominant powers.[4]

Antimilitarism was a central activity for many anarchists and syndicalists. Nieuwenhuis was perhaps its greatest exponent in Europe and the key figure in the International Anti-Militarist Union formed in 1904. A popular young Lutheran minister, Nieuwenhuis left the church in 1879 and joined the Social Democratic Union, which had been formed in 1881 and was modeled on the German SDP.[5] He was the first socialist senator in the Netherlands. When the Social Democratic Union split in 1893, with orthodox Marxists leading a breakaway Social Democratic Workers' Party, Nieuwenhuis and the majority of members remained loyal to the existing organisation. Like many in the Social Democratic Union, he moved toward anarchism by 1897. He published *De Vrije Socialist* ("The Free Socialist," which still exists as *De Vrije*, that is, "The Free") and wrote widely, dying in 1919.

The project of subversion was also linked to the view that it could lead to a split in the military when the revolution came; as the troops are "mostly working-men and in sympathy with the general strike," they could be "induced to join the ranks of their striking fellow workers." Therefore, antimilitarist work should encourage "working class soldiers not to shoot their brothers and sisters ... but, if need be, to shoot their own officers and to desert the army when the crucial moment arrives."[6] A masterpiece of this sort of appeal, stressing common class interests, is the "Don't Shoot" leaflet, also known as "An Open Letter to British Soldiers." Written by an anonymous British syndicalist, it got Tom Mann and several other syndicalists arrested for incitement to mutiny after it appeared in the British *Syndicalist* in the 1910s:

> Men! Comrades! Brothers!...
>
> You are Workingmen's Sons. When We go on Strike to fight to better Our lot, which is the lot also of your Fathers, Mothers, Brothers, and Sisters, YOU are called upon by your officers to MURDER US. Don't do it.... "Thou shalt not kill," says the Book. Don't forget that! It does not say, "unless you have a uniform on." No! MURDER IS MURDER, whether committed in the heat of anger on one who has wronged a loved one, or by clay-piped Tommies with a rifle.
>
> Boys, Don't Do It! Act the Man! Act the Brother! Act the Human Being! Property can be replaced! Human life, Never! The Idle Rich Class, who own and order you about, own and order us about also. They and their friends own the land and means of life of Britain.
>
> You don't! We don't! When We kick, they order You to murder Us. When You kick, You get court-martialled and cells. Your fight is Our fight. Instead of fighting Against each other, We should be fighting With each other.... You, like Us, are of the Slave Class. When We rise, You rise; when We fall, even by your bullets, Ye fall also.
>
> Comrades, have we called in vain? Think things out and refuse any longer to Murder your Kindred. Help US to win back the Britain for the British, and the World for the Workers.[7]

The history of the broad anarchist tradition is also replete with numerous examples of large-scale and effective antimilitarist campaigns, particularly in the glorious period. Some of the most important of these campaigns developed into revolts by the Western popular classes against colonialism. During the Cuban war of independence (1895–1904), the Spanish anarchists campaigned against Spanish intervention among the working class, peasantry, and military. "All Spanish anarchists disapproved of the war and called on workers to disobey military authority and refuse to fight in Cuba," leading to several mutinies among draftees.[8] The Spanish anarchists also opposed the intervention of the United States from 1898 onward. Michele Angiolillo, the insurrectionist anarchist who assassinated Spanish president Antonio Cánovas del Castillo in 1897, declared at his trial that the deed was in revenge for the repression of anarchists in Spain as well as for Spain's atrocities in its colonial wars in Cuba and the Philippines.[9]

The 1909 Tragic Week started as a popular revolt against conscription in the Spanish government's ongoing war in Morocco. It followed the decision by the Spanish government to call up army reservists, "most of whom were working-class family men, strongly anti-militarist ever since they, or their fathers, had returned starving, and ridden with malaria, from the colonial war with the United States in 1898."[10] Starting with a general strike on Monday, July 26, 1909, by Solidaridad Obrera ("Workers' Solidarity," the CNT's predecessor), the revolt escalated rapidly. By Tuesday, the working class was in control of Barcelona—halting troop trains, overturning trams, cutting communications, and erecting barricades. By Thursday, fighting broke out with government forces and over 150 workers were killed. For Henry W. Nevinson, a contemporary, the "refusal of the Catalonian reservists to serve in the war against the Riff mountaineers of Morocco" was "one of the most significant" events of modern times.[11]

The great significance of the Tragic Week was that "the proletariat *in Europe* rebelled and shed its blood against imperialism *in Africa*."[12] It was not an isolated incident. In 1911, the CNT marked its birth with a general strike in September, called in support of strikers in Bilbao and against the ongoing war in Morocco.[13] Again, in 1922, following a disastrous battle against the forces of Abd el-Krim in Morocco in August—a battle in which at least ten thousand Spanish troops died—"the Spanish people were full of indignation and demanded not only an end to the war but also that those responsible for the massacre and the politicians who favoured the operation in Africa be brought to trial," expressing their anger in riots and strikes in the industrial regions.[14]

It was by no means an isolated event, but rather one in an ongoing series of similar battles under anarchist and syndicalist influence. In Italy in the 1880s and 1890s, "anarchists and former anarchists" "were some of the most outspoken opponents of Italian military adventures in Eritrea and Abyssinia."[15] This opposition to colonialism was linked, via antimilitarism, to opposition to the use of the state's armed forces against the Italian popular classes; this related imperialism to the concrete conditions of the Italian working class, suggesting that it had no interest in such a policy. The Italian invasion of Libya on September 19, 1911, was another rallying point. The majority of PSI deputies voted for annexation.[16] Anarchists and syndicalists, on the other hand, organised demonstrations against the war and a partial general strike, and "tried to prevent troop trains leaving the Marches and Liguria for their embarkation points."[17]

Augusto Masetti, an anarchist soldier, shot and wounded a colonel addressing troops departing for Libya at a parade ground in Bologna, shouting, "Down with the War! Long Live Anarchy!" He became a popular symbol, and the anarchist journal *L'Agitatore* ("The Agitator") issued a special commemorative edition, claiming that "anarchist revolt shines through the violence of war."[18] This led to the arrest of anarchists and syndicalists; Borghi, one of the paper's editors, had a previous conviction for antimilitarist activity in 1902 and so he fled to Paris.[19] The war "stirred all the latent but deep anti-militarism of the peasant and working classes, imperfectly if at all integrated into the patriotism and nationalism which were universal among the middle and lower-middle classes," and it was the USI and the anarchists who captured the popular mood.[20] By 1914, an anarchist-led antimilitarist front, with twenty thousand adherents, was sufficiently powerful that top politicians feared it could lay the basis for a revolutionary "Red bloc."[21]

On June 7, 1914, the anarchist-led antimilitarists organised a national demonstration on Constitution Day against militarism, against special punishment battalions in the army, and for the release of Masetti.[22] With the spectre of the Red bloc in mind, the government ordered troops to prevent the protests.[23] Clashes with troops in the anarchist stronghold of Ancona following a rally addressed by Malatesta left three workers dead and sparked off the revolutionary crisis of the "Red Week" of June 1914, a mass uprising ushered in by a general strike.[24] Called by the PSI, the general strike was soon led by anarchists and the USI.[25]

Approximately a million workers participated in what became a working-class movement of unprecedented power.[26] Ancona was held by rebels for ten days, barricades went up in all the big cities, small towns in the Marche declared themselves self-governing communes, and everywhere the revolt took place "red flags were raised, churches attacked, railways torn up, villas sacked, taxes abolished and prices reduced."[27] The movement collapsed after the CGL called off the strike, but it took ten thousand troops to regain control of Ancona.[28]

Antimilitarism was widely adhered to elsewhere, always linked to a criticism of capitalism and the state. In France, anarchists like Michel called on conscripts to strike, forcing the ruling class "to go off to war by themselves."[29] The pre-First World War CGT had a long-standing tradition of antimilitarism. In 1900, the CGT and the Bourses du Travail decided to campaign among the military, with particular attention to young recruits, producing a seditious *Manuel du Soldat* ("Soldiers' Manual") for distribution among the soldiers and the public; the manual included a call for desertion. By 1906, two hundred thousand copies of the manual had been sold. By the early 1910s, antimilitarism constituted the "bulk of syndicalist activity."[30] In 1911, the CGT held an antiwar demonstration in Paris that attracted twenty thousand people, and a twenty-four-hour strike by eighty thousand workers in support of peace in 1913, and the state responded with massive raids, with syndicalists receiving a total of 167 months in jail. For the U.S. IWW, "the approved international policy of modern capitalism" was "but ruthless coercion in the pursuit of raw supplies and to secure export markets for capital and goods, all for the benefit of our economic overlords":

> The IWW favours a league of the world's workers against the world's ravishers. It favours the organisation of labour on the lines of world industry, to strike on such lines against war and the outrages against humanity arising from capitalism.... With corporations in existence having worldwide branches, with inventions like the steamship, wireless, aeroplane, eliminating distance, time and national barriers, the industrial organisation of labour on a world basis is not only possible but necessary.[31]

In South Africa, anarchists and syndicalists opposed the introduction of compulsory military service by the Defence Bill (passed in 1912), arguing that the legislation aimed to create an all-white army to crush African workers. A "native rising" would be a "wholly justified" response to "the cruel exploitation of South African natives by farmers, mining magnates and factory owners," and should receive the "sympathy and support of every white wage-slave."[32] For Shifu in China, "Our principles are communism, anti-militarism, syndicalism, anti-religion, anti-family, vegetarianism, an international language and universal harmony."[33]

In Japan, Kōtuku opposed the Russo-Japanese war from 1903 to 1905, and Ōsugi was jailed in 1907 for an antimilitarist article addressed to conscripts.[34] The Zenkoku Jiren, at its founding, declared that "we are opposed to imperialist aggression and we advocate the international solidarity of the working class."[35] Along with the Black Youth League (Kokushoku Seinen Renmai, better known as the Kokuren) anarchist group, the Zenkoku Jiren opposed Japan's 1927 intervention in Manchuria, and the Zenkoku Jiren responded to the 1931 invasion of Manchuria with a call for struggle against war and military production, a refusal to enlist, and general disobedience to officers.[36] When the Japanese army entered Mongolia in 1933, the anarchists called for mass struggle, strikes in munition plants, and mutinies.[37]

In 1907 and 1908, war threatened to break out between Brazil and Bolivia over the disputed territory of Acre, and a nine-year draft (seven in reserve forces) was instituted for male citizens aged twenty-one to forty-four. In response, the syndicalist Labour Federation of Rio de Janeiro established a Brazilian Anti-Militarist League, with chapters in coastal cities from Recife in the north to Porto Alegre in the south, and published *Não Matarás* ("Don't Kill").[38] In Rio Doce, women League activists destroyed a draft office and then telegraphed the minister of war to inform him of their actions—a pattern repeated in many other towns. The movement culminated in 1908 with a COB antiwar demonstration by five thousand people in Rio, backed by similar marches in other Brazilian cities as well as in Argentina and Uruguay, and a declaration that the revolutionary strike was the appropriate response to capitalist war. The Brazilians were represented at the 1913 International Syndicalist Congress held in London (a precursor of the IWA), where an opposition to war was reiterated.[39]

The outbreak of the First World War in August 1914 nonetheless saw a number of prominent anarchists—among them Cherkezov, Cornelissen, Grave, Guillaume, and Kropotkin—come out openly in support of the Allies, maintaining that a German victory must be avoided at all costs. The French CGT did likewise, joining with political socialists, the state, and the employers in a Sacred Union for the duration of the war. The great majority of sections of the Labour and Socialist International—with the notable exception of the Bolshevik wing of the RSDRP and a few minor affiliates like the Bulgarians—also rallied to the flag, throwing overboard their formal opposition to war and destroying the International. Lenin made great play of the capitulation of the "anarcho-trenchists," and suggested that anarchism had failed the test of war as badly as the Marxists.[40] Other writers speak in sweeping terms of the general crisis of the Left and the collapse of socialism in 1914, as "socialist leaders were either cowed or carried away by the wave of jingoism."[41]

In fact, the vast majority of anarchists and syndicalists rejected the war, and adopted the view that the war should be met with revolutionary struggle—a perspective that goes back to Bakunin.[42] Malatesta rebuked Kropotkin, called for resistance to the war, and called for a new socialist international.[43] He argued that the war was waged in the interests of the ruling classes, and declared,

> The war ought to have been prevented by bringing about the Revolution, or at least by threatening to do so. Either the strength or the skill neces-

sary for this has been lacking. Peace ought to be imposed by bringing about the Revolution, or at least by threatening to do so. To the present time, the strength or the skill has been wanting. Well! there is only one remedy: to do better in future. More than ever we must avoid compromise.... Long live the peoples, all the peoples![44]

Notwithstanding the great prestige of Kropotkin, his prowar position was extremely unpopular. The "immediate reaction" of the "vast majority" of British anarchists was "to reject the war and immediate steps were taken to propagandise against it."[45] No British syndicalist militant "actively supported the war," and Mann (who privately hoped for a German defeat) "never wavered" in his "fundamental opposition to the war."[46] Kropotkin was marginalised, as was Cornelissen, whose "very considerable" influence quickly "dwindled away to nothing."[47] In France, an antiwar faction quickly emerged in the CGT, coalescing into a Committee for Syndicalist Defence in 1916.[48]

A militarist group arose within the Italian USI and other sections of the Italian anarchist movement, but was soon defeated.[49] The anarchists and syndicalists generally maintained a consistently antiwar position, continuing into 1920, when they launched a mass campaign against the Italian invasion of Albania and the counterrevolutionary Western intervention against the Russian Revolution.[50] A militarist minority in Spain was also overwhelmingly defeated. In Germany, where the SDP had come out in support of the war effort and provided the crucial votes in parliament for war credits, the FVdG was "the only German workers' organisation to have adopted an internationalist rather than a patriotic response to the war."[51] The U.S. IWW declared itself among the "determined opponents of all nationalistic sectionalism or patriotism, and the militarism preached and supported by our one enemy, the Capitalist Class," and aimed at, "in time of war, the general strike in all industries."[52]

A number of anarchists and syndicalists, including FVdG representatives, attended the antiwar Zimmerwald congress organised by Lenin in September 1916, but this was not the start of anarchist participation in an international antiwar organisation. Five months earlier the Spanish anarchists organised the first antiwar international labour congress, at which 8 countries and 170 organisations were represented.[53] Held in El Ferrol, it was followed by a FORA mass rally in Buenos Aires in May. In Brazil, where antimilitarist activities revived with the outbreak of the First World War and the crushing of a peasant revolt in Paraná, the COB condemned all sides in the war between the great powers.[54] In 1915, it issued an antiwar manifesto in conjunction with other unions, held numerous antiwar rallies, published the antiwar *Guerra Sociale* ("Social War"), and held an International Peace Congress in Rio de Janeiro. This was organised through the anarchist People's Anti-War Agitational Commission—attended by delegates from Brazil, Argentina, Spain, and Portugal—which issued a manifesto calling for "permanent revolt."[55] Meanwhile, Goldman, Berkman, Malatesta, and other major figures issued an "International Anarchist Manifesto against War."[56]

Anarchists and syndicalists were subject to repression for their positions. While *Freedom* in London had printed Kropotkin's prowar position, it came out strongly against the war; its offices were raided, its press was seized, and its editor,

Tom Keell, was jailed.[57] Rocker, then resident in Britain, was interned as an "enemy alien." When the South African Labour Party and the orthodox unions came out in support of the British Empire, anarchists and syndicalists helped form a War-on-War League, held numerous antiwar meetings, and suffered ongoing arrests. In Cape Town, the anarchist Wilfred Harrison—a former soldier, carpenter, pioneer of interracial unionism, key figure in the local Social Democratic Federation, member of the War-on-War League, and later a founding member of the CPSA—was sentenced to six months for antimilitarist propaganda.[58] Slandered as "Imperial Wilhelm's Warriors"—as supporters of the German kaiser—the U.S. IWW faced "criminal syndicalism" laws in thirty-five states after 1914.[59] The repression increased dramatically after the United States entered the war in 1917, and was followed by the mass arrests and deportations of the Left during the subsequent Red Scare.

In Australia, where the IWW demanded, "Let those who own Australia do the fighting," twelve Wobblies were tried for an alleged plot to burn down Sydney, and another eleven for "seditious conspiracy."[60] With the passage of the December 1916 Unlawful Associations Act—which provided jail sentences of six months for anyone who advocated antimilitarism, direct action, or a change to the social order—more than one hundred Wobblies were subsequently imprisoned; others were deported, and the IWW press was suppressed. In Canada, the IWW was suppressed with the aid of the British North America Act of 1915, and a 1918 federal order-in-council made membership in either the Chicago or Detroit IWWs subject to a mandatory five-year prison term.[61] In Germany, syndicalist publications were suppressed and activists were arrested.[62] Undeterred, the new IWA included antimilitarism in its core principles, and founded an International Anti-Militarist Commission in 1926 to promote disarmament and gather information on war production.

If we have focused our account of anarchist and antimilitarism on developments in the glorious period, this is only because this era provides some of the most dramatic expressions of this tradition. The same commitment to antimilitarism can be found, however, throughout anarchist and syndicalist history, including opposition to the Anglo-Boer War (1899–1902), the annexation of Korea (1910), the invasion of Manchuria (1931), the Second World War (1939–1945), the Algerian War (1954–1962), the Vietnam War (1959–1975), the Gulf War (1990), the Russian war against Chechnya (starting in 1991), the invasion of Afghanistan (beginning in 2001), the occupation of Iraq (starting in 2003), and innumerable other conflicts.

Reforms, Laws, and Compromises

If the question of opposing war was fairly easily faced by the broad anarchist tradition, the daily struggle for immediate gains posed more complicated tactical issues. Mass anarchists assume that reforms are desirable, and recognise that the need for reforms is only removed with a revolution. Even a syndicalist union, based on a democratic structure, mobilised through direct action, and infused with radical ideas, must make numerous compromises with the ruling class in a prerevolutionary period, and engage in "negotiations, compromises, adjustments and contacts with the authorities and the employers."[63] (We leave aside here the insurrectionist view that reforms were worthless, and the claim that a programme of winning immediate gains was by definition "reformist" and therefore unacceptable.)[64] Unlike mass anarchism, insurrectionist anarchism refuses to deal with reforms, laws, and compromises.

However, the question for syndicalism is not whether to negotiate or make compromises with the class enemy but *how* to do so in a manner consonant with the syndicalist project. Most immediately and self-evidently, it follows from our discussion so far that, in situations falling short of revolution, negotiations and compromises must arise as the outcome of a struggle based on direct action, which forces the authorities and the employers to the negotiating table. It is in and around negotiations that complications arise, and specifically there are questions of *what* types of negotiations are acceptable, what compromises are possible, and which outcomes are compatible with the means and ends of a syndicalist union.

On one level, there is the issue of whether binding contracts could be entered into with employers. Syndicalists, given their stress on direct action and working-class autonomy, should evidently reject no-strike clause agreements as surrendering the vital weapon of direct action, and the politics of class struggle, in pursuit of an illusory class peace. But what of contracts—binding deals between labour and capital—as such?[65] The U.S. IWW reflected one view: "No contracts, no agreements, no compacts," said Haywood. "These are unholy alliances and must be damned as treason when entered into with the capitalist class."[66] Rather, victories should be enforced by the strength of the union.[67] For the IWW in New Zealand, "any understanding between workers and employers is only an armistice, to be broken, when convenient, by either side." The "Employing Class, as a whole, has always recognised and acted up to this," so it was "foolish" for workers to "keep to their side of contracts."[68] It was feared that formal agreements with employers would sap the fighting spirit of the union and prevent it from taking industrial action at will.

The difficulty, however, was that weaker syndicalist unions were often unable to enforce agreements, and hostile employers were able to grind away at concessions; moderate unions like the AFL, as some Wobblies admitted, were able to attract members as a result of recognition agreements with employers as well as binding contracts. Other syndicalists, bearing this in mind, were willing to accept formal contracts with employers as an outcome of strikes, so long as the contracts did not bind the union to particular courses of action for a set period.[69]

The ongoing development of official, statutory industrial relations systems, backed by law and including labour law courts, posed other issues. While such systems were absent or rudimentary in many places in the late nineteenth century, these systems evolved rapidly in the twentieth century, partly from the concern of elites for social order and partly under the impulse of social democratic movements. In 1904, for instance, the world's first Labour government was formed by the Australian Labour Party, which implemented suffrage and welfare reforms as well as immigration controls and a system of compulsory arbitration in labour disputes.[70] Similar models were adopted in New Zealand and elsewhere. In South Africa, major labour law reforms beginning in 1924, partly sponsored by the local Labour Party, created a whole system of negotiating forums at the level of industry; while generally avoiding compulsory arbitration, the new system (besides excluding large sectors of the working class) made legal strike action possible only after a lengthy set of negotiations and procedures had failed. Other reforms enabled unions to apply for statutory wage determinations, again a cumbersome process.

From the 1920s onward, many import-substitution industrialisation regimes and fascist states also created state-corporatist systems, in which unions were directly controlled by the state. From the 1940s onward, Keynesian welfare states established national-level, voluntary corporatist forums to negotiate policy, prices, and wages, and create binding social pacts between the classes, along with workplace forums to forge a consensus between unions and employers. Rather than decline with neoliberalism, voluntary corporatism and workplace forums have survived in the West as well as proliferated elsewhere.

Statutory industrial relations systems, of whatever type, pose a whole set of challenges. A consistent syndicalist might presumably reject direct participation in state-corporatist structures out of hand. Yet this still leaves the issue of whether it is possible to work at the grass roots of the state-controlled unions or employer-sponsored unions with the aim of fostering a syndicalist current of some sort. With the CNT surviving as a clandestine body following the establishment of the Miguel Primo de Rivera dictatorship in Spain in 1923, many activists entered the "free unions" promoted by employers (and tolerated by the new regime) to form "underground antidictatorial syndicalist nuclei."[71]

What of involvement in mechanisms that include compulsory arbitration? Historically, almost all syndicalists rejected these structures as both biased against labour and limiting the scope for direct action. The FORU in Uruguay, for example, rejected state arbitration in "the settlement of quarrels between capital and labour" as well as "draft legislation" to make such intervention mandatory.[72] The Mexican CGT refused to participate in the statutory Juntas de Conciliación y Abitraje (conciliation and arbitration councils), established in 1924 and designed to promote state-sponsored unions, and was thus declared an outlaw organisation.[73] Likewise, many French syndicalists refused to become entangled in collective bargaining machinery.[74]

Disillusionment with such systems played a key role in the life of the British syndicalist Mann. The son of a clerk at a colliery, Mann worked from a young age, became an engineer, converted to socialism in the 1880s, helped found the Independent Labour Party, and became a prominent trade unionist.[75] After immigrating to Australia in 1901, however, he was profoundly disillusioned with the system of compulsory arbitration and the Labour government; in conjunction with a rejection of craft unionism, this played a direct role in his shift to syndicalism. A pivotal event was the Broken Hill miners' strike, which was won after twenty-one weeks. The role of the Australian Labour Party, the labour laws, and state repression—and the failure of railway workers to prevent the police being transported in—convinced Mann of the need for revolutionary industrial unionism and the futility of "reliance on parliamentary action."[76] When he returned to Britain (visiting France and South Africa as well), he formed the Industrial Syndicalist Education League (ISEL) in 1910, led mass strikes in 1911, and published the *Industrial Syndicalist*. He later helped found the CPGB, heading its National Minority Movement union faction, and died in 1941.

For the IWW in New Zealand, the "evil effects of Arbitration on the workers generally" included "encouraging dependence on something outside themselves, taking the spine out of unionism, creating parasites in the shape of judges, lawyers, clerks, etc., opening the way to trickery on the part of union secretaries and others, in manipulating legal phraseology which the average worker has no time to unravel."[77] Arbitration could not protect workers from changes in capitalism, which continually undermined settlements, and it also legitimised exploitation under the cover of fairness.

The situation is more complicated with statutory negotiating forums and mechanisms for wage determinations that allow independent rather than state-run unions, and do not impose compulsory arbitration. Such systems certainly tend to push unions into official channels, foster a bureaucratic layer to work in these channels, and limit strike action, but they also provide unions with a degree of legal protection as well as determinations and regulations that can be used against employers and the state.

Compared with the alternative of crude repression, such systems have their attractions. Yet can they be effectively used in the mass anarchist project, and if so, which mechanisms can be engaged, and in which circumstances and with which qualifications? In Spain, where mixed labour commissions (representing unions and employers) and "parity committees" (which also included government representatives) emerged in 1919, the CNT briefly entered the former only to subsequently repudiate all such structures as corrupting, and the issue contributed to the subsequent split that saw a moderate faction, the *treintistas*, break away, form rival unions, and launch an electoral Syndicalist Party.[78] The moderate UGT, by contrast, became deeply immersed in such structures—a fact that accounts in part for its relatively high level of bureaucratisation.

These unresolved debates have been revived in Western Europe and elsewhere in the last quarter of the twentieth century, particularly around the statutory workplace forums established in many plants. Typically these allow workers to elect candidates, provide a mechanism for negotiating changes and disputes at work, and in some cases, supply the mechanism through which protected legal strikes may be authorised. Where the elections are individualised—that is, every worker, unionised or not, can elect candidates who stand on an individual basis—even orthodox unions have feared the possibility that the forums will duplicate union functions and render the union irrelevant by making free collective bargaining impossible. As a result of these concerns along with union pressures, workplace forums have therefore often been structured to allow unions to run candidates.

It is in such cases that the question of whether syndicalist unions should participate in workplace forums has been sharply posed, particularly in the late twentieth century. In Spain, the collapse of the Franco dictatorship in 1975 saw the CNT, suppressed for decades, rapidly reconstituted; its membership grew to three hundred thousand by 1978.[79] In 1979, the Spanish CNT began to split: there were a range of issues at stake, but one was certainly the question of participation in the post-Franco workplace forums.

The view of the official CNT was that such participation was incompatible with the syndicalist project, and that the forums should thus be boycotted. This position remains in force and is considered official IWA policy. It is clearly expressed by the Solidarity Federation, the IWA's current British affiliate, which argues that workplace forums would "control and pacify people at work," create an illusion of class partnership that leads workers and unions to take responsibility for the fortunes of the firm, undermines free collective bargaining, turns workers into a passive electorate, and detracts attention from the need to form strong union branches capable of direct action.[80] Where participation in forums is accompanied by the provision of subsidies, the problems are exacerbated by a growing union dependence on outside funding.[81]

An alternative position was represented by the main breakaway from the Spanish CNT, the Spanish CGT (it dropped the name CNT in 1989 after a lengthy and acrimonious dispute about which grouping constituted the "real" CNT), which argued for a critical and limited participation in the workplace forums. Currently, besides a formal membership of around sixty thousand, this union represents two million workers in terms of the workplace forums and other industrial relations structures, making it the third-largest union federation in the country and considerably larger than the official CNT.[82] The CGT has been accused of reformism by the IWA, which amended its statutes in 1996 to ban participation in workplace forums. The CGT's response has been that it remains loyal to syndicalism but has adapted its tactics to the new situation, and has done so to great effect. A similar split has played out in France in the 1990s, where the National Confederation of Labour (CNT), a syndicalist successor to the old CGT, split into two groups, a majority and a minority, based respectively in Paris and Bordeaux. The proparticipation CNT-Paris is substantially larger than the IWA section.

State welfare systems, which developed rapidly from the 1930s onward, also pose difficulties. Syndicalism stresses the importance of winning reforms, and much of the expansion of welfare is attributable, at least in part, to working-class struggles. Syndicalism also sees improvements in the material conditions of the working class in positive terms, and there is no doubt that state welfare systems have been critical, especially in the West, in improving the quality of popular life. Yet such welfare also serves to promote particular family structures (as, for example, when the state makes child support grants available to married women through their husbands) and foster a profound loyalty to the state as the benevolent representative of the public.

A case in point of some of the difficulties is presented by the Swedish SAC's situation; it was one of the only IWA affiliates still functioning as a union after 1945, in large part because Sweden had been relatively unaffected by the rise of dictatorships, fascism, and war elsewhere (although key members were interned during the war along with other "subversive elements"). By this time, the Swedish state was developing into a model of social democracy, introducing an extensive and expansive welfare system as well as a complicated system of collective bargaining. One aspect of this system (partly a concession to the Labour Organisation union federation, or LO, that was allied with the ruling Social Democratic Labour Party) was that the unions played a role in the administration of welfare, including the distribution of unemployment benefits.

Grappling with this issue, the SAC revised its programme in 1954 and decided to start distributing state unemployment funds to its members.[83] This was condemned by the IWA, and the SAC left in 1956, with many feeling that the union could not compete with the dominant Labour Organisation unless it also participated in the distribution of unemployment monies.[84] At the same time, while the SAC grew quickly, it also grew markedly moderate. Key SAC and SUF figures, notably the veteran activist Helmut Rüdiger (1903–1966), headed a "new orientation" current that articulated a programme that was not very different from that of mainstream social democracy; it included proposals for participation in municipal elections, stressed that the main struggle was against totalitarian systems, whether of the Left or Right, and is best considered in this period as a form of libertarian reformism, not anarchism or syndicalism.

From the 1970s onward, the SAC again swung to the Left and syndicalism—yet maintains participation in the unemployment benefits system to this day. The existence of state welfare was something that even large syndicalist unions, however purist, could not and cannot ignore. A whole range of issues arise here. Could a genuinely syndicalist union participate in a state welfare system? Could it even intervene in policy debates in order to change that system? Or were such forms of participation altogether incompatible with syndicalism? Finally, should state welfare be supported in the first place?

In the 1910s, many U.S. and British syndicalists distrusted state welfare schemes, arguing that these inculcated loyalty to the state machinery, sapped the fighting spirit of workers, and were reforms provided from above, rather than won from below.[85] The FORA even organised strikes against the introduction of such systems in the 1920s. On the other hand, even at that time some syndicalists approved of social reform laws like minimum wages and bans on child labour.[86] Where such social reform was introduced from below, the issues were not so complicated—they could be seen, like higher wages, as a consequence of syndicalist militancy and as compatible with the role of the syndicalist union—but in many cases, like in Argentina and Germany, the reforms were initiated and driven *from above*. Were they then acceptable? The contradictory character of state welfare is at the heart of these difficulties:

> But partly as a result of the effects of the proletariat's struggle, the State has taken on other roles apart from that of policeman and these roles, known by the general term "welfare state," have some very complex facets. On the one hand they have allowed the bosses to offload onto taxpayers (and thus mostly the workers themselves) part of the costs deriving from the greater security and well-being of those less well-off; a burden created through pressure from the workers has been offloaded onto the collectivity, which otherwise would form part of the cost of labour. On the other hand, though, these functions have enabled a minimum redistribution of wealth in favour of the workers; as the result of decades of struggles they have allowed the conflict to be regulated for the protection of the weakest, they have produced social institutions, such as education, healthcare and social insurance, with a high element of solidarity.[87]

The rise of neoliberalism, associated with a retreat of the welfare state, recasts the questions. The fear of an all-embracing state, incorporating the popular classes through its generosity, is being increasingly replaced by the fear of a lean capitalist state that enforces austerity, and the concern for many is, reasonably enough, less about defending the autonomy of the working class than it is about a larger defence of the popular classes against the neoliberal agenda. What the lean state of neoliberalism would like to get rid of, social reform, "is the very thing that the proletariat have an interest in maintaining."[88] The global rollback of welfare has given rise to significant popular resistance, playing a crucial role in the rise of the antiglobalisation movement, in which anarchists are often prominent, and there are many cases of syndicalists joining in struggles for the defence of welfare.[89] The complication here, however, is ensuring that the defence of welfare remains separated from calls for the return of Keynesianism, central planning, and import-substitution industrialisation regimes.

In summary, unlike principles and strategies, the development of appropriate tactics is not an easy matter. Depending on the context—for example, the rise of state welfare or its retreat—the tactics will be different. Principles and strategies provide a guide for the development of tactics, and set the boundaries on which ones are acceptable, but the continual emergence of new situations means that tactics must evolve continuously, are shaped by the context, and that there is no universal set of tactics applicable to every situation. Ultimately, while a clear analysis of particular historical conjunctures, knowledge of historical experiences, and understanding of the implications of principles and strategies can aid the development of tactics, it is practice that offers an effective adjudicator between different tactical approaches.

At present, the jury is still out. There is no consensus among syndicalists over issues of contracts in collective bargaining, participation in the statutory industrial relations machinery, and the issue of state welfare. One result has been a split in syndicalist ranks, leaving most syndicalists outside the IWA—including all of the largest syndicalist unions (with the exception of the Revolutionary Confederation of Anarcho-Syndicalists, RKAS, in Russia). One consequence has been the formation of the European Federation of Alternative Syndicalism (FESAL). Another has been the emergence of a new international formation also outside the IWA: established in Madrid in 2001, the International Libertarian Solidarity network includes dissident syndicalist unions like the Spanish CGT, the CNT-Paris, and the SAC as well as a number of other anarchist groups like the FdCA and the WSM along with the Italian formation, the Confederation of the Base. The latter is a revolutionary syndicalist body that emerged from the largely apolitical rank-and-file COBAS ("base committee") movement of the 1980s. Such initiatives have, perhaps understandably, not been welcomed by the IWA.

Boring from Within and Dual Unionism

The same *complexities* can be seen in relation to the question of how syndicalists would approach existing, established unions. Most immediately, there is the question of whether activists should aim to reform existing unions, "boring from within" to transform them into syndicalist unions, or take a "dual unionist approach," aiming at the creation of new and revolutionary unions outside the established bodies. The unions and groups linked to the IWA are strongly identified with dual unionism, as are all the main syndicalist unions that exist outside the IWA, such as the IWW, the SAC, the Spanish CGT, and the CNT-Paris. Such is the contemporary identity between syndicalism and dual unionism, that some current anarchist writing on syndicalism evidently assumes that syndicalism is necessarily dual unionist in character.[90]

Dual unionism is by no means a necessary feature of syndicalism, however. The question of whether it was an appropriate tactic was fiercely debated in the glorious period, for example, and many of the major syndicalist unions of the past were formed by boring from within. Both the Chicago IWW and the Detroit IWW adopted a strictly dual unionist perspective, but not all syndicalists held this view. The IWW was explicitly formed as an alternative to the conservative AFL, a body whose most powerful affiliates restricted their membership to skilled workers and whose activities were sectional in the extreme. In many cases, AFL unions explicitly excluded women, workers of colour, and immigrants from membership.

It was believed by the IWW founders that the AFL was incapable of reform and that the IWW would soon overtake the older body. Despite early successes, however, the IWW did not grow as quickly as was hoped, and it also lost key affiliates, like the Western Federation of Miners. At least some members thought that the policy of dual unionism was to blame—foremost among those was Foster. Foster had spent six months in France, studying under CGT militants like Monatte, before visiting Germany and Hungary.[91] He attended the 1911 IWW convention and recruited several activists to his position, including Ford, who came from Seattle. Foster's views were ridiculed by Vincent St. John, Trautmann, and other major figures, but he had enough support to be elected editor of the IWW's *Industrial Worker*. Foster used the *Industrial Worker* to promote the boring from within approach. The debate was also carried into the IWW's other paper, *Solidarity*, before being closed down, following which Foster pursued his case in the *Agitator*, through a tour of IWW locals, and then via the new SLNA.

Foster was profoundly impressed by the fact that the French syndicalists had captured the French unions by boring from within and came to view the IWW's dual unionism as a deviation from syndicalism itself, as well as an ineffective policy. He was also inspired by the example of the British syndicalists around Mann. Like Foster, Mann promoted boring from within existing unions. Foster, following this approach, made important criticisms of the IWW, which apply to the policy of dual unionism more generally.

Firstly, Ford and Foster considered the IWW's policy of dual unionism to be "a freak" with "no justification" and doomed to failure.[92] Even established moderate unions *could* evolve in a syndicalist direction. Implicit here was the view that even the most reactionary unions could not simply and repeatedly betray the working class; to survive, they must at least partially represent class interests.

The notion that the established unions could not evolve, and that the IWW alone was a real union and would inevitably replace the other ones, was for Foster an "IWW patriotism" with no basis in fact.[93] It was a caricature of other unions and ignored the fact that established unions retained the loyalties of existing members, who were not prepared to throw in their lot with an entirely new union: such obstacles to replacing existing unions were simply ignored by the IWW. Workers generally preferred to join established and proven unions, and the fact that the existing ones were often compelled to open their ranks to new categories of workers and reform their policies showed both their ability to change as well as their lasting appeal. Indeed, many ordinary workers rejected the IWW not so much because they disagreed with its ultimate aims but because they saw it as a threat to their existing unions.

In the second place, there were a number of negative features associated with dual unionism. One was a tendency to have a dogmatic and sectarian view of rival unions. As an example, Foster mentioned how the Western Federation of Miners had been unreservedly praised when affiliated to the IWW and then, following its withdrawal, was suddenly characterised as a fake union that should be "wiped out of existence"—even though the union had not really changed in any real way.[94] Another problem was that dual unionism divided the working class and hence undermined the very project of One Big Union. It is worth returning to Malatesta at this point, for he made a similar assertion. Malatesta noted that for a union to function, "it is necessary to bring together all workers, or at least all those who aim at improving their conditions," and it cannot therefore only recruit to its ranks those who embrace an anarchist programme. It is in this sense that he declared, "I do not ask for anarchist syndicates, which would immediately give legitimacy to social-democratic, republican, royalist and all other kinds of syndicates, and which would divide the working class more than ever against itself."[95]

Perhaps even more seriously, a policy of dual unionism effectively withdrew the radicals from the existing unions, isolating them in small rival dual unions that had (for all the reasons mentioned above) little chance of success. The IWW approach had led the best militants to withdraw from the existing unions into "sterile isolation." This was, Ford and Foster argued, a "calamity," a "desertion and disarming of their militants"; its result was that these unions were left in the "undisputed control of conservatives and fakers of all kinds to exploit as they see fit." Even the Western Federation of Miners, stripped of its best element, like Haywood, was degenerating into a "typical Socialist [Party] labour union-voting machine."[96]

On the other hand, even where dual unions did manage to grow, they failed to resolve the basic problem that bedeviled the existing unions: the lack of a radical political outlook and a cadre of revolutionary militants. Unable to challenge the existing unions effectively, the IWW turned to recruiting the unorganised workers ignored by the AFL. These workers, though, often joined the IWW because nothing else was available, not because they embraced its syndicalist vision; if the AFL had been on the scene and willing to open its doors, many would have joined it. Membership in the IWW did not imply agreement with the goals of the IWW; it would be a mistake to assume that twenty-five thousand IWW recruits were necessarily equivalent to twenty-five thousand syndicalists.

As Malatesta pointed out, the effect of such a recruiting strategy could be that the "original programme becomes an empty slogan which no one bothers about" and "tactics are readjusted to contingent needs"; the door was then opened for the union, formed on a radical platform, to evolve into an ordinary bread-and-butter union, whose leadership either adapts or "must make way for the 'practical' men."[97] The very success of the union could lead, in other words, directly to the destruction of its revolutionary aims as an ever-increasing number of members failed to share its original goals.

The third key contention in favour of boring from within was that it worked. Good examples, said Ford and Foster, were Britain, where Mann had been in the forefront of massive dock and railway strikes, the French CGT, and "Spain, Italy, Portugal."[98] There is certainly a great deal of evidence for this view. The Spanish CNT, for instance, had originally been formed as Solidaridad Obrera in 1907 by a coalition of anarchists and political socialists, but was captured by anarchists soon afterward.[99] Anarchists and syndicalists had likewise also taken hold of the Portuguese UON, while the roots of the Italian USI also lay in work within the CGL.

There are other examples, not cited by Ford and Foster, that indicate that boring from within was a common syndicalist tactic could bear real results. The CGOM in Mexico and the Federative Union of Metal Workers of America in the United States seem to have been taken over by boring from within. The Argentine Workers' Federation (FOA), founded in 1901 by a range of forces, was captured by anarchists by 1904 and renamed FORA, which then adopted an explicitly anarchist platform at the fifth congress in 1905. The situation in Brazil, Cuba, and Peru appears to have been similar.

In twentieth-century Greece, anarcho-syndicalists like Konstantinos Speras (1893–1943) focused their attention on trying to win over orthodox unions.[100] Born on the island of Serifos, Speras came into contact with anarchists in Egypt and then became active in Greece, where he was repeatedly arrested. In 1916, he set up the Union of Workingmen and Miners of Serifos, and was subsequently part of the anarcho-syndicalist minority in the Greek General Confederation of Labour, where he was elected to the supervising committee. He was involved in the Socialist Worker Party of Greece, which developed into the Communist Party of Greece (CPG), and in 1920 was prominent at the Greek General Confederation of Labour conference, where anarcho-syndicalists represented one-third of the delegates. In 1926, he was expelled from the union body at the behest of the CPG. By this time Greece was under a dictatorship, but Speras remained active. In 1943, he was murdered by CPG agents.

What was necessary, according to Ford and Foster, was the formation of an organised syndicalist "militant minority" in the existing unions. This would help conquer the unions "from within" and give a militant lead to the workers.[101] The IWW was faced with the problem of combining its union functions with its ideological one: it sought to grow by recruiting any worker available, and then had the problem of trying to educate raw recruits about its preestablished syndicalist programme. The militant minority had no such problem, Ford and Foster argued: based among *already* organised workers and strong union structures, it could concentrate on winning existing union members over to syndicalism.

From this perspective, while the ISEL in Britain had so far failed to conquer the existing unions, it had succeeded far better than the IWW (or its contemporary British section, which never really succeeded in forming unions) in influencing vast numbers of workers with syndicalism. Ford and Foster's view was then that the IWW should reorganise itself as a militant minority, join the AFL, and then conquer it. As for the unorganised workers, the reorganised IWW could set up special unions to cater to them; these would not face competition from the AFL, and as the IWW permeation of that body proceeded, the new unions could be amalgamated with it.[102]

The retort of the dominant IWW faction to such claims was predictable: the AFL could not be reformed, it was a waste of time and energy to bore from within its structures, controlled as they were by the labour fakers, and in any case, the IWW was obliged to recruit the unskilled, women, blacks, Mexicans, and immigrants excluded from the AFL.[103] As Haywood put it, "I do not give a snap of my finger whether or not the skilled workman joins this industrial movement at the present time. When we get the unskilled and labourer into this organisation the skilled worker will of necessity come here for his own protection."[104]

Many IWW stalwarts felt that it was simplistic to blame the IWW's continued minority status relative to the AFL on its dual unionist approach, as there were many millions of unorganised workers entirely ignored by the AFL. The obstacles to recruiting these workers were many: unskilled and migratory workers were always hard to organise, as were immigrants and oppressed nationalities like blacks; employers, the state, and vigilantes routinely attacked the IWW; the ruling class had far more resources than the syndicalist union and immigrants were often denied U.S. citizenship if they joined the IWW; IWW propaganda against patriotism and religion alienated many workers; and the SPA was often hostile as well.[105] For many, the prospect of dissolving the IWW into the AFL threatened to undermine its achievements in these trying circumstances.

There was, finally, an additional complication, touched on briefly in the IWW press: it was not always possible for even the most ardent advocate of the boring from within approach to make progress in the established unions without being "kicked out."[106] The Italian case, cited by Ford and Foster as an example of boring from within, in point of fact bears this out: the syndicalists in the CGL and PSI were eventually driven to establish the USI as a dual union by precisely the relentless campaign of expulsions and pressure by the political socialists. Mann's U.S. 1913 tour, which also stressed boring from within, left Haywood and others unmoved, and Foster and his faction left the IWW, while the SLNA worked within the AFL unions with some success.

Tactics in Context and Organisational Dualism

Several points in this debate bear some further exploration. First, both Malatesta and Foster emphasised organisational dualism in their discussions of syndicalism: the need for a strictly anarchist organisation or syndicalist militant minority besides the (syndicalist) union. Malatesta envisaged such a group working within the unions to promote the anarchist project and shift the unions toward a revolutionary goal; Foster doubted that a dual union could combine its ordinary union work and its syndicalist ideals, while his policy of boring from within required the constitution of a militant minority in the existing unions.

Both warned against the formation of dual unions on a radical platform, suggesting that such bodies were caught between a rock and a hard place: either they enforced a strict adherence to their revolutionary programme, in which case they must form small isolated bodies that masqueraded as unions while actually being close to a strictly anarchist or syndicalist political organisation, or they must open their doors to all, with the danger of evolving into an orthodox union as a result of the influx of workers who did not share their original aspirations. The rationale for a militant minority and the manner in which such a grouping should operate are contentious issues, to which we will return in a subsequent chapter.

Most immediately, however, it should be noted that bodies like the IWW tended to have their *own* informal militant minorities.[107] Even where a syndicalist union, formed by boring from within, emerges as a powerful force, it must confront the same problems as a dual union in raising the consciousness of the raw recruits. Where a syndicalist union is a major force, it will inevitably recruit many workers by virtue of its strength and record, rather than its politics. Education becomes crucial for any syndicalist union in order to prevent the dilution of union policies by the addition of new members.

The Mexican CGT faced precisely this problem: growing rapidly in the late 1920s, it was overwhelmed by an influx of members who did not share its anarcho-syndicalist position; by 1928–1929, the syndicalists were on the retreat, and the union split into rival federations along political lines.[108] Yet massive recruitment need not result in the collapse of the union's syndicalist commitment. By contrast, the Spanish CNT managed to win the battle of ideas by promoting a radical popular counterculture that infused the union with radicalism, which spread far beyond the union structures. That the CNT was successful in this is shown by the fact that its anarcho-syndicalist position was never seriously challenged at its congresses, despite a radically democratic practice, a minimal bureaucratic layer, and massive ongoing growth.

This success must be attributed in large part to its success in fostering a radical and popular counterculture as well as the role of the FAI, an anarchist political organisation formed in 1927, of which we will say more in the next chapter. This ability to combine union and ideological work shows some of the problems with the criticisms of syndicalism that "a union that accepts members irrespective of their politics is, by definition, not revolutionary," and "to have a mass base and therefore be effective in day to day struggles," a syndicalist union must have an open membership policy."[109] Rather, the question is what is to be done to educate the new members—an issue to which we will return.

The contemporary predominance of dual unionism in syndicalism should, in other words, be historicised and not projected back into the past as an inherent feature of syndicalism (or flaw, if the policy was rejected). The movement had and has an alternative tactical option in the form of boring from within. There are also many cases of syndicalist movements alternating between the two. While the French CGT was first made syndicalist through boring from within, the loss of syndicalist control in the 1910s saw two main responses: some French syndicalists broke away to form the CGT Revolutionary Syndicalist in 1921 as a minority union (this later evolved into the contemporary French CNTs); others, like Monatte, continued to bore from within the CGT, where they exerted some influence.

While boring from within could be effective, it is also necessary not to pose the choice between this approach and dual unionism on an abstract level. Circumstances matter greatly, as the cases of the USI and French CGT show. It is notable that many successful instances of boring from within took place in relatively young union bodies, which may suggest that the possibilities of conquering long-established unions with a well-entrenched bureaucracy could be far more limited. This observation may seem especially apposite where existing unions have long been entangled in statutory industrial relations machinery, particularly when participation in national-level social corporatist structures tends to generate a layer of union bureaucrats that operates outside the direct control of union members. Many unions are also controlled by political parties that do not tolerate rival factions operating in their ranks. The obstacles to capturing such unions are substantial.

Moreover, in most countries there are several union centres and a number of independent unions within different sectors, not to mention the fact that there are often different unions catering to different grades of workers: to which established unions, then, should anarchists or syndicalists convinced of boring from within direct their activities? If it is true that the Argentine FORA and Spanish CNT were both formed by boring from within, it is also the case that both unions were only a section of the larger labour movement. While the UGT in Argentina evolved into the syndicalist CORA, which eventually merged into the FORA, the CNT always faced a serious rival in the form of the UGT linked to by the Spanish Socialist Party. Even at its height in the 1930s, the CNT only organised half the working class; the UGT organised the other.

In a sense, then, the syndicalists in both these countries actually used both boring from within and dual unionism, showing that the picture is more complicated than a simple choice between two tactical approaches. Even the IWW was unable to maintain a strict dual unionism as it spread from the U.S. In Britain, the De Leonists operated a separate Industrial Workers of Great Britain, and distinct IWW unions were formed in Canada, Chile, Ecuador, and Mexico. In Australia and New Zealand, the IWW existed primarily as a vocal and influential current that overlapped with the established unions, rather than serving as a rival union centre. In South Africa, where the ideas of the IWW had a great influence, there was a separate IWW union from 1910 to 1912. There were also syndicalist attempts to penetrate the main unions through the formation in 1917 of a Solidarity Committee within the South African Industrial Federation, followed by the promotion of an independent shop stewards' movement from 1918 and involvement in the Cape Federation of Labour, alongside the formation of separate unions like the Industrial Workers of Africa, which organised workers of colour who were specifically excluded from both centres.

With the formation of the Comintern, Lenin harshly attacked dual unionism and the U.S. IWW, and made a principle of boring from within.[110] Context clearly matters; tactical issues cannot be made into abstract principles to be applied regardless of the situation. Thus, the USI in Italy was forced into a dual unionist position and the prospect of boring from within the CGL seemed unpromising. Furthermore, the USI developed into a powerful body that had at its height in 1920 about eight hundred thousand members, roughly half the size of the CGL.[111] To simply dissolve the USI back into the CGL posed serious problems: besides a disruption of the work achieved so far, there was the danger that a merger could easily mean surrender to the very officials who had made the formation of a dual union necessary. Given the considerations so far outlined, however, it is not surprising that practically no functioning syndicalist union accepted Lenin's advice and dissolved into the established nonsyndicalist unions.

Syndicalism and Rank-and-file Movements

A third syndicalist approach, which offers an alternative to both boring from within and dual unionism, is worth mentioning: the formation of independent rank-and-file movements within the established unions. This type of syndicalism can be anarcho-syndicalist, as was the case with the Union of Anarcho-syndicalist Propaganda and the Confederation of Russian Anarcho-syndicalists, or revolutionary syndicalist, as was the case with the Shop Stewards and Workers' Committee Movement in Britain, all active in the 1910s.

This approach does not seek to capture the union apparatus as such. This is where it differs from the boring from within of groups like the ISEL and the SLNA. It is an independent movement, it may overlap with the orthodox unions and participate in them, but it does not seek to capture them; instead, it aims at forming a movement of the union rank and file as well as the unorganised, based on regular mass meetings and delegate structures and infused with a radical programme that can operate independently of the unions where needed. The classic statement of its approach is as follows: "We will support the officials just so long as they rightly represent the workers, but we will act independently immediately they misrepresent them."[112]

A key example of this approach is the Shop Stewards and Workers' Committee Movement in Britain in the mid-1910s; we will examine the Russian case in the next chapter. An independent rank-and-file movement emerged spontaneously as a result of a range of factors, notably increasing wartime controls over industry, the dilution of skilled work, and the quiescence of the union bureaucracy.[113] Revolutionary syndicalists soon dominated it politically. In Scotland, the stronghold of the SLP in Britain, De Leonists like Gallacher found themselves playing a leading role in the first major initiative: the important Clyde Workers Committee.[114] Shifting away from their traditional dual unionism, they began to see a rank-and-file workers' movement, independent of the union leadership, yet overlapping with the unions, as the road to One Big Union. In England, IWW supporters won a number of workers' committees to the 1908 IWW *Preamble* from 1917 onward, and the centre of the movement shifted increasingly to Sheffield.[115]

By 1919, the emerging movement was evolving into a formal countrywide structure, with a national administrative committee headed by J. T. Murphy, and published *Solidarity* and *The Worker*.[116] The former had been established by syndicalists like Mann, and the latter was printed on the SLP press.[117] The movement held national conferences in 1919 and 1920 (taking care not to develop into a new dual union), and linked up with the syndicalist South Wales Unofficial Reform Committee, which worked within the miners' union.[118] It also formed close links with the Chicago IWW, including an arrangement for the interchange of membership cards.[119]

For the syndicalists involved in the Shop Stewards and Workers' Committee Movement, the movement ought to become "one powerful organisation that will place the workers in complete control of the industry."[120] When organised as a formal national body, it adopted as "its objective control of the workshop, control of the industry, the overthrow of the present capitalist system of society and the establishment of Industrial Democracy."[121] Yet, for all that, it did not aim to capture the existing unions or destroy them.[122] J. T. Murphy (1888–1966)—the leading figure in the Sheffield Workers' Committee, a prominent De Leonist, and later a CPGB founder—was widely regarded as the theorist of the Shop Stewards and Workers' Committee Movement. He advocated replacing the "territorially constructed State" with a "real democracy" based on industrial unionism and saw the committees an important step on the road to a "Workers' Republic."[123]

The Shop Stewards and Workers' Committee Movement was open to other currents as well; it should not be confused with a syndicalist militant minority like the SLNA or ISEL. Thus, it included numerous activists from the Independent Labour Party, a political socialist group, as well as the British Socialist Party, a Marxist party that emerged from the old Social Democratic Federation in opposition to that group's prowar position. MacLean, the Scottish Marxist, was another notable member. Still, the "chief sources of the ideology of the shop stewards' movement were the French and American doctrines of revolutionary syndicalism and Industrial Unionism."[124]

The rank-and-file syndicalist approach transcends, in key ways, both dual unionism and boring from within. On the one hand, it accepts the argument that dual unionism is likely to simply isolate militants in small separate unions and accepts the boring from within notion that even the conservative unions are basically working-class organisations. On the other hand, it also accepts the dual unionist claim that an established union bureaucracy is exceedingly difficult to overturn. The task, then, is not to capture the union as a whole but to build an independent workers' movement that *overlaps* with the unions and can itself undertake the role of the One Big Union.

Rank-and-file syndicalism converges in some respects with the workplace strategy of some contemporary anarchists.[125] The WSM argues that unions are nonetheless fundamentally working-class organisations and a necessary response to the class system: "No amount of conservatism, bureaucracy or backwardness within the unions can obliterate this essential fact."[126] It also objects to dual unionism (which it identifies as the hallmark of syndicalism), and sees work within the existing unions as making a major contribution to revolution. The unions are seen as internally contested, and shaped by ongoing struggles between the bureaucracy and the membership as well as competing ideas. What is needed is a rank-and-file opposition within the unions that is willing to defend the union while challenging the bureaucracy, and that is able to develop its own campaigns as well as support progressive union initiatives. The aim is neither to take over the union as a whole nor to withdraw from it; it is to promote a style of unionism that is "essentially the same" as syndicalism and can lay the basis for workers' councils:

> Trade unions will not become revolutionary organisations, they were never set up to be that. However from within trade union struggle will

arise the embryo of the workers' councils of the future. The early beginnings of this are seen wherever workers create their own rank & file organisation (without mediation or "all-knowing" leaders) to pursue their class interests.[127]

Anarchists can be elected to unpaid and accountable union posts, like shop steward positions, but should not get embroiled in the union bureaucracy.[128] The promotion of direct action, self-activity, and revolutionary ideas is central to the revolutionary project, and anarchists should thus also oppose engagement with corporatist structures and other types of centralised bargaining that remove initiative from the shop floor.[129] The rank-and-file movement should not be the property of any single political current, yet it should be broad enough to attract workers who are militant but would not see themselves as having a particular political outlook; while "we fight for our politics" in the rank-and-file movement, "the movement should be independent of any one political organisation," and its role is really "to provide a focus for workers moving to the left and wanting to fight."[130]

In Conclusion: Reform and Revolution

In this chapter, we have asserted that a historical approach to the broad anarchist tradition sheds a great deal of light on tactics. Simply adopting, for example, a mass anarchist strategy is only half the challenge facing an activist: the success of the strategy depends fundamentally on *tactical* choices. These should ideally be elaborated on the basis of a careful analysis of the situation in which the strategy is being applied, a careful consideration of the merits of different tactics in their own right, and the compatibility of a given tactic with the principles and strategy that it is meant to promote. Moreover, as circumstances change, tactics should also change.

Syndicalist boring from within, for instance, is a tactic with many arguments in its favour, but is not necessarily always applicable. The formation of a powerful union bureaucracy, entangled in the statutory industrial relations machinery or controlled by a hostile political party, can pose major obstacles to the success of this tactic. Indeed, it may certainly be doubted whether it would be successful in such circumstances, and whether an alternative approach may not be more effective.

A tactic cannot be made into a principle; different conditions merit different tactics. Issues of participation in statutory industrial relations machinery or dual unionism, or participation in welfare systems, are informed on one level by questions of principle; on another level, however, it is important to distinguish between principles, which are indispensable, and tactics, which are transitory, and not to make principles of particular tactics. The broad anarchist tradition suggests definite principles that must inform strategy and tactics, but no set of tactics is universally applicable. There is much that may be learned from the history of anarchism and syndicalism about the tactics that have been tried in the past, but the real challenge is always to develop tactics for the present.

Notes

1. Kropotkin, *War!*
2. Maximoff, *The Programme of Anarcho-syndicalism*, 45–46.

3. E. Goldman, "What I Believe," in *Red Emma Speaks: Selected Writings and Speeches*, ed. A. K. Shulman (1908; repr., New York: Vintage Books, 1972), 38, 41.

4. Rocker, *Anarcho-Syndicalism*, chapter 5.

5. See R. de Jong, "Ferdinand Domela Nieuwenhuis," in *Woordenboek van Belgische en Nederlands Vrijdenkers* (Brussels: Vrije Universiteit, 1979); G. Harmsen, "Nieuwenhuis, Ferdinand," in *Biografisch Woordenboek van het Socialisme an de Arbeidersbeweging in Nederland* (Amsterdam: International Institute of Social History, 1995); Nettlau, *A Short History of Anarchism*, 232–35.

6. Foster, *Syndicalism* pp. 9–13, 29–30.

7. Quoted in T. Mann, *Tom Mann's Memoirs* (1923; repr., London: MacGibbon and Kee, 1967), 236–38.

8. Casanovas, "Labour and Colonialism in Cuba in the Second Half of the Nineteenth-Century," 436.

9. Ibid., 436.

10. Kedward, *The Anarchists*, 67; see also Joll, *The Anarchists*, 236.

11. Quoted in P. Trewhela, "George Padmore, a Critique: Pan-Africanism or Communism," *Searchlight South Africa* 1, no. 1 (1988): 50.

12. Ibid., 50.

13. Bookchin, *The Spanish Anarchists*, 163.

14. Paz, *Durruti*, 39.

15. Levy, "Italian Anarchism," 56.

16. Williams, *A Proletarian Order*, 36–37.

17. Levy, "Italian Anarchism," 56; Williams, *A Proletarian Order*, 37.

18. Colombo, "Armando Borghi."

19. Ibid.

20. Williams, *A Proletarian Order*, 35–36.

21. Levy, "Italian Anarchism," 56; Bertrand, "Revolutionary Syndicalism in Italy," 145. See also G. Procacci, "Popular Protest and Labour Conflict in Italy, 1915–1918," *Social History*, no. 14 (1989).

22. Williams, *A Proletarian Order*, 56–57.

23. Bertrand, "Revolutionary Syndicalism in Italy," 145.

24. Levy, "Italian Anarchism," 56–57.

25. Williams, *A Proletarian Order*, 56; Woodcock, *Anarchism*, 333.

26. Bertrand, "Revolutionary Syndicalism in Italy," 145.

27. Levy, "Italian Anarchism," 56–57; Williams, *A Proletarian Order*, 51–52. The quote is from Williams.

28. Williams, *A Proletarian Order*, 36.

29. L. Michel, *The Red Virgin: Memoirs of Louise Michel*, ed. B. Lowry and E. E. Gunter (Tuscaloosa: University of Alabama Press, 1981), 129.

30. B. Mitchell, "French Syndicalism: An Experiment in Practical Anarchism," in *Revolutionary Syndicalism: An International Perspective*, ed. M. van der Linden and W. Thorpe (Otterup, Denmark: Scolar, 1990), 34–37; see also F. Feeley, "French School Teachers against Militarism, 1903–18," *Historian* 57, no. 2 (1994).

31. Industrial Workers of the World, *The IWW in Theory and Practice*.

32. Our Special Representative/Proletarian, "Sundry Jottings from the Cape: A Rebel's Review," *Voice of Labour*, December 1, 1911; see also P. R. Roux, "The Truth about the Defence Act: Straight Talk to Workers," *Voice of Labour*, October 11, 1912.

33. Quoted in Marshall, *Demanding the Impossible*, 521.

34. J. Crump, "Anarchist Opposition to Japanese Militarism, 1926–1937," *Bulletin of Anarchist Research*, no. 24 (1991): 34.

35. Quoted in ibid., 35.

36. Crump, *Hatta Shuzo and Pure Anarchism in Interwar Japan*, 95. The full statement is reproduced in Crump, "Anarchist Opposition to Japanese Militarism"; Zenkoku Jiren, "What to Do about War?" in *Anarchism: A Documentary History of Libertarian Ideas, Volume 1: From Anarchy to Anarchism, 300 CE to 1939*, ed. R. Graham (November 1931; repr., Montréal: Black Rose, 2005).

37. Crump, "Anarchist Opposition to Japanese Militarism," 36.

38. Gordon, "Anarchism in Brazil," 100–109.

39. Thorpe, "Keeping the Faith," 196. See also W. Thorpe, "The Provisional Agenda of the International Syndicalist Conference, London 1913," *International Review of Social History*, no. 36 (1981); W. Thorpe, "Towards a Syndicalist International: The 1913 London Congress," *International Review of Social History*, no. 23 (1978).

40. Lenin, "The State and Revolution," 309–10.

41. A. L. Morton and G. Tate, *The British Labour Movement, 1770–1920*, rev. ed. (London: Lawrence and Wishart, 1979), 255. See also N. Mackenzie, *Socialism: A Short History*, 2nd ed. (London: Hutchinson University Library, 1966), 130; C. Tsuzuki, *Tom Mann, 1856–1941: The Challenges of Labour* (Oxford: Clarendon Press, 1991), 177.

42. Notably Bakunin, "Letters to a Frenchman on the Current Crisis."

43. C. Levy, "Anarchism, Internationalism, and Nationalism in Europe, 1860–1939," *Australian Journal of Politics and History* 50, no. 3 (2004): 343.

44. E. Malatesta, "Anarchists Have Forgotten Their Principles," in *Errico Malatesta: His Life and Ideas*, ed. V. Richards (November 1914; repr., London: Freedom Press, 1965); E. Malatesta, "Pro-Government Anarchists," in *Errico Malatesta: His Life and Ideas*, ed, V. Richards (April 1916; repr., London: Freedom Press, 1965), 250–51.

45. Quail, *The Slow Burning Fuse*, 287.

46. Holton, *British Syndicalism*, 200; Tsuzuki, *Tom Mann*, 178.

47. Woodcock, *Anarchism*, 203, 413.

48. Mitchell, "French Syndicalism," 37.

49. Levy, "Anarchism, Internationalism, and Nationalism in Europe," 342.

50. See, inter alia, Levy, "Italian Anarchism," 64, 71.

51. Thorpe, "Keeping the Faith," 195.

52. Quoted in "The Deadly Parallel," *International Socialist Review* 17 (April 1917): 618.

53. W. Thorpe, "El Ferrol, Zimmerwald, and Beyond: Syndicalist Internationalism, 1914 to 1918" (paper presented at the European Social Science History conference, Amsterdam, March 22–25, 2006), 5–6.

54. Gordon, "Anarchism in Brazil," 108–12.

55. Reproduced in ibid., 311–13.

56. E. Goldman A. Berkman, E. Malatesta et al., "International Anarchist Manifesto against War," in *Anarchism: A Documentary History of Libertarian Ideas, Volume 1: From Anarchy to Anarchism, 300 CE to 1939*, ed. R. Graham (1915; repr., Montréal: Black Rose, 2005).

57. Quail, *The Slow Burning Fuse*, 291–93.

58. On these developments, see van der Walt, "Anarchism and Syndicalism in South Africa," chapters 3–5.

59. M. Dubofsky, "The Rise and Fall of Revolutionary Syndicalism in the United States," in *Revolutionary Syndicalism: An International Perspective*, ed. M. van der Linden and W. Thorpe (Otterup, Denmark: Scolar, 1990), 215.

60. See Burgmann, *Revolutionary Industrial Unionism*, chapters 1–14.

61. "The Class Struggle Declared Criminal," *The International*, January 4, 1918.

62. Thorpe, "Keeping the Faith."

63. Malatesta in Richards, *Errico Malatesta*, 126-27.

64. For an example of the latter view, see Crump, *Hatta Shuzo and Pure Anarchism in Interwar Japan*, 163.

65. F. Hanlon, "Industrial Unionism: The History of the Industrial Workers of the World in Aotearoa," in *Industrial Unionism: The History of the Industrial Workers of the World in Aotearoa: Aim, Form, and Tactics of a Workers' Union on IWW Lines* (1913; repr., Wellington, UK: Rebel Press, 2006), 22–23.

66. Quoted in Foner, *The Industrial Workers of the World*, 137.

67. Ibid., 137–38, 168–69, 470–72.

68. Hanlon, "Industrial Unionism," 23.

69. Hinton, *The First Shop Stewards Movement*, 312.

70. Mackenzie, *Socialism*, 132.

71. Bookchin, *The Spanish Anarchists*, 207.

72. Uruguayan Regional Workers' Federation, "Declarations from the Third Congress," 332.

73. Hart, *Anarchism and the Mexican Working Class*, 170–72.

74. Lambert, "Political Unionism in South Africa," 44.

75. See, inter alia, Tsuzuki, *Tom Mann*; Mann, *Tom Mann's Memoirs*.

76. T. Mann, "The Way to Win: An Open Letter to Trades Unionists on Methods of Industrial Organisation, by Tom Mann, Broken Hill, May 1909," *Voice of Labour*, December 31, 1909; Mann, *Tom Mann's Memoirs*, 193.

77. Hanlon, "Industrial Unionism," 21.

78. Bookchin, *The Spanish Anarchists*, 180, 183, 195, 201, 203, 206, 217, 231, 235; Peirats, *Anarchists in the Spanish Revolution*, 59–84. The moderates issued a manifesto in August 1931, signed by thirty people, hence the name *treintistas*.

79. L. Golden, "The Libertarian Movement in Contemporary Spanish Politics," *Antipode: A Radical Journal of Geography* 10–11, nos. 3 and 1 (1979): 116n3.

80. Solidarity Federation, *Out of the Frying Pan: A Critical Look at Works Councils* (Manchester, UK: Solidarity Federation, 1998), 2, 4, 8, 11–13.

81. Ibid., 12–13.

82. See *Alternative Libertaire*, "Spain."

83. M. Gardell, "A Conference in Spain," *SAC-Kontakt* (December 1992) (English translation; source unknown).

84. Golden, "The Libertarian Movement in Contemporary Spanish Politics," 18–19.

85. See Holton, "Syndicalist Theories of the State"; Haywood and Bohm, *Industrial Socialism*.

86. Holton, "Syndicalist Theories of the State," 8.

87. Craparo, *Anarchist Communists*, 76–77.

88. Ibid., 77.

89. Epstein, "Anarchism and the Anti-Globalisation Movement."

90. See, for example, Workers Solidarity Movement, *Position Paper*.

91. See Foner, *The Industrial Workers of the World*, chapter 18; Zipser, *Working Class Giant*, 27–87.

92. Ford and Foster, *Syndicalism*, 43.

93. Foner, *The Industrial Workers of the World*, 423–24.

94. Ibid., 424.

95. Malatesta in Richards, *Errico Malatesta*, 123–24; Malatesta, "Syndicalism," 220–21.

96. Ford and Foster, *Syndicalism*, 45–46.

97. Malatesta in Richards, *Errico Malatesta*, 123–24.

98. Ford and Foster, *Syndicalism*, 43.

99. Bar, "The CNT," 121.

100. L. Kottis, *Konstantinos Speras: The Life and Activities of a Greek Anarcho-syndicalist* (London: Kate Sharpley Library, 2000).

101. See Ford and Foster, *Syndicalism*, 43–47; Foner, *The Industrial Workers of the World*, 422–34.

102. Foner, *The Industrial Workers of the World*, 425–26.

103. Ibid., 418–22.

104. Quoted in ibid., 37.

105. Ibid., 462–71.

106. Ibid., 421–22.

107. Ibid., 147, asterisked footnote.

108. Hart, *Anarchism and the Mexican Working Class*, 156; Hart, "Revolutionary Syndicalism in Mexico," 200–1.

109. Made by the Anarchist Workers Group, "Anarchism in the Thatcher Years," *Socialism from Below*, no. 1 (August 1989). Available online at http://flag.blackened.net/revolt/awg/awg_thatcher1.html (accessed December 1, 2006).

110. V. I. Lenin, "'Left-wing Communism': An Infantile Disorder," in *Selected Works in Three Volumes*, ed. V. I. Lenin (1920; repr., Moscow: Progress Publishers, 1975), volume 3.

111. Williams, *A Proletarian Order*, 194–95.

112. J. T. Murphy, quoted in Hinton, *The First Shop Stewards Movement*, 119.

113. See ibid.

114. See ibid., 122–23.

115. A. E. Titley, "The IWW in England," *Workers' Dreadnought*, October 2, 1920.

116. S. Pankhurst, "Zinoviev to the Comintern: A 'Left' Wing View," *Workers' Dreadnought*, August 13, 1921.

117. Hinton, *The First Shop Stewards Movement*, 285n1; "Questions of the Day," *Workers' Dreadnought*, July 20, 1918.

118. Hinton, *The First Shop Stewards Movement*, 287; "Rank and File Convention," *Workers' Dreadnought*, February 14, 1920. For a statement of the committee's views, see Unofficial Reform Committee, *The Miner's Next Step: Being a Suggested Scheme for the Reorganisation of the Federation* (1912; repr., London: Germinal and Phoenix Press, 1991).

119. Thompson with Murfin, *The IWW*, 135.

120. Quoted in Hinton, *The First Shop Stewards Movement*, 129.

121. "The Workers' Committee," *Workers' Dreadnought*, March 9, 1918.

122. Hinton, *The First Shop Stewards Movement*, 290–93.

123. "Marxist Industrial Unionism," *Workers' Dreadnought*, October 19, 1918; J. T. Murphy, "The Embargo," *Workers' Dreadnought*, August 31, 1918.

124. Hinton, *The First Shop Stewards Movement*, 277; see also 290–93.

125. The FdCA has a similar position; see FdCA, *Towards a Programme of Conflictual, Class-Struggle Syndicalism*, 2005, available at http://www.fdca.it/fdcaen/labour/towards_a_platform.htm (accessed November 1, 2005).

126. Workers Solidarity Movement, *Position Paper*, section 2.1.

127. Ibid., section 11.1.

128. Ibid., section 7.4.

129. Ibid., section 7.6.

130. Ibid., sections 8.4. and 8.5.

Nestor Ivanovich Makhno (1889-1934) in Gulyai-Polye.

The central figure in the anarchist Ukrainian Revolution (1918–1921) and a brilliant guerrilla strategist, Makhno advocated the formation of a tight-knit anarchist political organisation to ensure that anarchism would "become the leading concept of revolution." His Revolutionary Insurgent Army of the Ukraine operated alongside the Nabat (Alarm) anarchist confederation, under the guidance of elected mass assemblies of peasants, workers, and insurgents.

T.W. Thibedi, Johannesburg.

"Bill" Thibedi was an important figure in the multi-racial revolutionary syndicalist movement in South Africa in the late 1910s. Active in the International Socialist League, he was also associated with the left-wing of the Transvaal Native Congress at this time. The outstanding black South African revolutionary of his age, Thibedi went on to help found the revolutionary syndicalist Industrial Workers of Africa along IWW lines in 1919.

CHAPTER 8

Militant Minority: The Question of Anarchist Political Organisation

The broad anarchist tradition has consistently stressed the significance of ideas for the libertarian and socialist reconstruction of society as well as the need for a *"fundamental transvaluation of values"* and the removal of the "authority principle" from the hearts and minds of the popular classes.[1] Even the insurrectionist anarchists, for example, saw armed action as important primarily for its educative function. The same concern with the centrality of ideas is seen in the mass anarchist strand, the promotion of revolutionary countercultures, Bakunin's emphasis on anarchism as a "new faith," Malatesta's stress on the "revolutionary imagination," the intellectual work of figures like Reclus, Foster's idea of a militant minority, and so on.

The issue that arises, however, is *how* best to spread the new faith, and it is here that we encounter a wide range of different tactical positions on a crucial question: Is it necessary for the militant minority of anarchists or syndicalists to form themselves into a specifically anarchist or syndicalist political organisation in order to promote their ideas and pursue their strategies? If so, how should such a group be organised?

There are a number of key positions. There is an "antiorganisationalist" one, which argues for an informal network of revolutionaries. There is the view of some syndicalists that a revolutionary union can undertake all the tasks of an anarchist or syndicalist political organisation, making such an organisation redundant. Finally, there is organisational dualism, which is the stance that there must be a specific and distinct anarchist organisation that would promote anarchist or syndicalist ideas. Yet even if organisational dualism is accepted, there is wide scope for disagreement over how much agreement, coherence, and discipline a group should adopt. We discuss these issues in this chapter, making the case that a coherent and specifically anarchist organisation, with a common analysis, strategy, and tactics along with a measure of collective responsibility, expressed in a programme, is the most effective of these approaches and arguably a necessary complement to a syndicalist strategy.

Insurrectionist Anarchists, Antiorganisationalism, and Stirner's Ghost

For insurrectionist anarchists, the role of the militant is to inspire the masses through exemplary actions, expose the inequities of the present, strike back at the ruling class, and disrupt the framework of class power through the "tactics of corrosion and continuous attack."[2] Besides opposing reforms and compromises of any sort, this type of anarchism is usually associated with a profound distrust of formal organisations. For Galleani, organisations with set political programmes, common strategies, and formal structures must be "modestly, but firmly" opposed. They involve a "graduated superstructure of bodies, a true hierarchy, no matter how disguised," and are united through a "single bond, discipline" that hampers initiative and "punishes infractions with sanctions that go from censure to excommunication, to expulsion." Galleani favoured a loose network of anarchists, with cells based on the affinity of different activists; "an organisation compatible with anarchist principles is not to be found," and an "anarchist party" must be a "government like any other government."[3] More recent insurrectionist anarchists have called for a "specific informal anarchist organisation" with "an insurrectional project," based on "autonomous base nuclei."[4]

It is possible that this antiorganisationalist approach, with its stress on a loose network of insurrectionary activists, was developed as an alternative to the authoritarian insurrectionism of earlier socialists like Louis Auguste Blanqui, who advocated a coup d'etat by a revolutionary conspiracy.[5] The Galleanist approach raises questions. Organised—even if informally—and bound by a definite programme, the Galleanists were essentially an "anarchist party" that was willing to enforce some sort of discipline and exclusion. A network is an organisation, as is a local cell, and the insurrectionist anarchist current was clearly characterised by a narrow set of shared analytic and strategic positions. If a network of individual affinity groups could operate in a nonauthoritarian manner and share common political positions, as the Galleanists believed, then there is no real reason to suppose that formal organisation must eventuate in "a true hierarchy," an authoritarian organisation; if not, then "antiorganisationalism" is also not a solution.

The Galleanists arguably did not recognise the dangers of informal organisation and the merits of formal organisation. The great problem of informal organisation is the development of informal and invisible hierarchies. By contrast, formal rules and procedures outlining responsibilities, rights, and roles enable a certain amount of accountability and transparency, and provide a safeguard against the "tyranny of structurelessness."[6] Thus,

> The absence of any formal structure not only does not guarantee greater internal democracy, but can also permit the creation of informal groups of hidden leaders. These groups come together on the basis of affinity, they can co-opt new adherents and they can generate an uncontrolled and uncontrollable leadership, hard to identify but nonetheless effective.[7]

If there is no necessary link between the formal character of an organisation and the rise of authoritarianism and hierarchy, it is also the case that an informal structure does not avoid such problems.

Antiorganisationalist currents were not restricted to insurrectionists, but also emerged among mass anarchists, though. In his exile in late nineteenth-century Argentina, for instance, Malatesta struggled against antiorganisationalist currents.[8] Isabel Meredith's semiautobiographical account of English anarchism in the late nineteenth century leaves no doubt that there were mass anarchists who stressed the right of every individual to do as they wished as well as the total autonomy of local groups, and opposed the development of any common analysis, strategy, and tactics.[9] While the Chinese anarchists were predominantly in favour of organisation, there were those who "believed that anarchism should not be organised, or that anarchist organisation had no room for discipline, rules, and regulations."[10] An "autonomist" faction within the IWPA accepted only the most loose-knit organisations, even distrusting the CLU.[11] The antiorganisationalist tendencies of many contemporary autonomist Marxists suggest that libertarian socialism—with its emphasis on individual freedom—is perhaps peculiarly vulnerable to the emergence of antiorganisationalist ideas in a way that political socialism is not.

Antiorganisationalist notions are also often associated with a very individualistic outlook, something that the rediscovery of the works of Stirner in the late nineteenth century reinforced. While Stirner's ideas were not integral to the broad anarchist tradition, they came to exercise a powerful attraction on antiorganisationalist anarchists. It was in these circles in particular that Stirner found a new audience; his ideas also attracted a number of mutualists, including Tucker.[12] Some anarchists were also attracted to Friedrich Nietzsche's doctrines of individualism and relativism. Besides being open to the tyranny of structurelessness, these approaches have another crucial limitation: they make consistent and coherent political work difficult, and hamper the promotion of the anarchist idea.

By the time of the 1907 Amsterdam Congress, antiorganisationalist currents were a serious problem. Not only did some self-described individualists disrupt the proceedings but a number of anarchists stayed away "because of their opposition to any organisation more elaborate than the loose local group."[13] The congress declared that "the ideas of anarchy and organisation, far from being incompatible, as has sometimes been pretended, in fact complement and illuminate each other," but antiorganisational and individualistic currents continued to grow.[14] Victor Serge (1890–1947) provided a vivid recollection of their impact in 1917 in Spain, at the time in the throes of preparations for a general strike:

> Andrés, an editor of the Confederation [CNT] paper, a thin swarthy Argentine with sharp, squarish features, a pointed chin, and a querulous look, held a pointed cigarette between purple lips.... Heinrich Zilz [a "French deserter "], his necktie carefully knotted ... was smoking with a smile on his face.... Hardly moving his lips, Andrés said:
>
> "The people over in Manresa have promised some grenades. Sabs, Tarrasa, and Granollérs are ready. Our pals in Tarrasa already have a hundred and forty Brownings. The Committee is negotiating with a junta of infantrymen. But what cowards those republicans are!"
>
> "So you're really itching to get yourselves chopped down, eh?" Zilz broke in, lighting another cigarette. "... you can count me out. My skin is worth more than a republic, even a workers' republic."

> A heavy silence fell over us.... We went out ... Andrés said what we
> were all thinking. "The ego-anarchist poison. People like that, you see,
> don't risk their necks anymore except for money."[15]

The impact of the "ego-anarchist poison" on the class struggle led Serge—
initially a supporter of the CNT—to abandon anarchism for Bolshevism, which
seemed to offer a more realistic conception of revolution; he was not the only anarchist to make this shift for these reasons.

Kropotkin also found it increasingly necessary to defend anarchism against
Stirnerite and Nietzschean ideas, which he believed provided a recipe for "the slavery and oppression of the masses."[16] He argued that anarchists were "individualists,"
but only in the sense that they advocated the free development of all people in a
democratic and egalitarian socialist order. In place of "misanthropic bourgeois individualism," he advocated "true individuality," which could only be realised "through
practising the highest communist sociability."[17] Rejecting relativism, he argued that:
"No society is possible without certain forms of morality generally recognised," and
"anarchist morality" was based on the principle of "solidarity."[18] Other anarchists
tried to deal with the destructive impact and troubling implications of Stirnerism
by rereading Stirner as compatible with anarchist views of freedom as the product,
not the antithesis, of society: Nettlau attempted unconvincingly to recast Stirner
as "eminently socialist"; Rocker tried to appropriate Stirner for mass anarchism
as a thinker who "impels powerfully to independent thinking"; and more recently
Guérin used the same approach.[19]

Developments in the 1920s showed that antiorganisationalist and individualistic attitudes continued to maintain their hold. If anything, the influence of these
views grew as the fate of the Russian Revolution convinced many anarchists that
attempts at establishing formal organisations were a form of creeping Bolshevism
that eventuated in Leninism and dictatorship. Camillo Berneri painted a depressing
picture of the effects on the anarchist movement by the 1930s:

> As for the unions, I believe that it is the only area in which we could build
> anything, although I cannot accept union officials and I can clearly see
> drawbacks and dangers in anarcho-syndicalism in practice. If I blame
> individualism, it is because, although less important numerically, it has
> succeeded in influencing virtually all of the movement.[20]

Born in Italy, Berneri had initially been affiliated with the PSI, left in 1915,
was drafted into the Italian army in 1917, became actively involved in the anarchist
press, and worked as a schoolteacher. Driven into exile by Mussolini, he suffered
arrests and expulsions from France, Switzerland, Germany, Belgium, Luxembourg,
and Holland. He was editor of the exiled USI paper *Guerra di classe* ("Class War"),
and was murdered in Spain in 1937 by Communist Party of Spain (PCE) agents.

Syndicalism and Anarchism without Adjectives

Some (but by no means all) syndicalists argued for an alternative approach to
spreading revolutionary ideas. Admitting the importance of and embracing formal
organisation, they claimed that there was no need for a specific political organisation to wage the battle of ideas within such a union. The syndicalist movement
was self-sufficient: based on a revolutionary platform, the union would inculcate

its membership with revolutionary ideals through systematic education. In other words, the syndicalist union would fulfill the tasks of both union and political group, and the case for a specific anarchist or syndicalist political organisation was therefore denied.

The basic problem with this approach is that it was not clear how syndicalism would be defended against rival political tendencies in the union. Workers, after all, join unions primarily with an eye on the "amelioration of the conditions of work."[21] They might join a syndicalist union simply because it was the only one available or the most effective union in a particular workplace. It is inevitable that a syndicalist union would continuously be infused with elements that did not share its official views. Building a mass syndicalist union must then inevitably pose the question of how best to defend the revolutionary project to which the union aspired.

Unless the union restricted its membership to convinced anarchists and syndicalists—in which case it would not be a union but a strictly anarchist or syndicalist political organisation masquerading as a union—it must open its doors and thereby continually place its syndicalist aims in jeopardy. The Mexican CGT, for example, grew from forty thousand to eighty thousand by 1928–1929, but this growth led to a substantial influx of members who did not share the union's anarcho-syndicalist aims and the CGT soon split along political lines into rival federations.[22]

As we have seen in the previous chapter, no syndicalists believed that the union struggle would spontaneously generate a revolutionary consciousness or counterculture. What they asserted instead was that the syndicalist union would be able to win new members over to its ideas. How should this programme of education be organised? It is here that the strand of syndicalism that denies the need for a specific political organisation falters. To operate a systematic programme of revolutionary education in a syndicalist union presupposes a group that is in agreement with those ideas, plays a central role in the union, and is willing to wage the battle of ideas against other ideologies. There is nothing otherwise to prevent the union being captured or split.

There is little doubt that even those syndicalists who denied the need for a separate political organisation in theory were compelled to organise one—even if only informally—in practice. This is shown by the experiences of the two major syndicalist formations that openly denied the need for a separate political organisation: the French CGT and the U.S. IWW. Public proclamations aside, the Wobblies embraced the theory that there must be a specific militant minority to "propagate revolutionary ideas, standardize their policies, instigate strike movements, and organise their attacks on the conservative forces in the unions," including the labour fakers.[23] In the French CGT, syndicalists organised "the most revolutionary elements among the masses" into "definite groups, *noyaux*, within the broad trade unions," and it was the noyaux network that provided the means for the initial anarchist takeover of the Bourses du Travail and the CGT.[24] The IWW operated Propaganda Leagues as auxiliaries to the union, and a network of convinced militants were key to driving the IWW's educational programme.[25] The question of the need for a separate anarchist or syndicalist political group was also posed elsewhere, notably when the revolutionaries were operating as a minority within existing unions or a rank-and-file movement.

In practice, then, it is difficult to avoid recognising the need for specific political organisations to supplement mass organisations—that is, the need for organisational dualism: the position that mass organisations like unions must be complemented by a specifically anarchist or syndicalist political organisation if they are to be revolutionary. As the *Platform* argued, "if trade unionism does not find in anarchist theory a support in opportune times it will turn, whether we like it or not, to the ideology of a political statist party."[26]

Organisational dualism has a long history within the broad anarchist tradition, and is distinct from both antiorganisationalism and the type of syndicalism that denies the need for specific political organisation. Nonetheless, there has never been a consensus over the way a specific anarchist grouping, based around anarchist ideas and focused on their propagation, should operate.

A common view, held by a vocal section of mass anarchists, was that while a specific anarchist political organisation was necessary, it should be structured loosely, seeking to unite all anarchists and syndicalists as far as possible. Thus, the specifically anarchist organisation should be open to all anarchists and syndicalists, and could and should not aspire to a close agreement on questions of analysis, strategy, and tactics. This approach is based on two ideas: that it is somehow authoritarian for an anarchist organisation to prescribe particular views and actions; and that it is more important that anarchists and syndicalists, in general, were united organisationally than share a programme based on clear positions.

The drive for anarchist unity, regardless of the major divisions within the broad anarchist tradition, can be traced to the 1890s, where it was often informed primarily by a concern with fostering cooperation between the advocates of collectivist and communist systems of distribution in the future society—a contentious issue in Spain and elsewhere.[27] Many anarchists felt such disputes were futile and could be resolved after the revolution. Malatesta held this view, as did Fernando Tárrida del Mármol (1861–1915), who advocated for unity on the basis of "anarchism without adjectives."[28] Born in Cuba, but mainly active in the Spanish movement, he was trained as a scientist and active in syndicalism; there is some evidence that his ideas on syndicalism were a crucial influence on Mann. One of those influenced by the call for unity was the U.S. anarchist de Cleyre.[29] Born to a poor family and initially intent on a religious career, she was radicalised by the Haymarket affair, influenced by the writings of Tucker, worked as a private tutor, wrote a number of important works, and was associated with Berkman, Kropotkin, Malatesta, Michel, and others. She maintained that an anarchist society would see "many different experiments" in social organisation "tried in various localities in order to determine the most appropriate form."[30]

While the idea of anarchism without adjectives was at first an argument for unity despite differences over the *future* society, it was expanded by the early twentieth century into a call for unity in the *present*, regardless of differences in analysis, strategy, and tactics. This was not Tárrida del Mármol's conception, for he argued for a well-organised anarchist grouping, with a "plan of struggle" to shape the "labour unions and societies of resistance."[31] For Nettlau, however, "all the anarchists" and "all freedom-loving human beings" must "become a united force, which, while preserving the autonomy of each of its members," would "practise mutual aid among all of them" as well as "advance liberty on a small scale and a large one."[32]

The same contentions were reiterated by the French anarchist Faure and became tied to the idea that an anarchist organisation should not in any way constrain the activities of its members. For Goldman, this was an issue of principle: "I will only accept anarchist organisation on one condition: it is that it should be based on absolute respect for *all* individual initiatives and should not hamper their free play and development. The essential principle of anarchism is individual autonomy."[33] Many of the "pure anarchists" in Japan wanted a loose organisational structure—some were even wary of federations—despite maintaining in practice a precise analysis and strategy.[34] For Voline, there was "validity in all anarchist schools of thought," and anarchists "must consider all diverse tendencies and accept them." To maintain that anarchism was "only a theory of classes" was "to limit it to a single viewpoint," for anarchism was "more complex and pluralistic, like life itself," and it was not the "anarchist way" to promote one view over another. An anarchist organisation was necessary, but it must accommodate all "opinions" and "tendencies," and be fairly loosely organised. A "harmonious anarchist organisation … does not have a formal character but its members are joined together by common ideas and ends," and it was a mistake to build a single anarchist organisation based on a unitary "ideological and tactical conception."[35]

There are a number of problems with this approach. Even if, as Goldman held, the essential principle of anarchism was individual autonomy, it simply did not follow that an anarchist organisation must tolerate all initiatives and views. An organisation is generally formed to allow people to cooperate in pursuit of common purposes, and there is no reason why individual initiatives should be at odds with those purposes, or why contradictory opinions and tendencies should be grouped together within a single organisation.

Nor is there any reason why an organisation should not develop a common programme, complete with close agreements on analysis, strategy, and tactics, so long as this is done democratically. Since the anarchists accept the idea that organisation should be voluntary, those who hold common views are entitled to exclude from their organisations those who express alternative ones. To insist that an organisation cannot exclude someone is to violate the principle of voluntary cooperation. Equally, those who hold alternative perspectives and who are excluded from one organisation are perfectly entitled to form their own groups, and the fact that other groups exist is no barrier to this free association. There is, in short, nothing authoritarian about forming a tight-knit group with a unitary "ideological and tactical conception," and nothing particularly libertarian about the stance that anarchists "must consider all diverse tendencies and accept them."

The view that anarchists and syndicalists will be strengthened by the formation of an organisation that is open to all anarchist currents is also open to question. Such unity, as Voline recognised, is only possible if the organisation highlights what the different currents share in common and ignores the points of division. This can be done in two ways: either by allowing every tendency "free play and development" within the loose framework of a common adherence to anarchism or by trying to develop a synthesis of views that enables the formulation of a common platform ac-

246 ... *Black Flame*

ceptable to the "entire movement." Goldman favoured the former approach; Voline proposed the latter "synthesist" approach, as did Faure: anarchism has "class elements as well as humanism and individualist principles," "its class element is above all its means of fighting for liberation; its humanitarian character is its ethical aspect, the foundation of society; its individualism is the goal of mankind."[36]

Examples of groups and federations that have sought to unite all self-declared anarchists on the basis of a common identity abound. A recent one was the now-defunct Social Revolutionary Anarchist Federation formed in the United States in 1972. The history of the broad anarchist tradition also provides many examples of a consciously "synthesist" approach, such as the Francophone Anarchist Federation (FAF) established in 1937 and the Italian Anarchist Federation formed in 1945, both of which are still active.

The problem, however, is that organisations formed in such ways often have difficulties in operating. While some issues can be deferred to a vague future, other points of division are not so easily sidestepped. An organisation that brought together insurrectionist anarchists, antisyndicalist mass anarchists, and syndicalists of various types would immediately be characterised by disagreements over fundamental issues. If the organisation used a loose definition of anarchism, it could also conceivably include in its ranks various nonanarchist currents, like Taoists, Stirnerites, and Tolstoyans. Propaganda and analysis would have to be vague; if all views are to be represented, publications must either carry a wide range of contradictory perspectives or focus on articles of a sufficiently abstract nature that avoid giving offence to different factions. The practical challenges of the class struggle pose further problems: for instance, faced with a bitter general strike by reformist unions, different members of the organisation would respond in radically different ways; the usefulness of the organisation would be doubtful.

The notion that bringing together all anarchists in a single organisation would strengthen the anarchist movement is arguably mistaken. Existing divisions within the broad anarchist tradition would simply be reproduced within the organisation, and the unity that was created would be nominal; once various nonanarchist tendencies are also allowed admission, this problem must be immeasurably more serious. Such an organisation must either have a fairly weak impact, even if numerically strong, or suffer serious splits.

In China, anarchism was a potent force in the first half of the twentieth century, but was often localised, uncoordinated, and made up of a wide variety of incompatible views.[37] This organisational chaos helps explain why the far better organised but initially far smaller CCP was able to make rapid gains against anarchism after 1921.[38] In the PLM, Flores Magón advocated "an activating minority, a courageous minority of libertarians," that would "move the masses ... despite the doubts of the incredulous, the prophecies of the pessimists, and the alarm of the sensible, coldly calculating, and cowardly."[39] Yet the PLM began as a Liberal party—"liberal" in the Latin American sense of a progressive, democratic, and modernising party—and its official platform remained Liberal until around 1911. When it moved into action during the Mexican Revolution (1910–1920) and adopted an openly anarchist programme, it was crippled by splits and secessions; many members were not in fact anarchists.[40] The same type of process took place in Japan, where the "pure anarchists" and the syndicalists split, followed by a split in the Zenkoku Jiren unions and the formation of the Nihon Jikyo.

The project of "synthesis" does not provide a solution to these difficulties. Voline was conscious of the limitations of a "mechanical alliance of different tendencies, each holding only to its own point of view," and it is partly for this reason that he favoured a synthesist approach. He was well aware that there were serious "contradictions" among the various currents of anarchism and syndicalism (among which he included Stirnerism), but optimistically believed these arose from misunderstandings along with the "vague and imprecise character of some of our basic ideas." In his view, synthesis would allow for unity as well as rectify "confusion in our ideas about a series of fundamental issues."[41]

The creation of a unifying synthesis is rather more difficult than this optimistic prognosis would suggest. Voline admitted that the points of "confusion" included "a series of fundamental issues, such as the conception of the social revolution, of violence, of the period of transition, of organisation," the means of "getting a large part of the population to accept our ideas," and the way to deal with "repression."[42] It is difficult to envisage an acceptable synthesis on these issues that would provide a basis for common work or "clarify" positions. The confusion about ideas that Voline mentioned would not be resolved but reproduced. It might seem self-evident that the unity of all anarchists must provide strength, but this is by no means the case:

> Whatever the level of theoretical unity may be (and it is never complete), the absence of any strategic unity means that any decisions taken need be observed only by those who agree with them, leaving the others to do as they please. This means that the decisions are of little value, that Congresses can make no effective resolutions, that internal debate is unproductive (as everyone maintains their own positions) and that the organisation goes through the motions of its internal rites without presenting a common face outside the organisation.[43]

An organisation aiming at synthesis through bringing together "heterogeneous theoretical and practical elements" can only result in a "mechanical assembly of individuals each having a different conception of all the questions of the anarchist movement, an assembly which would inevitably disintegrate on encountering reality."[44]

Bakuninism, the Organisation of Tendency, and the "Platform"

An alternative anarchist and syndicalist approach is represented by the "organisation of tendency," in which specifically anarchist or syndicalist political groups are formed on the basis of shared political positions, with a measure of organisational discipline.[45] The organisation has a shared analysis of the situation as well as an agreement on strategic and tactical issues expressed in a clear programme, and its members agree to carry out that programme and are held accountable for doing so. This approach can be traced back to the Alliance. The Alliance was formed in 1868, replacing the earlier International Brotherhood, and applied to join the First International.[46] At Marx's insistence, the Alliance was publicly dissolved, and its adherents entered the First International as individual members and branches.

This had little effect on the political views of the new adherents.[47] It is certain that the Alliance continued underground as a secret body, operating as a specifically anarchist political organisation that aimed to reshape the First International into an anarchist and syndicalist body.

When the First International began to split in the early 1870s, the continued existence of the Alliance despite the 1868 ruling provided the Marxists with a good deal of political ammunition. To the spurious charge that Bakunin was an advocate of "universal, pan destruction," "assassinations ... *en masse*," was added the claim that the International was being subverted by a sinister secret grouping, based on "blind obedience" to the personal dictatorship of "Citizen B," with designs on "barrack-room communism."[48] In response, the anarchists maintained that the Alliance no longer operated—a position that has frequently been accepted by later writers. What had been a flat denial by an emergent movement, caught in an obviously embarrassing position, became something of a dogma in later years and was incorporated into the literature. The result, reinforced by a hostile scholarship on Bakunin, has been that the significance of the Alliance has often been consistently underrated. Thus, Carr and Joll insist that the Alliance was an "imaginary" group, and explain this by reference to Bakunin's supposed mania for inventing nonexistent "secret societies."[49]

The evidence is rather different, though. When Bakunin's agent Giuseppe Fanelli (1827–1877) arrived in Spain in 1868 to help initiate what would become FORE, the largest section of the First International, he brought with him both the programme of the First International and the statutes of the Alliance.[50] The Alliance in Spain "worked within the organisation of workers against any possible antirevolutionary deviation" and played a critical role in shaping FORE. By 1870, there were "secret Bakuninist nuclei" of between twenty thousand and thirty thousand adherents in Spain, and an Alliance section was formed in Portugal in the following year.[51] The Alliance was also active in Italy and Switzerland; doubtless there were sections elsewhere. Bakunin himself referred to the Alliance in the present tense in 1872 and 1873, and Kropotkin joined the organisation as late as 1877.[52] As Malatesta, himself an Alliance member, would later comment:

> Why try to conceal certain truths now that they are in the domain of history and can serve as a lesson for the present and the future?... We, who were known in the International as Bakuninists and who were members of the Alliance made loud outcries against the Marxists because they tried to make their own particular programme prevail in the International. Yet, setting aside the question of the legality of their methods, which it is fruitless to dwell upon now, we did just what they did; we sought to make use of the International for our own party aims.[53]

Admitting to the existence of the Alliance, yet eager to deflect Marxist claims that the organisation was a sinister conspiracy, the anarcho-syndicalist Sam Dolgoff (1902–1990) insisted that the International Brotherhood and the Alliance were inoffensive and "quite informal fraternities of loosely organised individuals and groups."[54] This is not accurate: both the International Brotherhood and the Alliance had clearly set out programmes, rules, and criteria for membership.[55] Born in Russia to a Jewish family, Dolgoff grew up in the United States, where he worked on the docks and railroads, in lumber camps and factories, and painted houses. He became an anarchist, joined the IWW and a number of anarchist projects, devoted his life to the anarchist cause, edited the standard Bakunin anthology in English, and wrote important studies of Spain and Cuba as well as an interesting autobiography.[56]

For Bakunin, the Alliance was a "powerful but always invisible revolutionary association" that will "prepare and direct the revolution," "the invisible pilots guiding the Revolution ... the collective dictatorship of all our allies."[57] Bakunin saw the Alliance as a vehicle for mobilising and politicising the popular classes, rather than as a substitution for popular action or the instrument of a Blanquist-style dictatorship. The "*secret and universal association of the International Brothers*" would be "the life and the energy of the Revolution," composed of "men neither vain nor ambitious, but capable of serving as intermediaries between the revolutionary idea and the instincts of the people," and aiming at a revolution that "excludes any idea of dictatorship and of a controlling and directive power."[58]

The "invisible pilots" and "collective dictatorship" would "awaken and foment all the dynamic passions of the people," who would then organise from below upward, "spontaneously, without outside interference" or "official dictatorship."[59] The "sole purpose" of the Alliance was, Bakunin wrote, to "promote the Revolution; to destroy all governments and to make government forever impossible," to "give free rein to the ... masses ... voluntary federation and unconditional freedom," and to "combat all ambition to dominate the revolutionary movement of the people" by "cliques or individuals." Its power would not be based on official positions yet only the "*natural but never official influence* of all members of the Alliance."[60] Bakunin argued that the Alliance was "a secret society, formed in the heart of the International, to give it a revolutionary organisation, and to transform it and all the popular masses outside it, into a force sufficiently organised to annihilate political, clerical, bourgeois reaction, to destroy all religious, political, judicious institutions of states."[61]

The secrecy of the Alliance was, arguably, not an "authoritarian strategy" based on "manipulating others through secret societies."[62] The repressive conditions under which the early anarchists operated necessitated secrecy—a concern that revolutionaries of all types shared: for instance, it was a secret Communist League issued *The Communist Manifesto*.[63] Within these constraints, the anarchists sought to win the battle of ideas, not manipulate the popular classes through a conspiracy:

> The difference lay in the fact that we, as anarchists, relied chiefly on propaganda, and, since we wanted to gain converts for the anarchist cause, emphasised decentralisation, the autonomy of groups, free initiative, both individual and collective, while the Marxists, being authoritarians as they are, wanted to impose their ideas by majority strength—which was more or less fictitious—by centralisation and by discipline. But all of us, Bakuninists and Marxists alike, tried to force events rather than relying upon the force of events.[64]

The model of a specific anarchist political organisation of tendency developed by Bakunin and the Alliance as an alternative to Blanquist and classical Marxist conceptions—an anarchist organisation with a clear agenda, working within the movements of the popular classes, relating to their demands and striving to win the battle of ideas, rather than imposing its will by fiat or manipulation—has been a recurrent feature of mass anarchism. For Kropotkin, it was the "party which has made the most revolutionary propaganda and which has shown the most spirit and daring" that "will be listened to on the day when it is necessary to act, to march in front in order to realise the revolution."[65] He considered it essential "*to plan for the penetration of the masses and their stimulation by libertarian militants, in much the same way as the Alliance acted within the International.*"[66] Rejecting the notion that the unions were spontaneously revolutionary, Kropotkin maintained that "there is need of the other element Malatesta speaks of *and which Bakunin always professed.*"[67]

Malatesta had contended that "Bakunin expected a great deal from the International; yet, at the same time, he created the Alliance, a secret organisation with a well-determined programme—atheist, socialist, anarchist, revolutionary." This gave the "the anarchist impulse to one branch of the International just as the Marxists, on the other hand, gave the Social Democratic impulsion to the other branch."[68] While Malatesta flirted with the synthesist position on occasion, he more typically called for a "continuity of effort, patience, coordination and adaptability to different surroundings and circumstances," doubted the wisdom of "bringing together *all* anarchists into a single organisation," and argued for "cooperating in a common aim" as well as a "moral duty to see through commitments undertaken and to do nothing that would contradict the accepted programme."[69] He envisaged the ideal anarchist political organisation in fairly loose terms—congress resolutions were not, for instance, to be binding on those who disagreed with them—but was generally within the Bakuninist approach to organisational dualism.[70]

In Spain, the FORE was followed by the FTRE and then the Pact of Union and Solidarity, within which militants "committed to the need for political cadres and fearful of the reformist inclinations of organisations based on unions created ... the Anarchist Organisation of the Spanish Region."[71] In 1918, and again in 1922, anarchists committed themselves to working within the CNT to "bring their full influence to bear" and prevent a Bolshevik takeover.[72]

The National Federation of Anarchist Groups was followed in 1927 by the FAI, which was meant to operate in both Portugal and Spain, although it seems to have only been a serious factor in the latter. Explicitly modelled on the Alliance, the FAI was a clandestine organisation dedicated "to an intensification of anarchist involvement in the CNT," with the FAI viewing it as its "duty to guide the CNT from positions of responsibility."[73] For many veterans, the FAI "brought anarchist history full circle," with the Alliance again "revived to guide and to hasten the revolutionary action of anarcho-syndicalism."[74] It may have had nearly forty thousand members on the eve of July 19, 1936.[75] It was the FAI that played the key role in ousting the moderate *treintistas* from prominent positions in the CNT in 1931—a process during which the "leading trientistas were fired from their posts in publications and committees" and "expelled from the confederation."[76]

The FAI in Spain has been described as "a highly centralised party apparatus," but the position was more complicated.[77] It was tightly structured: based on small local bodies called "affinity groups," with a policy of carefully selecting members, it was organised into local, district, and regional federations, linked through mandated committees and based on regular mass assemblies; it also had a Peninsular

Committee that dealt with administrative questions, executed agreed policies, and issued public policy statements.[78] There is some evidence that significant sections of the organisation developed a cult of action in which politics was less important than doing something exciting and practical, regardless of its place in FAI strategy, yet the general impression is certainly that of political coherence and homogeneity.[79]

Durruti (1896–1936) exemplified the ideal FAI militant. The son of a railway worker, he became a mechanic on the railways at the age of fourteen, fled to France during the dramatic 1917 general strike, moved toward anarchism, and joined the CNT on his return in 1919.[80] He was active in union work, and in 1922 helped form the clandestine Los Solidarios anarchist group. The early 1920s saw a wave of assassinations of CNT militants by employer-hired killers and the police, and groups like Los Solidarios organised armed reprisals. Based in the CNT, these armed groups were qualitatively different from those of insurrectionist anarchists, for their actions were part of a mass struggle, not a substitute for it. In the same spirit, Durruti also robbed banks across Europe and Latin America to raise funds.

In 1931, Durruti joined the FAI, affiliated with the hard-line Nosotros ("We") tendency, and played a key role in the CNT's plans for revolution in 1932 and 1933, serving on its National Revolutionary Committee. With the outbreak of the Spanish Revolution, he opposed the Popular Front approach and took a leading part in the popular militia, heading what became known as the Durruti Column, which fought on the Aragon front and then in defence of Madrid. Durruti was shot on November 20, 1936, and two days later in Barcelona half a million people attended his funeral, the largest such procession in the city's history.

Woodcock's view that Spain provides "the only time in the history of anarchism" that "Bakunin's plan of a secret elite of devoted militants controlling [sic] a public mass organisation of partially converted workers came into being" is not accurate, for similar cases of the Bakuninist approach can be found elsewhere.[81] We have already touched on instances like the *noyaux*, the SNLA, the ISEL, the IWPA in Chicago, and the SLP.

In Mexico, the clandestine anarchist group La Social, first formed in 1865, played an active role in both the CGO and the CGOM, and aimed at establishing unions "similar in nature" to the Spanish CNT.[82] In 1912, this tradition was reinvigorated with the founding of Luz (renamed Lucha, or "Struggle," in 1913), a clandestine group that strived for the "creation of an anarcho-syndicalist labour front."[83] Its fiery manifesto declared that it would "enlighten an enslaved and ignorant people," "overthrow the tormentors of mankind," "devastate the social institutions generated by torturers and loafers," "use truth as the ultimate weapon against inequity," and march "toward the universal nation where all can live with mutual respect" and "absolute freedom."[84]

Besides promoting workers' schools and libraries, to be sponsored by the unions, Luz ran popular education classes, founded the COM and played a critical role in expanding the union, and also functioned within it "as a Bakuninist-type control [sic] group."[85] By 1914, it had become so difficult to distinguish the union's confederal committee from the Lucha group that the term Lucha even fell into disuse.[86] In 1917, a new Grupo Luz ("Light Group") was formed, and was critical in defending and strengthening syndicalism in the difficult years of 1917 to 1921, when it helped form the Mexican CGT.[87]

In China, Shifu's circle, the Society of Anarchist-Communist Comrades, pioneered union organising; "it was Sifu's [*sic*] group that first undertook such activity, propagated syndicalism in China, and, until the mid-twenties when they began to lose ground to the Communist Party, provided leadership in the labour movement."[88] By 1920 they had organised China's first May Day (in 1918), published the country's first magazine devoted to union work, *Laodong zazhi* ("Labour Magazine"), established nearly forty unions, and had played a similar role to groups like La Social and Luz. In Japan, the role of the Kokuren in the Zenkoku Jiren can be compared to that of the FAI in the CNT.[89] Formed in 1925, the Kokuren was an "inner core of battle-hardened militants" within the radical unions; it also operated in colonial Korea and Taiwan.[90]

In South Africa, the syndicalist political group, the International Socialist League, championed civil rights, promoted syndicalist ideas, distributed syndicalist materials, and worked within the mainstream unions, where it increasingly promoted rank-and-file syndicalism. It also formed a number of syndicalist unions like the Clothing Workers' Industrial Union, the Horse Drivers' Union, the Industrial Workers of Africa, and the Indian Workers' Industrial Union. The key figures in every single one of these syndicalist unions, like Thibedi, were members of the International Socialist League. Given that the mainstream unions, on the whole, did not admit workers of colour, the formation of new syndicalist unions operated in tandem with the promotion of rank-and-file syndicalism.

Nevertheless, while the International Socialist League aimed at operating as a politically cohesive and tight-knit formation, it tended to lack a clear and consistent programme of action that could foster unity around clear activities and targets, avoided hard choices regarding the use of limited resources in money, people, and time, and generally tried to organise every worker, everywhere, and all the time.[91] This meant that energies were often dissipated and breakthroughs were not always consolidated. Despite some influence in African and Coloured nationalist groups like the Transvaal Native Congress, there was no ongoing work in these bodies; likewise, the syndicalist unions were never linked together in a federation, nor coordinated with one another in other ways.

The Alliance and its successors in the Bakuninist tradition of organisational dualism proved to be successful in promoting and defending the ideas of the broad anarchist tradition in mass organisations, and were pivotal in fostering the successful implementation of the mass anarchist project. This track record arguably arises directly from its stress on shared perspectives and the carrying out of the programme that was adopted. In unifying anarchists around clear objectives, elaborating a shared set of strategic and tactical choices, orienting itself directly toward the popular classes as well as their struggles and organisations, adopting a possibilist outlook, taking decisions about priorities and avoiding the diversion of scarce resources, and uniting energies around a common programme and accepting the responsibility for carrying it out, a small Bakuninist organisation is invariably more effective than a large group that strives for a loose anarchism without adjectives.

From Bakunin to the "Platform"

In 1926, Makhno, Arshinov, and the other Paris-based editors of *Dielo Truda* issued the *Organisational Platform of the Libertarian Communists*, which argued for a specific anarchist political group with shared positions, a common programme, and a mandated executive.[92] The advocates of a loose conception of anarchist political organisation predictably responded with a series of scathing attacks. Voline led the assault, insisting that the *Platform* was "one step away from Bolshevism" and constituted an anarchist "revisionism toward Bolshevism." He asserted that the "Executive Committee of the Universal Anarchist Union" that would "assume the ideological and organisational direction of every organisation," and favoured "coercion, violence, sanctions," the suppression of "freedom of press and freedom of speech," a "centralised and planned" economy, and a "central army, with a central command ... and 'political direction'" would dominate the "mass organisations."[93] These charges—that the *Platform* was Leninist or Blanquist—have been uncritically accepted by many anarchists and syndicalists as well as by scholars today.[94] "It is difficult to see what the difference is between this concept and the Bolshevik idea of a revolutionary vanguard."[95] The strategy of the *Platform* "essentially consisted of adopting bolshevik means in order to compete more effectively with bolshevism."[96]

These claims, however, are rather a caricature of the *Platform*, which actually advocated "the total negation of a social system based on the principles of classes and the State, and its replacement by a free non-statist society of workers under self-management." The *Platform* called for a "General Union of Anarchists" that would aim at the "preparation of the workers and peasants for the social revolution" through "libertarian education," which required "the selection and grouping of revolutionary worker and peasant forces on a libertarian communist theoretical basis" in tandem with organising "workers and peasants on an economic base of production and consumption."[97]

As mass organisations like unions and peasant movements did not spontaneously generate a revolutionary consciousness, it was the "fundamental task" of the "General Union of Anarchists" to win the battle of ideas so that anarchism would "become the leading concept of revolution." This implied work in the unions: because it united "workers on a basis of production, revolutionary syndicalism, like all groups based on professions, has no determining theory," and "always reflects the ideologies of diverse political groupings notably of those who work most intensely in its ranks." Consequently, the "tasks of anarchists in the ranks of the [union] movement consist of developing libertarian theory, and pointing it in a libertarian direction, in order to transform it into an active arm of the social revolution." The organisation "aspires neither to political power nor to dictatorship" but attempts to "help the masses to take the authentic road to the social revolution" through popular bodies built "by the masses and always under their control and influence," thereby realising "real self-management."[98]

These tasks could not be fulfilled through an informal body, as suggested by antiorganisationalists, nor by a loose one structured along the lines of anarchism without adjectives, for the "masses demand a clear and precise response from the anarchists." "From the moment when anarchists declare a conception of the revolution and the structure of society, they are obliged to give all these questions a clear response, to relate the solution of these problems to the general conception of libertarian communism, and to devote all their forces to the realisation of these." As a result, the anarchist political organisation must have close agreement on its programme and project, collective responsibility to the organisation by its members, a federal structure, and an executive with tasks "fixed by the congress."[99] Overall, then, the *Platform* should be seen as a *restatement* of the Bakuninist approach, rather than an innovative one, let alone a "revisionism toward Bolshevism."

Like the AD's *Towards a Fresh Revolution*, the *Platform* emerged against the backdrop of revolution—in this case, the Russian and Ukrainian revolutions in the late 1910s. Although both Bakunin and Kropotkin came from Russia, their contribution to the anarchist movement took place mainly in Western Europe. Russia had perhaps the weakest of the European anarchist and syndicalist movements. Anarchism played a role in the narodnik movement, but the SRs that emerged from narodnism were mainly political socialists. Faltering in the late nineteenth century, the movement grew rapidly in the early twentieth century, particularly with the events of the 1905 Russian revolt.[100] Its ability to act effectively was hampered by the deep divisions between self-declared "Anarchist Communists," who were mainly insurrectionist anarchists, and mass anarchists, who were themselves deeply divided over issues of strategy and tactics. Besides these main currents, there was also a host of Stirnerites and other eccentrics, many of whom proclaimed themselves "individualist" anarchists.

By 1917, Voline recounts, anarchism and syndicalism were marginal and "nearly unknown" in Russia.[101] The socialist movement in Russia was dominated by the Mensheviks, who had developed into a social democratic current; the Bolsheviks, who were committed to classical Marxism; and the SRs, divided into moderate and radical wings. Anarchism and syndicalism grew rapidly with the Russian Revolution of 1917, but were never able to assume a leading role, despite the return from exile of leading figures like Berkman, Cherkezov, Goldman, Kropotkin, and Voline. *Golos Truda* was published in Russia starting in August 1917 by the Union of Anarcho-syndicalist Propaganda, and its editors included Maximoff and Voline.[102] The anarcho-syndicalists were highly critical of the Bolshevik regime, and despite ongoing repression, launched a Confederation of Russian Anarcho-syndicalists in November 1918.[103] Rather than try to capture the existing unions, controlled by political parties, and wary of the increasingly bureaucratic soviets, the anarcho-syndicalists adopted rank-and-file syndicalism, focusing on the factory committee movement that emerged in 1917.[104] The Anarchist Communists, meanwhile, continued their assassinations and "expropriations" (providing a ready pretext for the ongoing Bolshevik repression of the anarchists and syndicalists), while a significant section of the anarchists, disillusioned by the state of the movement, joined or otherwise actively supported the Bolsheviks; the latter were known as the "soviet-anarchists."

It was too little too late, and the movement was crushed and exiled by 1921. There was one important exception to this trend, and that was in the Russian territory of Ukraine; here, events took such a dramatically different path as to justify us speaking of a distinct Ukrainian Revolution. From 1917 onward, anarchists began to play a key role both in the urban centres, particularly the provincial capital Hul-yaypole (often called "Gulyai-Pole"), and among the peasants. Besides union work in industry, they formed the Union of Peasants, began promoting the expropriation of land and factories, and tried to destroy the state apparatus in 1917. In January and February of that year, they helped defeat an attempt by the Ukrainian nationalists to take power.

When the Bolsheviks handed the Ukraine to the German forces in the Treaty of Brest-Litovsk, these activities were disrupted. Yet the anarchists were able to or-ganise partisan detachments that were critical in expelling the invaders in 1918; these developed into a vast anarchist-led militia, the Revolutionary Insurgent Army of the Ukraine (RIAU). As the RIAU grew and expanded its control over territory, it created space for the blossoming of an anarchist revolution in a large part of the southern Ukraine. Based among poor peasants, but with a substantial degree of ur-ban support, the Ukrainian Revolution involved large-scale land expropriation, the formation of agrarian collectives, and the establishment of industrial self-manage-ment, all coordinated through federations and congresses of soviets. Voline, fleeing the oppressive climate of Petrograd, joined the movement and helped to establish the Nabat anarchist federation along with Arshinov—a federation that played a crit-ical role in Makhnovist education and propaganda.

The key figure in the movement was Makhno.[105] The son of poor peasants, he worked from a young age as a housepainter, cart driver, and then a labourer in a foundry, and joined an insurrectionist anarchist group in 1906. Involved in a number of terrorist actions, he was imprisoned in 1908, with a death sentence com-muted to hard labour, and then freed in 1917 during the political amnesties that followed the collapse of czarism. In prison, Makhno broke with insurrectionism, and after his release he organised the Group of Anarchist-Communists, became the leading union activist in Gulyai-Pole, also formed the Union of Peasants, and then became the main figure in the RIAU; it is no accident that the Ukrainian revolution-ary movement was widely known as the Makhnovists. In 1921, he fled into exile as the Bolshevik's Red Army crushed the Ukrainian Revolution, ending up in France, where he was involved in *Dielo Truda* and the Group of Russian Anarchists Abroad. He died in abject poverty in 1935.

Makhno's life cannot easily be disentangled from that of Arshinov, an anarchist metalworker. Arshinov came from the city of Ekaterinoslav in the Ukraine, and had been a prominent Bolshevik before his conversion to anarchism in 1906. Initially an insurrectionist anarchist, he was, like Makhno, involved in armed actions and sentenced to death. Arshinov escaped to Western Europe, but was extradited and retried, with his sentence changed to hard labour. In jail he met Makhno, and had a profound influence on the young activist. On his release in 1917, Arshinov initially went to Moscow, before returning to the revolutionary Ukraine. Like Makhno he had to flee abroad, and ended up in Paris. In 1931, Arshinov took a fateful deci-sion to return to Russia, hoping to form an underground anarchist group. Nettlau sneered at the time that Arshinov "was never really an anarchist" and that his deci-sion to enter the Soviet Union was merely a "homecoming."[106] Stalin obviously did not agree: Arshinov was executed in 1937 for anarchist activity.

Rethinking the "Platform" Debate

Makhno and Arshinov explicitly linked the *Platform* to the Bakuninist heritage. Bakunin's "aspirations concerning organisations, as well as his activity in the 1st IWMA [the First International] give us every right" to view him as an "active partisan" of the idea that anarchism "must gather its forces into one organisation, constantly agitating, as demanded by reality and the strategy of class struggle."[107] Likewise, they quoted Kropotkin with approval: "The formation of an anarchist organisation ... far from being prejudicial to the common revolutionary task ... is desirable and useful to the very greatest degree."[108] For the authors of the *Platform*, it was precisely the absence of a coordinated anarchist political group, with a common programme, that contributed to the Russian movement's crushing defeat by Bolshevism. Outside the Ukraine, Russian anarchism had been characterised by "inactivity and sterility," and "confusion in anarchist theory and organisational chaos in anarchist ranks"; indeed, most Russian anarchists had simply "*slept through*" the Ukrainian Revolution, a "mass movement of paramount importance."[109] It was during the Russian Revolution that "the libertarian movements showed the greatest degree of sectionalism and incoherence."[110]

This, of course, begs the question of why the *Platform* aroused so much controversy. On one level, it should be borne in mind that much of the debate over the *Platform* took place in the circles of the exiled Russian anarchists: such émigré milieus are notorious for their infighting, and it is not at all surprising to learn of an almost total breakdown of personal relations between Makhno and Voline, and between Arshinov and Berkman. Yet much of the debate was conducted in French and drew in anarchists well beyond the exiled Russian circles. Several other factors contributed to the vehemence with which many anarchists opposed the *Platform*—notaby, the rise of antiorganisationalism and the fear of creeping Bolshevism, expressed in the view that a tight-knit anarchist organisation must eventuate in Bolshevism.

Many of the criticisms of the *Platform* came from precisely the section of anarchism that rejected tight organisation on principle. For example, Maria Isidine (1873–1933), an anarchist and scientist of Russian and French descent, criticised the *Platform* in a paper that rejected in principle the view that an organisation should have shared political positions, a common strategy, a clearly structured federation, make binding decisions, or direct its press to promote particular stances.[111] In her opinion, even the synthesist position went too far: every individual, local group, and current should be free to act as it saw fit, as this was efficient, fostered unity, and did not violate the rights of dissenting minorities. Given such a perspective, it was inevitable that Isidine would baulk at the *Platform*'s proposals, which seemed to her a call for a "strong, centralised party" made of "new organisational formulas" that were "inspired" by Bolshevism.[112] (For Voline, too, the *Platform* was "only one step away from Bolshevism," and the "similarity between the Bolsheviks and the 'Platform anarchists' was frightening.")[113]

Such critics could not really explain why close agreement on analysis, strategy, and tactics was incompatible with anarchism. The view that a common programme violates the rights of those who cannot agree to that programme is surely weak. If there is a deep division, the minority can go along with the views of the majority, or if it is judged feasible, two divergent tactics could be permitted, or the minority could withdraw; the minority is neither punished for disagreeing nor brutalised into agreeing, and can leave freely at any time it wishes. The suggestion that the majority must, as a matter of principle, allow a dissident minority to do precisely as it pleases regardless of the fact of common membership in one organisation is also not without its problems. Besides dissipating limited resources, it can be problematic in other ways: the consequences of a group of insurrectionists engaging in assassinations while part of a group focuses on careful union work under difficult circumstances can readily be imagined, with obvious impacts on the individual freedom of the majority.

In caricaturing the *Platform*, critics like Isidine and Voline did anarchism a great disservice. Most important, they simply avoided the tough question posed by the *Platform*: the astounding failure of Russian anarchism. Voline purged anarchist and syndicalist history of experiences like the Alliance, and misrepresented the Ukrainian Revolution. The role of the Nabat would certainly seem to bear out the views of the *Platform*, so Voline presented it as a successful example of the synthesist approach. While the Nabat had started from an overtly synthesist view, it had quickly evolved in the "whirlwind of revolution" into a federation that rallied "the most determined, the most dynamic militants with an eye to launching a healthy, well-structured movement with the prospect of a standardised programme."[114] The Nabat practiced majority decision making and promoted a unitary "policy line," "a single, coherent platform":

> In short, it was a well-structured, well-disciplined movement with a leading echelon appointed and monitored by the rank and file. And let there be no illusions as to the role of that echelon [the secretariat]: it was not merely "technically" executive, as it is commonly regarded. It was also the movement's ideological "pilot core," looking after publishing operations, and propaganda activity, utilising the central funds and above all controlling and deploying the movement's resources and militants.

Why? As its press explained,

> Anarchism, which always leaned upon the mass movement of the workers, has to support the Makhno movement with all its power; it has to join this movement and close ranks with it. Hence we must also become a part of the leading organ of this movement, the army, and try to organise with the help of the latter the movement as a whole.[115]

Other Responses to the "Platform"

Still, not all criticisms of the *Platform* came from anarchists influenced by the ideas of antiorganisationalism and loose organisation, and these responses must be treated somewhat differently. It is necessary to distinguish between two types of responses by anarchists in the Bakuninist tradition of organisational dualism. Some were enthusiastic about the *Platform* and accepted its principles, with one French activist writing,

> If the Russian anarchists—like ourselves in fact—had had a serious organisation, had been grouped together, it would have been more diffi-

cult to defeat them, and something would have been left from the effort expended and the influence which they had acquired, because it would have been necessary to talk, to discuss, to deal with them, instead of exterminating them as the Bolsheviks, the Red Fascists, did.[116]

In 1927, the *Dielo Truda* group issued a call for an International Anarchist Communist Federation: its preliminary meeting in February and conference in April drew in Chinese, French, Italians, and Poles, but the conference was disrupted by the arrest of all those present.[117] The French Union Anarchiste initially incorporated some of the proposals of the *Platform*, but later repudiated them; the Revolutionary Anarcho-Communist Union also considered the *Platform* at its 1930 congress, but rejected it. The Group of Russian Anarchists Abroad itself fractured in 1927, and this also seems to have contributed to a split in the Federation of Anarcho-Communists in North America and Canada into advocates of tight organisation and antiorganisationalist *svobodnik* groupings.

In Italy, supporters of the *Platform* set up the short-lived Italian Anarchist Communist Union, while in Bulgaria, the FAKB incorporated the *Platform* into its constitution. The 1945 FAKB *Platform of the Federation of Anarchist Communists of Bulgaria* argued for an anarchist and communist future order. While rejecting the traditional political party as "sterile and ineffective," and "unable to respond to the goals and the immediate tasks and to the interests of the workers," it advocated syndicalist unions, cooperatives, and cultural and special organisations (like those for youth and women), and a specifically anarchist political group along the lines of the *Platform*:

> It is above all necessary for the partisans of anarchist communism to be organised in an anarchist communist ideological organisation. The tasks of these organisations are: to develop, realise and spread anarchist communist ideas; to study the vital present-day questions affecting the daily lives of the working masses and the problems of the social reconstruction; the multifaceted struggle for the defence of our social ideal and the cause of working people; to participate in the creation of groups of workers on the level of production, profession, exchange and consumption, culture and education, and all other organisations that can be useful in the preparation for the social reconstruction; armed participation in every revolutionary insurrection; the preparation for and organisation of these events; the use of every means which can bring on the social revolution. Anarchist communist ideological organisations are absolutely indispensable in the full realisation of anarchist communism both before the revolution and after.[118]

In Spain, the *Platform* was not available in translation at the time of the FAI's founding and thus was not discussed, although it was on the agenda; similar ideas to those of the *Platform* were nonetheless widely held in the FAI, and AD's *Towards a Fresh Revolution* was also widely regarded as an integral part of the Platformist tradition. The *Platform* also had some influence elsewhere in this period. In Brazil, for instance, Russian and Ukrainian immigrants, who had organised a self-managed farm in Erebango in Rio Grande do Sul state, were influenced by the example of the Ukrainian Revolution and received *Dielo Truda* starting in 1925.[119] In the period after 1945, Platformism underwent something of a revival, notably in Italy and

France. The Libertarian Communist Federation was formed in France, and it split from the FAF in 1952. Its history was marred by controversy, not least as a result of attempts to capture the FAF and by a decision to run in the 1956 elections, thereby reviving suspicions of the *Platform*.[120] Despite a decline in the late 1950s, the Libertarian Communist Federation left an important legacy in the form of the *Manifesto of Libertarian Communism*, written by George Fontenis and sometimes regarded as a key Platformist text.[121] The Anarchist Revolutionary Organisation, established in 1968 and splitting from the FAF in 1970, adopted elements of the *Platform*, leading to similar groups being formed in Denmark, Britain, and Italy (the latter evolving into the current FdCA).

The 1980s and 1990s saw a rapid spread of explicitly Platformist groups worldwide. These included the WSM in Ireland (formed in 1984), the Gaúcha Anarchist Federation in Brazil (FAG, formed in 1995), and the Workers Solidarity Federation in South Africa (formed in 1995). The controversial British Class War Federation also flirted with Platformism.[122] These developments will be examined more fully in volume 2. For now, it is worth noting that the postwar revival of Platformism was a response to a further upsurge of the doctrines of antiorganisationalism and loose federation in this period, with Platformism operating as a pole of attraction for anarchists in the Bakuninist tradition. For many—in part due to the weakness of anarchism in many countries by this time—the *Platform* was seen as something wholly new in anarchism. As organisations have developed, however, there is a growing recognition of its place in a larger Bakuninist tradition.[123]

The other response by anarchists in the Bakuninist tradition was substantially more critical of the *Platform*. Malatesta, who was under house arrest in Fascist Italy beginning in 1926, was sympathetic to the general project of the *Platform*, and also agreed with the view that a "large, serious and active organisation" was "necessary above all" to "influence the direction of the mass of the people." His criticisms were careful—he avoided Voline's wild accusations—but did make the suggestion that the "tendency" of the document was somewhat "authoritarian" and expressed some doubts about the wisdom of relying on majority rule principles.[124] Maximoff was rather more scathing, claiming that the *Platform* advocated the "Party structure of the Russian Bolsheviks," placed the "interests of the Party above the interests of the masses," and aimed at the forcible subjugation of the unions.[125]

As these criticisms did not proceed from a basic suspicion of organisation, they are of great interest and must be accounted for in other ways. In part, it is clear that we are dealing here with a problem of miscommunication, as the exchange with Malatesta revealed. Responding to Malatesta's initial input, Arshinov confessed his "perplexity" at the criticisms, for the "principles taken up by comrade Malatesta correspond to the principal positions of the *Platform*."[126] Makhno replied that Malatesta must either have "misunderstood the project for the 'Platform'" or rejected the principle of members having a responsibility to the organisation.[127] The latter, it turned out, was not the case: Malatesta responded with the statement that "anyone who associates and cooperates with others for a common purpose must feel the need to coordinate his actions with those of his fellow members and do nothing that harms the work of others," and that "those who do not feel and do not practice that duty should be thrown out of the association."[128]

Other misunderstandings were also evident. For example, Malatesta read the *Platform* as advocating an "Executive Committee to give ideological and organisational direction to the association," which he suggested might mean "a central body that would, in an authoritarian manner, dictate the theoretical and practical programme of the revolution." Yet as the authors of the *Platform* remarked, "Let it be said, first of all, that in our view, the Union's Executive Committee cannot be a body endowed with any powers of a coercive nature, as is the case with the centralist political parties." In case of a split in the organisation, "the question will be resolved, not by the Executive Committee which, let us repeat, is to be merely an executive organ of the Union, but by the entire Union as a body: by a Union Conference or Congress."[129] In a further reply, indeed, Malatesta conceded that "this is perhaps only a question of words ... reading what the comrades ... say ... I find myself more or less in agreement with their way of conceiving the anarchist organisation ... and I confirm my belief that behind the linguistic differences really lie identical positions."[130]

That misunderstandings could play so important a role—and it is clear that Maximoff also misinterpreted the *Platform* in many respects—points to a basic flaw of the document: many of its formulations are contradictory or lend themselves to misinterpretation. The *Platform*, for example, asserted that the "immutable principles and teachers" argued for a tight-knit group, a view held by "practically all active anarchist militants," and ascribed weak organisation to a "false interpretation" of anarchist ideas, yet also spoke of the movement as having an "absence of organisational principles and practices" as well as suffering from the "disease of disorganisation" for "dozens of years."[131] Likewise, as Arshinov suggested, the "absence of a homogeneous general programme has always been a very noticeable failing in the anarchist movement ... its propaganda not ever having been coherent and consistent in relation to the ideas professed and the practical principles defended."[132]

Such formulations, applied in a careless and indiscriminate manner to the whole of the broad anarchist tradition, served to alienate the very Bakuninists to whom the *Platform* might be expected to have the greatest appeal, for it dismissed a wide swath of anarchist history and theory. The bulk of Maximoff's angry retort to the *Platform*, for instance, arose from precisely this source. He expressed indignation that the *Platform* should be "credited with all kinds of achievements for which it was not responsible," and castigated its failure to acknowledge the achievements and policies of the anarchist First International, its ignorance of the history of syndicalism and the rise of the IWA, and its failure to give due credit to the role played by Russian groups like the Nabat and the Confederation of Russian Anarcho-syndicalists in combating "the chaotic, formless, disorganised and indifferent attitude then rampant among the Anarchists." The *Platform* was, Maximoff contended, characterised by an "ignorance of the history of our movement, or, more correctly, the notion that the history of our movement was ushered in by the 'Platform'"; that it "contains nothing original" and is marked by a "chronic ignorance."[133]

The tragedy of the situation was exemplified by Maximoff's rejection of the *Platform*'s proposals for anarchist organisation. Having alleged that the *Platform* was unduly influenced by Bolshevism, Maximoff went on to restate what he regarded as the principal anarchist positions on the relationship between the anarchist vanguard and the mass organisations of the popular classes—involvement in daily struggles, homogeneous national groups, work in the unions to win them to anarchism, work outside the unions, revolutionary reconstruction by the popular classes, armed self-defence, and so on—adding that there is "nothing 'anti-Anarchist' in a party organisation as such." "One must go into the masses oneself, work with them, struggle for their soul, and attempt to win it *ideologically* and give it guidance."[134] Anarchists must "organise their own associations," and consider "unification by ideological affinity" at all levels as "vitally important" in the field of "mass propaganda and the struggle against the political parties."[135]

Maximoff's views were not actually so different from those of the *Platform*. Like Bakunin, he openly argued that the anarchists must lead the masses, albeit in a libertarian way. The anarchists should not passively wait for the popular classes to call for assistance or provide only "ideological assistance." They must instead take steps to win the battle of ideas, and success in this task inevitably makes anarchists into leaders, and compels them to provide "guidance in action and struggle." If the popular classes were won to anarchism or syndicalism in large numbers, this would inevitably result in anarchists and syndicalists playing a key role in union structures, education, publishing, and so forth. It would be absurd, conversely, to take a principled opposition to such responsibilities; "logically it would be better not to mingle with the masses at all." In either case, the effect would be a de facto reservation of the role of leadership for nonanarchists. The "question is not the rejection of leadership, but making sure that it is *free* and natural."[136]

In other words, there is a place for a *libertarian* form of leadership, one compatible with anarchism, in which positions of responsibility are undertaken in a democratic and mandated manner, the influence of anarchism and syndicalism reflects its ideological influence yet is not imposed from above through coercion or manipulation, and leadership facilitates the self-emancipation of the popular classes, rather than substitutes for it. To refuse positions of responsibility can merely result in adopting an irresponsible position, as an incident from Voline's life shows. During the Russian revolt of 1905, Voline was apparently approached by a group of workers, who requested he take up the post of president of the Petrograd Soviet: citing his "scruples," he turned it down.[137] The post then went to Trotsky.

This followed from Voline's abstract views on the role of anarchists, including a repudiation of all "leadership." Voline maintained that anarchists "do not believe that the anarchists should lead the masses; we believe that our role is to assist the masses only when they need such assistance," and anarchists "can only offer ideological assistance, but not in the role of leaders." "The slightest suggestion of direction, of superiority, of leadership of the masses and developments inevitably implies that the masses must accept direction, must submit to it; this, in turn, gives the leaders a sense of being privileged like dictators, of becoming separated from the masses."[138]

In Conclusion: Militant Minority and Mass Movement

This chapter has examined the tactical issues that surround the question of how anarchists and syndicalists should organise themselves in order to reach their goals. It has surveyed insurrectionist anarchist approaches, syndicalist positions that deny the need for a specific anarchist or syndicalist political group, mass anarchist positions that advocate either antiorganisationalist approaches or loose organisation, and finally, Bakuninist positions that argue for a well-organised specifically anarchist political formation based on shared positions. These differences stem partly from different conceptions of the structure of the organisation; they also involve differences over the role of that organisation, and in particular, whether—or how—it can "lead" the popular classes. There has never been a consensus over these issues—a factor that has no doubt played a role in the fortunes of anarchism and syndicalism.

Several further points are worth noting. It is a mistake to contend that syndicalism as a whole rejects the need for a specific political group. There is certainly a current in syndicalism that holds this position, but there are many syndicalists from Bakunin onward who admitted—whether tacitly or openly—the need for organisational dualism. Inasmuch as the Platformist tradition is an example of the Bakuninist tradition of organisational dualism, and advocates something similar to that practiced by groups like the Alliance, Luz, La Social, the Society of Anarchist-Communist Comrades, the FAI, and other Bakuninist groups, and inasmuch as the core Platformist documents (the *Platform* and *Towards a Fresh Revolution*) supported syndicalism, setting up a sharp contrast between Platformism and syndicalism is not useful.

The survey of positions undertaken in this chapter raises a number of fundamental issues about the nature of social change as well as the relationship between society and the individual. An ideology's prospects rest in part on the strength of its basic ideas about the current society and its plans for the future. They also rest on the practical activity of its advocates, and the way in which they apply their ideas to economic and social realities. Ultimately, it is in the sphere of strategy and tactics that the fate of any movement is determined.

Any progressive movement for social change must inevitably confront the question of the relationship between the militant minority of conscious activists with a revolutionary programme and the broader popular classes. Should the revolutionaries substitute for the masses, as Blanqui suggested, or dominate them through a dictatorship, as Lenin believed? For the broad anarchist tradition, such positions are not acceptable, as they reproduce the very relations of domination and the oppression of the individual that the tradition rejects. It follows that the role of anarchists or syndicalists is to act as a catalyst for the self-emancipation of the masses, promoting both the new faith of which Bakunin spoke as well as popular self-organisation and participatory democracy.

There are various ways in which this can be done, and it is on this issue that the question of the need for a specific anarchist political organisation arises. There are a number of anarchist and syndicalist positions on this issue, as we have noted. The antiorganisationalist approach is flawed by its failure to consider the dangers of informal organisation and its dogmatic view that it is impossible to establish a formal organisation compatible with anarchist principles. The strand of syndicalism that denies the need for a specific anarchist or syndicalist political organisation fails to explain how a syndicalist union will be defended against the inevitable emergence of rival political currents within its ranks in the absence of such a body. The approach that calls only for a loose organisation that seeks to unite all anarchists and syndicalists, regardless of profound differences in outlook, on the basis of what they share does not provide a solution either: an organisation characterised by a wide diversity of views must lack a clear programme of action and fails to effectively coordinate the efforts of its militants in the battle of ideas; it is likely to split when confronted with situations that require a unified response. This approach also fails to explain why the unity of all anarchists should be seen as an end in itself and why a common programme should be seen as incompatible with anarchist principles.

The Bakuninist position, advocating an organisation of tendency with a shared analysis, strategy, and tactics, coordinated action, and an organisational discipline, seems the most effective approach. By coordinating activity, promoting common positions on the tasks of the present and future, and rallying militants around a programme, it offers the basis for consistent and coherent work, the direction of limited resources toward key challenges, and the defence and extension of the influence of anarchism. This approach, going back to the Alliance and expressed in the *Platform*, is probably the only way that anarchism can challenge the hold of mainstream political parties as well as nationalist, statist, and other ideas, and ensure that the anarchists' "new faith" provides a guide for the struggles of the popular classes. We turn now to an exploration of the class character and historical features of the broad anarchist tradition.

Notes

1. Goldman, "The Failure of the Russian Revolution," 159.

2. Galleani, *The End of Anarchism?*, 11.

3. Ibid., 44–45.

4. O. V., *Autonomous Base Nucleus*, n.d., available at http://www.geocities.com/kk_abacus/insurr2.html (accessed March 30, 2004).

5. A dedicated revolutionary, Blanqui spent forty of his seventy-six years in jail, being imprisoned by five successive French regimes. He believed that reforms were generally futile. Only a revolution could create a socialist order, but the masses were trapped in ignorance, which meant the key task was to form a hierarchical and disciplined secret society to seize state power. See A. B. Spitzer, *The Revolutionary Theories of Louis Auguste Blanqui* (New York: Columbia University Press, 1957), especially 95–105, 114, 128–44, 153, 157–79.

6. See J. Freeman, *The Tyranny of Structurelessness* (1970; repr., Hull, UK: Anarchist Workers' Association, n.d.).

7. Craparo, *Anarchist Communists*, 83.

8. See, for example, Yoast, "The Development of Argentine Anarchism," 155–56.

9. See, for example, I. Meredith, *A Girl among the Anarchists* (1903; repr., Lincoln: University of Nebraska Press, 1992), chapter 2. The author's name is a pseudonym.

10. Dirlik, *Anarchism in the Chinese Revolution*, 233.

11. Avrich, *The Haymarket Tragedy*, 150–52.

12. Tucker published an English translation of Stirner's *Ego and His Own* in 1907.

13. Woodcock, *Anarchism*, 251.

14. Quoted in ibid., 251.

15. V. Serge, *Birth of Our Power* (1931; repr., London: Writers and Readers Publishing Cooperative, 1977), 31.

16. Kinna, "Kropotkin's Theory of Mutual Aid in Historical Context," 268–69.

17. Kropotkin, "Letter to Nettlau," 296–97.

18. Kropotkin, "Anarchist Communism," 73; P. Kropotkin, "Anarchist Morality," in *Kropotkin's Revolutionary Pamphlets: A Collection of Writings by Peter Kropotkin*, ed. R. N. Baldwin (1890; repr., New York: Dover Publications, 1970), 97.

19. Nettlau, *A Short History of Anarchism*, 54–55; Rocker, *Anarcho-Syndicalism*, chapter 1; Guérin, *Anarchism*, chapters 1 and 2.

20. Quoted in F. Mintz, "Class War: The Writings of Camillo Berneri," *Cienfuegos Press Anarchist Review*, no. 4 (1978): 47.

21. Malatesta, "Syndicalism," 221–22.

22. Hart, *Anarchism and the Mexican Working Class*, 156; Hart, "Revolutionary Syndicalism in Mexico," 200–1.

23. Ford and Foster, *Syndicalism*, 44.

24. Foner, *The Industrial Workers of the World*, 417.

25. Ibid., 134.

26. Makhno, *The Organisational Platform of the Libertarian Communists*, 6–7.

27. See Nettlau, *A Short History of Anarchism*, 198.

28. Ibid., 166, 195, 198–201, 207.

29. Marshall, *Demanding the Impossible*, 392–93.

30. Ibid., 393.

31. Quoted in F. Castilla, *Anarchism without Adjectives: From Yesterday to Today*, January 23, 2007, available at http://www.anarkismo.net/newswire.php?story_id=4717&print_page=true (accessed January 24, 2007).

32. Nettlau, *A Short History of Anarchism*, 294–95.

33. Quoted in Joll, *The Anarchists*, 204. Also quoted in Darch, "The Makhnovischna," 499.

34. Crump, *Hatta Shuzo and Pure Anarchism in Interwar Japan*, 155–57, 159–60, 174–77.

35. S. Fleshin Voline, M. Steimer, Sobol, J. Schwartz, Lia, Roman, and Ervantian, *Reply to the Platform (Synthesist)*, 1927. Available online at http://www.nestormakhno.info/english/volrep.htm (accessed December 1, 2006).

36. Voline, *Reply to the Platform*.

37. Dirlik, *Anarchism in the Chinese Revolution*, 11–13. There were, for example, ninety-two different groups formed between 1919 and 1925, but no national federation.

38. Dirlik, *The Origins of Chinese Communism*, 215–16.

39. Quoted in D. Hodges, *Intellectual Foundations of the Nicaraguan Revolution* (Austin: University of Texas Press, 1986), 83–84.

40. MacLachlan, *Anarchism and the Mexican Revolution*, 32–38, 51, 113–14.

41. Voline, *Reply to the Platform*.

42. Ibid.

43. Craparo, *Anarchist Communists*, 83.

44. Makhno, *The Organisational Platform of the Libertarian Communists*, 1.

45. Craparo, *Anarchist Communists*, 83.

46. For a still-excellent history of the First International, albeit marred by overt hostility toward Bakunin, see Stekloff, *History of the First International*.

47. Woodcock, *Anarchism*, 156.

48. K. Marx and F. Engels, "The Alliance of Socialist Democracy and the International Working Men's Association," in *Marx, Engels, Lenin: Anarchism and Anarcho-syndicalism*, ed. N. Y. Kolpinsky (1873; repr., Moscow: Progress Publishers, 1972), 113, 116, 118, 120.

49. Carr insists that the Alliance was a figment of Bakunin's imagination. For Joll, Bakunin showed a lifelong "passion ... for establishing largely imaginary secret societies." See Carr, *Michael Bakunin*, 421–23; Joll, *The Anarchists*, 87.

50. Peirats, *Anarchists in the Spanish Revolution*, 237.

51. Bookchin, *The Spanish Anarchists*, 50, 52, 72; Woodcock, *Anarchism*, 168.

52. Bakunin, "Letter to *La Liberté*," 289; Nettlau, *A Short History of Anarchism*, 281.

53. Quoted in Nettlau, *A Short History of Anarchism*, 131.

54. S. Dolgoff, editorial comments to *Bakunin on Anarchy: Selected Works by the Activist-Founder of World Anarchism*, ed. S. Dolgoff (London: George Allen and Unwin, 1971), 182. Compare also to Joll, *The Anarchists*, 87–88, 91.

55. See, inter alia, Bakunin, "The Programme of the International Brotherhood"; Bakunin, "The Programme of the Alliance."

56. S. Dolgoff, *Bakunin on Anarchy*; Dolgoff, *Fragments*.

57. Quoted in S. Dolgoff, *Bakunin on Anarchy*, 10; M. Bakunin, "Letter to Albert Richard," in *Bakunin on Anarchy: Selected Works by the Activist-Founder of World Anarchism*, ed. S. Dolgoff (1870; repr., London: George Allen and Unwin, 1971), 180.

58. Bakunin, "The Programme of the International Brotherhood," 154–55.

59. Bakunin, "Letter to Albert Richard," 180–81.

60. M. Bakunin, "On the Internal Conduct of the Alliance," in *Bakunin on Anarchism*, ed. S. Dolgoff (Montréal: Black Rose, 1980), 387.

61. Alliance Syndicaliste Revolutionnaire et Anarcho-syndicaliste, "Putting the Record Straight on Mikhail Bakunin," *Libertarian Communist Review*, no. 2 (1976) (translated from the French by Nick Heath). Available online at http://flag.blackened.net/revolt/hist_texts/lcr_bakunin.html, Accessed March 8, 2000.

62. Marshall, *Demanding the Impossible*, 277.

63. See McLellan, *Karl Marx*, 167–88. The Communist League operated through a number of "front" organisations and emerged from the older secret society, the League of the Just. See also A. Flood, "Bakunin's Idea of Revolution and Revolutionary Organisation," *Red and Black Revolution: A Magazine of Libertarian Communism*, no. 6 (2002).

64. Quoted in Nettlau, *A Short History of Anarchism*, 131.

65. P. Kropotkin, "The Spirit of Revolt," in *Kropotkin's Revolutionary Pamphlets: A Collection of Writings by Peter Kropotkin*, ed. R. N. Baldwin (1880; repr., New York: Dover Publications, 1970), 43.

66. Nettlau, *A Short History of Anarchism*, 277.

67. Quoted in ibid., 281.

68. Quoted in ibid., 130.

69. Malatesta in Richards, *Errico Malatesta*, 181; Malatesta, "A Project of Anarchist Organisation," 97. On his flirtation with the synthesist position, see, for example, E. Malatesta, "Communism and Individualism," in *The Anarchist Revolution: Polemical Writings, 1924–1931: Errico Malatesta*, ed. V. Richards (April 1926; repr., London: Freedom Press, 1995).

70. Malatesta, "A Project of Anarchist Organisation," 98–99, 101–2.

71. Kaplan, *Anarchists of Andalusia*, 165.

72. Richards, *Lessons of the Spanish Revolution*, 200.

73. Joll, *The Anarchists*, 245; Peirats, *Anarchists in the Spanish Revolution*, 238–39.

74. Amsden, *Collective Bargaining and Class Conflict in Spain*, 18.

75. Bookchin, *The Spanish Anarchists*, 215.

76. Peirats, *Anarchists in the Spanish Revolution*, 81.

77. Morrow, *Revolution and Counter Revolution in Spain*, chapter 5.

78. Bookchin, *The Spanish Anarchists*, 213–14.

79. Richards, *Lessons of the Spanish Revolution*, 83–84. The same impression of sophistication is provided in Paz, *Durruti*, a book that offers some insight into the inner workings of the FAI.

For a somewhat different view, see S. Christie, *We, the Anarchists: A Study of the Iberian Anarchist Federation, 1927–1937* (Hastings, UK: Meltzer Press, 2000).

80. See Paz, *Durruti*.

81. Woodcock, *Anarchism*, 358.

82. Hart, *Anarchism and the Mexican Working Class*, 29, 47–48, 54, 58.

83. Ibid., 109, 192–93.

84. Quoted in ibid., 113.

85. Ibid., 109, 192–93

86. Ibid., 128.

87. Ibid., 156.

88. Dirlik, *Anarchism in the Chinese Revolution*, 128.

89. Crump, *Hatta Shuzo and Pure Anarchism in Interwar Japan*, 75.

90. Ibid.

91. Van der Walt, "Anarchism and Syndicalism in South Africa," 354–57, 507, 511–12, 582–83.

92. Makhno, *The Organisational Platform of the Libertarian Communists*.

93. Voline, *Reply to the Platform*.

94. "The unfortunate thing was that faced with two successful examples—the bolshevik party and the anarchist army—Arshinoff, Makhno and their group produced an organisational platform and politics incorporating the main features of both": 1987 preface to Maximoff, *Constructive Anarchism*, 4.

95. Darch, "The Makhnovischna," 500.

96. Crump, *Hatta Shuzo and Pure Anarchism in Interwar Japan*, 18–19.

97. Makhno, *The Organisational Platform of the Libertarian Communists*, 2, 3–4.

98. Ibid., 4–6.

99. Ibid., 5, 8–9.

100. See Avrich, *The Russian Anarchists*; P. Avrich, ed., *The Anarchists in the Russian Revolution* (London: Thames and Hudson, 1973).

101. Voline, *The Unknown Revolution*, 115.

102. Avrich, *The Russian Anarchists*, 135–51.

103. Ibid., 190–94.

104. Ibid., 140–45, 190–91.

105. For anarchist accounts of Makhno and Arshinov, see, inter alia, P. Arshinov, ed., *History of the Makhnovist Movement, 1918–1921* (1923; repr., London: Freedom Press, 1987), especially chapter 3; Voline, preface to *History of the Makhnovist Movement, 1918–1921*, ed. P. Arshinov (1923; repr., London: Freedom Press, 1987); Voline, *The Unknown Revolution*. For more scholarly works, see the definitive Makhno biography, now in English, A. Skirda, *Nestor Makhno: Anarchy's Cossack: The Struggle for Free Soviets in the Ukraine, 1917–1921* (1982; repr., Edinburgh: AK Press, 2003). See also the excellent, if fairly hostile, Darch, "The Makhnovischna." See also the more sympathetic Malet, *Nestor Makhno in the Russian Civil War*. There is also a useful chapter in Avrich, *Anarchist Portraits*.

106. N. Walter, "Preface to the British Edition," in *History of the Makhnovist Movement*, ed. P. Arshinov (London: Freedom Press, 1987), 5.

107. Makhno, *The Organisational Platform of the Libertarian Communists*, 1.

108. Kropotkin, quoted in ibid., 1.

109. Arshinov, *History of the Makhnovist Movement*, 242–44.

110. Makhno, *The Organisational Platform of the Libertarian Communists*, 1.

111. M. Isidine, *Organisation and Party*, first published in *Plus Lion*, nos. 36–37 (1928), available at http://www.nestormakhno.info/english/isidine.htm (accessed March 30, 2004).

112. Ibid.

113. Voline, *Reply to the Platform*.

114. Skirda, *Nestor Makhno*, 243–45.

115. Darch, "The Makhnovischna," 419.

116. Quoted in ibid., 502–3.

117. N. Heath, "Historical Introduction," in *The Organisational Platform of the Libertarian Communists*, ed. P. Archinov, N. Makhno, I. Mett, Valevsky, and Linsky (1989; repr., Dublin: Workers Solidarity Movement, 2001), ii–iii.

118. Federation of Anarchist Communists of Bulgaria, *Platform of the Federation of Anarchist Communists of Bulgaria*, 1945, available at http://www.anarkismo.net/newswire.php?story_id=2526 (accessed March 3, 2006).

119. E. Rodrigues, *Against All Tyranny!* 17–19.

120. See A. Skirda, *Facing the Enemy: A History of Anarchist Organisation from Proudhon to May 1968* (Edinburgh: AK Press, 2002).

121. G. Fontenis, *Manifesto of Libertarian Communism* (1953; repr., London: Anarchist Communist Federation, 1989).

122. See, for example, Class War Federation, *Unfinished Business: The Politics of Class War* (London: Class War Federation, 1992), chapter 7.

123. See, for example, the analysis provided by Saverio Craparo of the FdCA, which starts with Bakunin; Craparo, *Anarchist Communists*.

124. Malatesta, "A Project of Anarchist Organisation," 93–94, 98–101.

125. See Maximoff, *Constructive Anarchism*, 17–21.

126. P. Arshinov, *The Old and New in Anarchism*, May 1928, available at http://www.nestor-makhno.info/english/oldnew.htm (accessed March 15, 2004).

127. N. Makhno, "Letter to Errico Malatesta from Nestor Makhno," in *The Anarchist Revolution: Polemical Writings, 1924–1931: Errico Malatesta*, ed. V. Richards (1928; repr., London: Freedom Press, 1995), 103.

128. E. Malatesta, "Malatesta's Response to Nestor Makhno," in *The Anarchist Revolution: Polemical Writings, 1924–1931: Errico Malatesta*, ed. V. Richards (1929; repr., London: Freedom Press, 1995), 107–8.

129. Group of Russian Anarchists Abroad, *Supplement to the Organisational Platform (Questions and Answers)*, 1926, available at http://www.nestormakhno.info/english/supporg.htm (accessed March 15, 2004).

130. E. Malatesta, *On Collective Responsibility*, n.d., available at http://www.nestormakhno.info/english/mal_rep3.htm (accessed March 15, 2004).

131. Makhno, *The Organisational Platform of the Libertarian Communists*, 1.

132. Arshinov, *The Old and New in Anarchism*.

133. Maximoff, *Constructive Anarchism*, 12–13, 14, 16–17; see also 18, 20. Maximoff went on to criticise the *Platform* for ignoring a range of issues. This was not entirely fair (after all, the *Platform* was a brief document) but again reveals the same line of reasoning. For example, Maximoff's view that the *Platform* tended toward a reductionist class analysis was made on the grounds that the document was insufficiently aware of existing anarchist positions; see ibid., 16.

134. Ibid., 5–17; the quote is from 17.

135. Maximoff, *The Programme of Anarcho-syndicalism*, 57–58.

136. Maximoff, *Constructive Anarchism*, 19.

137. Recounted in Voline, *The Unknown Revolution*, 98–101.

138. Voline, *Reply to the Platform*.

3 SOCIAL THEMES

Li Pei Kan (1904-2005).

Better known by his pseudonym "Ba Jin" (derived from the Chinese names for Bakunin and Kropotkin), he was active in the Chinese anarchist movement from the 1920s onwards. Ranked among China's most famous novelists, Ba was persecuted during Mao Zedong's "Cultural Revolution", was later "rehabilitated," and died at the age of 100 in Shanghai.

IWW rally in Australia, date unknown.

The IWW was the most significant revolutionary current in Australia in the first two decades of the twentieth century, maintained contacts with Asian anarchists, and was fervently opposed to the "White Australia" policy that sought to prevent workers of colour entering the country. This anti-racist stance was echoed in IWW sections across the world and commended by African-American activist and writer W.E.B. du Bois. *Picture courtesy of Stewart Bird, Dan Georgakas and Deborah Shaffer.*

CHAPTER 9

The Class Character and Popular Impact of the Broad Anarchist Tradition

A s we have argued, the broad anarchist tradition looked to the working class and peasantry as the agents of an international social revolution. But just how much did anarchism and syndicalism actually influence the popular classes, through what means, and how do we explain this? The literature has often treated the broad anarchist tradition as "never more than a minority attraction," outside of Spain, supposedly the one country where it became "a major social movement" able to "threaten the State."[1] It has also been claimed by many writers (particularly classical Marxists) that anarchism and syndicalism were essentially non-proletarian in character, finding their support either amongst "petty bourgeois" peasantries and self-employed artisans facing ruin at the hands of the modern world, or amongst marginal modern groups, such as the lumpenproletriat.

This chapter questions these claims, suggesting that they seriously underestimate and misunderstand the enormous popular influence, and predominantly working-class character, of the broad anarchist tradition, particularly in the "glorious period" associated with syndicalism's second wave, from the mid-1890s to the mid-1920s. In the "glorious period," for example, the broad anarchist tradition achieved majority status in the labour movement of many countries. Contrary to the thesis of Spanish exceptionalism, it dominated the labour movement in Argentina, Brazil, Chile, Cuba, France, Mexico, the Netherlands, Peru, Portugal, and Uruguay. Large-scale anarchist peasant movements developed, inter alia, in Bulgaria, Manchuria, Mexico, and the Ukraine, as well as Spain. There were also innumerable local organising initiatives. And, as we highlight in chapter 11, significant anarchist and syndicalist influences—and organisations—can be found in the second half of the twentieth century. We will argue in volume 2 that these constituted further waves of anarchist and syndicalist activism.

Even where the broad anarchist tradition was a minority current in the organised labour movement, it could often exert an important influence on labour and the Left, especially through its promotion of a revolutionary counterculture. In Italy, where there was no national anarchist or syndicalist organisation from the days of the First International to 1912, the movement nevertheless exerted a powerful influence on the local level, particularly in central Italy.[2] Anarchist and syndicalist currents emerged in a number of parties of the Labour and Socialist International. They also played a part in, or influenced, many rural social movements—not all of which were wholly anarchist. For example, Augusto César Sandino (1895–1934), head of the peasant Army for the Defence of the National Sovereignty of Nicaragua (ED-SNN) formed in 1927, embraced an ideology founded in part on "radical anarchist communism."[3] The Industrial and Commercial Workers Union of Africa (ICU) spread across southern Africa in the 1920s and 1930s: its ideology was influenced by the IWW, and its support was largely drawn from farmworkers and peasants.

Contrary to the view that the broad anarchist movement was a revolt of classes doomed by modernity, a "reactionary" and "petty bourgeois" movement of ruined artisans and peasants, for whom it was a utopian secular religion promising salvation from modernity, we suggest that it was based first and foremost among the urban working class, followed by farmworkers, and then by peasants.[4] In the "glorious period," moreover, syndicalism's appeal was especially marked among workers affected by the Second Industrial Revolution starting in the 1890s, which involved the rise of the chemical and electric industries along with the extension of Taylorist and Fordist mass production techniques; among peasants, anarchism typically arose where capitalism—or imperial intrusion, or state formation—disrupted traditional agrarian relationships. There is an important history of peasants being recruited into syndicalist unions, and of grassroots anarchist work in the peasant heartlands. Yet, while it is often suggested that there is some sort of special affinity between anarchism and peasant interests and peasant cultures,[5] large and sustained peasant anarchist movements or revolts are, compared to anarchist labour movements, rather rare. This has often been obscured by the tendency of writers to group diverse rural popular classes as peasants (we use the term in the restricted sense of small family farmers), which leads to anarchist and syndicalist landless labourers and other rural workers being categorised as peasant anarchists.

There is no doubt that many major anarchist and syndicalist activists and ideologues had some tertiary education, or were drawn from the middle class (or even dissident ruling class) intelligentsia: Bakunin, Ervin Batthyány (1877–1945) of Hungary, John Creaghe (1841–1920) in Argentina and Britain, Guillaume, De Leon, Galleani, Guerrero, Hatta, Itō, Kropotkin, Flores Magón, Malatesta, Michel, Ōsugi, Reclus, Shifu, Shin, and Zalacosta as well as Pietro Gori (1865–1911) in Italy, Fábio Luz and Neno Vasco (1878–1920) in Brazil, Juan Francisco Moncaleano in Colombia and Mexico, González Prada in Peru, and Thibedi and S. P. Bunting (1873–1936) in South Africa. In this, the broad anarchist tradition was (and is) no different from other sections of the radical Left. Nonetheless, this does not detract from the basic point that the broad anarchist tradition has, historically, been fundamentally a movement of the working class and peasantry, and that many of its key activists and thinkers came from the popular classes, including imposing figures like Arshinov, Berkman, Connolly, Durruti, Foster, Goldman, Infantes, Makhno, Mann, Speras, Peirats Valls, and Manol Vassev Nicolev, the tobacco worker who helped organise the Vlassovden peasant movement in 1930s Bulgaria (see volume 2). And regardless of their class origins, most leading anarchist and syndicalist militants lived lives of privation and died before their time: exiled, jailed, executed, killed on the barricades or laid low by the diseases of crushing poverty.

The Case against "Spanish Exceptionalism"

It is a widely held position that anarchism "became a mass movement in Spain to an extent that it never did elsewhere," with Spain as "the only country in the 20th Century where Anarcho-communism and Anarcho-syndicalism were adopted extensively as revolutionary theories and practices," developing into "a major social movement" that could threaten the state.[6] This line of reasoning issues from a narrow framework of reference: Western Europe and the United States are the focus of analysis, and it is against other movements in this zone that Spanish anarchism is measured. Movements in other parts of the world—Africa, Asia, the Caribbean, the Middle East, and Latin America—are not really considered. It would be too generous to refer to this perspective as Eurocentric, for it generally ignored Eastern Europe as well.

A global perspective on the history of anarchism and syndicalism provides an important corrective to this perspective, for it draws attention to a host of mass anarchist and syndicalist movements outside Spain. The FOA, formed in Argentina in 1901, was under the control of the anarchists by 1904, and transformed into the anarchist FORA, unquestionably the dominant labour centre in the country. A smaller moderate rival centre controlled by political socialists, the UGT, was soon restructured into the revolutionary syndicalist CORA in 1909, which was later absorbed into the anarchist FORA, precipitating the latter's split into a hardline "anarchist-communist" FORA-V and the more conventionally anarcho-syndicalist FORA-IX. The impact of anarchist and syndicalist influence on unions in Argentina has been disputed by authors who point to union fragmentation and weakness, and who note that day-to-day union activities often focused on pragmatic goals like wage increases.[7] This misses the point, however, that the big battalions of the labour movement were all dominated by anarchism and syndicalism, and that successful syndicalists always mobilised around both immediate issues and revolutionary goals. Argentina provides a case where anarchist and syndicalist influence was so substantial that the main divisions in organised labour centred around tactics within the broader anarchist tradition, rather than divisions between the anarchists and syndicalists, on the one hand, and other union traditions, on the other.

If Argentina provides a striking case, it was by no means the only instance of an anarchist or syndicalist mass movement in the region. In Brazil, the COB/FORB was anarchist led from its inception; it was the main labour centre, and until the 1920s most Brazilian unions remained anarcho-syndicalist in orientation.[8] The FORU in Uruguay, also the main union federation, adopted an anarchist programme from the start. Anarchists were the leading figures in the early Mexican labour movement of the 1870s and 1880s through the CGOM, and its twentieth-century successors, COM and the CGT, were also the main Mexican labour centres; the main union body outside these centres was the Mexican IWW, which was especially strong in the growing oil industry.[9] In Peru, the anarchists formed the first unions and organised the national union centre, the syndicalist FORPe, in 1919.

From the 1880s, the Cuban anarchists advocated a union along the lines of the Spanish FORE, with early successes including the Artisans' Central Council, the Workers' Circle, the Tobacco Workers' Federation, and the Workers' Alliance, followed by the anarchist CTC in 1895.[10] Despite the apparent disintegration of the CTC after independence, anarchists continued to play a central role in strikes and other labour struggles, helping to form the FOH in 1921, followed in 1925 by CNOC, in which they held sway for years.[11] At the outbreak of the Cuban Revolution in 1952, anarchist militants played a leading role in both the legal and underground unions: we will examine this in volume 2.

In Chile, meanwhile, the anarchists, who were already a substantial force in the labour movement by the turn of the twentieth century, formed the Chilean Labourers' Federation in 1906. This body was followed in 1913 by the anarcho-syndicalist FORCh. Both federations failed to become truly countrywide organisations, but were the main force in the labour movement, and anarchism and syndicalism had a major influence in other unions; around this time, the Chilean IWW controlled the docks and had a significant role among the sailors.[12] In Japan, the syndicalists around the Shinyūkai printers' union, the Labour Movement circle, the Seishinkai newspaper union, and other groups initially played an important role in the Sōdōmei federation. In China, where anarchists and syndicalists founded the first modern labour unions in that country, there were at least forty anarchist-led unions in the Canton area by 1921, and "anarchist domination" of the unions in Canton and Hunan lasted into the mid-1920s, and there was also significant anarchist union influence in Shanghai for many years.[13]

A global perspective, then, shows that anarchist and syndicalist mass movements often existed outside of Spain. The notion of Spanish exceptionalism also pays insufficient attention to a number of important cases within Western Europe. In early twentieth-century France, the syndicalist CGT was the sole labour centre. In the Netherlands, the NAS, with a syndicalist platform, was the "most active and influential organisation among the Dutch trade unions" from 1893 to 1903.[14] It was the largest of several Dutch union centres, and reached its peak at nine thousand members. In Portugal, the anarcho-syndicalist CGT, which followed the UON— itself eventually taken over by anarchists—was the sole labour centre from 1919 to 1924.[15]

If we use the somewhat limited criterion of influence in the union movement to gauge the influence of the broad anarchist tradition on the working class, Argentina, Brazil, Chile, Cuba, France, Mexico, Peru, Portugal, and Uruguay all constitute countries in which anarchism and syndicalism were the dominant political force among organised workers; the Netherlands provides a case of central influence as well. Moreover, a case can be made that these movements were, when considered in relation to the union movement as a whole, *larger* than the Spanish CNT: while the Spanish CNT only represented half of the unionised workers (the moderate UGT represented the other half), the anarchist and syndicalist movements of Argentina, Brazil, Chile, Cuba, France, Mexico, Peru, and Portugal represented almost the entire union movement.

In *numerical* terms, the Spanish CNT, which had 1.7 million members at the time of the Zaragoza congress in May 1936, was the biggest syndicalist union ever.[16]

In *relative* terms—to the size of the working class and the structure of the union movement—it was by no means the largest of the syndicalist unions. Indeed, it was relatively smaller than its Spanish predecessors, FORE, the FTRE, and the Pact of Union and Solidarity, which faced no rival union centres; with 1.7 million members yet faced with an equally large UGT, it was smaller than the Portuguese CGT, with nearly 100,000 members but no union rivals. The notions that "anarchism lay outside the mainstream of events" and that in "no class, or economic grouping, outside of Spain, was anarchism the norm" is simply not accurate.[17] The history of labour and the Left in many parts of the world simply cannot be adequately understood if its anarchist and syndicalist currents are ignored or treated as unimportant.

Broader Impacts and Infusions

Even where the broad anarchist tradition was less influential than orthodox unionism or political socialism, its impact was often considerable; a minority status should not be conflated with insignificance. Some of the minority syndicalist unions were extremely large, at least in numerical terms: the Italian USI peaked at 800,000 in 1920, roughly half the size of the dominant CGL; Germany's FAUD was always overshadowed by the SDP-linked unions, but with perhaps 150,000 members at its height it can legitimately be considered something of a mass movement.[18] In interwar Japan syndicalism was by no means insignificant either. The Sōdōmei, the mainstream labour union, split in 1925. It retained 20,000 members, the breakaway Communist-led Nihon Rōdō Kumiai Hyōgikai had 12,500, members and the anarcho-syndicalist Zenkoku Jiren, formed the following year, claimed 15,000 members.[19]

Furthermore, care should be taken not to measure anarchist and syndicalist influence purely in terms of the numbers enrolled in syndicalist unions. As the single-largest formations established by the broad anarchist tradition, syndicalist unions and union federations undoubtedly provide a crucial indication of strength, but only an imperfect one. A purely numerical assessment of the movement takes insufficient account of anarchism and syndicalism as a radical proletarian counterculture that had an impact far beyond the confines of the movement's formal structures while also ignoring movements outside the workplace. We will address the question of anarchist peasant movements later in this chapter and in the next chapter; the next chapter will also examine anarchist and syndicalist initiatives outside the workplace.

Italy provides an important example of the need to take the cultural and informal impact of the broad anarchist tradition into account. The absence of a national anarchist or syndicalist organisation from the days of the First International to the launching of the USI in 1912 is easily interpreted as indicating the insignificance of the broad anarchist tradition. Such an approach follows from the tradition of "old labour history," with its stress on formal organisation and leadership.[20] "New labour history," which emphasises the social history of the popular classes and the need to examine popular movements from below upward, offers a needed corrective to such perspectives, for it directs attention to cultural forms and informal organisations.[21]

Using a social history approach, Carl Levy's groundbreaking work on Italian anarchism has suggested that the movement had a major impact on working-class culture and the Left on the local level, supplying much of its language, symbols, and tactics while influencing sections of the PSI and CGL.[22] Marxist scholars have tended to highlight the role of figures like Gramsci in the popular unrest that shook Italy in the 1910s, such as the insurrectionary Red Week of 1914 and the *bienno rosso* ("two red years") of 1919–1920, culminating in the 1920 factory occupation movement that involved hundreds of thousands of workers. One writer even describes Gramsci as the leader of the factory occupation movement and the "most capable of Turin's revolutionaries."[23]

As Levy shows, however, the Red Week emerged from a general strike led by anarchists and the USI, and demonstrated the ability of the broad anarchist movement to grow extremely rapidly. He adds that the Gramsci of 1920 was by no means a Leninist: his views were close to anarchism, the key figures in his circle, grouped around the fortnightly *L'Ordino nuovo* ("New Order"), were anarchists, and his then-libertarian ideas had an appeal precisely because of their resonance with Italian popular culture.[24] To this it might be added that the anarchists and revolutionary syndicalists have been judged the "most consistently and totally revolutionary group on the left" in 1920.[25] Indeed, Gramsci's *ordinovisti* were a "tiny group of socialists collected over several months" in Turin, and their paper was a fortnightly with a circulation of five thousand.[26] In contrast, the USI was approaching a membership of one million, the Italian Anarchist Union (UAI) formed in 1919 was growing rapidly as a national body, and Malatesta's anarchist daily *Umanita Nova* ("New Humanity") was moving fifty thousand copies at its peak.

The pull of syndicalism on figures like Connolly, De Leon, and Haywood also raises several important challenges to existing views on anarchist history. It is tempting yet mistaken to assume that the Labour and Socialist International was nothing but an outpost of political socialism. The relationship between the broad anarchist tradition and this grouping is typically seen in rather crude terms: with the return to mass anarchism, a significant number of anarchists and syndicalists attended its early congresses, but were expelled in 1891, and then excluded from membership by rule changes in 1893 and 1896; anarchist speakers were also physically attacked at the 1896 congress. In many accounts, this is where the story ends, with "no further question of unity" between libertarian and political socialists, and "no further attempts" by anarchists and syndicalists "to invade the Second International."[27]

Our account suggests something different, though. Syndicalist currents continued to emerge in many of the parties of the Labour and Socialist International in the twentieth century. Examples include the syndicalist faction in the Italian PSI, the Wobblies in the American SPA, the SLP's transformation into a syndicalist group, and the evolution of the CORA in Argentina into a syndicalist union. The French CGT was also an affiliate of the International's union wing. Kōtoku, founder of the Social Democratic Party in Japan, became a key Japanese anarchist figure; he was only one of a series of prominent Japanese anarchists who came from social democracy or classical Marxism. The Independent Irish Labour Party even adopted a syndicalist platform.[28] The political socialists had to wage an ongoing battle to drive such currents out of the International and its affiliates; that battle was certainly not won in 1896. It was really the 1913 International Syndicalist Congress in held in London, which aimed at creating a new international, that signaled the final break with the Labour and Socialist International.

It is also, finally, worth mentioning that anarchist and syndicalist ideas could infuse movements that were not, strictly speaking, primarily anarchist or syndicalist. The ICU, formed in 1919 in Cape Town, South Africa, amongst African and coloured dockworkers, provides an important example. The ICU not only spread rapidly across South Africa in the 1920s, growing to perhaps 100,000 members, but also developed into a transnational movement across southern Africa. In 1920, a section was formed in neighbouring South-West Africa (now Namibia), followed by sections in Southern Rhodesia (now Zimbabwe) in 1927, and Northern Rhodesia (now Zambia) in 1931. Although it had started as an urban union, the ICU drew an increasing part of its support, particularly in South Africa and Southern Rhodesia, from farm labourers and tenant farmers.

The ICU, headed by the charismatic Clements Kadalie (1896–1954), was noticeably influenced by IWW-style syndicalism.[29] The ICU aimed in 1920 to "form one great union of skilled and unskilled workers of South Africa, south of the Zambesi [sic]," "to bring together all classes of labour, skilled and unskilled, in every sphere of life whatsoever."[30] In 1921, it incorporated the Cape section of the syndicalist Industrial Workers of Africa, and in 1925 it adopted a version of the Chicago IWW *Preamble*:

> Whereas the interest of the workers and those of the employers are opposed to each other, the former living by selling their labour, receiving for it only part of the wealth they produce; and the latter living by exploiting the labour of the workers, depriving the workers of a part of the product of their labour in the form of profit, no peace can be between the two classes, a struggle must always obtain about the division of the products of human labour, until the workers through their industrial organisations take from the capitalist class the means of production, to be owned and controlled by the workers for the benefit of all, instead of for the profit of a few. Under such a system, he who does not work, neither shall he eat.... This is the goal for which the ICU strives along with all other organised workers throughout the world.[31]

While the ICU was definitely influenced by syndicalist ideas, imagery and anti-capitalism, and even aspired to a general strike that would transfer White-held land back to African communities, it would be an exaggeration to describe it as a truly syndicalist union. Its structures were loose, often undemocratic, and its leaders were often unaccountable to the membership. Equally importantly, its ideology was eclectic and unstable, drawing not only on syndicalism but also on Christianity, liberalism, Marxism, and Marcus Garvey's pan-Africanism. Even so, the ICU simply cannot be properly understood unless its syndicalist impulse is acknowledged.

The Sandino movement in Nicaragua provides another example. Sandino is today an icon of Nicaraguan anti-imperialism, and more particularly of radical nationalism. He is the symbol and namesake of the Sandinista National Liberation Front, that took state power in 1979, and still remains an active force. [32] Yet Sandino by no means a pure and simple nationalist as the following account will show.

The illegitimate son of a wealthy landowner and a Native American woman employed on his estate, Sandino was raised in desperate poverty until his father (a prominent Liberal) acknowledged him in 1911 and sent him to primary school. Trained in his father's grain business, he set up his own successful business in 1919 and became engaged to his childhood sweetheart. A fight with another young man, in which the latter was wounded, led Sandino to flee abroad. He worked first in Honduras as a mechanic, then as a farmworker for United Fruit in Guatemala, and starting in 1923 as a warehouse worker and mechanic in the Mexican oil port of Tampico, a stronghold of the Mexican IWW and CGT.

Sandino was profoundly opposed ongoing U.S. imperial intervention in his homeland: occupied by U.S. troops since 1909, the country was the site of numerous revolts led by modernising Liberals. Having returned to Nicaragua in 1926, Sandino was dismayed when the Liberals struck a deal in 1927 that left them in office, but granted the U.S. forces numerous military and political rights. A vociferous opponent of the settlement, Sandino was key in rallying a guerrilla force, the EDSNN, that began attacking army garrisons, and established a base of operations in the mountains and rain forests of the Las Segovias region. Sandino led the country's most sustained anti-imperial revolt, lasting from 1927 to 1933. In 1932, the U.S. forces were withdrawn, and the EDSNN came to a peace agreement with the new Nicaraguan government. The EDSNN was largely demobilised but its heartland, comprising roughly one-third of Nicaraguan territory and based in the province of Jintoega, was granted autonomous status; here Sandino established numerous collectives. The National Guard assassinated Sandino in 1934, and the autonomous zone was destroyed over the next three years.

Sandino "combined patriotic and anti-imperialist tenets directed mainly against U.S. intervention in Nicaragua with a deep concern for the lot of the Latin American peasant and working classes."[33] He was not an anarchist, perhaps, but he was certainly deeply influenced by anarchism. His forces flew the red-and-black flag, associated with Mexican and Spanish anarchism, and his politics incorporated a "peculiar brand of anarcho-communism," a "radical anarchist communism" rooted in the ideas of Proudhon and Flores Magón.[34] This was mixed with nationalist and religious ideas. If his views were based on the "most advanced and revolutionary social ideas of that epoch," they were also applied to "suit Nicaraguan reality," "assimilated ... in Mexico during the Mexican revolution, not in literary salons or in universities, but as a mechanic in oil fields owned by US firms" as a member of the syndicalist unions. His "political education in syndicalist ideology, also known as anarchosyndicalism, libertarian socialism, or rational communism," was always "framed in the ethnic pride so characteristic of the Mexican Revolution and this new generation of Latin Americans."[35] Sandino was influenced by anarchism; he was also deeply influenced by nationalist and religious ideas.[36] Like Kadalie, Sandino is an example of how far anarchist ideas could travel, and how wide their appeal could be.

The Class Character of the Broad Anarchist Tradition

Who exactly were the workers enrolled in the syndicalist unions? The classical Marxist tradition has typically described both anarchism and syndicalism as currents alien to the working class. Lenin sometimes suggested that the broad anarchist movement was capitalist in character; in 1918, for example, he charged that "anarchism and anarcho-syndicalism are *bourgeois* trends ... irreconcilably opposed ... to socialism, proletarian dictatorship and communism."[37] Bukharin would describe anarchism as the socialism of the lumpenproletariat.[38] More commonly, however, classical Marxists have portrayed anarchism as a petit bourgeois movement, the theory of peasant anticapitalist and antistatist movements, with anarcho-syndicalism a "petty bourgeois ideological expression produced by workers in small industry and artisan crafts" that exists "apart from the company of the broad masses, without the least contact with medium and large-scale industry."[39]

E. Yaroslavsky combined these various claims, arguing that peasants were born anarchists, and that anarchists were also drawn from the "children of ruined petty bourgeois, among the petty-bourgeois intellectuals, among the lumpenproletariat, and sometimes among real criminals."[40] In more recent years, such assertions were given an aura of respectability by Hobsbawm's analysis of Spanish anarchism, which depicted the anarchists as "primitive rebels" caught up in a quasi-religious revolt against the modern world, in a movement that was irrational, utopian, and doomed.[41] Underlying all of these somewhat inconsistent claims about the class character of anarchism and syndicalism is the classical Marxist conceit that it alone represents the authentic ideology of proletarian revolution: by definition, all other ideas *must* be nonproletarian in character.

The class character of the largest organisations formed by the broad anarchist tradition, the syndicalist unions, quickly highlights the inaccuracy of these claims. Two groups were particularly well-represented in syndicalism from the 1890s onwards: first, casual and seasonal labourers, such as construction workers, dockworkers, farmworkers, mariners, and gas workers, whose lives were characterised by instability, frequent job changes, and movement in search of work; and second, workers from light and heavy industry, such as factory workers, miners, and railway workers.[42] In addition to these main categories, there were also smaller numbers of white-collar workers and professionals, notably journalists, teachers, nurses, and doctors, in the syndicalist unions.

Country cases consistently demonstrate this pattern. In Germany, the FVdG was based largely among construction workers, while the FAUD was predominantly based among workers from the metal industry and the mines of the Rühr region.[43] In Britain, including Ireland, syndicalism also seems to have had a particular resonance among construction workers, metalworkers, miners, and transport workers.[44] In Peru, to give another example, anarchism and syndicalism were mainly based among "semi-skilled factory workers who championed collective, pragmatic action."[45] Mexican syndicalism drew significant support from skilled workers in small plants, but also had a mass base among factory workers (notably in textiles), oil workers and miners.[46] In South Africa, the small syndicalist unions of the 1910s were largely based among semiskilled and unskilled workers of colour, workers in manufacturing and services, such as dockworkers, clothing workers in large sweat-shops, and workers in food-processing factories.[47]

Much of the appeal of syndicalism lay precisely in its ability to respond to the concerns of the working class. For casual and seasonal labourers who worked in a range of jobs, the project of One Big Union was more practical than craft union-ism, the ties of loyalty to employers were minimal, and direct action was the best strategy given the limited periods of employment.[48] The workers in heavy industry were facing the host of changes brought about by the Second Industrial Revolution of the late nineteenth and early twentieth centuries, including the rise of the mass production assembly line, the de-skilling of skilled workers and mechanisation, the growing numbers of semiskilled workers, and Taylorist "scientific management" techniques.[49] These changes created a host of grievances such as speedups, de-skill-ing, increasingly intense supervision, and increasing casualisation, which unleashed a whole set of struggles around production while also breaking down traditional divisions among workers. This, too, facilitated a shift toward syndicalism even as the emergence of gigantic corporations provided a powerful impetus to attempts to create gigantic unions.

From 1909 to 1913, for instance, the U.S. IWW led a strike wave among the semiskilled workers of "industries being rationalised by scientific management and the introduction of new mass-assembly techniques," including the enormous auto-mobile plants of Ford in Detroit.[50] The Wobblies drew in the mass of unskilled and semiskilled industrial workers ignored by the AFL, with its craft unionism as well as nativist and racially exclusive practices, and in revolt against scientific management practices like efficiency payments, piecework, rationalisation, and assembly line speedups. It was precisely against such practices that much of the IWW's advocacy of industrial "sabotage" was directed.[51]

It would be a mistake to reduce the rise of the second wave of syndicalism in the glorious period to the changing labour process along with the growing concen-tration and centralisation of capital into huge firms, although such factors certainly played an important role. Syndicalism was also attractive in a context of growing popular radicalisation, partly expressed in a mass international strike wave in the 1910s that was perhaps only matched by the one of 1968–1974.[52] Facilitated by the growth of large workplaces and huge working-class neighbourhoods, this radicalisa-tion was reinforced by syndicalist ideas, corresponded to a growing disenchantment with the bureaucracy and moderation of orthodox unions and workers' parties, and was given further impetus by the growth of working classes sufficiently large and organised to successfully launch general strikes.[53] In this context, syndicalism "of-fered a powerful ... response" that "raised fundamental questions of socialist and democratic politics" while posing a radical alternative.[54]

A common explanation for the supposed Spanish exceptionalism is the claim that Spanish capitalism was relatively backward and its workers illiterate—an argu-ment that has some overlaps with the notion that anarchism and syndicalism were premodern or antimodern in character. Part of the problem with this notion is that these purported economic conditions were not unique to Spain, and the UGT and CNT support, respectively, did not correlate in any consistent way with the struc-ture or relative modernity of particular industries.[55]

It is also worth bearing in mind that twentieth-century Spain was hardly the economic backwater or "feudal fringe of Europe" that such explanations suggest.[56] The Spanish economy grew massively from the 1910s onward, particularly as a result of Spain's ability as a neutral country to sell supplies to all the belligerent powers in the First World War; massive industrial expansion took place, as the industries of the Second Industrial Revolution (metals, chemicals, and electricity) were established on a large scale; and Barcelona became one of the fastest-growing cities in Europe.[57] The rapid growth of the CNT in this period arose not against the backdrop of Spanish peculiarities but under conditions that were strikingly similar to those that fostered syndicalism elsewhere—so it is not surprising to find that the CNT organised major plants as well as small companies.

From the above discussion, several points stand out. The notion that syndicalism was somehow petit bourgeois is clearly not convincing. Leaving aside the rather facile idea that labour unions *can* represent the petit bourgeoisie, it is apparent that syndicalism in its glorious period was not a reaction against modernity isolated from the modern working class—it was a movement of waged workers, including those in the most advanced sites of industrial production. Speaking of the Spanish case, J. Romero Maura has argued that the appeal of the CNT has been obscured by the view that anarcho-syndicalism was an unrealistic and messianic doctrine unsuited to modern industrial conditions. On the contrary, he suggests, it was the ability of the CNT to mobilise workers—mainly industrial ones—around immediate grievances and militant practices, as well as revolutionary aims, that sustained the federation.[58]

This ability to relate the immediate concerns of workers to the ultimate goal of revolution would seem to be the necessary recipe for any successful syndicalist union movement; what it requires is the ability to relate to the working class in the here and now. The dramatic growth of syndicalism in its heyday is testament to the fact that not only did syndicalism recruit among the modern working class but it did so precisely because it was an effective and relevant type of unionism for workers in agriculture, industry, and the service sector. And, given the centrality of syndicalism to anarchist influence, it makes no sense to argue that anarchism and syndicalism were somehow atavistic, doomed, or nonproletarian.

Moreover, as the influence of syndicalism in contexts like Britain, France, Germany, and the United States attests, it was a movement perfectly capable of operating in the most advanced industrial countries. If anarchism and its progeny syndicalism emerged in the growing working-class movement represented by the First International, then, it is also the case that the majority of people organised by the broad anarchist tradition were ordinary wageworkers.

This does not mean that skilled workers played no role in the syndicalist movement. Skilled metalworkers were, for example, critical to British syndicalism. Nor is it to allege that craft union structures were always repudiated; unlike the IWW and the Spanish CNT, for instance, the Argentine FORA and the French CGT included a number of craft unions. What *was* striking was the ability of syndicalism to unite skilled, semiskilled, and unskilled workers into a unified labour movement. On the one hand, syndicalism brought the skilled workers, wherever possible, into larger general or industrial unions.[59] On the other hand, it linked different trades and industries as well as craft, general, and industrial unions into territorial structures like the IWW locals or French Bourses du Travail.[60] What it does mean is that the "artisans" (with the notable exception of shoemakers) who joined the anarchists and syndicalists were not self-employed craftworkers but skilled wage-earners. It was the latter who swelled the ranks of syndicalism; as a union movement, syndicalism offered little to the self-employed craftsperson.

The Broad Anarchist Tradition in the Countryside

The broad anarchist tradition consistently stressed the importance of uniting the popular classes in both town and country. Furthermore, it believed in the revolutionary potential of the peasantry in a way that classical Marxism did not, at least before Mao. Two main routes were taken into the countryside: syndicalist unionism among agricultural workers, particularly those employed on large estates and commercial farms, but which also sometimes recruited peasants; and anarchist organising in the villages. Given the different conditions of the two classes, anarchist organisations for workers and for peasants were often quite different.[61]

An early example of rural syndicalism was provided in Spain by the FORE, which drew mass support from among the *braceros*, the "landless, rural proletarians" of the large farms and great estates, or *latifundia*.[62] While, as we have mentioned, the FORE was an early syndicalist union, it should not be assumed that this meant it was an exclusively urban movement. It included a great many industrial and craft workers, but its rapid growth beginning in 1872 was partly a reflection of its spread into the rural areas of Andalusia and Catalonia.[63] The FORE had a number of agricultural sections from 1870 onward, and in 1872 helped found the Union of Rural Workers.[64] Interestingly, this recruited not only farm labourers but also peasants—the former around higher wages, and the latter around lower rents—and may have comprised between one-quarter and a half of the total FORE membership. The Union of Rural Workers was later revived by the FTRE, followed a similar approach, and was notable for its role in uniting Spanish workers and indentured Portuguese migrants.[65] An 1892 uprising in Andalusia, Spain, where four thousand farm labourers and peasants marched into Jerez—the main city in the latifundia-dominated Cádiz province—yelling "Long live Anarchy!" was a demonstration for the right to organise into unions.[66]

The second wave of syndicalism from the 1890s also set out to organise rural workers; in some cases, the syndicalist unions also organised peasants. The Spanish CNT was less successful than its predecessors in these ways; most farmworkers and small peasants enrolled in the UGT instead.[67] In Italy, the National Resistance Committee (CNR), the predecessor of the USI, faced its first major challenge in 1908 when landowners set out to destroy the Parma Chamber of Labour, a syndicalist stronghold that organised farmworkers.[68] The syndicalists responded with a two-month general strike, but lost the struggle which was seen by employers as the great showdown with syndicalism.[69] The U.S. IWW organised a multiracial Brotherhood of Timber Workers in Texas and Louisiana.[70] In 1917, the IWW organised a strike by twenty thousand lumber workers in the Pacific Northwest.[71] Its Agricultural Workers' Organisation, formed around 1915 and succeeded by the Agricultural

Workers' Industrial Union, claimed fifty thousand members by 1918, constituting roughly half of the entire IWW.[72] The French CGT organised workers on the farms and vineyards of the Aude province in the south, with over 143 strikes taking place between 1902 and 1914.[73] It also set up a peasant department in 1902. In Hungary the anarchist peasant-turned-railway worker Sándor Csismadia organised a Union of Rural Workers in 1905: this soon claimed seventy-five thousand members, but was banned 1908.

In Peru, the anarchists and syndicalists tried, with some success, to organise rural workers, particularly the labourers on the cotton and sugar estates in Chancay.[74] In the early twentieth century, the Cuban anarchists began to organise in the sugar industry.[75] In 1911, a Workers' Centre was organised in Cruces, a centre of sugar production, followed by the Cruces Congress of farmworkers and peasants, and various organising campaigns throughout the decade. In 1924 and 1925, strikes broke out in the sector, partly organised by the Northern Railway Union and backed by the CNOC. Anarchists were also central to the largely rural General Union of Labour of San Cristóbal. In Bolivia, anarchists strongly influenced the Departmental Agrarian Federation, which organised among the predominantly Indian peasants and farmworkers in the early 1930s, before the organisation was savagely repressed.[76]

While Argentine anarchism and syndicalism seems to have initially tended to ignore the countryside, they "made real inroads into rural labour during the early twenties," recruiting among farmworkers as well as employees of packing and processing facilities.[77] In 1920, the FORA-IX formed an alliance with the Agrarian Federation of Argentina, a peasant organisation linked to the Socialist Workers' Party, and began to systematically organise the countryside, sometimes organising small local revolts and several lengthy strikes. In 1922, union drive in the Patagonian region developed into a regional general strike that quickly escalated into a series of seizures of ranches and villages. The Patagonia rebellion was brutally crushed, with between one thousand and fifteen hundred workers killed.[78]

Behind the Rise of Peasant Anarchism

Despite the importance given to the peasantry in the discourse of the broad anarchist tradition—not to mention the tendency of both Marxists and others to suggest a natural affinity between anarchism and the peasantry—the fact is that large and sustained anarchist peasant movements or revolts are surprisingly rare.[79] The broad anarchist tradition tended to recruit workers more than peasants, and farmworkers more than small farmers. There were systematic and ongoing anarchist attempts to mobilise the peasantry, but this usually did not result in peasant mass movements; activity tended to be local, often quite informal, and sometimes very isolated. There were, of course, many important initiatives. In China, for example, the anarchists stressed the centrality of the peasantry and tried to organise model villages and rural militias, with varying success. In Japan, Zenkoku Jiren urged a united movement of workers and peasants, and a section of the "pure anarchists" formed the Farming Villages Youth Association (Nōson Seinen Sha); they met with limited success.[80] In Hungary, István Várkonyi organised a Peasant Alliance in 1896, which published the paper *A Földmüvelő* ("The Peasant"), and was outlawed in 1898 following the repression of a mass peasant strike.

Anarchists were also active in dramatic, if short-lived, peasant struggles. A case in point is the violent Greek peasant protests in the Peloponnese and Tesaly regions from 1895 onward. The peasants, mainly working in the vineyards, organised repeated demonstrations (often armed); a number of villages were occupied. Peasant hostility was directed against moneylenders, tax collectors, and large merchant companies. The anarchists of Patras, grouped around the paper *Epi ta Proso* ("Going Forward"), actively worked in the villages, as did the anarchists of Pyrgos, organised around the paper *Neo Fos* ("New Light"). No mass anarchist peasant organisation emerged, however, and much of the energy ended up channeled into appeals for tariff protection. The peasants were mainly producers of dried grapes—the country's main export crop—and the industry was ruined by the entry of major competitors into the market, combined with the imposition of tariffs by France.[81]

Yet, despite these innumerable efforts, mass anarchist peasant organisations or movements were quite unusual: the key cases were Macedonia, Manchuria, Mexico, Spain, and the Ukraine; Bulgaria is another with quite distinctive features, to which we return in volume 2. In Mexico, there was a long history of serious anarchist-led peasant risings, dating back to the 1860s and 1870s. The first was the uprising of Chávez López from 1867 to 1869. The son of poor peasants, Chávez López was educated in anarchism by activists like Zalacosta and Rhodokanaty. He organised a peasant militia in Chalco, Puebla, and Texaco that raided haciendas before being suppressed.[82] This was followed by Zalacosta's peasant revolt in 1878, discussed in chapter 6, and the anarchist-influenced uprising of General Miguel Negrete (who had actively assisted both Chávez López and Zalacosta) from 1879 to 1881.[83] In 1911, the PLM undertook a similar project, organising an armed revolt in the state of Baja California. The PLM had already tried to organise uprisings in 1906 and 1908. The 1911 revolt—initially planned by Praxedis G. Guerrero, who was killed the year before it started, and assisted by a U.S. IWW detachment—intended to establish a PLM zone on anarchist principles.[84] Guerrero, scion of a wealthy landed family and classically educated, joined the revolutionary movement, worked in industry, and organised unions, dying at age twenty-eight.

The Ukrainian Revolution, as noted earlier, was heavily based among the peasantry, although it included a substantial worker presence that should not be overlooked. In Spain, anarchist influence among the peasantry went back to the days of the First International, and the peasantry was a major force in the Spanish Revolution. In Macedonia, the anarchists drew in mass peasant support in the course of struggles in the early twentieth century against Ottoman imperialism (this is discussed in more detail in chapter 10).

The Kirin Revolution (1929–1931) in Manchuria was also primarily a peasant phenomenon. Korea, already increasingly subject to Japanese control in the late nineteenth century, was formally annexed in 1910. Influenced by Chinese and Japanese anarchism, anarchist currents emerged and the movement played an important role in the massive 1919 uprising against the Japanese occupation called the March 1st Movement. This was followed by a wave of anticolonial and radical activities and protests, including the establishment of a provisional Korean government in Shanghai in China, and the formation in 1919 of the Band of Heroes (Ŭiyŏltan) by anarchists and nationalists. It was in this period that anarchism really became a force in Korea.

The Ŭiyŏltan was influenced by the anarchist Yu Cha-myŏng (1891–1985), its "leading theorist," as well as by Chae-ho Shin.[85] It was followed by the Korean Anarchist Federation (KAF) and the Black Flag Alliance (Heuk Ki Yun Maeng) in 1924, and the League of Truth and Fraternity, or True Friends Alliance (Jin Wu Ryong Mong) and the Korean Artists' Proletarian Federation in 1925. KAF also set up sections in China (the KAF-C) and Manchuria (KAF-M) in 1929, and the Korean Anarcho-Communist Federation (KACF) the same year.

Many of the activities of the Korean anarchists took place outside peninsular Korea, particularly in China and Manchuria—the latter had over a million Koreans by the early 1930s.[86] Within Korea—after a brief period of liberalisation in the early 1920s—the Left and hard-line nationalists were heavily repressed, and attempts to launch the Korean Communist Party (KCP) within the country, to take one example, soon collapsed. One consequence seems to have been that the Left often played, at best, a limited role in the peasant and tiny labour movements in Korea itself.[87] Even moderate nationalists found it difficult to operate openly, especially after the establishment of the semifascist dictatorship in Japan in 1931. The significance of Manchuria to Korean resistance is also not surprising because the demarcation of the border was unclear and contested; an important strand of Korean thought, including Shin (before he became an anarchist), considered Manchuria to be part of a Greater Korea.[88] The conditions of turmoil and war in China and Manchuria created the space for radical opposition that was lacking in Korea, and it is worth mentioning that Korean anarchism seems to have been primarily a movement based among Korean émigrés.

From the late 1920s, the KCP was mainly active in Manchuria, where it was divided into guerrilla groups that fought independently or as Korean units of CCP forces, a notable veteran of the latter being Kim Il-Sung, later the dictator of North Korea.[89] Another major armed force was the Korean Independence Army (KIA), which was linked to the exiled Korean provisional government. An early success for the KIA was its defeat of a brigade of the Japanese Imperial Army in Manchuria in October 1920 at the battle of Ch'ing-Shan (Ch'uongsan-ri). The key figure in the KIA was the anarchist sympathiser Kim Jao-jin (Kim Jwa-Jin or Kim Chua-chin, 1889–1930), sometimes called a "Korean Makhno." Born to a wealthy family in Hongseong County, Chungcheong province, in Korea, he broke with his past when, at the age of eighteen, he released the family slaves and later threw himself into the struggle for independence.

Anarchists were involved in the administration of the Kirin province in southeastern Manchuria, an area effectively under the KIA's control starting in 1925. In 1925, with the backing of Kim Jao-jin, anarchists from the KAF-M and the KACF, notably Yu Rim (the *nom de guerre* of Ko Baeck Seong, 1894–1961), established the Korean People's Association in Manchuria, also known as the General League of Koreans (Hanjok Chongryong Haphoi). This was a delegate-based structure of councils similar to the soviet structures of the Ukrainian Revolution and perhaps not so different from the National Defence Council advocated by AD. The association provided education, social services, and military defence, and also promoted peasant cooperatives. The KAF-M, for its part, played a role similar to the Nabat in the Ukrainian Revolution. The Kirin Revolution came under attack from Japanese forces, the CCP and the KCP, and also the Chinese authorities, pressured by Japan. Kim Jao-jin was assassinated in 1930 while repairing a rice mill built by the KAF-M, and invasions and assassinations devastated the anarchist forces. By mid-1932, Kirin had been overrun and the anarchist movement driven underground.

An examination of the major anarchist peasant movements reveals several crucial features. These mass anarchist movements typically emerged in conditions of acute social instability and social conflict. Outside revolutionary situations, sustained mass anarchist peasant organisations or movements have been the exception rather than the norm. In periods of social peace, syndicalist unions emerged and competed with orthodox ones; under these conditions, though, peasant anarchism managed to form mass organisations that could rival bodies like the "populist" agrarian or peasant parties of Eastern Europe of the late nineteenth and twentieth centuries. The mass anarchist movements discussed here developed alongside popular uprisings with a decidedly anti-imperialist character (centred in the Macedonian case on the Interior Revolutionary Organisation of Macedonia and Adrianople or VMRO, the Korean People's Association in Manchuria, the Ukrainian Revolution, and the Sandino movement) or situations of class warfare (Mexico and Spain).

Under conditions of widespread unrest and upheaval, mass peasant movements where anarchists were central could emerge with incredible speed, organising village councils and soviets as well as peasant militias. Generally assuming the proportions of insurrection, such anarchist peasant movements' survival was shaped above all by their ability to mobilise armed force. In part, this insurrectionary character is linked to the nature of the peasantry. Waged workers are involved in fairly short production cycles, and able to disrupt production with dramatic and rapid effect. Peasants can refuse to sell produce, delay the harvest, and boycott rents and taxes, but the production cycle is set by the seasons, and a disruption of production risks a catastrophic loss of crops and income. The peasant parties of Eastern Europe were partly able to sustain themselves through concentrating on electoral politics.[90] Peasant anarchists struggle to build movements through ongoing direct action, except in revolutionary periods, where the social order totters and the possible gains of open revolt seem to dramatically outweigh the probable costs of defeat.

A closer examination of the major anarchist peasant movements that have been identified here helps us to understand the conditions under which such movements burst forth. One critical factor in the rise of mass anarchist peasant movements was the disruption of feudal and semifeudal agrarian relationships as capitalism penetrated the countryside, and production was restructured in ways conducive to profit and commodity production. On the one hand, this situation created an increasing pool of impoverished peasants who struggled to make a living; on the other hand, systems of feudal and semifeudal obligations in which large landowners were expected to provide a measure of charity and support for the poor broke down.

In Mexico, the rise of peasant anarchism in the nineteenth century was "deeply rooted" in a history of "land polarisation" that set "impoverished villages," often mainly Indian, against "the great estates," the haciendas or latifundia.[91] By the mid-nineteenth century, "free-contract and open-market sales" were replacing traditional systems of rights and obligations, while the rise of export-oriented commercial agriculture intensified the growth of haciendas and commercial farms owned by the bourgeoisie, threatening village communities. Massive transfers of land—sometimes through the market, sometimes by fraud, and sometimes by force—took place, and peasant villagers struggled desperately to avoid being pushed down into the rural proletariat. The centralisation of landholdings combined with peasant population growth created immense tensions. It was "within this milieu of the omnipresent great estate and the increasing impoverished and landless population in the countryside that agrarian turmoil developed."[92]

By the early twentieth century, the Ukraine was the richest farming region in the Russian Empire, accounting for 40 percent of the land under cultivation.[93] In 1914, the Ukraine produced around 20 percent of the world's wheat, and while "one-third of the wheat imports of Western Europe came from the Russian Empire," "nearly 90% of the empire's wheat exports" came from the Ukraine.[94] From the 1880s onward, farming in the Ukraine was increasingly commercialised, and other agricultural cash crops produced in the region included distilled alcohol, sugar, and tobacco. Farming for profit was encouraged by the state, which provided loans and reformed land tenure, and land was increasingly concentrated in the hands of emerging commercial farmers (*kulaks*) and rural capitalists. "Although the poorer peasants owned 57 percent of the farms in [the] Ukraine, they occupied only 12 percent of the land," and "one peasant in six had no land at all."[95] Ekaterinoslav province, the heartland of the Makhnovist movement, was characterised by large estates, a growing kulak and capitalist class, and "extremely hard" conditions for many peasants.[96] This in large part accounts for the area's long history of violent peasant rebellions.

Before the Japanese occupation, rural polarisation was already marked in feudal Korea, which was the site of numerous peasant revolts. Growing trade with Japan and the endogenous development of Korean agriculture provide some of the background for the Donghak ("Eastern Learning") peasant uprising in 1894.[97] Under the Japanese occupation, the rural areas were increasingly used for tax revenue, land tenure systems were reformed and various official moves to modernise farming took place, a degree of forced cash-cropping was enforced, and the countryside was increasingly commercialised as it attracted investments by the Korean elite and a growing number of Japanese farmers.[98] Rents, often paid in rice, rose sharply, landlords intervened increasingly in production, and costs like taxation (now calculated by land rather than harvest) were frequently shifted on to tenant farmers. Millions of people emigrated to Japan and Manchuria.[99] As a result of repression, poverty, or labour conscription, by 1945 nearly four million Koreans, around 16 percent of the total population, were working abroad within the Japanese Empire.[100]

While the Sandino movement in Nicaragua in the 1920s and 1930s was perhaps only partially anarchist in character, it exhibits some striking parallels. In the late nineteenth century, Nicaraguan agriculture had become increasingly commercialised by U.S. plantations as well as the local and "relatively dynamic new agro-exporting bourgeoisie" that took power through the Liberal regime established in 1893.[101] The United States, concerned about the security of the Panama Canal, installed a Conservative president in 1909. The new regime was backed by old-style latifundistas; unable to reassert premodern agrarian social relations, they clashed with the new bourgeoisie, and had to trade economic and political concessions to American political and economic interests in return for military backing. By 1920, coffee accounted for half of all export earnings in Nicaragua, and U.S. corporate enclaves produced bananas, gold, and rubber.[102] The other side of these developments was the expulsion of peasants from prime land by both latifundista Conservatives and modernising Liberals, and the creation of a rural working class. The Liberals' eventual accommodation with the United States in 1926 was partly a recognition of the growing economic ties between Nicaraguan and U.S. capitalists.[103]

In Spain, anarchism sank deep roots in the peasant villages of Andalusia and the Levant in the 1870s against the background of "chronic social upheaval" in the countryside. In previous times, access to communal lands helped offset land shortages, as did the "aristocratic pretensions and paternalism of the traditional nobility." By the 1860s, however, both church and "entailed lands" that were "mostly held communally by the villages and municipalities" were sold off, upsetting "the traditional equilibrium of the ruling classes and the oppressed of the region." Traditional obligations were increasingly being superseded by the ethos of a "grasping bourgeoisie."[104]

Given the background of restructuring and polarisation, it is not surprising that the anarchist agrarian programme, with its stress on land redistribution and the creation of democratic village self-government, had a powerful appeal to most peasants. The Mexican anarchist peasant revolts drew in thousands of peasants; testament to this was the use of a scorched-earth policy in the suppression of the Chávez López revolt. The VMRO, part of a sustained struggle from 1895 to 1903, was "almost exclusively" supported by frustrated peasants, although the national question—its area of operation was dominated by the Ottoman Empire—also played a role.[105] In Nicaragua, "thousands" of peasants flocked to the red-and-black banners of what Sandino called his "crazy little army."[106]

With the first phase of the Ukrainian Revolution in 1917, the amount of land under peasant control increased sharply from 56 to 96 percent of the total, administered by the traditional village body, the mir or commune.[107] In Kirin, the veteran Korean anarchist Ha Ki Rak (1912–1997) recalled, the proposal for a Korean People's Association in Manchuria met with a "warm welcome" from "the local people everywhere."[108] Nor is it startling that at least two thousand self-managed rural collectives formed during the Spanish Revolution, with over fifteen million acres of land expropriated between July 1936 and January 1938, and between seven and eight million people directly or indirectly affected by collectivisation in the nearly 60 percent of Spain's land area affected by this process.[109]

Yet structural changes in rural society cannot provide an adequate explanation of mass anarchist peasant movements. Peasant revolts have been a recurrent feature of modern history, and are only sometimes intertwined with anarchism. Many peasantries looked for salvation in conservative movements that sought to re-create an idealised feudal order For example, in Spain the impoverished peasantry of the northern provinces flocked to the banners of conservative "Carlist" monarchists; in Eastern Europe, peasants provided mass support to fascist movements like the Iron

Guard in Romania. Moreover, peasant revolts typically lacked the systematic project of social reconstruction undertaken in the Ukraine in the late 1910s, Shinmin in the late 1920s, and Spain in the late 1930s.

Two other factors are crucial. The first is the existence of a layer of anarchist militants based within the peasantry, able to promote their libertarian and revolutionary socialism, and mobilise and rally the peasantry. Such layers developed out of anarchist work amongst the peasantry. The second key factor in transforming peasant frustration and discontent into revolutionary action is the onset of a period of upheaval and instability. Where these two elements were combined, the results could be explosive. This was the context in which figures linked to anarchism like Chávez López, Zalacosta, Makhno, Kim Jong-jin (?–1931) of the KAFM, Kim Jao-jin, and perhaps Sandino came to the fore. Peasant uprisings may have taken place anyway, although without the anarchists, the history of these peasant movements would have been quite different: a massive wave of peasant land seizures swept the Russian Empire in 1917; it was in the Ukraine that a major anarchist revolution developed.

Ongoing and steady agrarian transformation never seems to have been enough to spark mass anarchist peasant revolt; a sudden change was vital. Struggles over land in Mexico and Spain, for instance, had been ongoing throughout the nineteenth century, but for much of this period were expressed in legal appeals and sporadic outbreaks of violence, and often enough a mood of fatalism and passive acceptance prevailed. Likewise, agricultural commercialisation was widespread in the Ukraine by the 1880s, yet the great anarchist peasant revolt only took place nearly forty years later. The "majority of villagers" in Spain "were never actively occupied with the Anarchist movement ... [and] in ordinary times they went about their daily business with very little interest in anarchistic tenets." It was only in times of "distress" or "hope" that the Spanish villagers could be "roused to action" *en masse* behind the anarchist nuclei.[110]

Sometimes the trigger was a local dispute. The Chávez López revolt in Mexico, for one, took place after a serious land dispute between a single village and hacienda. Sometimes a sudden change in the economy was the spark. The Greek peasant revolts of 1895 followed directly after a rapid decline in the price of the major crop, raisins, which led to mass unemployment of labourers and widespread foreclosures of farms. Sometimes a peasant revolt emerged from conditions of war and invasion. The economy of Russia and the Ukraine collapsed as a direct result of the First World War, and peasant households were crippled by the conscription of millions of men into the army. Production fell, as did exports, inflation rose, and peasants suffered further from government requisitions of livestock and the depredations of the invading forces.[111] This helped generate a radical mood among the peasantry, which responded enthusiastically to Makhno and the anarchists in 1917. The subsequent transfer of the Ukraine to the Germans forces by the Treaty of Brest-Litovsk, followed by the invasion of the reactionary White Army and nationalists, plus the forced grain requisitions of Bolshevik "War Communism," helped maintain the momentum of mass peasant struggle.

The case of Kirin should be situated in the larger context of war and instability in East Asia from the 1910s to the 1940s. The March 1st Movement opened up a period of mass unrest, frequently violent—early armed resistance in the 1910s had been ruthlessly crushed, but now new groups like Ŭiyŏltan waged an armed struggle, and the KIA and other forces emerged—while accelerating Japanese expansionism and the civil war in China created further conditions of instability. It also opened up a period of large-scale peasant struggles in Korea itself, often centred on tenant strikes around rents, the security of tenure, and taxation.[112] This developed into the "red peasant" unions of the early 1930s.[113] The sharp fall in rice prices in the late 1920s, coupled with rising costs, contributed directly to an upsurge in peasant struggles.[114] In tandem with increasing repression in Korea, these developments doubtless contributed to the appeal of the Korean People's Association in Manchuria project among the swelling Korean émigré population.

In Nicaragua, the Liberal settlement created a profound political crisis, which was followed soon after by a collapse in the coffee price as a result of the Great Depression. The use of bombing raids, the forced relocation of thousands of peasants in rebel areas to concentration camps, and the notorious brutality of the U.S. Marines and the Nicaraguan National Guard "served only to swell Sandino's forces, by increasing peasant hostility to the US presence and failing miserably in their [U.S.] military objectives."[115] Sandino's anti-imperialist programme, plus his experimentation with land redistribution and peasant cooperatives from an early stage in the war, followed by his Las Segovias project, assured him mass support.[116] In Spain, finally, Franco's attempted coup helped spark the revolution of 1936.[117]

In Conclusion: Labour Movements and Peasant Revolts

This chapter has argued that two main forms of mass movement emerged from the broad anarchist tradition: syndicalist unions, and anarchist peasant movements. Mass anarchist peasant movements or revolts—contrary to the view that anarchism was primarily "petty bourgeois" or that the peasantry had a natural affinity for anarchism—were in fact strikingly rare. The single most important and influential form of mass organisation in the broad anarchist tradition was syndicalist unionism, which dominated the labour movements in Argentina, Brazil, Chile, Cuba, France, Mexico, the Netherlands, Peru, Portugal, Spain, and Uruguay at different points. Contrary to the thesis of Spanish exceptionalism, anarchism and syndicalism became "a major social movement" that could "threaten the State" in a number of countries.[118] Even minority syndicalist currents (such as those of Britain, Germany, Japan, Italy, and the United States) could become critical social forces, while smaller movements (for instance, in South Africa) played a key role.

The view that anarchism was on the margins of major events and simply a minority attraction offers a misleading conception of the history of labour and the Left. Further, contrary to the notion that syndicalism was a petit bourgeois outlook generated by artisanal and cottage industry workers operating outside the broad masses and large industries it is clear that syndicalist unions were heavily based among casual and seasonal labourers, including farmworkers as well as industrial workers. Skilled workers played an important role in syndicalism, as did layers of semiprofessional workers like teachers. Yet above all, syndicalism was a movement of unskilled and semiskilled workers, many employed in large workplaces.

We have asserted at several points that the broad anarchist tradition must be historicised rather than treated as some form of universal phenomenon. The material discussed in this chapter supports this perspective. The broad anarchist tradition emerged—and developed into a powerful social force—in particular social and historical moments. It was not the product of a universal impulse in human nature, "a timeless struggle," or a "deeply felt human need."[119] It arose in modern capitalism from the period of the First International, and developed a mass character in specific historical conjunctures and class struggles. Mass anarchist peasant movements emerged under particular circumstances too—the capitalist penetration of the countryside, the disruption of older agrarian relations, crisis and war, and the existence of an anarchist cadre—and were central to the anarchist revolutions of the Ukraine, Manchuria, and Spain. Likewise, syndicalism derived much of its strength from its ability to respond to the needs of the modern working class in specific periods.

Finally, rural organising was a crucial part of syndicalism—rural syndicalism probably mobilised at least as many, and perhaps more, people in the countryside than peasant anarchism—but it seems that the centres of syndicalist strength were generally the urban areas. This was probably partly a function of the concentration of the working class in workplaces and neighbourhoods; farmlands are not as easily organised. The great strongholds of anarchist and syndicalist power, then, were typically urban industrial centres. If Barcelona was the "fiery rose" of anarchism, it should be seen as one of a number of important red-and-black cities, the foremost ranks of which include strongholds like Buenos Aires, Chicago, Havana, Lima, Lisbon, Montevideo, Mexico City, Rio de Janeiro, and São Paulo, followed by a second tier of cities where anarchists and syndicalists were not necessarily dominant but still influential, among which we could include Canton, Glasgow, Hamburg, Hunan, Santiago, Shanghai, and Tokyo.

Notes

1. Kedward, *The Anarchists*, 120; Marshall, *Demanding the Impossible*, 453.

2. Levy, "Italian Anarchism," 34–35.

3. Hodges, *Intellectual Foundations of the Nicaraguan Revolution*, 19, 49, 137; M. Navarro-Genie, "Sin Sandino No Hay Sandinismo: lo que Bendana pretende," mimeograph, n.d.

4. Stekloff, *History of the First International*, 312; Yaroslavsky, *History of Anarchism in Russia*, 26, 28, 41, 68–69; Hobsbawm, *Primitive Rebels*; Hobsbawm, *Revolutionaries*.

5. P. E. B. McCoy, "Social Anarchism: An Atavistic Ideology of the Peasant," *Journal of Inter-American Studies and World Affairs* 14, no. 2 (1972).

6. Joll, *The Anarchists*, 224; M. M. Breitbart, "Spanish Anarchism: An Introductory Essay," *Antipode: A Radical Journal of Geography* 10–11, nos. 3 and 1 (1979): 1; Marshall, *Demanding the Impossible*, 453.

7. R. Thompson, "The Limitations of Ideology in the Early Argentinean Labour Movement: Anarchism in the Trade Unions, 1890–1920," *Journal of Latin American Studies* 16 (1984).

8. Gordon, "Anarchism in Brazil," 155–63; Avrich, *Anarchist Portraits*, 255.

9. N. Caulfield, "Wobblies and Mexican Workers in Petroleum, 1905–1924," *International Review of Social History* 40 (1995).

10. Casanovas, "Slavery, the Labour Movement, and Spanish Colonialism in Cuba"; Casanovas, "Labour and Colonialism in Cuba in the Second Half of the Nineteenth-Century," especially chapters 6–9.

11. See Shaffer, "Purifying the Environment for the Coming New Dawn," especially chapters 1, 4, 7, and 8.

12. Shazo, *Urban Workers and Labor Unions in Chile*, 24, 76, 91–117, 129–41, 146–74, 180–88, 194–210.

13. Dirlik, *Anarchism in the Chinese Revolution*, 15, 27, 170; Dirlik, *The Origins of Chinese Communism*, 214–15.

14. Woodcock, *Anarchism*, 413.

15. For overviews, see J. Freire, *Freedom Fighters: Anarchist Intellectuals, Workers, and Soldiers in Portugal's History* (Montréal: Black Rose, 2001); van der Linden, "Revolutionary Syndicalism in Portugal."

16. Richards, *Lessons of the Spanish Revolution*, 163.

17. Kedward, *The Anarchists*, 28, 117–18.

18. Williams, *A Proletarian Order*, 194–95; Thorpe, "Keeping the Faith," 18, 18n76.

19. Ibid., 42, 78.

20. M. van der Linden, "Transnationalising American Labor History," *Journal of American History* 86, no. 3 (1999).

21. See ibid.; M. van der Linden, *Transnational Labour History: Explorations* (London: Ashgate, 2003).

22. Levy, "Italian Anarchism," 26, 29–30, 34–35, 44–45, 49.

23. "Under the leadership of Antonio Gramsci workers in Turin attempted to build a workers council movement ... an experiment in 'pure' council socialism"; D. Gluckstein, *The Western Soviets: Workers' Councils versus Parliament, 1915–1920* (London: Bookmarks, 1985), 162.

24. Levy, "Italian Anarchism," 54–58, 61, 70–71.

25. Williams, *A Proletarian Order*, 194–95.

26. Gluckstein, *The Western Soviets*, 239.

27. Woodcock, *Anarchism*, 248.

28. Ransome, *Connolly's Marxism*, 67–68; see also Allen, *The Politics of James Connolly*, 106–13.

29. van der Walt, "Anarchism and Syndicalism in South Africa," chapters 8 and 9.

30. Quoted in P. L. Wickens, "The Industrial and Commercial Workers' Union of Africa" (PhD diss., University of Cape Town, 1973), 145–46.

31. Industrial and Commercial Workers Union of Africa, "Revised Constitution of the ICU," in *From Protest to Challenge: A Documentary History of African Politics in South Africa, 1882–1964*, volume one, ed. G. M. Carter and T. Karis (1925; repr., Bloomington: Indiana University Press, 1972), 325–26.

32. See, inter alia, B. Marcus, ed., *Nicaragua: The Sandinista People's Revolution: Speeches by Sandinista Leaders* (New York: Pathfinder Press, 1985); C. Fonesca, T. Borge, D. Ortega, H. Ortega, and J. Wheelock, *Sandinistas Speak: Speeches, Writings, and Interviews with Leaders of Nicaragua's Revolution* (New York: Pathfinder Press, 1986).

33. R. E. Conrad, "Translators' Introduction," in *Sandino: The Testimony of a Nicaraguan Patriot, 1921–1934*, ed. S. Ramiréz and R. E. Conrad (Princeton, NJ: Princeton University Press, 1990), 17n39.

34. Hodges, *Intellectual Foundations of the Nicaraguan Revolution*, 19, 49, 137; Navarro-Genie, "Sin Sandino No Hay Sandinismo."

35. A. Bendana, "A Sandinista Commemoration of the Sandino Centennial: Speech Given on the 61 Anniversary of the Death of General Sandino, Held in Managua's Olaf Palme Convention Centre" (Managua: Centre for International Studies, 1995).

36. R. E. Conrad has disputed the extent to which anarchism influenced Sandino, pointing out the absence of explicit references to key anarchist figures in Sandino's writings. The absence of such names does not, however, demonstrate that anarchist ideas had no impact on Sandino's thinking; compare to Conrad, "Translators' Introduction," 17n39.

37. Lenin, "The Immediate Tasks of the Soviet Government," 599.

38. "*Lumpenproletarian socialism (anarchism)*.... They do not, for the most part, represent the interests and aspirations of the working class; they represent those of what is termed the lumpen-proletariat, the loafer-proletariat; they represent the interests of those who live in bad conditions under capitalism, but who are quite incapable of independent creative work"; Bukharin, *The ABC of Communism*, 77–78.

39. Stekloff, *History of the First International*, 312; Astrogilda Pereira, quoted in Gordon, "Anarchism in Brazil," 33.

40. Yaroslavsky, *History of Anarchism in Russia*, 26, 28, 41, 68–69.

41. Hobsbawm, *Primitive Rebels*; Hobsbawm, *Revolutionaries*.

42. See M. van der Linden and W. Thorpe, "The Rise and Fall of Revolutionary Syndicalism," in *Revolutionary Syndicalism: An International Perspective*, ed. M. van der Linden and W. Thorpe (Otterup, Denmark: Scolar, 1990), 7–12; L. Peterson, "The One Big Union in International Perspective: Revolutionary Industrial Unionism, 1900–1925," in *Work, Community, and Power: The Experiences of Labor in Europe and America*, ed. J. E. Cronin and C. Sirianni (Philadelphia: Temple University Press, 1983), 68–75. See also M. Davis, "The Stop Watch and the Wooden Shoe: Scientific Management and the Industrial Workers of the World," in *Workers' Struggles, Past and Present: A Radical America Reader*, ed. J. Green (Philadelphia: Temple University Press, 1984).

43. H. M. Bock, "Anarchosyndicalism in the German Labour Movement: A Rediscovered Minority Tradition," in *Revolutionary Syndicalism: An International Perspective*, ed. M. van der Linden and W. Thorpe (Otterup, Denmark: Scolar, 1990), 67–70.

44. See, for example, J. White, "Syndicalism in a Mature Industrial Setting: The Case of Britain," in *Revolutionary Syndicalism: An International Perspective*, ed. M. van der Linden and W. Thorpe (Otterup, Denmark: Scolar, 1990), 105–8.

45. Hirsch, "The Anarcho-Syndicalist Roots of a Multi-Class Alliance," 13, 15, 27, 30, 34, 47, 59, 169.

46. Hart, "Revolutionary Syndicalism in Mexico," 192–98.

47. Van der Walt, "Anarchism and Syndicalism in South Africa," 524–25, 589–91.

48. Thorpe, "The Rise and Fall of Revolutionary Syndicalism," 7–12.

49. Ibid., 7–12; Peterson, "The One Big Union in International Perspective," 68–75.

50. Davis, "The Stop Watch and the Wooden Shoe," 86–87.

51. Ibid., 91–95.

52. Thorpe, "The Rise and Fall of Revolutionary Syndicalism," 7–12; Peterson, "The One Big Union in International Perspective," 68–75.

53. Thorpe, "The Rise and Fall of Revolutionary Syndicalism," 7–12; Peterson, "The One Big Union in International Perspective," 68–75.

54. D. Howell, "Taking Syndicalism Seriously," *Socialist History* 16 (2000): 35–36.

55. As noted in Maura, "The Spanish Case," 62–63; see also 63n9.

56. Kedward, *The Anarchists*, 5.

57. Rider, "The Practice of Direct Action," 80–83.

58. Maura, "The Spanish Case," 71–80.

59. In Spain, the CNT organised a single union body in each workplace, thereby imposing "the militancy of the majority of unskilled workers on the labour aristocracy"; Maura, "The Spanish Case," 75.

60. "The real importance of the *Bourse*, however, lay in the sense of solidarity it established in its district. It united in common action workers of different trades, with different interests, who might otherwise have remained divided in their various *syndicates* [unions]"; Ridley, *Revolutionary Syndicalism in France*, 75.

61. For example, it is unfortunate that some sources treat rural workers and peasants as a single group; see, for instance, Molnár and Pekmez, "Rural Anarchism in Spain and the 1873 Cantonalist Revolution," 161.

62. Bookchin, *The Spanish Anarchists*, 89–110.

63. Molnár and Pekmez, "Rural Anarchism in Spain and the 1873 Cantonalist Revolution," 167.

64. Ibid., 172–84.

65. Kaplan, *Anarchists of Andalusia*, 143–55.

66. Kedward, *The Anarchists*, 59; Bookchin, *The Spanish Anarchists*, 118; T. Kaplan, "The Social Base of Nineteenth-Century Andalusian Anarchism in Jerez de la Frontera," *Journal of Interdisciplinary History* 6, no. 1 (1975): 67.

67. Richards, *Lessons of the Spanish Revolution*, 52–53.

68. T. S. Sykes, "Revolutionary Syndicalism in the Italian Labour Movement: The Agrarian Strikes of 1907–1908 in the Province of Parma," *International Review of Social History*, no. 21 (1976).

69. Thorpe, "*The Workers Themselves*," 36–37.

70. See, for example, J. R. Green, "The Brotherhood of Timber Workers, 1910–1913: A Radical Response to the Industrial Capitalism in the Southern U.S.A.," *Past and Present* 60 (1973).

71. Dubofsky, *"Big Bill" Haywood*, 102.

72. Ibid., 81, 95, 101.

73. L. Frader, "Socialists, Syndicalists, and the Peasant Question in the Aude," *Journal of Social History* 19, no. 3 (1985–1986): 457–58.

74. Hirsch, "The Anarcho-Syndicalist Roots of a Multi-Class Alliance," 13, 15, 27, 30, 34, 47, 59, 169.

75. Fernandez, *Cuban Anarchism*, chapter 2.

76. CNT, "The Libertarian Ideal in Bolivia," *Freedom: Anarchist Fortnightly*, June 12, 1999.

77. Yoast, "The Development of Argentine Anarchism," 226–30.

78. Ibid., 229.

79. See Stekloff, *History of the First International*, 312; writers quoted in Darch, "The Makhnovischna," 19n19; McCoy, "Social Anarchism: An Atavistic Ideology of the Peasant"

80. Crump, *Hatta Shuzo and Pure Anarchism in Interwar Japan*, 62–63, 78–79, 91–92, 104–5, 112–23, 141–51, 157, 159–60, 172–80.

81. A. L. Olmstead, P. W. Rhode, and J. Morilla Critz, "'Horn of Plenty': The Globalisation of Mediterranean Horticulture and the Economic Development of Southern Europe, 1880–1930," *Journal of Economic History* 59, no. 2 (1999): 316–18, 325–29, 337–38.

82. Hart, *Anarchism and the Mexican Working Class*, 32–42.

83. Ibid., 70–71, 81–82.

84. Ibid., 100–3; MacLachlan, *Anarchism and the Mexican Revolution*, 32–47. On Guerrero, see also W. S. Albro, *To Die on Your Feet: The Life, Times, and Writings of Praxedis G. Guerrero* (Fort Worth: Texas Christian University Press, 1996); R. Devis, "Praxedis Guerrero: Early Revolutionary; Revolution Is Beautiful," *Monthly Review* 37, no. 12 (1985); D. Poole, "The Anarchists in the Mexican Revolution, Part 2: Praxedis G. Guerrero,, 1882–1910," *Cienfuegos Press Anarchist Review*, no. 4 (1978).

85. Seo Dong-shin, "Korean Anarchists Pursuing Third Way," *Korea Times*, January 26, 2007, 310–11n54.

86. A. Buzo, *The Making of Modern Korea* (New York: Routledge, 2002), 36.

87. See, inter alia, Youn-tae Chung, "The Spread of Peasant Movement and Changes in

the Tenant Policy in the 1920's Colonial Korea," *International Journal of Korean History* 2 (2001); Gi-Wook Shin, *Peasant Protest and Social Change in Colonial Korea* (Seattle: University of Washington Press, 1996).

88. See A. Schmidt, "Rediscovering Manchuria: Sin Ch'aeho and the Politics of Territorial History in Korea," *Journal of Asia Studies* 56, no. 1 (1997); H. H. Em, "Nationalism, Post-Nationalism, and Shin Ch'ae Ho," *Korea Journal* 39, no. 2 (1999): 295.

89. Buzo, *The Making of Modern Korea*, 45–47.

90. G. D. Jackson, "Peasant Political Movements in Eastern Europe," in *Rural Protest: Peasant Movements and Social Change*, ed. H. A. Landsberger (London: Macmillan, 1974), 271, 283–309.

91. Hart, "Revolutionary Syndicalism in Mexico," 13–15, 35–37, 61–63, 85–87.

92. Ibid., 13–15, 35–37, 61–63, 85–87; see also Cockcroft, *Mexico*, chapter 3.

93. Darch, "The Makhnovischna," 136.

94. Ibid., 136, 138–39.

95. Ibid., 141.

96. Ibid., 146–48.

97. Ha Ki Rak, *A History of Korean Anarchist Movement* [*sic*] (Taegu, South Korea: Anarchist Publishing Committee, 1986), 10–18.

98. Chung, "The Spread of Peasant Movement and Changes in the Tenant Policy in the 1920's Colonial Korea," 160–62; Buzo, *The Making of Modern Korea*, 19–21, 26–27.

99. Ha, *A History of Korean Anarchist Movement* [*sic*], 33–34; see also Chung, "The Spread of Peasant Movement and Changes in the Tenant Policy in the 1920's Colonial Korea," 160–62.

100. Buzo, *The Making of Modern Korea*, 38.

101. G. Black, *Triumph of the People: The Sandinista Revolution in Nicaragua* (London: Zed Books, 1981), 6–10.

102. Ibid., 10–12.

103. Ibid.

104. Bookchin, *The Spanish Anarchists*, 92–104; see also Molnár and Pekmez, "Rural Anarchism in Spain and the 1873 Cantonalist Revolution," 168–71.

105. Jackson, "Peasant Political Movements in Eastern Europe," 279.

106. Black, *Triumph of the People*, 18–19.

107. Darch, "The Makhnovischna," 149.

108. Ha, *A History of Korean Anarchist Movement* [*sic*], 82.

109. Breitbart, "Spanish Anarchism," 60.

110. Bookchin, *The Spanish Anarchists*, 91–92.

111. Darch, "The Makhnovischna," 154.

112. Chung, "The Spread of Peasant Movement and Changes in the Tenant Policy in the 1920's Colonial Korea," 162–68.

113. See, in particular, Shin, *Peasant Protest and Social Change in Colonial Korea*.

114. Buzo, *The Making of Modern Korea*, 13–14.

115. Black, *Triumph of the People*, 18–19.

116. Ibid.

117. An important exception to this pattern seems to be 1930s Bulgaria, where the anarchists worked in traditional peasant cooperatives called *Vlassovden*, organising a *Vlassovden* Confederation with 130 sections during this time period. We will discuss this in volume 2.

118. Compare to Marshall, *Demanding the Impossible*, 453.

119. Marshall, *Demanding the Impossible*, xiv, 3–4.

Maria Lacerda de Moura (1887–1944)

A Brazilian militant involved in radical theatre, in the promotion of women's rights, and an active contributor to the anarchist and labour press, Lacerda de Moura exemplified the anarchist woman militant of the first half of the twentieth century. Involved in workers' education, in radical journalism, and in the promotion of gender equality, and a co-founder in the 1920s of the International Women's Federation and the Women's Anti-war Committee, her writings were widely read across Latin America and southern Europe. *Picture courtesy of the Centre for International Research on Anarchism.*

Shin Ch'aeho (1880–1936)

Korean anarchist and anti-colonial fighter. Author of the Korean Revolution Manifesto of 1923, he influenced the Ŭiyŏltan (Band of Heroes), and joined the transnational East Asian Anarchist Federation in 1927. Arrested in 1928, he died in a Japanese prison eight years later. The Korean anarchist movement, largely forced into exile in Manchuria by the 1910 Japanese invasion of Korea, created a substantial anarchist liberated zone in Manchuria between 1929 and 1931. *Picture courtesy of Dongyoun Hwang.*

CHAPTER 10

Anarchist Internationalism and Race, Imperialism, and Gender

The broad anarchist tradition, as we have noted, was an internationalist movement; it strove to unite the popular classes across state borders, stressed the common interests of the working class and peasantry of all countries, and aimed at an international social revolution. For Bakunin, it was only through the "association" of the masses of "all trades and in all countries" that "full emancipation" was possible.[1] The revolution required a "serious international organisation of workers' associations of all lands capable of replacing this departing world of *states*."[2] Bakunin looked toward "the spontaneous organisation of the working masses and ... the absolutely free federation, powerful in proportion as it will be free, of the working masses of all languages and nations."[3] This internationalist class politics directed the anarchists and syndicalists to overcome the divisions of gender and race. At the same time, the opposition of the broad anarchist tradition to all forms of social and economic inequality forced the movement to confront questions of oppression by gender and race, and develop a class analysis of the causes of such oppression.

In his classic *The Souls of Black Folk*, black American radical W. E. B. Du Bois famously asserted that "the problem of the Twentieth Century is the problem of the colour-line"; it was a century cast in the "shadow of a vast despair," "the burning of body and rending of soul."[4] If that was so, the broad anarchist tradition was one powerful response. As a movement that opposed racial prejudice and discrimination, it organised cross-racial movements of the popular classes and advocated a universal human community forged through class struggle. In the United States, for example, the IWW organised Asians, blacks, Hispanics, and whites, while in South Africa, syndicalists formed the first union for African workers, the Industrial Workers of Africa. For the broad anarchist tradition, popular racial prejudices undermined working-class and peasant solidarity, while racial discrimination was both unjust and against the interests of ordinary people of whatever background.

The contribution of anarchism and syndicalism to the development of multiracial popular movements has been obscured by the view that the internationalism of "the British and European labour movements" in the late nineteenth and early twentieth centuries was "an affair for 'Europeans only,'" and the related claim that "socialism only became definitely separated from racism through the actions of the international communist movement" from 1919 onward.[5] The Eurocentric and North Atlantic focus of most surveys of anarchism and syndicalism, and their tendency to ignore the question of race, has compounded the problem. In this chapter, by contrast, we demonstrate that the broad anarchist tradition was both opposed to the "colour-line" and in favor of a multiracial movement.

There was a profound feminist impulse in the broad anarchist tradition. It has become common in contemporary writings to label prominent anarchist and syndicalist women as "anarchist-feminists" or "anarcha-feminists," as we mentioned earlier. This approach has the merit of directing attention to the critical role played by women in raising questions of gender equality in the broad anarchist tradition, and helps delineate anarchist and syndicalist feminism from other types of feminism. We admit, however, to some discomfort with such labels. On the one hand, gender equality was a central principle of the broad anarchist tradition as a whole and was promoted by most male anarchists; on the other hand, anarchist and syndicalist women took on multiple roles in the larger movement, as writers, unionists, strike leaders, community organisers, and guerrillas, and it would be misleading to reduce their contribution to that of gender activists. Care should be taken, in short, not to assume that women activists are necessarily feminists or that feminists are necessarily women, or that anarchist and syndicalist women form a discrete category of "anarcha-feminists."

What distinguished the anarchist and syndicalist feminism of the anarchist tradition from mainstream liberal feminism (which sees women's equality as being realised through increasing the number of women at the helm of capital and the state) was its class politics. For the movement as a whole, the struggle for women's rights was part of the larger class struggle, and the women of the popular classes had far more in common with their male counterparts than with the women of other classes.

Yet there were important differences among both male and female anarchists and syndicalists regarding the meaning of women's emancipation as well as its practical implications for movement strategy. One thorny issue was the sexual division of labour: To what extent should traditional gender roles be changed? Should marriage and the family, as such, be abolished, or should they be restructured on a more equitable and voluntary basis? Another tricky issue was the question of separate organisation: Should women organise women-only anarchist groups, and if so, how would these interact with the larger emancipatory movement of the popular classes?

Anarchist Class Politics and Race

As we have seen in previous chapters, the broad anarchist tradition stressed class as its central organising principle, and also the common interests of the working class and peasantry worldwide. It was internationalist too, envisaging the struggle for a better society as taking place across state borders, and across the lines of nationality and race. Bakunin maintained that it was necessary to "rally not a few, but all, countries in a single plan of action," for an "international revolution," for a "universal, world-wide revolution" that supersedes all "particular interests ... vanities, pretensions, jealousies and hostilities within and among nations."[6] As part of this internationalism, he rejected doctrines of racial supremacy, arguing that "by respect for humanity" we "mean the recognition of human right and human dignity in every man, of whatever race" or "colour," for one's character is not due to "nature; it is solely the result of the social environment."[7]

For the anarchists and syndicalists, racial divisions undermined popular unity and prevented internationalism, the preconditions for fundamental social change. The "real definitive solution of the social problem," declared Bakunin, "can be achieved only on the basis of the universal solidarity of the workers of all lands; the Alliance rejects all policies based on the so-called patriotism and rivalry of nations."[8] The revolution must be "multi-national, multiracial," and "world-wide."[9] Racial divisions were of benefit only to the ruling classes. For Berkman,

> Capitalism thrives not so much on division of work as on division of the workers. It seeks to incite race against race, the factory hand against the farmer, the labourer against the skilled man, the workers of one country against those of another. The strength of the exploiting class lies in dis-united, divided labour. But the social revolution requires the *unity* of toiling masses.[10]

For Guerrero, racial and national divisions were deliberately promoted by the rich and powerful:

> Racial prejudice and nationality, clearly managed by the capitalists and tyrants, prevent peoples living side by side in a fraternal manner.... A river, a mountain, a line of small monuments suffice to maintain foreigners and make enemies of two peoples, both living in mistrust and envy of one another because of the acts of past generations. Each nationality pretends to be above the other in some kind of way, and the dominating classes, the keepers of education and the wealth of nations, feed the proletariat with the belief of stupid superiority and pride [and] make impossible the union of all nations who are separately fighting to free themselves from Capital.[11]

If racial prejudice was deliberately fostered from above as an ideological offensive against the popular classes, it followed that the project of building a revolutionary popular counterculture had to combat this prejudice. On one level, this meant challenging the doctrines of racial supremacy and emphasising class struggle. Reclus, for example, was a major opponent of nineteenth-century race doctrines, which he regarded as designed to justify imperialism and colonialism. Differing levels of development between regions resulted from historical and geographic factors, rather than the "racial features" of different peoples. As the world became ever more interconnected, Reclus predicted, people would increasingly recognise their common humanity and unite in a global revolt against capitalism.[12]

Rocker doubted that there was any evidence of major racial differences, pointing to the arbitrary and inconsistent ways in which races were classified, the evidence of common descent, and common abilities and aspirations, and remarked that "if one examines thoroughly the countless gradations of ... races one reaches a point at last where one cannot say with certainty where one race leaves off and the other begins." It was "monstrous" to infer "mental and spiritual characteristics" from physical appearances, and "deduce from them a judgement about moral worth," Rocker added. There were no pure races and no evidence that racial mixing was harmful, nor even a clear explanation for the "purely external characteristics like colour of hair and eyes." Rocker regarded doctrines of racial supremacy as an ideological justification for oppression, reflecting the ruling classes' "brutal spirit of mastery."[13] The South African syndicalists also regarded doctrines of inherent racial inequality and difference as "pure poppycock."[14] All "the fundamental phenomena and capabilities of man are rooted in ... humanity which is Black, White and Brown."[15]

The anarchist and syndicalist rejection of doctrines of racial inequality was closely intertwined with a critique of Social Darwinism. Charles Darwin's theory of evolution resounded across the world of the nineteenth century like a thunderbolt. Using paleontological evidence, Darwin contended that the development of life on Earth and the rise of increasingly sophisticated organisms were the result of natural adaptations to the changing environment. This thesis undermined religious arguments that the world was the result of a fairly recent creation, pointed to the immense age of life on Earth, stressed that humans were an advanced form of primate, and implied that humankind was not the result of intelligent design but of unpredictable natural processes. For Darwin, evolution involved an ongoing struggle to adapt to changing conditions, and those species that adapted best, prospered most.

This idea was summed up in the popular catchphrase "survival of the fittest." As the nineteenth century wore on, there were attempts to apply these ideas to human societies, which evolved into Social Darwinism by the 1870s. For Social Darwinists, human society was characterised by a relentless struggle between individuals, peoples, and races, and the survival of the fittest decreed that the domination of particular individuals, peoples, and races was a reflection of their inherent superiority, a testament to their victory in the harsh struggle for life. It followed directly that society was necessarily hierarchical and unequal, and that the existing social order was the inevitable and immutable result of the endless struggle to survive—a world that operated by the law of the jungle. These ideas had an enormous influence in Europe, the United States, East Asia, and elsewhere.[16]

Social Darwinist doctrines were easily intertwined with economic liberalism's stress on competition in the market and provided a ready justification for class inequality: the rich deserved their wealth, the outward sign of their innate superiority; the poor were an inferior people who had failed in life's grim struggle. While Darwin had believed that all human types shared a common ancestry, which was most likely in Africa, Social Darwinism was often associated with notions of inherent racial inequality. If human races were taken to be analogous to rival species, then conquests by superior races were both inevitable and justifiable; racial discrimination and segregation were also both necessary, for a superior racial stock must be protected from the degenerative influences of its natural inferiors.

Social Darwinism had alarming implications, and soon came under fire from anarchists and syndicalists. One such critic was González Prada. Born to a wealthy family in Lima, Peru, and a famous writer, he was himself something of a Social Darwinist in his early years. In the early twentieth century, however, he moved to an anarchist position, and came to believe that Social Darwinism was a rationale for "the suppression of the black man in Africa, the redskin in the United States, the

Tagalog in the Philippines and the Indian in Peru."[17] Within the "white race itself," such doctrines decreed the domination of some peoples and the suppression of others. Indeed, if "it can be said ... that in every nation, whatever its level of culture and its form of government, there are only two clearly defined social classes," and "money separates men more effectively than race, it's no exaggeration to say that *the poor are the blacks of Europe*."[18] Rejecting the powerful body of opinion in Peru that blamed the country's situation on racial mixing and degeneration, González Prada believed that the real question was not the racial divisions between Indians, mestizos, blacks, Asians, and Europeans but capitalism, which could only be overthrown by the united popular classes.[19] He was in favour of a world without borders, imperialism, or racial domination, a world with a harmonious mixture of races.

Kropotkin's *Mutual Aid: A Factor in Evolution* was, in large part, a direct critique of Social Darwinism.[20] Kropotkin believed that there "is no infamy in civilised society, or in the relations of the whites towards the so-called lower races, or of the strong towards the weak, which would not have found its excuse in this formula." On the contrary, Kropokin observed that while competition played a role in evolution, it largely took the form of competition between species rather than within them. He also claimed that cooperation between individuals within species was at least as important to evolution as competition and the success of humankind was in large measure due to its highly evolved mutual aid. In Kropotkin's view, competition was "not the rule either in the animal world or in mankind," and was "limited among animals to exceptional periods"; natural selection more typically proceeded through "mutual aid and mutual support."[21]

From the late 1880s on, Kropotkin began to issue the series of scientific articles that formed the basis of his book. His studies examined a wide range of animal species and human societies, argued that the Social Darwinists had caricatured Darwin, and suggested that human nature was entirely compatible with a society based on cooperation and freedom. Kropotkin's account was certainly influenced by the nineteenth-century evolutionary schema of human society progressing from "savage" hunter-gatherer societies to complex "barbarian" tribes to "civilized" society. Still, he underscored that all human societies had a tendency toward mutual aid, and his account presented "savage" and "barbarian" societies, among which he included the early Europeans, in a most favourable light: "When an intelligent man has stayed among them for a longer time, he generally describes them as the 'kindest' or 'the gentlest' race on the earth." He mocked European pretensions to superiority, stating that a man "brought up in ideas of a tribal solidarity in everything for bad and for good" is "incapable of understanding a 'moral' European" who can ignore the starving poor of one's own town.[22]

It could be argued that Kropotkin simply inverted Social Darwinism, replacing a "bio-social law of competition with his own bio-social law of cooperation," and thus dismissed as "'artificial' any instances of individualism."[23] This is not quite accurate. Kropotkin explicitly recognised both competition and cooperation as the "two dominant currents" of evolution, and asserted that he had emphasised cooperation as a corrective to accounts that stressed only conflict.[24]

While Kropotkin certainly held that there were continuities between nature and society, he drew a distinction between the two by noting the significance of social factors in determining whether cooperative or competitive impulses came to the fore: "Man is a result of both his inherited instincts and his education"; the "teachings of mutual hatred and pitiless struggle" undermined "institutions for mutual support"; narrow and "unbridled individualism is a modern growth, but it is not characteristic of primitive mankind."[25] Finally, while it has been claimed that "Kropotkin's ... contending 'laws' of mutual struggle and mutual aid have but little counterpart in Marx's theories of class struggle and unalienated cooperation," there can be little doubt that Kropotkin intended *Mutual Aid* to prove the possibility of a free socialist society, which was to be created by a class revolution.[26]

On another level, the struggle against racial prejudices required the promotion of internationalist sentiments and solidarity, a focus on the common interests of the popular classes worldwide, and organising across the lines of race. For Guerrero, "If all the workers of the different ... nations had direct participation in all questions of social importance which affect one or more proletarian groups these questions would be happily and promptly solved by the workers themselves."[27] In the words of the U.S. IWW, "All workingmen were considered equal and united in a common cause," and "the IWW is not a white man's union, not a black man's union, not a red or yellow man's union, but a workingman's union."[28] Further,

> We are "patriotic" for our class, the working class. We realize that as workers we have no country. The flags and symbols that once meant great things to us have been seized by our employers. Today they mean naught to us but oppression and tyranny. As long as we quarrel among ourselves over differences of nationality we weaken our cause, we defeat our own purpose.... Our union is open to all workers. Differences of colour and language are not obstacles to us. In our organisation, the Caucasian, the Malay, the Mongolian, and the Negro, are all on the same footing.[29]

Finally, the project of uniting the popular classes across racial lines also involved taking account of the specific experiences and forms of oppression faced by particular groups. For Berkman,

> Class-consciousness and solidarity must assume national and international proportions before labour can attain its full strength. Wherever there is injustice, wherever there is persecution and suppression—be it the subjugation of the Philippines, the invasion of Nicaragua, the enslavement of the toilers in the Congo by Belgian exploiters, the oppression of the masses in Egypt, China, Morocco or India—it is the business of workers everywhere to raise their voice against all such outrages and demonstrate their solidarity in the common cause of the despoiled and disinherited throughout the world.[30]

In other words, the revolutionary project was not simply a matter of struggling against the racial prejudices that permeated the working class and peasantry. It was also about revolting against the systematic racial discrimination practiced by the ruling classes, which was regarded as undermining the interests of *all* members of the popular classes. For the IWW, "All are workers and as such their interests are the same," and thus "an injury to them is an injury to us."[31]

Even in South Africa, where the majority of the working class was made up of unfree African workers, and where whites dominated skilled and supervisory positions, syndicalists argued along these lines. In their view, "If the natives are crushed the whites will go down with them," since the "stress of industrial competition" compels white workers to "accept the same conditions of labour as their black brethren."[32] Racial oppression was condemned in principle as unjust and incompatible with the creation of a revolutionary, class struggle position. What was required was a "new movement" that would overcome the "bounds of Craft and race and sex"; "founded on the rock of the meanest proletarian who toils for a master," the new movement must be "as wide as humanity" and "recognise no bounds of craft, no exclusions of colour."[33] For the De Leonist J. M. Gibson, writing for the International Socialist League's *The International*,

> Industrial Unionism is the only solution to the problem [of cheap labour], organised on the broad lines of no colour bar ... [because] the interests of the working class, irrespective of colour, are identical and irreconcilably opposed to the capitalist class.... The worker must organise to unite *all wage earners* to combat capital....
>
> The only hope for both races is to be united in an industrial organisation. They may then look at the future with confidence, pressing forward unitedly step by step towards the goal, the emancipation of labour from capital.
>
> To you the worker, no matter what your race or colour, belongs the future. You are the only class to take control of the disruption of society as presently formed. Yours is the historic mission to inaugurate the Cooperative Commonwealth, abolishing all class distinction, all class rule.[34]

This line of thought differs fundamentally from the analysis of race championed by nationalists, who claim that different races and nationalities have fundamentally incompatible interests. It also differs from modern "identity politics," which envisages society as fragmented into innumerable and irreconcilable strata with different "privileges" according to class, gender, nationality, sexual orientation, and race. In general, the focus is on identities that span classes. Identity politics generally does not take class seriously or see it as primary.

A particularly influential variant of this approach in recent years has been David Roediger, a U.S. academic. For him, all white workers benefit from a system of racial privileges, and they access these privileges by asserting a white rather than working-class identity. It follows that "it is not merely that whiteness is oppressive and false; it is that whiteness is *nothing but* oppressive and false." It is only through the "abolition of whiteness" and its privileges, then, that a unified working-class movement can be formed.[35] This would take place through people of colour resisting the system of white privilege, and whites rejecting their racial identity and the privileges that apparently come with it. Struggle is posed in racial terms, cutting across classes, rather than in class terms, cutting across races.

This reasoning draws heavily on two-stage Marxist theories of national liberation: a first stage of national liberation (in this case, meaning the abolition of whiteness) must be completed before a second stage of socialist struggle, where class is central, can begin. This link is sometimes quite direct. Noel Ignatiev, editor of *Race Traitor: Journal of the New Abolitionism*, which maintains "Treason to Whiteness is Loyalty to Humanity," is a former Maoist.[36] Yet there is a more basic affinity between identity politics and two-stage theory, which lies in their shared premise that struggles around social oppression by nationality, race, and so forth are, by their very nature, separated from class struggles against capitalism.

Such arguments are open to a number of serious objections, as an examination of the abolition of whiteness approach will show. The analysis is based on the notion that there are essential and immutable racial identities that define the politics and behaviour of those who hold them. Simply put, people's behaviour is regarded as being determined by their racial identity, racial identities are regarded as intrinsically connected to specific economic interests, and racial identities are viewed as also prescribing particular political choices.[37] Once this conflation of race, economics, and politics is in place, society is analysed as a set of competing races, and the analyst is free to imbue each race with particular virtues or vices.[38]

A basic problem with such approaches is that they ignore the complexities of racial identities. Racial identities can certainly be mobilised in pursuit of a politics of racial privilege, but to allege that everyone with a particular racial identity must share the same interests and outlook amounts to the crudest racial stereotyping. People as diverse as Albert Parsons and Lenin certainly identified themselves as whites, yet opposed racial supremacy and racial privileges, while Roediger's own work on the IWW shows that white identities were compatible with radical interracial politics.[39] People cannot simply reject their racial identities, as writers like Ignatiev and Roediger seem to suggest; in the race-conscious societies of the modern world, everyone is ascribed a racial identity regardless of their personal preferences. The project of new abolitionism falters at this point, while its two-stage conception of struggle—again, as racial liberation, followed later by class revolution—reproduces the problematic Marxist strategy of a national democratic revolution.

Finally, the view that workers of different races have fundamentally different interests is not something that the broad anarchist tradition would accept, and there is certainly solid evidence to support its stance that racial divisions worsen the overall conditions of the working class by dividing workers and disorganising labour movements.[40] This suggests the need for cross-racial popular movements, including mass unions, rather than an identity politics that makes a virtue of fragmentation and pitting different groups of workers against one another. Class politics indicates that the ruling class minority benefits from the exploitation of a working-class majority. The abolition of whiteness theory points toward the reverse: a racial majority of all classes exploits racial minorities of all classes. Besides ignoring the reality of class within races, such a perspective also fails to explain how exactly minorities that are—according to writers like Ignatiev and Roediger—defined precisely by their underemployment and concentration in the worst menial and manual jobs subsidise the majority of the working class.

By contrast, anarchist and syndicalist class politics, with its potential to unite people of different races, offers a path beyond the endless spiral of perpetual conflict that nationalism and identity politics must invariably generate and perpetuate. It is precisely such class unity that the abolition of whiteness perspective cannot provide. Applied to just about any Western country, it implies that the key task is to fight for *worse* conditions for the majority of the working class, who are seen as benefiting from white privilege. Problematic in itself, this position also shows the contradictions in the very project of abolishing whiteness: on the one hand, this project argues that the end of racial oppression requires massive defections from white privilege by whites; on the other hand, it also claims that the white working class benefits immensely from racial oppression—a position suggesting that a widespread rejection of white privilege is exceedingly unlikely. The broad anarchist tradition stresses, on the contrary, mobilising as many ordinary people as possible, across racial lines, to fight *in their own interests* for better conditions. This does not mean ignoring racial prejudice and discrimination; a revolutionary mass movement of the popular classes will succeed only to the extent that it combats racial prejudices and fights against racial discrimination.

Fighting prejudice is critical to defeating capitalism and the state. "The whole of the fight against capitalism is a fight with the prejudices and capitalist-engendered aversions of the workers," contended *The International* of Johannesburg. "Conquer these and capitalism is conquered."[41] But unity also required an active commitment to organising all workers and fighting against racial discrimination. It was necessary to "sweep away," *The International* added, in order to fight against the "chief barriers to efficient working class solidarity," such as the "denial of equal civil liberty to the natives" along with the cheap labour system based on compounds and indentured labour.[42]

An International and Internationalist Movement

Against this backdrop, it is not surprising to find that the anarchist and syndicalist movement before, during, and after the glorious period was a multiracial one opposed to racial prejudice and discrimination. "In conception and intent," for example, "syndicalism was an international movement," and syndicalists "conceived of their movement as international just as the working class was international, and therefore hoped to co-ordinate their struggle across national boundaries against an equally international capitalist system."[43] Moreover, "syndicalist movements probably belonged to those parts of the international labour movement which were the least sensitive to racism."[44]

In late nineteenth-century Cuba, the anarchist Workers' Circle was the "first working-class association ... that was explicitly antiracist and antinationalist." As their influence grew, the anarchists "successfully incorporated many nonwhites [*sic*] into the labour movement, and mixed Cubans and Spaniards in it," thereby "fostering class consciousness and helping to eradicate the cleavages of race and ethnicity among workers." The Workers' Alliance "eroded racial barriers as no union had done before in Cuba" in its efforts to mobilise the "whole popular sector to sustain strikes and demonstrations." Not only did blacks join the union in "significant numbers," but the union also undertook a fight against racial discrimination in the workplace. The first strike of 1889, for example, included the demand that "individuals of the coloured race [be] able to work there."[45]

This demand reappeared in subsequent years, as did the demand that blacks and whites have the right to "sit in the same cafés," which was raised at the 1890 May Day rally in Havana.[46] *El Productor* denounced "discrimination against Afro-Cubans by employers, shopowners and the administration specifically"; through campaigns and strikes involving the "mass mobilisation of people of diverse race and ethnicity," the syndicalist labour movement was able to eliminate "most of the residual methods of disciplining labour from the slavery era" such as "racial discrimination against non-whites and the physical punishment of apprentices and *dependientes*."[47]

In the United States, the founders of the IWPA included veterans of abolitionist and radical Republican circles, and the organisation's charter advocated "equal rights for all without distinction of race and sex"; the IWPA was vigorously opposed to racism, even if it had little impact among black Americans.[48] Nevertheless, it was able to unite the heavily immigrant working class of Chicago into a multiethnic mass movement, and was strongly opposed to the repression of Native Americans.[49] While working-class ethnic associations played an important role, they were linked to a larger movement that prided itself on its internationalism.[50] As an IWPA speaker at a mass rally put it,

> Our motto is liberty, equality, and fraternity. We do not believe in robbing or abusing a man because he is coloured, or a Chinaman, or born in this country or that. Our international movement is to unite all countries for the mutual good of all, and to do away with the robber class.[51]

In Paterson, New Jersey, anarchist silk workers were "deeply critical of the American racial hierarchy," and developed some of "the most sustained and detailed critique[s] of race in United States" by the Left.[52] Many joined the IWW, reputedly the "only federation in the history of the American labour movement never to charter a single segregated local," and that "united black and white workers as never before in American history and maintained solidarity and equality regardless of race or colour such as most labour organisations have yet to equal."[53] It "was one of the first (not specifically Asian) working-class organisations to actively recruit Asian workers," promoting interracial solidarity while opposing exclusion laws and the "Yellow Peril" climate of the Pacific coast.[54]

The IWW built a number of powerful and interracial unions in the U.S. South, the waterfront industry, and the shipping industry, attracting many blacks with its militancy, success, and "egalitarian racial policies."[55] In several cases, Wobblies were murdered for promoting interracial unionism.[56] The IWW's Marine Transport Workers' Industrial Union had branches worldwide; unlike many orthodox unions in shipping, which organised on racial lines and demanded job colour bars, it was an interracial union.[57] The IWW "from the very first ... maintained a definite stand against any kind of discrimination based on race, colour or nationality."[58] Even Du Bois would state that "we respect the Industrial Workers of the World as one of the social and political movements in modern times that draws no colour line."[59]

In Argentina, "socialism and anarchism ... caught the attention of the black community, particularly its working class," although the level of black involvement in the syndicalist movement is not clear.[60] In Brazil, where rapid industrialisation led to increasingly "strained" race relations in provinces like São Paulo in the early twentieth century, labour activists, "inspired by the egalitarian doctrines of socialism, anarchism and anarcho-syndicalism," actively struggled to forge an interracial labour movement.[61] They wished to overcome the divisions between native-born and immigrant workers as well as those between blacks and whites, and made explicit appeals to Afro-Brazilians.[62] This was not an easy task, given the fragility of the local unions, an oversupply of labour, and the fact that immigrants often under-cut the wages of Brazilians, including blacks.

In Australia, the IWW set out to organise all workers into the One Big Union and promoted for "the first time in the labour movement ... a coherent anti-racist viewpoint."[63] It opposed the "White Australia" policy of the Labour Party, championing free immigration and the rights of Asians and aboriginal workers, and maintained close links with anarchists and syndicalists in East Asia. In Ireland, likewise, Connolly and Larkin sought to unite workers across sectarian lines in the ITGWU.

In New Zealand, questions of race were posed by the existence of a large Maori population, which was increasingly part of the working class. IWW ideas spread into the country, notably in the "Red" Federation of Labour formed in 1908, and several IWW locals and Wobblies played an important role in a major strike in 1913 by miners and maritime workers.[64] "While there is no doubt" that the IWW "was made up of white men they did make an effort to reach out to Maori people," publishing articles in the Maori language in the *Industrial Unionist*, produced by the Auckland IWW.[65] During the 1913 strike, for example, the IWW specifically appealed for interracial solidarity, issuing a statement in Maori that proclaimed that all "workers ... suffer from the same affliction," capitalism. The "bosses ... confiscated your land ... shot your ancestors," so "do not help our mutual enemies" for we "are ever one tribe—the tribe of workers."[66]

Asian anarchist circles, in turn, promoted IWW literature, ideas, and organisation within Asia itself. In China before 1911, the overthrow of the Manchu dynasty was a central preoccupation for radicals, many of who saw the struggle in narrowly racial terms as between the Han and Manchus. Chinese anarchists generally supported the aim of overthrowing the Manchu emperor and creating a republic, but were "unwilling to condone the racism" that infused many "anti-Manchu arguments."[67] For instance, Li Shizeng (1881–1973)—a founder of Chinese anarchism who had studied in Paris—argued that while republicans "advocate overthrowing the Manchu government just because it is Manchu," anarchists "advocate overthrowing the Manchu government just because it is government."[68] Anarchists were also active in the anticolonial Taiwan Culture Association, founded in 1921, which struggled against discrimination in Taiwan, helped form the Black Labour Association (Kokurōkai) of Korean immigrant workers in Japan, and participated in the national organisation Suiheisha ("The Levelers"), which campaigned for the rights of the Burakumin caste.[69]

In Egypt, the Free Popular University drew in Egyptians and Syrians.[70] Anarchists there were involved in the formation of "international" unions, most notably the Ligue Internationale des Ouvriers Cigarretiers et Papetiers du Caire ("The International League of Cigarette Workers and Millers of Cairo"), which was "open to workers of all nationalities, Egyptians as well as foreigners," and included "production workers other than the skilled rollers."[71] In South Africa, where the early labour movement was formed by whites, was predominantly in favour of racial segregation, job colour bars, and Asian repatriation, and barred Africans from membership, anarchists and syndicalists pioneered socialism and labour unionism among workers of colour.[72] The General Workers' Union, organised by the anarchist Wilfred Harrison in 1906, and the local IWW formed in 1910, were probably the first unions in Britain's African empire to aim to recruit across the colour line.

The South African IWW and SLP, however, were really organisations of white workers, and their principled internationalism remained somewhat abstract, in part because they did not position themselves as champions of the rights of people of colour.[73] When the International Socialist League was formed in 1915, it was also predominantly an organisation of white workers. Yet in 1916, the League began to recruit people of colour like Reuben (Alfred) Cetiwe, Johnny Gomas (1901–1979), Hamilton Kraai, R. K. Moodley, Bernard L. E. Sigamoney (1888–1963), and T. W. Thibedi to its ranks. In Cape Town, the Industrial Socialist League, a separate group, enrolled "coloured and Malay comrades in our propaganda—amongst the coloured and native workers."[74] Unlike the earlier IWW and SLP, these new groups made systematic efforts to recruit people of colour, and many of these activists were drawn from the syndicalist unions formed among Africans, Coloureds, and Indians from 1917 onward.

The systematic and specific attention that the syndicalists gave to the question of racial oppression in South Africa from 1915 onward played a role in making syndicalism attractive to people of colour.[75] At a time when the local African, Coloured, and Indian nationalist groups shied away from demanding universal suffrage, the International Socialist League adopted a specific programme of African rights that declared "the abolition of the Native Indenture, Passport and Compound Systems and the lifting of the Native Workers to the Political and Industrial Status of the White is an essential step towards the Emancipation of the Working-class in South Africa." Insisting that "one section of the workers cannot benefit itself at the expense of the rest without betraying the hope of the children," the programme asserted that the "tyrant laws" of segregation and unfree labour must be "swept away" through a struggle for the "complete political equality" of all races. "Only thus can the whole of the working class, white and black, march unitedly forward to their common emancipation from wage slavery."[76]

In the Ukraine, where anti-Semitism was rife within the peasantry and frequently used to stir up pogroms, anarchists like Makhno regarded "the Jewish bourgeoisie" as enemies, but "it was their class, not their 'race' that made them so."[77] Poor Jews were, he insisted, the natural allies of Ukrainian peasants and workers. The RIAU and the larger Makhnovist movement included many prominent Jews, among them Voline and Elena Keller of the Nabat, secretary of the RIAU's cultural and educational section. The RIAU's head of counterespionage was a Jew, L. Zin'kovsky (Zadov), and the militia included Jewish detachments.[78] The RIAU also provided guns and ammunition to Jewish communities for self-defence, and militia members found guilty of persecuting Jews were promptly executed. The Makhnovist Revolutionary Military Council and the Nabat put it this way:

> Peasants, workers and insurgents! You know that the workers of all nationalities—Russians, Jews, Poles, Germans, Armenians, etc.—are equally imprisoned in the abyss of poverty.... We must proclaim everywhere that our enemies are exploiters and oppressors of various nationalities....
> At this moment when the international enemy—the bourgeoisie of all countries—hurries to ... create nationalist hatred ... to ... shake the

very foundation of our class struggle—the solidarity and unity of all workers—you must move against conscious and unconscious counter-revolutionaries who endanger the emancipation of the working people from capital and authority. Your revolutionary duty is to stifle all nationalist persecution by dealing ruthlessly with all instigators of anti-Semitic pogroms.[79]

It has often been said that at best, the Left before Bolshevism ignored issues of race; at worst, it was Eurocentric and racially prejudiced, "an affair for 'Europeans only.'"[80] According to this line of reasoning, for example, the "American socialist tradition" was one of "relative indifference to the situation of African Americans" before the rise of the CPUSA.[81] It is also claimed that "socialism only became definitely separated from racism through the actions of the international communist movement: this is one of the enduring (but largely unnoted) contributions of communism to socialism more generally."[82] The history of the broad anarchist tradition casts serious doubts on such assertions. Anarchism and syndicalism played a crucial role in developing a serious theory and practice of fighting racial prejudice and discrimination, and developed into a multinational and multiracial movement that contributed to the history of unionism, peasant movements, and the Left among people of colour.

Imperialism and National Liberation

The broad anarchist tradition was hostile to imperialism. This followed from its antistatist outlook, and opposition to social and economic inequality. Bakunin had a "strong sympathy for any national uprising against any form of oppression," affirming the right of "every people to be itself ... no one is entitled to impose its costume, its customs, its languages and its laws."[83] Setting the pattern for other anarchists and syndicalists, he did not favour the statist path involving the establishment of separate national states, as these would only reproduce the class system and generate new wars, because wars arose from the political and economic interests of the ruling classes.[84]

Only a social revolution could abolish class and imperialism, and such a revolution must be "international in scope"; Bakunin argued that oppressed nationalities "must therefore link their aspirations and forces with the aspirations and forces of all other countries."[85] Maximoff added that the new states would also create new national questions, as they persecuted minority nationalities within their own borders in the name of "nation building." The "anarchists demand the liberation of all colonies and support every struggle for national independence," and deny "the usefulness to the proletariat, not of self-determination as such, but of self-determination according to State concepts."[86] For Rocker, a new national state would either become a new imperial power or the vassal of an existing one. And "if smaller states, due to their numerically inferior population, do not act in the same way, their alleged virtuous behaviour is, as Bakunin once remarked, due mainly to their impotence."[87]

Indeed in Bakunin's view, national liberation had to be achieved "as much in the economic as in the political interests of the masses," or become a "retrogressive, disastrous, counter-revolutionary movement."[88] He noted that "there is no greater enemy for a nation than its own State." Bakunin drew a basic distinction between the nation and the state, believed that "nations existed for their members," not for states, and argued that "the redemption of nationality through the establishment of a state was not a valid emancipatory goal."[89] The ultimate aim had to be universal federation, embracing all nationalities, and organised around a planned international economy. Rocker concurred:

> What we seek is not world exploitation but a world economy in which every group of people shall find its natural place and enjoy equal rights with all others. Hence, internationalisation of natural resources and territory affording raw materials is one of the most important prerequisites for the existence of a socialistic order based on libertarian principles.... We need to call into being a new human community having its roots in equality of economic conditions and uniting all members of the great cultural community by new ties of mutual interest, disregarding the frontiers of the present states.[90]

While anarchists and syndicalists celebrated the diversity of cultures and nationalities, they refused to entertain the politics of uncritically defending particular cultures. Aiming to create an international and internationalist movement, and a universal human community, using class struggles and popular education, they could not accept the notion that cultures were monolithic or unchanging, or the claim made by some nationalists that certain rights are alien to their cultures and therefore unimportant or objectionable. As Bakunin remarked, "We should place human, universal justice above all national interests," while for Maximoff, the "fact" of nationality was always less important than universal principles:

> The right to be oneself ... is a natural consequence of the principles of liberty and equality.... International freedom and equality, world-wide justice, are higher than all national interests. National rights cease to be a consequence of these higher principles if, and when, they place themselves against liberty and even outside liberty.[91]

This still left open the question of exactly how anarchists and syndicalists should relate to struggles for national liberation. Such struggles were frequently infused with nationalism—a politics of uniting a whole nationality regardless of class in order to take state power—which anarchists and syndicalists found highly objectionable. Anarchists and syndicalists responded in several ways.

One anarchist and syndicalist approach was to support nationalist currents fairly uncritically, regarding their struggles as a step in the right direction. For some, this meant supporting the formation of small states in preference to large ones—a view that most anarchists rejected.[92] For others, this meant supporting the creation of new national states as a partial break with imperialism. The opposite approach was to simply reject all participation in national liberation struggles on the grounds that such struggles were irredeemably tainted by nationalism and must always fail to deliver genuine freedom to the popular classes. National liberation struggles were viewed as futile, and national questions as something to be resolved in the course of a world revolution.

The third, more sophisticated approach was to participate in national liberation struggles in order to shape them, win the battle of ideas, displace nationalism with a politics of national liberation through class struggle, and push national liberation struggles in a revolutionary direction. Underlying this approach is the view that nationalism is only *one* current in national liberation or anti-imperialist struggles, and not necessarily the dominant one, and that national liberation struggles could develop into a variety of outcomes. For some who take this position, the emergent national ruling class is regarded as unable to truly break with the power of the imperialist rulers; for others, it is possible that it can make such a break, but that the results will, for the mass of the people, fall short of a genuine popular liberation.

Such positions may be usefully compared with those taken by classical Marxism. Before the Comintern, classical Marxism paid little attention to struggles in colonial and semicolonial countries, with the notable exceptions like Ireland and Poland. Marx believed that the more industrialised countries with stronger states were the key agents of historical change. Thus, he supported the German side in the Franco-Prussian War of 1870–1871; if "the Prussians are victorious the centralisation of state power will be helpful to the centralisation of the German working class" and "German predominance will shift the centre of gravity of the Western European labour movements from France to Germany."[93]

Believing that the completion of the capitalist stage was a precondition for socialism, Marx and Engels looked somewhat favourably on Western imperialism as a means of spreading capitalism. Humankind could not "fulfil its destiny without a social revolution in the state of Asia," and whatever "the crimes of England, she was the unconscious tool of history in bringing about the revolution," the conquest of Algeria was a "fortunate fact for the progress of civilisation," "magnificent California has recently been snatched from the inept Mexicans [and] ... 'independence' might suffer.... But what can be done in the face of ... universal history?"[94] National rights were secondary to the development of the forces of production. For many in the Labour and Second International, including Engels, this implied a progressive colonial policy, and the colonies "inhabited by a native population" "must be taken over" by the Western proletariat in the event of revolution and then "led as rapidly as possible towards independence."[95] Once certain states were seen as progressive, and certain peoples as revolutionary and progressive, and others were viewed as what Engels called "counterrevolutionary nations," it followed that working-class politics should be aligned to particular states.[96]

One obvious consequence of this strict stress on stages, and the inability of colonial and semicolonial countries to move toward socialism, was the marginalisation of Marxism in these regions. The Argentine socialists, "profoundly affected by the reigning political theories of the Second International," held that only the growth of the economy would lead to the possibility of socialism, placed their faith in elections, were "averse to massive organisation of workers on the shop floor" and political strikes, ignored the immigrant majority, and were a negligible force.[97] (It is most inaccurate to claim that these socialists had "overtaken" the anarchists "by the second decade of the twentieth century.")[98] One of the major differences between the Labour and Socialist International and the broad anarchist tradition in the late nineteenth and early twentieth centuries was that the anarchists and syndicalists had a mass base in what is now thought of as a "third world," whereas the political socialists did not; the domination of Argentine labour by anarchism and syndicalism in the early twentieth century is a case in point.

This situation began to change with the rise of Bolshevism and the establish-ment of the Comintern. Lenin revised the classical Marxist approach to the colonial and semicolonial world in two important ways: on the one hand, he argued that im-perialism undermined the development of the forces of production and must there-fore be opposed; on the other hand, he thought that capitalism had developed into a global system, which meant that a revolution in a less developed country could take place, inasmuch as it was assisted by revolutions in highly industrialised countries that could transfer the forces of production. Marx saw the colonial and semicolonial world as a stagnant object of history; Lenin pioneered a Marxist understanding that saw that world as a subject of history.[99]

As discussed earlier, these theses developed into a two-stage strategy for the struggles in colonial and semicolonial countries: first, a struggle for national libera-tion, understood as the creation of a national state that could develop a modern economy and remove national oppression; and second, a stage of socialist struggle against capitalism. Here, national liberation struggles, organised around national-ism, would focus on bourgeois or national democratic revolutions that break with imperialism, and would lay the basis for subsequent proletarian and socialist revo-lutions.[100] Essentially, it amounted to the view that the immediate task for Commu-nists was to promote national liberation through a class alliance aimed at a national state, to break with imperialism and complete the capitalist stage. This helped break classical Marxism out of its ghetto in the advanced industrial countries, while main-taining the traditional Marxist theory of history as moving through unavoidable stages. In practice, it usually meant that Communist parties in the less developed countries were directed to ally with nationalists, rather than focus on building an independent and revolutionary working-class movement. In some cases, such as Egypt and Indonesia, this incorporation had tragic results, when the nationalists massacred their former allies after taking state power.

Socialism, in such cases, was tied to a national rather than an international project, and identified with particular states and peoples. In many cases, this led to a loss of political independence by the Communist parties, which became loyal members of nationalist movements struggling for a different capitalism, with com-munism relegated to rhetoric and a vague future. Thus, Guevara, attending the 1965 meeting of the Organisation of Afro-Asian Solidarity, could argue that "Cuba is attending this conference to raise on her own the voice of the *peoples* of America," and that "Cuba speaks both in her capacity as an underdeveloped *country* and as a country building socialism." Cuba shared with other countries the desire for "the defeat of *imperialism* ... liberation from *colonial* or *neocolonial* shackles.... Freedom is achieved when *imperialist economic domination* is brought to an end," laying the basis for the "path that ends in communism" through "industrial development."[101] There is nothing in this address about class struggle or capitalism as such, only "monopoly capital," meaning imperialism; internationalism is presented here as economic and political international solidarity between countries and peoples; the popular classes disappear and are replaced by nationalist regimes as the agents of history.[102] This approach is often coupled with the view that Western workers ben-efit from imperialism through a "higher standard of living."[103]

In the first phase of classical Marxism—where its adherents were unable to relate effectively to anti-imperialist demands, and unwilling to raise a socialist banner that took the local popular classes seriously—the small Marxist circles in the colonial and semicolonial world were easily overtaken by the anarchists and syndicalists, who were unencumbered by Marxist stage theory. With the rise of the Comintern, anarchists and syndicalists began to face a powerful Marxist rival on the Left, in the countries in which they had previously held sway, and different strands in the broad anarchist movement responded in different ways.

The anarchists and syndicalists who saw nationalism as progressive, and the creation of independent states as a step forward, wished to simultaneously organise the working class and peasantry for the anarchist revolution. Like their Communist Party rivals, however, they faced the very real danger of being incorporated into nationalism. Those anarchists and syndicalists who distrusted national liberation movements often failed to directly address issues of imperialism, and the specifically national questions that directly affected particular sections of the larger working class and peasantry of the world. As such, they struggled to compete effectively with Communists, who raised such issues directly.

What both perspectives shared with Lenin was the identification of national liberation with *nationalism*. Such an identity is not as self-evident as it may seem: struggles against imperialism and for national liberation have assumed a variety of forms, ranging from religious millenarianism, to liberalism, to socialism. Thus, the particular politics of nationalism can be distinguished from the project of national liberation, and the possibility of a range of types of national liberation can then be considered. The third and most sophisticated anarchist and syndicalist approach to national liberation and anti-imperialist struggles was based on precisely this conceptual distinction. It aimed to engage seriously with national liberation struggles, and at supplanting nationalism, radicalising the struggle, and merging the national and class struggles in one revolutionary movement.

Just as anarchists and syndicalists rejected the view that racial prejudice and discrimination benefited any section of the popular classes, so too did the great majority reject the idea that Western workers were a labour aristocracy that benefited from imperialism. Such a position follows in part from Marxist economics. If the rate of exploitation of a worker consists of the difference between wages and output, then the highly productive worker in the mechanised industries of the industrialised countries could be *more* exploited than a worker in a low-value-added industry in a nonindustrial country. Given that such a worker can produce a relatively larger total mass of surplus value, even if the rate of profit per individual commodity falls, it was possible to win relatively higher wages through class struggles in such contexts than elsewhere. Consequently, uneven levels of wages between different countries can be explained by dynamics within each country, rather than through some sort of nebulous notion that wealth is transferred from one set of peoples to another.

At the same time, imperialism has many negative consequences for the working classes of dominant countries, in the form of war spending, militarism, the creation of national divisions and hatreds, the strengthening of the state machinery, and the deaths of millions on the battlefields. It was such concerns that led anarchists and syndicalists in imperialist powers to wage the dramatic antimilitarist and anti-imperialist campaigns that were discussed in chapter 8, and it is the claim that the popular classes had no stake in the wars of their rulers that underlay their opposition to modern wars.

Rocker was one of the few anarchists and syndicalists to suggest that "some small comforts may sometimes fall to the share of the workers when the bourgeoisie of their country attain some advantage over that of another country." He failed to see how such a claim undermines the case against war, or his own view that "the workers in every country" must "understand clearly that their interests are everywhere the same, and ... learn to act together" and lay an "effective basis" for the "international liberation of the working class."[104] His analysis also failed to show how exactly "small comforts" were to be gained from the great wars of the twentieth century, which he believed were driven by rival imperialisms, and could not account for the fact that the most dramatic advances in the conditions of the Western working classes took place post-1945 alongside and after the collapse of imperialism. Most important, Rocker failed to see that the argument that workers in imperialist countries benefited from imperialism must undermine international unity, for it must inevitably pit the popular classes of different countries against one another.

Anarchists and Syndicalists in Anti-imperialist Struggles

In this section, we will examine some of the most dramatic instances of anarchist and syndicalist involvement in national liberation struggles. Our focus will be on the struggles waged *within* countries subject to imperialist domination. This is only half of the story of anarchist and syndicalist participation in anti-imperialist struggles, for a significant part of the broad anarchist tradition's history of anti-imperialism took place through antimilitarist struggles within the imperialist countries themselves; again, these were discussed in chapter 8, where we looked at anarchist opposition to war and conquest. When we speak here of struggles against imperialism, then, we do not wish to suggest that they can only take place within countries under imperialist domination or only concern peoples in such countries. It should also be noted that while we will concentrate on countries under direct imperialist domination, imperialism is understood here in the broad sense of the external domination of the ruling class of one country over all the classes of another country; it may be more or less formal, depending on the situation. Finally, national liberation struggles are also often partly struggles against racial discrimination and prejudice, for such practices are frequently critical components of imperialism.

The Mexican case is a good illustration of these points. While Mexico was formally independent from the early nineteenth century on, the country was increasingly subject to the informal imperialism of the United States. Porfirio Díaz, the dictator who ruled Mexico from 1876 to 1911, sought to industrialise the country through attracting foreign investment and modernising agriculture, and his policies were influenced by Social Darwinist ideas. The period, known as the *Porfiriato*, was one of rapid growth in the economy and advances in state power, but also rapidly increasing foreign control of industry. By 1911, U.S. investments were greater than those of the Mexican capitalists, double that of all other foreign investors combined, and dominant in sectors like mining and oil; only six of the eighty largest commercial and industrial establishments were owned by Mexicans; up to 20 percent of the land surface was foreign owned.[105] Class polarisation, an economic crisis from 1907 that saw a large faction of the ruling class turn toward economic nationalism and back Francisco Madero against Díaz, as well as the PLM's strikes and armed revolts, helped break the regime's "stability and claims to legitimacy," and open the Mexican Revolution.[106]

During this tumultuous period combining features of class war and anti-imperialist revolt, Madero was succeeded by a range of other leaders, peasant revolts swept the country, COM organised a revolutionary strike, and U.S. forces intervened. Infused with hostility toward both the U.S. and Mexican ruling classes, the PLM rejected nationalism even as it sought to struggle against both capitalism and imperialism, and regarded the resistance in Mexico as part of a global class struggle. In its "Manifesto to the Workers of the World," the PLM stressed that "our cause is yours: it is the cause of the silent slave of the soil, of the pariah of the workshop and the factory, of the galley-slave of the sea, of the hard labour convicts of the mines, of all those who suffer from the inequity of the capitalist system."[107] "We do not appeal to you to help US" but to "help YOURSELVES," for our "success means your success."[108] The Mexican struggle was "not a national problem, but a universal conflict" and a "crushed revolution means a victorious capitalism," in which U.S. workers will find their factories and firms have "closed down" and been moved to cheaper Mexico.[109]

After the PLM was crushed, the peasant revolutionary Emiliano Zapata, influenced by agrarian anarchism, helped organise a large libertarian zone in Morelos. Meanwhile, the emphasis of the syndicalist unions like COM and the Mexican IWW on "'bread and butter' issues combined with the promise of future workers' control struck a responsive chord among workers caught up in a nationalist revolution that sought to regain control from foreigners of the nation's natural resources, productive systems and economic infrastructure." The syndicalist movement opposed the "wage disparity between Mexicans and North Americans," and "discriminatory practices by foreign managers."[110]

The inability of most of the remnants of the PLM to ally with the Zapatistas, the Zapatistas' own inability to win over urban workers, and the urban workers' alienation from peasant armies like those of Pancho Villa that were notorious for their looting all contributed to a tragic situation in 1915.[111] Judging the Constitutionalist forces of Alvaro Obregón and Venustiano Carranza to offer the best option for the advancement of the working class in a situation of civil war, COM, which already had a militia of its own, raised "Red Battalions" to help the Constitutionalists drive back the peasant armies from Mexico City. They hoped to use this participation to build their organisation, push the Constitutionalists to the Left, and expropriate local and foreign businesses.[112] After the fighting ended in mid-1915, COM grew dramatically, rallying vast crowds, joined by Red Battalion veterans. "No era in the history of labour in the western hemisphere has witnessed the working-class belligerence that the Casa members ... demonstrated in 1915 and 1916."[113] The COM's successor, the CGT, was "deeply aware of and concerned with Yankee imperialism," arguably far more so than its predecessor.[114]

The Mexican case seems to exemplify an anarchist and syndicalist willingness to engage in anti-imperialist struggle, without accepting nationalism, and in the hope of merging anti-imperialist and class struggle. Among those influenced by the Mexican Revolution and the Mexican anarchists was Sandino; as we have contended in a previous chapter, the Nicaraguan struggle against U.S. imperialism was definitely influenced by anarchism. In this case, however, Sandino's eclectic views—which included a strong dose of nationalism—made it difficult to see much in the way of a distinction being drawn between anarchism and nationalism.

In Cuba, anarchist and syndicalist opinion was deeply divided over the question of separatism. Roig de San Martín refused to support the separatist cause, believing that the Cuban nationalists aimed to create a capitalist republic that would be as repressive as Spanish rule.[115] Yet an 1892 anarchist congress declared support for "the collective liberty of a people, even though the collective liberty desired is that of emancipation from the tutelage of another people."[116] It added that the struggle for independence must not be fought at the expense of the class struggle, though, and prompted nationalists like José Martí to adopt a far more pro-labour stance than traditional separatists.[117] Anarchists made a "huge" contribution to the Cuban independence struggle, including its military aspects; the Cuban struggle attracted the support of the Spanish anarchists, while in France the Committee for a Free Cuba was composed principally of anarchists.[118]

With the 1898 Treaty of Paris, Spain effectively ceded Cuba, Puerto Rico, and the Philippines to the United States. Cuban anarchists and syndicalists opposed the U.S. intervention in the war, which was followed by a military occupation from 1899 to 1902.[119] They were also highly critical of the postcolonial Cuban state—whose constitution made no provision for labour rights (but granted the United States the right to intervene militarily)—organised the first general strike under the republic, and used the occasion of the republic's first anniversary celebrations to criticise the new regime. They presented themselves as the true heirs and made Martí, who died early in the war, into an anarchist symbol.[120]

Cuba remained nominally independent, but Puerto Rico became a U.S. protectorate. Here some anarchists argued for both national and class liberation. Ramón Romero Rosa, a printer and leading labour activist, cofounded the weekly *Ensayo Obrero* ("Workers' Trial"), which "began openly stating the need to transform society, and its prerequisite: a union of all the workers." The paper was imbued "with the ideas—mainly of the anarchist strain—of European workers."[121] For Romero Rosa, the colonial system worked for the "direct or indirect benefit of the dominant, exploiting class," but an independent state would not resolve the issue of class exploitation and domination: "The exploiting class is the dominant one under any form of government.... Capitalists of the whole world are represented in a nation whatever its form of government." He advocated instead a "true Fatherland" that was not "the exclusive property of a few"; there must be the "social ownership" of property" and the abolition of "the barbaric system of man's enslavement by man."[122]

In Eastern Europe, anarchists and syndicalists were also active in national liberation struggles. We have already discussed the Ukrainian Revolution in the previous chapter and will not recapitulate its history. What is important to stress in the current context is that the Makhnovist movement was both a revolutionary movement of the popular classes, and one fighting for Ukrainian independence against its traditional Austrian and Russian overlords, and subsequently the German forces. National liberation was viewed in revolutionary terms, as the movement's Revolutionary Military Council made clear in 1919:

> When speaking of Ukrainian independence, we do not mean national independence in [Symon] Petliura's sense but the social independence of workers and peasants. We declare that Ukrainian, and all other working people have the right to self-determination not as an "independent nation," but as "independent workers."[123]

Not only did it strive to mobilise the multinational peasantry and working class of the region, and repel the White Army, but it also opposed the incipient Ukrainian national states like the *Rada* ("Council") and the Directory, and the Petliuraist nationalists. While the Makhnovist movement showed evidence of national feeling, it consistently allied with the Bolsheviks rather than the nationalists.[124]

There were antecedents for this outlook in the Ukraine. In the 1880s, Mikhailo Drahomanov and Ivan Franko "echoed" Bakunin's views on national liberation in "the international socialist movement and formulated programmes" that "drew considerably from Bakuninist tenets."[125] Partly due to the influence of Drahomanov's anarchist viewpoints, it would take many years before the goal of Ukrainian national liberation became identified with the creation of a Ukrainian state.[126] Anarchists were also active in the 1873 uprisings in Bosnia and Herzegovina against the Austro-Hungarian Empire.[127] They participated in the independence movements against Ottoman Empire in Bulgaria and Macedonia, which took place against the backdrop of growing conflict between Russia and the Ottomans, in which the anarchist Khristo Botev (1849–1876) was killed. Bulgaria became independent in 1879.

Between 1880 and 1894, the anarchist Alexandre Atabekian published the Armenian-language journal *Hamaink* ("Commonwealth"), with an anarchist analysis of the Armenian national question, linking this to the social revolution. Atabekian was instrumental in founding the Dashnaktsutiun (Revolutionary Armenian Federation), which fought against Ottoman imperialism, in 1890 in Tbilisi, Georgia. In 1893, the Bulgarian Macedonian Edirne Revolutionary Committee was formed in Thessaloniki, followed in 1898 by the Macedonian Clandestine Revolutionary Committee (MTRK), which had as its mouthpiece *Otmastenie* ("Revenge"). MTRK founders included anarchists like Mikhail Gerdzhikov, a guerrilla commander in its armed wing, and an anarchist influence was becoming increasingly central by the turn of the century. By this stage *Otmastenie* rejected the nationalisms of the ethnic minorities of the Ottoman Empire, favouring alliances with ordinary Muslim people against the sultanate and Balkan federation.

In July 1903, the MTRK staged a revolt against the Ottoman authorities in Thrace, based itself among the Bulgarian peasants, and "believed that the struggle for national liberation presented an opportunity to further the cause of libertarian communism."[128] Gerdzhikov's forces, numbering about two thousand and poorly armed, managed to establish the "Kruševo Commune." The Thracian uprising was timed to coincide with a Macedonian one by the VMRO, which drew much of its support from the Bulgarian and Slavic peasants, and included many anarchists.[129] The VMRO set up a guerrilla force, sought to organise across ethnic lines, and established the "Kruševo Commune." The Thracian and Macedonian uprisings lasted around two months before being defeated, and the hopes of some partisans that independent Bulgaria would intervene were dashed.

How did these Thracian and Macedonian anarchists approach national liberation? It is not difficult to find at least some anarchists who exhibited a nationalist approach at times. Gerdzhikov, normally an internationalist, reportedly told some of his forces that "every Turk shall be greeted not with the customary Muslim greeting but with knife and bullet until our land is purged of the enemy, or until they submit to our way and begin to live a new life ... as peace-loving Thracians with equal rights and responsibilities."[130] Other statements, however, show an attempt to push national liberation in the direction of revolutionary class struggle across ethnic boundaries. For example, the revolutionary Thracian military command declared in a communiqué that "we are taking up arms against tyranny and inhumanity; we are fighting for freedom and humanity; our cause is thus higher than any national or ethnic differences ... we express our solidarity with all others who suffer in the Sultan's dark Empire," including "ordinary Turkish villagers."[131]

In Ireland, the syndicalist Connolly opposed the nationalist dictum that "labour must wait," arguing that there would be little difference if the unemployed were rounded up "to the tune of 'St. Patrick's Day'" and the bailiffs wore "green uniforms and the Harp without the Crown, and the warrant turning you out on the road will be stamped with the arms of the Irish Republic."[132] In the end, he insisted, "the Irish question is a social question, the whole age-long fight of the Irish people against their oppressors resolves itself, in the final analysis into a fight for the mastery of the means of life, the sources of production, in Ireland." Connolly flatly denied that Irish capital could ever fight consistently against imperialism; it had "bowed the knee to Baal," and had "a thousand economic strings ... binding them to English capitalism as against every sentimental or historic attachment drawing them toward Irish patriotism," and so "only the Irish working class remain as the incorruptible inheritors of the fight for freedom in Ireland."[133]

Connolly was executed in 1916 following his involvement in the Easter Uprising. Irish Republicans, joined by a section of the Irish Citizens Army—a workers' militia linked to the ITGWU that had been formed during the Dublin Lockout of 1913 and was headed at the time by Connolly—seized key buildings in Dublin and proclaimed Irish independence, before being crushed. Despite the involvement of Connolly, the uprising was not really influenced by socialist ideas; Connolly put his class politics on the back burner and placed his faith in nationalism. For Berkman, the repression that followed "was entirely in keeping with the character and traditions of the British government." The uprising failed, in his view, precisely because it did not move beyond nationalism: "The precious blood shed ... will not have been in vain if the tears of their great tragedy will clarify the vision of the sons and daughters of Erin and make them see beyond the empty shell of national aspirations toward the rising sun of the international brotherhood of the exploited in all countries and climes combined in a solidaric struggle for emancipation from every form of slavery, political *and* economic."[134]

In North Africa, Malatesta had been involved in the 1882 "Pasha Revolt" that followed the 1876 takeover of Egyptian finances by an Anglo-French commission representing international creditors, and he aimed to pursue "a revolutionary purpose" when he "fought with the Egyptians against the British colonialists."[135] From Paris, the Algerian anarchist Saïl Mohamed Ameriane ben Amerzaine (1894–1953) sought to mobilize against French colonialism in his homeland. He launched the Indigenous Algerian Defence Committee and the Anarchist Group of the Indigenous Algerians, was secretary of the Algerian Defence Committee against the Provocations of the Centenary, held meetings in French and Arabic, edited the North African edition of *Terre Libre* ("Free Land"), and was active in the CGT-SR.[136] The Anarchist Union, the CGT-SR, and the Association of Anarchist Federations issued a joint statement on the centenary of the French occupation in 1930, denouncing the conquest as "murder."[137] For Saïl Mohamed, the indigenous Algerians, "a people enslaved," were the "brothers" of the French workers, facing "one enemy—the masters."[138] The Algerian anarchist group also called for class unity while advocating Algerian freedom: "Come towards your brothers in poverty who, without distinction of race, will struggle with you for an absolute brotherhood and equality."[139]

In the early weeks of the Spanish Revolution, the CNT was "preparing with certain Moroccan groups an insurrection in Spanish Morocco."[140] Franco's troops were largely made up of North Africans under Spanish officers (together with the Spanish Foreign Legion), and the Francoist uprising was launched from Spanish Morocco. A Moroccan uprising certainly had the potential to immeasurably strengthen the revolutionaries in Spain. Yet these plans were put on hold as the anarchists and syndicalists moved toward the Popular Front. In September 1936, Pierre Besnard, the international secretary of the IWA, again advised the CNT to ensure the success of the revolution by the internationalisation of the struggle through promoting rebellion against the pro-Franco regime in Portugal and fomenting a Moroccan uprising.[141] He recommended rescuing Abd el-Krim from Reunion and returning him to Morocco, and then declaring the independence of that country. Berneri, then resident in Spain, counseled a similar approach: promote Moroccan independence and "release revolt throughout the Arab world."[142] The retreat on the Moroccan question, part of the broader retreat from revolution by the CNT and the FAI necessitated by their entry into the Popular Front, was tragic; here was a case where the class revolution in Europe required national liberation in Africa.[143]

In the colonial and semicolonial countries of East Asia, the anarchist and syndicalist rejection of imperialism and Social Darwnism played a critical role in winning adherents to the movement. This was, for instance, the case with the Korean anarchist Shin. Given a classical education by his grandfather, he entered the state-run Confucian academy at the age of eighteen, earning a doctorate in 1905.[144] Over the next few years, he immersed himself in the emerging Korean nationalist movement, became profoundly nationalist, and left the country on the eve of the Japanese annexation in 1910. Shin continued his activities in exile (he never returned to Korea except for a brief period in 1916) and helped to form the Korean provisional government in Shanghai.

Disgusted with the gradualism and diplomatic strategies of the Korean provisional government, Shin withdrew, throwing himself instead into historical and political studies. He was increasingly influenced by the Chinese anarchists, and became an anarchist in the early 1920s. It was Shin who wrote the 1923 "Korean Revolution Manifesto," the founding document of the Band of Heroes. The manifesto called for both national liberation and class revolution:

> Today's revolution is one that the masses make for themselves.... De-
> struction by the masses and for the masses of all obstacles ... that stand
> in the way of improving the masses' livelihood is the only way to "awaken
> the masses." ... The reasons why we are to destroy the Japanese forces
> are ... [to] destroy the rule of a foreign race ... overthrow the privileged
> class ... destroy the system of economic exploitation ... destroy social in-
> equality ... destroy servile cultural thoughts ... [and] construct an ideal
> Korea in which one human being will not be able to oppress other hu-
> man beings and one society will not be able to exploit other societies.[145]

In 1927 Shin joined the East Asian Anarchist Federation, which linked anarchists in China, Korea, Japan, Taiwan (Formosa), Vietnam, and apparently India. He was arrested in 1928, and died in a Japanese prison eight years later.

Kropotkin's *Mutual Aid* was decisive in Shin's shift to anarchism. In his nationalist phase, Shin was deeply influenced by Social Darwinism and aimed at modernising Korean national power in order to secure the country's survival. In accepting the Social Darwinist outlook of the Japanese ruling class, however, Shin removed the basis for his own opposition to imperialism: if survival and success depended on national power, and the world was characterised by the endless struggle between fit and unfit, then the victory of Japanese imperialism was proof of its own superiority and was, from a Social Darwinist perspective, beyond reproach.[146] Kropotkin offered an alternative model of history that offered a solution to this dilemma, and placed its faith in the popular classes and direct action against imperialism. Shin "found in anarchism the anti-imperial critical stance that Social Darwinism did not provide," and "what attracted Shin to Kropotkin was not simply the idea of social revolution, but the Russian's alternative to the primacy of struggle as the determinant of the fate of nations."[147]

In colonial Korea, national liberation took centre stage, and anarchists had to define their positions on this question. Some, like Ha, Yu Cha-myŏng, and Yu Rim, seem to have openly embraced nationalism. Yu Cha-myŏng and Yu Rim were elected to the parliament of the Korean provisional government, and after independence a substantial section of the movement—perhaps even a majority—formed an Independent Workers and Peasants Party; while the party had a fairly radical platform in some respects, it aimed to participate in elections as a conventional party. Yu Rim argued, with some sophistry, that "we Korean Anarchists are not literal non-governmentists but non-hetero-governmentists, in other words, auto-governmentists," and "want to establish an independent and democratic unified government."[148]

This uncritical support for nationalism and a Korean state has sometimes been explained as a consequence of the fact that "national liberation became the overriding goal of the Korean anarchists," leading to an embrace of "any strategy which can be justified as in terms of bring[ing] closer a unified and independent Korean nation."[149] The implication is that any significant anarchist movement in a colonial territory will evolve toward nationalism and participation in conventional politics.[150] This reasoning is not satisfactory. On the one hand, it assumes, with Lenin, that national liberation must take the form of nationalism, ignoring the possibility that national liberation could mean more than wanting "a unified and independent Korean nation"; on the other hand, it ignores the current in anarchism that aims to merge national liberation and class struggle. Such a current certainly existed among the Korea anarchists. Shin and the Band of Heroes leaned sharply in this direction. The KAF-C likewise aimed "to give back to the oppressed classes of the Korean masses a colony, called Korea," but rejected "coming to terms with the capitalist class of our native country" in a "national united front"; rather, "we are going to wipe out the present bourgeoisie and capitalist society."[151]

In China, a section of the anarchists, including Li Shizeng, joined the nationalist Guomindang in the late 1920s. Some hoped to use it to spread anarchism; others seem to have supported the nationalist project of forming a unified Chinese state as progressive.[152] The National Labour University was one result of this collaboration. Most of the Chinese anarchists rejected collaboration with the Guomindang. For the anarcho-syndicalist Shen Zhongjiu, the Guomindang and the anarchists shared the goal of crushing the warlords and ending imperialism, but the anarchists could not accept Guomindang nationalism and statism.[153] Li Pei Kan (1904–2005), better known by his pseudonym Ba Jin (derived from the Chinese names for Bakunin and Kropotkin), saw all anti-imperialist movements and struggles, including the nationalist movement, as progressive when compared to imperialism. Nonetheless, he believed the anarchists must win the popular classes away from the Guomindang, push demands far beyond the Guomindang programme, and link current class struggles directly to the struggle for social revolution.[154]

Michel, the most prominent woman anarchist in nineteenth-century France, also played a role in anti-imperialist struggles. A schoolteacher of rural origins, Michel took an active part in the 1871 Paris Commune, for which she was sentenced to lifetime servitude in the penal colony of New Caledonia in the South Pacific.[155] She was converted to anarchism en route, and during her years of servitude aligned herself to the struggles of the indigenous Kanaks against French demands for land and labour (and, apparently, women); during the Kanak uprising of 1878, two of the Kanak fighters wore pieces of her red Communard scarf.[156] "The Kanakas," she believed, "were fighting for the same liberty we sought in the Commune."[157]

Michel's role in this struggle is not as well documented as might be hoped, and her memoirs hint "broadly that she knows more than she chooses to tell."[158] Unlike a number of former Communards, who joined the French forces in suppressing the uprising, Michel showed the rebels how to cut the island's telegraph lines to hamper the authorities.[159] She returned to Europe after the 1880 amnesty of the Communards, was jailed in 1882 and again in 1883, spent several years in England, and spoke out against French colonialism in Algeria, anti-Semitism, and militarism. Michel died in Marseilles in 1905, and her funeral in Paris—held on January 20, the day that the 1905 Russian Revolution began—was the largest since that of the famous author Victor Hugo twenty years earlier.

Anarchism, Syndicalism, and Women's Emancipation

Class was central to the anarchist and syndicalist perspectives on race: on the one hand, members of the same race were divided by class; and on the other hand, racial prejudice and discrimination were best fought as part of a larger interracial and multinational class struggle. Likewise, national liberation was often seen as requiring a revolutionary class struggle.

The movement's perspectives on women's emancipation followed a similar logic of trying to find a means of linking struggles against the specific problems faced by women within the larger project of revolutionary class struggle. In line with its commitment to economic and social inequality as well as individual freedom, the anarchist tradition aimed to create equality between the sexes as part of its project of creating a new society. For Bakunin, women in general were oppressed by the current social order: "In the eyes of the law, even the best educated, talented, intelligent woman is inferior to even the most ignorant man," and within the family, women were the "slaves of their husbands." Even the "upper/middle class woman" was not allowed to develop her "faculties on an equal basis with men," but was forced to live out her life with the permission of the men of her family, and was driven into marriages where "true passion" was only "rarely found." For the women of the popular classes, these gender inequalities were compounded by those of class: "hunger and cold," the ever-present threat of sexual harassment by employers and officials, the grim spectre of prostitution, and children "deprived of a decent education condemned to a brutish life of servitude and degradation."[160]

The Alliance sought not just the "complete and definite abolition of classes" but the "economic, political and social equality of both sexes."[161] Only a libertarian and socialist society could genuinely ensure that "equal rights ... belong to both men and women," and make women economically independent, "free to forge their own way of life." In the anarchist society, the "authoritarian juridical family would disappear" along with private property and the state, people would be able to live together "without civil and religious marriage," and the "old impediments to the full sexual freedom of women" would no longer exist.[162]

The new society would recognise the right of all people to "unite and separate as they please," in relationships based on "absolute liberty"; neither "violence nor passion nor rights surrendered in the past can justify an invasion by one of the liberty of another, and every such invasion shall be considered a crime." The economic dependence of women on men would be abolished by a system that guaranteed the "right of every man and woman, from birth to adulthood," to "complete upkeep ... at the expense of society." Children "belong to themselves and to their own future liberty." While raised in the family until old enough to take care of themselves, children could be removed by the commune in cases of abuse or treatment that hinders their "physical and mental development"; at adolescence, they must be allowed to freely choose their careers, "supported by society."[163]

Bakunin did not directly address the question of housework, although his proposals pointed to the need to restructure it in a fundamental way. Kropotkin, by contrast, addressed the issue squarely, advocating the abolition of "domestic slavery," the "last form of slavery, perhaps the most tenacious because it is also the most ancient." He chided those socialists who assumed traditional domestic roles should continue in the postrevolutionary society: "Servant or wife, man always reckons on woman to do the housework," but "woman, too, at last claims her share in the emancipation of humanity" and "no longer wants to be the beast of burden of the house":

> Why has woman's work never been of any account? It is because those who want to emancipate mankind have not included woman in their dream of emancipation, and consider it beneath their superior masculine dignity to think "of those kitchen arrangements," which they have put on the shoulders of that drudge—woman.[164]

Many household tasks could be mechanised (Kropotkin was writing on the eve of the new electric household appliances), and others could be carried out on a socialised basis: cooking, laundry, lighting, and heating could all be organised on a large scale and provided to every home. This would free women "from the brutalising toil of kitchen and washhouse," and avoid the situation under capitalism where the "'emancipated' woman" of the higher classes threw "domestic toil on to another woman," her servant.[165]

Such perspectives were widely accepted in the broad anarchist tradition, which "held out to women the opportunity (and, in some degree, the possibility) of participating actively in a movement for equality and human solidarity."[166] For Grave, for instance, "Woman is the equal of man; woman is a human being who has a right to the full satisfaction of all her mental and physical needs; the absolute right to do with herself as she desires, to her fullest possible development; that is the right and duty of every being, male or female."[167] In Li Shizeng's view, "Women are unequal to men purely because of the techniques of the oppressors and not because of nature."[168]

For González Prada, the revolution required the "revolution of the philosopher against the absurdities of dogma, the revolution of the individual against the omnipotence of the state, the revolution of the worker against the exploitations of capital, the revolution of women against the tyranny of men, the revolution of one sex or another against the enslavement of love and the prison of matrimony; in short, the revolution of everyone against everything" inequitable.[169] Guerrero believed that women were trapped by class, custom, and discrimination, and "women and men must struggle for ... rational equality, harmonising of individual and collective happiness, because without it the home will always nurture the seeds of tyranny, slavery, and social misery."[170]

As Louis Lingg of the IWPA and CLU asserted, "A woman has a right to all positions which she can administer, and in a free society she will know how to exercise the right, too." In the free society, a woman "will no longer be the mere servant, the cookmaid of her spouse, but the equal of him" and "absolutely independent."[171] The anarchists, Maximoff declared, "beginning with the fundamental concept of liberty and equality, are opposed to marriage by compulsion, and raise the banner of the free union of the sexes."[172]

Women, Class, and Counterculture

The broad anarchist tradition embedded its feminism within its class framework. This class perspective distinguished anarchism from late nineteenth-century mainstream feminism, which focused primarily on suffrage and legal equality, opposed revolutionary socialism, and drew much of its support from the middle and upper classes.[173] For Goldman, equal legal rights were important, as men should not have rights denied to women. Still, the great majority of women were trapped in struggling households, faced lower wages than men, sweated in deadening work in the factories and professions, and feared that children would cost both their income and independence.[174] Many hoped that marriage would free them from wage labour, only to find themselves economically dependent on their husbands as well as subject to their wills, and now working a double shift of wage labour and domestic work.[175]

Yet Goldman insisted that women should not see their "slavery apart from the rest of [the] human family" but rather link their struggles to the larger one for a new society.[176] Underlying the class framework through which the anarchists viewed the question of women's emancipation were several key points. Critically, the oppression of women was firmly entrenched in both traditional and modern societies, and was closely intertwined with the class system. The Chinese anarchist He Zhen, for instance, developed this argument. She is known by her writings along with her editorship in the Tokyo-based *Tianyi bao* ("Journal of Natural Justice"), the Society for the Study of Socialism, and the Women's Rights Recovery Association (Nüzi Fuquan Hui) in the early twentieth century. Little is known of her life, other than that she was born to a family of some means in Jiangsu and became involved in radical politics.[177]

Like other Tokyo-based Chinese anarchists, such as Liu Shipei (1884–1919, also her partner), Li Shizeng, and Wu Zhihui (1865–1953), He tied the unequal position of women to the class system. It was the poverty of the women of the popular classes that forced them to become maids, factory workers, and prostitutes, and trapped in unhappy marriages; "you women allow people to mistreat you" because "you depend on others to eat," and you do not "have food to eat" because "the rich have stolen our property and walk over the majority of the people." She "firmly linked women's liberation to the notion of revolution, a remaking of society in political, economic, and class terms," and argued that women's liberation "depended on the liberation of all." This led He to the second crucial point that underlay the anarchists' class framework for women's emancipation: the idea of class solidarity and revolution, in which women "unite with men and completely overthrow the upper classes and the rich!"[178]

Class divisions meant that while women—as women— shared many common experiences, they were deeply divided by class. He "paid attention to poor women, or poor and middle-class women, not the rich," and stressed their common interests with the "overwhelming majority of men." If women were "uniquely oppressed" by gender, they were "not oppressed in unique ways"; the oppression of peasant and working-class women was integrally connected to their positions in class society, while most men were also oppressed by the same economic system that made women economically dependent.[179]

For Flores Magón, likewise, "Women's position ... varies according to their social stature; but in spite of the refinements of customs and the progress of philosophy, women continue to be subordinated to men by tradition and laws." In wage labour, "though women work more than men, they are paid less, and misery, mistreatment, and insult are today as yesterday the bitter harvest," forcing women into prostitution or the "marketplace of marriage." The road to liberation was the class struggle, which united men and women: "The solution is here on earth! That solution is rebellion."[180] Similarly, Bakunin maintained that the women of the popular classes had far more in common with the men in those classes than they did with ruling class women: "Oppressed Women! Your cause is indissolubly tied to the common cause of all the exploited—men and women! Parasites of both sexes! You are doomed to disappear!"[181] In the new society, argued He, there would be "equality of the sexes," and men will "no longer to be oppressed by other men and women no longer to be oppressed by other women."[182] Goldman contended that women could only be free when men were free as well.[183]

In other words, for the anarchists and syndicalists, the struggle for women's freedom should not be waged with a narrow focus on women alone but should be part of a larger emancipatory project that struggled against exploitation and domination more generally; women's oppression was not the sole oppression, and it was necessary to avoid a crude bifurcation of gender and class oppression. As de Cleyre put it, "The tyranny of the State" was that it denies, to "both woman and man, the right to earn a living, and rents it as a privilege to a favoured few."[184]

This line assumes that ordinary men do not fundamentally benefit from the oppression of women. Even if they benefited in some ways, such as being freed from housework, they lost out in many more ways. Low wages for women, for example, were the logical consequence of gender inequality, and undermined both men's wages and the income of families as a whole.[185] Divisions between men and women undermined the class struggle and the revolution, but were not a problem for these reasons alone. Inequitable gender relations between men and women in the popular classes also crippled the revolutionary project of forging a movement of the popular classes that carries within it the organisational and cultural values of the new society. Without free association and real solidarity between men and women, a truly anarchist society could never emerge. As Kropotkin observed,

> Only let us fully understand that a revolution, intoxicated with the beautiful words, Liberty, Equality, Solidarity, would not be a revolution if it maintained slavery at home. Half humanity subjected to the slavery of the hearth would still have to rebel against the other half.[186]

The question of culture and ideology was a particularly significant one. In an 1884 analysis, Engels had asserted that the roots of women's subjugation could be found in the rise of private property, itself only possible when early societies first began to generate an economic surplus due to farming, metalworking, and weaving. These riches passed into the "private possession of families," and men, "according to the custom of society at that time," controlled the most important new sources of wealth. The men then "seized the reins in the house" and established patriarchal systems to ensure that their property passed only to legitimate heirs.[187]

If, however, "custom" is the decisive factor in determining what Engels called the "world-historic defeat of the female sex," then the subjugation of women cannot be explained simply as the product of changes in the material basis of society. Nor can it be comfortably assumed, with Engels, that the "predominance of the man in marriage is simply a consequence of his economic predominance and will vanish with it automatically."[188] Culture and ideas play a critical and irreducible role in explaining gender inequality, and the struggle for women's emancipation must therefore also involve a cultural and ideological struggle. The creation of an egalitarian and socialist order might be a necessary step toward gender equality, but it is not a sufficient one.

It is here that the broad anarchist tradition is especially interesting. On the one hand, while anarchists and syndicalists saw class and gender inequality as intertwined, they did not reduce women's oppression to a shadow cast by the class system or a functional imperative of that system, somehow required to keep it operating effectively. For Flores Magón, the subordination of women was partly based in laws and customs that predated the class system.[189] Michel spoke of "human stupidity" throwing "old prejudices" over women like a "winding sheet."[190] Likewise, anarchists in Argentina and Spain did not reduce women's oppression to the operations of capitalism but also developed "a radical critique of the family, *machismo*, and authoritarianism in general."[191]

In Li Shizeng's view, women's oppression was certainly shaped by the class system, but was not reducible to it. Much of the blame had to be placed at the door of superstition and a "false morality," promoted by men to enforce their power over women, as well as by authoritarian philosophies like Confucianism.[192] This was a view shared by Goldman, who condemned the "stupid social customs" and sexual double standards that made women's lives a misery.[193] For de Cleyre, "the priests" had long "taught the inferiority of woman," an idea created in "the womb of Fear" with "the fatherhood of Ignorance"; in "one form or another through the various mythical legends of the various mythical creeds, runs the undercurrent of the belief in the fall of man through the persuasion of woman, her subjective condition as punishment, her natural vileness, total depravity, etc."[194] The traditional family was identified by the broad anarchist tradition as a major site of women's oppression— de Cleyre forthrightly described women submitting to sex against their will in marriage, for whatever reason, as rape—and regarded as the place where traditional attitudes suppressed women and hierarchical relationships prepared the popular classes for the tyranny of the ruling class.[195]

On the other hand, and as a result, the broad anarchist tradition linked women's emancipation to the larger project of promoting a revolutionary counterculture. Anarchists and syndicalists advocated free love and free unions. Some saw in this the possibility of plural and "open" relationships along with an end to monogamy.[196] The great majority, though, believed that committed and long-term relationships were more fulfilling, and that few people would be able to tolerate a situation where partners were involved sexually with other people. As such, they favoured a new type of family, based on faithful couples with equal rights, free of official restrictions, sanctions, or controls, and united by love rather than economic necessity. This recognised that the family was the basic unit of peasant and working-class life, and indicated that revolutionising the family was an essential component of the broader revolution.[197]

As Bakunin put it,

> In abolishing religious, civil and juridical marriage, we will return life,
> reality and morality to natural marriage, based solely on the mutual re-

spect and the freedom of two people, man and woman who love each other; in recognizing for each of them the right to separate from the other whenever he desires, without requiring for this the permission of anyone, in denying also the need for permission in the joining of two people, and in rejecting all interference of any institution whatsoever, in their union, we shall make their relations with each other even firmer, truer and more sincere.[198]

The UAI's programme, written by Malatesta, called for the "reconstruction of the family, as will emerge from the practice of love, freed from every legal tie, from every economic and physical oppression, from every religious prejudice."[199] Explained Pelloutier, "With regard to the union of the sexes we are simply asking for the liberty that we were claiming yesterday and that we will claim tomorrow for all manifestations of individuality."[200] The self-activity of women—and in the behaviour of both men and women—was also regarded as essential to their emancipation. In twentieth-century Cuba, similarly, anarchists generally envisaged the family as a site of lived communist relations and an important sphere in which to inculcate the young with libertarian values.[201]

The creation of a revolutionary movement involved a revolutionary process of creating new values and new ways of life, even before the revolution, and this required that women, too, become actively involved in reshaping the world. Goldman observed that

the right to vote, or equal civil rights, may be good demands, but true emancipation begins neither at the polls nor in courts. It begins in woman's soul. History tells us that every oppressed class gained true liberation from its masters through its own efforts. It is necessary that women learn that lesson, that she realise her freedom will reach as far as her power to achieve her freedom reaches.[202]

Likewise, Michel remarked that

the first thing that must change is the relationship between the sexes. Humanity has two parts, men and women, and we ought to be walking hand in hand; instead there is antagonism and it will last as long as the "stronger" half controls the "weaker" half.... We women are not bad revolutionaries. Without begging anyone, we are taking our place in the struggle; otherwise we could go ahead and pass motions until the world ends and gain nothing.[203]

Given these perspectives—free associations in love, the abolition of the traditional family, economic independence for women, the equality of rights, sexual freedom, fundamental changes in the domestic and cultural spheres, attention to women's needs as individuals and as mothers, and the importance of women themselves struggling for equality—it would be misleading to suggest that the anarchist tradition, or its founders, Bakunin and Kropotkin, were unconcerned with the emancipation of women.

There were, of course, cases where anarchist and syndicalist men did not live up to their formal commitments to women's emancipation, and those who used the ideal of free love to avoid responsibility for the children that resulted from sexual liaisons. This hypocrisy attracted the scorn of anarchist and syndicalist women, such as those grouped around the Buenos Aires paper *La Voz de la Mujer* ("The Voice of the Woman"), which denounced "the Corruptors of the Ideal." Thus, *La Voz de la Mujer* championed a class-based feminism that fought for women's emancipation while advising strikers to "knock off" the police; its "fiery feminist radicalism" was "reserved exclusively for working-class and poor women." If *La Voz de la Mujer* was "one of the first recorded instances in Latin America of the fusion of feminist ideas with a revolutionary and working-class orientation," it was part of a substantial anarchist press, including men in its ranks, which took the same line.[204]

The point is that the broad anarchist tradition had, starting in the 1860s, a principled commitment to women's emancipation. This commitment was held by both men and women, contrary to the notion that it was "anarchist women" who added a "new dimension ... [to] anarchist theory" at the turn of the twentieth century by highlighting the "personal and psychological dimensions of life," like "families, children, [and] sex."[205] The tendency of many writers to label women anarchists and syndicalists "anarchist-feminists" or "anarcha-feminists" is therefore problematic, as mentioned earlier, since both male and female anarchists and syndicalists generally advocated a feminist position.[206]

The feminism of anarchism was in advance of the views of many of its contemporaries. It is a mistake to suggest that the anarchist critique of the authoritarian family was "taken over" from Engels's writings, for it preceded these writings by a decade and a half.[207] Anarchism and syndicalism made an important contribution to challenging traditional gender relations, notably by linking issues of class and gender oppression, directing attention to the way in which personal lives were shaped by the larger social systems, and recognising that domination was also internalised in people's consciousness and had to be confronted through developing a new personal ethics.[208]

It is not reasonable, then, to suggest like John Hutton that behind a "rather thin veneer" of egalitarian rhetoric, anarchism concealed a "deeply-rooted antifeminism" and "full-blown misogyny." Hutton's analysis presents anarchism as the ideology of a declining petty bourgeoisie with a "horror of industrialisation," to be contrasted unfavourably with the feminism of classical Marxism.[209] Hutton's line of argumentation—which conflates mutualism and anarchism, and presents socialist antifeminism as a uniquely anarchist phenomenon—not only misrepresents the class character of the broad anarchist tradition but also ignores the feminist impulse within anarchism and the significant break that this entailed with Proudhon's misogyny. (In all fairness, it should also be added that many mutualists, not least the U.S. current associated with Tucker, embraced the cause of women's rights.)[210]

Anarchist and Syndicalist Women's Activism

Still, there were limitations to the feminism of many of the early anarchists and syndicalists. The question of the larger sexual division of labour in society was one area where the anarchist and syndicalist imagination of the glorious period tended to be somewhat circumscribed. While early twentieth-century Brazilian anarchists and syndicalists recognised "how victimised woman was by the social system," many adherents—women included—did not "propose liberation through struggle for jobs and equality, but rather through a reinstatement of woman's natural role as companion, mother and educator."[211] The Spanish anarchists were "more sensitive to the connections between socialism and the liberation of women from tyrannical sexual and family relationships than any other European political group," yet there were certainly some who believed that women would be returned to the household after the revolution.[212] Pouget and Pataud envisaged women grouped "like men into Trade Unions," playing an active role "in social administration" as well as having "material and moral independence" after the revolution. Nevertheless, they still believed that certain occupations would remain "undertaken by women," with "special colleges where women's occupations were taught."[213] This sort of thinking was fairly common on the Left as a whole before the 1960s, when second-wave feminism challenged the notion that there was some sort of specifically "women's work."

Bakunin called on women to actively participate in the class struggle, as did anarchist and syndicalist organisations like the PLM and the IWPA.[214] Kropotkin appealed to "men and women, peasants, labourers, artisans, and soldiers" to "work with your brethren in the preparation of that revolution ... which shall at length establish true liberty, real equality [and] ungrudging solidarity throughout human society."[215] Like working-class and peasant movements more generally, however, women have often been underrepresented in the mass organisations of the broad anarchist tradition.

To some extent, this has been the result of attitudes in the anarchist and syndicalist movement. While the PLM press called on women to become architects of their own destiny, Flores Magón could still tell women, "Your duty is to help man; to be there to encourage him when he vacillates; stand by his side when he suffers; to lighten his sorrow; to laugh and to sing with him when victory smiles," so demand that "your husbands, brothers, fathers, sons and friends pick up the gun."[216] Such ideas were contested and frequently defeated. In France, there were certainly some syndicalists who doubted that women could (or should) play a role in the labour movement, but many others disagreed fundamentally.[217] Yet the "Proudhonist antifeminism of some male workers was always mitigated by the libertarians' call for the establishment of a non-authoritarian society," the logic of syndicalist action, which required unity and equality between men and women workers, and the feminist component of anarchism.[218] Starting in 1900, the CGT was urging its members to recruit women, and by 1912 the syndicalists "were less concerned about sending women back to their firesides than they were in attracting them to the union halls."[219]

Another critical factor that limited women's participation was that both females and males have tended to define women's lives largely in terms of familial relationships and responsibilities, and these obligations have often restricted women's ability to participate in larger movements.[220] The relatively limited participation of women in wage labour also affected their ability to engage in the syndicalist unions, which as a result tended to be preponderantly male. Thus, the IWW was only open to wageworkers, thereby debarring the majority of women in Australia and the United States; while the question of recruiting the wives of wageworkers was debated on several occasions, the existing membership criteria were upheld.[221]

It would be a mistake, however, to underestimate the role of women in the broad anarchist tradition. The notion that syndicalism was a highly gendered and predominantly masculine movement, for example, is something of a caricature.[222] It downplays women's contributions, and adopts a narrow view of anarchism and syndicalism that ignores the way in which syndicalist unions were typically embedded in a rich associational and cultural life that went well beyond the workplace. Where women were able to join syndicalist unions, they did so in great numbers, and also played an important part in anarchist and syndicalist organisations as well as struggles based in working-class and peasant neighbourhoods.

Local union centres, workers' halls, and anarchist schools provided a crucial space for women's participation in the movement, where women were able to challenge the dominant culture. "The Anarchist movement in Spain, and particularly in Barcelona," for instance, "did not ... limit itself to the domain of trade-union action.... [F]or many workers in Barcelona, Anarchism and Anarcho-syndicalism could best be described as a way of life that permeated beyond the male-dominated trade unions and brought together both sexes of the city's proletariat."[223] Anarchist women often baptised their children at the anarchist local rather than at the church. For example, in 1873 at the Sanlúcar de Barrameda FORE local, a boy was named "Gateway to Human Progress" and a girl was named "Anarchist Europe."[224] The anarchist ateneus also drew in large numbers of women. They provided a place where women activists from the communities and the unions could immerse themselves in anarchist culture, offered a nexus where community struggles (often led by women) and union struggles (frequently led by men) could be connected, and played a central role in the development of female activists.[225]

As we have seen, one of the virtues of general strikes was their ability to draw the unwaged, including housewives, into confrontations with the ruling class. The U.S. IWW, for example, was able to reach out "in an extraordinarily sensitive way to women in many strike situations, leading vast uprisings of the entire working-class community—men, women, and children—in isolated, poverty-stricken, one-industry textile or mining towns." The union had a "keen appreciation of the fighting qualities of women," regularly "proved its ability to mobilise masses of women during strikes," and thereby created an opportunity for them to come out of the isolation of the kitchen. It is unfair to describe the IWW as "economistic" on questions of gender.[226] The union, which hoped to draw women into the public political arena, developed some analysis of the specific problems faced by females.[227] In France, the CGT tried to mobilise women by stressing the "moral and non-violent nature" of the general strike, urging women to run strike offices and join picket lines during strikes, and reaching out to mothers, who typically "opposed the extension of military service and the use of troops to break up labour demonstrations."[228]

Women played a prominent role in anarchist and syndicalist activities outside the workplace, such as during rent strikes. For example, the 1922 rent strike in Veracruz, Mexico, was described by contemporaries as a "women's rebellion," and anarchist women like María Luisa Marín were central in organising the tenant committees and demonstrations.[229] Marín had arrived in Veracruz in 1922, along with her brothers Esteban and Lucio, intending to organise workers. She formed the Federation of Libertarian Women, which organised opposition to evictions and also tried to pull together a domestic workers' union. The federation played a key role in the Revolutionary Syndicate of Tenants as well. In 1922, Marín was sent to jail for eleven months for her activities, and from there she continued to aid the tenants' movement and even organised a strike by female prisoners. By 1926, the authorities felt that the only way to break the movement was to expel Marín, then secretary of the Revolutionary Syndicate of Tenants, from Veracruz altogether.

The broad anarchist tradition was generally opposed to the development of a separate women's movement outside the larger popular one for class revolution. Many worried that separate groups for youth and women could divide the popular classes.[230] Some anarchists like Goldman also doubted the value of women's groups.[231] Nonetheless, the movement often involved women's groups and sections as part of the larger revolutionary movement. The syndicalist movement included women's sections within the unions or even unions specifically for women, such as the IWW Women's Committee in Australia.[232]

In 1927, for example, anarchist women like Catalina Mendoza, Rosa Rodríguez de Calderón, Susana Rada, and Felipa Aquize formed the General Women Workers' Union as part of the syndicalist FOL in Bolivia.[233] This union was supported by the overwhelmingly male FOL leadership, but alienated from the mainstream women's movement; dominated by the Creole upper class, this sat uncomfortably with the union's constituency of working-class *chola* (Native American) women. The General Women Workers' Union grew rapidly—it was particularly noteworthy for successfully organising domestic workers and market women as well as workers in industry—and was restructured as the Women Workers' Federation (FOF), with sixty affiliates. Infantes, the head of the important Cooks' Union, was a leading figure in the FOF, which organised "child care, literacy courses, numerous cultural events, and a library, all of which were designed to meet the needs of working *cholas*."[234]

Anarchist and syndicalist women also formed women's groups at local anarchist and syndicalist centres as well as in their communities. An instance of the former was the Women's Action Group, based at the Agrupación Cultural Faros, one of the main ateneus in Barcelona, which was linked to the CNT.[235] Examples of the latter include the Women's Anarchist Centre in Buenos Aires in the early twentieth century, organised by Virginia Bolten, Maria Collazo, and Teresa Caporaletti, and the Libertarian Women's Union in Chile and the Federation of Libertarian Women in Mexico in the 1920s, all of which took the lead in anarchist and syndicalist rent strikes.[236] While violent confrontations usually decreased women's participation in mass struggles, anarchist women were keenly aware that police and soldiers were often reluctant to fire on women and children, and used this knowledge to hamper the security forces. During food protests in Barcelona in 1918 and the Spanish anarchist rent strikes of the early 1930s, women utilized this insight to play a key role in preventing evictions.[237]

The best-known anarchist women's organisation is probably Mujeres Libres in Spain. Founded in 1936 in Barcelona and Madrid, Mujeres Libres held the view that women needed a specific organisation that could raise their consciousness and empower them to fill an equal role in the larger anarchist and syndicalist movement along with the society that it wished to create.[238] "From now on," its journal argued, "every woman must transform herself into a defined and defining being; she must reject hesitation, ignorance."[239] While the attitudes of male activists influenced the decision to form the organisation, its founders insisted that it was part of the larger revolutionary movement, alongside the CNT, the FAI, the FIJL, and Libertarian Youth. It "saw itself as a political movement ideologically linked to anarchism" and the class struggle.[240] As Suceso Portales of Mujeres Libres contended, "It's necessary to work, to struggle, *together* because if we don't, we'll never have a social revolution."[241]

Mujeres Libres, which grew to over twenty thousand members, set up daycare centres in order to involve more women in CNT activities, published a journal and regular columns in other anarchist papers to raise women's consciousness, ran radio broadcasts, and provided traveling libraries, propaganda tours, and literacy programmes.[242] It also stressed child and maternal health, birth control, and education regarding sexuality, and formed the Institute of Maternal and Childcare in Barcelona, named after Michel. Mujeres Libres was actively involved in the collectivisations of the Spanish Revolution, in which women were extremely engaged, and specifically sought to include women in work outside the home through vocational education and apprenticeship programmes, organised in conjunction with the CNT.

Besides their significant involvement in community organising, anarchist and syndicalist women were also leading speakers, writers, union organisers, and militia fighters, with notable examples including Choi, de Cleyre, Goldman, He, Infantes, and Marín. There are many others worth mentioning. In Japan, for instance, Itō translated the writings of Goldman and was involved in anarchist organising before her murder in 1923. Kanno Sugako (1881–1911), born in Osaka and raised in an unhappy home, became a socialist at a young age, was associated with Kōtuku's circle, and shifted toward anarchism.[243] Following the June 1908 Red Flags Incident—in which scores of anarchists and socialists who staged a public rally were arrested and tortured by the police—Kanno was jailed for two months for visiting the prisoners. As a result, she embraced revolutionary anarchism: "It is necessary to arouse the people of society by instigating riots, undertaking revolutionary action, and engaging in assassinations."[244] In 1909, she began to publish *Jiyu Shiso* ("Free Thought") with Kōtuku and was again arrested. She was a prime mover in the High Treason Incident and was among the twelve anarchists hanged in 1911.

Another notable Japanese woman anarchist was Takamure Itsue (1894–1964), who was born on the Japanese island of Kyūshū to a middle-class family and was fairly well educated despite her family's limited means.[245] After working as a teacher's assistant, in 1920 she moved to Tokyo, where she established herself as a writer and poet, and moved toward anarchism's antiauthoritarian aims and views on women. Takamure joined the anarchist Proletarian Women Artists' League (Musan Fujin Geijutsu Renmei), which published *Fujin sensen* ("The Woman's Front") from 1930 to 1931, and made contact with female factory workers. She spent the remainder of her life developing an anarchist analysis of the history of Japanese women and related topics.

In Brazil, the writer, journalist, and educator Lacerda de Moura was a leading anarchist propagandist, whose works gained wide popularity throughout Latin America and southern Europe.[246] Born on a farm in Manhuaçu in Minas Gerais state, she trained as a primary school teacher, and in 1915 set up the League against Illiteracy. By 1918, Lacerda de Moura was moving toward anarchism. Working as a private tutor, she began giving lectures to anarchist unions, cultural centres, and theatre groups, and writing for the anarchist press. She was a cofounder in this period of the International Women's Federation and the Women's Anti-War Committee, and in 1923 launched an anarchist monthly review called *Renascença* ("Renaissance"), which was distributed internationally and promoted her feminist ideas. In 1927, she embarked on a speaking tour of Latin America and then remained active in various ways for the remainder of her life.

Other anarchist and syndicalist women were prominent union leaders. María Hernandez Zarco (1889–1967) was a founding member of the COM. In Puerto Rico, Capetillo was a legendary figure in the labour movement, addressing countless meetings all over the country in the late nineteenth and early twentieth centuries, and championing women's rights as well as preaching free love.[247] She worked as a *lector* in cigar-making factories, organised workers in Cuba, the Dominican Republic, Tampa (Florida), New York, and Puerto Rico, wrote numerous essays dealing with labour and women, and edited *La Mujer* ("The Woman"), which she founded in 1910. In 1919, she created a sensation after she arrested for wearing trousers in public.

Lucy Parsons's early life is shrouded in mystery. Born in Texas, she claimed to be of Indian and Mexican descent, but may have been a former slave.[248] In 1872, she married Albert Parsons, who was then a Radical Republican. The couple had to flee Texas for Chicago as the white supremacist backlash against Reconstruction headed by the Ku Klux Klan grew. By 1883, Lucy was actively involved in the anarchist movement, helping to found the IWPA, writing for the *Alarm*, and addressing meetings. When Albert was blacklisted for union activities, she supported the family by opening a dress shop, and played a central role in the campaign against his execution. When she visited him for one last time, she was arrested and held while he was hanged. Living in extreme poverty and facing continual official harassment, Lucy remained an active speaker and publisher, producing papers like *Freedom* in the 1890s, the *Liberator* from 1905 to 1906, and the *Alarm* in the 1910s. A founding member of the IWW, she advocated the revolutionary general strike. In the 1920s and 1930s, as the U.S. anarchist and syndicalist movement declined, Lucy found herself working alongside the CPUSA on many occasions, but never joined the party. She died at the age of eighty-nine in an accidental fire, and the FBI reportedly destroyed her papers after her death.

Annie Westbrook, May Ewart Wilson, and Violet Clark Wilkins were prominent women in the Australian IWW. In the United States, Flynn became a socialist at the age of sixteen, and her political activities led to her expulsion from school.[249] In 1907, she became a full-time organiser for the IWW, organising among garment and textile workers, miners and restaurant workers, and was arrested ten times. Flynn was expelled from the IWW in 1916 after a botched legal case in which three miners were jailed. She was also a founding member of the American Civil Liberties Union, a champion of women's rights and birth control, and joined the CPUSA in 1936, running for Congress in 1942, and was jailed in the 1950s' Red Scare.

Anarchist and syndicalist women were in the movement's militias as well. They played an active part in the Irish Citizen's Army, for example, and participated in the 1916 Easter Uprising. There were also "women within the *magonista* movement from the very beginning," such as the sisters Teresa and Andrea Villarreal González, who came from Lampazos in the state of Nueva León.[250] When the PLM leadership was located in Saint Louis, Missouri, the sisters became well-known thanks to frequent appearances in the local press. Andrea Villarreal González was part of the PLM junta, and argued that "the real revolution will envelop Mexico in a whirlwind." She added, "I am a woman, and I hate bloodshed and violence. But if it became necessary I could myself use the dagger or the torch."[251] Andrea went on to edit *Mujer Moderna* ("Modern Woman") and Teresa *El Obrero* ("The Worker").[252]

When Ekaterinoslav in the Ukraine was occupied by the anarchists in 1919, an observer was "curious to find some young Amazons, dressed in black, entering the town along with the bulk of the Makhnovist troops," who he described as "intellectual anarchists."[253] Leah Feldman (1899–1993) was one of the prominent anarchist women in the movement. Perhaps the foremost Makhnovist female guerrilla was Maroussia "Maria" Nikiforova, a working-class woman sentenced to death for terrorist activities in 1905. Escaping abroad, she returned to Alexandrovsk, helping to form the anarchist Black Guard. Beginning in 1919, she was an active fighter in the RIAU, and "in the autumn of 1921, we find a certain 'Maroussia' heading a detachment fighting against the Reds…. [S]he is sometimes depicted as dressed entirely in black, and galloping on a white horse at the head of 1,500 fanatical horsemen."[254] In the Spanish Revolution, there were women in the anarchist militias; their numbers were limited, although Mujeres Libres provided some military training. Concha Perez, the daughter of an anarchist militant, and an FAI militant, herself, participated in the anarchist uprisings of 1934, was active in the street fighting in Barcelona in July 1936, and was a notable militia member. Few women commanded militia detachments during the Spanish Revolution, it is true, but among them was Mika Etchebéhère who captained the 14th Division, 70th Brigade, of the Republican army.

In Conclusion: Class Politics and Human Emancipation

In this chapter, we have examined the ways in which the broad anarchist tradition engaged with questions of race, national and gender oppression, and imperialism. The record is an impressive one overall, and its rediscovery sheds new light on the relationship between socialist movements and racial oppression, socialist views on the national question, and the politics of gender on the Left and in popular culture. The pioneering role of anarchism and syndicalism in revolutionary peasant and working-class movements in the colonial and postcolonial world directs attention to a revolutionary tradition of internationalism and anti-imperialism that has been ignored by analyses of leftist history that take classical Marxism, nationalism, and social democracy as their focus. The history of the broad anarchist tradition reveals a strategy of struggling against national and racial oppression that avoids the two-stage approaches of classical Marxism and, more recently, new abolitionism— one that repudiates nationalism while opposing imperialism and national oppression.

The approach of the broad anarchist tradition toward oppression by race, nationality, imperialism, and gender was structured by a class framework that sought to fuse various struggles into a larger internationalist and international movement of the popular classes for a new world of equality and solidarity. Rather than defer the resolution of these oppressions to a postcapitalist future, the movement aimed to construct a revolutionary working-class and peasant movement that was premised on striving for egalitarian relations between the nationalities, races, and genders in the present in order to prefigure the new world. At the same time, it typically rejected labour aristocracy theories, according to which one group of the popular classes exploits another, stressing the common interests of "ordinary" people worldwide in a global struggle for economic and social justice.

Class, from this perspective, provides the basis for uniting diverse demands and constituencies into a larger struggle for human emancipation more generally, and the basis for identifying the role of the class system in both creating nonclass oppressions and shaping the experience of those oppressions. From this viewpoint, race, gender, national, and imperial oppression can only be fundamentally ended by a social revolution that creates a society that emancipates the majority of people; at the same time, opposition to such oppressions in the present is a necessary component of the project of creating the revolutionary counterpower and counterculture that makes the revolution possible.

Notes

1. Bakunin, "Geneva's Double Strike," 148.

2. Bakunin, "The Policy of the International," 174.

3. Bakunin, "Internationalism and the State," 43.

4. W. E. B. DuBois, *The Souls of Black Folk*, based on the 1953 rev. ed. (1903; repr., New York: Bantam, 1989), xxxi, 7–8.

5. P. van Duin, "South Africa," in *The Formation of Labour Movements, 1870–1914*, ed. M. van der Linden and J. Rojahn (Leiden: E. J. Brill, 1990), 624–25; Krikler, *Rand Revolt*, 110.

6. M. Bakunin, "The National Catechism," in *Bakunin on Anarchy: Selected Works by the Activist-Founder of World Anarchism*, ed. S. Dolgoff (1866; repr., London: George Allen and Unwin, 1971), 99; Bakunin, *Statism and Anarchy*, 49; Bakunin, "The Revolutionary Catechism," 95–96.

7. Bakunin, "Federalism, Socialism, Anti-Theologism," 147. There are, it must be noted, Bakunin passages that show an unmistakeable tendency towards crude national and racial stereotypes. If Marx often showed a certain "Russophobia" and anti-Slavic prejudice, then Bakunin expressed on several occasions a definite bias against Germans and Jews. Both Marx and Bakunin sometimes ascribed peculiarly revolutionary properties to their own nationalities. For Marx, most Slav nationalities "never had a history," the German conquest of Eastern Europe was "in the interest of civilisation"; for Bakunin, the worship of authority was "absorbed into the entire life, flesh and blood of every German," while the "Slavs were pre-eminently peaceable and agricultural" and statism was "wholly contrary" to their "passions." See Bonanno, *Anarchism and the National Liberation Struggle*, 13–15; Bakunin, *Statism and Anarchy*, 39, 45, 105. On Marx's Russophobia, see McLellan, *Karl Marx*, 202–3, 261–62, 288, 362, 377, 389, 438–39. It could, of course, be argued that neither Marx nor Bakunin made recourse to biological explanations for these supposed national characteristics and were speaking of mutable political cultures. There is some merit in this approach, but this does not excuse their prejudices. It is more useful to admit their flaws, noting that their prejudices contradicted their larger doctrines and hopes. For example, having stereotyped the Germans, Bakunin went on to assert that "the time will come when the German proletariat itself, having better understood ... its own interests (which are inseparable from the interests of the proletariat of all other countries)" would join with the "Slavic prole-

tariat," which must itself learn that internationalism provided "the sole path to … liberation";
Bakunin, *Statism and Anarchy*, 51.

8. Bakunin, "Preamble and Programme of the International Alliance of the Socialist Democracy," 427–28.

9. Bakunin, *Statism and Anarchy*, 45.

10. Berkman, *The ABC of Anarchism*, 45–46; see also 53.

11. Quoted in Poole, "The Anarchists in the Mexican Revolution," 71.

12. Fleming, *The Anarchist Way to Socialism*, 239–44.

13. Rocker, *Nationalism and Culture*, 40, 298–99, 303, 313, 317, 320, 40.

14. "Notes on Natives, No. 1," *The International*, March 16, 1917.

15. "The Great Unskilled," *The International*, February 9, 1917.

16. Dong-hyun Huh, "Forms of Acceptance of Social Darwinism by the Korean Progressives of the 1880s–1890s:on the Materials of Yu Giljun and Yun Ch'iho," *International Journal of Korean History* 2 (2001).

17. M. González Prada, "Our Indians," in *Anarchism: A Documentary History of Libertarian Ideas, Volume 1: From Anarchy to Anarchism, 300 CE to 1939*, ed. R. Graham (1904; repr., Montréal: Black Rose, 2005), 321. For a useful introduction and anthology, see also D. Sobrevilla, ed., *Free Pages and Other Essays: Anarchist Musings: Manuel González Prada* (New York: Oxford University Press, 2003).

18. M. González Prada, "The Two Nations," in *Free Pages and Other Essays: Anarchist Musings: Manuel González Prada*, ed. D. Sobrevilla (New York: Oxford University Press, 2003), 270.

19. See J. Delhom, "Ambiguïtés de la Question Raciale dans les Essais de Manuel González Prada," in *Les Noirs et le Discours Identitaire Latino-américain*, ed. V. Lavou (Perpignan, France: CRILAUP-Presses Universitaires de Perpignan, 1997).

20. Kropotkin's *Mutual Aid* was compiled in 1902 from a series of articles on evolution, nature, and society dating back to 1890. It was intended as a critique of social Darwinism and extreme individualism, stressing the central role of cooperation in both animal and human evolution. See P. Kropotkin, *Mutual Aid: A Factor of Evolution* (1902; repr., New York: Penguin Books, 1939).

21. Kropotkin, *Memoirs of a Revolutionist*, 299.

22. Kropotkin, *Mutual Aid*, 84, 94–95.

23. D. A. Stack, "The First Darwinian Left: Radical and Socialist Responses to Darwin, 1859–1914," *History of Political Thought* 21, no. 4 (2000): 699; see also P. Mattick, "Kropokin on *Mutual Aid*: Review," *Western Socialist* (February 1956).

24. Kropotkin, *Mutual Aid*, 231–32.

25. Ibid., 82, 218, 229.

26. H. Cleaver, "Kropotkin, Self-Valorization, and the Crisis of Marxism" (Paper presented at the conference on Pyotr Alexeevich Kropotkin organized by the Russian Academy of Science on the 150th anniversary of his birth, Moscow, December 8–14, 1992).

27. Quoted in Poole, "The Anarchists in the Mexican Revolution," 71.

28. Quoted in Foner, *The Industrial Workers of the World*, 123, 125.

29. G. H. Perry, *The Revolutionary IWW* (Chicago: IWW Publishing Bureau, 1913), 7–8.

30. Berkman, *The ABC of Anarchism*, 55–56.

31. Perry, *The Revolutionary IWW*, 7–8.

32. "The Problem of Coloured Labour," *Voice of Labour*, October 27, 1911.

33. "The Wrath to Come," *The International*, December 3, 1915.

34. J. M. Gibson, "Race Prejudice," *The International*, February 23, 1916.

35. D. Roediger, *Towards the Abolition of Whiteness: Essays on Race, Politics, and Working Class History* (London: Verso, 1994), 13.

36. For a representative collection from the journal, see N. Ignatiev and J. Garvey, ed., *Race Traitor* (London: Routledge, 1996).

37. Thus, for Roediger, European immigrants defined themselves as white once on U.S. soil in order to access "the particular public and psychological wages whiteness offered"; D. Roediger, *The Wages of Whiteness: Race and the Making of the American Working Class* (London: Verso, 1991), 136–37. The same contention can be found in N. Ignatiev, *How the Irish Became White* (New York: Routledge, 1995). The logic is clear: race, economic interests, and politics are all conflated in such an analysis. There is, it is worth noting, little solid evidence for claims that the groups like the Irish were only considered white in the United States after long struggles; see, for example, R. Jensen, "'No Irish Need Apply': A Myth of Victimisation," *Journal of Social History* 36, no. 2 (2002).

38. For instance, the black nationalist Cedric Robinson argued that "the persistent and continuously evolving resistance of African peoples to oppression," expressed in a "single historical identity," is the "negation" of capitalism" rather than the "European proletariat"; C. J. Robinson, *Black Marxism: The Making of the Black Radical Tradition* (London: Zed Books, 1983), 2–5. White right-wing theories of capitalism as "Jewish" follow the same logic.

39. The data deployed in Roediger's analysis of the racial politics of IWW's multiracial Brotherhood of Timber Workers, for instance, suggests that the union regarded white identity as perfectly compatible with radical politics and interracialism, and advicated a revolutionary working class white identity aimed at universal working-class unity; Roediger, *Towards the Abolition of Whiteness*, 127–80.

40. Examining the United States, Al Szymanski found that the narrower the gap between the wages of whites and people of colour, the higher white earnings were relative to white earnings elsewhere, and that the wider the gap, the higher the inequality among whites. This was because white workers' racial prejudices prevented the rise of strong labour movements, while systematised racial discrimination drove down the wages and bargaining position of people of colour, undermining the conditions of white workers. See A. Szymanski, "Racial Discrimination and White Gain," *American Sociological Review*, no. 41 (1976): 403–414. It follows that interracial labour movements and the struggle against racial discrimination *benefit* white workers—this is the reverse of what is suggested by the "abolition of whiteness" analysis.

41. "Disunity of Labour," *The International*, September 22, 1916.

42. "Mineworkers and Political Action," *The International*, February 25, 1916.

43. Thorpe, "*The Workers Themselves*," 1.

44. M. van der Linden, "Second Thoughts on Revolutionary Syndicalism: Keynote Address" (Paper presented at the Syndicalism: Swedish and International Historical Experiences conference, Stockholm University, March 13–14, 1998), 15.

45. Casanovas, "Labour and Colonialism in Cuba in the Second Half of the Nineteenth-Century," 302–3, 8, 366, 367.

46. Ibid., 381, 393–94.

47. Casanovas, "Slavery, the Labour Movement, and Spanish Colonialism in Cuba," 381–82. These struggles are detailed in Casanovas, "Labour and Colonialism in Cuba in the Second Half of the Nineteenth-Century," chapters 8 and 9.

48. Clause 5 of the 1883 "Pittsburgh Manifesto," cited in Avrich, *The Haymarket Tragedy*, 75.

49. For details of the Chicago anarchists' general opposition to national and racial prejudice, and the multiethnic composition of their movement, see ibid., 75–76, 79–98, 106–8, 111, 115–16, 144–48, but compare to 126–27.

50. Bekken, "The First Daily Anarchist Newspaper."

51. Avrich, *The Haymarket Tragedy*, 144–45.

52. S. Salerno, "Paterson's Italian Anarchist Silk Workers and the Politics of Race," *Working-USA: The Journal of Labour and Society* 8 (September 2005): 612, 619–20.

53. See P. S. Foner, *Organised Labour and the Black Worker, 1619–1973* (New York: International Publishers, 1974), 111, 119; see also P. S. Foner, "The IWW and the Black Worker," *Journal of Negro History* 55, no. 1 (1974).

54. D. Rosenberg, "The IWW and the Organisation of Asian Workers in Early 20th Century America," *Labour History*, no. 36 (1995): 77–79.

55. L. McGirr, "Black and White Longshoremen in the IWW: A History of the Philadelphia Marine Transport Workers Industrial Union Local 8," *Labour History*, no. 36 (1995): 401. On these unions, see also M. R. Brown, "The IWW and the Negro Worker" (PhD diss., Ball State University at Muncie, 1968); Foner, *The Industrial Workers of the World*; Foner, *Organised Labour and the Black Worker*; J. R. Green, "The Brotherhood of Timber Workers, 1910–1913: A Radical Response to Industrial Capitalism in the Southern U.S.A.," *Past and Present*, no. 60 (1973).

56. Levy, "Anarchism, Internationalism, and Nationalism in Europe," 338.

57. J. Bekken, "Marine Transport Workers IU 510 (IWW): Direct Action Unionism," *Libertarian Labour Review*, no. 18 (1995); H. Rubner, "Occupational Culture, Conflict Patterns, and Organisational Behaviour: Perspectives of Syndicalism in 20th Century Shipping" (Paper presented at the Syndicalism: Swedish and International Historical Experiences conference, Stockholm University, March 13–14, 1998).

58. Brown, "The IWW and the Negro Worker," 30.

59. Quoted by Foner, *Organised Labour and the Black Worker*, 159.

60. G. R. Andrews, "Race versus Class Association: The Afro-Argentines of Buenos Aires, 1850–1900," *Journal of Latin American Studies* 11, no. 1 (1979): 27. Andrews's study unfortunately ends before the rise of FORA.

61. Ibid., 37; G. R. Andrews, "Black and White Workers: São Paulo, Brazil, 1888–1928," *Hispanic American Historical Review* 68, no. 3 (1988): 497–98.

62. Andrews, "Black and White Workers," 497–500, 511.

63. Burgmann, *Revolutionary Industrial Unionism*, 81.

64. See E. Olsen, *The Red Feds: Revolutionary Industrial Unionism and the New Zealand Federation of Labour, 1908–14* (Auckland: Oxford University Press, 1988).

65. P. Steiner, "Industrial Unionism: The History of the Industrial Workers of the World in Aotearoa," in *Industrial Unionism: The History of the Industrial Workers of the World in Aotearoa:Aim, Form, and Tactics of a Workers' Union on IWW Lines* (Wellington: Rebel Press, 2006), 6–7.

66. Quoted in F. Prebbles, *"Trouble Makers": Anarchism and Syndicalism: The Early Years of the Libertarian Movement in Aotearoa/New Zealand*, available at http://www.takver.com/history/nz/tm/tm10.htm (accessed June 15, 2005).

67. Dirlik, *Anarchism in the Chinese Revolution*, 94.

68. Quoted in Zarrow, *Anarchism and Chinese Political Culture*, 179.

69. See M. Turner, *Meseifushugi: A Brief History of Anarchism in Pre-war Japan* (Christchurch: Libertarian Press, n.d.), 19–21.

70. Gorman, "Anarchists in Education"; see also I. Khuri-Makdisi, "Levantine Trajectories: The Formulation and Dissemination of Radical Ideas in and between Beirut, Cairo, and Alexandria, 1860–1914" (PhD diss., Harvard University, 2003), 229–77, 336–54.

71. J. Beinin and Z. Lockman, *Workers on the Nile: Nationalism, Communism, Islam, and the Egyptian Working Class, 1882–1954* (London: I. B. Tauris and Co., 1988), 51n9, 52; see also Khuri-Makdisi, "Levantine Trajectories," 336–54.

72. See van der Walt, "'The Industrial Union Is the Embryo of the Socialist Commonwealth'"; van der Walt, "Bakunin's Heirs in South Africa"; van der Walt, "Anarchism and Syndicalism in South Africa."

73. Also see L. J. W. van der Walt, "Reflections on Race and Anarchism in South Africa, 1904–2004," *Perspectives on Anarchist Theory*, no. 1 (2004).

74. M. Lopes, "Letter from Manuel Lopes," *Workers' Dreadnought*, August 7, 1920.

75. See van der Walt, "Reflections on Race and Anarchism in South Africa."

76. Management Committee of the International Socialist League, "International Socialism and the Native: No Labour Movement without the Black Proletariat," *The International*, December 7, 1917.

77. Darch, "The Makhnovischna," 206.

78. See, for example, Arshinov, *History of the Makhnovist Movement*, 209–19.

79. Quoted in ibid., 216.

80. Compare to Duin, "South Africa," 624–25.

81. Compare to O. Berland, "The Emergence of the Communist Perspective on the 'Negro Question' in America: 1919–1931, Part One," *Science and Society* 63, no. 4 (1999–2000): 413. For a similar argument, see Foner, *Organised Labour and the Black Worker*, 49–50.

82. Compare to Krikler, *Rand Revolt*, 110.

83. Bakunin, quoted in Guérin, *Anarchism*, 68.

84. Cipko, "Mikhail Bakunin and the National Question," 9–11.

85. Bakunin, "Statism and Anarchy," 342–43; see also 341.

86. Maximoff, *The Programme of Anarcho-syndicalism*, 468, 49.

87. Rocker, *Nationalism and Culture*, 552–53, 550.

88. Bakunin, quoted in Guérin, *Anarchism*, 68.

89. Quoted in Forman, *Nationalism and the International Labor Movement*, 37, 36.

90. Rocker, *Nationalism and Culture*, 527.

91. Bakunin, quoted in appendix to Bonanno, *Anarchism and the National Liberation Struggle*, 20; Maximoff, *The Programme of Anarcho-syndicalism*, 47.

92. Nettlau, *A Short History of Anarchism*, 247–48. For Bakunin, "Powerful States can maintain themselves only by crime, little States are virtuous only from weakness"; quoted in Eltzbacher, *Anarchism*, 83.

93. Karl Marx, letter to Friedrich Engels, July 20, 1870, quoted in Rocker, "Marxism and Anarchism," 85. Also quoted in Rocker, *Nationalism and Culture*, 234–35; Mehring, *Karl Marx*, 438.

94. Quoted in Warren, *Imperialism*, 40–41, 44; Bonanno, *Anarchism and the National Liberation Struggle*, 14.

95. Quoted in Warren, *Imperialism*, 44.

96. Forman, *Nationalism*, 58.

97. J. Adelman, "Socialism and Democracy in Argentina in the Age of the Second International," *Hispanic American Historical Review* 72, no. 2 (1992): 213, 223.

98. For a contrary view, see Molyneux, "No God, No Boss, No Husband," 140.

99. Seth, *Marxist Theory and Nationalist Politics*, 24, 32–34, 39–41, 44.

100. See, for example, Lenin, "Two Tactics of Social-Democracy in the Democratic Revolution."

101. C. Guevara, "At the Afro-Asian Conference," in *Ché Guevara Speaks: Selected Speeches and Writings*, ed. J. Hansen (London: Pathfinder Press, 1967), 106–7, 109, 111, 114–15 (emphasis added).

102. Guevara's two-stage approach was very much in the tradition of post-1919 Leninism, as was his vanguardism: there is "one possible strategic end—the seizure of power"; "To be a vanguard party means to stand in the forefront of the working class in the struggle for the seizure of power"; "the guerrilla nucleus ... begins the construction of the future state apparatus"; the "mass carries out with matchless enthusiasm and discipline the tasks set by the government ... [and] initiative generally comes from Fidel or from the Revolutionary High Command," and is "subjected to stimuli and pressures ... [with] the dictatorship of the proletariat operating ... on individuals of the victorious class." See C. Guevara, "Guerrilla Warfare: A Method," in *Ché Guevara Speaks: Selected Speeches and Writings*, ed. J. Hansen (London: Pathfinder Press, 1967), 75, 83–84;

C. Guevara, "Notes on Man and Socialism in Cuba," in *Ché Guevara Speaks: Selected Speeches and Writings*, ed. J. Hansen (London: Pathfinder Press, 1967), 123, 127, 129. There is no real evidence for the view that Guevara was a "new Bakunin" or that his thought and action "keeps alive a libertarian strand in Cuban communism"; for a contrary view, see Marshall, *Demanding the Impossible*, 517. His strategy of constructing the vanguard party as a guerrilla formation was Maoist, not anarchist, and his "foci" idea of organising by a guerrilla nucleus was simply a variant of the mainstream Marxist theory of the vanguard party.

103. See, for example, Guevara, "At the Afro-Asian Conference," 107; Guevara, "Notes on Man and Socialism in Cuba," 125.

104. Rocker, *Anarcho-Syndicalism*, chapter 4.

105. Cockcroft, *Mexico*, 93, 103.

106. Ibid., 94.

107. Organising Junta of the Mexican Liberal Party, "Manifesto to the Workers of the World," in *Land and Liberty: Anarchist Influences in the Mexican Revolution: Ricardo Flores Magón*, ed. D. Poole (April 8, 1911; repr., Orkney, Scotland: Cienfuegos Press, 1977), 95.

108. R. Flores Magón, "Labour's Solidarity Should Know neither Race nor Colour," in *Land and Liberty: Anarchist Influences in the Mexican Revolution: Ricardo Flores Magón*, ed. D. Poole (April 29, 1911; repr., Orkney, Scotland: Cienfuegos Press, 1977), 90.

109. E. Flores Magón, R. Flores Magón, L. Rivera, A. De P. Araujo, and A. L. Figueroa, "To the Workers of the United States," in *Anarchism and the Mexican Revolution: The Political Trials of Ricardo Flores Magón in the United States*, ed. C. M. MacLachlan (April 7, 1914; repr., Berkeley: University of California Press, 1991), 123.

110. Caulfield, "Wobblies and Mexican Workers in Petroleum," 52, 54, 56, 64–65, 67–68, 70–72.

111. MacLachlan, *Anarchism and the Mexican Revolution*, 55–56.

112. Hart, "Revolutionary Syndicalism in Mexico," 194–96.

113. Ibid., 197.

114. See Hart, *Anarchism and the Mexican Working Class*, 160.

115. Fernandez, *Cuban Anarchism*, chapter 1.

116. Ibid.; see also Casanovas, "Labour and Colonialism in Cuba in the Second Half of the Nineteenth-Century," 413–23, 433–42.

117. See G. E. Poyo, "The Anarchist Challenge to the Cuban Independence Movement, 1885–1890," *Cuban Studies* 15, no. 1 (1985): 39–41.

118. Casanovas, "Labour and Colonialism in Cuba in the Second Half of the Nineteenth Century," 424; Fernandez, *Cuban Anarchism*, chapter 1.

119. Fernandez, *Cuban Anarchism*, chapter 2.

120. Shaffer, "Purifying the Environment for the Coming New Dawn."

121. A. Quintero Rivera, ed., *Workers Struggle in Puerto Rico: A Documentary History* (London: Monthly Review Press, 1976), 17–19, editor's notes.

122. R. Romero Rosa, "The Social Question and Puerto Rico: A Friendly Call to Intellectuals," in *Workers Struggle in Puerto Rico: A Documentary History*, ed. A. Quintero Rivera (1904; repr., London: Monthly Review Press, 1976), 20, 28–29, 33–34.

123. Arshinov, *History of the Makhnovist Movement*, 209; see also N. Makhno, "A Few Words on the National Question in the Ukraine," in *The Struggle against the State and Other Essays by Nestor Makhno*, ed. A. Skirda (December 1928; repr., Oakland: AK Press, 1996).

124. Darch, "The Makhnovischna," 6–7.

125. Cipko, "Mikhail Bakunin and the National Question." 11–12.

126. See J. P. Himka, "Young Radicals and Independent Statehood: The Idea of a Ukrainian Nation-state, 1890–1895," *Slavic Review* 41, no. 2 (1982): 219–21, 223–24, 227–29.

127. This account of struggles in Armenia, Bulgaria, and Macedonia is drawn from Balkanski, *Liberation nationale et revolution sociale: a l'example de la Revolution Macedonienne* (Paris: Volon-

te Anarchiste, 1982); V. Bojanev, "Bulgaria: The History of the Bulgarian Anarchist Movement," *Raven* 4, no. 1 (1991); G. Khadziev, *"Down with the Sultan, Long Live the Balkan Federation!" The 1903 Risings in Macedonia and Thrace*, 1992, available at http://flag.blackened.net/revolt/bulgaria_1903.html (accessed January 10, 2003); Nettlau, *A Short History of Anarchism*, 256–58.

128. Bojanev, "Bulgaria," 32.

129. Jackson, "Peasant Political Movements in Eastern Europe," 279.

130. Khadziev, *"Down with the Sultan, Long Live the Balkan Federation!"*

131. Ibid.

132. Connolly, *Socialism Made Easy*, 28.

133. J. Connolly, *Labour in Irish History* (Cork: Corpus of Electronic Texts, 1910), 183, 25.

134. A. Berkman, "The Only Hope of Ireland," *Blast!* no. 13, May 15, 1916, 2.

135. Marshall, *Demanding the Impossible*, 347; D. Poole, "About Malatesta," in *Fra Contadini: A Dialogue on Anarchy*, ed. E. Malatesta (London: Bratach Dubh, 1981), 42.

136. S. Boulouque, "Saïl Mohamed ou la Vie et la Révolte d'un Anarchiste Algérien," in *Saïl Mahomed: Appels aux Travailleurs Algériens*, ed. S. Boulouque, trans. David Short (Paris: Volonte Anarchiste, 1994).

137. Ibid.

138. S. Mohamed, "Peuple algérien, debout!" in *Saïl Mahomed: Appels aux Travailleurs Algériens*, ed. S. Boulouque, trans. provided by Martin Howard (1932; repr., Paris: Volonte Anarchiste, 1994): 12; S. Mohamed, "A l'opinion Publique," in *Saïl Mahomed: Appels aux Travailleurs Algériens*, ed. S. Boulouque, trans. provided by Martin Howard (1930; repr., Paris: Volonte Anarchiste, 1994): 11–12.

139. S. Mohamed, "Un Appel du Groupe Anarchiste aux Indigènes Algériens," in *Saïl Mahomed: Appels aux Travailleurs Algériens*, ed. S. Boulouque, trans. provided by Martin Howard (1935; repr., Paris: Volonte Anarchiste, 1994): 16–17.

140. Paz, *Durruti*, 258–59; see also 262n9.

141. Ibid.; see also 262n9, 258–59.

142. C. Berneri, "Open Letter to Comrade Federica Montseny," *Cienfuegos Press Anarchist Review*, April 14, 1937, 58–59. See also N. Chomsky, *American Power and the New Mandarins* (New York: Penguin, 1970), 91–93.

143. Trewhela, "George Padmore," 45–52.

144. See Em, "Nationalism, Post-Nationalism, and Shin Ch'ae Ho," 289n13.

145. Shin Ch'aeho, "Declaration of the Korean Revolution," in *Anarchism: A Documentary History of Libertarian Ideas, Volume 1: From Anarchy to Anarchism, 300 CE to 1939*, ed. R. Graham (1923; repr., Montréal: Black Rose, 2005), 373–76.

146. Em, "Nationalism, Post-Nationalism, and Shin Ch'ae Ho," 311–12n56.

147. Allen, "Ambivalent Social Darwinism in Korea," 14, 18–19.

148. Quoted in Ha, *A History of Korean Anarchist Movement* [*sic*], 144

149. J. Crump, "Anarchism and Nationalism in East Asia," *Anarchist Studies* 4, no. 1 (1996): 52, 59.

150. Ibid., 60–61.

151. Talhwan, "What We Advocate," in *Anarchism: A Documentary History of Libertarian Ideas, Volume 1: From Anarchy to Anarchism, 300 CE to 1939*, ed. R. Graham (June 1928; repr., Montréal: Black Rose, 2005), 382–83.

152. Crump, "Anarchism and Nationalism in East Asia," 47–48; Dirlik, *Anarchism in the Chinese Revolution*, chapter 11.

153. Dirlik, *Anarchism in the Chinese Revolution*, 253–55.

154. See Li Pei Kan, "Anarchism and the Question of Practice," in *Anarchism: A Documentary History of Libertarian Ideas, Volume 1: From Anarchy to Anarchism, 300 CE to 1939*, ed. R. Graham (1927; repr., Montréal: Black Rose, 2005).

155. For her memoirs up to 1886, see Michel, *The Red Virgin*. For more details about her life, see B. Lowry and E. E. Gunter, "Translators' Introduction," in *The Red Virgin: Memoirs of Louise Michel*, ed. B. Lowry and E. E. Gunter (Tuscaloosa: University of Alabama Press, 1981); Gunter, "Epilogue."

156. See Michel, *The Red Virgin*, 105–14.

157. Ibid., 112.

158. Lowry and Gunter, "Translators' Introduction," xiv.

159. K. Hart, "Oral Culture and Anti-Colonialism in Louise Michel's *Memoires* (1886) and *Légendes et chants de gestes* (1885)," *Nineteenth-Century French Studies* 30, no. 2 (2001): 107–8.

160. M. Bakunin, "Manifesto of the Russian Revolutionary Association to the Oppressed Women of Russia: On Women's Liberation," in *Bakunin on Anarchism*, ed. S. Dolgoff (Montréal: Black Rose, 1980), 396, 397.

161. Bakunin, "Preamble and Programme of the International Alliance of the Socialist Democracy," 427.

162. Bakunin, "Manifesto of the Russian Revolutionary Association to the Oppressed Women of Russia," 397.

163. Bakunin, "The Revolutionary Catechism," 79, 93–95.

164. Kropotkin, *The Conquest of Bread*, 123, 124–25, 127–28.

165. Ibid., 127–28.

166. J. Hutton, "Camile Pissarro's *Turpitudes Sociales* and Late Nineteenth-Century French Anarchist Anti-Feminism," *History Workshop: A Journal of Socialist and Feminist Historians*, no. 24 (1987): 38.

167. Quoted in ibid., 38.

168. Quoted in P. Zarrow, "He Zhen and Anarcho-Feminism in China," *Journal of Asian Studies* 47, no. 4 (1988): 804.

169. M. González Prada, "Revolution," in *Free Pages and Other Essays: Anarchist Musings: Manuel González Prada*, ed. D. Sobrevilla (1907; repr., New York: Oxford University Press, 2003), 262.

170. Quoted in B. Ortiz, "Forerunner of Feminism: Praxedis Guerrero, Mexican Writer and Revolutionary," *Monthly Review* 37, no. 12 (1985): 45–46.

171. Quoted in Avrich, *The Haymarket Tragedy*, 479n29.

172. Maximoff, *The Programme of Anarcho-syndicalism*, 55–56.

173. On "bourgeois feminism," see M. Kennedy and C. Tilly, "Socialism, Feminism, and the Stillbirth of Socialist Feminism in Europe, 1890–1920," *Science and Society* 51, no. 1 (1987): 9–17.

174. See E. Goldman, "The Tragedy of Women's Emancipation," in *Red Emma Speaks: Selected Writings and Speeches*, ed. A. K. Shulman (1911; repr., New York: Vintage Books, 1972), 135–42.

175. E. Goldman, "Marriage and Love," in *Red Emma Speaks: Selected Writings and Speeches*, ed. A. K. Shulman (1911; repr., New York: Vintage Books, 1972), 159–66.

176. Wexler, *Emma Goldman*, 197; A. R. Wexler, "Emma Goldman and Women," in *The Anarchist Papers*, ed. D. I. Roussopoulus (Montréal: Black Rose, 1986), 153.

177. Zarrow, "He Zhen and Anarcho-Feminism in China," 799–800.

178. Quoted in ibid., 802.

179. Ibid., 802.

180. R. Flores Magón, "*A La Mujer* [To Women]," *Regeneración*, September 24, 1910.

181. Bakunin, "Manifesto of the Russian Revolutionary Association to the Oppressed Women of Russia," 397–98.

182. Quoted in Zarrow, "He Zhen and Anarcho-Feminism in China," 810.

183. Wexler, "Emma Goldman and Women," 157.

184. V. de Cleyre, *Sex Slavery*, April 28, 1907, available at http://dwardmac.pitzer.edu/Anarchist_Archives/bright/cleyre/sexslavery.html (accessed March 15, 2000).

185. See, for example, Pelloutier's analysis in Jennings, "The CGT and the Couriau Affair," 323–24.

186. Kropotkin, *The Conquest of Bread*, 124–25, 127–28.

187. F. Engels, *The Origin of the Family, Private Property, and the State* (1884; repr., Moscow: Progress Publishers, 1948), 54–59, 75–76, 81–83.

188. Ibid., 57, 82. A notably less reductionist Marxist analysis was provided in A. Bebel, *Woman under Socialism*, trans. D. de Leon (1891; repr., New York: New York Labor Press, 1904).

189. Flores Magón, "*A La Mujer* [To Women]."

190. Michel, *The Red Virgin*, 140; see also 59.

191. Molyneux, "No God, No Boss, No Husband," 142.

192. Zarrow, "He Zhen and Anarcho-Feminism in China," 803–5, 807.

193. E. Goldman, "The Traffic in Women," in *Red Emma Speaks: Selected Writings and Speeches*, ed. A. K. Shulman (1911; repr., New York: Vintage Books, 1972), 150.

194. V. de Cleyre, *Those Who Marry Do Ill*, available at http://dwardmac.pitzer.edu/Anarchist_Archives/bright/cleyre/theywhomarry.html (accessed March 15, 2000).

195. Ibid.; Kaplan, "Other Scenarios," 404. See also C. H. Palczewski, "Voltairine de Cleyre: Sexual Slavery and Sexual Pleasure in the Nineteenth Century," *NWSA Journal* 7 (1995).

196. This is, for example, suggested by E. Goldman, "Jealousy: Causes and a Possible Cure," in *Red Emma Speaks: Selected Writings and Speeches*, ed. A. K. Shulman (1912; repr., New York: Vintage Books, 1972). Pelloutier also believed that monogamy was not natural or normal; see Jennings, "The CGT and the Couriau Affair," 323.

197. By contrast, de Cleyre favoured "unions rare and impermanent," believing, rather like Godwin, that a "permanent dependent relationship … is detrimental to the growth of individual character"; de Cleyre, *Sex Slavery*.

198. Quoted in Maximoff, *The Programme of Anarcho-syndicalism*, 55.

199. Malatesta in Richards, *Errico Malatesta*, 182.

200. Quoted in Jennings, "The CGT and the Couriau Affair," 323.

201. See Shaffer, "Purifying the Environment for the Coming New Dawn."

202. Goldman, "The Tragedy of Women's Emancipation," 142.

203. Michel, *The Red Virgin*, 139.

204. Molyneux, "No God, No Boss, No Husband," 119–20, 127–29, 131–32, 141–42.

205. Compare to E. Leeder, "Let Our Mothers Show the Way," in *Reinventing Anarchy, Again*, ed. H. J. Ehrlich (Edinburgh: AK Press, 1996), 143.

206. For example, "The majority of the anarchist-feminists … were largely anonymous women…. To the extent that such ideas appear to have been widely shared by women anarchists of the rank-and-file, anarchist-feminism may be said to have been a grass roots phenomenon"; M. S. Marsh, "The Anarchist-Feminist Response to the 'Woman Question' in Late Nineteenth-Century America," *American Quarterly* 30, no. 4 (1978): 538. Here, the conflation of the categories "anarchist-feminists" and "women anarchists" is inescapable.

207. For a contrary view, see Molyneux, "No God, No Boss, No Husband," 133.

208. On the latter point, see M. Hewitt, "Emma Goldman: The Case for Anarcho-feminism," in *The Anarchist Papers*, ed. D. I. Roussopoulos (Montréal: Black Rose, 1986), 169–70.

209. For a contrary view, see Hutton, "Camille Pissarro's *Turpitudes Sociales* and Late Nineteenth-Century French Anarchist Anti-Feminism," 38–44, 53–54.

210. See, for example, Marsh, "The Anarchist-Feminist Response to the 'Woman Question' in Late Nineteenth-Century America."

211. Gordon, "Anarchism in Brazil," 135.

212. Kaplan, "Other Scenarios," 402, 406–11.

213. Pouget and Pataud, *How We Shall Bring about the Revolution*, 183, 229–31.

214. On the PLM, see C. Lomas, "Transborder Discourse: The Articulation of Gender in the Borderlands in the Early Twentieth Century," *Frontiers* 24, no. 2–3 (2003): 61–62. On the IWPA, see, for example, Avrich, *The Haymarket Tragedy*, 143.

215. Kropotkin, "An Appeal to the Young," 281–82.

216. Lomas, "Transborder Discourse," 62; Flores Magón, "*A La Mujer* [To Women]."

217. Jennings, "The CGT and the Couriau Affair," 321–24, 331–35.

218. Mitchell, "French Syndicalism," 35–36. See, for example, Jennings, "The CGT and the Couriau Affair," 324–25, 330–35.

219. Mitchell, "French Syndicalism," 35–36.

220. Kaplan, "Other Scenarios," 404–5.

221. Burgmann, *Revolutionary Industrial Unionism*, 92–93.

222. See, for instance, ibid., 92–97; Kaplan, "Other Scenarios"; F. Shor, "Masculine Power and Virile Syndicalism: A Gendered Analysis of the IWW in Australia," *Labour History*, no. 63 (1992); van der Linden, "Second Thoughts on Revolutionary Syndicalism," 13–15.

223. Hadfield, "Politics and Protest in the Spanish Anarchist Movement," 1.

224. See Kaplan, "Other Scenarios," 413.

225. Hadfield, "Politics and Protest in the Spanish Anarchist Movement"; Ackelsberg, *Free Women of Spain*, 84–85.

226. M. Tax, *The Rising of the Women: Feminist Solidarity and Class Conflict, 1880–1917* (New York: Monthly Review Press, 1980), 126–27, 162–63.

227. See, for example, Burgmann, *Revolutionary Industrial Unionism*, 97, 102–10.

228. Mitchell, "French Syndicalism," 35.

229. Wood, "Postrevolutionary Pioneer," 3–6, 13–35.

230. Peirats, *Anarchists in the Spanish Revolution*, 265; see also Ackelsberg, "Revolution and Community."

231. Wexler, "Emma Goldman and Women," 157.

232. Kaplan, "Other Scenarios," 414–15; Burgmann, *Revolutionary Industrial Unionism*, 101.

233. CNT, "The Libertarian Ideal in Bolivia"; Horn, *Organising Informal Women Workers*; M. Stephenson, *Gender and Modernity in Andean Bolivia* (Austin: University of Texas Press, 1999), chapter 1.

234. Stephenson, *Gender and Modernity in Andean Bolivia*, 12.

235. Hadfield, "Politics and Protest in the Spanish Anarchist Movement," 4–5.

236. Baer, "Strength in Numbers," 869, 874–75.

237. Hadfield, "Politics and Protest in the Spanish Anarchist Movement," 1–2; Rider, "The Practice of Direct Action," 97–98.

238. Ackelsberg, *Free Women of Spain*, 147–54.

239. Quoted in Ackelsberg, "Models of Revolution," 370.

240. Carpena, "Spain 1936," 49.

241. Quoted in Ackelsberg, *Free Women of Spain*, 23–24.

242. See Ackelsberg, "Revolution and Community; Ackelsberg, "Separate and Equal?"; Ackelsberg, "Models of Revolution"; Ackelsberg, *Free Women of Spain*; Carpena, "Spain 1936"; Kaplan, "Other Scenarios"; Ortiz, "*Mujeres Libres*."

243. See M. Hane, ed., *Reflections on the Way to the Gallows: Voices of Japanese Rebel Women* (New York: Pantheon Books, 1988).

244. Ibid., 53.

245. See E. P. Tsurumi, "Feminism and Anarchism in Japan: Takamure Itsue, 1894–1964," *Bulletin of Concerned Asian Scholars* 17, no. 2 (1985).

246. E. Rodrigues, *Against All Tyranny!* 23–25.

247. See Rivera, *Workers Struggle in Puerto Rico*, 40–50.

248. There is surprisingly little written about Lucy Parsons, despite her almost sixty years of activism in a wide range of important movements. Some material is provided in Avrich, *The Haymarket Tragedy*; Nelson, *Beyond the Martyrs*; Rosemont, *Haymarket Scrapbook*. See also G. Ahrens, ed., *Lucy Parsons: Freedom, Equality, Solidarity* (Chicago: Charles H. Kerr, 2003); C. Ashbaugh, *Lucy Parsons: American Revolutionary* (Chicago: Charles H. Kerr, 1976); J. McKean, "A Fury for Justice: Lucy Parsons and the Revolutionary Anarchist Movement in Chicago" (PhD diss., Columbia University, 2006). The literature is also uneven; for instance, for a denial that Parsons was an anarchist—a claim that surely cannot be taken too seriously—see Ashbaugh, *Lucy Parsons*.

249. See E. G. Flynn, *The Rebel Girl: An Autobiography, My First Life (1906–1926)*, rev. ed. (New York: International Publishers, 1973). For another interesting work, see E. G. Flynn, "Memories of the Industrial Workers of the World (IWW)," *Original Occasional Papers Series, American Institute for Marxist Studies*, no. 24 (1977). See also R. Fraad Baxandall, ed., *Words on Fire: The Life and Writing of Elizabeth Gurley Flynn* (New Brunswick, NJ: Rutgers University Press, 1987).

250. Albro, *To Die on Your Feet*, 78.

251. Ibid., 81.

252. See Lomas, "Transborder Discourse."

253. Skirda, *Nestor Makhno*, 313.

254. Ibid., 318.

Anarcho-syndicalist demonstration, 1 May 2000, Paris.

The rally drew 6,000 people, and followed the Pour un Autre Futur ("For Another Future") international syndicalist conference, which drew together many of the main syndicalist unions formed or revived since the 1970s, new syndicalist formations from countries like Russia, and anarchist political organisations from Africa and Latin America. The conference laid the groundwork for the International Libertarian Solidarity network founded in Madrid in 2001. *Picture courtesy of the Le Combat Syndicaliste, Paris.*

Strike by the anarcho-syndicalist Union of Plasterers in Resistance (URE), Chile, 1947.

The broad anarchist tradition remained a significant force in many countries after the Second World War, notably in France, Italy, Cuba, Argentina, Chile, China and Korea. It revived in the 1960s and resurged after the collapse of Francoist fascism in Spain in 1975. The most important post-war growth of the movement would, however, begin in the 1990s after the collapse of the USSR and the East Bloc. *Picture courtesy of José Antonio Gutierrez Dantón.*

CHAPTER 11

Conclusion to Volume 1 and Prologue to Volume 2

In volume 1, we have examined the core ideas of the broad anarchist tradition, discussed key features of its history and practice, and suggested its relevance to contemporary struggles against neoliberalism. While we have paid a great deal of attention to the movement before the 1940s—particularly because it is so rich in examples of the application of anarchist and syndicalist theory to practical situations— we do not wish to create the impression that the movement went into a steep decline with the rise of Bolshevism in the 1920s or died out with the defeat of the Spanish Revolution in 1936. A number of substantial movements continued to operate from the 1940s onward: these are just some illustrations drawn from a rich history that will be discussed in more depth in volume 2. While the Bolivian FOL went into decline in the 1940s as a result of repression and competition from new unions led by political parties, the FOF continued operate under anarcho-syndicalist leadership until 1953, when it joined the COB.[1] In Argentina and Brazil, anarchists and syndicalists continued to play a key role in the labour movement into the 1950s, notably. In Chile, anarchists were among the national leadership of the Chilean Workers' Central formed in 1953, breaking away to establish a CNT in 1960.

In China, the anarchist Chu Cha-pei waged guerrilla war in southern Yunan in the 1940s and 1950s, launching attacks against the Maoist regime from the mountains.[2] In Cuba, where CNOC had been heavily repressed from 1927 onward, a CGT was formed in 1931; banned in 1938, it continued to operate, as did the Libertarian Association of Cuba. Syndicalists "stood at the helm of several industrial unions" in the 1950s, and the CGT, the Libertarian Association of Cuba, and other anarchist and syndicalist groups made a substantial contribution to the struggle against the Fulgencio Batista regime, proving a thorn in Fidel Castro's side until they were suppressed in the 1960s.[3] In Russia, a libertarian group emerged in Moscow in 1950 that argued for "Soviets, not Party": its members were shipped off to gulags.[4] Spanish anarchists and Ukrainian prisoners were prominent in the uprising at the Karaganda gulag in Kazakhstan that broke out after the news of Stalin's death in 1953; black flags, an anarchist symbol, were flown in the 1953 revolts at the gulags of Norilsk and Vorkuta. In Southern Rhodesia, the syndicalist-influenced ICU was revived by Charles Mzingeli in the 1940s and remained active into the 1950s.[5]

In Uruguay, the Uruguayan Anarchist Federation (FAU) was established in 1956. Like anarchists in Argentina, China, Spain, and elsewhere who were waging guerrilla war against dictatorships into the 1970s, the FAU embarked on an armed struggle, organising the Revolutionary Popular Organisation-33 (OPR-33). The global revolts of 1968 meanwhile spurred a revival of interest in anarchist and syndicalist ideas in many countries, and the collapse of the Franco regime in 1975 and the rebirth of the CNT helped lay the basis for the massive upsurge of anarchism and syndicalism in the 1990s. In the late 1980s and early 1990s, there were signs of an upsurge in interest in anarchism in China that "may be compared" to that in Europe "following the events of May 1968 in France."[6] The rise of profoundly libertarian movements in the 1990s, such as the Zapatistas in Mexico, the rebirth of syndicalist unionism, and the rise of anarchism in the "antiglobalisation" movement show that the contemporary resurgence of the broad anarchist tradition and its aspirations is far from over.

The twenty-first century is a time of both despair and hope: despair at the evils of contemporary society, and hope that a new world is possible. The ideas of the broad anarchist tradition have, we believe, much to contribute to creating such a world, and the record of the anarchist and syndicalist movement has much to offer in the way of inspiration and experiences. At the same time, the ability of contemporary anarchists and syndicalists to make a meaningful contribution to current struggles depends very much on their ability to organise as an effective force. We close volume 1 on this note and invite readers to join us in volume 2, where we will provide a global history of the 150 years of the broad anarchist tradition, and move from exploring the black flame of the revolutionary anarchist idea to looking at the global fire that anarchism and syndicalism ignited.

Notes

1. Horn, *Organising Informal Women Workers*.

2. Interview with H. L. Wei, in Avrich, *Anarchist Portraits*, 214ff.

3. A. Souchy, *Beware! Anarchist! A Life for Freedom: The Autobiography of Augustin Souchy*, trans. T. Waldinger (Chicago: Charles H. Kerr, 1992), 142–50, 154.

4. P. Ruff, *Anarchy in the USSR: A New Beginning* (London: ASP, 1991), 8–10.

5. See B. Raftopolous, "Nationalism and Labour in Salisbury, 1953–1965," in *Sites of Struggle: Essays in Zimbabwe's Urban History*, ed. B. Raftopolous and T. Yoshikuni (Harare, Zimbabwe: Weaver Press, 1999).

6. Dirlik, *Anarchism in the Chinese Revolution*, 7.

Bibliography

Abse, T. "The Rise of Fascism in an Industrial City." In *Rethinking Italian Fascism: Capitalism, Populism, and Culture*, edited by D. Forgacs. London: Lawrence and Wishart, 1986.

Ackelsberg, M. A. "Revolution and Community: Mobilization, De-politicisation, and Perceptions of Change in Civil War Spain." In *Women Living Change*, edited by S. C. Bourque and D. R. Divine. Philadelphia: Temple University Press, 1985.

———. "'Separate and Equal'? Mujeres Libres and Anarchist Strategy for Women's Emancipation." *Feminist Studies* 11, no. 1 (1985).

———. "Models of Revolution: Rural Women and Anarchist Collectivisation in Spain." *Journal of Peasant Studies* 20, no. 3 (1993).

———. *Free Women of Spain: Anarchism and the Struggle for the Emancipation of Women*. Rev. ed. Oakland: AK Press, 2005.

Adelman, J. "Socialism and Democracy in Argentina in the Age of the Second International." *Hispanic American Historical Review* 72, no. 2 (1992): 211–38.

Ahrens, G., ed. *Lucy Parsons: Freedom, Equality, Solidarity*. Chicago: Charles H. Kerr, 2003.

Albert, M. *Parecon: Life after Capitalism*. London: Verso, 2003.

Albro, W. S. *To Die on Your Feet: The Life, Times, and Writings of Praxedis G. Guerrero*. Fort Worth: Texas Christian University Press, 1996.

Allen, J. M. "History, Nation, People: Past and Present in the Writing of Sin Ch'aeho." PhD diss., University of Washington, 1999.

———. "Ambivalent Social Darwinism in Korea." *International Journal of Korean History* 2 (2002).

Allen, K. *The Politics of James Connolly*. London: Pluto Press, 1987.

Alliance Syndicaliste Revolutionnaire et Anarcho-syndicaliste. "Putting the Record Straight on Mikhail Bakunin." *Libertarian Communist Review*, no. 2 (1976). Translated from the French by Nick Heath.

American Continental Workers' Association. "American Continental Workers' Association." In *Anarchism: A Documentary History of Libertarian Ideas, Volume 1: From Anarchy to Anarchism, 300 CE to 1939*, edited by R. Graham. 1929. Reprint, Montréal: Black Rose, 2005.

Amsden, J. *Collective Bargaining and Class Conflict in Spain*. London: Weidenfeld and Nicholson, 1972.

Anarchist Workers Group. "Anarchism in the Thatcher Years." *Socialism from Below*, no. 1 (August 1989).

Anderson, B. *James Connolly and the Irish Left*. Dublin: Irish Academic Press, 1994.

———. *Under Three Flags: Anarchism and the Anti-colonial Imagination*. London: Verso, 2006.

Andrews, G. R. "Race versus Class Association: The Afro-Argentines of Buenos Aires, 1850–1900." *Journal of Latin American Studies* 11, no. 1 (1979), 19–39.

———. "Black and White Workers: São Paulo, Brazil, 1888–1928." *Hispanic American Historical Review* 68, no. 3 (1988), 491–524.

Anonymous. *Chile: The IWW and FORC*. Sydney: Rebel Worker, 1983.

Archinov, P., N. Makhno, I. Mett, Valevsky, and Linsky. *The Organisational Platform of the Libertarian Communists*. 1926. Reprint, Dublin: Workers Solidarity Movement, 2001.

Aroni-Tsichli, E. "The Crisis of Currant in Greece: Protectionism and Social Conflicts, 1892–1905." Paper presented at the European Social Science History conference, Amsterdam, March 22–25, 2006.

Arshinov, P. *History of the Makhnovist Movement, 1918–1921*. 1923. Reprint, London: Freedom Press, 1987.

———. *The Old and New in Anarchism*. May 1928. Available at http://www.nestormakhno. info/english/oldnew.htm (accessed March 15, 2004).

Ashbaugh, C. *Lucy Parsons: American Revolutionary*. Chicago: Charles H. Kerr, 1976.

Avrich, P. *The Russian Anarchists*. Princeton, NJ: Princeton University Press, 1967.

———. "The Legacy of Bakunin." In *Bakunin on Anarchy: Selected Works by the Activist-Founder of World Anarchism*, edited by S. Dolgoff. London: George Allen and Unwin, 1971.

———, ed. *The Anarchists in the Russian Revolution*. London: Thames and Hudson, 1973.

———. Introduction to *The Anarchists in the Russian Revolution*, edited by P. Avrich. London: Thames and Hudson, 1973.

———. *The Modern School Movement: Anarchism and Education in the United States*. Princeton, NJ: Princeton University Press, 1980.

———. *The Haymarket Tragedy*. Princeton, NJ: Princeton University Press, 1984.

———. *Anarchist Portraits*. Princeton, NJ: Princeton University Press, 1988.

———. *Sacco and Vanzetti: The Anarchist Background*. Princeton, NJ: Princeton University Press, 1991.

Baer, J. A. "Tenant Mobilization and the 1907 Rent Strike in Buenos Aires." *Americas* 49, no. 3 (1993).

Bakunin, M. "The National Catechism." In *Bakunin on Anarchy: Selected Works by the Activist-Founder of World Anarchism*, edited by S. Dolgoff. 1866. Reprint, London: George Allen and Unwin, 1971.

———. "The Revolutionary Catechism." In *Bakunin on Anarchy: Selected Works by the Activist-Founder of World Anarchism*, edited by S. Dolgoff. 1866. Reprint, London: George Allen and Unwin, 1971.

————. "Federalism, Socialism, Anti-Theologism." In *Bakunin on Anarchy: Selected Works by the Activist-Founder of World Anarchism*, edited by S. Dolgoff. 1867. Reprint, London: George Allen and Unwin, 1971.

————. "Preamble and Programme of the International Alliance of the Socialist Democracy." In *Bakunin on Anarchism*, edited by S. Dolgoff. 1868. Reprint, Montréal: Black Rose, 1980.

————. "Geneva's Double Strike." In *Mikhail Bakunin: From out of the Dustbin: Bakunin's Basic Writings, 1869–1871*, edited by R. M. Cutler. 1869[?]. Reprint, Ann Arbor, MI: Ardis, 1985.

————. "The Policy of the International." In *Bakunin on Anarchy: Selected Works by the Activist-Founder of World Anarchism*, edited by S. Dolgoff. 1869. Reprint, London: George Allen and Unwin, 1971.

————. "The Programme of the International Brotherhood." In *Bakunin on Anarchy: Selected Works by the Activist-Founder of World Anarchism*, edited by S. Dolgoff. 1869. Reprint, London: George Allen and Unwin, 1971.

————. "Letter to Albert Richard." In *Bakunin on Anarchy: Selected Works by the Activist-Founder of World Anarchism*, edited by S. Dolgoff. 1870. Reprint, London: George Allen and Unwin, 1971.

————. "Letters to a Frenchman on the Current Crisis." In *Bakunin on Anarchy: Selected Works by the Activist-Founder of World Anarchism*, edited by S. Dolgoff. 1870. Reprint, London: George Allen and Unwin, 1971.

————. "Representative Government and Universal Suffrage." In *Bakunin on Anarchy: Selected Works by the Activist-Founder of World Anarchism*, edited by S. Dolgoff. 1870. Reprint, London: George Allen and Unwin, 1971.

————. *The Capitalist System*. 1871. Reprint, Champaign, IL: Libertarian Labor Review, 1993.

————. "God and the State." In *Bakunin on Anarchy: Selected Works by the Activist-Founder of World Anarchism*, edited by S. Dolgoff. 1871. Reprint, London: George Allen and Unwin, 1971.

————. "The Paris Commune and the Idea of the State." In *Bakunin on Anarchy: Selected Works by the Activist-Founder of World Anarchism*, edited by S. Dolgoff. 1871. Reprint, London: George Allen and Unwin, 1971.

————. "The Programme of the Alliance." In *Bakunin on Anarchy: Selected Works by the Activist-Founder of World Anarchism*, edited by S. Dolgoff. 1871. Reprint, London: George Allen and Unwin, 1971.

————. "Three Lectures to Swiss Members of the International." In *Mikhail Bakunin: From out of the Dustbin: Bakunin's Basic Writings, 1869–1871*, edited by R. M. Cutler. 1871. Reprint, Ann Arbor, MI: Ardis, 1985.

————. "The International and Karl Marx." In *Bakunin on Anarchy: Selected Works by the Activist-Founder of World Anarchism*, edited by S. Dolgoff. 1872. Reprint, London: George Allen and Unwin, 1971.

————. "Letter to *La Liberté*." In *Bakunin on Anarchy: Selected Works by the Activist-Founder of World Anarchism*, edited by S. Dolgoff. 1872. Reprint, London: George Allen and Unwin, 1971.

————. "Worker Association and Self-Management." In *No Gods, No Masters: An Anthology of Anarchism, Book One*, edited by D. Guérin. January 3, 1872. Reprint, Oakland: AK Press, 1998.

———. "Statism and Anarchy." In *Bakunin on Anarchy: Selected Works by the Activist-Founder of World Anarchism*, edited by S. Dolgoff. 1873. Reprint, London: George Allen and Unwin, 1971.

———. *Statism and Anarchy*. 1873. Reprint, Cambridge: Cambridge University Press, 1990.

———. "Manifesto of the Russian Revolutionary Association to the Oppressed Women of Russia on Women's Liberation." In *Bakunin on Anarchism*, edited by S. Dolgoff. Montréal: Black Rose, 1980.

———. "On the Cooperative Movement." In *Bakunin on Anarchism*, edited by S. Dolgoff. Montréal: Black Rose, 1980.

———. "On the Internal Conduct of the Alliance." In *Bakunin on Anarchism*, edited by S. Dolgoff. Montréal: Black Rose, 1980.

———. "Internationalism and the State." In *Marxism, Freedom, and the State*, edited by K. J. Kenafick. London: Freedom Press, 1990.

———. "On Cooperation." In *No Gods, No Masters: An Anthology of Anarchism, Book One*, edited by D. Guérin. Oakland: AK Press, 1998.

Balkanski, G. *Liberation Nationale et Revolution Sociale: A l'example de la Revolution Macedonienne*. Paris: Volonte Anarchiste, 1982.

Bar, A. "The CNT: The Glory and Tragedy of Spanish Anarchosyndicalism." In *Revolutionary Syndicalism: An International Perspective*, edited by M. van der Linden and W. Thorpe. Otterup, Denmark: Scolar, 1990.

Baxandall, R. Fraad, ed. *Words on Fire: The Life and Writing of Elizabeth Gurley Flynn*. New Brunswick, NJ: Rutgers University Press, 1987.

Bayerlein, B., and M. van der Linden. "Revolutionary Syndicalism in Portugal." In *Revolutionary Syndicalism: An International Perspective*, edited by M. van der Linden and W. Thorpe. Otterup, Denmark: Scolar Press, 1990.

Bebel, A. *Woman under Socialism*. Translated by D. De Leon. 1891. Reprint, New York: New York Labor Press, 1904.

Beinin, J., and Z. Lockman. *Workers on the Nile: Nationalism, Communism, Islam, and the Egyptian Working Class, 1882–1954*. London: I. B. Tauris and Co., 1988.

Bekken, J. "The First Daily Anarchist Newspaper: The *Chicagoer Arbeiter-Zeitung*." *Anarchist Studies*, no. 3 (1995).

———. "Marine Transport Workers IU 510 (IWW): Direct Action Unionism." *Libertarian Labor Review*, no. 18 (1995): 12–25.

Bendana, A. "A Sandinista Commemoration of the Sandino Centennial: Speech Given on the 61 Anniversary of the Death of General Sandino, Held in Managua's Olaf Palme Convention Centre." Managua: Centre for International Studies, 1995.

Berkman, A. "The Only Hope of Ireland." *Blast!* no. 13, May 15, 1916.

———. *The Bolshevik Myth (Diary, 1920–1922), including the "Anti-Climax."* 1925. Reprint, London: Pluto Press, 1989.

———. *The ABC of Anarchism*, 3rd ed. 1929. Reprint, London: Freedom Press, 1964.

———. *What Is Communist Anarchism?* 1929. Reprint, London: Phoenix Press, 1989.

Berland, O. "The Emergence of the Communist Perspective on the 'Negro Question' in America: 1919–1931, Part One." *Science and Society* 63, no. 4 (1999–2000): 411–32.

Berneri, C. "Open Letter to Comrade Federica Montseny." *Cienfuegos Press Anarchist Review*, April 14, 1937.

Bernstein, E. *The Preconditions for Socialism*. Edited and translated by H. Tudor. 1899. Reprint, Cambridge: Cambridge University Press, 1993.

Bernstein, H. "Farewells to the Peasantry." *Transformation: Critical Perspectives on Southern Africa*, no. 52 (2003).

Bertrand, C. L. "Revolutionary Syndicalism in Italy." In *Revolutionary Syndicalism: An International Perspective*, edited by M. van der Linden and W. Thorpe. Otterup, Denmark: Scolar Press, 1990.

Beyer-Arnesen, H. "Anarcho-syndicalism: A Historical Closed Door ... or Not?" *Libertarian Labor Review* (Winter 1997–1998).

Black, G. *Triumph of the People: The Sandinista Revolution in Nicaragua*. London: Zed Books, 1981.

Bock, H. M. "Anarchosyndicalism in the German Labour Movement: A Rediscovered Minority Tradition." In *Revolutionary Syndicalism: An International Perspective*, edited by M. van der Linden and W. Thorpe. Otterup, Denmark: Scolar Press, 1990.

Bojanev, V. "Bulgaria: The History of the Bulgarian Anarchist Movement." *Raven* 4, no. 1 (1991).

Bonanno, A. M. *A Critique of Syndicalist Methods*. 1975. Available at http://www.geocities.com/kk_abacus/ioaa/critsynd.html (accessed March 25, 2005).

———. *Anarchism and the National Liberation Struggle*. 2nd ed. London: Bratach Dubh, 1976.

Bookchin, M. *The Spanish Anarchists: The Heroic Years, 1868–1936*. New York: Harper Colophon Books, 1977.

———. "Deep Ecology, Anarchosyndicalism, and the Future of Anarchist Thought." In *Deep Ecology and Anarchism: A Polemic*, edited by G. Purchase, M. Bookchin, B. Morris, and R. Aitchley. London: Freedom Press, 1993.

———. *To Remember Spain: The Anarchist and Syndicalist Revolution of 1936: Essays by Murray Bookchin*. Oakland: AK Press, 1994.

———. *Social Anarchism or Lifestyle Anarchism: An Unbridgeable Chasm*. Oakland: AK Press, 1995.

Boulouque, S. "Saïl Mohamed ou la Vie et la Révolte d'un Anarchiste Algérien." In *Saïl Mohamed: Appels aux Travailleurs Algériens*, edited by S. Boulouque. Paris: Volonte Anarchiste, 1994.

Bourdieu, P. "Utopia of Endless Exploitation: The Essence of Neo-liberalism." *Le Monde Diplomatique*, December 8, 1998.

Breitbart, M. M. "Spanish Anarchism: An Introductory Essay." *Antipode: A Radical Journal of Feography* 10–11, nos. 3 and 1 (1979).

Bricianer, S. *Pannekoek and the Workers' Councils*. Saint Louis, MO: Telos Press, 1978.

Brissenden, P. *The IWW: A Study in American Syndicalism*. New York: Columbia University Press, 1920.

Brogan, D. W. *Proudhon*. London: H. Hamilton, 1934.

Brown, G. Introduction to *How We Shall Bring about the Revolution: Syndicalism and the Co-operative Commonwealth*, edited by E. Pataud and E. Pouget. London: Pluto Press, 1990.

Brown, M. R. "The IWW and the Negro Worker." PhD diss., Ball State University at Muncie, 1968.

Brown, T. *The Social General Strike*. Durban: Zabalaza Books, n.d.

Buhlungu, S. M. "Democracy and Modernisation in the Making of the South African Trade Union Movement: The Dilemma of Leadership, 1973–2000." PhD diss., University of the Witwatersrand, 2000.

Bukharin, N. *The ABC of Communism*. 1922. Reprint, Ann Arbor: University of Michigan Press, 1966.

Burgmann, V. *Revolutionary Industrial Unionism: The IWW in Australia*. Cambridge: Cambridge University Press, 1995.

Buzo, A. *The Making of Modern Korea*. New York: Routledge, 2002.

Cahm, C. *Kropotkin and the Rise of Revolutionary Anarchism, 1872–1886*. Cambridge: Cambridge University Press, 1989.

Carey, G. W. "The Vessel, the Deed, and the Idea: Anarchists in Paterson, 1895–1908." *Antipode: A Radical Journal of Geography* 10–11, nos. 3 and 1 (1979).

Carpena, P. "Spain 1936: *Free Women*, a Feminist, Proletarian, and Anarchist Movement." In *Women of the Mediterranean*, edited by M. Gadant. London: Zed Books, 1986.

Carr, B. "Marxism and Anarchism in the Formation of the Mexican Communist Party, 1910–19." *Hispanic American Historical Review* 63, no. 2 (1983).

Carr, E. H. *Michael Bakunin*. Rev. ed. Basingstoke, UK: Macmillan, 1975.

Carter, A. *The Political Theory of Anarchism*. London: Routledge and Kegan Paul, 1971.

Casanovas, J. "Labour and Colonialism in Cuba in the Second Half of the Nineteenth-Century." PhD diss., State University of New York, 1994.

———. "Slavery, the Labour Movement, and Spanish Colonialism in Cuba, 1850–1890." *International Review of Social History* 40 (1995).

Castilla, F. *Anarchism without Adjectives: From Yesterday to Today*. January 23, 2007. Available at http://www.anarkismo.net/newswire.php?story_id=4717&print_page=true (accessed January 24, 2007).

Caulfield, N. "Wobblies and Mexican Workers in Petroleum, 1905–1924." *International Review of Social History* 40 (1995).

Chaplin, R. *The General Strike*. 1933. Reprint, Chicago: IWW, 1985.

Chomsky, N. *American Power and the New Mandarins*. New York: Penguin, 1970.

Christie, S. *We, the Anarchists: A Study of the Iberian Anarchist Federation, 1927–1937*. Hastings, UK: Meltzer Press, 2000.

Cipko, S. "Mikhail Bakunin and the National Question." *Raven* 3, no. 1 (1990).

Clark, J. P. *The Philosophical Anarchism of William Godwin*. Princeton, NJ: Princeton University Press, 1977.

"The Class Struggle Declared Criminal." *International*, January 4, 1918.

Class War Federation. *Unfinished Business: The Politics of Class War*. London: Class War Federation, 1992.

Cleaver, H. "Kropotkin, Self-Valorization, and the Crisis of Marxism." Paper presented at the conference on Pyotr Alexeevich Kropotkin organized by the Russian Academy of Science on the 150th anniversary of his birth, Moscow, December 8–14, 1992.

CNT. "The Libertarian Ideal in Bolivia." *Freedom: Anarchist Fortnightly*, June 12, 1999.

Cockcroft, J. D. *Mexico: Class Formation, Capital Accumulation, and the State*. New York: Monthly Review Press, 1968.

Colombo, M. "Armando Borghi." *Le Monde Libertaire*, November 10, 1988.

Comintern. "Theses on the National and Colonial Question Adopted by the Second Comintern Congress." In *The Communist International, 1919–1943: Documents*, edited by J. Degras. 1920. Reprint, London: Frank Cass and Co., 1971.

———. "Theses on the Eastern Question Adopted by the Fourth Comintern Congress." In *The Communist International, 1919–1943: Documents*, edited by J. Degras. 1922.

Reprint, London: Frank Cass and Co., 1971.

Connolly, J. *Socialism Made Easy*. Chicago: Charles H. Kerr, 1909.

———. *Labour in Irish History*. Cork: Corpus of Electronic Texts, 1910.

Conrad, R. E. "Translators' Introduction." In *Sandino: The Testimony of a Nicaraguan Patriot, 1921–1934*, edited by S. Ramiréz and R. E. Conrad. Princeton, NJ: Princeton University Press, 1990.

Cook, P. J. "Robert Michels's *Political Parties* in Perspective." *Journal of Politics* 33, no. 3 (1971).

Craparo, S. *Anarchist Communists: A Question of Class; Studies for a Libertarian Alternative Series*. Italy: Federazione dei Comunisti Anarchici, 2005.

Crump, J. "Anarchist Opposition to Japanese Militarism, 1926–1937." *Bulletin of Anarchist Research*, no. 24 (1991).

———. *Hatta Shuzo and Pure Anarchism in Interwar Japan*. New York: St. Martin's Press, 1993.

———. "Anarchism and Nationalism in East Asia." *Anarchist Studies* 4, no. 1 (1996), 45–64.

Darch, C. M. "The Makhnovischna, 1917–1921: Ideology, Nationalism, and Peasant Insurgency in Early Twentieth Century Ukraine." PhD diss., University of Bradford, 1994.

Davis, M. "The Stop Watch and the Wooden Shoe: Scientific Management and the Industrial Workers of the World." In *Workers' Struggles, Past and Present: A Radical America Reader*, edited by J. Green. Philadelphia: Temple University Press, 1984.

———. "Planet of Slums: Urban Involution and the Informal Proletariat." *New Left Review* 26 (2004): 5–34.

"The Deadly Parallel." *International Socialist Review* 17 (April 1917).

de Cleyre, V. de. *Sex Slavery*. April 28, 1907. Available at http://dwardmac.pitzer.edu/Anarchist_Archives/bright/cleyre/sexslavery.html (accessed March 15, 2000).

———. *Those Who Marry Do Ill*. Available at http://dwardmac.pitzer.edu/Anarchist_Archives/bright/cleyre/theywhomarry.html (accessed March 15, 2000).

de Jong, R. "Ferdinand Domela Nieuwenhuis." In *Woordenboek van Belgische en Nederlands Vrijdenkers*. Brussels: Vrije Universiteit, 1979.

De Leon, D. *The Preamble of the Industrial Workers of the World, Address Delivered at Union Temple, Minneapolis, Minnesota, July 10, 1905*. 1905. Reprint, Edinburgh: Socialist Labour Press, n.d.

———. "With Marx for Text." *Daily People*, June 29, 1907.

——— [Socialist Labour Party, pseud.]. *The Socialist Labour Party: Its Aims and Methods*. Edinburgh: Socialist Labour Press, 1908.

———. "Syndicalism." *Daily People*, August 3, 1909.

———. "Getting Something Now." *Daily People*, September 6, 1910.

———. "Industrial Unionism." *Daily People*, January 20, 1913.

Delhom, J. "Ambiguïtés de la Question Raciale dans les Essais de Manuel González Prada." In *Les Noirs et le Discours Identitaire Latino-américain*, edited by V. Lavou. Perpignan, France: CRILAUP-Presses Universitaires de Perpignan, 1997.

De Shazo, P. *Urban Workers and Labor Unions in Chile, 1902–1927*. Madison: University of Wisconsin Press, 1983.

Devis, R. "Praxedis Guerrero: Early Revolutionary; Revolution Is Beautiful." *Monthly Review* 37, no. 12 (1985).

Dirlik, A. *The Origins of Chinese Communism*. Oxford: Oxford University Press, 1989.

———. *Anarchism in the Chinese Revolution*. Berkeley: University of California Press, 1991.

"Disunity of Labour." *International*, September 22, 1916.

Dolgoff, S., ed. *Bakunin on Anarchy: Selected Works by the Activist-Founder of World Anarchism*. London: George Allen and Unwin, 1971.

———. Introduction to *Bakunin on Anarchy: Selected Works by the Activist-Founder of World Anarchism*, edited by S. Dolgoff. London: George Allen and Unwin, 1971.

———. *Fragments: A Memoir*. London: Refract Publications, 1986.

Dong-hyun Huh. "Forms of Acceptance of Social Darwinism by the Korean Progressives of the 1880s–1890s." *International Journal of Korean History* 2 (2001): 41–63.

Drinnon, R. *Rebel in Paradise: A Biography of Emma Goldman*. Chicago: University of Chicago Press, 1961.

Dubofsky, M. "The Origins of Western Working-Class Radicalism." *Labour History*, no. 7 (1966).

———. *We Shall Be All: A History of the IWW*. Chicago: Quadrangle Books, 1969.

———. *"Big Bill" Haywood*. Manchester: Manchester University Press, 1987.

———. "The Rise and Fall of Revolutionary Syndicalism in the United States." In *Revolutionary Syndicalism: An International Perspective*, edited by M. van der Linden and W. Thorpe. Otterup, Denmark: Scolar Press, 1990.

DuBois, W. E. B. *The Souls of Black Folk*. Based on 1953 rev. ed. 1903. Reprint, New York: Bantam, 1989.

Duin, P. van. "South Africa." In *The Formation of Labour Movements, 1870–1914*, edited by M. van der Linden and J. Rojahn. Leiden: E. J. Brill, 1990.

Dutch, R. A. *Roget's Thesaurus of English Words and Phrases*. Rev. ed. London: Longmans, Green and Co., 1962.

Edwards, O. D., and B. Ransome. Introduction to *James Connolly: Selected Political Writings*, edited by O. D. Edwards and B. Ransome. London: Jonathan Cape, 1973.

Edwards, S., ed. *Selected Writings of Pierre-Joseph Proudhon*. Basingstoke, UK: Macmillan, 1969.

Eltzbacher, P. *Anarchism: Exponents of the Anarchist Philosophy*. 1900. Reprint, London: Freedom Press, 1960.

Em, H. H. "Nationalism, Post-Nationalism, and Shin Ch'ae Ho." *Korea Journal* 39, no. 2 (1999).

Engels, F. "Letter to C. Cuno in Milan." In *Marx, Engels, Lenin: Anarchism and Anarcho-syndicalism*, edited by N. Y. Kolpinsky. January 24, 1872. Reprint, Moscow: Progress Publishers, 1972.

———. "The Bakuninists at Work: An Account of the Spanish Revolt in the Summer of 1873." In *Marx, Engels, Lenin: Anarchism and Anarcho-syndicalism*, edited by N. Y. Kolpinsky. 1873. Reprint, Moscow: Progress Publishers, 1972.

———. "On Authority." In *Marx, Engels, Lenin: Anarchism and Anarcho-syndicalism*, edited by N. Y. Kolpinsky. 1873. Reprint, Moscow: Progress Publishers, 1972.

———. *Socialism: Utopian and Scientific*. 1883. Reprint, Chicago: Charles H. Kerr, 1917.

———. *The Origin of the Family, Private Property, and the State*. 1884. Reprint, Moscow: Progress Publishers, 1948.

Epstein, B. "Anarchism and the Anti-Globalisation Movement." *Monthly Review* 53, no. 4 (2001).

Ettor, J. J. *Industrial Unionism: The Road to Freedom.* Cleveland, OH: IWW Publishing Bureau, 1913.

Farmer, D. "Emma Goldman: A Voice for Women?" *Raven* 23, no. 6 (1993).

FdCA. *Towards a Programme of Conflictual, Class-Struggle Syndicalism.* 2005. Available at http://www.fdca.it/fdcaen/labour/towards_a_platform.htm (accessed November 1, 2005).

Federation of Anarchist Communists of Bulgaria. *Platform of the Federation of Anarchist Communists of Bulgaria.* 1945. Available at http://www.anarkismo.net/newswire.php?story_id=2526 (accessed March 3, 2006).

Feeley, F. "French School Teachers against Militarism, 1903–18." *Historian* 57, no. 2 (1994).

Fernandez, F. *Cuban Anarchism: The History of a Movement.* Chapter 1. Tucson, AZ: See Sharp Press, 2001. Available at http://www.illegalvoices.org/bookshelf/cuban_anarchism/chapter_1_colonialsm_and_separatism_1865-1898_.html (accessed June 27, 2006).

———. *Cuban Anarchism: The History of a Movement.* Chapter 2. Tucson, AZ: See Sharp Press, 2001. Available at http://www.illegalvoices.org/bookshelf/cuban_anarchism/chapter_2_intervention_and_republic_1899-1933_.html (accessed June 27, 2006).

Feyerabend, P. *Against Method: Outline of an Anarchistic Theory of Knowledge.* London: New Left Books, 1975.

Fine, B. *Marx's "Capital."* London: Macmillan, 1975.

Fischer, A. "Adolph Fischer." In *Anarchism: Its Philosophy and Scientific Basis*, edited by Albert R. Parsons. 1887. Reprint, New York: Kraus Reprint Co., 1971.

Fleming, M. *The Anarchist Way to Socialism: Elisée Reclus and Nineteenth-Century European Anarchism.* London: Croom Helm, 1979.

Fleshin, S., Voline, M. Steimer, Sobol, J. Schwartz, Lia, Roman, and Ervantian. *Reply to the Platform (Synthesist)*, 1927.

Flood, A. "Bakunin's Idea of Revolution and Revolutionary Organisation." *Red and Black Revolution: A Magazine of Libertarian Communism*, no. 6 (2002).

Flynn, E. G. "Memories of the Industrial Workers of the World (IWW)." 1962. Reprint, *Original Occasional Papers Series, American Institute for Marxist Studies*, no. 24 (1977).

———. *The Rebel Girl: An Autobiography, My First Life (1906–1926).* Rev. ed. New York: International Publishers, 1973.

Foner, P. S. *The Industrial Workers of the World, 1905–17.* New York: International Publishers, 1965.

———. "The IWW and the Black Worker." *Journal of Negro History* 55, no. 1 (1974): 45–64.

———. *Organised Labour and the Black Worker, 1619–1973.* New York: International Publishers, 1974.

Fonesca, C., T. Borge, D. Ortega, H. Ortega, and J. Wheelock. *Sandinistas Speak: Speeches, Writings, and Interviews with Leaders of Nicaragua's Revolution.* New York: Pathfinder Press, 1986.

Fontenis, G. *Manifesto of Libertarian Communism.* 1953. Reprint, London: Anarchist Communist Federation, 1989.

Foot, D. *Red Prelude: A Life of A. I. Zhelyabov.* London: Cresset Press, 1968.

Ford, E. C., and W. Z. Foster. *Syndicalism.* Facsimile copy with new introduction by J. R. Barrett. 1912. Reprint, Chicago: Charles H. Kerr, 1990.

Forman, M. *Nationalism and the International Labor Movement: The Idea of the Nation in Socialist and Anarchist Theory*. University Park: Pennsylvania State University Press, 1998.

Foster, W. Z. *The Railroaders' Next Step*. Chicago: Trade Union Educational League, Labor Herald Pamphlets, no. 1, 1921.

———. *From Bryan to Stalin*. London: Lawrence and Wishart, 1936.

Fowler, R. B. "The Anarchist Tradition of Political Thought." *Western Political Quarterly* 25, no. 4 (1972).

Frader, L. "Socialists, Syndicalists, and the Peasant Question in the Aude." *Journal of Social History* 19, no. 3 (1985–1986).

Freeman, J. *The Tyranny of Structurelessness*. Hull, UK: Anarchist Workers' Association, 1970.

Freire, J. *Freedom Fighters: Anarchist Intellectuals, Workers, and Soldiers in Portugal's History*. Montréal: Black Rose, 2001.

Friedman, M., with R. Friedman. *Capitalism and Freedom*. Chicago: University of Chicago Press, 1962.

Friends of Durruti. *Towards a Fresh Revolution*. 1938. Reprint, Durban: Zabalaza Books, 1978.

Fukuyama, F. "The End of History?" *National Interest* (Summer 1989).

Gallacher, W. *Revolt on the Clyde*. 4th ed. 1936. Reprint, London: Lawrence and Wishart, 1978.

Galleani, L. *The End of Anarchism?* 1925. Reprint, Orkney, Scotland: Cienfuegos Press, 1982.

Gallin, D., and P. Horn. *Organising Informal Women Workers*. March 2005. Available at http://www.streetnet.org.za/english/GallinHornpaper.htm (accessed September 2006).

Gardell, M. "A Conference in Spain." *SAC-Kontakt* (December 1992).

Gerber, J. *Anton Pannekoek and the Socialism of Workers' Self-Emancipation, 1873–1960*. Dordrecht: Kluwer Academic Publishers, 1989.

Giddens, A. *Capitalism and Modern Social Theory: An Analysis of the Writings of Marx, Durkheim, and Max Weber*. Cambridge: Cambridge University Press, 1971.

Gi-Wook Shin. *Peasant Protest and Social Change in Colonial Korea*. Seattle: University of Washington Press, 1996.

Gluckstein, D. *The Western Soviets: Workers' Councils versus Parliament, 1915–1920*. London: Bookmarks, 1985.

Godwin, W. *Enquiry concerning Political Justice, with Selections from Godwin's Other Writings*, edited and abridged by K. Cordell Carter. 1798. Reprint, London: Clarendon Press, 1971.

Golden, L. "The Libertarian Movement in Contemporary Spanish Politics." *Antipode: A Radical Journal of Geography* 10–11, nos. 3 and 1 (1979).

Goldman, E. "What I Believe." In *Red Emma Speaks: Selected Writings and Speeches*, edited by A. K. Shulman. 1908. Reprint, New York: Vintage Books, 1972.

———. "Marriage and Love." In *Red Emma Speaks: Selected Writings and Speeches*, edited by A. K. Shulman. 1911. Reprint, New York: Vintage Books, 1972.

———. "The Traffic in Women." In *Red Emma Speaks: Selected Writings and Speeches*, edited by A. K. Shulman. 1911. Reprint, New York: Vintage Books, 1972.

———. "The Tragedy of Women's Emancipation." In *Red Emma Speaks: Selected Writings and Speeches*, edited by A. K. Shulman. 1911. Reprint, New York: Vintage Books, 1972.

————. "Jealousy: Causes and a Possible Cure." In *Red Emma Speaks: Selected Writings and Speeches*, edited by A. K. Shulman. 1912. Reprint, New York: Vintage Books, 1972.

————. *Syndicalism: The Modern Menace to Capitalism*. New York: Mother Earth Publishing Association, 1913.

————. *My Disillusionment in Russia*. New York: Doubleday, Page and Company, 1923.

————. "The Failure of the Russian Revolution." In *The Anarchist Reader*, edited by G. Woodcock. 1924. Reprint, Glasgow: Fontana/Collins, 1977.

————. *Living My Life*. 2 vols. 1931. Reprint, London: Pluto Press, 1988.

————. *Trotsky Protests Too Much*. Anarchist Communist Federation, 1938. Available at http://sunsite.berkeley.edu/Goldman/Writings/Essays/trotsky.html (accessed February 19, 2004).

Goldman, E., A. Berkman, E. Malatesta et al. "International Anarchist Manifesto against War." In *Anarchism: A Documentary History of Libertarian Ideas, Volume 1: From Anarchy to Anarchism, 300 CE to 1939*, edited by R. Graham. 1915. Reprint, Montréal: Black Rose, 2005.

Gombin, G. *The Radical Tradition: A Study in Modern Revolutionary Thought*. London: Methuen and Co., 1978.

González Prada, M. "Our Indians." In *Anarchism: A Documentary History of Libertarian Ideas, Volume 1: From Anarchy to Anarchism, 300 CE to 1939*, edited by R. Graham. 1904. Reprint, Montréal: Black Rose, 2005.

————. "Revolution." In *Free Pages and Other Essays: Anarchist Musings: Manuel González Prada*, edited by D. Sobrevilla. 1907. Reprint, New York: Oxford University Press, 2003.

————. "The Two Nations." In *Free Pages and Other Essays: Anarchist Musings: Manuel González Prada*, edited by D. Sobrevilla. New York: Oxford University Press, 2003.

Gordon, E. A. "Anarchism in Brazil: Theory and Practice, 1890–1920." PhD diss., Tulane University, 1978.

Gorman, A. "Anarchists in Education: The Free Popular University in Egypt (1901)." *Middle Eastern Studies* 41, no. 3 (2005).

Gouldner, A. W. *The Two Marxisms: Contradictions and Anomalies in the Development of Theory*. Vol. 11. Houndmills, UK: Macmillan, 1980.

————. "Marx's Last Battle: Bakunin and the First International." *Theory and Society* 11, no. 6 (1982).

Graeber, D. "The New Anarchists." *New Left Review* 13 (2002).

Graham, R., ed. *Anarchism: A Documentary History of Libertarian Ideas, Volume 1: From Anarchy to Anarchism, 300 CE to 1939*. Montréal: Black Rose, 2005.

————. Preface to *Anarchism: A Documentary History of Libertarian Ideas, Volume 1: From Anarchy to Anarchism, 300 CE to 1939*, edited by R. Graham. Montréal: Black Rose, 2005.

"The Great Unskilled." *International*, February 9, 1917.

Green, J. R. "The Brotherhood of Timber Workers, 1910–1913: A Radical Response to Industrial Capitalism in the Southern U.S.A." *Past and Present*, no. 60 (1973).

Gregor, A. J. *Young Mussolini and the Intellectual Origins of Fascism*. Berkeley: University of California Press, 1979.

Group of Russian Anarchists Abroad. *Supplement to the Organisational Platform (Questions and Answers)*. 1926. Available at http://www.nestormakhno.info/english/supporg.htm (accessed March 15, 2004).

Guérin, D. *Anarchism: From Theory to Practice*. New York: Monthly Review Press, 1970.

———. "Marxism and Anarchism." In *For Anarchism: History, Theory, and Practice*, edited by D. Goodway. London: Routledge, 1989.

———, ed. *No Gods, No Masters: An Anthology of Anarchism, Book One*. Oakland: AK Press, 1998.

Guevara, C. "At the Afro-Asian Conference." In *Ché Guevara Speaks: Selected Speeches and Writings*, edited by J. Hansen. London: Pathfinder Press, 1967.

———. "Guerrilla Warfare: A Method." In *Ché Guevara Speaks: Selected Speeches and Writings*, edited by J. Hansen. London: Pathfinder Press, 1967.

———. "Notes on Man and Socialism in Cuba." In *Ché Guevara Speaks: Selected Speeches and Writings*, edited by J. Hansen. London: Pathfinder Press, 1967.

Guillamón, A. *The Friends of Durruti Group, 1937–1939*. Oakland: AK Press, 1996.

Guillaume, J. "On Building the New Social Order." In *Bakunin on Anarchy: Selected Works by the Activist-Founder of World Anarchism*, edited by S. Dolgoff. 1876. Reprint, London: George Allen and Unwin, 1971.

———. "A Biographical Sketch [Bakunin]." In *Bakunin on Anarchy: Selected Works by the Activist-Founder of World Anarchism*, edited by S. Dolgoff. London: George Allen and Unwin, 1971.

Guillen, A. *Anarchist Economics: The Economics of the Spanish Libertarian Collectives, 1936–39*. Durban: Zabalaza Books, 1992.

Ha Ki Rak. *A History of Korean Anarchist Movement* [*sic.*]. Taegu, South Korea: Anarchist Publishing Committee, 1988.

Hadfield, R. "Politics and Protest in the Spanish Anarchist Movement: Libertarian Women in Early Twentieth-Century Barcelona." *University of Sussex Journal of Contemporary History*, no. 3 (2001).

Hane, M., ed. *Reflections on the Way to the Gallows: Voices of Japanese Rebel Women*. New York: Pantheon Books, 1988.

Hanlon, F. "Industrial Unionism: The History of the Industrial Workers of the World in Aotearoa." In *Industrial Unionism: The History of the Industrial Workers of the World in Aotearoa: Aim, Form, and Tactics of a Workers' Union on IWW Lines*. 1913. Reprint, Wellington: Rebel Press, 2006.

Harman, C. *A People's History of the World*. London: Bookmarks, 1999.

Harmsen, G. "Nieuwenhuis, Ferdinand." In *Biografisch Woordenboek van het Socialisme an de Arbeidersbeweging in Nederland*. Amsterdam: International Institute of Social History, 1995.

Harper, C. *Anarchy: A Graphic Guide*. London: Camden Press, 1987.

Hart, J. *Anarchism and the Mexican Working Class, 1860–1931*. Austin: University of Texas Press, 1978.

———. "Revolutionary Syndicalism in Mexico." In *Revolutionary Syndicalism: An International Perspective*, edited by M. van der Linden and W. Thorpe. Otterup, Denmark: Scolar Press, 1990.

———. *Plotino Rhodakanaty: The Actions of a Greek Anarchist in Mexico*. East Brunswick, Australia: No God, No Master Anarchist Pamphlets, n.d.

Hart, K. "Oral Culture and Anti-Colonialism in Louise Michel's *Memoires* (1886) and *Légendes et chants de gestes* (1885)." *Nineteenth-Century French Studies* 30, no. 2 (2001): 107–20.

Hatta Shuzo. "On Syndicalism." In *Anarchism: A Documentary History of Libertarian Ideas, Volume 1: From Anarchy to Anarchism, 300 CE to 1939*, edited by R. Graham. 1927. Reprint, Montréal: Black Rose, 2005.

Hayek, F. A. von. *The Road to Serfdom*. London: Routledge, 1944.

Haywood, W. D., and F. Bohm. *Industrial Socialism*. Chicago: Charles H. Kerr, 1911.

Heath, N. "Historical Introduction." In *The Organisational Platform of the Libertarian Communists*, edited by P. Archinov, N. Makhno, I. Mett, Valevsky, and Linsky. Dublin: Workers Solidarity Movement, 2001.

Hewitt, M. "Emma Goldman: The Case for Anarcho-feminism." In *The Anarchist Papers*, edited by D. I. Roussopoulus. Montréal: Black Rose, 1986.

Himka, J. P. "Young Radicals and Independent Statehood: The Idea of a Ukrainian Nation-state, 1890–1895." *Slavic Review* 41, no. 2 (1982), 219–35.

Hinton, J. *The First Shop Stewards Movement*. London: George Allen and Unwin, 1973.

Hirsch, S. J. "The Anarcho-Syndicalist Roots of a Multi-Class Alliance: Organised Labor and the Peruvian Aprista Party, 1900–1933." PhD diss., George Washington University, 1997.

Hirst, P. "The Global Economy: Myths and Realities." *International Affairs* 73, no. 3 (1977).

Hobsbawm, E. *Primitive Rebels: Studies in Archaic Forms of Social Movement in the 19th and 20th Centuries*. 3rd ed. Manchester: Manchester University Press, 1971.

———. *The Age of Capital, 1848–1875*. London: Abacus, 1977.

———. *Revolutionaries*. London: Abacus, 1993.

Hodges, D. *Intellectual Foundations of the Nicaraguan Revolution*. Austin: University of Texas Press, 1986.

Hoffman, R. Introduction to *Anarchism*, edited by R. Hoffman. New York: Atherton Press, 1970.

Holloway, J. *Change the World without Taking Power: The Meaning of Revolution for Today*. Rev. ed. London: Pluto Press, 2005.

Holton, R. J. *British Syndicalism: Myths and Realities*. London: Pluto Press, 1976.

———. "Syndicalist Theories of the State." *Sociological Review* 28, no. 1 (1980).

Hopkins, A. G. "The History of Globalisation—and the Globalisation of History?" In *Globalisation and World History*, edited by A. G. Hopkins. London: Pimlico, 2002.

Horowitz, I. L. *Radicalism and the Revolt against Reason: The Social Theories of Georges Sorel*. London: Humanities Press, 1961.

Howell, D. "Taking Syndicalism Seriously." *Socialist History* 16 (2000).

Hutton, J. "Camillo Pissarro's *Turpitudes Sociales* and Late Nineteenth-Century French Anarchist Anti-Feminism." *History Workshop: A Journal of Socialist and Feminist Historians*, no. 24 (1987), 32–61.

Hyman, R. *Marxism and the Sociology of Trade Unionism*. London: Pluto Press, 1971.

Ignatiev, N. *How the Irish Became White*. New York: Routledge, 1995.

Ignatiev, N., and J. Garvey, ed. *Race Traitor*. London: Routledge, 1996.

Industrial and Commercial Workers Union of Africa. "Revised Constitution of the ICU." In *From Protest to Challenge: A Documentary History of African Politics in South Africa, 1882–1964*, edited by G. M. Carter and T. Karis. 1925. Reprint, Bloomington: Indiana University Press, 1972.

Industrial Workers of the World. *What Is the IWW? A Candid Statement of Its Principles, Objects, and Methods.* 2nd ed. Chicago: IWW Publishing Bureau, 1924. Available at http://www.workerseducation.org/crutch/pamphlets/whatistheiww.html (June 15, 2004).

―――. *The IWW: What It Is and What It Is Not.* Chicago: IWW Publishing Bureau, 1928.

―――. *The IWW in Theory and Practice.* 5th rev. ed. Chicago: IWW Publishing Bureau, 1937. Available at http://www.workerseducation.org/crutch/pamphlets/ebert/ebert_5th.html (accessed July 20, 2004).

International Working People's Association. "The Pittsburgh Proclamation." In *Anarchism: A Documentary History of Libertarian Ideas, Volume 1: From Anarchy to Anarchism, 300 CE to 1939,* edited by R. Graham. 1883. Reprint, Montréal: Black Rose, 2005.

Isidine, M. *Organisation and Party.* First published in *Plus Lion,* nos. 36–37 (1928). Available at http://www.nestormakhno.info/english/isidine.htm (accessed March 30, 2004).

"Italian Syndicalism and Fascism." *Black Flag: For Anarchist Resistance,* no. 217 (1999).

Ivanova, G. M. *Labor Camp Socialism: The Gulag in the Soviet Totalitarian System.* New York: M. E. Sharp, 2000.

Jacker, C. *The Black Flag of Anarchy: Antistatism in the United States.* New York: Charles Scribner's Sons, 1968.

Jackson, G. D. "Peasant Political Movements in Eastern Europe." In *Rural Protest: Peasant Movements and Social Change,* edited by H. A. Landsberger. London: Macmillan, 1974.

Jennings, J. R. *Georges Sorel: The Character and Development of His Thought.* Basingstoke, UK: Macmillan, 1985.

―――. "The CGT and the Couriau Affair: Syndicalist Responses to Female Labour in France before 1914." *European History Quarterly* 21 (1991).

Jensen, R. "'No Irish Need Apply': A Myth of Victimisation." *Journal of Social History* 36, no. 2 (2002), 405–29.

Johanningsmeier, E. P. "William Z. Foster and the Syndicalist League of North America." *Labour History* 30, no. 3 (1985).

Johnpoll, B. K., and L. Johnpoll. *The Impossible Dream: The Rise and Decline of the American Left.* Westport, CT: Greenwood Press, 1981.

Joll, J. *The Anarchists.* London: Methuen and Co., 1964.

―――. *The Second International, 1889–1914.* New York: Harper Colophon Books, 1966.

Kaplan, T. "The Social Base of Nineteenth-Century Andalusian Anarchism in Jerez de la Frontera." *Journal of Interdisciplinary History* 6, no. 1 (1975).

―――. *Anarchists of Andalusia, 1868–1903.* Princeton, NJ: Princeton University Press, 1977.

―――. "Other Scenarios: Women and Spanish Anarchism." In *Becoming Visible: Women in European History,* edited by R. Bridenthal and C. Koonz. Boston: Houghton Mifflin Co., 1977.

Kedward, R. *The Anarchists: The Men Who Shocked an Era.* London: Library of the Twentieth Century, 1971.

Kelly, A. *Mikhail Bakunin: A Study in the Psychology and Politics of Utopianism.* Oxford: Clarendon Press, 1982.

Kenafick, K. J. "The Life of Bakunin." In *Marxism, Freedom, and the State,* edited by K. J. Kenafick. London: Freedom Press, 1990.

Kennedy, M., and C. Tilly. "Socialism, Feminism, and the Stillbirth of Socialist Feminism in Europe, 1890–1920." *Science and Society* 51, no. 1 (1987): 6–42.

Khadziev, G. *"Down with the Sultan, Long Live the Balkan Federation!" The 1903 Risings in Macedonia and Thrace*. 1992. Available at http://flag.blackened.net/revolt/bulgaria_1903.html (January 10, 2003).

Khuri-Makdisi, I. "Levantine Trajectories: The Formulation and Dissemination of Radical Ideas in and between Beirut, Cairo, and Alexandria, 1860–1914." PhD diss., Harvard University, 2003.

Kinna, R. "Kropotkin's Theory of Mutual Aid in Historical Context." *International Review of Social History* 40, part 2 (1995).

Knowles, R. "Political Economy from Below: Communitarian Anarchism as a Neglected Discourse in Histories of Economic Thought." *History of Economics Review*, no. 31 (2000).

Kostick, C. *Revolution in Ireland: Popular Militancy 1917 to 1923*. London: Pluto Press, 1996.

Kottis, L. *Konstantinos Speras: The Life and Activities of a Greek Anarcho-syndicalist*. London: Kate Sharpley Library, 2000.

Krikler, J. *Rand Revolt: The 1922 Insurrection and Racial Killings in South Africa*. Cape Town: Jonathon Ball, 2005.

Kropotkin, P. "Prisons and Their Moral Influence on Prisoners." In *Kropotkin's Revolutionary Pamphlets: A Collection of Writings by Peter Kropotkin*, edited by R. N. Baldwin. 1877. Reprint, New York: Dover Publications, 1970.

———. "An Appeal to the Young." In *Kropotkin's Revolutionary Pamphlets: A Collection of Writings by Peter Kropotkin*, edited by R. N. Baldwin. 1880. Reprint, New York: Dover Publications, 1970.

———. "The Spirit of Revolt." In *Kropotkin's Revolutionary Pamphlets: A Collection of Writings by Peter Kropotkin*, edited by R. N. Baldwin. 1880. Reprint, New York: Dover Publications, 1970.

———. *The Place of Anarchism in Socialistic Evolution*. 1886. Reprint, Cyrmu: Practical Parasite Publications, 1990.

———. "Anarchist Communism: Its Basis and Principles." In *Kropotkin's Revolutionary Pamphlets: A Collection of Writings by Peter Kropotkin*, edited by R. N. Baldwin. 1887. Reprint, New York: Dover Publications, 1970.

———. *In Russian and French Prisons*. 1887. Reprint, New York: Schocken Books, 1971.

———. "Anarchist Morality." In *Kropotkin's Revolutionary Pamphlets: A Collection of Writings by Peter Kropotkin*, edited by R. N. Baldwin. 1890. Reprint, New York: Dover Publications, 1970.

———. *The Conquest of Bread*. 1892. Reprint, London: Elephant Editions, 1990.

———. *Memoirs of a Revolutionist*. 1899. Reprint, New York: Dover Publications, 1980.

———. "Letter to Nettlau." In *Selected Writings on Anarchism and Revolution: P. A. Kropotkin*, edited by M. A. Miller. March 5, 1902. Reprint, Cambridge, MA: MIT Press, 1970.

———. *Mutual Aid: A Factor of Evolution*. 1902. Reprint, New York: Penguin Books, 1939.

———. "Anarchism." In *Kropotkin's Revolutionary Pamphlets: A Collection of Writings by Peter Kropotkin*, edited by R. N. Baldwin. 1905. Reprint, New York: Dover Publications, 1970.

———. *The Great French Revolution, 1789–1973, Volume 1*. Introduction by Alfredo M. Bonanno. 1909. Reprint, London: Elephant Editions, 1986.

———. "Modern Science and Anarchism." In *Kropotkin's Revolutionary Pamphlets: A Collection of Writings by Peter Kropotkin*, edited by R. N. Baldwin. 1912. Reprint, New York: Dover Publications, 1970.

———. *War!* William Reeves, 1914. Available at http://dwardmac.pitzer.edu/Anarchist_Archives/kropotkin/War!/war!1.html (accessed April 1, 2000).

———. "Letter to the Workers of Western Europe." In *Kropotkin's Revolutionary Pamphlets: A Collection of Writings by Peter Kropotkin*, edited by R. N. Baldwin. April 28, 1919. Reprint, New York: Dover Publications, 1970.

Kropotkin, P., and H. Glasse. *Organised Vengeance, Called "Justice"/The Superstition of Government*. London: Freedom Press, 1902.

Krugman, P. "For Richer." *New York Times Magazine*, October 20, 2002.

Kubo Yuzuru. "On Class Struggle and the Daily Struggle." In *Anarchism: A Documentary History of Libertarian Ideas, Volume 1: From Anarchy to Anarchism, 300 CE to 1939*, edited by R. Graham. 1928. Reprint, Montréal: Black Rose, 2005.

Lambert, R. V. "Political Unionism in South Africa: The South African Congress of Trade Unions, 1955–1965." PhD diss., University of the Witwatersrand, 1988.

Lavrin, J. *Tolstoy: An Approach*. London: Methuen and Co., 1944.

Leeder, E. "Let Our Mothers Show the Way." In *Reinventing Anarchy, Again*, edited by H. J. Ehrlich. Oakland: AK Press, 1996.

Lehning, A. "Cornilessen, Christian." In *Biografisch Woordenboek van het Socialisme en de Arbeidersbeweging in Nederland*. Amsterdam: International Institute of Social History, 1987.

Lenin, V. I. "What Is to Be Done? Burning Questions of Our Movement." In *Selected Works in Three Volumes*, edited by V. I. Lenin. 1902. Reprint, Moscow: Progress Publishers, 1975.

———. "Two Tactics of Social-Democracy in the Democratic Revolution." In *Selected Works in Three Volumes*, edited by V. I. Lenin. 1905. Reprint, Moscow: Progress Publishers, 1975.

———. "The State and Revolution: The Marxist Theory of the State and the Tasks of the Proletariat in the Revolution." In *Selected Works in Three Volumes*, edited by V. I. Lenin. 1917. Reprint, Moscow: Progress Publishers, 1975.

———. "The Immediate Tasks of the Soviet Government." In *Selected Works in Three Volumes*, edited by V. I. Lenin. 1918. Reprint, Moscow: Progress Publishers, 1975.

———. "'Left-wing Communism': An Infantile Disorder." In *Selected Works in Three Volumes*, edited by V. I. Lenin. 1920. Reprint, Moscow: Progress Publishers, 1975.

Levine, L. *Syndicalism in France*. 2nd ed. New York: Columbia University Press, 1914.

Levy, C. "Italian Anarchism, 1870–1926." In *For Anarchism: History, Theory, and Practice*, edited by D. Goodway. London: Routledge, 1989. .

———. "Anarchism, Internationalism, and Nationalism in Europe, 1860–1939." *Australian Journal of Politics and History* 50, no. 3 (2004).

Li Pei Kan. "Anarchism and the Question of Practice." In *Anarchism: A Documentary History of Libertarian Ideas, Volume 1: From Anarchy to Anarchism, 300 CE to 1939*, edited by R. Graham. 1927. Reprint, Montréal: Black Rose, 2005.

Lipset, S. M. *Union Democracy: The Internal Politics of the International Typographical Union*. Glencoe, IL: Free Press, 1956.

Lomas, C. "Transborder Discourse: The Articulation of Gender in the Borderlands in the Early Twentieth Century." *Frontiers* 24, no. 2–3 (2003).

Lopes, M. "Letter from Manuel Lopes." *Workers' Dreadnought*, August 7, 1920.

Lorwin, L. "Syndicalism." In *Encyclopaedia of the Social Sciences*. New York: Macmillan, 1959.

Lowry, B., and E. E. Gunter. Epilogue to *The Red Virgin: Memoirs of Louise Michel*, edited by B. Lowry and E. E. Gunter. Tuscaloosa: University of Alabama Press, 1981.

———. "Translators' Introduction." In *The Red Virgin: Memoirs of Louise Michel*, edited by B. Lowry and E. E. Gunter. Tuscaloosa: University of Alabama Press, 1981.

Mbah, S., and I. E. Igariwey. *African Anarchism: The History of a Movement*. Tucson, AZ: See Sharp Press, 1997.

Mackenzie, N. *Socialism: A Short History*. 2nd ed. London: Hutchinson University Library, 1966.

MacLachlan, C. M. *Anarchism and the Mexican Revolution: The Political Trials of Ricardo Flores Magón in the United States*. Berkeley: University of California Press, 1991.

MacLean, J. "A Scottish Communist Party." In *John MacLean: In the Rapids of Revolution: Essays, Articles, and Letters*, edited by N. Milton. December 1920. Reprint, London: Allison and Busby, 1978.

MacNally, D. *Against the Market: Political Economy, Market Socialism, and the Marxist Critique*. London: Verso, 1993.

Magón, E. F., R. F. Magón, L. Rivera, A. De P. Araujo, and A. L. Figueroa. "To the Workers of the United States." In *Anarchism and the Mexican Revolution: The Political Trials of Ricardo Flores Magón in the United States*, edited by C. M. MacLachlan. April 7, 1914. Reprint, Berkeley: University of California Press, 1991.

Magón, R. F. "*A La Mujer* [To Women]." *Regeneración*, September 24, 1910.

———. "Labour's Solidarity Should Know Neither Race Nor Colour." In *Land and Liberty: Anarchist Influences in the Mexican Revolution: Ricardo Flores Magón*, edited by D. Poole. April 29, 1911. Reprint, Orkney, Scotland: Cienfuegos Press, 1977.

———. "*Sin Jefes* [Without Bosses]." *Regeneración*, March 21, 1914.

Makalsky, L. "To the Worker." In *The Anarchists in the Russian Revolution*, edited by P. Avrich. December 19, 1917. Reprint, London: Thames and Hudson, 1973.

Makhno, N. "A Few Words on the National Question in the Ukraine." In *The Struggle against the State and Other Essays by Nestor Makhno*, edited by A. Skirda. December 1928. Reprint, Oakland: AK Press, 1996.

———. "Letter to Errico Malatesta from Nestor Makhno." In *The Anarchist Revolution: Polemical Writings, 1924–1931: Errico Malatesta*, edited by V. Richards. 1928. Reprint, London: Freedom Press, 1995.

Malatesta, E. *Fra Contadini: A Dialogue on Anarchy*. 1883. Reprint, London: Bratach Dubh, 1981.

———. *Errico Malatesta: His Life and Ideas*, edited by V. Richards. London: Freedom Press, 1965.

———. *The Anarchist Revolution: Polemical Writings, 1924–1931: Errico Malatesta*, edited by V. Richards. London: Freedom Press, 1995.

———. *On Collective Responsibility*, n.d. Available at http://www.nestormakhno.info/english/mal_rep3.htm (March 15, 2004).

Malet, M. *Nestor Makhno in the Russian Civil War*. London: London School of Economics and Political Science, 1982.

Management Committee of the International Socialist League. "International Socialism and the Native: No Labour Movement without the Black Proletariat." *International*, December 7, 1917.

Mann, T. "The Way to Win: An Open Letter to Trades Unionists on Methods of Industrial Organisation, by Tom Mann, Broken Hill, May 1909," *Voice of Labour*, December 31, 1909.

———. *Tom Mann's Memoirs*. 1923. Reprint, London: MacGibbon and Kee, 1967.

Mao Tsetung. "Report on an Investigation of the Peasant Movement in Hunan." In *Selected Readings from the Works of Mao Tsetung*, edited by Editorial Committee for Selected Readings from the Works of Mao Tsetung. 1927. Reprint, Peking: Foreign Languages Press, 1971.

———. "The Chinese Revolution and the Chinese Communist Party." In *Revolutionary Thought in the Twentieth Century*, edited by B. Turok. 1939. Reprint, Johannesburg: Institute for African Alternatives, 1990.

———. "On the People's Democratic Dictatorship: In Commemoration of the Twenty-eighth Anniversary of the Communist Party of China." In *Selected Readings from the Works of Mao Tsetung*, edited by Editorial Committee for Selected Readings from the Works of Mao Tsetung. 1949. Reprint, Peking: Foreign Languages Press, 1971.

———. "On the Correct Handling of Contradictions among the People." In *Selected Readings from the Works of Mao Tsetung*, edited by Editorial Committee for Selected Readings from the Works of Mao Tsetung. 1957. Reprint, Peking: Foreign Languages Press, 1971.

Marcus, B., ed. *Nicaragua: The Sandinista People's Revolution: Speeches by Sandinista Leaders*. New York: Pathfinder Press, 1985.

Marsh, M. S. "The Anarchist-Feminist Response to the 'Woman Question' in Late Nineteenth-Century America." *American Quarterly* 30, no. 4 (1978).

Marshall, P. *Demanding the Impossible: A History of Anarchism*. London: Fontana Press, 1994.

Martin, J. J. Introduction to *The Ego and His Own*, by M. Stirner. 1844. Reprint, New York: Libertarian Book Club, 1963.

———, ed. "Editor's Preface." In *Anarchism: Exponents of the Anarchist Philosophy*, by P. Eltzbacher. London: Freedom Press, 1960.

Marx, K. *The Eighteenth Brumaire of Louis Bonaparte*. 1852. Reprint, Moscow: Progress Publishers, 1983.

———. *A Contribution to the Critique of Political Economy*. 1859. Reprint, London: Lawrence and Wishart, 1971.

———. *Value, Price, and Profit: Addressed to Working Men*. 1865. Reprint, Chicago: Charles H. Kerr, n.d.

———. *Capital: A Critique of Political Economy*. 1867. Reprint, New York: Penguin, 1976.

———. "Letter to Paul Lafargue in Paris." In *Marx, Engels, Lenin: Anarchism and Anarcho-syndicalism*, edited by N. Y. Kolpinsky. April 19, 1870. Reprint, Moscow: Progress Publishers, 1972.

———. *The Gotha Programme*. 1875. Reprint, New York: Socialist Labour Party, 1922.

Marx, K., and F. Engels. *The Communist Manifesto*. 1848. Reprint, Chicago: Henry Regnery Company, 1954.

———. "From the Resolutions of the General Congress Held in the Hague." In *Marx, Engels, Lenin: Anarchism and Anarcho-syndicalism*, edited by N. Y. Kolpinsky. 1872. Reprint, Moscow: Progress Publishers, 1972.

———. "The Alliance of Socialist Democracy and the International Working Men's Association." In *Marx, Engels, Lenin: Anarchism and Anarcho-syndicalism*, edited by N. Y. Kolpinsky. 1873. Reprint, Moscow: Progress Publishers, 1972.

"Marxist Industrial Unionism." *Workers' Dreadnought*, October 19, 1918.

Mattick, P. "Kropokin on *Mutual Aid*: Review." *Western Socialist* (February 1956).

Maura, J. R. "The Spanish Case." In *Anarchism Today*, edited by D. Apter and J. Joll. London: Macmillan, 1971.

Maximoff, G. P. [M. Sergven, pseud.]. "Paths of Revolution." In *The Anarchists in the Russian Revolution*, edited by P. Avrich. September 16, 1918. Reprint, London: Thames and Hudson, 1973.

———. *The Programme of Anarcho-syndicalism*. 1927. Reprint, Sydney: Monty Miller, 1985.

———. *Constructive Anarchism*. 1930. Reprint, Sydney: Monty Miller, 1988.

———. *The Guillotine at Work: Twenty Years of Terror in Russia: The Leninist Counter Revolution*. 1940. Orkney, Scotland: Cienfuegos Press, 1979.

McCoy, P. E. B. "Social Anarchism: An Atavistic Ideology of the Peasant." *Journal of Inter-American Studies and World Affairs* 14, no. 2 (1972).

McGirr, L. "Black and White Longshoremen in the IWW: A History of the Philadelphia Marine Transport Workers Industrial Union Local 8." *Labour History*, no. 36 (1995), 377–402.

McKean, J. "A Fury for Justice: Lucy Parsons and the Revolutionary Anarchist Movement in Chicago." PhD diss., Columbia University, 2006.

McKee, D. K. "The Influence of Syndicalism upon Daniel De Leon." *Historian*, no. 20 (1958).

———. "Daniel De Leon: A Reappraisal." *Labour History*, no. 1 (1960).

McLellan, D. *Karl Marx: His Life and Thought*. Frogmore, UK: Paladin, 1976.

McNally, D. *Socialism from Below*. 2nd ed. Chicago: International Socialist Organisation, 1984.

———. *Against the Market: Political Economy, Market Socialism, and the Marxist Critique*. London: Verso, 1993.

Mehring, F. *Karl Marx: The Story of His Life*. 1936. Reprint, London: George Allen and Unwin, 1951.

Mendel, A. *Michael Bakunin: Roots of Apocalypse*. New York: Praeger, 1981.

Meredith, I. *A Girl among the Anarchists*. 1903. Reprint, Lincoln: University of Nebraska Press, 1992.

Michel, L. *The Red Virgin: Memoirs of Louise Michel*, edited by B. Lowry and E. E. Gunter. 1886. Reprint, Tuscaloosa: University of Alabama Press, 1981.

Michels, R. *Political Parties: A Sociological Study of the Oligarchical Tendencies of Modern Democracy*. 1915. Reprint, New York: Free Press, 1962.

Miliband, R. *Marxism and Politics*. Oxford: Oxford University Press, 1977.

Miller, D. *Anarchism*. London: J. M. Dent and Sons, 1984.

Miller, M. A. Introduction to *Selected Writings on Anarchism and Revolution: P. A. Kropotkin*, edited by M. A. Miller. Cambridge, MA: MIT Press, 1970.

———. *Kropotkin*. Chicago: University of Chicago Press, 1976.

Milton, N. Introduction to *John MacLean: In the Rapids of Revolution: Essays, Articles, and Letters*, edited by N. Milton. London: Allison and Busby, 1978.

"Mineworkers and Political Action." *International*, February 25, 1916.

Mintz, F. "Class War: The Writings of Camillo Berneri." *Cienfuegos Press Anarchist Review*, no. 4 (1978).

Mintz, J. R. *The Anarchists of Casas Vejas*. Chicago: University of Chicago Press, 1982.

Mises, L. von. *Socialism*. 1922. Reprint, Indianapolis, IN: Liberty Classics, 1981.

Mitchell, B. "French Syndicalism: An Experiment in Practical Anarchism." In *Revolutionary Syndicalism: An International Perspective*, edited by M. van der Linden and W. Thorpe. Otterup, Denmark: Scolar Press, 1990.

Mohamed, S. *Appels aux Travailleurs Algériens*, edited by S. Boulouque. 1930. Reprint, Paris: Volonte Anarchiste, 1994.

Molnár, M., and J. Pekmez. "Rural Anarchism in Spain and the 1873 Cantonalist Revolution." In *Rural Protest: Peasant Movements and Social Change*, edited by H. A. Landsberger. London: Macmillan, 1974.

Molyneux, M. "No God, No Boss, No Husband: Anarchist Feminism in Nineteenth-Century Argentina." *Latin American Perspectives* 13, no. 1 (1986).

Monatte, P. "Syndicalism: An Advocacy." In *The Anarchist Reader*, edited by G. Woodcock. 1907. Reprint, Glasgow: Fontana/Collins, 1977.

Moody, K. *Workers in a Lean World: Unions in the International Economy*. London: Verso, 1997.

Morris, B. *Bakunin: The Philosophy of Freedom*. Montréal: Black Rose, 1996.

Morrow, F. *Revolution and Counter Revolution in Spain*. 1938. Reprint, London: New Park Publications, 1963. Available at http://www.marxists.org/archive/morrow-felix/1938/revolution-spain/ (accessed June 30, 2006).

Morton, A. L., and G. Tate. *The British Labour Movement, 1770–1920*. Rev. ed. London: Lawrence and Wishart, 1979.

Most, J. J. *Revolutionare Kriegswissenschaft, together with The Beast of Property*. New York: Kraus Reprint Co., 1983.

Munck, R. *Argentina: From Anarchism to Peronism: Workers, Unions, and Politics, 1855–1985*. London: Zed Books, 1987.

Murphy, J. T. "The Embargo." *Workers' Dreadnought*, August 31, 1918.

National Confederation of Labour. *Resolution on Libertarian Communism as Adopted by the Confederacion Nacional del Trabajo, Zaragoza, 1 May 1936*. May 1, 1936. Reprint, Durban: Zabalaza Books, n.d.

Navarro-Genie, M. "Sin Sandino No Hay Sandinismo: lo que Bendana pretende." Mimeo, n.d.

Nelson, B. C. *Beyond the Martyrs: A Social History of Chicago's Anarchists, 1870–1900*. New Brunswick, NJ: Rutgers University Press, 1988.

Nettlau, M. *A Short History of Anarchism*. 1934. Reprint, London: Freedom Press, 1996.

Nohara Shirō. "Anarchists and the May 4 Movement in China." *Libero International*, no. 1 (January 1975).

"Notes on Natives, No. 1." *International*, March 16, 1917.

Novak, D. "The Place of Anarchism in the History of Political Thought." In *Anarchism*, edited by R. Hoffman. 1958. Reprint, New York: Atherton Press, 1970.

O'Connor, E. *Syndicalism in Ireland, 1917–1923*. Cork: Cork University Press, 1988.

Olmstead, A. L., P. W. Rhode, and J. Morilla Critz. "'Horn of Plenty': The Globalisation of Mediterranean Horticulture and the Economic Development of Southern Europe, 1880–1930." *Journal of Economic History* 59, no. 2 (1999).

Olsen, E. *The Red Feds: Revolutionary Industrial Unionism and the New Zealand Federation of Labour, 1908–14*. Auckland: Oxford University Press, 1988.

Organising Junta of the Mexican Liberal Party. "Manifesto to the Workers of the World." In *Land and Liberty: Anarchist Influences in the Mexican Revolution: Ricardo Flores Magón*, edited by D. Poole. April 8, 1911. Reprint, Orkney, Scotland: Cienfuegos Press, 1977.

Ortiz, B. "Forerunner of Feminism: Praxedis Guerrero, Mexican Writer and Revolutionary." *Monthly Review* 37, no. 12 (1985): 43–47.

Ortiz, V. "*Mujeres Libres*: Anarchist Women in the Spanish Civil War." *Antipode: A Radical Journal of Geography* 10–11, nos. 3 and 1 (1979).

Our Special Representative/Proletarian, "Sundry Jottings from the Cape: A Rebel's Review." *Voice of Labour*, December 1, 1911.

O. V. *Autonomous Base Nucleus*, n.d. Available at http://www.geocities.com/kk_abacus/in-surr2.html (accessed March 30, 2004).

Palczewski, C. H. "Voltairine de Cleyre: Sexual Slavery and Sexual Pleasure in the Nineteenth Century." *NWSA Journal* 7 (1995).

Pankhurst, S. "Zinoviev to the Comintern: A 'Left' Wing View." *Workers' Dreadnought*, August 13, 1921.

"The Pass Laws: Organise for Their Abolition." *International*, October 19, 1917.

Pataud, E., and E. Pouget. *How We Shall Bring about the Revolution: Syndicalism and the Co-operative Commonwealth*. 1909. Reprint, London: Pluto Press, 1990.

Paz, A. *Durruti: The People Armed*. Montréal: Black Rose, 1987.

Peirats, J. *Anarchists in the Spanish Revolution*. 1964. Reprint, London: Freedom Press, 1990.

Pelloutier, F. "Anarchism and the Workers' Union." In *No Gods, No Masters: An Anthology of Anarchism, Book Two*, edited by D. Guérin. 1895. Reprint, Oakland: AK Press, 1998.

Pengam, A. "Anarcho-Communism." In *Non-Market Socialism in the Nineteenth and Twentieth Centuries*, edited by M. Rubel and J. Crump. Basingstoke, UK: Macmillan, 1987.

Perlin, T. M. *Contemporary Anarchism*. New Brunswick, NJ: Transaction Books, 1979.

Perry, E. J. *Shanghai on Strike: The Politics of Chinese Labor*. Stanford, CA: Stanford University Press, 1993.

Perry, G. H. *The Revolutionary IWW*. Chicago: IWW Publishing Bureau, 1913[?].

Peterson, L. "The One Big Union in International Perspective: Revolutionary Industrial Unionism, 1900–1925." In *Work, Community, and Power: The Experiences of Labor in Europe and America*, edited by J. E. Cronin and C. Sirianni. Philadelphia: Temple University Press, 1983.

Petrograd Union of Anarcho-syndicalist Propaganda. "Declaration of the Petrograd Union of Anarcho-syndicalist Propaganda." In *The Anarchists in the Russian Revolution*, edited by P. Avrich. June 4, 1917. Reprint, London: Thames and Hudson, 1973.

Philips, M. P. "The Russian Class Struggle: Bolshevik Syndicalism Leading." In *Dispatches from the Revolution: Russia, 1916–1918: Morgan Price Philips*, edited by T. Rose. December 5, 1917. Reprint, London: Pluto Press, 1997.

Poole, D., ed. *Land and Liberty: Anarchist Influences in the Mexican Revolution: Ricardo Flores Magón*. Orkney, Scotland: Cienfuegos Press, 1977.

———. "The Anarchists in the Mexican Revolution, Part 2: Praxedis G. Geurerro, 1882–1910." *Cienfuegos Press Anarchist Review*, no. 4 (1978).

———. "About Malatesta." In *Fra Contadini: A Dialogue on Anarchy*, edited by E. Malatesta. London: Bratach Dubh, 1981.

Possony, S. T. Introduction to *The Communist Manifesto*, edited by K. Marx and F. Engels. Chicago: Henry Regnery Company, 1954.

Pouget, E. *Direct Action*. London: Fresnes-Antony Group of the French Anarchist Federation, n.d. English translation by Kate Sharpley Library.

Poyo, G. E. "The Anarchist Challenge to the Cuban Independence Movement, 1885–1890." *Cuban Studies* 15, no. 1 (1985), 29–42.

Prebbles, F. *"Trouble Makers": Anarchism and Syndicalism: The Early Years of the Libertarian Movement in Aotearoa/New Zealand*, n.d. Available at http://www.takver.com/history/nz/tm/tm10.htm (accessed June 15, 2005).

Procacci, G. "Popular Protest and Labour Conflict in Italy, 1915–1918." *Social History*, no. 14 (1989).

Proletarian. "The Problem of Coloured Labour." *Voice of Labour*, October 27, 1911.

Purchase, G. *Evolution and Revolution: An Introduction to the Life and Thought of Peter Kropotkin*. Persham, UK: Jura Media, 1996.

Quail, J. *The Slow Burning Fuse: The Lost History of the British Anarchists*. London: Paladin, 1978.

"Questions of the Day." *Workers' Dreadnought*, July 20, 1918.

"Race Prejudice." *International*, February 23, 1916.

Radcliff, P. B. *From Mobilization to Civil War: The Politics of Polarization in the Spanish City of Gijon, 1900–1937*. Cambridge: Cambridge University Press, 1996.

Raftopolous, B. "Nationalism and Labour in Salisbury, 1953–1965." In *Sites of Struggle: Essays in Zimbabwe's Urban History*, edited by B. Raftopolous and T. Yoshikuni. Harare: Weaver Press, 1999.

Ramos R., E. Rodrigues, and A. Samis. *Against All Tyranny! Essays on Anarchism in Brazil*. London: Kate Sharpley Library, 2003.

"Rank and File Convention." *Workers' Dreadnought*, February 14, 1920.

Ransome, B. *Connolly's Marxism*. London: Pluto Press, 1980.

Ravindranathan, T. R. "Bakunin in Naples: An Assessment." *Journal of Modern History* 53, no. 2 (1981).

Regional Workers' Federation of Uruguay. "Declarations from the Third Congress." In *Anarchism: A Documentary History of Libertarian Ideas, Volume 1: From Anarchy to Anarchism, 300 CE to 1939*, edited by R. Graham. 1911. Reprint, Montréal: Black Rose, 2005.

Richards, V, ed. *Errico Malatesta: His Life and Ideas*. London: Freedom Press, 1965.

———. *Lessons of the Spanish Revolution*. Rev. ed. London: Freedom Press, 1983.

———, ed. *The Anarchist Revolution: Polemical Writings, 1924–1931: Errico Malatesta*. London: Freedom Press, 1995.

Rider, N. "The Practice of Direct Action: The Barcelona Rent Strike of 1931." In *For Anarchism: History, Theory, and Practice*, edited by D. Goodway. London: Routledge, 1989.

Ridley, F. F. *Revolutionary Syndicalism in France: The Direct Action of Its Time*. Cambridge: Cambridge University Press, 1970.

Rivera, A. Q., ed. *Workers Struggle in Puerto Rico: A Documentary History.* London: Monthly Review Press, 1976.

Roberts, D. *The Syndicalist Tradition and Italian Fascism.* Chapel Hill: University of North Carolina Press, 1979.

Robinson, C. J. *Black Marxism: The Making of the Black Radical Tradition.* London: Zed Books, 1983.

Rocker, R. "Marxism and Anarchism." In *The Poverty of Statism: Anarchism versus Marxism*, edited by A. Meltzer. 1920. Reprint, Orkney, Scotland: Cienfuegos Press, 1981.

———. *Nationalism and Culture.* 1937. Reprint, Saint Paul, MN: Michael E. Coughlin, 1978.

———. *Anarcho-Syndicalism.* Oakland: AK Press, 2004. Available at http://www.spunk.org/library/writers/rocker/ (accessed November 12, 2000).

Roediger, D. 1991, *The Wages of Whiteness: Race and the Making of the American Working Class.* London: Verso, 1991.

———. *Towards the Abolition of Whiteness: Essays on Race, Politics, and Working Class History.* London: Verso, 1994.

Roediger, D., and F. Rosemont, eds. *Haymarket Scrapbook.* Chicago: Charles H. Kerr, 1986.

Rogers, J. A. "Peter Kropotkin, Scientist and Anarchist." PhD diss., Harvard University, 1957.

Rosa, R. R. "The Social Question and Puerto Rico: A Friendly Call to Intellectuals." In *Workers Struggle in Puerto Rico: A Documentary History*, edited by A. Q. Rivera. 1904. Reprint, London: Monthly Review Press, 1976.

Rosenberg, D. "The IWW and the Organisation of Asian Workers in Early 20th Century America." *Labour History*, no. 36 (1995), 77–87.

Rothbard, M. "Milton Friedman Unveiled." *Journal of Libertarian Studies* 16, no. 4 (1971).

———. *Ludwig von Mises: Scholar, Creator, Hero.* Auburn, AL: Ludwig von Mises Institute, 1988. Available at http://www.mises.org/rothbard/scholarhero.pdf (accessed June 30, 2006).

Roux, P. R. "The Truth about the Defence Act: Straight Talk to Workers." *Voice of Labour*, October 11, 1912.

Rubner, H. "Occupational Culture, Conflict Patterns, and Organisational Behaviour: Perspectives of Syndicalism in 20th Century Shipping." Paper presented at the Syndicalism: Swedish and International Historical Experiences conference, Stockholm University, March 13–14, 1998.

Ruff, P. *Anarchy in the USSR: A New Beginning.* London: ASP, 1991.

Rühle, O. *The Struggle against Fascism Begins with the Struggle against Bolshevism.* 1939. Reprint, London: Elephant Editions, 1981.

Russell, B. *Roads to Freedom.* 1920. Reprint, London: Routledge, 1993.

Salerno, S. "The Impact of Anarchism on the Founding of the IWW: The Anarchism of Thomas J. Hagerty." In *Haymarket Scrapbook*, edited by D. Roediger and F. Rosemont. Chicago: Charles H. Kerr, 1986.

———. *Red November, Black November: Culture and Community in the Industrial Workers of the World.* Albany: State University of New York Press, 1989.

———. "Paterson's Italian Anarchist Silk Workers and the Politics of Race." *WorkingUSA: The Journal of Labor and Society* 8 (September 2005), 611–25.

Saul, J. S., and C. Leys. "Sub-Saharan Africa in Global Capitalism." *Monthly Review* 51, no. 3 (1999): 13–30.

Schechter, D. *Radical Theories: Paths beyond Marxism and Social Democracy*. Manchester: Manchester University Press, 1964.

Schmidt, A. "Rediscovering Manchuria: Sin Ch'aeho and the Politics of Territorial History in Korea." *Journal of Asia Studies* 56, no. 1 (1997).

Schram, S. R. "General Introduction: Mao Zedong and the Chinese Revolution, 1912–1949." In *Mao's Road to Power: Revolutionary Writings, 1912–1949*, edited by S. R. Schram. New York: M. E. Sharpe, 1992.

Seo Dong-shin. "Korean Anarchists Pursuing Third Way." *Korea Times*, January 26, 2007.

Seretan, L. G. *Daniel De Leon: The Odyssey of an American Marxist*. Cambridge, MA: Harvard University Press, 1979.

Serge, V. *Birth of Our Power*. 1931. Reprint, London: Writers and Readers Publishing Cooperative, 1977.

Sergven, M. *See* Maximoff, G. P.

Seth, S. *Marxist Theory and Nationalist Politics: The Case of India*. New Delhi: Sage, 1995.

Shaffer, K. R. "Purifying the Environment for the Coming New Dawn: Anarchism and Counter-cultural Politics in Cuba, 1898–1925." PhD diss., University of Kansas, 1998.

Shin Ch'aeho. "Declaration of the Korean Revolution." In *Anarchism: A Documentary History of Libertarian Ideas, Volume 1: From Anarchy to Anarchism, 300 CE to 1939*, edited by R. Graham. 1923. Reprint, Montréal: Black Rose, 2005.

Shipway, M. "Council Communism." In *Non-Market Socialism in the Nineteenth and Twentieth Centuries*, edited by M. Rubel and J. Crump. Basingstoke, UK: Macmillan, 1987.

———. *Anti-Parliamentary Communism: The Movement for Workers' Councils in Britain*. Basingstoke, UK: Macmillan, 1988.

Shor, F. "Masculine Power and Virile Syndicalism: A Gendered Analysis of the IWW in Australia." *Labour History*, no. 63 (1992).

———. "Left Labor Agitators in the Pacific Rim in the Early Twentieth Century." *International Labor and Working Class History*, no. 67 (2005).

Skirda, A. *Nestor Makhno: Anarchy's Cossack: The Struggle for Free Soviets in the Ukraine, 1917–1921*. 1982. Reprint, Oakland: AK Press, 2003.

———. *Facing the Enemy: A History of Anarchist Organisation from Proudhon to May 1968*. Oakland: AK Press, 2002.

Smart, D. A., ed. *Pannekoek and Gorter's Marxism*. London: Pluto Press, 1978.

Smith, A. *An Inquiry into the Nature and Causes of the Wealth of Nations, Volume 2 of the Glasgow Edition of the Works and Correspondence of Adam Smith*. 1776. Reprint, Indianapolis, IN: Liberty Fund, 1981.

Sobrevilla, D., ed. *Free Pages and Other Essays: Anarchist Musings: Manuel González Prada*. New York: Oxford University Press, 2003.

Socialist Labour Party. *See* De Leon, Daniel.

Solidarity Federation. *Out of the Frying Pan: A Critical Look at Works Councils*. Manchester: Solidarity Federation, 1998.

Sorel, G. *Reflections on Violence*. London: Allen and Unwin, 1915.

Souchy, A. *Beware! Anarchist! A Life for Freedom: The Autobiography of Augustin Souchy*, translated by T. Waldinger. Chicago: Charles H. Kerr, 1992.

"Spain: CGT Is Now the Third Biggest Union." *Alternative Libertaire*, November 2004. Translated by N. Phebus.

Spitzer, A. B. *The Revolutionary Theories of Louis Auguste Blanqui.* New York: Columbia University Press, 1957.

———. "Anarchy and Culture: Fernand Pelloutier and the Dilemma of Revolutionary Syndicalism." *International Review of Social History* 8 (1963).

Stack, D. A. "The First Darwinian Left: Radical and Socialist Responses to Darwin, 1859–1914." *History of Political Thought* 21, no. 4 (2000): 682–710.

Stalin, J. *Economic Problems of Socialism in the USSR.* 1951. Reprint, Beijing: Foreign Languages Press, 1972.

Statz, M., ed. *The Essential Works of Anarchism.* New York: Bantam, 1971.

———. Introduction to *The Essential Works of Anarchism*, edited by M. Statz. New York: Bantam, 1971.

———. Introduction to *Statism and Anarchy*, by M. Bakunin. Cambridge: Cambridge University Press, 1990.

Steenson, G. P. *Karl Kautsky, 1854–1938: Marxism in the Classical Years.* 2nd ed. Pittsburgh, PA: University of Pittsburgh Press, 1991.

Steiner, P. "Industrial Unionism: The History of the Industrial Workers of the World in Aotearoa." In *Industrial Unionism: The History of the Industrial Workers of the World in Aotearoa; Aim, Form, and Tactics of a Workers' Union on IWW Lines.* Wellington: Rebel Press, 2006.

Stekloff, G. M. *History of the First International.* Rev. ed. London: Martin Lawrence, 1928.

Stephenson, M. *Gender and Modernity in Andean Bolivia.* Austin: University of Texas Press, 1999.

Stevis, D. "International Labor Organizations, 1864–1997: The Weight of History and the Challenges of the Present." *Journal of World-Systems Research* 4, no. 1 (1998): 52–75.

Stirner, M. *The Ego and His Own.* 1844. Reprint, New York: Benjamin R. Tucker Publishers, 1907.

Sykes, T. S. "Revolutionary Syndicalism in the Italian Labour Movement: The Agrarian Strikes of 1907–1908 in the Province of Parma." *International Review of Social History*, no. 21 (1976).

Szymanski, A. "Racial Discrimination and White Gain." *American Sociological Review*, no. 41 (1976): 403–14.

Talhwan. "What We Advocate." In *Anarchism: A Documentary History of Libertarian Ideas, Volume 1: From Anarchy to Anarchism, 300 CE to 1939*, edited by R. Graham. June 1928. Montréal: Black Rose, 2005.

Tasuro Nomura. "Partisan Politics in and around the I.W.W: The Earliest Phase." *Journal of the Faculty of Foreign Studies*, no. 1 (1977).

Tax, M. *The Rising of the Women: Feminist Solidarity and Class Conflict, 1880–1917.* New York: Monthly Review Press, 1980.

Teitelbaum, K., and W. J. Reese. "American Socialist Pedagogy and Experimentation in the Progressive Era: The Socialist Sunday School." *History of Education Quarterly* 23, no. 4 (1983).

Thompson, F., with P. Murfin. *The IWW: Its First Seventy Years, 1905–1975.* Chicago: IWW, 1976.

Thompson, R. "The Limitations of Ideology in the Early Argentinean Labour Movement: Anarchism in the Trade Unions, 1890–1920." *Journal of Latin American Studies* 16 (1984).

Thorpe, W. "Towards a Syndicalist International: The 1913 London Congress." *International Review of Social History*, no. 23 (1978).

———. "The Provisional Agenda of the International Syndicalist Conference, London 1913." *International Review of Social History*, no. 36 (1981).

———. "*The Workers Themselves*": Revolutionary Syndicalism and International Labour, *1913–23*. Dordrecht: Kulwer Academic Publishers, 1989.

———. "Keeping the Faith: The German Syndicalists in the First World War." *Central European History* 33, no. 2 (2000).

———. "El ferrol, Zimmerwald, and beyond: Syndicalist Internationalism, 1914 to 1918." Paper presented at the European Social Science History conference, Amsterdam, March 22–25, 2006.

Titley, A. E. "The IWW in England." *Workers' Dreadnought*, October 2, 1920.

Tolstoy, L. "The Kingdom of God Is within You." In *The Essential Works of Anarchism*, edited by M. Statz. 1893. Reprint, New York: Bantam, 1971.

Trautmann, W. E. *One Great Union*. Detroit: Literature Bureau of the Workers' International Industrial Union, 1915.

Trewhela, P. "George Padmore, a Critique: Pan-Africanism or Communism." *Searchlight South Africa* 1, no. 1 (1988).

Trotsky, L. *The Revolution Betrayed*. London: New Park, 1967.

———. *Writings of Leon Trotsky, 1936–37*. 2nd ed. New York: Pathfinder Press, 1975.

———. *The Lessons of October*. 1924. Reprint, London: Bookmarks, 1987.

Tsurumi, E. P. "Feminism and Anarchism in Japan: Takamure Itsue, 1894–1964." *Bulletin of Concerned Asian Scholars* 17, no. 2 (1985).

Tsuzuki, C. *Tom Mann, 1856–1941: The Challenges of Labour*. Oxford: Clarendon Press, 1991.

Tucker, B. R. "State Socialism and Anarchism: How Far They Agree, and Wherein They Differ." In *Selections from the Writings of Benjamin R. Tucker*, edited by B. R. Tucker. 1926. Reprint, Millwood, NY: Kraus Reprint Company, 1973.

Turner, M. *Meseifushugi: A Brief History of Anarchism in Pre-war Japan*. Christchurch: Libertarian Press, n.d.

United Nations Development Programme. *Human Development Report*. New York: United Nations, 1996.

Unofficial Reform Committee. *The Miner's Next Step: Being a Suggested Scheme for the Reorganisation of the Federation*. 1912. Reprint, Sheffield, UK: Phoenix Press, 1991.

Vallance, M. "Rudolf Rocker: A Biographical Sketch." *Journal of Contemporary History* 8, no. 3 (1973).

van der Linden, M. "Second Thoughts on Revolutionary Syndicalism: Keynote Address." Paper presented at the Syndicalism: Swedish and International Historical Experiences conference, Stockholm University, March 13–14, 1998.

———. "Transnationalizing American Labor History." *Journal of American History* 86, no. 3 (1999).

———. *Transnational Labour History: Explorations*. London: Ashgate, 2003.

van der Linden, M., and W. Thorpe. "The Rise and Fall of Revolutionary Syndicalism." In *Revolutionary Syndicalism: An International Perspective*, edited by M. van der Linden and W. Thorpe. Otterup, Denmark: Scolar Press, 1990.

van der Walt, L. J. W. "'The Industrial Union Is the Embryo of the Socialist Commonwealth': The International Socialist League and Revolutionary Syndicalism in South Africa, 1915–1919." *Comparative Studies of South Asia, Africa, and the Middle East* 19, no. 1 (1999).

———. "Bakunin's Heirs in South Africa: Race, Class, and Revolutionary Syndicalism from the IWW to the International Socialist League." *Politikon* 30, no. 1 (2004).

———. "Reflections on Race and Anarchism in South Africa, 1904–2004." *Perspectives on Anarchist Theory*, no. 1 (2004): 1, 14–16.

———. "Anarchism and Syndicalism in South Africa, 1904–1921: Rethinking the History of Labour and the Left." PhD diss., University of the Witwatersrand, forthcoming

Vizetelly, E. A. *The Anarchists: Their Faith and Their Record*. Edinburgh: Turnbull and Spears Printers, 1911.

Voline. Preface to *History of the Makhnovist Movement, 1918–1921*, edited by P. Arshinov. 1923. Reprint, London: Freedom Press, 1987.

———. *The Unknown Revolution, 1917–1921*. 1947. Reprint, Montréal: Black Rose, 1990.

Voss, K., and R. Sherman. "Breaking the Iron Law of Oligarchy: Union Revitalization in the American Labor Movement." *American Journal of Sociology* 106, no. 2 (2000).

Walker, J. L. Introduction to *The Ego and His Own*, by M. Stirner. New York: Benjamin R. Tucker Publishers, 1907.

Walter, N. "Preface to the British Edition." In *History of the Makhnovist Movement, 1918–1921*, by P. Arshinov. London: Freedom Press, 1987.

Warren, B. *Imperialism: Pioneer of Capitalism*. London: Verso, 1980.

Wetzel, T., *Workers' Power and the Spanish Revolution*, 1987. Available at http://www.uncanny.net/~wsa/spain.html (accessed September 10, 2004).

———. *Looking Back after 70 Years: Workers Power and the Spanish Revolution*, n.d. Available at http://www.workersolidarity.org/Spanishrevolution.html#power (accessed June 15, 2005).

Wexler, A. R. *Emma Goldman: An Intimate Life*. New York: Pantheon Books, 1984.

———. "Emma Goldman and Women." In *The Anarchist Papers*, edited by D. I. Roussopoulus. Montréal: Black Rose, 1986.

"What's Wrong with Ireland." *International*, May 5, 1916.

White, J. "Syndicalism in a Mature Industrial Setting: The Case of Britain." In *Revolutionary Syndicalism: An International Perspective*, edited by M. van der Linden and W. Thorpe. Otterup, Denmark: Scolar Press, 1990.

Wickens, P. L. "The Industrial and Commercial Workers' Union of Africa." PhD diss., University of Cape Town, 1973.

Williams, G. *A Proletarian Order: Antonio Gramsci, Factory Councils, and the Origins of Italian Communism, 1911–21*. London: Pluto Press, 1975.

Wolff, R. P. *In Defence of Anarchism*. New York: Harper and Row, 1970.

Wood, A. G. "Postrevolutionary Pioneer: Anarchist María Luisa Marín and the Veracruz Renters' Movement." *A Contracorriente* 2, no. 3 (2005).

Wood, A., and J. A. Baer. "Strength in Numbers: Urban Rent Strikes and Political Transformation in the Americas, 1904–1925." *Journal of Urban History* 32, no. 6 (2006).

Woodcock, G. *Anarchy or Chaos*. London: Freedom Press, 1944.

———. *Anarchism: A History of Libertarian Ideas and Movements*. Rev. ed. New York: Penguin, 1975.

Woodcock, G., and I. Avakumovic. *The Anarchist Prince*. London: Boardman, 1950.

Woodruff, A. E. *The Advancing Proletariat: A Study of the Movement of the Working Class from Wage Slavery to Freedom*. Chicago: IWW Publishing Bureau, 1919.

"The Workers' Committee." *Workers' Dreadnought*, March 9, 1918.

Workers Solidarity Movement. *Position Paper: The Trade Unions*. Dublin, 2005.

"The Wrath to Come." *International*, December 3, 1915.

Yaroslavsky, E. *History of Anarchism in Russia*. London: Lawrence and Wishart, 1937[?].

Yates, M. D. "Poverty and Inequality in the Global Economy." *Monthly Review* 55, no. 9 (2004): 37–48.

Yoast, R. A. "The Development of Argentine Anarchism: A Socio-Ideological Analysis." PhD diss., University of Wisconsin at Madison, 1975.

Youn-tae Chung. "The Spread of Peasant Movement and Changes in the Tenant Policy in the 1920's Colonial Korea." *International Journal of Korean History* 2 (2001).

Zarrow, P. "He Zhen and Anarcho-Feminism in China." *Journal of Asian Studies* 47, no. 4 (1988).

———. *Anarchism and Chinese Political Culture*. New York: Columbia University Press, 1990.

Zenkoku Jiren. "What to Do about War?" In *Anarchism: A Documentary History of Libertarian Ideas, Volume 1: From Anarchy to Anarchism, 300 CE to 1939*, edited by R. Graham. November 1931. Reprint, Montréal: Black Rose, 2005.

Zipser, A. *Working Class Giant: The Life of William Z. Foster*. New York: International Publishers, 1981.

Index

About the Authors

Michael Schmidt is a Johannesburg-based investigative journalist and journalism trainer. He has twenty years' experience in the field as a writer and columnist for South Africa's leading newspapers including the *Sunday Times* and *ThisDay*. His work in conflict and post-conflict zones has taken him from Chiapas and the Guatemalan Civil War, to the Democratic Republic of Congo, Mozambique, Rwanda, Darfur, and Lebanon during the Summer War. A co-editor of the anarkismo.net news and analysis website and writer for the anarchist press, his lifelong passion for grassroots democracy has seen him involved in volunteer advocacy that has included work as a trade unionist, as a member of the Workers' Library and Museum committee, and also as a delegate to international civil society summits such as the Another Future conference in France and the First Encounter of Latin American Autonomous Popular Organisations in Brazil.

Lucien van der Walt is based at the University of the Witwatersrand, Johannesburg, where he teaches in development, economic sociology and labour studies. His recently completed PhD on the history of anarchism and syndicalism in early twentieth-century southern Africa was awarded the *Labor History* journal's prestigious international prize for best doctoral thesis of 2007. Van der Walt also researches contemporary working-class struggles against neo-liberal restructuring, and the relationship between race and class. He has presented at more than forty conferences on these subjects, written several book chapters, and published in numerous scholarly journals, magazines, and newspapers, including *Archiv für die Geschichte des Widerstandes und der Arbeit*, *African Studies*, *Capital and Class*, *Comparative Studies of South Asia, Africa and the Middle East*, *Labor History*, *Perspectives on Anarchist Theory*, *Politikon*, *Society in Transition*, *Southern Africa Report*, and the *South African Labour Bulletin*. He has also served as a media officer for the Anti-Privatisation Forum, on the executive of the Workers' Library and Museum, been an organiser for the Workers' Bookshop, and remains involved in education workshops for community organisations and unions.